Serious ADO:
Universal Data Access
with Visual Basic

ROB MACDONALD

Serious ADO: Universal Data Access with Visual Basic

Copyright ©2000 by Rob Macdonald

ISBN (pbk): 1-893115-19-4

Printed and bound in the United States of America 12345678910

Technical Reviewer: Russ Lewis

Editors: Andy Carroll and Grace Wong

Production Services, Page Composition, and Icon Trainer: Susan Glinert

Artist: Karl Miyajima

Indexer: Nancy Guenther

Cover and Interior Design: Derek Yee Design

Distributed to the book trade in the United States by Springer-Verlag New York, Inc.,

175 Fifth Avenue, New York, New York, 10010

and outside the United States by Springer-Verlag GmbH & Co. KG, Tiergartenstr. 17,

69112 Heidelberg, Germany

In the United States, phone 1-800-SPRINGER; orders@springer-ny.com; www.springer-ny.com

Outside the United States, contact orders@springer.de; www.springer.de; fax +49 6221 345229

For information on translations, please contact Apress directly at 901 Grayson Street, Suite 204, Berkeley, California, 94710

Phone: 510-549-3930; Fax: 510-549-3939; info@apress.com; www.apress.com

Contents at a Glance

Contents

Chapter 8   Recordset Recursion
                  and Data Shaping

Chapter 9   Working with Documents—
                  Records and Streams

Introduction

YOU'LL HAVE HEARD OF ADO (ActiveX Data Objects) before picking up this book. It's quite likely you'll have written some ADO code, possibly a fair bit. At one level, ADO needs no introduction—it's already well established as Microsoft's flagship product for database access. However, it's a great deal more than a new syntax for talking to databases. One of the major themes of this book is to make this point come alive—not only to show you how to write the best possible database access programs, but also to show you how ADO can work with many sources of data apart from your familiar relational database, and how ADO was designed to make it easy to develop component-based systems and Web applications, once you know how.

I have assumed you are an experienced Visual Basic programmer, and so I haven't wasted pages on the basic knowledge that all VB programmers have. I have also assumed you know a little bit about databases—enough at least to know the difference between a table and a query, and a SELECT statement and an UPDATE statement.

But I haven't made any assumptions about your knowledge of ADO. I have tried to cover the basics at a brisk pace, but with enough examples to keep newcomers to ADO fully in touch. At the other end of the spectrum, I really believe I have covered more advanced issues in more detail than any other ADO book available. Even if you are an ADO expert, if you don't start finding new things pretty early on, my guess is you have already written an ADO book, or maybe even written ADO!

How the Book Is Structured

This introduction aside, *Serious ADO* is divided into two parts.

Part One is "ADO in Depth." Its aim is to go beyond the syntax of ADO to help you develop a thorough understanding of the components that make up ADO, what they can do for you, and how to make them sing. Its chock full of code snippets, with explanations of exactly what is going on at each stage. Where appropriate, I have included sections that explain some of the key concepts that ADO programming is based on: locking and transactions, connection pooling, marshalling, and Inter-Process Communication, among others. In addition to the code samples in the text, the accompanying CD contains VB programs to complement each chapter. These allow you to explore the samples in the text in the context of a working program.

"ADO in Depth" is designed to work both as a book to be read and as a reference source. To make it easy to find relevant topics, the outer margin contains the name of the ADO object method or property being introduced.

Part Two is "ADO At Large." This part is all about using ADO in real-world development situations. It discusses creating user interfaces by binding Recordsets to controls and shows you new ways to take control of the binding process. It explains how the Data Environment concept introduced in VB6 makes it easy to apply your hard-earned ADO knowledge. It deals with using ADO in Internet and data mining scenarios.

Central to many VB projects these days is the use of Microsoft Transaction Server or COM+ applications to create transactional component-based systems. "ADO At Large" takes this topic head-on, explaining what these environments are really for and how to use ADO to write components that really benefit from MTS and COM+.

Data Sources Used in Code Samples

To demonstrate ADO in action requires some actual data to process. I didn't want to invent a make-believe business and develop applications to support its operation. This would require you spending time learning about a make-believe business and not ADO. Nor did I want to use a sample database supplied with Microsoft SQLServer, because you may be using Oracle, Sybase, DB2 or one of many other databases, and not have access to a Microsoft teaching database.

Therefore I have taken the text from Shakespeare's *Much ADO about Nothing* and converted it into a database. Yes, I know it's corny, but it results in a simple data model with one large table (>10,000 records) and three small tables and is perfect for teaching purposes.

More importantly, it allows me to use the raw text of the play to explore ADO Data Sources that are not relational in nature, such as a Web site's directory structure or search engine. (Just as important, it gave me ready access to a large lump of data with no copyright issues!). The accompanying CD explains how to re-create the sample data sources in your own environment.

For your information, I am no Shakespeare expert, so I want no emails complaining that introducing Bart Simpson in Act 1, Scene 1 destroys the textural harmony of the play's sub-context or distresses its dialectic integrity (whatever that means).

Conventions Used in This Book

When referring to the methods and properties of ADO objects, I have frequently used a two-letter abbreviation to refer to the object or class name (or three-letter abbreviations for collection classes). For example, rs.Open refers to the Open method of a Recordset object, while cn.Open refers to the Open method of a Connection object. In the same way, fds.Count refers to Count property of the

Fields collection. The same notation is used to refer to variable names in code, except where additional clarity is required.

Code samples are shown in the following typeface:

```
Dim rd As New Record
Dim rs As Recordset

rd.Open "Act 1/", "URL=http://POLECAT/MuchADO/"
Set rs = rd.GetChildren
While Not rs.EOF
  Print rs!RESOURCE_DISPLAYNAME, _
        rs!RESOURCE_ISCOLLECTION, _            ◄─────── a selection of Provider-
        rs!RESOURCE_STREAMSIZE                          supplied Fields for Document
  rs.MoveNext                                           Source Providers
Wend
```

and frequently have arrows pointing to key parts of the code, with explanatory text. Where code samples have printed output (as in the example above), the results are shown like this:

```
Act 1 Scene 2.htm        False        4665
Act 1 Scene 2.doc        False        19968
Act 1 Scene 1.htm        False        34454
Act 1 Scene 1.doc        False        50688
Act 1                    True         0
```

How to Use the CD

The CD is self-explanatory. It contains all the data needed to re-create the sample data stores used in the book, with advice on how to set them up. It also contains a directory for each chapter in the book, where you can get hold of the sample programs. There will also be updates and further information on the Apress Web site at www.apress.com.

Feedback and Further Information

I'd love to hear from you if you have comments or suggestions concerning anything to do with this book. You can email me at rob@salterton.com.

You can get further information from the Apress Web site (URL above) or from my Web site at www.salterton.com/hill.

Acknowledgments

I'd like to thank Karen Watterson for introducing me to Apress, and Gary Cornell and Dan Appleman for having the nerve to start up a publishing house that believes that authors and readers are actually an important part of the publishing process.

Thanks also to all the staff at Apress and elsewhere, including but not limited to Grace Wong, Andy Carroll, Susan Glinert, Karl Miyajima, and Sarah Jaquish, who listened patiently to all my wild demands (well, nearly all), and have done such a fine job of turning words into a book .

The credit (and the responsibility!) for technical accuracy and clarity never rests entirely on the shoulders of the author, and I am indebted to Russ Lewis for his many, many suggestions, which have improved the original draft immeasurably. Finding a reviewer whose technical expertise spans both ADO and the Simpsons was a tall order. Also, special thanks to Reuben Wells for so kindly taking on the role of "advanced novice" and giving me such helpful feedback as a result.

I'd also like to express my gratitude to the many organizations who have placed full-text versions of Shakespeare's plays on the Web for people to download. This book must surely represent one of the more unexpected applications of these efforts.

You can write books by picking up a help file and translating it into slightly less obscure English, but you need to have suffered on real-life, grown-up projects before you can genuinely feel you have something to write about. Therefore, I'd like to express my gratitude to the following fine people at Morgan Stanley Dean Witter & Co. in London and New York: Simon Burgess, Demian Duh, Albert Ho, Claire Lecourtier, Alec Nelson, Mehrdad Nourshargh, Mark Rice, Joli Riley, Karen Rossi, Karwoo Tang, Paul Tilleray and Cuneyt Varol. You have given me tough problems to solve in tight situations. You have also been a pleasure to work with.

Most importantly of all, there aren't words to express what I owe to Margaret Feetham, my lifelong partner who has cheerfully accepted the reclusive-obsessive behavior that accompanies my forays into writing (or maybe I'm always like that). You have suffered enough. I'll stop writing now.

CHAPTER 1
ADO's Big Idea

The Look and Feel of ADO

ADO Components and Libraries

Summary

WHILE CARS RUN ON GASOLINE, computer programs run on data. They really can't do much without it. Whereas the pumps at the gas station provide the driver with a simple, uniform approach to selecting one from a handful of fuel types, getting data in and out of computer programs has consumed the time and energy of millions of computer programmers struggling to understand the thousands of interfaces to the hundreds of types of data stores available.

Data is absolutely essential to computer programs, and yet there isn't a computer programmer alive who knows one-tenth of one percent of what there is to know about data access. It's no surprise then, that the topic of how computer programs use data is such a big deal. It's almost as though whenever a new type of data comes along, experienced programmers become novices all over again when trying to make use of it.

ADO's big idea is to change all of that. ADO wants to make all data look the same, so that programmers can spend their time creating new applications instead of poring over technical specs and writing test programs. Of course, wanting to do something isn't quite the same as achieving it. It would be marvelous to think that hooking up to a data store was as simple as selecting a nozzle. The reality is that data access is too big a topic for it to ever be quite that simple.

For one thing, applications have such a wide range of needs. Some just need simple, read-only access to a local data store created for a single user. Other applications are expected to give blistering performance, processing a multi-gigabyte data store located on a remote computer accessed by thousands of users at the same time.

For another thing, computer programs don't just consume data; they generate and modify data too. They have to do real-world things like transfer money between bank accounts with the same reliability and guarantees you would expect from the most trusted bank official.

Applications demand a great deal of flexibility when working with data. They expect to be able to sort it, filter it, and scroll through it easily and efficiently.

1

They expect data to perform just as well on a local network as it does over the Internet (ever wondered why you can't fill your tank up from www.fill-me-up.com?). And they expect it to deal with new innovations and trends as they come along: new types of data, new ways of transmitting data, new ways of presenting data.

For all these reasons and more, data access will never be as simple as buying gasoline. You can't learn it in one day—or twenty-one days for that matter. But with ADO, you can learn it once. Period. ADO provides the same interface for many, many different data stores—not just relational databases, but email systems, Web servers, search engines, and OLAP (On Line Analytical Processing) cubes. ADO is simple enough to be appropriate for straightforward desktop applications and basic Web pages, yet sufficiently efficient and sophisticated for the needs of complex systems serving millions of transactions a day, running in environments such as Microsoft Transaction Server (MTS) and COM+. In short, ADO provides Universal Data Access . This book shows you how.

The Look and Feel of ADO

You can neither see nor touch ADO. Yet experienced users know that ADO has a certain style. Compared to earlier Microsoft data access technologies, ADO has a looser, more convenient feel to it. It manages to be more flexible and powerful, but has fewer objects and needs fewer lines of code. It lets you do the same thing a number of different ways. In this respect, a certain care is needed, because while some of these alternatives are simply a matter of preference, others can have a major performance impact. You'll be seeing which is which in later chapters.

At the heart of ADO is the Recordset object. It represents a set of related records, which are usually the result of a query. First-time users of Recordsets sometimes find them a little unnerving because a Recordset represents all the records it contains *and* one particular record (the current record) at the same time. This split personality becomes very familiar very quickly, and represents the optimal combination of ease of use and efficiency.

Recordsets are intelligent. They know how to call on other ADO objects (such as Connection and Command objects) when they need them. This means you can write whole ADO applications using Recordsets alone. Alternatively, you can create additional ADO objects explicitly if you need the extra control and functionality they can provide when programmed directly.

Recordsets are efficient. They can sort and filter data faster than any code you could write. They are cleverly constructed to be able to update databases using pretty much the same SQL you would use if you wrote it yourself. And just in case you disagree, they provide options to allow you to control their work.

Recordsets are versatile. They can be bound to standard VB/ActiveX controls, or to Dynamic HTML elements in Web pages. They can be passed around networks and internetworks effortlessly and efficiently. They can be combined with each other or doubled-back on themselves to create the "data shapes" needed by your users. They can be used in the place of many traditional data structures to save time for both you and your users. They can represent many types of data—not just the results returned from a relational database.

Prior to ADO 2.5, all the other ADO objects existed pretty much to help in the process of creating and using Recordsets and the Field objects used to represent each column of data in a Recordset. Recordsets and Fields are perfect for working with any sort of tabular data, such as that returned by relational databases and search engines. As ADO has matured and its role has expanded, other objects have been added into ADO to handle data requirements that go beyond this two-dimensional view of data. These include the Record and Stream objects introduced in ADO 2.5 to allow ADO to work with "document-type" data such as that found in file systems and email message stores, as well as the Cellset object introduced in multidimensional ADO (ADOMD), which allows data to be viewed in the three- and four- (or more) dimensional structures often found in data mining applications.

ADO doesn't stand still. But as it grows, the new features build upon and integrate with the core ADO features.

ADO Components and Libraries

Microsoft has been generous in the creation of abbreviations and sound bytes to describe its flagship data access technology. The purpose of this section is to find a path through the terminology and identify the actual technology of interest to us developers.

Much of Microsoft's publicity surrounding data access has come under the general banner of Universal Data Access (UDA). This isn't so much a technology as a strategic vision—the goal of providing a standard access layer for all kinds of data stores. This shouldn't be dismissed as pure marketing speak —Microsoft's vision differs strongly from that of its main competitors in the data management arena. For companies like Oracle and Informix, the future lies in using a powerful data store capable of supplying a wide range of data needs, from relational tables to Web pages and emails. In contrast, UDA is about standardizing the access layer, with best of breed data stores for each type of data living behind the data access software. Of course, it's no surprise that the Oracle and Informix approaches require customers to make strategic commitments to data servers, while the Microsoft approach requires a strategic commitment to an operating system with built-in data access software. The important point is that the two strategies present very different technical challenges, opportunities, and risks.

The vision of UDA is delivered through the Microsoft Data Access Components, typically referred to as MDAC. MDAC contains the run-time components required to support several different but related data access technologies.

Before defining these technologies, it's worth making two points about getting access to MDAC. The first is that MDAC is provided as a distinct installable module only for Windows NT and 9x. In Windows 2000, MDAC is considered to be built into the operating system and is therefore not available as a separate product. New releases of these components on Windows 2000 will be made available through operating system service packs. The second point is that in addition to the MDAC run-time components, there is a whole suite of documentation, sample programs, and test programs historically known as the Data Access Software Developer's Kit (SDK). More recently, the Data Access SDK has been built into the much broader Platform SDK which provides developer support for the entire Windows platform.

MDAC contains the following technologies :

- **ActiveX Data Objects**: ADO is the subject of this book. It's the primary technology used by applications programmers to write data access programs for programs running on any Windows operating system. ADO will connect applications to a wide range of data stores by communicating through OLE DB.

- **OLE DB**: OLE DB is the low-level technology upon which ADO is based. OLE DB defines the specification that is used by "OLE DB Providers" to connect programs to data stores. OLE DB Providers perform a real-time translation service, translating OLE DB instructions into the target language used by the data store, and vice versa. They are, therefore, an essential part of nearly all ADO and OLE DB applications. It's rare for applications to talk directly to OLE DB, as it's a far more complex interface than ADO, and it isn't designed for use with languages such as VB. ADO translates application program requests into instructions to OLE DB. ADO was specifically designed for application programmers—regardless of the language they use.

- **Remote Data Services**: RDS was originally developed to enable programs running on remote computers to communicate with each other by exchanging Recordsets. In particular, RDS enables communication over HTTP and HTTPS enabling Web-based exchange of Recordsets between clients and servers. These days, RDS functionality is almost entirely built-in to standard ADO objects.

- **Open Data Base Connectivity**: ODBC was Microsoft's first serious attempt at creating a generic interface for data access. It has been extremely successful and remains the cornerstone of many client-server database applications. However, ODBC was designed for relational database access rather than universal data access, and it has certain restrictions that make it less appropriate for modern system designs than approaches based on ADO and OLE DB. ODBC can still operate as a component in ADO and OLE DB applications, meaning that existing ODBC drivers can be used as part of an ADO solution.

- **ADO Extensions for Data Definition and Security**: ADOX is a separate ADO library that complements the main ADO objects. It provides a set of objects that can be used to describe the structure of a database and to control its security. The standard ADO Connection object provides much of what ADOX can do, but ADOX presents the information in a more palatable fashion and is especially of interest to users of Microsoft Access migrating from DAO to ADO.

- **Multidimensional ADO**: ADOMD is a version of ADO designed to work with OLAP applications and data warehouses. These systems typically present data to users in the form of multidimensional "cubes" that can be cut and sliced in many different ways to allow flexible data analysis at a management level.

- Various OLE DB Providers and ODBC drivers, including the Microsoft OLE DB Provider for SQLServer and the Microsoft OLE DB Provider for Oracle.

The relationship between ADO, OLE DB, and ODBC is explored in more detail in Chapter 3 (Recordsets with SQL Data Sources). RDS is discussed in Chapter 15 (RDS and DHTML) while Chapter 16 (Multidimensional ADO) covers ADOMD. ADOX is described in Chapter 10 (The ADO Data Definition Language and Security Model [ADOX]).

ADO, ADOMD, and ADOX each have their own object model—which is linked by the ADO Connection object. The relevant chapters on ADOMD and ADOX describe their respective object models.

The object model of the main ADO library is relatively simple to look at, and it's shown in Figure 1-1. Learning all of its capabilities is a different matter, and the next eight chapters are devoted to exploring it in full. Every ADO programmer should carry in her or his head a picture similar to Figure 1-1. Knowing the different ADO objects and how they relate to each other is absolutely essential.

For the record, it should be mentioned that there are two ways of referencing the ADO object model (that is, it has two type-libraries). The most frequently used type-library is called ADODB, and it contains all the objects shown in Figure 1-1. A cut-down version, known as ADOR, exposes only the Recordset object. It should be noted that since ADO 2.0, both ADODB and ADOR refer to exactly the same code base, and therefore, there is no reason to use ADOR any more. The ADOR Recordset and the ADODB Recordset are identical.[1] In earlier versions of ADO, ADOR had a separate library with a smaller footprint, and you may still encounter computers that have ADOR installed, but not the full ADODB library. Both options are available to VB programmers through the Project-References dialog. Since ADO 2.0 however, ADOR has been provided only for backwards compatibility.

---

1. Bemused readers should note that there is still a DLL called msador15.dll that represents ADOR. However, it contains no Recordset code and merely passes on any requests to msado15.dll, which contains the ADODB code. Microsoft hasn't renamed DLLs with each release of ADO, so ADO 2.5 code is stored in a DLL called msado15.dll.

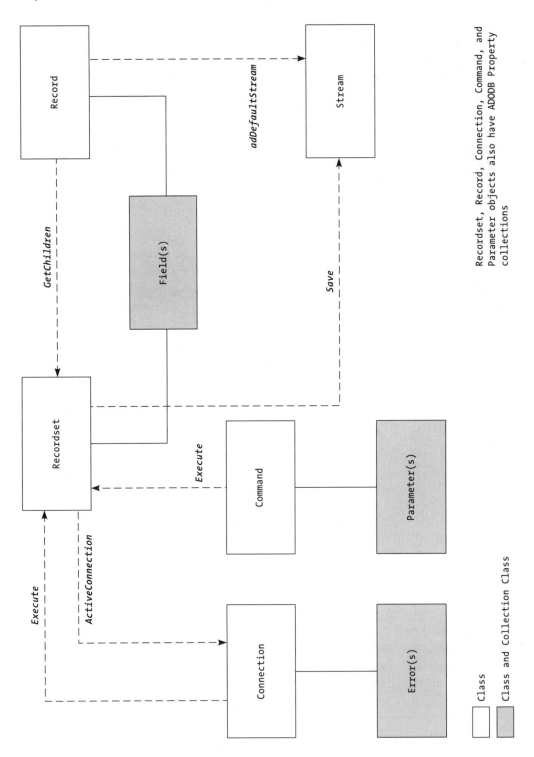

Recordset, Record, Connection, Command, and Parameter objects also have ADODB Property collections

Class

Class and Collection Class

Figure 1.1. ADO Object Model

Summary

In this chapter we:

- Looked at what ADO hopes to achieve and at some of the challenges that such ambitions present.

- Learned something of the programming style supported by ADO.

- Saw how ADO is packaged.

- Discussed technologies and components related to ADO.

The best introductions are short. It takes time for the full picture of ADO to develop, and rather than indulge in generalizations now, we'll take time out over the forthcoming chapters to step back and reflect on how the different parts of ADO fit together and how they deliver Universal Data Access.

I am sure you are eager to get your hands dirty. I, for one, already have my sleeves rolled up.

Part One

ADO IN DEPTH

CHAPTER 2

ADO Unplugged

Recordset and Field Objects

Look, No Connection!—Creating a Standalone Recordset

Basic Recordset Navigation

Find, Sort, and Filter

Working with Pages

Modification Operations

ADO Data Types and Attributes

Introducing Property Objects

Recordset Optimizations

Cloning

Recordset Error Handling

Recordsets Compared to Other Data Structures

Summary

To GET TO THE ESSENCE of a thing you need to isolate it. You can then explore it completely as a solo instrument, before placing it back in the orchestra to see how it performs as part of the whole. Right at the very heart of ADO is the Recordset and its collection of Field objects. In a very real sense, virtually all the other ADO objects play only a supporting role—they exist solely to create and save Recordsets—so it makes sense to focus first on the star performer.

There will be little mention of Providers, SQL, databases or anything else in this chapter—just Recordsets. You may well be itching to hook up to your favorite server as soon as possible, but please bear with me. For one thing, spending time on this chapter will make sure you exploit your server to the full. And for another, you might see that your ADO knowledge can be applied to a far wider range of tasks than you had thought possible.

Recordset and Field Objects

At its most basic, a *Recordset* is a two-dimensional data structure, consisting of rows (referred to as *records*) and columns (referred to as *Fields*). You may well expect a Recordset to be accessed in the same way as you would access a two-dimensional array, for example:

```
'This is not valid code
rs(iRow, iCol) = x
```

But this isn't the case. Instead, the Recordset is based on a cursor model—you only see one record at a time, and you position a cursor to identify the current row. As a result some operations that apply to Recordsets and Fields actually only operate on a single row, while others operate on the entire data structure.[1] Microsoft has used this technique before, so there is every chance you are familiar with it, but if you have never worked this way, you'll find that it becomes second nature amazingly quickly.

As an example, consider the following table of data, containing some of the characters from Shakespeare's *Much ADO about Nothing*.

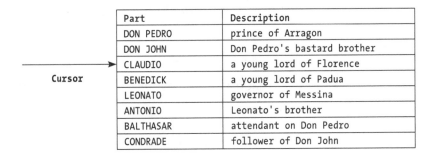

Figure 2-1. A set of records

rs.Fields
fd.Name
fd.Value

In Figure 2-1, the cursor is pointing at the third record. In ADO, a single Recordset would represent this table. Every Recordset has a property called *Fields*, which is a collection of Field objects—one Field object for each field or column of data in the table. For our table, there would be two Field objects. We could write the following code to print out the current record (this code is in ADO "longhand" to make everything explicit—we'll see how to streamline the coding shortly):

---

1. Recordsets represents a fruitful marriage of the mathematical Set theory, which underlies relational technologies and the ease-of-use of object orientation. It seems as if the Recordset contains a collection of many Record objects, only one of which is exposed at a time. However, the internal data structure is far more efficient than could ever be achieved with a collection of objects, and it provides "set manipulation" features as an added bonus.

```
'assumes we have a Recordset called rs
'assumes we have set a reference to the ADODB library
Dim colFields As Fields
Dim f1 As Field                              get hold of the Fields collection
Dim f2 As Field
Set colFields = rs.Fields
Set f1 = colFields("part")             ◄─┐   get hold of each Field object
Set f2 = colFields("description")      ◄─┘
Print f1.Name, f1.Value
Print f2.Name, f2.Value
```

which prints

part	CLAUDIO
description	a young lord of Florence

In other words, we are printing the names and values of two Field objects in the Recordset for the current record.

The following code advances the cursor onto the next record:

```
rs.MoveNext
Print f1.Name, f1.Value
Print f2.Name, f2.Value
```

and prints

part	BENEDICK
description	a young lord of Padua

There are three key points to draw from the previous example.

1. All the data for the Recordset is retrieved using the Field objects. This is the most common approach in ADO coding.

2. Calling a navigational method (such as MoveNext) on the Recordset affects the properties of the Field objects; these objects access the same internal data structure. Note that the *Name* property applies to the entire Field, whereas the *Value* property applies to the current record only. The Value changes as we move the cursor.

3. We had to type an awful lot of code just to print one record.

We'll return to the first two points later in the chapter when I discuss optimization techniques for Recordsets. My guess is you want me to address the last point right now!

For starters, we can avoid declaring explicit object variables for the Fields collection and the Field objects. Assuming we are still pointing at the third record, using the following code will print the record out just as before:

```
Print rs.Fields("part").Name, rs.Fields("part").Value
Print rs.Fields("description").Name, rs.Fields("description").Value
```

We can also exploit the fact that rs.Fields is the default property on the Recordset object (if we don't specify a property, the default one is used), as follows:

```
Print rs("part").Name, rs("part").Value
Print rs("description").Name, rs("description").Value
```

and use the shorthand technique provided by Visual Basic (but not VBScript) for accessing a collection object using its key:

```
Print rs!part.Name, rs!part.Value
Print rs!description.Name, rs!description.Value
```

Finally, we can exploit the fact that fd.Value is the default property on the Field object, as follows:

```
Print rs!part.Name, rs!part
Print rs!description.Name, rs!description
```

You'll spend far more of your time using the fd.Value property of a Field than any other property. Therefore, by exploiting this last shortcut, you can make your code very concise.

A warning is required at this point: When you use default properties, it's not always clear whether you are referring to the default property or the object itself. For example, assume you wanted to put the name and description of the current record into your own VB collection. You might write code like this:

```
Dim colRecordData As New Collection
colRecordData.Add rs!part, "part"                    ◄──────┐   Add some things
colRecordData.Add rs!Description, "desc"             ◄──────┘   to a collection

Print colRecordData("part"), colRecordData("desc")
rs.MoveNext
Print colRecordData("part"), colRecordData("desc")
```

You may well expect both print statements to generate the same output. (Haven't you just copied the data into the collection, so the MoveNext will have no effect?) However, ask yourself whether rs!part returns a string or a Field object. This code prints as follows:

```
CLAUDIO                     a young lord of Florence
BENEDICK                    a young lord of Padua
```

The code added a reference to each Field object into the collection, rather than to each Fields' value. Therefore, the Print statements print whatever data the Field object contains in its fd.Value property at the time it was accessed and not the static data you might have expected. The confusion occurs because rs!part is ambiguous. It could mean the value contained in a Field object or it could mean the Field object itself. Much of the time, VB makes the choice you expect it to because the context determines which to use. If you are assigning something to a string, the "something" is clearly not going to be an object. But if you are adding something to a collection, then it's more likely to be an object than not.

You can avoid this ambiguity and related problems by explicitly referring to fd.Value when accessing the Value property of a Field object. Some folks do this as a matter of course.

In This Section

We established the relationship between the Recordset object, the Fields collection object, and Field objects. Every Recordset is built in this way. The rest of this chapter will explore how to exploit this fundamental ADO structure.

Look, No Connection!– Creating a Standalone Recordset

The previous section discussed a theoretical Recordset. For the rest of this chapter we'll work with two real Recordsets, which means we'll have to create them. The first Recordset will contain the characters from *Much ADO about Nothing* (we'll turn our previous theory into practice). It has only a couple of dozen records, so it will be easy enough to build up in memory. The second one contains all the words from the play. It has over 12,000 records. The program that creates it from the text of the play is surprisingly simple, but we'll work with a ready-made Recordset. This will allow us a glimpse of how a Recordset can be made to be self-persisting;

rs.State

in this case, storing itself in a file. We'll return to Recordset persistence in Chapter 7.

We've seen that Recordsets are constructed out of records and Fields. Another important Recordset feature is its *state*. Typically a Recordset is either open or closed, and this distinction is enough to define its state. However, when Recordsets are being created asynchronously (see Chapter 6), other states are possible, and the Recordset can be in more than one state at a time. Therefore, you should always use a **bitmask** when testing for any state other than closed. The following code shows a correct way and a not-so-correct way of testing whether a Recordset is open:

```
Print "Closed", rs.State = adStateClosed
rs.Open
Print "Open (hopefully)", rs.State = adStateOpen 'may not work
Print "Open (definitely)", (rs.State And adStateOpen) <> 0
```

It prints

Closed	True
Open (hopefully)	True
Open (definitely)	True

rs.Open
rs.Close

The State property is read-only. Recordsets are opened and closed using the Open and Close methods, which change the State property internally.

Once a Recordset is open, its records are available for manipulation, but the Field objects and most of their properties (excluding the Value property) are read-only. When a Provider builds the Recordset (which is typically the case), the Provider creates the required Field objects in response to your command. This happens *during* the rs.Open method call, after which the Fields collection is read-only. When you generate the Recordset yourself (as we are about to do), you create the Field objects before opening the Recordset. A Recordset you have generated yourself is often called a *fabricated Recordset*.

So let's see how to fabricate a Recordset that contains every character from *Much ADO about Nothing*.

```
Public Function getParts() As Recordset
Dim rs As New Recordset

Dim varrFields As Variant
With rs.Fields
    .Append "part", adChar, 20                      create the Fields
    .Append "description", adVarChar, 50, adFldIsNullable
    End With
```

```
varrFields = Array("part", "description")
With rs
  .Open                    ◄─────────────────────── open the Recordset

  .AddNew varrFields, Array("DON PEDRO", "prince of Arragon")
  .AddNew varrFields, Array("DON JOHN", "Don Pedro's bastard brother")
  .AddNew varrFields, Array("CLAUDIO", "a young lord of Florence")
  .AddNew varrFields, Array("BENEDICK", "a young lord of Padua")
  .AddNew varrFields, Array("LEONATO", "governor of Messina")
  .AddNew varrFields, Array("ANTONIO", "Leonato's brother")
  .AddNew varrFields, Array("BALTHASAR", "attendant on Don Pedro")
  .AddNew varrFields, Array("CONRADE", "follower of Don John")
  .AddNew varrFields, Array("BORACHIO", "follower of Don John")
  .AddNew varrFields, Array("FRIAR FRANCIS", Null)
  .AddNew varrFields, Array("DOGBERRY", "a constable")
  .AddNew varrFields, Array("VERGES", "a headborough")
  .AddNew varrFields, Array("SEXTON", Null)
  .AddNew varrFields, Array("BOY", Null)
  .AddNew varrFields, Array("LORD", Null)
  .AddNew varrFields, Array("HERO", "daughter to Leonato")
  .AddNew varrFields, Array("BEATRICE", "niece to Leonato")
  .AddNew varrFields, Array("MARGARET", "gentlewoman attending on Hero")
  .AddNew varrFields, Array("URSULA", "gentlewoman attending on Hero")
  .AddNew varrFields, Array("MESSENGER", Null)
  .AddNew varrFields, Array("WATCHMAN", Null)
  .AddNew varrFields, Array("FIRST WATCHMAN", Null)
  .AddNew varrFields, Array("SECOND WATCHMAN", Null)
End With                              reposition the cursor
rs.MoveFirst        ◄───────────────── to the first record
Set getParts = rs   ◄───────────────── return the fabricated Recordset
End Function
```

fd.Append

Prior to the rs.Open call in the previous example, the code adds two columns to the Recordset using the Append method on the Fields collection. The Append method's full definition is as follows:

Sub Append(Name As String,
             Type As DataTypeEnum,
             [DefinedSize As Long],
             [Attrib As FieldAttributeEnum = adFldUnspecified],
             [FieldValue])[2]

---

2. FieldValue was introduced in ADO 2.5. It's mostly of use when using the Record object, rather than the Recordset object (see Chapter 9).

17

ADO supports a wide range of data types, as we'll see later in "ADO Data Types and Attributes." DefinedSize is only required for those data types that don't define their own size in bytes, such as variable length character fields. Attrib specifies one or more of a set of attributes defined by an enumeration called FieldAttributeEnum. We've just used one attribute to specify that the description field can be set to Null, although multiple values from the enumeration can be linked together with Or.

fd.Attributes

Once the Recordset is open, the attributes can be read using the Recordset's Attribute property and an appropriate bitmask. Attributes will also be discussed more fully later in "ADO Data Types and Attributes."

rs.AddNew

Appending Field objects can only be done before the Recordset is opened. When a fabricated Recordset is first opened it's empty, so we need to use the AddNew method to start adding records to it. AddNew is defined as follows:

```
Sub AddNew(    [FieldList],
               [Values])
```

AddNew takes two optional arguments in the form of Variant arrays, one containing the list of fields being inserted and one containing a value for each field in the field list. You don't have to provide all the fields, and the fields can be in any order, but (it almost goes without saying) the two lists must match up. This approach is rather like the way the SQL INSERT statement works, but readers who have used other Microsoft data access libraries such as ***Data Access Object (DAO)*** or ***Remote Data Object (RDO)*** will be more familiar with the following approach, which is also valid:

```
rs.AddNew
rs("part").Value = "DON PEDRO"
rs("description").Value = "prince of Arragon"
```

While this approach works, it isn't as efficient as providing the information as arguments to AddNew, so if you are writing code that will add a lot of rows, it's better to use the "new" ADO syntax based on providing arguments to AddNew, especially if you predefine the FieldList array, as we did above.

rs.Open

There is one other way of creating and saving Recordsets without directly invoking a Provider, and that is by reading and writing to and from a file.[3] If you happen to have a Recordset stored in a file, you can open it very easily:

```
rs.Open FILE_SOURCE_PATH & "words.rs"
```

---

3. I've chosen my words carefully here because this operation does in fact use a Provider— the OLE DB Persistence Provider that is built into MDAC—even though it isn't invoked directly. We will discuss its hugely important role in Chapter 7, but for now, we'll treat it as a convenient way of storing Recordsets in files.

I've conveniently created a Recordset and saved it in a file called "words.rs." You can find it in the Data directory on the companion CD. This Recordset stores every word from *Much ADO about Nothing*, and has well over 10,000 records. I'll hold back the temptation to list them here; instead, I will just show you the schema for the Recordset in Table 2-1.

Table 2-1. Schema for Words Recordset

FIELD	TYPE	SIZE	DESCRIPTION
Word	adVarChar	50	A word from the text.
Part	adVarChar	20	Part or Character speaking the word.
Act	adChar	5	Act in which the word appears.
Scene	adChar	5	Scene in which the word appears.
Count	adInteger		Number of times word appears for Part, Act, or Scene.
Length	adInteger		Number of characters in Word.

rs.Save

As well as being able to open Recordsets from files, Recordsets can also be saved to a file. The syntax for saving a Recordset is

Sub Save([Destination],
             [PersistFormat As PersistFormatEnum = adPersistADTG])

An example is

```
rs.Save FILE_SOURCE_PATH & "words.xml", adPersistXML
```

Note that the destination is optional. For a Recordset that has already been saved, you can omit the destination and it will be saved back to where it came from, without requiring you to delete the file first.

There are two options for the format used to persist the Recordset. The default is Microsoft's own Advanced Data TableGram (ADTG) format, which is only for use with ADO functions that understand it. However, since ADO 2.1, it has also been possible to read and write Recordsets using *Extensible Markup Language (XML)*, as shown previously. The use of XML provides some exciting possibilities, especially in conjunction with Internet Explorer 5. At the same time, ADTG is more efficient.

We've seen how Recordsets can be fabricated in memory and stored in a file, and in the next section we'll start looking at how you can move around inside a Recordset and do things with individual records. Let's finish this section by looking at a couple of interesting operations that can be applied to whole Recordsets.

rs.GetString However wonderful Recordsets may be (and they are pretty wonderful), there are times when you'll want the data in a different format to serve a specific purpose. There are two Recordset functions, GetString and GetRows, which allow you to turn Recordsets into strings or arrays with very little effort.

Function GetString([StringFormat As StringFormatEnum =
     adClipString],
    [NumRows As Long = -1],
    [ColumnDelimeter As String = vbTab],
    [RowDelimeter As String = vbCr],
    [NullExpr As String = ""])
    As String

Using GetString with no arguments yields convenient results:

```
Dim rs As Recordset
Set rs = getParts

Print rs.GetString
```

This code prints

DON PEDRO	prince of Arragon
DON JOHN	Don Pedro's bastard brother
CLAUDIO	a young lord of Florence
BENEDICK	a young lord of Padua

and so on.

However, you can very easily do far more interesting things, such as generating HTML tables, by providing arguments. For example, once the following code has executed:

```
Dim rs As Recordset
Dim sHTML As String
Set rs = getParts
rs.Move 10, adBookmarkFirst 'we'll look at the Move method soon
sHTML = "<HTML><BODY><TABLE BORDER=1><TR><TD>" & vbCrLf

sHTML = sHTML & rs.GetString(, 4, _          ◄──── this many rows
          "</TD><TD>", _                      ◄──── column delimiter
          "</TD></TR><TR><TD>" & vbCrLf, _    ◄──── row delimiter
          "unknown")                          ◄──── use in place of Nulls
sHTML = sHTML & "</TD></TR></TABLE></BODY></HTML>"
```

sHTML will contain

```
<HTML><BODY><TABLE BORDER=1><TR><TD>
DOGBERRY          </TD><TD>a constable</TD></TR><TR><TD>
VERGES            </TD><TD>a headborough</TD></TR><TR><TD>
SEXTON            </TD><TD>unknown</TD></TR><TR><TD>
BOY               </TD><TD>unknown</TD></TR><TR><TD>
</TD></TR></TABLE></BODY></HTML>
```

which will look predictably like a standard HTML table when loaded into a browser.

GetString has been defined to allow different string formats to be provided via the first argument. Currently however, only the default value is supported. This otherwise very handy function has one other limitation—you can't control which Fields to use.

rs.GetRows

The related GetRows function is nicer than GetString in this respect. Its definition is

Function GetRows([Rows As Long = -1],
                    [Start],
                    [Fields])

GetRows returns a zero-based, two-dimensional *Variant array*. Be aware that this array has the rows and columns transposed. The first dimension correlates to the Recordset's Fields while the second dimension correlates to its records, which is the opposite of what you would expect.[4] So the following row-and-column counting code

```
Dim rs As Recordset
Dim vData As Variant
Set rs = getParts
vData = rs.GetRows
Print rs.RecordCount, rs.Fields.Count
Print UBound(vData, 1) + 1, UBound(vData, 2) + 1
```

prints

23	2
2	23

---

4. There is a good reason for this, and it relates to how dynamic arrays work. With a two-dimensional dynamic array, only the last dimension can be extended without losing existing data. Changing any other dimension corrupts the internal structure of the array. In a Recordset, Fields are fixed in number, but records can be added or removed, so it makes sense for the last (dynamic) dimension to be used to represent records.

This is counterintuitive. Believe me, it takes some getting used to.

Incidentally, I subtly introduced the RecordCount property in the previous code sample. When you are using fabricated Recordsets, this property can always be relied upon. However, when you are working with regular Providers there are situations when you can't depend on Record-Count (more on this in Chapter 3).

Sadly, there is no consistency between the arguments of GetString and GetRows. GetRows allows you to specify a start position (in the form of a bookmark; these are described in the next section), whereas GetString always begins from the current cursor location. They use different names for the argument that determines how many rows to return, although at least both default to –1, which means "get all rows after the starting position." ADO defines a constant called adGetRowsRest for this purpose, which can only legitimately be used with GetRows.

What makes GetRows really different is the Fields argument. This is either a single field name (as a string) or a Variant array of field names from the Recordset, providing full control over which fields you use and their order. There is no obvious performance penalty for specifying Fields. If you want half the fields, GetRows takes half the time to build the array—regardless of the field order. I've only got two fields in my simple Recordset. But I can show you how to reverse the field order:

```
Dim rs As Recordset
Dim vData As Variant
Dim i As Integer

Set rs = getParts
vData = rs.GetRows(5, adBookmarkFirst, Array("description", "part"))
For i = 0 To UBound(vData, 2)
  Print vData(0, i), vData(1, i) 'the args are the right way round
  Next
```

This prints the description field before the part field:

```
prince of Arragon              DON PEDRO
Don Pedro's bastard brother DON JOHN
a young lord of Florence     CLAUDIO
a young lord of Padua        BENEDICK
governor of Messina          LEONATO
```

In This Section

You saw how to create fabricated Recordsets, and open and save them from and to a file. You also learned that Recordsets have a State, which is usually either open or closed, and a RecordCount that tells you how many records there are. Finally, you looked at two methods for processing whole Recordsets, GetString and GetRows.

Basic Recordset Navigation

rs.MoveNext
rs.MovePrevious
rs.MoveFirst
rs.MoveLast

Usually, you'll want to operate on one record at a time. The process of locating the required record is called *navigation*.[5] The following four methods are simple to use and will meet 90% of your navigational needs:

> rs.MoveNext
>
> rs.MovePrevious
>
> rs.MoveFirst
>
> rs.MoveLast

There is one key point to bear in mind when using these (or any) navigational methods. The only method that is guaranteed to behave as you might expect is MoveNext. Once upon a time (before ADO), Recordsets were always assumed to come from relational databases, and early relational databases only supported fetching the next record; they wouldn't allow you to move backward or jump to the end. For many data sources, using only the MoveNext method is still the most efficient way to navigate a Recordset, and Recordsets that only support MoveNext (known as forward-only Recordsets) are the often the default type returned by the data source.

rs.Supports

The navigational functionality of a Recordset depends more than anything on its CursorType, a topic I address in detail in Chapter 3. Our fabricated Recordset is completely functional, but always bear in mind that you aren't guaranteed the full monty when working with other Recordsets. You can check just what functionality a Recordset provides by using the Supports method.

rs.BOF
rs.EOF

One of the few guarantees that ADO does provide is that if you call MoveNext enough times, you'll eventually run out of records. Life's like that. To prevent run-time errors when navigating, ADO provides two

---

5. The maritime metaphor is actually quite appropriate. Most of the time, navigation is plain sailing, but there are occasions when you'll feel decidedly seasick.

properties, BOF (Beginning of File) and EOF (End of File). These properties tell you when you are at one end of a Recordset, as shown next.[6]

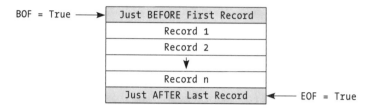

Figure 2-2. Cursor position when BOF and EOF are True

When you are pointing at the last record, both BOF and EOF are False. If you then call MoveNext, EOF will become True. This isn't an error state, even though you aren't pointing at a record. An error will occur if you try to access this record's fields, or if you call MoveNext again, but not if you try and move somewhere else. The same reasoning applies at the other end of the Recordset when using BOF and MovePrevious.

rs.RecordCount

If both BOF and EOF are True, then there are no records in your Recordset. This is a better way of testing for an empty Recordset than using the RecordCount property, as it's always reliable. Depending on the data source and the type of Recordset created, the RecordCount property may return −1, which means that the RecordCount isn't supported. We'll come back to this issue in Chapter 3.

We are now able to review the classic ADO code fragment for opening a Recordset and iterating through to the end:

```
Dim rs As Recordset
Set rs = New Recordset

rs.Open FILE_SOURCE_PATH & "words.rs"
While Not rs.EOF
    Print rs("word").Value, rs("length").Value
    rs.MoveNext
Wend
```

---

6. "What file?" you ask. Even though we can store a Recordset in a file, it's quite rare for a Recordset to represent the contents of a file. BOF and EOF are misnomers—for which the only excuse is backwards familiarity—Microsoft has been using BOF and EOF for years and didn't want to introduce new property names in ADO for the petty purpose of being accurate.

Although this code is the ADO equivalent of "Hello World" it's actually rather elegant. Open leaves you pointing at the first record (if there is one), so no initial positioning is required. If the Recordset is empty, no error will occur because the EOF test will drop straight out of the loop without ever executing it.

It's quite easy to take for granted the fact that Open positions the cursor for you, especially when you start getting Recordsets by other means (such as fabrication) and the code that creates them for you leaves the cursor pointing at the last record. If you are writing code that returns Recordsets for others to use, have a heart—do a MoveFirst before you return it.[7] Of course, you would only do this if your Recordset supports MoveFirst!

There are times when you'll really need more flexible navigation techniques. You may wish to move to a specific record for example. ADO provides two basic approaches for doing this: identifying a record by position in the Recordset or identifying a record by using bookmarks.

rs.AbsolutePosition

Navigation by position is achieved using either the AbsolutePosition property or the Move method (see later). Nothing could seem simpler than moving to the twenty-third record by executing

```
rs.AbsolutePosition = 23
```

The problem is that what may have been the twenty-third record a few moments ago may now be in a completely different position. Not only do operations such as deleting a record affect the absolute position of all records that come after it in the Recordset, but also seemingly benign operations such as sorting or filtering a Recordset also affect each record's position. To use this approach, you either must know exactly what you are doing or enjoy living dangerously.[8]

When you read the AbsolutePosition property, you may not always get a positive number back. Three other possible values exist for which the following constants in the PositionEnum enumeration have been defined:

adPosUnknown

adPosBOF

adPosEOF

---

7. While this assumes your cursor supports MoveFirst, it's highly unlikely you would write code that returned Recordsets that didn't have an appropriate cursor.

8. Programmers sometimes get dispirited at the idea of not using record numbers when working with Recordsets, but it's usually easy to get used to. Mathematicians will recognize that the "set" in Recordset has a specific meaning. In math, the concept of position in a set is actually meaningless.

These cover the situations when either BOF or EOF are True or when the position can't be determined, which usually occurs because the Recordset doesn't support using AbsolutePosition (which you can test using the Supports method, which we'll explore in Chapter 3).

rs.Bookmark

A better way to navigate to a particular record is to use a Bookmark. The name "Bookmark" is meant to suggest how bookmarks work, but in my opinion, "paper clip attached to a specific page in a ring binder" would be a more illustrative name. No matter how you shuffle and sort the pages in a ring binder, the paper clip will still be attached to that page. In a Recordset, a Bookmark consistently and uniquely identifies a specific record regardless of any change in the record's position and is, therefore, very much like the paper clip. (I concede that bookmark is a catchier name).

A Bookmark is a Variant, and you can get a Bookmark for the current record by simple assignment:

```
Dim vBMK as Variant
vBMK = rs.Bookmark
```

Anytime while the Recordset is still open you can return to the record like so:

```
rs.BookMark = vBMK
```

(This may not look like a "move" operation, but it most certainly is.)

Bookmarks are really useful if you want to allow users to identify one or more records, and then when they have finished browsing, to apply an operation on all the selected records that requires moving to each record in turn. They are also very useful when working with Recordset Clones, as you'll see later in this chapter.

rs.CompareBookmarks

Many Bookmarks are actually numerical, and you may be tempted to exploit this fact. Please don't. Bookmarks are allowed to be other types of data as well, and Providers are entitled to change how they create Bookmarks. That said, you can compare Bookmarks, but not by using standard relational operators. Instead, use the CompareBookmarks method. This method takes two Bookmarks from the same Recordset and returns one of the following values from the CompareEnum enumeration:

adCompareLessThan

adCompareEqual

adCompareGreaterThan

adCompareNotEqual

adCompareNotComparable

If ADO knows that two Bookmarks aren't equal but cannot determine their order, it will return adCompareNotEqual. Not all Recordsets support Bookmarks; the Supports method will throw light on this.

Bookmarks are only valid for the Recordset you read them from. Using them with other Recordsets, even ones created by reexecuting the same command, will disappoint.

rs.Move

Bookmarks and numerical positioning can be combined using the Move method, which has the following defintion:

```
Sub Move(      NumRecords As Long,
               [Start = adBookmarkCurrent])
```

Move causes the cursor to be moved forward or backward a specified number of records relative to the current position or to a Bookmark if one is specified as the optional Start argument. Positive numbers are used to move forward (toward the end of the Recordset), while negative numbers move the cursor backward. The BookmarkEnum enumeration defines some standard Bookmarks, which include:

adBookmarkFirst

adBookmarkLast

In This Section

You saw how to move around inside Recordsets. The standard Move methods will meet most of your needs, but you can use either absolute positioning or the more reliable Bookmark approach to achieve other types of navigation. In the next section, we'll look at some more advanced techniques for manipulating Recordsets so that you can work on them in different ways.

Find, Sort, and Filter

You are most likely aware of the features provided by SQL for finding, sorting, and filtering data. All of these operations are completely valid when using ADO and should be used for all the well-known and correct reasons. However, the ADO Client Cursor Engine also provides its own version of these functions. There are several reasons why the functionality is duplicated.

- Not all OLE DB Providers support SQL or equivalent functionality.

- After the Recordset retrieves an initial set of records, it can often be more convenient to use client-side features to narrow down the Recordset further, rather than issue additional SQL statements and work with multiple Recordsets.

- Your Recordset may be disconnected from its original Provider, yet you still want to sort, filter, and find records. This is particularly likely in n-tier application designs.

- It can be more efficient to do these operations in the client, as it reduces network and server load.

It's worth knowing that applying client indexes can considerably optimize all the operations discussed in this section. See "Recordset Optimizations" for more details. We'll work with our smaller "parts" Recordset in this section, and use the larger "words" Recordset when exploring optimization.

rs.Find

Find and Filter both provide ways of finding records that meet certain criteria. Find is the easier of the two to understand and will appear familiar to DAO programmers, but Filter is far more powerful and flexible and is preferable in nearly all circumstances. Let's look at Find first. Here's its definition:

Sub Find(Criteria As String,
            [SkipRecords As Long = 0],
            [SearchDirection As SearchDirectionEnum = adSearchForward],
            [Start As Variant = adBookmarkCurrent])

Criteria is the condition you are searching for. The following diagram illustrates the function of the other arguments, all of which are optional.

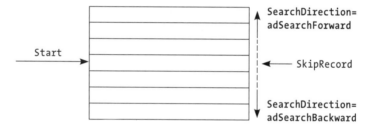

Figure 2-3. Purpose of the optional arguments to rs.Find

For example

```
Dim rs As Recordset
Set rs = getParts

rs.Find "part > 'T'", , , adBookmarkFirst
While Not rs.EOF
    Print rs("part"), rs("description")
    rs.Find "part > 'T'", 1        ◄─────────────  skip 1 record
Wend
```

prints

VERGES	a headborough
URSULA	gentlewoman attending on Hero
WATCHMAN	Null

Note that the SkipRecords argument is used in this code to ensure that the current record isn't included in the Find within the loop. If we omitted SkipRecords, this code would loop forever. When Find doesn't locate a match, the cursor is left in the BOF or EOF state, according to the direction of the search.

When using Find, the comparison operator in criteria may be >, <, =, >=, <=, <> or LIKE. LIKE is used for pattern matching. Null can be used as a value, and strings should be single-quoted, as if being used in an SQL WHERE clause. There are two gotchas you should be aware of when using Find:

1. You can't create compound criteria using And or Or. If you need more power than this, use the Filter property.

2. When using the LIKE operator, you use * or % (any characters) and _ (any single character) as wildcards. The wildcards * and _ are *not* the standard wildcards used in nearly every database in existence.[9]

rs.Filter

The Filter property is an altogether more wonderful thing than the Find method. It allows a Recordset to appear as though it only has a subset of the actual records it contains. Operations applied to the Recordset work on the filtered subset of records until another filter is applied or the existing one is removed.

---

9. Why this discrepancy? I can only guess, but I suspect it's done this way for the benefit of Access programmers. Find is a familiar type of operation for DAO and Access, and the Jet database engine uses the same nonstandard wildcards.

Filter scores over Find for at least two reasons:

1. You can create compound And and Or filters, allowing you to search on multiple fields.

2. You can identify (and count) all the records that meet the search criteria in one go.

The Filter property is a Variant, and can take one of the following three types of values:

1. A search string. This, with some restriction, is very much like an SQL WHERE clause.

2. An array of bookmarks.

3. A filter constant from the FilterGroupEnum enumeration.

Figure 2-4 shows the effect of applying a filter to a Recordset. The Recordset cursor is repositioned, and only those records that meet the Filter criteria are visible.

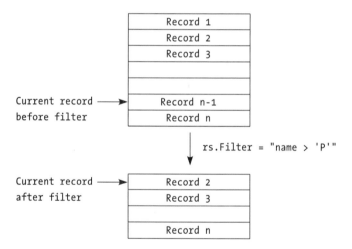

Figure 2-4. A Filter exposes a subset of a Recordset's records.

Following is a code example that shows the use of an array of Bookmarks. In this example, we iterate through the "parts" Recordset randomly selecting three records (simulating user interaction) and then list the selected records.

```
Dim rs As Recordset
Dim vArray(0 To 2) As Variant
Dim i As Integer
Set rs = getParts
rs.MoveFirst
While Not rs.EOF And i < 3
    If (Rnd < 0.25) Then ' 1 in 4 chance
        vArray(i) = rs.Bookmark
        i = i + 1
        End If
    rs.MoveNext
Wend
'apply the filter here
rs.Filter = vArray

While Not rs.EOF
    Print rs("part"), rs("description")
    rs.MoveNext
Wend
Print rs.RecordCount
```

Construct an array of Book-arks, selected at random from the Recordset. This simulates a user selecting records via a user interface.

Use the array as the Filter.

The code prints

BALTHASAR	attendant on Don Pedro
DOGBERRY	a constable
MARGARET	gentlewoman attending on Hero
3	

Once the Filter is applied, the Recordset behaves as though it only ever had those three records. Also note that the big-hearted Filter property leaves the cursor pointing at the first record that meets the Filter criteria. If there were no such records, EOF and BOF would be True.

You can remove a Filter by applying the adFilterNone constant from the FilterGroupEnum enumeration as follows:

```
rs.Filter = adFilterNone
```

This is the only value from the enumeration that we'll cover in this chapter, although it will receive more attention in Chapter 6.

The most commonly used type of Filter will be of the "WHERE clause" variety. Here's an example that combines a compound And, a Null value, and a wildcard:

```
Dim rs As Recordset

Set rs = getParts
rs.Filter = "part like 'B%' and description <> Null"

While Not rs.EOF
   Print rs("part"), rs("description")
   rs.MoveNext
Wend
Print rs.RecordCount
```

This example prints

BENEDICK	a young lord of Padua
BALTHASAR	attendant on Don Pedro
BORACHIO	follower of Don John
BEATRICE	niece to Leonato
4	

As you'll see later in the chapter, once the Recordset has been optimized, searching with Filter is amazingly efficient and convenient. I routinely use this technique, for example, when I want to identify those records in one Recordset with a foreign key that matches the primary key of a record in another Recordset. This works even when the key is a compound one because I can create a compound And statement using Filter. If, like me, you end up with a set of standard Filter-based functions, remember that it's considered polite to return a Recordset as you found it. This means making sure the Filter and current record are reset. Here's my template Filter modification function, stripped of its specific functionality (and its error handling):

```
Private Sub doSomething(rs As Recordset)
Dim vFilter As Variant
Dim vBookmark As Variant
vFilter = rs.Filter
vBookmark = rs.Bookmark
rs.Filter = <apply my filter>
'do my operation
rs.Filter = vFilter
rs.Bookmark = vBookmark
End Sub
```

It's very annoying when you are debugging your code and you find that a function you called changed the Filter property on your Recordset. If anything, this exemplifies one of the potential pitfalls of ADO—its power makes it all too easy to leave something in an unexpected state.

rs.Sort

One of VB's weakpoints over the years has been its lack of decent sorting capabilities.[10] It may please you to know that Recordsets have excellent built-in sorting—so good in fact, that you may be tempted to fabricate Recordsets simply in order to sort data.

Just as applying a Filter is rather like specifying an SQL-like WHERE clause, sorting is achieved by assigning an SQL-like ORDER BY clause to the Sort property. This means you can apply multiple sort columns and determine the direction of the sort using "ASC" and "DESC" as qualifiers (ASC is the default).

Sorting can be as simple as

```
rs.Sort = "part"
```

after which, iterating will reveal records in alphabetical order.

More complex sorting can be achieved. The following example is combined with a Filter:

```
rs.Filter = "part < 'D' and description <> Null"
rs.Sort = "description, part DESC"
```

If this were printed, the result would be:

CLAUDIO	a young lord of Florence
BENEDICK	a young lord of Padua
BALTHASAR	attendant on Don Pedro
CONRADE	follower of Don John
BORACHIO	follower of Don John
ANTONIO	Leonato's brother
BEATRICE	niece to Leonato

These results are sorted by description (first), but the two followers of Don John are sorted in descending order by part. If DESC was removed or replaced with ASC, these two records would be reversed.

When you set the Sort property, ADO builds a temporary index in client memory which is then used when working with records. In other words, the data itself isn't physically sorted, rather, the index is used to

---

10. OO languages with inheritance have the edge over VB6 when it comes to sorting because it's so easy to create data structures that can inherit and then specialize sorting functionality.

provide the required order. The index construction is very efficient and makes ADO sorting a pleasant experience. You can also optimize the Recordset so that the index is preconstructed (see the later section on "Recordset Optimizations"), making the sort operation appear faster still.

In This Section

We saw some of the features that make Recordsets an extremely powerful data structure to work with. The Find feature provides a standard search operation, similar to the Find methods in DAO. The more impressive Filter and Sort provide a great deal of power for client-side data manipulation, placing on the desktop functionality that previously required additional database queries or (for nondatabase data) that was only achievable through complex and inefficient client-side code.[11]

Working with Pages

rs.PageSize
rs.PageCount
rs.PageSize
rs.AbsolutePage

Paging is a navigational technique that allows you to split a Recordset into pages for presentation purposes. It doesn't do anything that can't be achieved using AbsolutePosition and RecordCount, but it does save the tedious arithmetic otherwise involved. Three properties are involved in Recordset paging:

1. **PageSize**: You set this property to specify how many records should appear on a page.

2. **PageCount**: This read-only property tells you how many pages there are. It's based on dividing PageSize by RecordCount.

3. **AbsolutePage**: You set this property to turn to a particular page. It's equivalent to AbsolutePosition, but with page-granularity instead of record-granularity.

---

11. There is an interesting design issue here. Does *fat client* mean too much processing on the client, or too much *custom* processing on the client? Fancy client-side custom processing raises all kinds of issues about software management and deployment. However, if your code uses heavy client-side processing based on built-in functionality (as provided by the ADO Client Cursor Engine) does that make it a fat client in the negative sense of the phrase? The ADO angle is that you can offload server processing without increasing the complexity of the client by using standard, powerful functions such as Sort and Filter. These days, most desktops are more than capable of performing these functions, so why not increase scalability and response times by delegating these tasks to the client computer? We'll return to this issue again, in particular when we look at Browser functionality.

The following code, which prints random pages, shows you all there is to know about paging.

```
Dim rs As Recordset
Dim iRecs As Integer

Set rs = getParts
rs.Sort = "part"                    typically, these three lines would
rs.PageSize = 4                     only execute once

                                                     assigns a random
Cls                                                  page number
rs.AbsolutePage = CInt(Rnd * (rs.PageCount - 1)) + 1

Print "Page: " & rs.AbsolutePage
For iRecs = 1 To rs.PageSize
   Print rs("part"), rs("description")
   rs.MoveNext
   If rs.EOF Then Exit For
Next
```

It prints (for example)

Page: 5	
MARGARET	gentlewoman attending on Hero
MESSENGER	Null
SECOND WATCHMAN	Null
SEXTON	Null

Note that the `AbsolutePage` property is another Move method in disguise. The `Exit For` is required because the last page may not contain exactly the number of records as defined by PageSize.

In This Section

We looked at how ADO makes it easy to split a Recordset into pages for more convenient presentation.

Modification Operations

Reading data is easy. Making changes to data is far more complex and the cause of much woe. If only all programs could be read-only, programmers would be held in higher regard and the software industry would be in much better shape.[12] Here are just a few of the things that account for this complexity:

1. When data is static, the data on your user interface, in your Recordset, and in your data source will all be the same. As soon as anything changes, you have to take responsibility for the way these layers are synchronized (and we all hate responsibility).

2. Users change their mind. They like to be able to cancel everything halfway through an update (users pay our salaries, so we have to pander to their foibles).

3. Things go wrong at crucial points. If all we ever do is read data it's easy enough to repeat the process, but repeating a partially successful multirecord update, such as a typical banking transaction, is unlikely to put things right.

4. Just as you are about to do your update, some other user goes and changes one of the records that matters to you, making your update unsafe. Sorting this out is your responsibility too.

5. Users always seem to want to do all their updates at the same time. Therefore, we have to ensure our system runs efficiently at peak throughput, rather than just average throughput. Peak throughput can easily be ten times the average.

The good news is that the software industry has come up with some very good ideas to tackle these problems, and the even better news is that ADO uses (or can be used with) all of them. The bad news is that the problem is still complex, and large chunks of this book will deal with it. In this section, we'll only cover the basic operations.

The first thing you need to be aware of when dealing with modifications is the many different states that your system might be in, all of which impact your modification strategy.

1. **Transactional/Non-Transactional**: If you are making modifications within a ***transaction***, then all changes are deferred until the transaction commits (if it commits). We'll deal with transactions in Chapters 4 and 14.

---

12. There is a flaw in this logic.

2. **Multiuser/Single User:** Systems that only allow a single user to perform updates are fairly simple. When multiple users might update at the same time, you have to handle the implications of this. We'll start looking at these issues in Chapter 3.

rs.LockType

3. **Batch/Immediate:** The usual mode of operation with ADO is known as Immediate mode. In Immediate mode, modifications take place on a row-by-row basis. As soon as you update a row, the data source (if there is one) is notified of the change. However, by changing the LockType property, you can have the Recordset keep track of all changes without troubling the data source. At the appropriate time, you can issue a single instruction to update the data source with all the changes made. This mode of operation is called Batch. Batch mode is becoming increasingly important, as it allows updates to be made even when there is no connection to the data source. A connection is only required when the batch update takes place, dramatically reducing the number and duration of connections required by the application (which is a good thing). The difference between the two modes is very important when working with a data source. Chapter 3 will deal with Immediate mode updating when using an SQL data source, and Chapter 6 will deal with Batch mode.

It so happens that when you create a fabricated Recordset, its default mode of operation is Batch. For the purpose of this section we want to work in Immediate mode, so we'll use a function called getPartsImmediate that creates the same data as getParts, but overrides the default behavior of a fabricated Recordset to use a LockType that provides Immediate mode updating. The first three lines of this function are

```
Public Function getPartsImmediate() As Recordset
```

```
Dim rs As New Recordset
rs.LockType = adLockOptimistic          ⟵——————  this is the only line that
                                                 differs from getParts
```

We'll talk more about the LockType property in later chapters. It can have one of several values, only one of which (adLockBatchOptimistic) places the Recordset in Batch mode. By selecting adLockOptimistic, we are selecting a value that supports updates in Immediate mode.

rs.Update

There are ways you can change data in a Recordset. You can modify an existing record, delete an existing record, or add new records. We'll begin with modifying existing records. In the "parts" Recordset we've been using, the character VERGES is described as a headborough. No, I don't know what it means either, but my dictionary defines a *headborough* as a petty constable.[13] So I'm going to update VERGES' description to be a bit more meaningful. I hope he doesn't mind. The definition of Update is as follows:

Sub Update([Fields],
                 [Values])

Syntactically, Update is very similar to AddNew, and we can use it in a number of different ways. The following technique will be more familiar to DAO and RDO programmers:

```
Dim rs As Recordset
Set rs = getPartsImmediate
rs.Filter = "description = 'a headborough'"
rs!Description = "a petty constable"  ←——————  assign new value
rs.Update                                        to the Field
Print rs("part"), rs("description")
```

This prints

VERGES	a petty constable

In this example, field-specific changes are made to the current record, and then Update is called explicitly to trigger the update process. ADO also allows you to supply arguments to the Update method, in which case you can provide one or more field names and field values, as the following examples show:

```
'update a single column of current record
rs.Update "description", "a petty constable"

'update multiple columns of current record
rs.Update Array("part", "description"), _     ←——— field name array
          Array("DIBBLE", "an officer")       ←——— field value array
```

If you choose to use this approach, be sure that you include all changes to the same row in a single Update statement. The reason for this is that each call to Update will involve a call to your data source (if you have one) unless you are in Batch mode.

Because ADO lets you assign directly to a Field, you may be wondering what happens if you don't call Update after making changes, and what

---

13. True, this is only marginally more meaningful, but it's an improvement. I am no historian, but I understand that folks used to organize themselves into groups of ten households and elect a representative or leader—a headborough.

sort of state the record is in prior to calling Update. To understand this, we need to meet some new properties.

rs.EditMode

EditMode is a property of a Recordset, but it applies to the current record. Its data type is the EditModeEnum enumeration that has the following values:

0: adEditNone

1: adEditInProgress

2: adEditAdd

4: adEditDelete

fd.Value
fd.OriginalValue
fd.UnderlyingValue

Field objects have the following properties that are extremely useful when you are making any sort of modification:

Value

OriginalValue

UnderlyingValue

You have already met Value, and you know that even if you don't type it that often, this is the property that actually lets you access the data that the Recordset contains. OriginalValue contains the value that the Field held prior to any edits within this Recordset. UnderlyingValue contains the value currently held in the data source the Recordset was built from, including changes made by other users since we opened the Recordset. As our Recordset is fabricated, we won't pay much attention to it right now.

The following program traces the state of a record at different stages during the update.

```
Dim rs As Recordset
Set rs = getPartsImmediate
With rs.Fields("description")
  rs.Filter = "description = 'a headborough'"

  Print "EM = " & rs.EditMode, "V = " & .Value, _
      "OV = " & .OriginalValue
  rs!Description = "a petty constable"        ◄──────  make the change
  Print "EM = " & rs.EditMode, "V = " & .Value, _
      "OV = " & .OriginalValue
  rs.Update                                   ◄──────  call Update
  Print "EM = " & rs.EditMode, "V = " & .Value, _
      "OV = " & .OriginalValue
End With
```

EM = EditMode
OV = OriginalValue

39

It prints

EM = 0	V = a headborough	OV = a headborough
EM = 1	V = a petty constable	OV = a headborough
EM = 0	V = a petty constable	OV = a petty constable

In other words, as soon as one field value on the record has changed, the record automatically enters edit mode (adEditInProgress), and the original value is maintained in the OriginalValue property. Once Update is called, the edit mode is reset (adEditNone), and the original value is lost. It's important to realize that this is the process for Immediate update mode. As you'll see in Chapter 6, it works quite differently in Batch update mode.

rs.CancelUpdate

There are actually three different ways in which you can "round off" an update:

1. Explicitly use Update (as discussed previously, with or without arguments).

2. Call CancelUpdate. This restores the original value for all fields in the Recordset and sets EditMode back to adEditNone.

3. Move off the current record. This triggers an implicit Update if any fields have changed. This is the opposite behavior from using DAO or RDO, where moving off the current record triggers an implicit CancelUpdate.

Update, CancelUpdate, EditMode, and the properties of the Field object provide the tools to take control of the Update process. You can offer users a very versatile interface for updating records based on this model.

rs.AddNew

Adding records to a Recordset is similar in many ways to updating existing records. You have already seen enough of the AddNew method to know that it can be used with field and value arguments, or with the more traditional approach of direct assignment to fields.

When AddNew is used without arguments, a new record is created, and EditMode assumes the value of adEditAdd (2). EditMode will keep this value until either Update or CancelUpdate is called or the current record is changed. If CancelUpdate is called, the new record is deleted and the cursor resets to the record it was pointing at prior to the call to AddNew.

rs.Delete

Deleting records is achieved using the Delete method, which has the following definition:

Sub Delete([AffectRecords As AffectEnum = adAffectCurrent])

The usual way of using Delete is simply to remove the current record from the Recordset. Poor old VERGES is having a bad day because he is just about to be removed from the play. (This is only temporary as there is no data source at present, and the only way you could make the change persistent would be to save the entire Recordset to a file, as discussed early on in this chapter).

```
Dim rs As Recordset
Set rs = getPartsImmediate
Print rs.RecordCount

rs.Filter = "description = 'a headborough'"
rs.Delete                          ◄——————— delete the current record
rs.Filter = adFilterNone
Print rs.RecordCount
```

prints

```
23
22
```

When operating on the current record, the record remains current even after the Delete method is called, although there is very little you can do with it, and the best policy is to reposition the cursor after a delete. Full marks if you recall that the EditModeEnum contains a value called adEditDelete. How, you may be wondering, can I access a deleted field? Well, you can, under special circumstances, when operating in Batch mode. All will be revealed in due course.

In This Section

We tool a first look at modification and learned the major distinction between Immediate mode and Batch mode updating. Understanding the state model of a modification operation gives you a high degree of control over what happens during Updates, AddNews, and Deletes. This is a topic that will receive much greater attention later.

ADO Data Types and Attributes

We've played quite a bit with the data in a Recordset without worrying too much about what sort of data it is. Field objects and the data they provide access to can behave quite differently depending on the nature of the data within. It's not only the standard notion of data types (such as Char, Integer, or Double) that accounts for these differences. Fields can also have "attributes" that give them special behaviors.

Data Types

We'll look at data types first. ADO defines at least 40 data types, a number which has swelled to include not only a comprehensive range of database-oriented data types, but also explicit support for COM objects and *Unicode*, as well as a Variant data type. This is more data types than are defined in VB, which limits the extent to which we can exploit all these data types when using fabricated Recordsets. We'll see how VB handles data types returned from SQL-based Providers in Chapter 3.

The Value property of a Field is always a Variant. While this places a performance penalty on all ADO operations, it makes life very convenient. It allows the same property to be used regardless of the data type and provides a means for handling Null values,. Nevertheless, VB Variants have subtypes that define the type of data currently being held in the Variant. It is illuminating to look at the subtypes (and other data type information) reported from VB when using the more common ADO data types. To create the following table, I defined a Recordset where each field is of a different data type. I then ran the following code:

```
rs.Open
rs.AddNew

For Each f In rs.Fields
  f.Value = 0
  Print f.Name, f.Type, TypeName(f.Value), _
        f.DefinedSize, f.ActualSize
Next
```

fd.Type
fd.DefinedSize
fd.ActualSize

This code introduces three properties of the Field object that we haven't paid much attention to yet. Type is the ADO data type created, and the values come from the DataTypeEnum as defined by ADO. DefinedSize is the number of bytes allocated to the Field, while the ActualSize is the number of bytes actually used. In this example, 0 has been assigned to each Field's value to produce the following results:

Field.Name	Field.Type	TypeName	Defined Size	Actual Size
adChar	129	String	12	12
adVarChar	200	String	12	1
adLongVarChar	201	String	12	1
adInteger	3	Long	4	4
adSmallInt	2	Integer	2	2
adBigInt	20	Decimal	8	8
adSingle	4	Single	4	4
adDouble	5	Double	8	8
adDecimal	14	Decimal	16	16
adNumeric	131	Decimal	19	19
adCurrency	6	Currency	8	8
adBoolean	11	Boolean	2	2
adDate	7	Date	8	8
adDBDate	133	Date	6	6
adDBTime	134	Date	6	6
adDBTimeStamp	135	Date	16	16

A number of useful guidelines for ADO data type processing can be extracted from this example:

1. A Field defined as adChar will always have the same number of characters in it, regardless of what you assign to it. ADO will pad the field out with blanks. Ignoring the data source implications of choosing between adChar and adVarChar, it's nearly always the case that adVarChar fields are easier to process in VB code. For example, any string you create to compare to an adChar field (for example, in a Find or Filter operation) will need to be padded out to the same length.

2. An ADO Integer is *not* the same as a VB Integer. The former is 4 bytes while the latter is 2 bytes. Therefore, if your Field is defined as adInteger, use a VB Long to hold its value, not an Integer variable.[14]

3. Numbers that are too big to store in a Double or Long can still be processed in VB. Such numbers can be handled by the Decimal subtype of a Variant. Decimal doesn't exist as its own data type in VB, so you must use a Variant to handle really big numbers. See the later section on "Decimal and Numeric Data Types" for more on Decimals.

14. VB is still haunted by its 16-bit past.

Attributes

fd.Attributes

There are many things about a piece of data that aren't necessarily encapsulated by its data type.[15] The data type doesn't tell you whether the data can be updated or whether it forms part of a record's ***primary key***. There are other useful bits of information that you may be able to deduce from the data type, such as whether the field has a fixed size length, but it's simpler to get the information directly. This is what the Attributes property is for. We met Attributes when first creating a fabricated Recordset. We can specify Attributes when creating a Field before the Recordset is open. Once the Recordset has been opened, we can read the attributes of a Field through the read-only Attributes property. Just like the State property, the Attributes property is overloaded with many values and must be accessed using a bitmask. Some of the common bitmasks (which are defined in the FieldAttributeEnum enumeration) are listed in Table 2-2.

Table 2-2. Bitmask Constants for the fd.Attributes Property

BITMASK CONSTANT(S)	DESCRIPTION
adFldFixed	True for fixed size data types.
adFldUpdatable, adFldUnknownUpdatable	Provide information about whether the field can be updated.
adFldIsNullable, adFldMayBeNull	Provide information about whether you are able/required to handle Nulls.
adFldKeyColumn, adFldRowID, adFldRowVersion	Provide information about fields used to uniquely identify records or to track updates. These will be discussed further in Chapter 3.
adFldLong, adFldMayDefer, adFldCacheDeferred	Fields that contain large amounts of binary data can and often should be handled differently from other Fields. These attributes help you identify such Fields and will be discussed further in Chapter 3.
adFldNegativeScale	See the following section on "Decimal and Numeric Data Types."

---

15. A piece of data is, of course, a datum. However, it sounds plain wrong using such a word when writing about computers.

Decimal and Numeric Data Types

To store numbers that aren't integers, it's standard practice to use a single- or double-precision floating point number and live with rounding errors. When rounding errors can't be accepted, many databases support special data types known as Numeric or Decimal. Visual Basic is capable of handling these numbers using Variants with a subtype of Decimal. Decimals in VB are stored as 12-byte signed integers scaled by a variable power of 10. The power of 10 scaling factor determines the number of digits to the right of the decimal point, and ranges from 0 to 28.

fd.Precision
fd.NumericScaleADO provides two Field properties for working with Decimals: Precision and NumericScale. These properties let you use noninteger numbers with a known level of accuracy. Precision specifies the total number of digits to be used to store a number on either side of the decimal point. NumericScale determines just the number of decimal places. In theory at least, NumericScale could be negative (meaning numbers are accurate to some multiple of ten), in which case the adFldNegativeScale bitmask could be used with the Attributes property to test if this capability is supported. In practice, it rarely is.

You can specify fd.Precision and fd.NumericScale for Decimal or Numeric fields created in fabricated Recordsets. Once the Recordset is open, they become read-only properties. Here's an example:

```
Dim rs As New Recordset
rs.Fields.Append "adPi", adDecimal
rs.Fields("adPi").Precision = 6          ⟵——————  maximum number of digits
rs.Fields("adPi").NumericScale = 3       ⟵———————  maximum number
rs.Open                                              of decimal places
rs.AddNew "adPi", 3.1415926535
Print rs.Fields("adPi").Value
```

which prints

```
3.141
```

This field will maintain three decimal places (the value of NumericScale).

In This Section

We addressed several properties of the Field object that relate to data that it stores, most notably, the Type and Attributes properties. We have also seen how ADO and VB handle Decimal data.

Introducing Property Objects

ADO has been designed to support a huge range of different types of data sources and to allow new types of Providers to be developed as required. While some properties are required on ADO objects regardless of the source of data, ADO was designed with the principle that Providers should be able to define new properties as required.

rs.Properties
fd.Properties

As you have seen, there is a range of properties built into the Recordset and Field objects, and the properties are accessed using the "object.property" notation. These are sometimes called the *static* properties of an object. An even wider range of properties is available in the form of Property objects, belonging to the Properties collection of each of the major ADO objects. Property objects are added to the Properties collections by the Provider or by ADO services such as the Client Cursor Engine. Because Property objects aren't predefined by ADO, they are also known as *dynamic* properties. You should employ defensive programming techniques when testing for specific dynamic properties because different Providers are free to provide different dynamic properties, so if you change Providers, the dynamic property you are looking for may no longer be there.

py.Name
py.Type
py.Value
py.Attributes

All dynamic properties are objects with a Name, a Type, a Value, and an Attributes property.[16] The Attributes property should be accessed using bitmasks from the PropertyAttributesEnum, which defines the following values:

adPropNotSupported

adPropRequired

adPropOptional

adPropRead

adPropWrite

Using dynamic properties is generally very simple, as long as you know the name of the property you want. For example

```
Print rs.Properties("Cursor Engine Version")
```

prints

25

indicating that I am using version 2.5 of the ADO Client Cursor Engine.

---

16. It's easy to get confused when discussing the properties of a Property object (which isn't a property but a member of a Properties collection, which itself not only has properties (which aren't Property objects), but is a property of a non-Property object (which is any ADO object that isn't itself a Property or Properties object). I hope I've cleared this up.

Some dynamic properties are more complex and use overloaded values, so bitmasks are required. Many of the more complex properties give you access to underlying OLE DB information and are defined by OLE DB, rather than ADO enumerations and data types. As a taste of what is available if you are prepared to look for it, many Providers support the Filter Operations property which informs you which operations can be used in a Filter property assignment. For example

```
Print rs.Properties("Filter Operations").Value
```

prints

```
27
```

This means nothing until you refer to the OLE DB documentation, which defines the OLE DB enumerations shown in Table 2-3 for this property.

Table 2-3. Bitmask Constants for Filter Operations

CONSTANT	VALUE	DESCRIPTION
DBPROPVAL_CO_EQUALITY	1	Supports LT, LE, EQ, etcetera
DBPROPVAL_CO_STRING	2	Supports Beginswith operations
DBPROPVAL_CO_CASESENSITIVE	4	Case sensitive search
DBPROPVAL_CO_CASEINSENSITIVE	8	Case insensitive search
DBPROPVAL_CO_CONTAINS	16	Supports "contains" and "not contains" operations
DBPROPVAL_CO_BEGINSWITH	32	Supports "Beginswith" and "not Beginswith" operations

From this definition, it's possible to deduce certain capabilities of the Filter operation for the Provider. For example, by working out which combination of bitmask constants add up to 27, you can work out which Filter Operations are supported by the ADO Client Cursor Engine.

You'll meet many other Property objects as I address specific ADO functionality throughout the book.

We looked at ADO's dynamic property objects. .

Recordset Optimizations

No matter how fast computers become, good developers are always interested in writing efficient code. A great deal of the scope for optimizing ADO
applications concerns the mode of interaction with data sources, and
Chapter 3 addresses optimization issues for SQL data sources.

Regardless of the data source however, there are several ways in which
you can exploit your knowledge of the Recordset and Field objects to
enhance performance. We'll look at some of these in this section.

fd.Value

One of the most effective ways in which Recordset usage can be optimized is by tuning the most heavily used operation—basic data retrieval
from fields. Right at the beginning of this chapter, you saw that there are
several ways in which a Field's value can be retrieved. In most cases, the
following listing achieves the same end:

```
x = rs.Fields("part").Value
x = rs!part
```

If you are completely aware of how these operations work, you can
exploit this fact to improve performance. For example, it's quite common
to iterate through a Recordset, retrieving or operating on one or more
fields in each row. Each time you call rs!part, you know that behind the
scenes, ADO is retrieving the Fields collection, getting the Field object
keyed by "part" from that collection, and accessing the Value property
on that Field object. In a Recordset of 10,000 records, ADO is doing this
10,000 times for each Field accessed during a complete iteration.

Most of these lookups can be avoided by setting an explicit reference
to the Field objects prior to the iteration. Compare the two approaches in
the following code, which iterates through the "words" Recordset (which
contains over 12,000 records) and assigns values from two of its fields to
local variables:

```
Dim rs As Recordset
Dim t As Double
Dim sWord As String
Dim lLength As Long
Set rs = New Recordset
```

```
rs.Open FILE_SOURCE_PATH & "words.rs"
rs.MoveFirst
t = Timer                    ◄─────────  using the Timer function gives
                                         reasonable accuracy for this operation
While Not rs.EOF
    sWord = rs!word          ◄─────────  ADO's convenient syntax hides the amount
                                         of work really going on here
    lLength = rs!length
    rs.MoveNext
Wend
t = Timer - t
Print "Slow Method", Format(t, "0.00")


Dim fdWord As Field
Dim fgLength As Field
rs.MoveFirst
t = Timer
Set fdWord = rs("word")
Set fdlength = rs("length")
While Not rs.EOF
    sWord = fdWord.Value      ◄─────────  this approach involves a bit more
    lLength = fdlength.Value             typing, but is considerably faster
    rs.MoveNext
Wend
t = Timer - t
Print "Fast Method",Format(t, "0.00")
```

It prints

Slow Method	0.47
Fast Method	0.30

For any Recordset of more than a few dozen records, the second approach is 50% to 100% faster.

rs.Collect

In order to understand ADO, it's important to appreciate that in nearly all circumstances, you access the data in a Recordset via a Field object, even if it's implicit.

This isn't the case for GetString and GetRows. There is one other feature, which is rarely mentioned, and this is the Collect property.

```
x = rs.Collect("part")
rs.Collect("part") = x
```

Collect allows you to access the data in a specific field of a record without involving a Field object. When you are operating on multiple records it's still not as efficient as the fast method in the Fast/Slow comparison we examined, but it's very efficient when you only want to access a single record, which would be the case when you are retrieving records using a unique key, for example.

The Collect property is marked as hidden in the ADO Recordset definition, which is why it won't appear in VB IntelliSense or in the Object Browser. But if you use a tool like the OLE COM Viewer, you'll see that it has been part of the Recordset's definition since (at least) ADO 1.5. It can't be removed from ADO without breaking COM's compatibility rules.

rs.AddNew

It's also possible to optimize the AddNew method, if you are likely to perform a large number of inserts on an open Recordset (although if you are working with an SQL data source, it's often better to perform inserts using a stored procedure, as you'll see in Chapter 5). We looked at this optimization earlier in this chapter, but it's worth repeating here for completeness. It's measurably more efficient to add rows by passing data as arguments to the AddNew method, as opposed to calling AddNew with no arguments, and then setting values individually on the newly created record. The optimization is enhanced if you declare the array of field names once, and then use it in each AddNew statement. As a reminder, this is how that efficient syntax looks:

```
varrFields = Array("part", "description")
rs.ddNew varrFields, Array("DON PEDRO", "prince of Arragon")
rs.AddNew varrFields, Array("DON JOHN", "Don Pedro's bastard brother")
```

rs.Find
rs.Filter

If you are planning on using the Find or Filter features of ADO Recordsets, there is an optimization technique that can have a significant impact on your performance. The ADO Client Cursor Engine has the built-in capability to create local indexes on the fields of a Recordset. These indexes have nothing to do with any indexes maintained by the Provider you are using, and must be created each time you open the Recordset, but they will give you the same kind of performance gain on client-side operations as traditional database indexes do to server-side searches.

fd.Properties

When the ADO Client Cursor Engine is being used, a dynamic property called "OPTIMIZE" appears in the Properties collection of each Field object. By setting this property to True or False you can create and destroy client-side indexes on a Field-by-Field basis. If the OPTIMIZE property is True, ADO will automatically use these indexes when Find and Filter operations are applied, and the performance gains can be staggering.

The following example shows how to use this feature, and it's followed by some indicative times. This code applies a Filter and retrieves the Record-Count of the filtered Recordset. The Filter used identifies 42 records from the original 12,000. The Filter is applied 100 times to get an accurate figure. The entire loop is executed twice. The OPTIMIZE property is set to True between the executions to reveal the time difference.

```
Dim rs As Recordset
Dim t As Double
Dim i As Integer
Dim sWord As String
Dim lLength As Long
Set rs = New Recordset


rs.Open FILE_SOURCE_PATH & "words.rs"
rs.MoveFirst
t = Timer
For i = 1 To 100
rs.Filter = "length > 12"          ◄────────  apply the filter to an
lLength = rs.RecordCount                       unoptimized Field
rs.Filter = ""
Next
t = Timer - t
Print "Slow Method", Format(t, "0.00")
                                              ─────────── optimize the Field
t = Timer                          ▼
rs("length").Properties("OPTIMIZE") = True
Print "Time to build index = ", Format(Timer - t, "0.00")
For i = 1 To 100
rs.Filter = "length > 12"          ◄────────  apply the filter to an
lLength = rs.RecordCount                       optimized Field
rs.Filter = ""
Next
t = Timer - t
Print "Fast Method", Format(t, "0.00")
```

It prints

```
Slow Method    4.01
Time to build index =          0.06
Fast Method    0.09
```

What's important about these times is their relative magnitude. I am not claiming to have a clinical benchmarking rig, but I do know that I get similar results in a whole range of real life system configurations.

The most impressive aspect of this process is the speed with which the indexes are constructed. This makes it entirely reasonable to use the technique in a totally dynamic, "on demand" fashion. If you are going to carry out even a few Filter or Find operations, it's well worth constructing a client index by using the dynamic OPTIMIZE property.

As mentioned in the section "Find, Sort, and Filter," client-side index construction is also applied when you use the Sort property on a Recordset. If an index has not already been created, setting the Sort property will cause ADO to create an index, which is then used to make iteration on the sorted Recordset efficient. One word of warning is required, however. When a Sort criterion has been applied, the client-side indexes are no longer used for Find and Filter purposes, and the performance of these operations goes back to unoptimized levels. This can be remedied by setting the Sort property back to an empty string. If you don't want to lose the sort order, but want to regain the performance, consider using a Clone (see the following section on "Cloning").

It's very important to remember that the indexing, sorting, and searching are performed entirely in client memory—there is no server or network involvement at all. On client PCs with a reasonable specification, this fact can significantly improve the scalability of your applications by relieving servers and networks of unwanted loading. Such thinking takes the idea of optimization into new dimensions, which will be explored in later chapters.

In This Section

We saw how to optimize data retrieval from Recordsets by holding direct references to Field objects instead of referencing them indirectly via the Recordset itself. We also looked at how the Collect and AddNew methods can be used to enhance performance. Finally, we saw how client-side indexes can be applied using the OPTIMIZE property to enhance Find and Filter operations.

Cloning

What science-fiction predicts, ADO delivers. Cloning in ADO allows you to create multiple Recordset objects representing the same Recordset data. What this means is that Clone is a bad name for this feature, because a Clone is a physical copy of a thing, not an alternative reference to it. To understand how cloning works, it's important to separate out the actual data in a Recordset (which is private to ADO) and the objects (and their properties) we use to access that data. Figure 2-5 shows you what I mean.

rs.Clone

Figure 2-5 shows a Recordset object, its associated fields, and a variable called rsOriginal that points to the Recordset. These objects refer

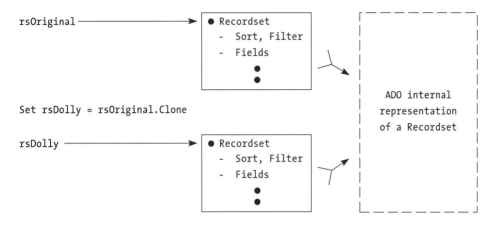

Figure 2-5. Two Clones sharing the same internal representation

rs.Sort
rs.Filter
rs.Find
rs.Bookmark

into an internal Recordset data structure, visible only to ADO. We don't know what is inside this data structure (and because Microsoft could change it any time, it would be dangerous to assume too much), but from what we know of the different ways we can access this data, we can infer that it isn't contained either in a Recordset object or in Field objects directly.

When you create a Clone, copies of these objects are created, but both the original and the Clone point at the same internal data structure. What this means is that properties of the objects, such as the current record and the Sort and the Filter properties, behave independently, but changes made to the data are seen by all Clones.

The following code sample illustrates a number of the characteristics of cloning:

```
Dim rs As Recordset
Dim rsDolly As Recordset
Set rs = New Recordset
Set rs = getParts

rs.Sort = "part desc"
Set rsDolly = rs.Clone              ⟵———— Dolly is a clone
rsDolly.Filter = "part > 'M'"
Print , "Original", "Clone"
Print "Records:", rs.RecordCount, rsDolly.RecordCount
Print "Sort:", rs.Sort, rsDolly.Sort
Print "Filter:", rs.Filter, rsDolly.Filter
Print "Current:", rs!part, rsDolly!part
```

```
Print
rs!Description = "A watchman"  ◄──────── change some data through rs
                                         which will be visible via Dolly

rsDolly!Description = "a petty constable"  ◄──────  change some data
rs.Bookmark = rsDolly.Bookmark            ◄──────   through Dolly which
Print rs!Description, rsDolly!Description            will be visible via rs

                                         make both objects point
Print                                    at the same physical
While Not rsDolly.EOF                     record using Bookmarks
  Print rs!Description, rsDolly!part, rsDolly!Description
  rsDolly.MoveNext          ◄──────────  iterate through Dolly's
Wend                                     view of the data
```

It prints

```
Original      Clone
Records:      23            7
Sort:         part desc
Filter:       0             part > 'M'
Current:      WATCHMAN      VERGES


a petty constable      a petty constable

a petty constable      VERGES           a petty constable
a petty constable      SEXTON           Null
a petty constable      MARGARET         gentlewoman attending on Hero
a petty constable      URSULA           gentlewoman attending on Hero
a petty constable      MESSENGER        Null
a petty constable      WATCHMAN         A watchman
a petty constable      SECOND WATCHMAN  Null
```

There is a fair bit to extract from these results. The first point is that Filter, Sort, and the current record act entirely independently, and this is regardless of whether they are set before or after the Clone is created. After the first set of print statements, rsDolly is pointing at VERGES (which will be the first record in the set created by the filter) while rs is pointing at WATCHMAN (because this is the first record on rs, after applying the reverse sort). Clones allow you to have multiple "current" records on the same Recordset.

At this point, the description associated with WATCHMAN is Null, but the code then alters this via rs. Although the new value adds little in the form of description, we should expect to see this value when later we iterate through Dolly's records.

When the description of Dolly's current record (VERGES) is set, you are able to see that the two Clones share the same Bookmarks. This is the only time when it's safe to apply the Bookmark from one Recordset to another, and helps to reinforce the point that two Recordset Clones point to the same underlying data representation (and its Bookmarks), held in memory by ADO.

Finally, we've iterated through the records as seen by Dolly. Satisfy yourself that the Filter, sort order, and the description values for VERGES and WATCHMAN are as you might expect.

Cloning may seem a bit esoteric, but it does have a number of practical applications. Perhaps its most common usage is it allows applications to maintain two "current" cursors on the same Recordset. While this effect can be simulated through the use of Bookmarks, cloning does make it easier. But perhaps more powerful is its ability to maintain completely different views of the same data.

With Clones, you can safely apply sorts and filters to a Recordset without affecting anyone else's view of it. For example, imagine that a user is looking at a large set of records, and she is using a filter to screen out those that aren't important to her. Whenever she makes a change, the application needs to recalculate some statistics based on the entire Recordset and display a warning if certain thresholds are exceeded. But you don't want to remove her filter, even temporarily, as this would certainly affect the display if she was using data-bound controls. Cloning provides you with an efficient way to solve this problem, as you can create a Clone with completely different navigational properties.

One final feature of Clones becomes apparent as soon as you look at the Clone function's formal definition:

Function Clone ([LockType As LockTypeEnum = adLockUnspecified])
                As Recordset

By default, the LockType of a clone is the same as the original Recordset. However, you can also provide the value adLockReadOnly. This allows you to stop Clones from being able to update the Recordset data and should make you feel comfortable about using Clones for a wide range of Recordset manipulation tasks.

In This Section

Cloning allows you to create Recordset objects based on the same Recordset data, which allows you to maintain multiple views of the same records.

Recordset Error Handling

ADO errors come in two forms. There are those generated by ADO itself and those generated by a Provider or some other underlying component supporting ADO.

ADO's own errors are handled by the error handling mechanism of the language in question—in our case, VB. Other errors are added as Error objects into the Errors collection of the ADO Connection object. These errors may or may not raise a VB error, depending on their severity. Error objects often provide far more information than the more simple ADO errors and we'll investigate this mechanism in detail in Chapter 4. Even when you haven't explicitly created a Connection object, there is often one available on the ActiveConnection property of the Recordset that can be used to provide detailed error information.

If, however, you have set this property to Nothing, or you are using fabricated Recordsets (as we are in this chapter), then the Errors collection isn't available, and you have to rely on VB trappable errors as raised by ADO.

A small set of error codes is defined in the ErrorValueEnum enuneration in ADO. While these cover many common errors, others can also arise, and they don't always come with any obvious documentation or explanation. Fortunately, you can query the Microsoft MSDN Knowledge Base with query number Q168354 for an additional list of common ADO error codes, and impress your friends with your sad but useful knowledge. Another option is to set a reference to the "OLE DB Errors Type Library." This defines OLE DB constants for a much wider set of common errors reported by ADO.

When the Connection object's Errors collection isn't available, use the VB Err object to query error information, in the time-honored VB way. For completeness, the following code sample shows VB error handling being used to trap ADO errors:

```
On Error GoTo ErrH
Dim rs As Recordset
Set rs = getParts
Do
  Print rs!part
  rs.MoveNext
Loop
Exit Sub
ErrH:
  Print Err.Number
  Print Err.Description
  Print Err.Source
  Print "Next time, remember to test for EOF!"
  Exit Sub
```

which prints

```
3021
Either BOF or EOF is True, or the current record has been deleted; the
operation requested by the application requires a current record.
ADODB.Field
Next time, remember to test for EOF!
```

We saw how to handle simple ADO errors when no ADO Connection object is available to provide more detailed error information.

Recordsets Compared to Other Data Structures

In this chapter, I've deliberately examined the Recordset as a standalone data structure and showed you the basic techniques available to manipulate it. I did this, in part, so you would become familiar with the basics of Recordsets, in isolation from the many different roles they perform.

But there is another reason for focusing on Recordsets alone. Many computer programs still manipulate internal data structures and commonly represent two-dimensional data structures. Reflect for a moment on the following list of techniques available for doing this:

- Two-dimensional array (typically of Variants)

- Array of User-defined Types

- Collection or Dictionary of objects

- Property Bag

- Recordset

Now consider the following list of operations commonly performed on such structures:

1. Navigation

2. Reading and writing values

3. Adding and removing rows

4. Searching and filtering

5. Sorting

6. Saving to and reading from files

7. Saving to and reading from databases

8. Passing as arguments within a process

9. Passing as arguments between processes

10. Binding to user interfaces

11. Raising events when changed

You can see what's coming. You have seen already how convenient Recordsets are for items 1 to 6. We'll explore throughout the rest of the book how Recordsets leave all the other options standing when considering items 7 to 11.[17]

From the perspective of ease of use, power, and flexibility, I contend that for all the previous operations, Recordsets are at least as good, and in most cases, far, far better than any of the other representations available. You might be able to argue for one or two exceptions, but in general, I am confident that you'll tend to agree.

The Data Structure Performance "Shoot-out"

When wise developers are offered something easier and more fun than what they are used to, their first question concerns performance. In order to find out how Recordsets measure up against some of our other favorite data structures I put together a performance shoot-out. In the shoot-out, each data structure was subjected to the same performance tests which represented common operations performed on two-dimensional data structures. When reviewing the following numbers, remember that I tested Recordsets on their weakest ground. We already accept that they are generally much easier to use and far more powerful than the other candidates.

---

17. This is no accident, nor is it the outlandish claim of an obsessive ADO-crazed author. Microsoft has deliberately made it so, as a result of massive investment.

I defined some data with four columns or fields in each row or record:

- Unique String (different for each record/row)

- Non-unique String

- Unique Long

- Non-unique Long

and implemented it using the following data structures:

- A fabricated, indexed Recordset

- A keyed Collection

- An array of User-Defined Types

- A Variant array

I created 10,000 records for each data structure in order to put the data structures under pressure. Each data structure had the four fields/columns mentioned previously. Some of the shoot-out tests were run 100 times to get accurate numbers, in which case I recorded the total, not the average, time. The full code for all these tests can be found on the companion CD. Once again, these are indicative numbers, not definitive benchmarks.

Performance Tests Applied in the "Shoot-out"

Here are details of each test applied:

1. **Create data.** Before you use a data structure, you need to be able to populate it. Each of the following tests placed the "same" data into the data structures.

2. **Iterate through data**. The code looped through each record or row, copying its four fields into local variables.

3. **Find one record based on one criteria.** The test created a random string (known to be one of those used in the data structure) and searched the unique string field of each data structure for that string. The test was repeated 100 times.

4. **Find *n* records based on one criteria.** The non-unique Long field of each record/row holds a random Long between 1 and 1/10 of the data set size. Therefore, there were about ten records matching each possible value. This means that an iterative search can't stop on the first hit—it must search right through the data set to find all the matches. The test was repeated 100 times.

5. **Find one record based on two criteria.** Both of the string fields were used in this search. Because of the way the data was populated, there was no guarantee that a match would be found; in fact, in 100 iterations an average of about 20 matches were made.

6. **Sort.** All records were sorted using the non-unique Long field.

The "Shoot-out" Results

Tables 2-4 and 2-5 show the results for all tests, for both uncompiled and compiled VB6 code.

Table 2-4. Shoot-out Results for Uncompiled Code with 10,000 Records

TEST	DESCRIPTION	ITERATIONS	RECORDSET	COLLECTION	UDT ARRAY	VNT ARRAY
1	Create	1	2.32s	1.26s	0.03s	0.46s
2	Iterate	1	0.58s	0.06s	0.02s	0.06s
3	Find 1 (1 field)	100	0.02s	0.02s	0.45s	1.15s
4	Find All (1 field)	100	0.09s	2.91s	0.43s	1.27s
5	Find 1 (2 fields)	100	0.07s	4.84s	1.55s	4.38s
6	Sort	1	0.66s	> 1 hour	54.33s	82.27s

Table 2-5. Shoot-out Results for Compiled Code with 10,000 Records

TEST	DESCRIPTION	ITERATIONS	RECORDSET	COLLECTION	UDT ARRAY	VNT ARRAY
1	Create	1	2.03s	1.03s	0.02s	0.16s
2	Iterate	1	0.52s	0.05s	0.02s	0.05s
3	Find 1 (1 field)	100	0.02s	0.01s	0.26s	0.88s
4	Find All (1 field)	100	0.08s	3.16s	0.03s	0.82s
5	Find 1 (2 fields)	100	0.07s	5.16s	0.88s	3.52s
6	Sort	1	0.59s	> 1 hour	5.88s	27.03s

Recordsets are very definitely slower to create and iterate through than any of the other data structures. This is explainable by the richness of the Recordset data structure, but might lead you to think that Recordsets are too inefficient for general data storage purposes. On the other hand, once you start manipulating data, the picture starts looking very different indeed. Overall, Recordsets are the most efficient. (I'm ignoring the fact that the Recordset sort required one line of code, while the Quick-Sort algorithm for array sorting was around fifty lines.) A keyed collection is efficient at searching, as long as you can search by its key, which is frequently not possible. Sorting collections is notoriously slow. There may be better algorithms than the one I used, but I used a standard one from a good text.[18] Arrays of User-defined Types are generally fast, although they are hard to work with (try supporting adds and deletes!), and each one requires custom coding to exploit its performance potential. Variant arrays are comparatively sluggish all round, even though they improve markedly by compiling.

Ten thousand records is a large data set, and it's safe to assume that for more typical data sets of less than a few hundred records that performance isn't that much of an issue (in client processes at least), unless you need to support a great deal of sorting. In this case, a powerful, general purpose, and easy-to-use data structure must be the highest priority. When performance is an issue, you can decide for yourself whether the sort and search capabilities of Recordsets make up for their comparatively slow creation and iteration.

In This Section

We compared the use of fabricated Recordsets to more traditional approaches to representing two-dimensional data. The comparison is highly favorable.

Summary

In this chapter I covered the basic machinery of Recordset and Field objects, using fabricated Recordsets. This approach allows you to ignore the impact of specific Providers as you come to terms with how Recordsets work. We:

- Looked at Recordset navigation techniques in depth.

- Began the exploration of how to use Recordsets to modify data.

---

18. I stopped my timing after one hour. For all I know, if I hadn't, it would still be running now.

- Introduced the idea of persisting Recordsets.

We also covered some fairly advanced topics, such as:

- The immediate mode update model.

- The use of Clones.

- Optimization techniques.

You should now have a clearer view of Recordsets as a powerful and efficient data structure—a far more powerful technique for data management than just a new syntax for working with databases.

As ADO develops and matures, the areas in which it is applied will undoubtedly broaden as the promise of "Universal Data Access" moves closer and closer to reality.

Right now however, ADO is still used more for relational database work than any other form of data, and the next chapter will take you into the heart of using Recordsets with SQL data sources.

Recordsets with SQL Data Sources

ADO and ODBC

The Open Method

Staying Connected—Cursor Control

Staying Connected—Lock Control

Examining the Fields Collection

Modifications and Locking with Client-side Cursors

Resynchronizing Connected Recordsets

Using Index and Seek

Processing Multiple Recordsets

Optimizations When Working with SQL Data Sources

Summary

IN THE PREVIOUS CHAPTER we looked in depth at the structure of a Recordset. In this chapter we'll deal exclusively with creating and using Recordsets generated by relational (SQL-based) databases. While there are many other sources of Recordsets, databases are the most common, and for developers already experienced in DAO (Data Access Objects) or RDO (Remote Data Objects), this will be the source of data they are most familiar with.

You have already seen that any Recordset can be in one of two distinct modes—Immediate or Batch—and that the mode has a big impact on how modifications to the Recordset work. There is another major distinction that affects Recordsets, which is related to, but separate from, these modification modes. When working with a data source such as a relational database, a Recordset can be either connected or disconnected. *Connected* Recordsets are what most database developers are used to—they allow you to maintain a live connection to the database while you are working with the Recordset. A *disconnected* Recordset shares some of the characteristics of the fabricated Recordsets you saw in the previous chapter, but the two shouldn't be confused. A disconnected Recordset is created from a data source and can be connected back to the data source at any time. It's just that you can release the live connection as soon as the Recordset has been created and continue using pretty much all the Recordset's functionality in disconnected mode. How and why you should find this useful is the subject of Chapter 7. In this chapter, we focus solely on connected Recordsets.

This chapter uses a database design with four tables based on the contents of Shakespeare's *Much ADO about Nothing*. The database schema is shown in the following diagram. Both the Scenes and the Parts tables are very small. The Words table contains over 10,000 records. The SceneContents table contains the entire text of the play, stored using one record per scene. This data has been loaded into both SQLServer 7 and Access 2000. Instructions for re-creating the database can be found on the CD which accompanies this book.

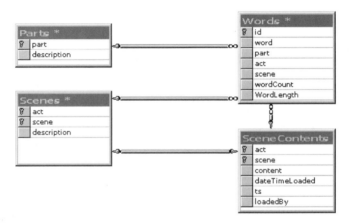

Figure 3-1. Data model for the MuchADO database

Opening and using a Recordset should be a very straightforward task, and it is. As you'll see however, there are many options available, which can greatly impact the performance and functionality of your programs, and it's worth spending time becoming familiar with these options and what they mean. Most of this chapter addresses these details. To make the most of it, I invite you to use the companion application (which is also on the accompanying CD) which I developed to create and test the examples presented in this chapter, and which you can use to explore the features of your own data sources.

ADO and ODBC

ADO does *not* require ODBC in order to access relational databases. In fact, ODBC will slowly and gracefully retire from the scene over the next few years. Why then do I begin a chapter on ADO and SQL by discussing the relationship between ADO and ODBC? There are various reasons:

- ODBC was the dominant data access technology throughout the 1990s. The development of ADO and OLE DB has been strongly influenced by the strengths and weaknesses of ODBC.

- ADO *can* be used with ODBC, and right now, many existing ADO applications exploit the maturity of ODBC drivers to deliver data access. For many people starting on new ADO applications, the use of ODBC remains a sensible option.

- It's easy to be confused about this relationship.

ODBC filled a vital gap in getting Windows applications to talk to databases. For example, getting VB to work with a relational database requires three things:

1. Queries or statements constructed using SQL or stored procedures that the database can execute.

2. A means of moving the queries or statements to the database and moving any results back to the VB program. Typically this means the use of some network protocol capable of moving data between VB client and database server, but in the simplest case (such as when working with a Jet [Access] database), this means nothing more than a function call into a DLL running in the VB client's *process*.

3. An interface that allows VB to interact with the database (for example, the interface must specify what function(s) should be called to cause an SQL statement to be executed and how the results should be retrieved into VB).

Database vendors have tended to implement more or less standard SQL in their products, at least as far as simpler queries are concerned. They have also provided *DLLs* that can be installed on PCs to take care of network communications, so that developers need only call the DLLs to do database work. The problem is that when most of the big database vendors started building their products there was no acceptable standard way of providing the interface for programmers to use, and so they all developed their own variations on a theme that covered connecting and disconnecting, executing statements, retrieving results, controlling transactions, setting and reading database properties and schema details, and processing errors.

ODBC was created to isolate programs and programmers from the differences between these interfaces, or APIs (Application Program Interfaces), so that programmers wouldn't need to write different bits of code for each database they wished to work with, or learn new interfaces each time they faced a new database. Just as important, it means that the same program can be connected to many different database engines, so long as they use the same database design.

ODBC achieves this isolation using exactly the same technique that is used to isolate programs from the differences between printers, graphic devices or many other computer subsystems. ODBC defines a single standard interface, and then allows drivers to be written to translate between the ODBC standard and the interface of any specific database. The general ODBC model can be shown graphically as follows:

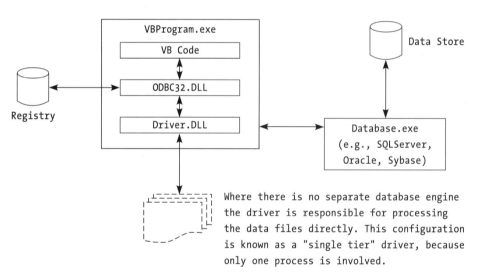

Figure 3-2. The architecture of an ODBC application

Client programs using ODBC always make calls through the ODBC Driver Manager, which (for 32-bit Windows) is a DLL called ODBC32.DLL that gets mapped into the client program's process. The Driver Manager has a published API that all client programs use. The client program passes a DSN (Data Source Name) into the Driver Manager to identify the database with which it wants to connect. This is the only information the client program needs to use that is specific to the database in question. The Driver Manager uses the DSN to query the Registry on the local machine to find out which driver to use, where the database is physically located, and other vital connection information.[1]

The Driver Manager loads the driver, which is then responsible for all communication with the database and translation to and from ODBC standards. From this point on, the Driver Manager simply routes client program calls to the correct driver and applies basic error trapping and reporting.

ODBC doesn't care how the driver performs its tasks, so long as it does them properly. Therefore, suppliers of ODBC middleware were able to produce many different driver "architectures," and Figure 3-2 and its description are only representative of the general arrangement.

Very few VB programmers program directly with the ODBC API.[2] Instead, most VBers use one or more of the approaches shown in Figure 3-3, based either on the DAO or RDO object libraries.

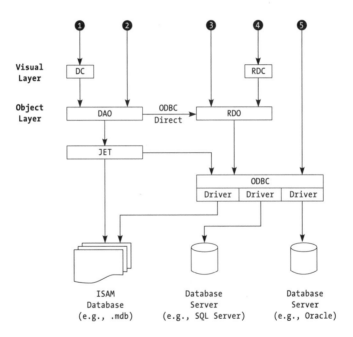

Figure 3-3. Visual Basic database access options prior to ADO

VB3 introduced DAO and its associated visual programming layer, ❶ the Jet Data Control (DC), which supported data-aware controls via data

---

1. This process requires that the information about the DSN is entered into each client computer's Registry. While DSNs provided an elegant way to hide all the connection information for a database behind a simple string, the need to hold information in the local Registry has proved a shortcoming of ODBC. Later versions of ODBC overcame this shortcoming, and the lessons learned have been adopted in ADO and OLE DB.

2. I was one of those few, on occasion. You could get incredible performance gains, especially in 16-bit environments where RDO could not be used. It was hard work though.

binding. ❷ DAO provides an object layer for interfacing to the Jet data access engine, which is primarily designed for working with .mdb database files as used by Access.[3]

A small corner of the Jet engine could act as an ODBC client program, and this facility opened up the potential for creating client-server database applications, with VB3 driving Jet, and Jet driving ODBC. Many people built such applications. Many people became despondent. In truth, many of these applications were successful, but they all suffered from far below optimal performance. ODBC was generally blamed for this poor performance, but the fact is that Jet used ODBC in an extremely inefficient way.

While Jet's ability to control ODBC did improve over time, Microsoft acknowledged that Jet was the culprit, and released ❸ RDO with the 32-bit Enterprise version of VB4. RDO looked and felt rather like DAO, but operated directly on the ODBC API, bypassing Jet. RDO proved much more efficient than DAO for working with relational databases, although it was slower than DAO when working with Jet .mdb files. RDO had its own visual component, ❹ the Remote Data Control (RDC) that could work with all existing data-aware controls. Later, Microsoft even released ODBCDirect—a bridging layer that allowed DAO programs to avoid the Jet engine when working with relational databases.[4] ODBCDirect was for the benefit of Access developers, many of whom were building applications which connected both to Jet data sources and SQL data sources. Microsoft's licensing of RDO prevented its distribution with Access applications and ODBCDirect provided a way around the licensing problem.

This then, was how things looked prior to the arrival of ADO. ODBC had matured into an efficient and robust open data access layer from which dozens of vendors made a living selling drivers for hundreds of databases. Thousands upon thousands of critical applications depended on ODBC. VB developers had a choice of data programming models. In some ways this choice was good, but in other ways, it left developers confused and forced into choosing between a model that was good for relational databases (RDO) or a model that was good for Access and other ISAM (Indexed Sequential Access Method) databases (DAO). Neither RDO nor DAO were appropriate for data sources that didn't fit one of these two basic models. ❺ Programming directly to the ODBC API was efficient but too much like hard work.

I've already discussed the reasons for the development of ADO (see Chapter 1), one of which was to solve the problems just stated. Undoubtedly, ADO is making life simpler for developers, but its immediate effect has been to add yet more choices to an already oversized list.

---

3. Users of Jet will be aware that the name "Jet" should not be taken to imply that it goes very fast. Jet is an acronym for "Joint Engine Technology."

4. ODBCDirect is one of the grosser misnomers of our time. It doesn't talk directly to ODBC at all. Instead, it maps DAO calls onto equivalent RDO calls, and thus, communicates with ODBC via RDO.

The introduction of ADO adds three new programming models for VBers to consider. ❻ The ADO Data Control (ADC) and ❼ the Data Environment provide two alternative visual models based on ADO, and will be covered in Part Two of this book. ❽ The ADO object model itself is the stuff of this and other chapters in Part One. It's anticipated that these ADO-based options will completely replace the DAO and RDO options over the course of the next few years.

As we know, ADO itself is an object model that simplifies access to OLE DB (in much the same way that RDO simplified access to ODBC[5]). OLE DB interacts with Providers that retrieve data from data sources. The choice of the term "Provider" isn't just new jargon for the sake of it. OLE DB Providers often play a far more active role in generating data than ODBC drivers and the new title reflects this more elevated status.

Microsoft has grown rich because of its marketing panache, and a major element of its genius has been a determination to provide users of existing technology with a smooth pathway to becoming users of new technology.[6] When ADO first appeared, there were huge numbers of tested and proven ODBC drivers and no OLE DB Providers for any specific database. This would hardly have given developers confidence to adopt ADO but for one reason—Microsoft produced a special Provider that would work with any existing ODBC driver. This Provider, called MSDASQL, takes the place of the ODBC Driver Manager when used with ADO, allowing the number of software layers to be kept to a minimum.

What this means is simple—if you have ODBC, you can use ADO. Period. MSDASQL makes this possible, and because it's highly optimized, it's as likely to improve your system's performance as not. All early adopters of ADO used MSDASQL to gain ADO functionality through their existing ODBC driver. Over time, as more and more developers adopt native OLE DB Providers for their databases, the role of MSDASQL will become less important. But please don't forget, the smooth transition to ADO would never have occurred but for the selfless performance of this heroic …[7]

As a nice touch, Microsoft has made MSDASQL the default Provider for ADO. Typically, when creating an ADO connection, you need to specify a Provider name and supply any other connection information required by the Provider (see the later section on "The Open Method" and also Chapter 4 for more details). For example, to use an existing ODBC DSN called "MuchADO," your connection string might be

```
"Provider=MSDASQL;DSN=MuchADO;UID=sa;PWD=;"
```

---

5. However, RDO was targeted at VB developers, whereas ADO is language neutral.

6. Windows is often accused of being clunky—in part because it continues to support DOS programs. This is also a major factor behind its success—a lesson that IBM failed to heed when promoting the technically superior failure code-named OS/2.

7. Oh no! I am romanticizing a piece of software. If I do it again, email me.

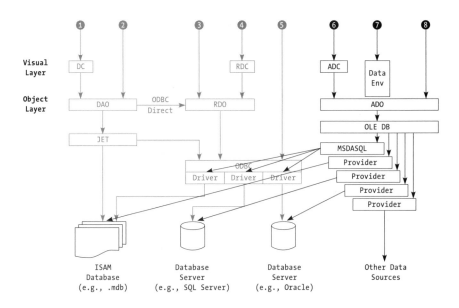

Figure 3-4. Visual Basic database access options after the release of ADO

However, if you omit the Provider name, the default Provider is used, in which case, your ADO connection string can be simplified to

```
"DSN=MuchADO;UID=sa;PWD=;"
```

If you have used ODBC before, you will instantly recognize this as a standard ODBC connection string. When used to create an ADO connection, the default Provider (MSDASQL) will use this string to connect to the database using your existing ODBC driver, reading the DSN information from the Registry, exactly as an RDO- or a DAO-based program would. Welcome home!

In This Section

We examined the need for data access software in the relational database world and saw how ODBC developed to meet this need. ADO can be used either to exploit existing ODBC investment or to avoid using ODBC altogether.

The Open Method

rs.Open

In its simplest form, the process of requesting a Recordset from a relational database involves calling the Recordset's Open method along with two arguments, one specifying the command (such as an SQL string) and one specifying connection details for the target database. You'll soon see that there is often a bit more to it than this, but let's start with this simple model.

Assuming that we have a table called "Scenes" in a database for which we have an ODBC data source called MuchADO[8] and a valid logon, we can create a Recordset as follows:

```
rs.Open "SELECT act, scene, description FROM Scenes", "DSN=MuchADO;"
```

The Recordset is now open, pointing at the first record. We can use the techniques learned in Chapter 2 to print the records out, which yields:

1	1	Before LEONATO'S house.
1	2	A room in LEONATO's house.
1	3	A room in LEONATO's house.
2	1	A hall in LEONATO'S house.
2	2	A hall in LEONATO'S house.
2	3	LEONATO'S orchard.
3	1	LEONATO'S garden.
3	2	A room in LEONATO'S house
3	3	A street.
3	4	HERO's apartment.
3	5	Another room in LEONATO'S house.
4	1	A church.
4	2	A prison.
5	1	Before LEONATO'S house.
5	2	LEONATO'S garden.
5	3	A church.
5	4	A room in LEONATO'S house.

In this example, all the steps involved in creating a Recordset are accomplished with one line of code. If you are more used to working with other data access libraries this comes as a pleasant surprise. With ADO, you don't have to explicitly create Connection or Command objects. While there are times when it's useful to create your own ADO Connection and Command objects, you'll see that much of the time it's actually best not to. Many of the reasons for creating the equivalent of Connection objects with DAO and RDO (such as Database, Connection, or rdoConnection objects) disappear because of the power of ADO and its relationship with Windows.

rs.ActiveConnection
rs.ActiveCommand

This doesn't mean that the ADO Recordset has all the connection and command functionality built into it. In fact, the ADO design would be pretty poor if this was the case. Instead, the Recordset object is smart enough to

8. I am assuming you know how to create an ODBC data source using the ODBC Applet in the Control Panel. There is more information on setting up connections in Chapter 4.

know when Command or Connection objects are required, and it creates them for you implicitly. You can access these objects and use them in your programs via the ActiveConnection and ActiveCommand properties on the Recordset. For example

```
Dim rs As New Recordset

rs.Open "SELECT act, scene, description FROM Scenes", _
    "DSN=MuchADO;"
Print rs.ActiveCommand.CommandText
Print rs.ActiveConnection.ConnectionString
rs.Close
```

prints (when using a SQLServer 7 database on a server called POLECAT)

```
SELECT act, scene, description FROM Scenes
Provider=MSDASQL.1;Extended Properties="DSN=MuchADO;UID=sa;PWD=;APP=Visual
Basic;WSID=POLECAT;DATABASE=MuchADO;Trusted_Connection=Yes
```

or if I change the DSN to MuchADOJet (which uses a local Access 2000 database), it prints

```
SELECT act, scene, description FROM Scenes
Provider=MSDASQL.1;Connect Timeout=15;Extended
Properties="DSN=MuchADOJet;DBQ=D:\ADOBook\Data\muchado.mdb;DriverId=25;
FIL=MS Access;MaxBufferSize=2048;PageTimeout=5;";Locale Identifier=2057
```

rs.Close   There are two things worth noting in this example. First, notice that the full connection string as reported by the Connection object contains the name of the Provider, MSDASQL, which routes the connection through ODBC. In other words, in the absence of an explicit Provider, ADO adds the default Provider name. The second thing is that I explicitly close my Recordset once I am done with it. You should get into the habit of doing this, as it helps ADO provide better optimization and resource management services to your program. If you just let the variable go out of scope, you won't enjoy these benefits.

You'll learn a great deal more about the Connection and Command objects in Chapters 4 and 5. Just like the ADO Field objects, it's important to know the role of these objects, even if you don't explicitly create them that often.

Microsoft supplies native OLE DB Providers for both SQLServer 7 and Access 2000, so there is generally no need to use ODBC connections. OLE DB connection strings can get quite long and cumbersome (and definitely tedious to type). Fortunately, there are easy ways to generate connection strings, as you'll see in Chapter 4. For now, here are the pure OLE DB connection strings that I used when writing this chapter:

For SQLServer 7 using Windows Integrated Security:

```
"Provider=SQLOLEDB;Data Source=POLECAT;Integrated Security=SSPI;
Initial Catalog=MuchADO;"
```

For SQLServer 7 with a specific user name (sa) and a blank password:

```
"Provider=SQLOLEDB;Data Source=POLECAT;User ID=sa;Password=;
Initial Catalog=MuchADO;"
```

For Access 2000 (Jet 4):

```
"Provider=Microsoft.Jet.OLEDB.4.0;Data Source=D:\Data\muchado.mdb;"
```

Connection strings are notoriously fussy about syntax, so be sure not to add unwanted spaces (or to leave out required spaces and semicolons). For databases other than SQLServer or Access, the connection string syntax could be quite different. You'll need to refer to Provider vendor details or use a graphical tool to build the required string.

The Recordset created in the examples just shown uses a read-only, forward-only, server-side cursor. Precisely what this means will be covered later in the chapter, but for the time being, take it on trust that while this is a sensible default, there are many, many times when the default type of Recordset won't do. It's time to see how to control the type of Recordset we create.

As with many things in ADO, you can choose from a range of ways of achieving the same end. For example, here's the full syntax of the Recordset's Open method:

Sub Open   ([Source As Variant],
             [ActiveConnection As Variant],
             [CursorType As CursorTypeEnum = adOpenUnspecified],
             [LockType As LockTypeEnum = adLockUnspecified],
             [Options As Long = -1])

and here's a list of properties that can be set before the Open method is called:[9]

Source As Variant

ActiveConnection As Variant

---

9. More precisely, all of these properties can be set on a closed or unopened (State = adStateClosed) Recordset. Only the ActiveConnection and CacheSize can be set on open Recordsets. The ActiveCommand property that we met earlier is read-only at all times.

> CursorType As CursorTypeEnum
>
> LockType As LockTypeEnum
>
> CursorLocation As CursorLocationEnum
>
> MaxRecords As Long
>
> CacheSize As Long

Note that all the arguments to Open are optional. The four most common characteristics of a Recordset can be specified either by setting properties or supplying arguments. It makes little difference which approach you choose. Because of this overlap there are eight different characteristics available. Let's review them.

rs.Source

1. **Source**: This is either a command string or an ADO Command object. The command string can be SQL, a stored procedure, or a table name. To use either a stored procedure or table name you should specify the command type via the Options argument.

rs.ActiveConnection

2. **ActiveConnection**: This is either an OLE DB connection string or an ADO Connection object. If a connection string is supplied, a new ADO Connection object will implicitly be created, which may create a new live database connection. For more details, see Chapter 4.

rs.CursorType

3. **CursorType**: Determines the type of cursor. See the later section on "Staying Connected—Cursor Control."

rs.LockType

4. **LockType**: Determines how database locking is controlled, and must be set if the Recordset is to support modifications. See the later section on "Staying Connected—Lock Control."

5. **Options**: This argument is used to set the command type and also to enable asynchronous Recordset creation. Command type is discussed further in Chapter 5. Asynchronous processing is discussed in Chapter 6.

rs.CursorLocation

6. **CursorLocation**: Determines where the Recordset cursor is created (on the client or the server). The default is to use server-side cursors. See the later section on "Staying Connected—Cursor Control."

rs.MaxRecords

7. **MaxRecords**: Places an upper limit on the number of records returned by the data source. MaxRecords can be very useful if your program allows users to make choices that affect the "WHERE" clause of a large query, because you can make sure they don't bring the network down by retrieving a million-record Recordset.

8. **CacheSize**: While the ADO programmer only ever sees one record at a time, the number of records retrieved by the Provider each time it accesses the database can be controlled by setting the CacheSize property. This can have very significant performance implications. See the section on "Optimizations for SQL Data Sources."

You can use any of the following techniques to create a static server-side cursor with pessimistic locking on a Recordset containing all the scenes in Act 2 of *Much ADO About Nothing,* based on my SQLServer 7 database. The differences are purely in programming style.

Example 1: All properties

```
Dim rs As New Recordset
rs.Source = "SELECT act, scene, description FROM Scenes WHERE act = 2"
rs.ActiveConnection = "Provider=SQLOLEDB;Data Source=POLECAT;" & _
                      "Integrated Security=SSPI;Initial Catalog=MuchADO;"
rs.CursorType = adOpenStatic
rs.LockType = adLockPessimistic
rs.Open
```

Example 2: All arguments

```
Dim rs As New Recordset
rs.Open "SELECT act, scene, description FROM Scenes WHERE act = 2", _
        "Provider=SQLOLEDB;Data Source=POLECAT;" & _
        "Integrated Security=SSPI;Initial Catalog=MuchADO;", _
        adOpenStatic, adLockPessimistic
```

Example 3: A combination

```
Dim rs As New Recordset
rs.Source = "SELECT act, scene, description FROM Scenes WHERE act = 2"
rs.ActiveConnection = "Provider=SQLOLEDB;Data Source=POLECAT;" & _
                      "Integrated Security=SSPI;Initial Catalog=MuchADO;"
rs.Open , , adOpenStatic, adLockPessimistic
```

One thing all these options have in common is an excessively long connection string. It makes sense to store the string in a global variable or constant, but you can also hold connection string details in a file called a Data Link File (as you'll see in Chapter 4).

Before we finish with the Open method, this seems like a good place to make a crucial statement about OLE DB Providers: NOT ALL PROVIDERS, OR EVEN ALL DATABASE PROVIDERS, PROVIDE THE SAME FUNCTIONALITY.

You can often control the functionality provided by a Recordset by setting the properties just discussed, effectively trading features for performance, but there are some features you can't get from a given Provider regardless of how you configure it. There will be times when you'll need a way of finding out which features a given Recordset supports.

As you saw in Chapter 2, the Properties collection on Recordset and Field objects can be used to provide a great deal of information about the objects' capabilities. In most cases however, a more convenient approach is to use the Supports method. For example

```
Dim rs As New Recordset

rs.Source = "SELECT * FROM Words"
rs.ActiveConnection = "Provider=SQLOLEDB;Data Source=POLECAT;" & _
                      "Integrated Security=SSPI;Initial Catalog=MuchADO;"
rs.CursorLocation = adUseClient
rs.Open , , adOpenStatic, adLockPessimistic

Print "AddNew            ", rs.Supports(adAddNew)
Print "ApproxPosition    ", rs.Supports(adApproxPosition)
Print "Bookmark          ", rs.Supports(adBookmark)
Print "Delete            ", rs.Supports(adDelete)
Print "Find              ", rs.Supports(adFind)
Print "HoldRecords       ", rs.Supports(adHoldRecords)
Print "Index             ", rs.Supports(adIndex)
Print "MovePrevious      ", rs.Supports(adMovePrevious)
Print "Notify            ", rs.Supports(adNotify)
Print "Resync            ", rs.Supports(adResync)
Print "Seek              ", rs.Supports(adSeek)
Print "Update            ", rs.Supports(adUpdate)
Print "UpdateBatch       ", rs.Supports(adUpdateBatch)
```

will print

AddNew	True
ApproxPosition	True
Bookmark	True
Delete	True
Find	True
HoldRecords	True
Index	False
MovePrevious	True
Notify	True
Resync	True

Seek	False
Update	True
UpdateBatch	True

The different values you can use with Supports are defined by the CursorOptionsEnum. I configured my Recordset to support just about all the options available. However, if I don't need these options, I could be losing performance by requesting them. Try as hard as you can and you won't get SQLServer 7 to support the Index and Seek methods (you'll see why later in the chapter), whereas they can be made to work with Access under certain circumstances.

Microsoft has put a great deal of effort into making the SQLServer Provider as fully functional as possible, but not all Providers are this obliging. There is a lesson here. If you are writing an ADO application that is designed to work with a range of different Providers or data sources, spare some time to investigate which ADO features they support. It's not a bad idea to call the Supports method in your program so that you can test to see whether the Provider will do what you require of it. You can then act defensively and avoid nasty bugs.[10]

While Supports will tell you if a Provider has a certain capability, it doesn't go into detail. For example, a Recordset may be updateable, even if some of its fields aren't. You can check individual Field objects to find out more.

In This Section

We looked at the Open method for creating Recordsets. There are many different ways of creating Recordsets and several properties or arguments that you must understand in order to use Recordsets correctly. We also saw how the Supports method can be used to examine the features a Recordset provides.

Staying Connected—Cursor Control

Now that you have seen how to open a Recordset with default properties, it's time to explore some of the options available. One of these is the type of cursor our Recordset uses.

What exactly is a cursor? Well, a *set* is something that contains zero, one, or more elements, and a Recordset is something that contains zero, one, or

---

10. It's easy for an author to say this kind of thing, but it's much more difficult to decide how you are going to handle this issue. If your aim is to cover a wide range of data sources, you should either consider using the more straightforward ADO features or use client-side cursors for which ADO provides functionality through the Client Cursor Engine that may be missing in certain Providers.

more records. The concept of a set of records is convenient in many ways, but more often than not, we want to be able to work with one record at a time and navigate through our Recordset. A cursor provides us with the ability to do this.

This sounds fairly simple (and it is), but there are numerous options concerning how the cursor works. Cursors are like everything else in computing: the more power you want, the more expensive it is to create the cursor. Consider the following questions:

1. Do you just want to move in a forward direction through the Recordset or do you want full scrolling capability so that you can move any number of records in any direction?

2. Do you want a rich supply of metadata describing the Recordset or do you just want raw data?

3. Do you want to be able to see changes that others may be making to the data you requested or do you want a fixed view of the data?

4. Do you want to stay connected to the server for a significant length of time?

5. Where should the cursor (and the resources it consumes) be created (in the client process or in the data source)?

rs.CursorLocation
rs.CursorType

In ADO, cursor characteristics are controlled by two properties, Cursor-Location and CursorType.

The cursor location determines whether the cursor service (the software that manages the cursor functionality) is provided by ADO on the client (via the ADO Client Cursor Engine) or by the data source itself. The values for CursorLocation are provided by the CursorLocationEnum enumeration, which contains the values adUseClient and adUseServer. Two other values are also supported (adUseNone and adUseClientBatch) for backward compatibility but have no relevance to contemporary ADO programs.

The cursor type is one of the following values, as defined by the Cursor-TypeEnum enumeration:

adOpenForwardOnly (default)

adOpenStatic

adOpenKeyset

adOpenDynamic

adOpenUnspecified

In order to make cursor issues clearer, I'll use some structural diagrams. The purpose of these diagrams is to make it easier for you to picture how

ADO and Providers work together to provide Recordset functionality. Please don't assume that they represent physically how your particular configuration works. The implementation details vary from vendor to vendor. However, in many cases, the diagrams are close to physical reality.

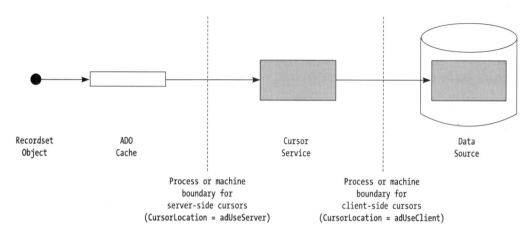

| Recordset Object | ADO Cache | Cursor Service | Data Source |

Process or machine boundary for server-side cursors (CursorLocation = adUseServer)

Process or machine boundary for client-side cursors (CursorLocation = adUseClient)

Figure 3-5. The different structures involved in maintaining a Recordset

In this diagram, an open Recordset object is pointing at a single current record in a cache of current records maintained by ADO. By default, there is only one record in the cache at any time, but this can be controlled programmatically by setting the CacheSize property. The cache maintains one or more current records, whereas the cursor service represents the entire Recordset. The cursor service will be managed by ADO in your client process if you ask for a client-side cursor, or managed by the data source if you ask for a server-side cursor and the data source supports the type of cursor you request. Typically, the data source is running on a separate computer or at least in a process separate from your application. However, this won't be the case if you are using a desktop (ISAM) database such as Access.[11]

If you request a client-side cursor, the cursor type is always set to adOpenStatic by ADO (even if you ask for a different type). When you *open* a client-side cursor, ADO copies all the results from your query into your client process as part of the Open method. If the Recordset is large or your network is slow, this task can cause a measurable delay.[12] It can also put a strain on your client computer if it's memory constrained. The upside of this is that once the Open method has completed, all the data is readily available.

11. This is true even if your .mdb file is located on a remote file server.

12. However, client-side cursors generally use highly efficient forward-only server cursors to create this client-side copy, therefore, a client-side static cursor can be more efficient than a server-side static cursor overall.

It also means you can disconnect from the database and continue using the Recordset.

Figure 3-5 presents a general model of the relationship between the Recordset, ADO Cache, cursor service, and data source. Important differences appear depending on the type of cursor service selected. Apart from performance considerations, the cursor type affects two important characteristics of a Recordset:

1. **Record Membership**: During the time you have a Recordset open other users may make changes (particularly deletions and additions) to the database that affect which records meet the criteria to belong in your Recordset, and which order they appear in. You may or may not want to see these changes in membership.

2. **Record Data**: Regardless of whether the membership changes, you may or may not want to see changes that other users make to the values of fields of records in your Recordset.

For example, consider the following query against the MuchADO data source:

```
SELECT * FROM Scenes WHERE act = 3 order by description
```

This will return the following records:

act	scene	description
3	2	A room in LEONATO'S house
3	3	A street.
3	5	Another room in LEONATO'S house.
3	4	HERO's apartment.
3	1	LEONATO'S garden.

Now, suppose that after you open your Recordset, but before you close it, a modernizing stage director decides that Scene 1 should be set in a Jacuzzi and that Scene 4 should be scrapped to make the play a bit shorter. Once the changes have been made, reexecuting the query will return

act	scene	description
3	1	A Jacuzzi
3	2	A room in LEONATO'S house
3	3	A street.
3	4	Another room in LEONATO'S house.

What should your Recordset see after the changes have been made, before you close the Recordset? The answer depends on the membership and data characteristics of the Recordset, which are in turn determined by the cursor type.

Forward-Only Cursor

The cursor service performs a minimal role with a forward-only cursor. As a result, it can be very fast (because no cursor management features are created).[13] Generally speaking, only MoveNext navigation is supported, however. You can use the Move method, but only to achieve the same effect as a MoveNext.

Membership and data concerns don't really apply to forward-only cursors because you only visit each record once.

rs.CacheSize

When your navigation happens to fall within the records in the ADO Cache, there is no server intervention. A consequence of this is that if your cache size is greater than 1, other arguments to the Move method (such as using –1 to move to the previous record) are allowed, even though Move-Previous always creates an error with a forward-only cursor. Unless you keep a very careful track of where you are within the current cache, exploiting this functionality can prove dangerous.

By experimentation or otherwise, you may know that you can call Move-First on a forward-only Recordset and reposition the cursor on the first record. If you have no real cursor service, how can this be? What happens is that ADO reexecutes your SQL statement and leaves you positioned on the first record. Depending on your point of view, this is either

- extremely convenient, or

- potentially dangerous and expensive.[14]

Forward-only cursors are useful when you only need to iterate through a Recordset once and then throw it away. This is very often the case, and it makes sense to use forward-only cursors if you don't need the functionality offered by cursor types.

rs.RecordCount

Because only a limited cursor service is provided, a forward-only cursor doesn't provide a RecordCount. If you ask for one, the answer will be –1.

---

13. SQLServer's forward-only cursors pipe data directly from the server to your application in a highly optimized fashion and are sometimes referred to as "firehose" cursors.

14. Personally, I wouldn't choose to do it. Whereas it's an inexpensive operation against a small Access table, it can really throw performance on large, high-demand systems or queries. If I want to execute a query, I choose to do it explicitly.

Static Cursor

Once you have opened a static cursor, the contents look the same, regardless of what other people do to the underlying data. In other words, both the membership and data of a static Recordset are fixed for the lifetime of the Recordset. Diagrammatically, this works as follows:

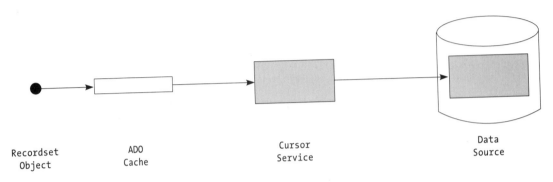

Recordset Object	ADO Cache	Cursor Service	Data Source

Figure 3-6. The structure of a static cursor

The static cursor creates a complete copy of all the data requested in the query and holds it as a separate structure. That's why the cursor service and data source have the same size gray blocks in the diagram.[15] This is physically what happens when you request a client-side cursor. It's also physically what happens when you request a server-side cursor using SQLServer, which holds the copy in tempdb. Other databases that provide server-side static cursors probably work in the same way, but they could use a different scheme (based on locks for example) to keep the Recordset static.

rs.RecordCount

Static cursors are extremely flexible and easy to work with. Full scrolling and navigational support are provided and the RecordCount property can be relied upon. There is a cost associated with creating the copy of the data, which is noticeable (sometimes very noticeable with large Recordsets), and you should evaluate the impact of this cost if you expect to create Recordsets of more than a few hundred records.

Because the data and membership is fixed, you don't need to apply too much defensive programming (which keyset and dynamic cursors demand). And it can be very convenient to know that changes made by other users won't affect the consistency of your data. For example, if you iterate through the Recordset multiple times performing financial calculations, it's helpful to know that the numbers won't change between iterations.

---

15. This doesn't mean that the cursor service copies the entire database or even entire tables. It just copies the records that meet the query's WHERE clause. It almost goes without saying that you should only ever request the records and Fields that you need, regardless of the cursor being used.

On the other hand, don't keep a static cursor open for long if the underlying data is highly volatile, as would be the case in a ticket reservation application, for example. Once the Recordset is created, you would never know if a seat that appears free in your Recordset has subsequently been booked, just as the modernizing director's changes in the example just shown are not visible to a static cursor. The data in static cursors can become stale very quickly.

Keyset Cursor

Keyset cursors have a fixed membership, but the data is dynamic.

Microsoft pioneered the concept of a keyset cursor with DAO's Dynasets, and ODBC's keyset-driven cursors, and this highly useful type of cursor has found its way into ADO. Like static cursors, keyset cursors are based on the concept of making a copy of data, but unlike static cursors, only the ***primary key*** for each record is copied, instead of the whole record. Theoretically, this should make opening a keyset cursor faster, but more important is the fact that with a keyset cursor, you can see changes made by others to your Recordset, even after the Recordset has been opened.

As you read data from the Recordset, the cursor service uses the keyset as a lookup table to read the actual data from the data source's tables each time. As a result, keyset cursor data doesn't get stale like static cursor data does.

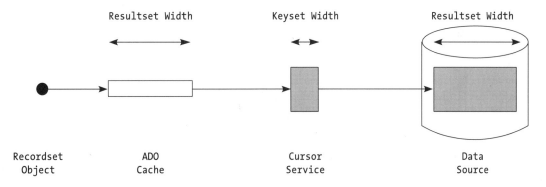

Figure 3-7. The structure of a keyset cursor

Two factors limit the dynamic nature of keyset cursor's data. First, although the data is read freshly each time it is accessed the keyset created by the cursor service remains fixed. As a result, membership and ordering won't be affected.

Because membership is fixed, you'll always see the same records in the Recordset, even if data changes made by other users mean that existing records no longer meet the query conditions. Also, you won't see new records added by other users after the Recordset was opened.

The most difficult issue to address is what happens if another user deletes a record in the Recordset. A problem occurs because there is still an entry in your (fixed) keyset, even though the real record in the data source no longer exists. Technically speaking, the keyset contains a "hole," and ADO raises an error with error number –2147217885 when this occurs.[16] Your Provider should allow you to navigate to this record but raise the error when you try to access a value. In practice, behavior varies widely among Providers.

The Jet native Provider behaves as expected. I will demonstrate. Assume you have just opened the Recordset discussed previously and the modernizing director's changes are made immediately afterward. To handle the possible error triggered by the hole that these changes have left in the Recordset, I used the following code with the Jet native Provider:

```
On Error GoTo ErrH
Const RECORD_DELETED As Long = -2147217885
Dim fd As Field
Dim rs As Recordset
Set rs = <create the Recordset with keyset cursor>
rs.MoveFirst

While Not rs.EOF
  For Each fd In rs.Fields
    Print fd.Value,
  Next
  Print
ResumeFromNextRecord:
  rs.MoveNext
Wend

Exit Sub
ErrH:
If Err.Number = RECORD_DELETED Then
    Print Err.Description
    GoTo ResumeFromNextRecord
End If
```

---

16. ADO doesn't provide a predefined constant for this error, although OLE DB does.

I am no fan of labeled "gotos," but this code does let you clearly see what happens. An error occurs on the first `Print fd.Value` executed for the hole. The results are

```
3              2         A room in LEONATO'S house
3              3         A street.
3              4         Another room in LEONATO's house
Record is deleted.
3              1         A Jacuzzi
```

Note that Scene 1 has had its description updated, but the ordering hasn't been affected (because the keyset is fixed). Also note that the hole caused an error to be raised.

The same code executed against the SQLServer native Provider (under the same contrived circumstances) produces the following results:

```
3              2         A room in LEONATO'S house
3              3         A street.
3              4         Another room in LEONATO'S house.
3              1         A Jacuzzi
```

In this case, although the ordering clearly indicates a keyset cursor, the hole doesn't appear. The SQLServer Provider handles the error for you, so that you don't have to handle it in code. (I'll address how to test for this behavior later in this section). The ODBC Provider behaves differently again.

rs.CacheSize
The second factor that affects the dynamic nature of a keyset cursor is the CacheSize. When you are navigating around records in the cache, the cursor service isn't affected, so data changes by other users will not be made visible. The closer the value of CacheSize gets to the RecordCount, the more like a static cursor a keyset cursor appears. Even with a CacheSize of 1, there is still one record in the cache. You won't see changes made by others to this record unless you move off it and move back again (although there are ways to resynchronize a Recordset, which you'll see later in the chapter).

Keyset cursors provide an efficient and easy way to create Recordsets that provide you with a partially dynamic view of the database, without any of the programming complexities introduced by dynamic cursors. They are traditionally used by developers who want to perform cursor-based updates on an open Recordset.

Dynamic Cursor

When using a dynamic cursor, both membership and data are dynamic. There are no holes, and inserts by other people become visible as you scroll around within the Recordset.

rs.CacheSize   Conceptually at least, a dynamic cursor also uses a keyset. However, instead of creating a key in the keyset for each record in the Recordset with a dynamic cursor, the number of keys in the keyset matches the CacheSize. New keysets are built dynamically as and when needed, and old ones are thrown away.

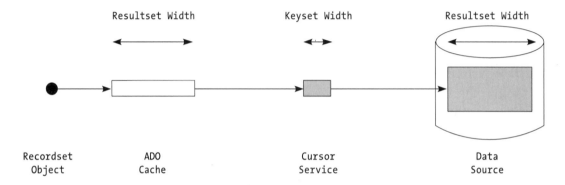

Figure 3-8. The structure of a dynamic cursor

rs.RecordCount   Because the keyset is constructed dynamically, there is no messing around with holes as can occur with keyset cursors.

However, dynamic cursors aren't as easy as they seem. A record you were looking at a moment ago may disappear without trace when you go back to find it, and new records can appear at any time. A RecordCount (if it's provided) will be expensive to generate and unreliable.

Few Providers offer a complete implementation of dynamic cursors. Consider the following example, based on the SQLServer native Provider. Assume that the trendy director, having made his changes to the play, is smugly examining a Recordset created using a dynamic cursor, based on the same query as I was using:

```
SELECT * FROM Scenes WHERE act = 3 order by description
```

Unknown to him, I have uncovered his plot and changed the data back to its previous state. Iterating through his Recordset now yields

3	1	LEONATO'S garden.
3	2	A room in LEONATO'S house.
3	3	A street.
3	4	HERO's apartment.

This looks suspiciously like a keyset cursor—there is no sign that a scene has been added back. It turns out that the SQLServer Provider won't show inserts made by others if your query uses an "order by" clause based on a varchar field. Just about any other data type is fine; for example

```
SELECT * FROM Scenes WHERE act = 3 order by scene
```

provides the expected results

3	1	LEONATO'S garden.
3	2	A room in LEONATO'S house.
3	3	A street.
3	4	HERO's apartment.
3	5	Another room in LEONATO'S house.

Very soon we'll see how to determine which behavior to expect.

Use dynamic cursors if you want to keep a cursor open for some period of time, and yet still be able to see changes made by other users.[17]

Unspecified Cursor

Given that cursor type can have a profound effect on how a Recordset behaves, it may seem that creating a Recordset with an unspecified cursor type is a rather reckless action. However, ADO allows you to specify the functionality you require of a cursor, and leave it to the Provider to decide how to configure the cursor service. This is achieved through the following set of dynamic ADO properties[18]:

Scroll Backwards

Others' Inserts Visible

---

17. Typically, programmers only use dynamic cursors if they really need them. While the functionality sounds attractive, they can prove quite hard to work with.

18. You met dynamic properties in Chapter 2. Dynamic properties are Provider-specific. Therefore, there is no guarantee that a given Provider will support these properties.

Others' Changes Visible

Own Inserts Visible

Own Changes Visible

Remove Deleted Rows

For example, a cursor created with the following dynamic property assignment (but without setting any of the others) does a very good impersonation of a static cursor:

```
rs.Properties("Scroll Backwards") = True
```

These properties can only be set before the Open method is called. If the Provider cannot supply the specified cursor characteristics, then either an error will occur or the best-fitting cursor will be created instead. As a result, it's a good idea to check the properties after the Recordset has been opened, because there is no guarantee that you'll get what you asked for.

You can read these properties even if you created the cursor by setting the CursorType property. For example, you can use this facility to test whether a dynamic cursor actually allows you to see rows inserted by other users, as it is meant to.

In This Section

We saw how changing the cursor type of a server-side cursor has a huge impact, not only on how the Recordset works under the covers, but also on how programs behave. Knowledge of the underlying technology helps us predict expected behavior in many different circumstances. Client-side cursors always use a static cursor, managed in the client process by the ADO Client Cursor Engine.

Staying Connected—Lock Control

rs.LockType

The LockType property/argument can be used to control how updates take place through an ADO Recordset. Back in Chapter 2 I mentioned that there are a number of states that need to be considered when discussing any kind of modification. They are:

- Transactional/Non-transactional

- Multiuser/Single User

- Batch/Immediate

Our focus in this chapter is on non-transactional Immediate mode modifications suitable for both single and multiuser applications. I'll discuss the other situations in due course.

There are different views as to how relational database updates should be performed. Some people argue that all modifications should be performed by generating SQL UPDATE/INSERT/DELETE statements, while others prefer the simpler approach of making updates into a Recordset (by assigning to a field on the current record, as discussed in Chapter 2).

The first of these approaches is often called "searched update" because it requires the specification of an SQL WHERE clause to search for the required record before modifying it.

For example, you could use the following searched update to modify the description of the VERGES record in the Parts table:

```
Dim rs As New Recordset
Dim sSQL As String
rs.ActiveConnection = <A valid connection string>
sSQL = "UPDATE Parts SET description = 'a petty constable'" & _
"WHERE part = 'VERGES'"rs.Open sSQL
```

Here rs.Open is used to execute an SQL statement that doesn't return a Recordset. In this case, after calling rs.Open, the value of rs.State will be adStateClosed.

The second approach is known as "positioned update" because the update is performed using a cursor positioned on the current row. The pros and cons of these approaches will occupy our minds at various points in the chapter.

To perform positioned updates, you need to set the LockType property on the Recordset, as discussed later.

LockType can have one of the following values, as defined by the Lock-TypeEnum enumeration:

adLockReadOnly

adLockPessimistic

adLockOptimistic

adLockBatchOptimistic

adLockUnspecified

Locking is a complex issue, and before rushing headlong into which option gives us the most power, it's worth taking a few minutes to consider why we need locks and why they are a big issue in any multiuser application.

If someone is paying you to create a data-based computer program, it must be because they place some value on the data it uses. Therefore, it's important to make sure that the data is consistent and represents the way things work in the real world.

Suppose it's your birthday, and a kindly aunt is paying $1,000 into your bank account. Here's some SQL that might accomplish this:

```
UPDATE Account SET Balance = Balance + 1000.00 WHERE id = ???
```

Let's forget that this statement may be part of a bigger transaction and all that that entails. Even this simple statement, considered in isolation, involves a read and a write operation separated in time by some countable number of clock cycles. So let's say the database has done the read, and your current balance is $0.04.[19] But just before the database writes $1000.04 back into the table, a check from another kindly, but less wealthy, aunt begins processing with

```
UPDATE Account SET Balance = Balance + 50.00 WHERE id = ???
```

This processing also reads your balance as $0.04 (you can see where this is leading). The first update completes, writing $1000.04 back into the database, and is immediately followed by the second update writing $50.04 over the top of it. Happy?

Even though the time between the reads and writes here is small, this situation will occur. It will occur even more often when the update is done through a Recordset because the time between the original read and the execution of the update is much greater.

To stop such financial injustices, databases use locks. I'll present a simple model of locking based on one type of lock, known as an exclusive lock (XL). Real implementations may do things differently.[20] Databases typically have multiple operations running in parallel. Only one operation may have an XL on a particular record, and an XL is required to read or write a record.[21]

The longer an XL is held, the more chance there is that an operation wishing to perform an update will fail or be blocked. In this sense, locks are rather like red traffic lights. They are essential to maintain safety and sanity, but we want them to be on as little as possible.

We can now consider the different options available for the LockType property. The sample application for this chapter (which is on the companion

---

19. We authors are often criticized for creating unrealistic examples. I am trying to make amends here.

20. This model is good enough to explain the principles of locking as seen by ADO. Databases may use more complex models, however. For example, SQLServer 7 uses five different types of locks.

21. It's becoming more common for databases to apply locks on individual records. Many databases however still lock "pages" instead of records, where a page is fixed size chunk of data (typically 2KB, 4KB, or 8KB), and a lock applies to all records on a page. Oracle and SQLServer 7 are examples of databases with record-level locking. SQLServer 6.x uses page-level locking, which means that a single record operation can lock out dozens of records.

CD) allows you to create Recordsets with any lock type, position to particular rows, and attempt updates. By running two instances of this program it's easy to simulate multiuser scenarios.

The examples that follow are based on using the Jet native OLE DB Provider with a static server-side cursor. Different Providers will exhibit different behaviors while sticking (or at least sticking closely) to the rules defined for each lock type. I am creating a Recordset with just one record, based on the SQL

```
SELECT * FROM Parts WHERE part = 'VERGES'
```

which I will use to redefine his description.

Read-Only Lock

The default value for the LockType property is adLockReadOnly. It never uses XLs, and therefore, does not permit updates through the Recordset. Attempting the following update

```
On Error GoTo ErrH
rs!Description = "a petty constable"
rs.Update
Exit Sub
ErrH:
Print Err, Error
```

results in

```
3251        The operation requested by the application is
not supported by the Provider.
```

The built-in ADO error value, adErrFeatureNotAvailable, equals 3251.

Using a read-only locking scheme doesn't mean that your application needs to be read-only. As you have seen, you can always perform searched updates via SQL.

Pessimistic Lock

Pessimistic locks are useful when the chances of two operations contending for the same resource are high, and resolving contentions is complex or expensive. Pessimistic locking works by acquiring XLs early (typically when an edit begins) and holding on to them until the update has completed. So long as it was possible to acquire the lock, the update will succeed because you have exclusive access to the record.

ADO doesn't allow pessimistic locking with client-side cursors. If you ask for one, ADO will substitute another lock type.

```
On Error GoTo ErrH
rs!Description = "a petty constable"        ◄————————  XL acquired
<other operations?>
rs.Update                        ◄————————————————————  XL released
Print "done"
Exit Sub
ErrH:
Print Err, Error
```

In a single-user application, this code will always succeed, as there is no chance that another user has an XL on this record. Let's see what happens when two users attempt to acquire XLs on the same record. In the following code, only the code shown in black actually executes. Remember, this example uses the Jet native OLE DB Provider. You can try this out using the sample program on the companion CD.

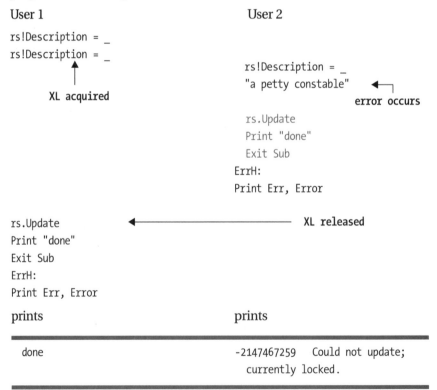

User 2 attempted to acquire an XL and failed (because User 1 had that record locked at the time) before any serious work was done.

Error handling with pessimistic locks is quite easy (because errors occur before any changes have been made to the Recordset), and therefore, it's tempting to use them. However, there is quite a high price to pay. Early locking prevents other users from making changes they want to make, thereby reducing the *concurrency* of the entire system.

SQLServer 7 behaves rather differently from Jet. Before throwing an error, it will wait for a significant timeout period for the lock to be released. If the delay before the lock is released is short, this is convenient, because the program will continue running without having to have retry code. However, if the delay is long, users will assume their program has crashed.[22] If you choose to use SQLServer 7 with pessimistic locking and a keyset or static cursor, you should be aware that SQLServer 7 will acquire XLs when the Recordset opens, not just when an edit begins. This effectively means that you can't have two pessimistic keyset or static cursors open at the same time if they share any records. If you choose to use pessimistic locking be sure to keep those WHERE clauses tight!

Optimistic Lock

Use optimistic locking if the chance of record contention is low. Optimistic locking acquires an XL only when the Update statement executes. This means that locks are held for a much shorter period of time than pessimistic locks.

```
On Error GoTo ErrH
rs!Description = "a petty constable"
<other operations?>

rs.Update                                          XL acquired
Print "done"                                       XL released
Exit Sub
ErrH:
Print Err, Error
```

While this sounds a bit reckless, optimistic locking won't allow you to update a record if another user has changed a value since you read it. It doesn't conflict with our desire to keep the database consistent, but it does mean that you might have to handle an error after you have set all the fields on a record, and you might have to throw all these changes away. Let's see this

---

22. Studies have shown that users are very consistent. Anything that takes more than two seconds is slow. Anything that takes more than fifteen seconds is broken.

in action. Once again, we are using the native Jet Provider, and only the code in black gets executed.

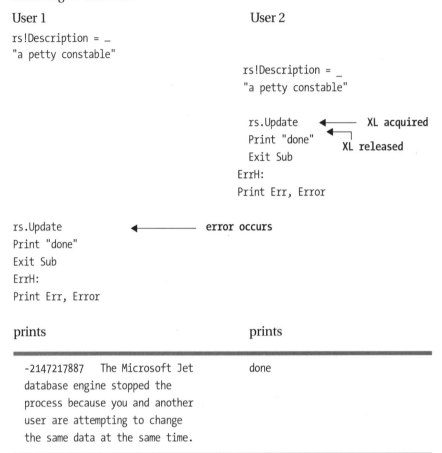

User 1

```
rs!Description = _
"a petty constable"
```

User 2

```
                              rs!Description = _
                              "a petty constable"

                              rs.Update        ◄──────  XL acquired
                              Print "done"         ┐
                                                   XL released
                              Exit Sub
                              ErrH:
                              Print Err, Error
```

```
rs.Update              ◄───────────  error occurs
Print "done"
Exit Sub
ErrH:
Print Err, Error
```

prints   prints

-2147217887 The Microsoft Jet database engine stopped the process because you and another user are attempting to change the same data at the same time.	done

Using SQLServer 7 in otherwise identical circumstances, User 1 gets the following error:

-2147217887   Errors occurred.

It's the same error number, but a less helpful message.

Batch Optimistic Lock

Scrolling around in a Recordset performing updates in Immediate mode as and when you or your user pleases is very convenient. However, this approach suffers from two drawbacks:

1. Each update, delete, or insert requires a roundtrip to the server, and may result in additional requests for metadata from the server, which adds additional costs to the process.

2. It assumes that a database connection is maintained the entire time the Recordset is open. As you'll see in later chapters, making this assumption is becoming increasingly frowned upon (and unnecessary), and in some circumstances, isn't possible (for example, when the Recordset is open inside a Web browser).

Batch optimistic locking has evolved as a technique that maintains the convenience of Recordset updating (as opposed to generating SQL in your code), but without the limitations just mentioned.

These days, it's most widely used with disconnected Recordsets, which are the subject of Chapter 7; we'll look at batch updating in detail in that chapter. For this reason, I won't say any more about this locking strategy at this point.

In This Section

We came to terms with the need for locks when updating databases. We discussed the locking options provided by ADO and explored what happens when two users attempt to update the same record. ADO doesn't allow pessimistic locking with client-side cursors.

Examining the Fields Collection

We explored the static properties of Field objects in Chapter 2, where we saw that in addition to having a value, Field objects carry type and other metadata about each field in a Recordset. We also saw one dynamic property that is available with client-side cursors, the Optimize property. Together, the static properties (including the Attribute property) and the dynamic properties provide an enormous amount of information about each Field object in a Recordset.

If you know inside-out the design of the database and the details of every field in each query you are using, then much of this information is of only background interest. However, if you are writing more generic software, where the user has some control over the fields (or even tables or databases!) they are using, you may need all kinds of information about the fields you use in order to create robust software. Either way, a deeper look at field information will allow us to explore some valuable ADO programming techniques.

fd.Attributes   Let's look first at the information available through the Attributes property. As you may remember, the Attributes property is an overloaded property, and a bitmask should always be used when reading it. The Field-AttributeEnum enumeration defines all the bitmasks available for use with the Attribute property. We'll take a look at how the Attributes property helps us deal with three important programming tasks: handling Null values, reading "large" data types (typically large binary or text fields), and handling special columns.

Handling Null Data

When defining a database table, the designer specifies whether the fields can hold Null values. Given a Field object, fd, the following code will tell you whether the Field might contain Nulls when you read it and whether you are allowed to assign Null values to the Field:

```
Print "MayBeNull", CBool(fd.Attributes And adFldMayBeNull)
Print "IsNullable", CBool(fd.Attributes And adFldIsNullable)
```

Handling Null values in VB code can be problematic. For example, if you have a database field defined as adInteger and you want to copy this value into a variable, there are many reasons why you might want to define that variable as a Long. However, if the field allows Nulls, this might prove to be a dangerous decision because a Long variable cannot hold a Null value. You have the following options:

1. *Declare the variable as a Variant.* Variants can hold Nulls, so this is safe. However, if you intend to use this variable in a calculation later in your program, you are only putting off the time when you'll need to address the problem, and at the same time, you are missing out on the blistering speed of compiled VB's Long arithmetic.

2. *Test the value of the field each time you need to read it (hopefully only once) using the IsNull function.* Safe—but tedious. Also, you have to decide what to do if you find a Null. It may be appropriate to set the variable to 0, but then again, it may not.

3. *Place* On Error Resume Next *at the top of each procedure to skip past the error.* You don't really want to do this, do you?[23]

---

23. This isn't a book about VB programming, so I won't harp on about the dangers of this kind of error handling. Let me just remind you though, that in a compiled VB program, any procedure that contains a Resume or Resume Next statement performs like it's running through maple syrup.

Nulls are the hot potatoes of VB programming. Use any relational or logical operator (such as >= or Not) in a statement where one variable is set to Null, and the result will be Null rather than True or False. The only safe way to handle anything that may be Null is to test it with the IsNull function.

Handling Large Data Fields

Most of the data types used in databases result in fairly small fields. However, there are times when you'll need to store large amounts of text in a single field, or large binary objects such as images or serialized COM objects.[24] There are reasons why these data types might need special treatment.

1. Because such fields may contain very large amounts of data, we may not want them to be retrieved every time you refill the ADO Cache with records. We may only want to retrieve the data when or if the specific field is requested.[25]

2. Even when reading or writing an individual field, we may want to break the operation into several stages or chunks, instead of transferring a huge lump of data in one go. Doing so will put less strain on our server, the network, and our client memory.

3. RDO programmers were forced to process large fields in chunks. They may want to continue using their battle-hardened skills in ADO.

I have a large field called "contents" in the SceneDetails table. This table has a record for each scene, which contains the entire text of *Much ADO about Nothing* for that scene.[26] While this table has a one-to-one relationship with the Scenes table (and I could therefore hold all the data in a single table) many developers and database designers choose to hold Long data types in separate tables. For a whole range of reasons, this usually means

---

24. Such data is often referred to as BLOBs (Binary Large Objects).

25. I was once called to a client to work out why a window that used to take two seconds to fill with data suddenly started taking several minutes. The window used a SELECT * FROM employee-type of query. We finally found that someone had decided to add a new field to the employee table to hold each employee's ID card photo image. Although the window didn't use this new field, the query was now reading several thousand bitmaps across a highly segmented network. Rewriting the query to return only the required fields corrected the problem. There are many lessons here, but telling them is too painful.

26. In SQLServer, the Text data type is used to create very large character-based fields. Access uses the Memo data type for this purpose. Just to be difficult, while every other database in the world uses char or varchar to hold standard-length character fields, Access calls this data type Text. One of the most common mistakes that Access programmers make when moving to SQLServer is to use the Text data type for standard length strings.

that queries and updates to the "main" table (the one without the Long field) will run faster.

When fd refers to this contents field, and I am using SQLServer with a server-side cursor, the following code

```
Print "Long", CBool(fd.Attributes And adFldLong)
Print "MayDefer", CBool(fd.Attributes And adFldMayDefer)
Print "CacheDeferred", CBool(fd.Attributes And adFldCacheDeferred)
```

prints

```
Long           True
MayDefer       True
CacheDeferred False
```

Here, MayDefer tells me that retrieving this field's data is deferred until it's actually needed. Not surprisingly, if I changed the cursor location to client-side, MayDefer would become False. If CacheDeferred were True, it would mean that, once read, this deferred field's value would be held by the Provider in cache.

In an attempt to confuse VB programmers, database jargon often uses the word "long" to refer to large data types. This is what adFldLong means (it doesn't mean 4-byte integer). If adFldLong is True, I know that I can read and write this field's value in chunks, using the Field object's GetChunk and AppendChunk methods. Both these methods work in a similar way and can be used with either text or binary long data. Normally, you would choose a chunk size of 1KB or 2KB, but in order to show you how it works without reproducing most of Shakespeare's output, my example uses a chunk size of 72 characters. It assumes a Recordset has been opened on the SceneContents table.

```
Const LINE_LENGTH As Integer = 72
Dim sText As String
Dim lFieldLength  As Long
Dim lCharsRead As Long
Dim lCount As Long

Dim fd As Field
Set fd = rs("content")          ←————   get a reference
lCount = 0                               to a Field object
rs.Filter = "act = 3 and scene = 1"
```

```
lFieldLength = fd.ActualSize
lCharsRead = 0
While lCharsRead < lFieldLength
  sText = fd.GetChunk(LINE_LENGTH)
  Print CStr(lCount) & Space(8 - Len(CStr(lCount))) & sText
  lCharsRead = lCharsRead + LINE_LENGTH
  lCount = lCount + 1
Wend
```

call GetChunk, passing the
chunk size as an argument

This code prints each chunk on a separate line, prefixed with an eight-character-line header containing a line number. Here, for the benefit of FORTRAN programmers everywhere, are the first few lines of this printout, in which Hero addresses Margaret at the opening of Act 3, Scene 1:

```
0       HERO Good Margaret, run thee to the parlor; There shalt thou find my cou
1       sin Beatrice Proposing with the prince and Claudio: Whisper her ear and
2       tell her, I and Ursula Walk in the orchard and our whole discourse Is al
3       l of her; say that thou overheard'st us; And bid her steal into the plea
4       ched bower, Where honeysuckles, ripen'd by the sun, Forbid the sun to en
5       ter, like favourites, Made proud by princes, that advance their pride Ag
6       ainst that power that bred it: there will she hide her, To listen our pu
7       rpose.  This is thy office; Bear thee well in it and leave us alone.
```

Handling Special Columns

Certain columns in database tables have special properties that affect how they should be handled.

On any table, one or more columns should be identified as the primary key. The primary key uniquely identifies a record, and you can always generate a WHERE clause that will identify one row (and one row only) if you know which field(s) constitute(s) a table's primary key.

Primary keys are specified when a record is created. You should think hard about whether you want to modify the primary key of an existing record. It's generally better not to.

Databases such as SQLServer support what are sometimes called timestamp fields. These do not hold a date or time, however. Instead, the timestamp field holds some form of number, which is incremented whenever a record is updated. Timestamp fields can be used to provide an efficient form of optimistic locking. When an update takes place, the database can compare the timestamp field currently in the database with the value when the updating process reads the record. If the two values differ, another user or process has updated the record since it was read, and the update will be rejected.[27] ADO identifies such columns as RowVersion columns. You shouldn't attempt to update these explicitly—it's the database's job to increment them.

The following code tests for these two types of special fields on a Field object called fd:

```
Print "KeyColumn", CBool(fd.Attributes And adFldKeyColumn)
Print "RowVersion", CBool(fd.Attributes And adFldRowVersion)
```

You should only rely on this code for an updateable client-side cursor. For other cursors, the required metadata is typically not available, so you may incorrectly get a value of False.

A closely related issue is that of AutoIncrement keys that allocate system-generated primary keys when a new record is inserted. These are discussed later in this section.

Dynamic Field Properties

fd.Properties

The remainder of this section looks at the dynamic properties that you can expect to find on Field objects derived from relational databases. Because these properties are added dynamically to the Properties collection, different Providers vary in the quantity of information available. For example, the MSDASQL (ODBC) Provider generates twenty dynamic properties for each field, while the Jet OLE DB Provider generates only five. To provide some consistency, I will only present the properties generated when using client-side cursors (that use the ADO Client Cursor Engine) which provides nine dynamic properties. If you are considering writing applications that use dynamic properties heavily and you want to be database independent, I strongly recommend using client-side cursors at all times.

Even when using the same Provider, the dynamic properties that are created won't be assigned values in all circumstances. Because retrieving metadata has an associated cost, ADO only retrieves it when it's likely to be needed. If you are only reading data, you are likely to need less metadata than if you are writing back to the database.[28] In practice, this means that the metadata is not retrieved when the Recordset is opened with a read-only LockType.

Given a client-side cursor using SQLServer 7 and a Field object, fd, representing the "part" field in the Parts table, the following code

---

27. If your database doesn't have this facility, you can simulate it using database triggers.

28. The same is true for ADO itself. If you want it to generate update instructions for you, it needs enough metadata to get the update correct.

```
Dim py As Property
For Each py In fd.Properties
    Print py.Name, py.Value
Next
```

produces these results with a read-only lock type:

BASECOLUMNNAME	Null
BASETABLENAME	Null
BASECATALOGNAME	Null
BASESCHEMANAME	Null
KEYCOLUMN	False
ISAUTOINCREMENT	False
RELATIONCONDITIONS	Null
CALCULATIONINFO	Null
OPTIMIZE	False

and these results with any other lock type:

BASECOLUMNNAME	part
BASETABLENAME	Parts
BASECATALOGNAME	MuchADO
BASESCHEMANAME	Null
KEYCOLUMN	True
ISAUTOINCREMENT	False
RELATIONCONDITIONS	Null
CALCULATIONINFO	Null
OPTIMIZE	False

Not only are many of the properties not supplied when a read-only lock type is used, but those defined as Booleans default to False, which can be misleading.

This kind of information can help resolve a problem you may encounter from time to time. Let's say that I want to find out all the parts that speak in Act 1, Scene 1, and get a description of the part and the scene. To do this with my data model, three tables will need to be joined using SQL; for example:

```
SELECT DISTINCT
    Scenes.act, Scenes.scene, Scenes.description,
    Parts.part, Parts.description
FROM Parts INNER JOIN Words ON Parts.part = Words.part, Scenes
WHERE (Words.act = 1) AND (Words.scene = 1) AND
    (Scenes.scene = Words.scene) AND
    (Scenes.act = Words.act)
```

This query will yield eight records, the first three of which are

```
1    1    Before LEONATO'S house    BEATRICE    niece to Leonato
1    1    Before LEONATO'S house    BENEDICK    a young lord of Padua
1    1    Before LEONATO'S house    CLAUDIO     a young lord of Florence
```

A problem arises when I start using the description field in code, because I have two fields called description! If my cursor is on the first record of this Recordset, guess which description I get when I execute

```
Print rs!description
```

The answer of course is

```
niece to Leonato
```

If you got this right, don't feel too smug—it's more than likely your answer was based on a guess. If you can avoid this problem by using field name aliases, fine. But if you can't, then iterating through all the fields and checking the BASETABLENAME dynamic property may be your only salvation.[29]

KEYCOLUMN and ISAUTOINCREMENT dynamic properties allow you to handle primary keys correctly, and are especially important for insert operations or for automatically generating WHERE clauses for SQL-based updates and deletes. To identify the primary key for a record, you need to scan the entire Fields collection in case compound keys are being used.

If you are performing an insert (such as rs.AddNew) you shouldn't provide values for any field where ISAUTOINCREMENT is True, as these keys will be assigned by the database.[30] There are many times when you'll need to know the value that the database has assigned to an AutoIncrement field (for example, you may want to use this value as a foreign key in another table). This wasn't always easy with earlier versions of ADO, but since ADO 2.1, it has been possible to read an AutoIncrement field after an update in order to retrieve the assigned key value, with both client-side and server-side cursors. SQLServer 7 and Access 2000 provide full support for this feature—with other

---

29. There is an example of how to do this later in the chapter.

30. AutoIncrement fields are useful when there is no "natural" primary key available for a table, as they leave it up to the database engine to create a value that is guaranteed unique for each record, but is otherwise without meaning. Access calls such fields AutoNumber, while SQLServer calls them Identity fields. Most databases provide a similar facility. Problems can arise should you need to merge records from different physical databases as there is scope for duplicate AutoIncrement field values to occur. SQLServer provides a failsafe solution to this problem by providing a "uniqueidentifier" data type based on *GUID*s.

databases you may find only certain cursor types or locations will provide access to an AutoIncrement value for a newly inserted record.

In This Section

We examined the metadata associated with Field objects and what use we can make of it. In the next section, we'll begin to see how ADO makes use of the metadata on our behalf.

Modifications and Locking with Client-Side Cursors

This section looks in greater detail at what ADO does on your behalf when you perform a modification operation on a Recordset. The update process works very differently depending on whether you have a client-side or a server-side cursor.[31] We'll also explore how well Recordset operations work when the Recordset is based on an SQL join.

When you use a server-side cursor the database engine maintains resources on your behalf while you have a Recordset open. In particular, the server knows which record you are currently pointing at in your Recordset.[32] This is very handy when you perform an update or a delete on your Recordset because the server can operate directly on the current record. What's more, the server is able to handle the pessimistic or optimistic locking requirements of your Recordset using its own lock management schemes.

None of this applies to client-side cursors. Remember that all client-side cursors are static, and there is no pessimistic locking. Once the Open method on a Recordset with a client-side cursor returns, the only server reference that is retained is the server connection (and even that is released for a disconnected Recordset). Any server-side locks or cursor features used to create the Recordset are freed up.

This begs the question: How does the Recordset know how to update a record if there is no server cursor to act on its behalf? This is one area where ADO behaves very differently from its DAO and RDO forerunners. Microsoft has learned a lot. The new ADO mechanism works very nicely, although right now unless you are using SQLServer, there are a few potential problem areas to be aware of, which I will address shortly.

To show you how client-side updating works, I have created a Recordset, rs, with a client-side optimistic-locking cursor based on `select * from Parts`.

---

31. I performed low-level analysis for this section by studying ODBC traces when using the MSDASQL Provider. This enabled me to compare Access and SQLServer behavior and exploit the relative maturity of ODBC tools. I found the external behavior of native OLE DB Providers to be very similar to that of ODBC-based connections.

32. Strictly speaking, this is only true when the CacheSize is 1. However, the model differs only in detail for a larger CacheSize.

I am going to make DON PEDRO (the first record to appear in this query) into a far more aromatic character, as follows:

```
Print rs!Description
rs.Update "description", "prince of Tarragon"
Print rs!Description
```

This prints

```
prince of Arragon
prince of Tarragon
```

No big surprise here, and when I check the database, DON PEDRO is appropriately flavored.

When I study the SQL trace generated by this process, I find the following statement:

```
UPDATE 'Parts' SET 'description'=? WHERE 'part'=? AND 'description'=?
```

In other words, the ADO Client Cursor Engine has turned my positioned update into a searched update. The previous listing is a parameterized SQL statement, in which actual values from the current record are substituted for the question marks when the update executes. ADO terminology calls this technique "Query Based Update" (QBU).

With such a small table, it isn't immediately obvious how this SQL was generated. Understanding it will draw on all our knowledge of ADO Field objects.

- The table name is derived from the BASETABLENAME dynamic property.

- The elements of the SET part of the update are derived by looking at all the Value and UnderlyingValue properties of each Field. Where the values differ, a SET element is generated.

- There are two parts to the WHERE clause. First, the primary key is used to identify the record uniquely, translating our positioned update into an equivalent searched update (QBU). However, the WHERE clause also includes the description field, which isn't part of the primary key. Its purpose is to simulate optimistic locking. If the field I am updating has changed, the WHERE clause will be unable to locate a record and the update will fail with the following message:

```
-2147217864   Row cannot be located for updating. Some values
may have been changed since it was last read.
```

This describes how the Client Cursor Engine works when handling updates. It's not only elegant, but it's fairly efficient, especially when you perform multiple updates with the same basic structure.

rs.Attributes

Generating the WHERE clause based on primary keys and changed field values works well in many cases. However, there are situations in which you might want the WHERE clause to be constructed differently. ADO allows you to control this by setting the "Update Criteria" dynamic property on the Recordset, using values from the ADCPROP_UPDATECRITERIA_ENUM enumeration, any time before the rs.Update statement executes.

Consider the SceneContents table, introduced earlier in the chapter. It has the fields shown in the table.

Table 3-1. Fields of the SceneContents Table

FIELD NAME	DATA TYPE	COMMENT
act	tinyint	Primary key
scene	tinyint	Primary key
content	text	'long' data type
datetimeloaded	datetime	--
loadedby	varchar(20)	--
ts	timestamp	RowVersion field

Assuming that the LoadedBy Field is changed, the "Update Criteria" property will affect the SQL generated by a Recordset Update in the following ways.

rs.Properties("Update Criteria") = adCriteriaKey

```
UPDATE "Scenecontents" SET "loadedBy"=? WHERE "act"=? AND "scene"=?
```

Only primary keys are used in the WHERE clause. Another user's changes would be overwritten when this statement executes, so there is no optimistic locking effect.

```
rs.Properties("Update Criteria") = adCriteriaAllCols
```

```
UPDATE "Scenecontents" SET "loadedBy"=? WHERE "act"=? AND "scene"=? AND
"dateTimeLoaded"=? AND "ts"=? AND "loadedBy"=?
```

Here, all fields are included in the WHERE clause, whether or not they have been modified and the optimistic locking effect is achieved. Note that "all columns" does not include long data types. This would be true even if the long data type was being modified.

```
rs.Properties("Update Criteria") = adCriteriaUpdCols
```

```
UPDATE "Scenecontents" SET "loadedBy"=? WHERE "act"=? AND "scene"=? AND
"loadedBy"=?
```

This is the default option. Any modified fields are added to the primary keys. This applies optimistic locking of a sort. However, optimistic locking is generally considered a record-level issue, while the optimistic locking applied by adCriteriaUpdCols only checks fields that have been changed in the Recordset. It's just possible that another user has modified the same record, but none of the fields that you have changed. In this case, the update will succeed, even though the integrity of the record may have been compromised. While you could use the "all columns" approach to prevent this from happening, it's a cumbersome solution that will generate unnecessary network and database load. If your table supports row versioning (which the SceneContents table does, as it has a timestamp field), the following approach can be used instead.

```
rs.Properties("Update Criteria") = adCriteriaTimeStamp
```

```
UPDATE "Scenecontents" SET "loadedBy"=? WHERE "act"=? AND "scene"=? AND "ts"=?
```

Note that only the primary key and the timestamp field are included in the WHERE clause. This is all that is required to achieve record-level optimistic locking.

Overcoming Missing Fields

So far in this chapter, the examples have assumed that all the required fields were available. If the data isn't in your Recordset, you might think that it can't be included in the SQL statement that the Client Cursor Engine generates. In this case, you would have no guaranteed means of identifying a unique record.

To explore this possibility, I'll switch back to using Access and the Parts table, and use the following query to create my Recordset: `select description from Parts where part = 'BORACHIO'`. Then I'll introduce some Mafia spice by changing BORACHIO's description from "follower of Don John" to "follower of Don Corleone." This should be easy.

```
On Error GoTo ErrH
Print rs!Description
rs.Update "description", "follower of Don Corleone"
Print rs!Description
Exit Sub
ErrH:
 Print Err.Number, Err.Description
```

This prints

```
 follower of Don John
 -2147467259   Key column information is insufficient or incorrect.
 Too many rows were affected by update.
```

Even though my Recordset has only one record, there are two followers of Don John in the underlying table. ADO recognizes that my update would affect more than one record and returns the error shown. It doesn't matter what setting I use for "Update Criteria"—because there is only one field in the query, ADO generates the following SQL:

```
UPDATE 'Parts' SET 'description'=? WHERE 'description'=?
```

which of course will hit any record with a description of Don John. Unfortunately, ADO only notices that more than one record is affected *after* the update has taken place, so although I get a warning error, all records in my table that meet the WHERE clause are updated![33]

The implication of this is very important. Generally speaking, when using client-side cursors for updating purposes, you should make sure that the query includes the entire primary key of the table you are working on. I said "generally speaking" for a reason. Let's see the UPDATE statement that SQLServer (as opposed to Access) generates in the exact same circumstances:

```
UPDATE "Parts" SET "description"=?
WHERE "part"=? AND "description"=?
```

---

33. However, in a properly written MTS or COM+ transactional application, the error would cause the update to roll back.

Here, the query includes the part Field, even though it doesn't appear in the Recordset. If your Recordset supports updates, but its query doesn't contain the primary key of the table being updated, SQLServer adds the primary key fields to the data it returns when the Recordset is opened, but marks them as hidden, so that they don't appear as part of the Recordset itself. However, ADO can see these columns, and so it can include them in the WHERE clause if appropriate. You can prove to yourself that hidden columns are used by reading the "Hidden Columns" dynamic property available on client-side cursor Recordset objects after the Recordset has been opened. It will always return 0 for "select * ..." queries, but the number goes up as you leave out primary key fields, so long as the Recordset is updateable. The same is true for RowVersion fields. SQLServer automatically includes them as hidden columns if they do not form part of your query and you ask for an updateable cursor.

At the time of this writing, SQLServer appears to be the only database that provides this feature. However, there is no reason why other Providers or databases won't offer this in the future.

Modifications Applied to Joins

Understanding how modifications apply to Recordsets based on single tables is a start. But to give the topic the treatment it deserves, at least some discussion of what happens when the Recordset is based on an SQL join is required.

I am going to explore the one-to-many relationship between the Parts and Words tables, using the SQLServer ODBC route. For example

```
SELECT * FROM Parts, Words WHERE Parts.part = 'BOY'
and Parts.part = Words.Part
```

will yield the following data:

part	description	id	word	part	act	scene	wordCount	WordLength
BOY	Null	11406	Signior	BOY	2	3	1	1
BOY	Null	3472	I	BOY	2	3	1	1
BOY	Null	3473	am	BOY	2	3	1	2
BOY	Null	3474	here	BOY	2	3	1	4
BOY	Null	3475	already	BOY	2	3	1	7
BOY	Null	3476	sir	BOY	2	3	1	3

The fields are drawn from two tables, and just for kicks, there are two fields called "part".

Just to remind you, the primary key of the Parts table is "part" and the primary key of the Words table is "id".

Let's take a look at the SQL generated when I try to make some changes to the first record in this Recordset. Here's what happens when I change the description field and call rs.Update:

```
UPDATE "Parts" SET "description"=?
WHERE "part"=? AND "description" IS NULL
```

and when I change wordCount and call rs.Update:

```
UPDATE "Words" SET "wordCount"=?
WHERE "id"=? AND "wordCount"=?
```

and if I change both wordCount and the description and then call rs.Update:

```
UPDATE "Words" SET "wordCount"=?
WHERE "id"=? AND "wordCount"=?

UPDATE "Parts" SET "description"=?
WHERE "part"=? AND "description"=?
```

No problem. In each case, the Client Cursor Engine creates exactly the required SQL.

The fun begins when I call rs.Delete:

```
DELETE FROM "Words" WHERE "id"=?
DELETE FROM "Parts" WHERE "part"=?
```

The chance of this being the result I want is remote. Not only does a record get deleted from the Words table (I probably did want this to happen), but also the "BOY" record is deleted from the Parts table. If my database were enforcing referential integrity I would receive an error at this point. As my particular database doesn't, I now have a bunch of records in the Words table that refer to a part that doesn't exist (I am not happy). We'll see how to resolve this in a moment. But first let's see what happens when I try an insert.

I have a burning desire to use this same Recordset to introduce Rhett Butler, quoting his most famous line, right at the end of Act 1, Scene 2. The code for this is a bit more interesting than you might think because we have to deal with two fields called "part". Here it is:

```
With rs
 .AddNew
 For Each fd In .Fields
  If fd.Name = "part" Then
    fd.Value = "RHETT BUTLER"
  End If
 Next
  !Description = "dashing soldier of fortune"
  !word = "Frankly"
  !act = 1
  !scene = 2
  !wordCount = 1
  !wordLength = 7
 .Update
End With
```

which generates the following SQL:

```
INSERT INTO "Words" ("word","part","act","scene","wordCount","WordLength")
VALUES (?,?,?,?,?,?)

INSERT INTO "Parts" ("part","description") VALUES (?,?)
```

As this is the first word Rhett speaks, it may be convenient to have a record inserted into Parts, as well as into Words. It certainly won't be convenient when I start adding "my", "dear", "I", and the rest of Rhett's first line, because I will start getting errors if I attempt to create duplicate records in the Parts table.[34]

It looks like I may have the same problem I had with Delete, but in fact this isn't so. If I only assign values to the Fields whose base table is Words, then only the Words table insert is generated. Therefore, as long as I am careful, I can control which table the insert applies to.[35]

Specifying a Unique Table

The only conclusion you can draw from the prior discussion is that the modification functionality for Recordsets based on joins is incomplete.

---

34. Note that ADO has correctly identified the AutoIncrement field in the Words table and handled the insert appropriately.

35. This still isn't ideal. If I can't write data into the fields that belong to a table I don't want to update, then any code that reads my Recordset will get incomplete data.

Updates are fine. Inserts are achievable, but with some problems. Deletes are impossible to perform safely.

Fortunately, Microsoft knew about this, and with ADO 2.1, a solution appeared. The idea is that you nominate one base table and that all modification operations only apply to this "unique" base table. Any changes to fields with a different base table are ignored. There must be a one-to-one correlation between records in the Recordset and records in the unique table. In the example just discussed, this would mean that Words could be a unique table, but Parts could not be.

This is a pragmatic and valuable solution, which solves the major problem of dealing properly with deletes, and provides a means for making inserts behave correctly. In reality, it doesn't work quite like this, and it certainly doesn't work as documented—but once you understand what it does do, you can make the model work perfectly correctly.

rs.Properties

The unique table is specified by setting one or more of the following dynamic Recordset properties available for client-side cursors (collectively known as the Unique* properties):

> Unique Catalog
>
> Unique Schema
>
> Unique Table

Providers have different ideas about which ones you should set. The safest approach is to identify a field belonging to the correct table and assign each Unique* property as follows:

```
If Not(IsNull(rs("word").Properties("BASECATALOGNAME")) Then
    rs.Properties("Unique Catalog") = _
rs("word").Properties("BASECATALOGNAME")
End If
```

Doing this for each of the three properties will ensure that the unique table is correctly specified.

Once you have specified the unique table, the rs.Delete method begins to work in the way you would want it to. Using the following code with SQLServer (where I don't need to specify the "Unique Schema" property):

```
rs.Properties("Unique Catalog") = rs("word").Properties("BASECATALOGNAME")
rs.Properties("Unique Table") = rs("word").Properties("BASETABLENAME")
rs.Delete
```

generates the following SQL:

```
DELETE FROM "Words" WHERE "id"=?
```

It would be nice if the Unique* approach guaranteed that only the unique table could be affected by inserts and updates as well as deletes. It doesn't. For both inserts and updates, it's your responsibility to provide values only for those tables you want to be affected. This means that some fields may not contain values that reflect the database contents accurately. To make updates and inserts work consistently for Recordsets based on joins, further effort is expected from you. The next section completes this picture.

In This Section

We came to terms with how updateable Recordsets work in real-world scenarios. The Client Cursor Engine is a sophisticated tool, and to get the most out if it, you need to understand exactly how it works. One of the big changes in ADO 2.1 was a decent model for Recordsets based on joins. Another valuable feature, available when using SQLServer, is the use of hidden columns to ensure you can safely update Recordsets that aren't based on "select * from" queries.

Resynchronizing Connected Recordsets

A universal fact about Recordsets is that they are never up-to-date.[36] Server-side cursors (except static ones) are reasonably up-to-date, especially if CacheSize is 1. But even in this case, once data has been read into the ADO Cache, it will become out-of-date when another user changes the underlying data source. With client-side cursors, the freshness of the data is always in question.

Optimistic locking prevents us from making dangerous updates when our data is stale. But it doesn't help to make the data we are presenting to users up-to-date. Furthermore, on the basis that prevention is better than a cure, we may want to check the freshness of our data before performing an update in order to avoid an optimistic locking collision.

In the case where we are doing inserts to join-based Recordsets, as we saw in the last section, we must avoid providing values for any fields that belong to tables that we don't want to be affected by the QBU. Typically, this means fields from the master table of a master-detail query—when we insert into the Recordset, it's usually only the detail table that we want to change. However, the fields from the master table should have valid values in the new record—values they would have if we had requested the data from the data source or if we had been allowed to fill in all the fields.

---

36. Arguably, a pessimistically locked Recordset could be up-to-date, but only because updates that would keep the database up-to-date with the real world have been prevented.

rs.Requery

In such cases, we could simply close the Recordset and reopen it using the same command, or call the rs.Requery method, which effectively does the same thing. However, this is not only wasteful, it might have unwanted effects on those parts of our program that use that Recordset.

rs.Resync

To address all of these issues, ADO provides resynchronization functionality through the Resync method. Resync isn't supported by all Providers or with all cursor types[37], although it's available with client-side cursors. You can test for the availability of Resync functionality through the Supports method.

The syntax of the Resync method is:

Sub Resync([AffectRecords As AffectEnum = adAffectAll],
        [ResyncValues As ResyncEnum = adResyncAllValues])

The arguments to Resync are mostly used with disconnected or hierarchical Recordsets, which are not the focus of this chapter, so we'll just use the default values for the time being.

fd.Value
fd.UnderlyingValue

When using a server-side cursor, calling Resync will update the current ADO Cache with the latest values based on the contents of the database. The latest values are then available in the fd.Value property. This is far more efficient than reexecuting the query and is also more convenient. ADO performs a similar task when you access the fd.UnderlyingValue property. In this case, the cache is refreshed, but the new values appear in the UnderlyingValue property rather than the Value property of each relevant Field object.

For example, in the following code based on the Parts table and a server-side, keyset cursor, VERGES' description is changed by another user at the point shown:

```
Print "Value", "Underlying", "Original"

With rs("description")
   Print .Value, .UnderlyingValue, .OriginalValue



   Print .Value, .UnderlyingValue, .OriginalValue
   rs.Resync
   Print .Value, .UnderlyingValue, .OriginalValue
End With
```

←   database update from other user occurs here

---

37. With SQLServer, the only server-side cursors that support Resync are keyset cursors.

It prints

Value	Underlying	Original
a petty officer	a petty officer	a petty officer
a petty officer	a headborough	a petty officer
a headborough	a headborough	a headborough

If the record is deleted instead of updated, then the Underlying property will throw an error prior to the Resync, equivalent to the identification of a hole in the keyset.[38]

With client-side cursors, there is no server-side cursor support, so reading the fd.UnderlyingValue property doesn't give you an instant view of what is happening in the database. It simply tells you what the database contained for the field the last time you accessed the database using rs.Open or rs.Resync.

Calling Resync generates an SQL statement based on the primary key of the current record, which results in the all the fd.Value properties being updated. Just as with QBUs, issues arise when the primary key is not part of the query. If the Provider and data source support hidden columns, there will be no problem resyncing a client-side cursor. If hidden columns aren't supported, you must ensure that the primary key is present in the Recordset if you want to allow resyncing.

When the Recordset is based on a join, the Client Cursor Engine will create and execute an SQL statement for each table. If this brings back haunting memories of the previous section (concerning updating joins), don't be surprised—the issues are very much the same. Once again, ADO 2.1 and later versions provide a solution that is not only useful if we want to resync, but also allows us to address the limitations concerning inserts that were uncovered in the last section.

rs.Properties   ADO 2.1 allows you to specify a customized resynchronization command. If you have specified a unique table, then you can provide a command to execute when resyncing occurs by setting the "Resync Command" dynamic Recordset property. The command will only be used when you have properly specified a unique table; it must:

1. Return columns in exactly the same order as the Recordset contains them.

2. Contain command parameters that match the primary keys of the unique table in both number and order.

---

38. See previous discussion of keyset cursors.

For example, if my Recordset was created using the following SQL:

```
SELECT * FROM Parts, Words WHERE Parts.part = 'BOY'
and Parts.part = Words.Part
```

then my Resync Command could be

```
SELECT * FROM Parts, Words WHERE Parts.part = 'BOY'
and Parts.part = Words.Part and Words.id = ?"
```

or

```
SELECT * FROM Parts, Words WHERE
Parts.part = Words.Part and Words.id = ?"
```

or even just

```
SELECT 'BOY', Null, id, word, part, act, scene, wordCount,
wordLength" FROM Words WHERE id = ?"
```

All of these SQL statements meet the criteria. The last one avoids performing a join and works if I know the values that I want to have in the two fields from the Parts table. In all cases, ADO provides the parameter values based on the primary key value(s) for the current record. Stored procedures are also permitted.

You get full marks if you have now worked out how to correct the problem I was having with the insert into a join-based Recordset in the previous section. I was forced to avoid providing values for the two fields from the Parts table because I only wanted to add a new record to the Words table, not Parts. As a result, those two fields of my new record were empty and would not look correct if displayed anywhere. However, by resyncing the record after the AddNew/Update, I can restore the missing values via a customized Resync Command.

Even better, I can ask ADO to perform an implicit Resync after my modification operation by setting yet another dynamic Recordset property provided by the Client Cursor Engine, the "Update Resync" property. It can have one of the following values defined by the CEResyncEnum enumeration:

adResyncNone

adResyncAutoIncrement

adResyncConflicts

adResyncUpdates

adResyncInserts

adResyncAll

This is a bitmasked property, so values can be "Anded" together. It gives fine control over which modifications trigger resyncs.

Based on what you have learned since I first attempted to add Rhett Butler's words into Act 1, Scene 2, you should now be able to make the whole operation work successfully. Remember this is a client-side cursor based on a join between the Words and the Parts tables. Rhett has already been created as a part. Here's the complete code:

```
Dim fd As Field

With rs

    '********** this code need only run once ***********
    .Properties("Unique Catalog") = "MuchADO"
    .Properties("Unique Table") = "Words"
    .Properties("Resync Command") = _
            "select 'RHETT BUTLER', " & _
            "'dashing soldier of fortune',id, word,part,act, " & _
            "scene, wordCount, WordLength from Words where id = ?"
    .Properties("Update Resync") = adResyncAll


    '******* this code runs for each new record ******
    .AddNew
    For Each fd In .Fields
        If fd.Name = "part" And _
            fd.Properties("BASETABLENAME") = "Words" Then
            fd.Value = "RHETT BUTLER"
        End If
    Next

    !word = "Frankly"
    !act = 1
    !scene = 2
    !wordCount = 1
    !wordLength = 7
    Print !part, !Description
    .Update
    Print !part, !Description
End With
```

set all the dynamic rs properties

make sure the part field from the Words table gets updated, and the one from the Parts table doesn't which prints

```
RHETT BUTLER    Null
RHETT BUTLER    dashing soldier of fortune
```

Before the update, the description field has no value. After the update, the custom resynchronization ensures that it does. If you are wondering why the part field has a value before the update, ask yourself which part field is being displayed.

In This Section

We explored the Resync capabilities of ADO for both single-table and join-based Recordsets. We also saw how custom resynchronization can be used to provide full power when updating join-based Recordsets.

Using Index and Seek

Most relational database programmers use SQL to retrieve data. SQL is known as a "non-navigational" means of data retrieval. This means that you tell the database what data you require (via an SQL query) and the database engine works out the most efficient strategy to find its way around the physical data to create the Recordset you requested. Database engines use optimizers to do this, which exploit any available database indexes to come up with the best query execution plan. If new indexes are created, the same query could run much faster without requiring any coding changes.

rs.Index
rs.Seek

However, some programmers feel more comfortable with "navigational" techniques which require an explicit reference to an index in program code in order to locate a desired record efficiently. ADO provides the Index property and Seek method to support this approach, although most Providers don't support it. In fact, I have only seen this functionality supported by the Jet Provider, and only in certain circumstances.

When using the navigational programming style, you specify the table you want to use (joins are not allowed) and select a predefined index to provide an ordering on the table. You then use a Seek command to find a record that meets a certain set of criteria, providing a value for the columns defined in the index. If the index is non-unique, you need to use MoveNext or MovePrevious to go to the next record in "index order" in order to identify other records meeting the same criteria.[39]

To use Index and Seek, you must specify a server-side cursor and specify a command type of adCmdTableDirect[40] via the Options argument to rs.Open.

You can use the Supports method to tell whether your Recordset supports Index and Seek.

In *Much ADO about Nothing*, Beatrice utters the underused word "noisome" in Act 5, Scene 2. Let's look for it. In order to do this, I have added an index called "WordUnique" to the Words table[41], based on the columns word, part, act, and scene.

```
Dim rs As New Recordset

rs.ActiveConnection = "Provider=Microsoft.Jet.OLEDB.4.0;" & _
          "Data Source=D:\ADOBook\Data\muchado.mdb;"
rs.Source = "Words"
rs.CursorLocation = adUseServer
rs.Open Options:=adCmdTableDirect

If rs.Supports(adSeek) And rs.Supports(adIndex) Then
  rs.Index = "WordUnique"
  rs.Seek Array("noisome", "BEATRICE", 5, 2)      ◄────   search criteria
                                                          specified here

  If rs.EOF Then
    Print "not found"
  Else
    Print rs!word, rs!part, rs!wordCount, rs!WordLength
  End If

End If
```

which prints

noisome	BEATRICE	1	7

Note that the source isn't SQL, it's a table name. This is what the adCmd-TableDirect command type expects. Also notice that the values forming the search criteria are turned into an array, using a field ordering as defined by the index. You don't have to provide a value for each field, but you can't skip fields—you can only leave them off the end. I was searching an index

---

39. This approach is very similar to using Find and Sort on a client-side cursor. However, Find and Sort are more flexible, as they don't require an index to physically exist on the database, and will work on the results of joins. Even so (and as discussed in Chapter 2), the Filter property is more powerful and easy to use than Find.

40. We'll discuss command type in Chapter 5.

41. An Index must exist before it's used with the Index and Seek approaches. Indexes are usually created using database administration tools, but you can use ADO to create indexes programmatically (see Chapter 10), if your Provider supports this functionality.

comprising the fields: word, part, act, scene, so I supplied "Array("noisome", "BEATRICE", 5, 2)." Finally note the use of EOF. If the requested record can't be found, EOF becomes True. Here's the full syntax for the Seek method:

Sub Seek (KeyValues as Variant,
          [SeekOption As SeekEnum = adSeekFirstEQ])

    The SeekEnum provides a number of choices for specifying the SeekOption. This allows you to navigate the index from either end, or if there is no record exactly matching your criteria, to locate the first record before or after the place where such a record would be if it existed. These options basically equate to >, >=, <, and <=, duplicating the Seek functionality of DAO.

    If you are porting an existing DAO application to ADO, you can use Index and Seek to keep the code changes to a minimum. Otherwise, you are more likely to use SQL combined with client-side navigation.

In This Section

You learned how to use the Index and Seek navigational techniques.

Processing Multiple Recordsets

There are two situations in which calling the rs.Open method can return more than one Recordset:

1. When you provide a compound command such as "SELECT * FROM Parts; SELECT * FROM Scenes". Here, two separate SQL statements are joined together into a single command using a semicolon as a delimiter.

2. When you call a stored procedure that generates multiple result sets.

    The latter case is a valuable technique that we'll return to in Chapter 5 when I discuss stored procedures. The former technique can be useful when you have a batch of commands that can be executed together. However, it can also make your code more obscure and limit the number of Providers your code will work with.

rs.NextRecordset   ADO lets you process multiple result sets returned from a single command by using the NextRecordset method, which is defined as follows:

Function NextRecordset([RecordsAffected]) As Recordset

Here's some code using this technique:

```
Dim rs1 as New Recordset
Dim rs2 as Recordset
rs1.CursorLocation = adUseClient
rs1.Open "SELECT * FROM Parts;" & _
        "DELETE FROM Words where wordCount > 15;" & _
        "SELECT * FROM Scenes", "DSN=MuchADO"
Set rs2 = rs1.NextRecordset
```

The first Recordset, rs1, is opened using a compound command string. It contains a Recordset based on "SELECT * FROM Parts;". Calling NextRecordset on rs1 will return a new Recordset, which I can either assign to rs1, or to a new Recordset variable. Some Providers will allow you to operate on both Recordsets at the same time, while others will automatically close the first one.

There are two things to note here. The first is that I could have achieved the same results with clearer code by processing each statement separately. The second is that my second statement is non-row–returning, even though a Recordset object is created. There are three valid outcomes from calling NextRecordset:

1. There is no next Recordset. In this case, NextRecordset returns Nothing.

2. The statement is non-row–returning. In this case, a Recordset is returned, but it's closed.

3. A Recordset is returned with zero or more records. In this case, the Recordset is open.

You can easily test for each of these outcomes.

If the current Recordset has an edit pending, such as rs.EditMode <> adEditNone, an error will occur.

Contrary to some of the current ADO documentation, the compound command string is passed directly to the server when the first Recordset is opened. However, until NextRecordset is called, only the first Recordset is retrieved from the server.

In This Section

You learned how to process multiple Recordsets returned by compound commands.

Optimization for SQL Data Sources

It was very straightforward discussing optimization with standalone Record-sets in Chapter 2. There is little more to it than identifying those situations where, for a little more effort, we can give ADO a helping hand to squeeze extra performance out of our code. When working with SQL Recordsets, optimization can sometimes be this cut-and-dry, but usually there are many more factors to consider.

By far the best way to optimize performance with an SQL data source is to really understand both the standard theory of relational databases and the particular approach of the database you are using. As far as the former is concerned, a database that is well-designed (both logically and physically) will give the best combination of performance and protection of your code from future changes in requirements, while knowing SQL in depth will allow you to write optimal queries. Understanding how your particular database handles indexes, query optimization, caching, locking and lock escalation, and knowing how to exploit stored procedures (if your database supports them) is, generally speaking, more important than the material I am presenting in this section from a performance viewpoint. Of course, if you are targeting multiple data sources, then there is less that you can do to exploit these specifics, but this simply increases the importance of understanding relational theory and how databases in general go about implementing it.

However, there are still plenty of issues to address when considering what you can achieve in ADO code to optimize your application. One of the most important questions to ask yourself is, What are you trying to optimize?

It may be that you are aiming to optimize portability between databases. If this is the case, you are likely to abandon server-side cursors and stored procedures in favor of the greater conformity offered by client-side cursors and standard SQL.

If performance is your primary goal, then you need to consider the circumstances in which you want to achieve optimal performance. There is more to optimization than performance alone. Performance targets have to be tempered by safety and robustness concerns. The use of locking and trans-actions slow down database operations, but without them, no one would have any faith in the programs we write.

As an example of the complexity of performance issues, consider the performance tradeoffs of server-side and client-side cursors.

A server-side cursor is fast to open because the data is not copied into your client process at the time the Recordset is opened. This is particularly true when forward-only cursors are used. Updates are faster through server-side cursors because a direct reference is held in the server to your current record. For example, when using the ODBC Provider, a server-side update translates into a single ODBC API call for many databases. It couldn't be much faster. Server-side cursors can also give you better exposure to changes in the underlying data when using keyset or dynamic cursors. This is not only convenient, but it can reduce the number of update collisions due to optimistic locking, which itself will improve the performance of the system.

However, client-side cursors also have their advantages, even from a performance perspective. Although a server-side cursor opens quickly, it does so before all your data is available in your client program. As you scroll through the data, you may be delayed by fetches from the network as the server-side cursor is asked to deliver the next cacheful of records. However, once a client-side cursor is open, all the data is immediately available in your client programs, so scrolling will always be instantaneous, regardless of the network or server load. Your users may be willing to wait for the initial Open method to execute, in return for immediate scrolling.[42]

Updates through client-side cursors are undoubtedly slower than those executed through server-side cursors, although batch updates improve matters for client-side cursors (see Chapter 7). Also, the searched update generated by the Client Cursor Engine may be slower than a positioned update.

While individual updates are faster using server-side cursors, you need to consider the cost of maintaining the server-side cursor features. This can include the maintenance of locks[43] and keysets the entire time the Recordset is open. For small numbers of users, this won't cause a problem, but once the number of users starts to exceed a few dozen, the *scalability* offered by client-side cursors can start to become more important. Client-side cursors are scalable because they place minimal demands on the server, so increasing the number of users by a factor of five or ten is less likely to suddenly turn the server into a bottleneck.[44]

For another example of the complexity of performance issues, consider the type of operation you want to optimize. Doing updates by writing your own SQL is a lot faster than doing them through server-side cursors (because you can read all data through a fast forward-only, read-only cursor), which in turn is faster than using client-side cursors. Using stored procedures is faster still. However, for most interactive applications on a private network, update traffic is tiny when measured as a percentage of system load, and few users notice the time it takes to update a few records unless there are locking or indexing problems on the database. If you are writing a batch process to insert thousands of records, or keeping a world-beating Web site alive, then it's well worth using the most highly-tuned techniques. These tend to involve not using Recordsets for modifications,

---

42. Arguably, if immediate return from the Open method is essential, you should consider using asynchronous techniques (see Chapter 6).

43. SQLServer applies locks on all records in a Recordset for optimistic and pessimistic locking. For pessimistic locking these locks are exclusive, but for optimistic locking "shared" locks are used.

44.4 The scalability of client-side cursors is increased further when they are disconnected (see Chapter 7).

and you'll meet them in later chapters. But otherwise, it may be better to focus on good database design and efficient use of SQL.[45]

While most performance issues are complex and multifaceted, there are two basic techniques that can make a major performance difference in many scenarios: the use of append-only Recordsets and the correct use of rs.CacheSize.

Append-only Recordsets

rs.Properties

If your only task is to add records to a database, and you want to do this using a Recordset approach, how might you proceed? Let's say I want to add some words to the Words table. What sort of query might I use as the Recordset source? The most obvious choice is "SELECT * FROM Words", but this is also the most dangerous. There are over 10,000 records in this table. I don't want to cache them all just to do a few inserts. Any other query I can think of is likely to be either arbitrary or obtuse. Fortunately, I can ask for an append-only Recordset and avoid such dilemmas. Here's how:

```
rs.CursorLocation = adUseClient
rs.LockType = adLockOptimistic
rs.Properties("Append-Only Rowset") = True
rs.Open "SELECT * FROM Words"
```

The server executes the statement, but no data is retrieved and the RecordCount is initially 0. This can make a huge difference for client-side cursors (the "Append-Only Rowset" property is created by the Client Cursor Engine, so it's unlikely to be present on a server-side Recordset). However, I can happily add records and scroll around to see what I have added.

Cache Size

rs.CacheSize

The most dramatic and easily achieved optimization that can be applied purely by ADO coding is probably that of CacheSize adjustment. By understanding CacheSize there are many situations in which you can reduce the time it takes to iterate through a Recordset by a factor of five or more.

The impact of CacheSize is most impressive on server-side scrollable cursors. With client-side or forward-only cursors the impact will typically be less dramatic, but still desirable.

---

45. We've talked a great deal about cursors, metadata, and locks in the chapter. This is a good basis for thinking about which types of Recordset are the most resource-intensive. The major issue we haven't addressed yet is connection management, which is covered in Chapter 4.

The role of the ADO Cache was discussed earlier in the chapter with cursor types. By default, a Recordset's CacheSize property is set to 1. This means that the ADO Cache holds one record at a time and each rs.MoveNext or rs.MovePrevious will cause the ADO Cache to be loaded with more data from the cursor service.

By increasing the CacheSize property to 100, the ADO Cache is loaded with 100 records at a time.[46] There is an overhead each time the ADO Cache is loaded, so loading it less frequently (by having a higher CacheSize) yields better performance. When the ADO Cache is loaded across a network (for instance, by a server-side cursor), this overhead is relatively high. When it's loaded from a client-side cursor, the overhead is lower (because the data is already in memory), but it's still measurable.

When a forward-only cursor is used, even though there is no "real" cursor service, a cache is still maintained, and therefore, there is still scope for optimization.

There is no scientific way to determine the optimal CacheSize, but many people have found 100 to be a good value. If you are using a server-side cursor, it's important to remember that increasing the CacheSize reduces your Recordset's sensitivity to changes in the underlying database. The reason for this was presented earlier in the chapter.

When you are retrieving only a very small number of records, there is a small overhead in having a CacheSize other than 1, so it makes sense to stick with the default value.

In This Section

On the whole, simplistic statements about performance fail to tell the whole story. Controlling CacheSize is one obvious optimization technique all ADO programmers should consider, but otherwise, it's far more important to be an informed and environmentally friendly consumer of data resources than to hope for quick fixes and hot tips.

Summary

In this chapter, I built on techniques described in Chapter 2 by explaining in detail the use of Recordsets based on SQL-based data sources. At a basic level, using Recordsets is all too easy—provide a command string and a connection string to the Open method and "presto!" However, once you start taking an interest in what you are *really* doing, or start using Recordsets for real-world tasks such as updating join-based Recordsets, a new level of

---

46. This assumes there are 100 records available to load. If there are less than 100 records the cache will be partially filled.

complexity arises. This isn't to say SQL programming with Recordsets is hard—you can still achieve astonishing things with a few lines of code. It's more the case that ADO is powerful, and controlling power properly requires understanding.

In particular, we

- Looked at the different cursor and locking models used by ADO.

- Considered the differences between client-side and server-side cursors.

- Examined the differences between Providers and learned how to check whether the functionality we require is actually there. You can smooth out many of these differences by using client-side cursors.

- Explored how Query Based Updates and resynchronization work, and how to control the techniques.

- Learned how to exploit hidden columns when the Provider supports them.

- Saw how Recordsets based on joins can be modified safely.

Finally, we discussed optimization. There are some smart techniques for making queries work faster, but there are also more subtle ways to achieve optimization . A prime example of this is the use of connections. Only a few years ago, the idea of "creating" a new connection for each new Recordset would have seemed an insane waste of system resources. These days however, the approach seems more reasonable, not because computers are faster, but because of the advanced connection management that is built into ADO. How this works and how to exploit it is just one of the topics of the next chapter.

Explicit Connections

ADO USES CONNECTION OBJECTS to establish and maintain a session between a client program and a data source. It used to be that the first task of any data access program was to create some form of Connection object (in traditional DAO, the Database object fulfills this role), which was then used as the basis for all interaction between the program and its server. As explained in the previous chapter, this is no longer necessary, and the issue of when it is or isn't appropriate to use explicit Connection objects remains the topic of a healthy debate. I will hold off from entering into this debate until later in the chapter. Instead, let's begin by exploring what to do with Connection objects on the assumption that you use them.

I've already introduced the idea of connection strings, but only in the limited sense of using them to create direct connections to relational databases. In this chapter I expand on connection strings and how to manage them.

We'll continue to use the MuchADO database, but as we are no longer confining ourselves to relational data sources, we'll also make use of Microsoft Indexing Services (and its OLE DB Provider). In addition to having the text of *Much ADO about Nothing* loaded into a database, I also have it in free text format in my file system, with a separate HTML document for each

Scene. Indexing Services automatically indexed these documents without any work on my part, other than copying them onto my hard disk.[1]

Creating and Using Connections

cn.Open

Connection objects are opened by calling the Open method. Here's its syntax:

Sub Open([ConnectionString As String],
             [UserID As String],
             [Password As String],
             [Options As Long = -1])

Just as with the Recordset object, all the arguments to Open are optional, which means you can choose to set properties before calling the method if you wish. Before exploring these in detail, let's take a look at some examples.

rs.ActiveConnection

In the first example, I used an ODBC-based SQLServer connection and assigned it to the ActiveConnection property of a Recordset that is counting occurrences of the word "toothache" in the MuchADO database.

```
Dim cn As New Connection
Dim rs As New Recordset
cn.Open "DSN=MuchADO"    ◄─────────────────  Connection opened here
rs.Source = "SELECT  S.act, S.scene, S.description," & _
    " sum(W.wordCount) as hits" & _
    " FROM Scenes as S, Words as W WHERE W.word = 'toothache'" & _
    " and S.scene = W.scene and S.act = W.act " & _
    " group by S.act, S.scene, S.description"
Set rs.ActiveConnection = cn   ◄─────────────  Connection assigned
rs.Open                                          to Recordset here
While Not rs.EOF
    Print rs!act, rs!scene, rs!Description, rs!hits
    rs.MoveNext
Wend
rs.Close
cn.Close                       ◄──────────  Connection and Recordset
                                             closed here
```

---

1. Windows 2000 Indexing Services is an improved version of the impressive Index Server available for NT4. In addition to having a richer command language, Indexing Services automatically catalogues the entire file system, not just the Virtual Web directories. Both products are free to use.

This prints

5	1	Before LEONATO'S house.	1
3	2	A room in LEONATO'S house	3

The equivalent task using Microsoft Indexing Services[2] is

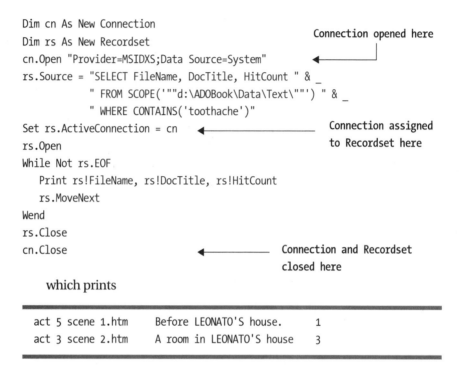

```
Dim cn As New Connection
Dim rs As New Recordset                        Connection opened here
cn.Open "Provider=MSIDXS;Data Source=System"
rs.Source = "SELECT FileName, DocTitle, HitCount " & _
            " FROM SCOPE('""d:\ADOBook\Data\Text\""') " & _
            " WHERE CONTAINS('toothache')"
Set rs.ActiveConnection = cn                   Connection assigned
rs.Open                                        to Recordset here
While Not rs.EOF
    Print rs!FileName, rs!DocTitle, rs!HitCount
    rs.MoveNext
Wend
rs.Close
cn.Close                                       Connection and Recordset
                                               closed here
```

which prints

act 5 scene 1.htm	Before LEONATO'S house.	1
act 3 scene 2.htm	A room in LEONATO'S house	3

By assigning a Connection object to the ActiveConnection property of the Recordset (or the equivalent argument of the rs.Open method) instead of providing a connection string directly to the Recordset, you can exploit any property settings made on the Connection object and ensure that multiple Recordsets all share the same Connection object. Whether this gives you any performance benefits is a question I will answer later.

Now that you have seen a Connection object in action, let's take a closer look at how you can construct connection strings. A connection string is made out of keywords and values, and each pair is separated by a semicolon. The connection string must contain enough information to identify the

2. My purpose in this book is to write about ADO rather the command syntax used by Providers, and as such, I am much more interested in the similarities in these two code samples, than in the differences between the connection strings and the command language. Microsoft Indexing Services supports three different access languages, all of which generate ADO Recordsets. This example uses an extended form of SQL.

connection required and may also contain additional information used to
configure the connection or to provide security validation details.

In Chapter 3, we saw just how hideous connection strings can be,
for example:

```
"Provider=SQLOLEDB;Data Source=POLECAT;
User ID=sa;Password=;Initial Catalog=MuchADO;"
```

This connection string contains the Provider name, the data source (in this
case, the name of the computer running SQLServer), the logical database (initial catalog) within that server that we wish to use, and a user ID and password.

cn.Provider
cn.Connection-
String
cn.DefaultDatabase

When using a Connection object, you can make the task of connecting
more approachable. For example, instead of passing the previous string to
the cn.Open method (or assigning it to cn.ConnectionString), you could
achieve the same with:

```
cn.Provider = "SQLOLEDB"
cn.ConnectionString = "Data Source=POLECAT"
cn.Open , "sa", ""
cn.DefaultDatabase = "MuchADO"
```

The default database can be changed any time after the connection is
open, to switch between different logical databases.

cn.Properties

As an alternative to connection strings, you can do the whole thing using
dynamic connection properties once you have identified the Provider,
for example:

```
cn.Provider = "SQLOLEDB"
cn.Properties("Data Source") = "POLECAT"
cn.Properties("Initial Catalog") = "MuchADO"
cn.Properties("User ID") = "sa"
cn.Properties("Password") = ""
cn.Open
```

Some of the dynamic properties are, of course, Provider-specific.
However, the same is true of the keywords in a connection string, so the
choice of connection technique is entirely up to you. ADO ignores most of
this connection information, passing it straight through to the Provider.
Connecting is one area where you must always be sensitive to the differences
between Providers.[3]

---

3. There are some "standard" dynamic properties defined for Connection objects. These
are discussed more in the "Connection Properties" section, later in this chapter.

There are currently three situations in which it's valid *not* to specify a Provider when connecting using a Connection object[4]:

1. When `File Name=` is used to refer to a Data Link File containing connection information (see later).

2. When `URL=` is used to refer to a Web-based resource. This is a short-hand means of referring to the Microsoft OLE DB Provider for Internet Publishing (MSDAIPP.DSO); it's discussed in Chapter 9.

3. When neither of the above nor a Provider is explicitly referenced, in which case, the entire connection string will be passed to MSDASQL, the ODBC Provider.

One standard dynamic Connection property that is particularly useful during the connecting process is the Prompt property, which controls whether users are prompted for logon information. Although it's a dynamic property rather than a standard Connection property, there is an enumeration (ConnectPromptEnum) defined for it in ADO with the following values:

adPromptAlways: Always prompts the user for initialization information.

adPromptComplete: Prompts the user only if more information is needed.

adPromptCompleteRequired: Prompts the user only if more information is needed. Doesn't allow the user to enter optional information.

adPromptNever (default): Doesn't prompt the user.

For embedded or Web-based applications, the default is quite obviously the most sensible value. For applications in which the Connection object is created in the client program, the following is the most common setting:

```
cn.Properties("Prompt") = adPromptCompleteRequired
```

Data Link Files

Connection strings can be long, and different Providers require different connection information, so Microsoft has provided a graphical way of constructing connection strings that is simpler than typing them out manually.

---

4. Some documentation implies that "Remote Provider" and "Remote Server" can also be used in place of "Provider" when using a Connection object. This is not the case. These terms refer to dynamic properties of the "MS Remote" Provider (see Chapter 15).

Connection strings created this way can be saved in a file called a Data Link File, which has a .udl extension.

Data Link Files were introduced with ADO 2.0 and have been extended in ADO 2.5. They are in many ways the OLE DB equivalent of the ODBC Administrator Applet. This Applet appears in the Control Panel and is used to define ODBC DSNs. However, Data Link Files avoid using the Registry for storing connection configuration information, and therefore, are a good deal more flexible.

The user interface for Data Link Files is based on Property Pages, and there are three main pages in the Data Link Properties dialog:

1. **Provider**: Lists all the OLE DB Providers known to your system.

2. **Connection**: Allows you to specify connection information. A default display is provided by OLE DB, which can be customized by individual Providers. The connection information allows you to save a password. This isn't a good idea. It's better to use the User ID and Password arguments of cn.Open (or thse Prompt dynamic property) and keep security information separate from connection information.

3. **All Properties**: Allows you to set any dynamic initialization property for the selected Provider.

You can see these three tabs in Figure 4.1, which show the settings for the SQLServer native OLE DB Provider.

The Data Link Properties window is used by VB's Data Environment to provide a graphical way of specifying connection properties. Alternatively you can create .udl files using Windows Explorer. Prior to Windows 2000, you could create a Data Link File just by right-clicking in the file pane of Windows Explorer, and selecting New ➤ Data Link File. For Windows 2000, Microsoft decided that unsophisticated users might be confused by the notion of Data Link Files, so this option is no longer available by default. Therefore, you need to create an empty text file with a .udl extension by some other means. Once created however, you can double-click the file to bring up the graphical display.

Visual Basic programs can create files with a .udl extension programmatically and can then shell the file using the Windows API function ShellExecute. Keeping connection information separate from your programs can be advantageous, as it allows connections to be modified without needing

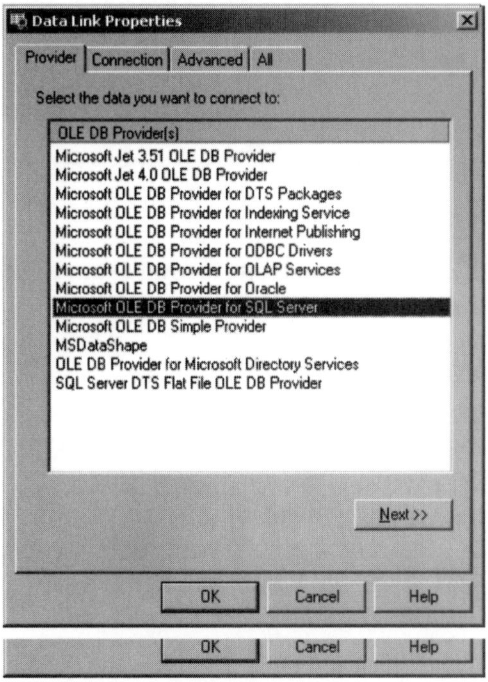

A. The Provider tab

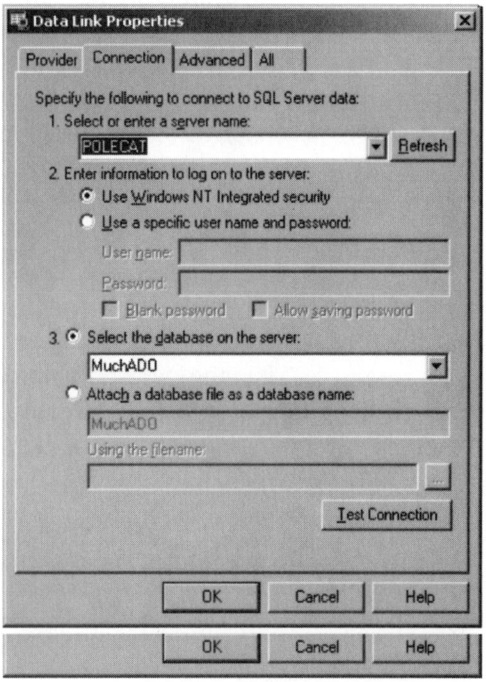

B. The Connection tab

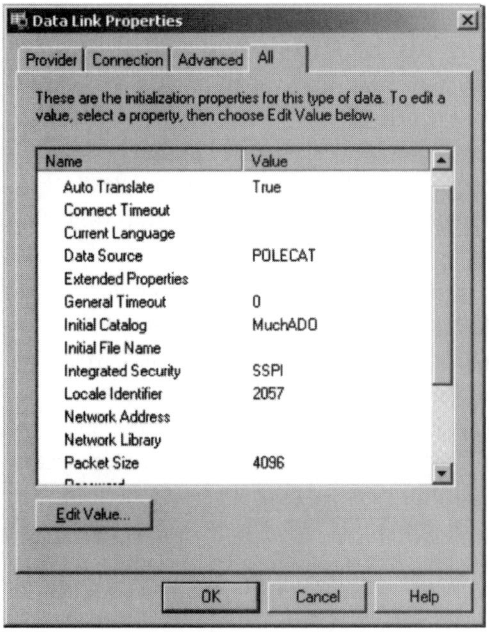

C. The All Properties tab

Figure 4-1. The Data Link Properties window

to recompile. The following sample shows how to connect using a file in a directory designated by Microsoft for the storage of Data Link Files[5]:

```
Dim cn As New Connection
cn.Open "File Name=C:\Program Files\Common Files" & _
        "\SYSTEM\ole db\Data Links\MuchADO.udl"
```

dl.PromptNew

Even if you don't like the idea of Data Link Files, you can use the graphical tool to generate connection strings that you can then paste into your code. Alternatively, you can make use of the Microsoft OLE DB Service Component library. This an OLE DB Core component, so you can safely set a reference to it in the knowledge that wherever OLE DB is installed (as least version 2 or greater) this library will be available. Once referenced, you can create an instance of a DataLinks object and call its PromptNew method. This displays the Data Link Properties window which the user can use to build a connection string graphically. When the user closes the window, the function returns a closed Connection object with its ConnectionString property initialized according to the user's choices. Here's the code (assuming the reference has been set):

```
On Error GoTo ErrH:
Dim dl As New MSDASC.DataLinks
Dim cn As Connection

Set cn = dl.PromptNew
If Not cn Is Nothing Then cn.Open
Exit Sub
ErrH:
  MsgBox "Could not connect to:" & vbCrLf _
         & cn.ConnectionString
```

If the user presses the Cancel button on the Data Link Properties window, PromptNew returns Nothing, so it's important to test for this. Equally, there is no guarantee that the user will have tested the connection details that they select, so you need to error handle the Open method.

dl.PromptEdit

The DataLinks class also supports a PromptEdit method that takes an existing Connection object as an argument and allows its connection string to be edited graphically.

---

5. There is no obligation to store Data Link Files in this directory. The benefit of doing so is that you can't be accused of using them just to avoid typing long connection strings.

Other Properties Used When Connecting

cn.Connection-
TimeOut

To round off our discussion of connecting, there are one or two other Connection object properties worth mentioning. By default, ADO will wait 15 seconds for a connection request to return. If this is an inappropriate amount of time, you can set the ConnectionTimeout property to a value of your choice. Setting it to 0 means that the connection request will never time out.

cn.CursorLocation

The Connection object has a CursorLocation property. By setting this once you can ensure that all Recordsets created using the connection will use this setting, unless it's specifically overridden. This is very useful if you adopt a policy of using client-side cursors for all your Recordsets, if only because you can't provide cursor location as an argument to rs.Open.

cn.Mode

Some data sources (such as Jet) respond to the Mode property. This can be used to control your mode of access to the entire database (for example, adModeRead for read-only access) or even to control all others' access rights (such as adModeShareDenyWrite). This is an extreme form of pessimistic locking (perhaps it should be called depressive locking) that is appropriate if you are knowingly writing an application either for a single user or to allow only one user to perform updates at a time. The ConnectModeEnum enumeration defines the possible values.

cn.State
cn.Version

Finally, the Connection object has a State property that uses the same enumeration as the Recordset object and for the same purpose (see Chapter 2), and a Version property to return the version number of the ADO implementation.

In This Section

We explored the process of connecting to a data source using the Open method and either a connection string or connection properties. You learned how to use Data Link Files to keep connection information separate from our programs and to provide a convenient graphical interface for gathering connection information. Finally, you saw some of the standard static properties of the Connection object.

The Execute Method

The Execute method provides a direct way to create Recordsets and also to execute non-row–returning commands[6], such as INSERT, UPDATE, and DELETE SQL statements.

---

6. There is no consensus over whether to use "row" or "record" when referring to databases. DAO used "record," while RDO used "row." ADO uses "record," while OLE DB uses "row" to refer to the exact same structure. I've used "record" except where ingrained usage dictates the use of "row," but both terms can be considered synonymous.

cn.Execute

Whereas the last chapter presented Recordsets as the focus for creating ADO-based applications, the Execute method features strongly in applications centered on Connection objects. In this style of application, all Recordsets are read-only, and updates are performed by SQL statements, supported by optimistic locking based on a RowVersioning mechanism such as SQLServer's timestamp fields. This technique has been prized as a high-performance model for heavy-duty applications for some years. Both Recordset and Connection-oriented approaches are valid, and we'll be comparing them directly at the end of the chapter.

The syntax of the Execute method is:

Function Execute(CommandText As String,
                    [RecordsAffected As Long],
                    [Options As Long = -1]) As Recordset

When used to create Recordsets, a row-returning command string (typically a SELECT statement or a row-returning stored procedure call) is supplied as the first argument, while the second argument is ignored.

All Recordsets created using Execute are read-only and use a forward-only cursor unless the cn.CursorLocation has been set to adUseClient, in which case the cursor is read-only, static, and client-side. Other types of Recordset must be created using rs.Open.

As with the Options argument to rs.Open, the values for the Options argument to cn.Execute are drawn from the CommandTypeEnum and ExecuteOptionEnum enumerations. Command type will be discussed in detail in Chapter 5, while Chapter 6 addresses the asynchronous features enabled using the ExecuteOptionEnum enumeration.

Here's an example using Microsoft Indexing Services to locate the famous quote from *Much ADO about Nothing* concerning toothache and philosophers. It assumes an existing connection.

```
Dim rs As Recordset
Dim sCommand As String

sCommand = "SELECT FileName, DocTitle, Size " & _
            " FROM SCOPE('""d:\ADOBook\Data\Text\""') " & _
            " WHERE CONTAINS('toothache NEAR philosopher')"

Set rs = cn.Execute(sCommand)    ⟵————————    Execute returns a Recordset

While Not rs.EOF
   Print rs!FileName, rs!DocTitle, rs!Size & " bytes"
   rs.MoveNext
Wend
rs.Close
```

It prints

---

act 5 scene 1.htm   Before LEONATO'S house.   35060 bytes

When executing non-row–returning commands, the following code exploits the Execute method to send a haughty message to the lesser actors (we are back with SQLServer now):

```
Dim lAffected As Long
cn.Execute " UPDATE Parts set description = 'minor part' " & _
         " WHERE description Is Null", _
         lAffected, adExecuteNoRecords
```

The optional RecordsAffected argument is an output parameter rather than an input parameter. After the call to Execute, it will contain the number of records that the command changed. If it's 0, the WHERE clause missed its target.

It's common to include adExecuteNoRecords as an option for non-row–returning commands. If you don't specify this option, Execute will generate a Recordset object as a return value, even though to do so would be meaningless, and you probably would choose to ignore the return value anyway. This is untidy and theoretically wasteful, although you are unlikely to be able to measure the performance gain.

cn.Command-
TimeOut

By default, Execute will time out after thirty seconds if the call doesn't return. You can control this period by setting the cn.CommandTimeOut property. This setting also applies to rs.Open, when a Connection object is passed as the ActiveConnection argument. This provides one way to protect against lock or deadlock problems, as the command will eventually time out if it can't access the records it needs.

ADO is much more consistent than its DAO and RDO predecessors, which required use of different method calls for row-returning and non-row–returning commands. There was never a good reason for this, and the ADO approach has a better feel to it. As with all functions in VB, you just have to remember to bracket the arguments if you want a return value, or leave them naked if you don't.

In This Section

You learned how to use the Execute method. This is a technique that works well in applications where you keep a connection open throughout a session, and it allows you to directly fire off SQL and other commands.

Getting Schema Information

It's frequently useful to be able to find out information about a data source's schema—its tables, columns, procedures, and the like. Unlike DAO or RDO, the standard ADO object model provides no explicit objects to represent a "database design," partly because there is no assumption that a data source will always conform to a standard based on a relational model. However, ADO has two models for schema information access:

1. **cn.OpenSchema method**: This model provides read-only access to a wide range of schema information. It offers all that is required for many applications.

2. **ADOX object model**: This is a broader, more elaborate model, which is intended to support schema creation and modification as well as just reading, although only Jet supports modification at present. You must set a reference to the ADOX library to access these objects.

You'll see the ADOX objects in Chapter 10. In this section we'll focus on the cn.OpenSchema method.

cn.OpenSchema

OpenSchema is extremely easy to use, as all results are presented as Recordsets. Its definition is

Function OpenSchema(Schema As SchemaEnum,
                       [Restrictions],
                       [SchemaID]) As Recordset

The only required argument is Schema, which is defined by the SchemaEnum enumeration. This enumeration has over thirty predefined options and also supports Provider-specific schema information. The companion CD contains a program that allows you to experiment with all these options. Here's a list of some of the more frequently used ones:

adSchemaCatalogs
adSchemaColumns
adSchemaProcedures
adSchemaSchemata
adSchemaTables
adSchemaProviderTypes
adSchemaProcedureParameters
adSchemaForeignKeys
adSchemaPrimaryKeys
adSchemaProcedureColumns
adSchemaDBInfoKeywords

For each option, there is a defined set of fields that is returned, and a defined set of constraints that can be applied to filter out unwanted records. Constraints are applied via the Restrictions argument. Let's take a look at the basic operation of cn.OpenSchema before seeing how to use constraints. The fields and constraints for adSchemaTables and adSchemaColumns are shown in the following tables.

Table 4-1. adSchemaTables Fields and Constraints

FIELDS	CONSTRAINTS
TABLE_CATALOG	TABLE_CATALOG
TABLE_SCHEMA	TABLE_SCHEMA
TABLE_NAME	TABLE_NAME
TABLE_TYPE	TABLE_TYPE
TABLE_GUID	
DESCRIPTION	
TABLE_PROPID	
DATE_CREATED	
DATE_MODIFIED	

Table 4-2. adSchemaColumns Fields and Constraints

FIELDS	CONSTRAINTS
TABLE_CATALOG	TABLE_CATALOG
TABLE_SCHEMA	TABLE_SCHEMA
TABLE_NAME	TABLE_NAME
COLUMN_NAME	COLUMN_NAME
COLUMN_GUID	
COLUMN_PROPID	
ORDINAL_POSITION	
COLUMN_HASDEFAULT	
COLUMN_DEFAULT	
COLUMN_FLAGS	
IS_NULLABLE	

Table 4-2. adSchemaColumns Fields and Constraints (Continued)

FIELDS	CONSTRAINTS
DATA_TYPE	
TYPE_GUID	
CHARACTER_MAXIMUM_LENGTH	
CHARACTER_OCTET_LENGTH	
NUMERIC_PRECISION	
NUMERIC_SCALE	
DATETIME_PRECISION	
CHARACTER_SET_CATALOG	
CHARACTER_SET_SCHEMA	
CHARACTER_SET_NAME	
COLLATION_CATALOG	
COLLATION_SCHEMA	
COLLATION_NAME	
DOMAIN_CATALOG	
DOMAIN_SCHEMA	
DOMAIN_NAME	
DESCRIPTION	
SS_DATA_TYPE	

For example

```
Dim cn As New Connection
Dim rs As Recordset
cn.Open "DSN=MuchADO"
Set rs = cn.OpenSchema(adSchemaTables)

While Not rs.EOF
  If rs!TABLE_TYPE = "TABLE" Then          table type can be "TABLE,"
    Print rs!TABLE_NAME, rs!TABLE_TYPE     "VIEW," or "SYSTEM TABLE"
  End If
  rs.MoveNext
Wend
```

prints

Parts	TABLE
SceneContents	TABLE
Scenes	TABLE
Words	TABLE

This code makes sure that we only print tables we've defined in the database, ignoring system tables and views. However, a more elegant and efficient solution would use constraints. When you use constraints, you ask the Provider to filter out unwanted records, instead of writing code to do it. This is not only more convenient for you, it's also more efficient. Constraints are specified by constructing an array with an element for each constraint defined for the schema option. Table 4-1 shows you that there are four constraints defined for use with adSchemaTables. Empty values are used when a constraint isn't required. The results just presented are better achieved using

```
Dim cn As New Connection
Dim rs As Recordset
cn.Open "DSN=MuchADO"
Set rs = cn.OpenSchema(adSchemaTables, _
             Array(Empty, Empty, Empty, "TABLE"))
```
constraint position must match the defined position in the constraint list

```
While Not rs.EOF
  Print rs!TABLE_NAME, rs!TABLE_TYPE
  rs.MoveNext
Wend
```

If the constraint of interest doesn't fall at the end of the list of defined constraints, the full array doesn't have to be specified. For example, the following code lists all the fields in the Words table[7]:

```
Dim cn As New Connection
Dim rs As Recordset
cn.Open "DSN=MuchADO"
Set rs = cn.OpenSchema(adSchemaColumns, _
    Array(Empty, Empty, "Words"))
```
Recall the adSchemaColumns definition and its four constraints. We aren't interested in the last one, so we can ignore it.

---

7. ADO and OLE DB have the same identity crisis with "field" and "column" as they do with "record" and "row."

```
While Not rs.EOF
  Debug.Print rs!COLUMN_NAME
  rs.MoveNext
Wend
```

The SchemaID argument is used only when the Schema option is adSchemaProviderSpecific, in which case the Provider's documentation must be consulted to identify valid schemas and their fields and constraints.

In This Section

The OpenSchema method provides a simple, flexible way of getting schema information when the full capabilities of ADOX are not needed.

Connection Properties

Connection objects carry a large number of dynamic properties. Some of these are standard and can therefore be expected to be available on any Provider (even though you may not be able to change them). Others are Provider-specific and are described in vendor documentation.[8]

cn.Properties   There are three categories of dynamic properties for the Connection object:

1. **Initialization properties**: These expose settings for opening a connection to a data source, and can usually be used as connection string keywords. The standard Initialization properties are shown in Table 4-3.

Table 4-3. Standard Initialization Properties

Cache Authorization	Encrypt Password	Mask Password
Password	Persist Encrypted	Persist Security Info
User ID	Asynchronous Processing	Data Source
Window Handle	Locale Identifier	Mode
Prompt	Extended Properties	

2. **Data Source Information properties**: These provide information about the behavior or capabilities of the Provider and data source.

---

8. The Jet Provider, in particular, has a huge number of Provider-specific properties in order to allow the phasing out of DAO.

The standard Data Source Information properties are shown in Table 4-4.

Table 4-4. Standard Data Source Information Properties

Active Sessions	Asynchronous Abort	Asynchronous Commit
Pass By Ref Accessors	Catalog Location	Catalog Term
Column Definition	Null Concatenation Behavior	Data Source Name
Read-Only Data Source	DBMS Name	DBMS Version
Data Source Object Threading Model	Group By Support	Heterogeneous Table Support
Identifier Case Sensitivity	Maximum Index Size	Maximum Row Size
Maximum Row Size Includes BLOB	Maximum Tables in SELECT	Multiple Parameter Sets
Multiple Results	Multiple Storage Objects	Multiple Table Update
NULL Collation Order	OLE Object Support	Order By Columns in Select List
Output Parameter Availability	Persistent ID Type	Prepare Abort Behavior
Procedure Term	Provider Name	OLE DB Version
Quoted Identifier Sensitivity	Rowset Conversions On Command	SQL Support
Structured Storage	Subquery Support	Transaction DDL
Isolation Levels	Isolation Retention	Table Term

3. **Session properties**: These expose database engine initialization settings for the current session. There is only one standard Session property: Autocommit Isolation Levels.

These properties are fully documented and it's not my intention to expend more paper describing each one. You have already seen how to use the Initialization properties. The Data Source Information properties are extremely useful if you are writing applications that are meant to connect to a range of Providers, as they can be used defensively to avoid a whole range of errors. At the very least, you could provide a simple function on the Help menu that allows all the relevant properties to be listed. That way, if a bug is encountered with a new Provider, it becomes a simple task to check any suspected Provider properties.

In This Section

We examined the many dynamic properties of ADO Connection objects, some of which can be used during the process of connecting to a data source, while others provide useful information about a data source's capabilities.

ADO and Transactions

In Chapter 3 we saw how locks are used to protect a single update statement such as

```
UPDATE Account SET Balance = Balance + 1000.00 WHERE id = ???
```

This statement involves two physical disk operations, a read and a write. Logically however, it's a single operation, and locks ensure that it's treated as such. While the record being updated is locked, no other process or user can interfere.

In database terminology, any set of operations that are logically a single unit of work is called a *transaction*. Managing a transaction that consists of operations on a single row is a fairly straightforward process. However, logical units of work can be far more complex. The classic example of a transaction is a bill payment. This involves moving money from one account to another. For simplicity, let's assume that both accounts are in the same table.[9] The logical unit of work looks like this:

```
UPDATE Account SET Balance = Balance - 1000.00 WHERE id = X
UPDATE Account SET Balance = Balance + 1000.00 WHERE id = Y
```

---

9. In a more complex situation, the two accounts would be in different databases in different parts of the world. The same logic applies, but sorting out problems becomes a vastly more elaborate chore.

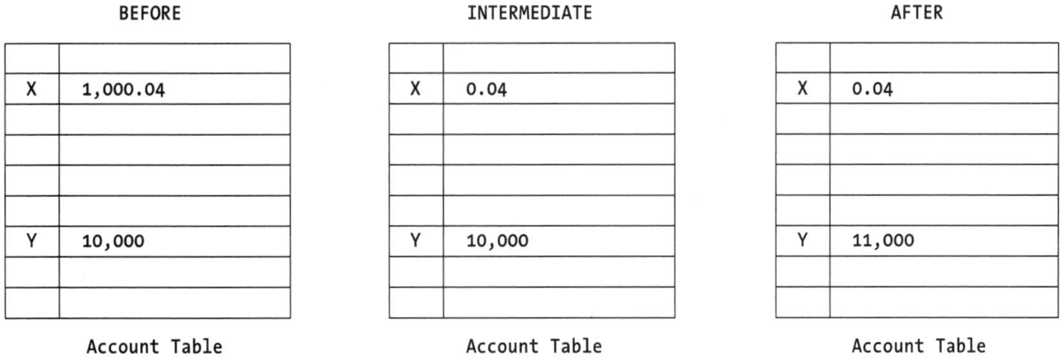

	BEFORE		INTERMEDIATE		AFTER
X	1,000.04	X	0.04	X	0.04
Y	10,000	Y	10,000	Y	11,000
	Account Table		Account Table		Account Table

Figure 4-2. Three different internal states of a simple transaction

There are three scenarios to consider:

1. What happens if the process fails at the intermediate point (that is, after the first UPDATE completes, but before the second begins)?[10]

2. Even if both UPDATEs succeed, what happens if another process reads the table at the intermediate point?[11]

3. What happens if the server fails after the operations complete, destroying all the evidence of the transfer?

By default, ADO will treat each of these UPDATEs as separate units of work, so the three scenarios are real concerns for any busy database. Clearly, we need a way of treating any number of operations as a single, logical unit of work—we need transactions.

There is a more formal way of defining a transaction than as a logical unit of work, which is the ACID (Atomic, Consistent, Isolated and Durable) test.

Atomic: The word "atom" means something that can't be divided. Many individual operations make up a transaction, but they are treated as a single unit of work that can't be divided. Either all the operations succeed or they all fail; partial success (as in Scenario 1) isn't possible.

---

10. It would look as though money had disappeared into thin air. In the real world, only taxation can achieve this.

11. The other process would see the world in an inconsistent state (one which could never really happen) and might take inappropriate action as a result.

Consistent: Money disappearing into thin air isn't consistent with the laws of economics. A consequence of atomicity is that transactions move the system (in this case the "system" is the total amount of money in the world) from one consistent state to another, preventing inconsistencies resulting from partial success of a unit of work

Isolated: Transactions need to be isolated from each other, so that one transaction can't see the intermediate workings of another (in order to avoid Scenario 2).

Durable: Once a transaction is complete, its effects must be permanent, even if the system fails (in order to avoid Scenario 3)—which all sounds wonderful, but trying to write code that achieves this would consume most of our lifetimes. One of the great advances in computing is that we can now expect our databases, or even our operating systems, to do all the hard work for us. Our task is simply to say when a transaction should begin, when it should end, and whether it should succeed (meaning that all the changes we've made since starting the transaction are fine, so they should be permanently committed to the data store) or fail (meaning that something went wrong, so everything should be rolled back to the beginning of the transaction).

Programming Transactions with ADO

There are two main ways of using transactions with ADO:

1. Use the transaction features of the Connection object.

2. Use the transaction features of Microsoft's Distributed Transaction Coordinator (DTC), either via COM+ in Windows 2000, or via MTS with earlier versions of Windows.

Using the DTC provides far more power and flexibility to your transactions (for example, you can create transactions that use multiple databases on different servers), but also requires that you design your system using an n-tier architecture and run all your data source access code (but not necessarily all your ADO code) either as COM+ Applications (under Windows 2000) or MTS Packages.

cn.BeginTrans
cn.CommitTrans
cn.RollbackTrans

We'll spend some time dealing with what all this means in Chapter 14. In this chapter, we'll focus on the transactional features of the ADO Connection object. This is the appropriate technique to use for a standard "two-tier" application in which all your code is compiled into a single VB EXE, or possibly in database stored procedures.[12]

There are three ADO methods that are used for defining transaction boundaries, cn.BeginTrans, cn.CommitTrans, and cn.RollbackTrans.[13]

As an (imaginary) theater director, I'm tired of plays in which every scene is acted out in chronological order, so I've decided to create a "Swap Scene" function, which allows me to completely swap any two scenes of my choice (in the example that follows, I have dealt only with the Words table—in reality, my code would need to be a little more complex). In order to do this, I temporarily assign 0 to the act and scene numbers for one scene in my swap, and then set them to their new location afterward. This is definitely a procedure that I don't want to go wrong halfway through, so transaction processing is a must.

```
Public Function swapScene(iActA As Integer, iSceneA As Integer, _
                iActB As Integer, iSceneB As Integer) As Boolean
On Error GoTo ErrH

Dim lSetToZero As LongDim lSetFromZero As Long


cn.BeginTrans                    ◄——————  begin transaction here
cn.Execute "UPDATE Words SET act = 0, scene = 0 WHERE act = " & _
            iActA & " and scene = " & iSceneA, lSetToZero
cn.Execute " UPDATE Words SET act = " & iActA & _
            ", scene = " & iSceneA & " WHERE act = " & _
            iActB & " and scene = " & iSceneB
cn.Execute " UPDATE Words SET act = " & iActB & _
            ", scene = " & iSceneB & " WHERE act = 0 " & _
             " and scene = " & 0, lSetFromZero


If lSetToZero = lSetFromZero Then
    cn.CommitTrans               ◄——————  commit if everything is OK
Else
    cn.RollbackTrans    ◄——————  roll back if you are not happy
    Err.Raise vbObjectError + 1000
End If
```

---

12. It's not an appropriate technique to use for writing code that runs on a Web server, unless your database is not compliant with the DTC.

13. When BeginTrans is called within an existing transaction, it returns a value that is the nesting level of the new transaction. Few databases support nested transactions. One exception is Jet, which supports transactions up to five levels deep.

```
swapScene = True
Exit Function
ErrH:

End Function
```

There is one danger with changing act and scene to 0 during this operation. It's possible that there may already be records in the Words table with those values, even though there shouldn't be. When I reassign all my records back to their new act and scene, I will pick up any errant records as well as my own. To handle this, I have used the RecordsAffected argument on cn.Execute to hold the number of records affected by each transfer. If the two numbers don't match, I simply roll back the entire transaction, as though nothing ever happened. Imagine trying to write your own code to handle this sort of mess, and you'll come to love transaction processing systems.

A matching CommitTrans or RollbackTrans must follow every BeginTrans. Closing a connection mid-transaction will raise an error, although dereferencing a Connection object mid-transaction will quietly cause a roll back.

Transactions can be arbitrarily complex. However, there are two things to bear in mind about any transaction:

- During the transaction, the data source is managing all the information required to either commit or roll back the transaction at any stage. Huge transactions put a heavy demand on the server, which is fully justified if you have a large logical unit of work, but unjustified otherwise.

- Databases need to lock all resources used in a transaction, which (as you'll see shortly) can include every record you read during a transaction, as well as every one you modify. Extensive, long-lived transactions seriously reduce the concurrency of applications using your data source.[14]

Concurrency and Isolation

Full isolation of a transaction requires heavy use of locking, which can impact concurrency in a major way. For example, if I have a statistics-gathering query that I run against some large tables on a routine basis, and I am reading every record in a busy table, the chance of being blocked by open transactions is very high. Transactions need to protect uncommitted records with exclusive locks, so that other business-critical transactions don't see inconsistent

---

14. Large transactions are sometimes used as an optimization technique. While it's true that performance can be improved by wrapping many operations into a transaction, doing so is not without its penalties. Personally, I only use transactions to apply the ACID principles to a logical unit of work.

data or read values that might get rolled back (and therefore should never "really" be in the database).

However, if my statistical query isn't business-critical—it's just useful— I'd rather have a small amount of inaccuracy if it means that my query will run in a few seconds instead of consistently timing out as a result of being blocked by complex transactions.

cn.IsolationLevel

You can control the tradeoff between transaction isolation and concurrency by setting the cn.IsolationLevel property. The options available are defined by the IsolationLevelEnum enumeration. This enumeration actually contains some synonyms because there are two established naming schemes for the same concepts. I will use the official ANSI SQL-92 names and show the alternatives in parentheses.

> **Read Uncommitted (Browse)**: Read Uncommitted is generally considered the lowest isolation level.[15] It ignores all locks, allowing you to see uncommitted changes made by other users (known as a *dirty read)*. This should only be used when you are prepared to accept inconsistencies and should never be used as part of an update process. At this isolation level the following scenario can occur: User A begins a transaction and after applying an exclusive lock, changes a value. User B then reads that value, ignoring the exclusive lock. However, User A doesn't commit the transaction, instead she rolls it back. The value is changed back to the original and User B has read a value that never really existed.

> **Read Committed (Cursor Stability)**: The read is blocked by exclusive locks to prevent reading uncommitted data. At any point during the transaction, the database appears consistent, but rereading a record might yield a new value if another user has committed a new value to that record in-between reads (in other words, the read isn't always repeatable). This is the default isolation level used by ODBC, SQLServer, and ADO and is considered a good tradeoff in most scenarios.

> **Repeatable Read**: Places a "read lock" on every record read during the transaction, preventing any other user from changing the records until the transaction completes. This means that you can go back and repeat a read on any record and always see the same values, but it doesn't prevent new records inserted during the transaction from affecting your results. For example, if you execute SELECT * FROM Parts twice during a transaction, another user might insert a new Part in-between your two reads (there is no lock to prevent them from inserting a new record, even though all existing records are

---

15. There is an isolation level even more relaxed than Read Uncommitted called Chaos. Draw your own conclusions.

read-locked) and you would get different results the second time. Such inserts are called phantoms. Phantoms mean that you are not completely isolated from other transactions.

Serializable (Isolated): Has the effect of locking every table touched during the transaction, in order to prevent phantoms. You are now completely isolated from all other transactions. This isolation level is called *serializable* because transactions running at the same time are guaranteed to produce results that would have appeared if all the individual transactions were run one after the other, serially, with no possible interaction between them. Serializable is the highest level of transaction isolation.

You can test the difference between Read Uncommitted and Read Committed using the CD's companion program to this chapter. It allows you to stop the swapScene function immediately after the first update and then complete the transaction at your leisure. By running a second instance of the program at this intermediate point, you can try using different isolation levels when creating the "Word Count" report that executes the following query:

```
cn.BeginTrans
Set rs = cn.Execute("SELECT act, scene, & _
            "sum(wordCount) as WordCount" & _
            " FROM Words group by act, scene order by act, scene")

While Not rs.EOF
  Print rs!act, rs!scene, rs!wordCount
  rs.MoveNext
Wend
cn.CommitTrans
```

With Read Committed (or higher isolation levels), the query is blocked until the "Swap Scene" transaction completes or the command times out.[16] However, with Read Uncommitted, the function completes immediately. The first few lines of its output are

0	0	1327
1	1	2464
1	2	215

---

16. This is a good way to test the cn.CommandTimeOut property.

Midway through a transaction, "dirty" data is clearly visible—you can see that some words have Act 0, Scene 0 values. However, the query does complete. Whether you accept this tradeoff is up to you.

You may have noticed that I wrapped this report with transaction delimiters, even though I was only doing a read operation. IsolationLevel only applies during a transaction explicitly started with a BeginTrans and finished with a CommitTrans or a RollbackTrans.

Any operation that takes place outside of an explicit transaction is treated as a separate transaction running in "autocommit" mode. The Provider fixes the transaction isolation level used in autocommit mode, although you can read the level it uses using a standard dynamic property as follows:

```
cn.Properties("Autocommit Isolation Levels")
```

The value this code returns can be compared with the IsolationLevel-Enum values to identify the isolation level that applies. Yet another property can be used to identify which transaction isolation levels a Provider supports:

```
cn.Properties("Isolation Levels")
```

This is an overloaded property, so the IsolationLevelEnum values should be treated as bitmasks.[17]

In practice, it isn't that common for developers to modify isolation levels. However, it's common for applications to run into locking problems as the number of users scale up. Understanding the way transactions work and the extent to which you can control this process plays a key role in writing heavy-duty ADO applications. Simple transactions don't often revisit the same record, and therefore, Read Committed is adequate for most purposes. More ambitious transactions often require a more isolated transaction.

In This Section

We looked in detail at transaction handling within ADO. When appropriate, you should consider using the DTC for transaction processing, but otherwise, the Connection object provides a familiar and powerful set of transaction features. An understanding of isolation levels can help you make sense of locking issues on your databases.

---

17. If you ask for an isolation level that isn't supported, the closest fit will be substituted. All the above examples use SQLServer because it supports all the available options, while Jet supports only Read Committed.

ADO and Errors

You have already seen that error situations encountered by ADO result in trappable errors that can be handled in the time-honored VB way. The most common errors are defined by the ErrorValueEnum enumeration, but a much larger set of errors is defined in OLE DB documentation.

However, when you have an open Connection object (either as an explicit reference or via the ActiveConnection property of a Recordset, Record, or Command object), you have access to a wider range of error information generated by Providers; in particular:

1. Multiple errors can be generated by a single ADO instruction, which can provide error information at different levels of detail.

2. Additional error information can be provided for each error, including non-ADO error codes, and links to help files can be provided where appropriate.

3. Warnings that don't raise errors but still contain error-related information can be generated by specific methods.

cn.Errors

Provider-generated errors are available after any ADO instruction in the Errors collection, which is a property of the Connection object. The Errors collection contains Error objects with the following properties:

er.Description

- **Description**: Contains a textual description of the error.

er.Number

- **Number**: Contains an ADO or OLE DB error constant.

er.Source

- **Source**: Identifies the object that raised the error.

er.SQLState

- **SQLState**: Provides an ANSI standard error code for SQL data sources.

er.NativeError

- **NativeError**: Helps identify the error data-source–specific documentation,

er.HelpFile
er.HelpContext

- **HelpFile, HelpContext**: Helps provide access to more detailed help.

It's common practice to write a simple piece of code that iterates the Error collection, presenting the information in a standard dialog that provides access to each error. This code can then be called whenever `cn.Errors.Count > 0` inside a VB error handler. The error description won't mean much to users, but if they can use the dialog to add some situational commentary and then print, log, or email the result back to you, you'll save the time invested in building the dialog after just a few support calls.

We examined the ADO Errors collection and Error objects.

Connection Pooling

There are two important facts about server connections: they are expensive to create, and they are expensive to maintain. This is much more true about a connection to a heavyweight resource such as SQLServer, Oracle, or DB2 than it is about a Jet connection, for example, but it remains a significant factor in the design of any ADO program.

Ever since developers have been writing programs that connect to servers they have faced a dilemma about how to manage connections.

1. *Do you create the connection at the beginning of a session and hold on to it for as long as possible?* This way, you only have to wait once to create the connection, but it means you hold on to an expensive server resource that you probably use for less than 5% of the time you are holding it.[18]

2. *Or do you create a new connection each time you have a server operation to perform and release it immediately afterward?* This is kind to servers in that it keeps the number of live connections they need to maintain down to a minimum. However, it's tough on your users as they have to wait for a new connection to be established each time they need server resources. The time it takes to create a new connection may be subsecond, but all too often isn't. And if you are executing several queries in quick succession, subsecond isn't fast enough—even hundredths of a second can have a noticeable impact.

Neither of these options is ideal. What we really need is some sensitivity to the demand we place on servers. When we are using a connection frequently, we want each request for a connection to be near instantaneous. When server demand is light, we want server resources to be managed conservatively.

---

18. What server resources do I mean? Only a general answer is possible because each server is different. Most servers maintain a lump of information about each connection that typically ranges between 10KB and 100KB in size. They also maintain a pool of threads the size of which is related to the number of live connections. When you have a connection open, it's very easy to keep Recordsets open that may consume their own resources and hold locks on the server. Finally, there is a licensing issue. Many servers are sold based on a maximum number of live connections—the more connections, the higher the price. This is where "expensive" has a meaning everyone can understand!

Connection pooling provides this sensitivity. ADO will manage a pool of connections on our behalf. The size of the pool is demand-sensitive, meaning that it will be empty when nothing has happened for a while, and it may contain several live connections in a busy middle-tier application or Web site. When you ask for a new connection, a pooled connection will be given to you if it matches your requirements, otherwise, a new connection will be created. When you release a connection, it will be pooled. It will remain pooled until either it's reused or released from the pool because there is insufficient demand to justify keeping it open. All this pool management is handled automatically on our behalf.

Conceptually, this is very simple and amazingly convenient. However, as is so often the case, the devil is in the detail, and there is good deal of misunderstanding about pooling at present. The pooling issue is complicated by

- Multiple levels of pooling software (OLE DB, ODBC, COM+/MTS) that all work in different ways and potentially compete with each other, and use different terminology.

- Different versions of pooling software which work in different ways.

- Traditional programming styles which tend to prevent pooling from working correctly.

- A lack of standard features to verify that pooling is working properly.

Let's begin by looking at the different technologies and their terminology. ODBC introduced Connection Pooling with version 3. By default it was disabled, and it was enabled by making Registry changes or when using MTS. By version 3.51, ODBC Connection Pooling was easily configured using the ODBC Control Panel Applet, and it provided graphical monitoring via the NT Performance Monitor.

In OLE DB, the term "Session Pooling" (or sometimes Resource Pooling) was used to highlight the fact that OLE DB Providers could provide all kinds of services aside from database connections. However, in ADO terms, Session Pooling still meant creating pools of Connection object resources. Session Pooling became a part of ADO with version 2.0, but ADO continued to use ODBC Connection Pooling when the MSDASQL Provider was used. This changed with ADO 2.1, so that Session Pooling was used instead of ODBC Connection Pooling. However, Session Pooling can still be disabled when it still makes sense to use the ODBC approach.

COM+ and MTS provide genuine Resource Pooling. They are able to manage pools of any kind of resource, including (in COM+) ActiveX components. Resource Pooling works differently from Session Pooling and Connection

Pooling, and the difference affects the way you'll write code for ASP (Active Server Pages) applications or any other server running under COM+/MTS/IIS.

From the perspective of this book, regardless of the technology being used, we'll be pooling ADO connections, so I will use "ADO connection pooling" as the general term, unless I specifically want to address one of the three technologies just mentioned.

You should keep in mind the following four points when considering ADO connection pooling:

1. Strictly speaking, it isn't ADO Connection objects that are being pooled, it's the OLE DB Provider connections that ADO manages on our behalf.

2. ADO connection pooling doesn't work on Windows 9x. It works on NT4 and Windows 2000.

3. Connections are *not* shared between processes. Each application uses its own connection resources. However, connections are shared between threads in multithreaded applications.

4. You'll only be given a pooled connection if it precisely matches the requirements you have requested. In most cases this means user name and password[19], which must match for obvious security reasons[20], but it also means other connection properties, such as ConnectionTimeOut.

In the examples that follow, I used SQLServer 7 and the SQLServer 7 Performance Monitor options. Most databases have their own way of monitoring the number of live connections. Let's consider two common scenarios:

- A traditional two-tier, multiuser application in which Connection objects are created on each user's desktop computer.

- The middle tier of an n-tier application running under COM+/MTS. In this case, the code will be ASP running under IIS, but the same techniques would apply to any COM+/MTS application.

---

19. And server/Provider of course!

20. While this is obvious, it does impose a design constraint. If you are used to writing server applications that connect to databases using the logon of each different user, you will not get full benefit out of pooling because a different pool will be used for each logon. It's easier to exploit pooling by using a single logon from middle-tier systems, regardless of who the end user is. While this may sound reckless, COM+/MTS security features are designed to overcome this problem, although it does mean you need to reconsider the use of database logging techniques based on logons.

A Two-Tier Pooling Scenario

Traditionally, two-tier programs have created a Connection object at startup and held on to it until they are closed. However, we've seen that ADO Recordsets can be created that don't require an explicit Connection object. While this is convenient for coding, it traditionally has been expensive because of the need to create a connection for each Recordset.

By exploiting pooling, we can use avoid using explicit Connection objects, and make our applications resource-efficient. Many users keep applications open all day, although they may use the program in intensive bursts, with periods of inactivity ranging from a few minutes to a few hours.[21] Connection pooling means that the pool will release the connection during these periods of inactivity, at the cost of a once-only connection overhead when activity starts up. Your database administrator will be highly appreciative. Let's see how this works.

Here's the code for a complete application. I have added a time delay of eight seconds into the function to make it easier to interpret the SQLServer Performance Monitor Trace.

```
Private Sub cmdDoSomething_Click()
Dim rs As New Recordset
Dim dTime As Double
rs.Open "SELECT * FROM Parts", "MuchADO"
dTime = Timer
Do
Loop Until Timer - dTime > 8
rs.Close
End Sub
```

Clicking the cmdDoSomething button eight times in five minutes produced the trace shown in Figure 4-3, showing the number of live connections on my otherwise unused server (vertical axis) against time (horizontal axis).

It's very clear from this trace that no connection pooling took place! Each request started a brand new Connection object that was closed when the request completed.

---

21. I am not suggesting that users are inactive, just that they may be doing things other than using my system. Your experience may differ here.

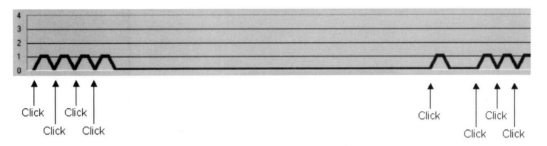

Figure 4-3. Connection activity with no pooling

A standard response is to believe that ADO connection pooling doesn't work and to change the code to

```
Dim cn As Connection

Private Sub cmdDoSomething_Click()
Dim rs As New Recordset
Dim dTime As Double
rs.Open "SELECT * FROM Parts", cn  ◄——————  reuse the same
                                            open Connection object
dTime = Timer                               each time
Do
Loop Until Timer - dTime > 8
rs.Close
End Sub

Private Sub Form_Load()
Set cn = New Connection
cn.Open "MuchADO"
End Sub
```

This, of course, is the traditional approach of hogging a connection all through the application session. It produces the following trace:

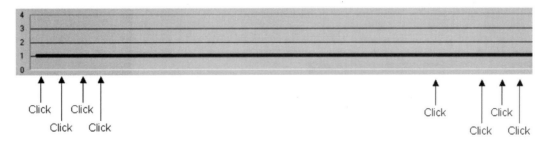

Figure 4-4. Traditional connection hogging

To make pooling work, we have to apply Rule Number 1 of OLE DB Session Pooling:

> *To keep a Session Pool alive, you must maintain a reference to an ADO Connection object for the lifetime of your application. This Connection does not need to be kept open.*

In other words, you need to "prime" the pool and then keep it live with a dormant Connection object. Here's how:

```
Dim cn As Connection

Private Sub cmdDoSomething_Click()
Dim rs As New Recordset
Dim dTime As Double
rs.Open "SELECT * FROM Parts",  "MuchADO"   ◄─── Use a connection string
dTime = Timer                                    to create a new
Do                                               Connection object.
Loop Until Timer - dTime > 8
rs.Close
End Sub


Private Sub Form_Load()
Set cn = New Connection
cn.Open "MuchADO"
cn.Close        ◄───────────
End Sub
```

Here's the difference—
the Connection object is closed.

Don't set the cn variable to Nothing or allow it to go out of scope, as this will dereference the entire pool.

This is the resulting trace:

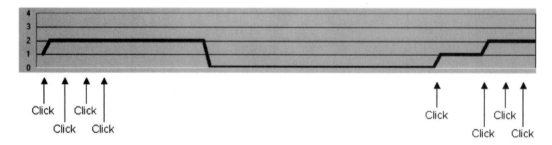

Figure 4-5. Connection activity with pooling

Here, the total number of connection requests was four, and we averaged about one connection over the five-minute period. It's a fact that ADO connection pooling prefers having two connections open rather than one. For two-tier applications, you need to balance the connection cost over the lifetime of a typical application session. When the application is in use, it's quite likely that two connections will be live. However, in those long dormant periods, the pool will be empty. You can be more aggressive about releasing connections from the pool. ADO allows you to control how long a pool keeps connections open. The default is sixty seconds, but by adding a DWORD property called SPTimeOut to the Registry key for a Provider[22], you can provide an alternative value.

You can also control whether pooling is enabled. This is set on a Provider-by-Provider basis according to the OLEDB_SERVICES property on the Provider's Registry entry. However, you can override this setting for individual connections by including "OLE DB Services" as either a keyword in the connection string or as a dynamic property set prior to opening the connection.

A value of –1 ensures pooling is enabled, while –2 ensures it's disabled.[23]

An N-Tier Pooling Scenario

Pooling differs in one big way when your code is running as a COM+ Application or an MTS Package. This, of course, includes any ASP page or component running under IIS4 or later.[24]

Rule Number 1 of OLE DB Session Pooling doesn't apply because COM+/MTS provides its own Resource Pooling. As an example, here's a simple ASP page:

```
<HTML>
<BODY>
<%
set rs = Server.CreateObject("ADODB.RecordSet")
rs.Open "SELECT * FROM Parts", "DSN=MuchADO;"
Response.Write "<BR>"

rs.MoveFirst
while not rs.EOF
    Response.Write  rs("part") & "  " & _
                    rs("description") & "<BR>"
    rs.MoveNext
wend
```

---

22. Searching the Registry for the Provider name will quickly identify the GUID required. This feature was new to ADO 2.5. In earlier versions, it wasn't possible to configure pooling.

23. OLE DB Services can also be used to control other general services, such as availability of the Client Cursor Engine.

24. These topics are covered in their own chapter later in the book. The material here concerns only the mechanics of ADO connection pooling.

```
rs.Close
%>
</BODY>
</HTML>
```

This listing uses a server-side connection to generate a Web page with now familiar output. Here's the trace that results if I simulate ten concurrent requests[25] for the page, followed by the same burst of activity about two minutes later:

Figure 4-6. Connection Pooling doesn't require priming under MTS and COM+

One trap that developers can fall into is to believe it makes sense to store Connections or Recordsets in ASP Session objects. This is rarely a good thing to do, because it creates a separate Connection for each concurrent user. By adding

```
Set Session("rs") = rs
```

to the previous Web page, the trace changes to

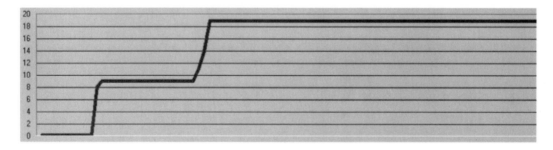

Figure 4-7. The effect of creating a separate Connection for each user

---

25. The simulation launches ten separate browsers on the same machine, configured to automatically navigate to the same page at the same time based on a timer event. The timer interval is ten milliseconds.

Compare the different scale of Figures 4-6 and 4-7. In Figure 4-7, the large number of connections will remain open until the ASP Sessions time out.

Generally speaking, ADO connection pooling is very easy to use, and is safer and more efficient than any other tricks or techniques available for reducing connection requests. Most of the problems experienced with connection pooling result either from code that isn't releasing resources when it should or from failure to apply Rule Number 1 when it's needed.

Keep in mind that using pooling is never quite the same as using a dedicated Connection all of your own. Connections coming from a pool may be used by other users (in n-tier applications), and you are by no means guaranteed to always get the same connection. You should be aware of the following implications of pooling:

- *When using the ADO Connection object for transaction management, don't release a Connection object during a transaction.* There are two techniques available for transaction processing when pooling is used. The first is to create a Connection object explicitly and hold on to it throughout the transaction. The second is to use the DTC via COM+/ MTS to handle the transaction. The DTC will correctly manage transactions when they use multiple connections to different servers, so it can handle multiple connections to the same server without getting out of bed.

- *Avoid creating prepared statements or temporary stored procedures.* These create server resources attached to a specific connection. Because you might not get the same connection from the pool next time you ask for one, you lose the benefit of creating them in the first place. Worse, because the connection may reside in the pool for a long time, it can get clogged up with the useless but expensive server resources created by each "user" that creates them. We'll look at this issue in more detail in the next chapter.

- *Take care when using temporary tables.* Make sure they are destroyed before releasing the connection back to the pool.

- *If you change the logical database on a Connection object (for example by setting cn.DefaultDatabase) remember to reset it before releasing it back to the pool.*

In This Section

We saw how ADO connection pooling provides a demand-sensitive way of conserving connection resources, while minimizing connection requests. When you use connection pooling you should release connections as soon as possible. When COM+/MTS Resource Pooling isn't available, it's important to prime a connection pool. Connection pooling can be a benefit to standard desktop applications as well as to n-tier DCOM and Web applications.

Summary

The Connection object plays an important role in ADO programming, and in this chapter, we explored the traditional functionality one might expect of Connection objects.

Traditionally, Connection objects have been important for a couple of reasons:

- The high cost of creating connections has encouraged developers to create a single connection and hold on to it throughout an application.

- Connection objects have been necessary to create transactions consisting of multiple separate instructions.

These days, such requirements are less important for a few reasons:

- Connection pooling means that you don't need to hold a connection open throughout a session. When you need instantaneous access to a connection, ADO automatically provides one via a pool. When this isn't really necessary, ADO automatically releases the connection resource, freeing up the server.

- Transaction processing is now available in many scenarios through the Distributed Transaction Coordinator which doesn't require you to use the same physical connection for all elements of a transaction. When NT4 is being used as a server or Windows 2000 is being used either as a server or desktop, DTC functionality is usually readily available.

As a result of these advances, we often have little need of an explicit, permanent Connection object.

This isn't to say that the traditional model is no longer valid—it's certainly unlikely to do any harm when you have a relatively small, known number of concurrent users. At the same time, ADO encourages us, through an attractive combination of a simpler programming model and more efficient functionality, to think differently about how we use Connection objects.

When you want to use transactions without using the DTC or have a need to work with the Connection object's Errors collection, then an explicit Connection object is required. When you don't have these needs, you can work directly with Recordsets. And in all cases, pooling means that holding permanent connections looks more and more like an outdated "gas-guzzling" programming model.

CHAPTER 5

Explicit Commands

Why Use Command Objects?

Parameters and Parameter Objects

Working with Stored Procedures

Command Optimizations

Summary

WE'VE COME A LONG WAY without explicitly using Command objects and their associated Parameters collection. About the only thing you simply can't do without using Command objects is to execute commands such as stored procedures that may have output parameters. For this reason alone, it's important to understand Command and Parameter objects, but they also have wider reaching benefits for data access design.

It's also important to realize that although we haven't explicitly created any Command objects yet, just about every operation we've performed so far has used a Command object (you can prove this by checking the Active-Command property of most Recordsets). Therefore, just like Connection objects, implicit Command objects are created and destroyed by ADO on our behalf—a fact we can sometimes exploit as long as we know they are there.

As before, we'll spend most of our time working with the MuchADO database, but we'll also look briefly at a completely different Provider, the OLE DB Provider for Microsoft Directory Services. I won't go into significant detail on this Provider, which allows us to use ADO to access ADSI-compliant Directory Services such as Windows 2000's Active Directory. The main purpose for using it is to make sure that we don't lose sight of the fact that ADO reaches out far beyond relational data.

Why Use Command Objects?

Command objects have the following uses:

1.   They provide the best way to call stored procedures and the only way to call stored procedures that return output parameters.

2. They provide the only way in ADO to make use of prepared SQL statements in situations where prepared statements are advantageous.

3. They allow developers to work directly with tables as an alternative to SQL.

4. They allow developers to use parameterized SQL, so that once a command has been created, it can be called multiple times simply by substituting parameters with new field values. This approach can make code considerably neater by removing the need to use multiple string concatenations to create SQL statements dynamically.

Command objects make it possible to organize data access in a central-ized way. This means that Command objects can be created in one module within an application, with all the SQL, stored procedure calls, properties, and connection details hidden within the module. Other parts of the appli-cation can then execute the Command objects to gain access to Recordsets, without needing to know the implementation details. This concept is taken to its logical conclusion with the Data Environment designer (introduced in VB6), which provides a graphical way to centralize all data access for one or more applications in a related group of Command objects. Chapter 13 will explore the Data Environment in detail.

Let's take a look at a Command object in action. We'll use an SQL state-ment that returns a word count for each word spoken by DON PEDRO in the entire play. To sort out the wheat from the chaff, we'll ignore all words of less than five characters, and only list words that appear at least five times. We'll declare the Command object as a module-level variable and initialize it in `Form_Load` as follows:

```
Private cd As Command

Private Sub Form_Load()
sSQL = "SELECT Words.word, SUM(Words.wordCount) AS total " & _
    "FROM Words INNER JOIN Parts ON Words.part = Parts.part " & _
    "GROUP BY Words.word, Parts.part, Words.WordLength " & _
    "HAVING (Parts.part = 'DON PEDRO') AND " & _
      "(SUM(Words.wordCount) > 4) AND (Words.WordLength > 4) " & _
    "ORDER BY SUM(Words.wordCount) DESC"

Set cd = New Command
cd.CommandText = sSQL
cd.CommandType = adCmdText
End Sub
```

cd.CommandText
cd.CommandType
cd.ActiveConnection
cd.Execute

Note that the previous listing doesn't execute anything or connect to any database; we've simply set the CommandText and CommandType properties of a Command object. Each time we wish to execute this command, the following code can be used:

```
cd.ActiveConnection = "File Name=c:\MuchADO.udl"

Set rs = cd.Execute          ←———————————    Command is submitted to the
While Not rs.EOF                              database for execution here
    Print rs!word, rs!total
    rs.MoveNext
Wend
Set cd.ActiveConnection = Nothing
```

which prints

Benedick	20
shall	14
would	12
Signior	9
heart	8
Leonato	8
Beatrice	7
indeed	6
Claudio	6
What''s	6
great	5
other	5
brother	5

Apart from the obvious neatness of being able to execute the same command multiple times with a simple code segment, there are a number of points to note about this example. This code sets and unsets the Active-Connection each time the command is executed. Whether or not this causes a new physical connection to be created each time depends on the use of Connection Pooling. An alternative would be to use an ADO Connection object which could be assigned once when the Command object is first used, or set and unset much as in the example just shown. It's quite possible to assign a connection to a different data source each time, as long as each connection's database schema will support the SQL.

The second thing to note is the use of the CommandType property. This is defined by the CommandTypeEnum emuneration, which has the following values:

adCmdUnspecified

adCmdUnknown (default)

adCmdText

adCmdTable

adCmdStoredProc

adCmdFile

adCmdTableDirect

adCmdURLBind

In addition to being used with the CommandType property of Command objects, any of these values can be used in the Options argument of cd.Execute, cn.Execute, or rs.Open to provide ADO with additional information about how to interpret a command string. When an SQL statement is being used as the command string, it's quite safe to leave the default value (adCmdUnknown). It's arguably clearer to specify adCmdText, and there is supposed to be a performance gain, although it would be hard to measure it.

However, for all other types of commands, there are definite benefits in specifying the CommandType.[1] adCmdFile can be used when opening a Recordset from a persisted file, a topic which I will address in Chapter 7. adCmdStoredProc makes calling stored procedures more convenient, and we'll meet it later in this chapter. adCmdURLBind is used mostly with semi-structured data, and it's covered in Chapter 9.

Let's look at adCmdTable and adCmdTableDirect now. When adCmdTable is used as the CommandType, the CommandText should be a table name instead of an SQL statement. The Command object converts the table name into an SQL statement and then executes the full SQL statement, rather than the table name. This means that adCmdTable can be used against any SQL data source; for example

```
cd.ActiveConnection = "File Name=c:\MuchADO.udl"
cd.CommandType = adCmdTable
cd.CommandText = "Parts"
Set rs = cd.Execute
Print cd.CommandText
```

prints

```
SELECT * FROM Parts
```

---

1. The command might fail unless you specify the correct type.

It shows that the CommandText has been converted into an SQL statement. This isn't especially useful functionality, but it exists to make ADO a little more palatable to developers who are not used to working with SQL. It's worth noting the general point that setting the CommandType can result in the CommandText being modified by the Provider to a syntax more suited to the data source.

The adCmdTableDirect constant is a little more interesting. It doesn't convert the table name into an SQL string, meaning that it can only be used with data sources that can accept raw table names. As you saw in Chapter 3, this command type is required in order to use the Index and Seek Recordset features supported by the Jet Provider. What makes this command type interesting[2] is that it doesn't work with Command objects! In fact, when used as an argument to rs.Open, ADO creates the Recordset directly, instead of creating an implicit Command object, and therefore, the ActiveCommand property of the Recordset will equal Nothing. For example, the following code

```
On Error GoTo ErrH
Dim cd As New Command
Dim rs As New Recordset
cd.ActiveConnection = "File Name=c:\MuchADOJet.udl"
cd.CommandType = adCmdTableDirect   ◄────────
rs.ActiveConnection = "File Name=c:\MuchADOJet.udl"
rs.Open "Parts", , , , adCmdTableDirect
Print "No Command?", rs.ActiveCommand Is Nothing
Exit Sub
ErrH:
  Print Err.Description
  Resume Next
```

An error occurs here. This command type is not valid for a Command object!

prints

```
Arguments are of the wrong type, are out of acceptable range, or are in
conflict with one another.
No Command?    True
```

One thing that may not be obvious about the examples just presented is that there is little scope for controlling the properties of the Recordset created by cd.Execute. By default, the Recordset has the same properties as those created by cn.Execute: server-side Recordsets are forward-only, while client-side Recordsets are static. Both types are read-only.

---

2. Maybe this should read "frustrating."

ADO 2.5 introduced a cute solution to the limitations just described. It allows you to pass a Command object as the Source argument to rs.Open. This means that you can configure the Recordset's properties as you would like. The following example shows how to create an updateable, scrollable, server-side Recordset using a Command object as its source:

```
Dim cd As New Command
Dim rs As New Recordset

cd.CommandText = "SELECT * FROM Parts"
cd.ActiveConnection = "File Name=c:\MuchADO.udl"
rs.CursorType = adOpenKeyset
rs.LockType = adLockOptimistic
rs.Open cd                          ◄─────────── use the Command object as the
rs.MoveLast                                      Source argument to rs.Open
rs!Description = "Some value"
rs.Update
```

An interesting but generally neglected property of Command objects is the Name property, and to explore this, we'll make use of the OLE DB Provider for Microsoft Directory Services. As mentioned in the introduction , this Provider provides ADO access to ADSI, and from ADSI into Active Directory, NT4, and other Directory Services. Directory Services are a huge topic, to which I won't even attempt to do justice. It's enough for you to know that a Directory Service provides access to a wide range of information about all manner of resources available in a system domain. In ADO terms, this means you can easily retrieve Recordsets listing the computers on your network, the users or groups defined for security administration, and a great deal more.

The Directory Services Provider name is "ADSDSOObject," and I can use it to execute SQL-like statements like

```
SELECT Name, Description FROM 'LDAP://DC=Salterton,DC=local'
WHERE objectCategory=  <Category Name>
```

in which <Category Name> can include "Computer," "Group," "Person" or "Container," among many other options. The rather strange looking FROM clause is based on an industry standard protocol called LDAP (Lightweight Directory Access Protocol), and in this case, it's extracting details from the private domain in my office called "Salterton.local." If you are using Windows 2000 with Active Directory, you could substitute your domain name here. The syntax for NT4 is slightly different.

The following example shows how to use ADSDSOObject directly from a Recordset (we'll get on to cd.Name shortly!):

```
Dim rs As New Recordset
rs.ActiveConnection = "Provider=ADSDSOObject;"
rs.Open "SELECT Name, Description " & _
        "FROM 'LDAP://DC=Salterton,DC=local' " & _
        "WHERE objectCategory='Computer'"
```

```
While Not rs.EOF
  Print rs!Name, rs!Description(0)
  rs.MoveNext
Wend
```
← the description field is a Variant array—not something you would find returned from a relational database

which prints

POLECAT	W2000 Advanced Server
STOAT	Old trusty laptop (W95)
BADGER	NT4 Server
WEASEL	W2000 laptop

cd.Name

By using Command objects, we can exploit a convenient feature afforded by the Name property. If you give a Command object a name and leave its ActiveConnection set, you can treat the Command's name as though it were a method on the Connection object. The method won't appear in VB's IntelliSense, but it's otherwise perfectly valid.

For example, the following code sets up three "Commands as Methods:"

```
Private cn As New Connection
Private cd(2) As New Command
```
← an array of Command objects

```
Private Sub Form_Load()
cn.Open "Provider=ADSDSOObject"
cd(0).Name = "Computers"
cd(0).ActiveConnection = cn
cd(0).CommandText = "SELECT Name, Description " & _
        "FROM 'LDAP://DC=Salterton,DC=local' " & _
        "WHERE objectCategory='Computer'"
cd(1).Name = "Groups"
cd(1).ActiveConnection = cn
cd(1).CommandText = "SELECT Name, Description " & _
        "FROM 'LDAP://DC=Salterton,DC=local' " & _
        "WHERE objectCategory='Group'"
```
← Name must be assigned before setting the ActiveConnection

```
cd(2).Name = "Users"
cd(2).ActiveConnection = cn
cd(2).CommandText = "SELECT Name, Description  " & _
        "FROM 'LDAP://DC=Salterton,DC=local' " & _
        "WHERE objectCategory='Person'"
End Sub
```

The "Users" command can then be executed as follows:

```
Dim rs As New Recordset
cn.Users rs
While Not rs.EOF
  Print rs!Name, rs!Description(0)
  rs.MoveNext
Wend
```

The first few records are

```
Administrator  Built-in account for administering the computer/domain
Guest          Built-in account for guest access to the computer/domain
TsInternetUser This user account is used by Terminal Services.
```

cd.Execute

Note that the Recordset is passed as an argument to the "Command as Method" call. When the commands have parameters, the parameters can also be passed as arguments to the method. They must come before the Recordset which is always the last argument. We'll see an example of this shortly. Let's conclude this section by looking at the formal definition of the Execute method:

Function Execute([RecordsAffected As Long],
                   [Parameters As Variant],
                   [Options As Long = -1]) As Recordset

The RecordsAffected argument works in the same way as it does for cn.Execute and exposes the fact that Command objects can be used for non-row–returning commands that make changes to one or more records. We'll take a look at the use of the Parameters argument in the next section. Options can be one or more values from the CommandTypeEnum or ExecuteOption-Enum enumerations, the latter of which provides asynchronous functionality as described in Chapter 6.

cd.Command-
TimeOut

Finally, you may have noticed that the Command object has a Command-TimeOut property. This has a default of thirty seconds and is in no way affected by the CommandTimeOut property of the active connection. If you want to change the time out used by a Command object, you must set its CommandTimeOut explicitly.

Parameters and Parameter Objects

Command objects come into their own when used with parameters. Parameters can be used either in SQL statements or stored procedures. While you can expect any SQL data source to support parameterized commands, you are less likely to find the technique supported by other types of Providers.

In the previous section, there was an SQL statement that provided a word count for DON PEDRO. Realistically, you would want to be able to use this query with any character in the play. There are two ways of achieving this:

1. Hold the part name in a variable and use string concatenation to build a new SQL string each time you call it.

2. Use a parameter in the SQL string and supply the parameter value in time for each execution.

The second approach is a neater and more readable solution. Here's what the SQL would look like:

```
SELECT Words.word, SUM(Words.wordCount) AS total
    FROM Words INNER JOIN Parts ON Words.part = Parts.part
    GROUP BY Words.word, Parts.part, Words.WordLength
    HAVING (Parts.part = ?)     ◄─────────────     parameter place marker
      AND (SUM(Words.wordCount) > 4)
      AND (Words.WordLength > 4)
    ORDER BY SUM(Words.wordCount) DESC
```

cd.Parameters

Before executing a parameterized statement, the Command object requires a Parameter object for each parameter (our example has one parameter). The Parameter objects, which are stored as a collection in the cd.Parameters property, have the following properties:

Name
Direction
Value
Attributes
Precision
NumericScale
Size
Type

As Parameter objects typically represent a field in a query, it's no surprise that most of these properties have the same or similar meanings to a Field object's properties of the same name. The differences to note are as follows:

pm.Name

- **Name:** This is a name given to the Parameter, which can be used to refer to it in the Parameters collection of the Command object. It need not be the name of the field the Parameter represents.

pm.Direction

- **Direction:** This property specifies whether the parameter is an input, output, input/output, or return value. For SQL queries it's always input, which is the default.

pm.Size

- **Size:** For Parameters with a variable length data type (such as a dVarChar), Size must always be set to the actual length of an input parameter (actually, there is one exception to this rule, which will be explained shortly).

pm.AppendChunk

Parameter objects also have an AppendChunk method, which serves the same purpose as it does for Field objects.

pms.Refresh

There are two ways to construct the Parameters collection:

1. You can construct it yourself (possibly with some help from ADO).

2. You can ask the Provider to construct the Parameters collection for you and set any properties on the Parameter objects before calling Execute. You can achieve this by calling the Refresh method on the Parameters property of the Command object. The Refresh method is triggered automatically when you read the Parameters.Count property or attempt to access a Parameter object that you haven't explicitly added to the Parameters collection yourself.

3. If Refresh is called after setting the cd.ActiveConnection property and before calling cd.Execute, the Provider will be asked to build the Parameters collection. Calling Refresh after calling Execute has no effect.

Calling or triggering the Refresh method during development can be a convenient way of finding out about a parameterized query of stored procedure. Calling it in a finished application is best avoided for two reasons:

1. Your code will run more slowly if you ask the Provider to do work you could do yourself.[3] Even the best Providers are rarely optimized for this particular task.

2. Many Providers can't supply this information, so you compromise the portability of your application by expecting the Provider to oblige.

---

3. This age-old programmer's dilemma is as true today as ever.

Let's take a look at some different ways of constructing the Parameters collection and executing a parameterized statement. In the examples that follow, assume that sSQL is a string containing the SQL statement introduced at the beginning of this section, and cn is an open Connection object.

The Lazy Way to Use Parameters

```
Dim cd As New Command
Dim rs As Recordset
cd.CommandText = sSQL
cd.ActiveConnection = cn
Set rs = cd.Execute(, "DON PEDRO")
Set cd.ActiveConnection = Nothing
While Not rs.EOF
    Print rs!word, rs!total
    rs.MoveNext
Wend
```

Here, the Parameter is supplied as an argument to the Execute method. ADO builds the Parameter objects for you.

Although this is a "lazy" approach, it doesn't result in the Provider being asked to supply any parameter information, and so it's perfectly efficient. Instead, ADO uses the argument you supply as the Value property of the Parameter object and works out the Type and Size properties for you from the Value. The only downside of this technique is that it assumes the parameter is an input parameter, and therefore, it won't work with any other parameter direction.

Note that the Recordset is still connected even after Set cd.Active-Connection = Nothing.

The Inefficient Way to Use Parameters

```
Dim cd As New Command
Dim rs As Recordset
Dim sParam As String
cd.CommandText = sSQL
cd.ActiveConnection = cn
sParam = "DON PEDRO"
cd.Parameters(0).Value = sParam
Print "Before setting Size", cd.Parameters(0).Size
cd.Parameters(0).Size = Len(sParam)
Print "After setting Size", cd.Parameters(0).Size
Set rs = cd.Execute
Set cd.ActiveConnection = Nothing
```

referencing the Parameters collection causes Parameters.Refresh to be called implicitly

```
While Not rs.EOF
   'Print rs!word, rs!total
   rs.MoveNext
Wend
```

prints

Before setting Size	20
After setting Size	9

Two print statements make this code longer than it needs to be, but even without them, this approach requires more coding for less efficiency. In this code, when we first reference the Parameters collection ADO has no knowledge about what parameters there should be, so it triggers the Refresh method, which asks the Provider to supply details about the parameters. The first print statement is proof of this, because ADO now knows that this Parameter's size is 20, this being the size defined in the database for Parts.part. However, this is not the size of the parameter we'll be supplying, so we have to override this value with the actual size of DON PEDRO.[4]

It's hard to think of a good reason to use this technique, at least with standard SQL statements.

Using Explicit Parameter Objects Efficiently

The lazy way to use parameters doesn't suit everyone, and it doesn't give you complete control over use of parameters. The key to using Parameter objects efficiently is to avoid triggering a Refresh method.[5] This means building Parameter objects and then appending them to the cd.Parameters collection.

There are two ways of doing this, each equally valid:

```
Dim sParam As String
Dim pm As New Parameter
sParam = "DON PEDRO"
pm.Name = "Character"
pm.Type = adVarChar
pm.Direction = adParamInput
pm.Size = Len(sParam)
```

Here, Name is optional and Direction (if omitted) will default to adParamInput. All other properties are mandatory and an error occurs in the Append method if any are missing.

(Size is only mandatory for variable length data types.)

---

4. In fact, working with SQLServer7 and an adVarChar field means that you can get away without setting the Size property, but you shouldn't rely on this.

5. There are several ways to check this out. My preferred way is to use an ODBC-based connection and look in the ODBC trace for calls to the ODBC functions SQLNumParams and SQLDescribeParam.

```
pm.Value = sParam
cd.Parameters.Append pm
```

◄——————— Append to the Parameters collection here.

or

```
Dim sParam As String
Dim pm As Parameter
sParam = "DON PEDRO"
Set pm = cd.CreateParameter("Character", adVarChar, _
               adParamInput, Len(sParam), sParam)
cd.Parameters.Append pm
```

cd.CreateParameter

The CreateParameter method simply provides a more concise way of setting the properties of a Parameter object. You might expect that it would automatically append the Parameter to the Parameters collection, but it doesn't. Its formal definition is

Function CreateParameter([Name As String],
                                   [Type As DataTypeEnum = adEmpty],
                                   [Direction As ParameterDirectionEnum = adParamInput],
                                   [Size As Long],
                                   [Value]) As Parameter

After constructing the Parameters collection, you can simply execute the command

```
Set rs = cd.Execute
```

to get the desired Resultset.

You only need to create the Parameter objects once (which can be done at the same time the Command object is initialized). Next time you want to execute the command, the following code will suffice:

```
sParam = "FRIAR FRANCIS"
cd("Character").Size = Len(sParam)
cd("Character").Value = sParam
Set rs = cd.Execute
```

This example uses the Name property to identify the Parameter. The Parameter's ordinal position (0) is equally valid. Note that it's important to change the `Size` property before assigning a new value, otherwise an error will occur if the new string is larger than the previous one.

Commands with Multiple Parameters

Our SQL query would be more flexible if we could specify the filters used on word count and word length instead of being stuck with the hard-coded numbers. This means using three parameter place markers in the command string, as follows:

```
SELECT Words.word, SUM(Words.wordCount) AS total
      FROM Words INNER JOIN Parts ON Words.part = Parts.part
      GROUP BY Words.word, Parts.part, Words.WordLength
      HAVING (Parts.part = ?)AND (SUM(Words.wordCount) > ?)
         AND (Words.WordLength > ?)
      ORDER BY SUM(Words.wordCount) DESC
```

When using explicit Parameter objects, using this command string is simply a matter of working with three Parameter objects instead of one. When appending Parameters to the collection, it's important to append them in the same order as the parameter markers appear in the query, as the Parameter objects are ultimately matched to their respective markers based on ordinal position.

With multiple parameters, the code becomes verbose quite quickly, although you can reduce its size slightly by omitting the Size property for the two Parameters with adInteger data types, as the Size property is ignored for fixed-size data types.

The lazy approach can still be used with multiple parameters, although it is easy to get the syntax wrong. The Parameters argument of the Execute method is a Variant. When there is only one parameter you can simply use the parameter value as shown previously, but when there is more than one argument a ***Variant array*** must be supplied, containing all the parameter values (a conventional array will not do). The easiest way to create a Variant array is by using the Array function in VB.[6] For example

```
cd.ActiveConnection = cn
Set rs = cd.Execute(, Array("MARGARET", 3, 4))  ⟵——— a Variant array of
Set cd.ActiveConnection = Nothing                       Parameter values
While Not rs.EOF
   Print rs!word, rs!total
   rs.MoveNext
Wend
```

---

6. Another very convenient approach is to use the ParamArray keyword to exploit VB's ability to define procedures which take a variable number of arguments. The argument list appears to the VB procedure as a Variant array, which can be passed directly to cd.Execute.

will print

think	10
Troth	4
would	4

Working with Stored Procedures

Many databases provide a commonly used feature called stored procedures. *Stored procedures* are much like any other type of procedure (such as a VB Sub or Function) except that they are stored in the database and are executed by the database in its own process on its server. Stored procedures can contain SQL statements, but they also support standard programming features such as variables, loops, and branching. They have names and argument lists just as any type of procedure does and can return Recordsets, output parameters, or return values, or even all three. The attributes of stored procedures include:

1. *They can provide significant performance benefits.* This is partly because stored procedures are (more or less) compiled, and therefore, the server doesn't have to convert raw SQL statements into a binary format that it can execute each time the stored procedure is called. Stored procedures can also help you reduce network traffic. This can happen when you need to execute several SQL statements to produce a single result. When you do this from VB code, all the intermediate Recordsets need to be passed across the network to the VB program so that it can create the final result. When all of this work is done inside a stored procedure, only the final result needs to be sent across the network.

2. *They allow you to centralize functionality in a server.* Developers can call complex SQL-based functions simply by knowing the function name and arguments. Stored procedures can be managed centrally and modified without needing to compile and distribute application code.

3. *They frequently tie your application to a specific database.* There are no standards for databases to adhere to for stored procedure syntax and functionality.[7]

---

7. This is one reason why database vendors are so keen for you to use stored procedures. You must always be aware of this constraint when using stored procedures, although it shouldn't necessarily prevent you exploiting their significant benefits.

ADO provides a standardized way of calling stored procedures and processing their results, regardless of the data source. However, databases differ in their stored procedure capabilities. Some can only return output parameters or return values, while others can only return Recordsets. Some can do either but not both. All of the examples in this section are based on SQLServer 7, which has full stored procedure capabilities . If you are using a different database, you may need to consult its documentation concerning stored procedure capabilities.

SQLServer 7 provides a language called Transact-SQL (T-SQL) which you can use to write stored procedures., T-SQL is a superset of the SQL that can be used from client programs. If you take the query from the previous section and convert it into T-SQL, it looks like this:

```
CREATE PROCEDURE sp_WordList (@part varChar(20),
                             @wordCount Int, @wordLength Int )
AS
SELECT Words.word, SUM(Words.wordCount) AS total
    FROM Words INNER JOIN Parts ON Words.part = Parts.part
    GROUP BY Words.word, Parts.part, Words.WordLength
    HAVING (Parts.part = @part)
       AND (SUM(Words.wordCount) > @wordCount)
       AND (Words.WordLength > @wordLength)
    ORDER BY SUM(Words.wordCount) DESC
```

This code creates a stored procedure called sp_WordList with three arguments. The arguments are named and prefixed with @. Remember that this stored procedure must be created inside SQLServer (typically using SQLServer tools) and not in VB code, although you can use the VB6 Data View window to create SQLServer stored procedures from within the Visual Studio Development Environment.

Either of the following approaches can be used to call this stored procedure:

```
Dim rs As New Recordset
      rs.Open "sp_Wordlist ('VERGES',2,2)", cn, , , adCmdStoredProc
```

or

```
Dim cd As New Command
Dim rs As Recordset
Set cd.ActiveConnection = cn
cd.CommandType = adCmdStoredProc
cd.CommandText = "sp_WordList"
Set rs = cd.Execute(, Array("VERGES", 2, 2))
Set cd.ActiveConnection = Nothing
```

Command type is set for stored procedures

In either case, the resulting Recordset can be treated exactly as if it were created using an SQL statement in VB.[8]

So far, we have only considered input parameters. To explore other types of parameters, we'll write a stored procedure that returns the length of the longest word spoken by a given character. Of course, this stored procedure could be written to return a Recordset, as follows:

```
CREATE PROCEDURE sp_LargestWord1 (@part varChar(20))
  AS
SELECT MAX(wordLength) as LargestWord
       FROM Words WHERE part = @part
```

and called from VB using

```
Dim lResult as Long
cd.CommandText = "sp_LargestWord1"
Set rs = cd.Execute(, "DON PEDRO")
lResult = rs("LargestWord").Value
```

Here, the Recordset returned has a single record with one column. If the column name is known, it can be used to extract the value, otherwise, an ordinal position can be used. This code works fine, but a reasonable amount of time is spent creating a Recordset structure just to hold a single value. It's considerably more efficient to use an output parameter instead of a Recordset. The following code shows a stored procedure coded to return an output parameter:

```
CREATE PROCEDURE sp_LargestWord2 (
            @part varChar(20),
            @LargestWord Int OUTPUT)
  AS
 SELECT @LargestWord = MAX(wordLength)
        FROM Words WHERE part = @part
```

parameter is defined as OUTPUT
(default is INPUT) ←

this T-SQL SELECT statement assigns a value to the output parameter

---

8. In this particular case, the SQL is too complex to allow updates to be performed on the Recordset. However, for a stored procedure with a simpler query, the Recordset can be updated as long as the appropriate lock type is set. (Note that while this is true of SQLServer7, it's not true of all databases.)

It can be called using

```
Dim lResult As Long
Dim pm As Parameter
cd.CommandText = "sp_LargestWord2"
Set pm = cd.CreateParameter("Part", adVarChar, , 20, "DON PEDRO")
cd.Parameters.Append pm
Set pm = cd.CreateParameter("Largest", adInteger, adParamOutput)
cd.Parameters.Append pm
cd.Execute
lResult = cd("Largest").Value    ◀─────────── result is read from the
                                               OUTPUT Parameter object
```

This code uses no Recordset! The information requested from the database is passed back directly via the stored procedure parameter. Even when the stored procedure executes a fairly expensive query, the performance advantage gained by using an output parameter is significant. It's more significant still if your code only creates the Parameter objects once. When the query itself is very fast, using output parameters can easily be several times more efficient than a "singleton" Recordset.

As well as wanting to know the length of the longest word, you may also wish to know which words spoken by the character have that length. Your first thought may be to use another output argument. However, there could be several words of the same length. The best way to handle this requirement is to create a stored procedure that returns a Recordset and has an output parameter. The following stored procedure does all this, and it also takes an additional argument that allows you to specify whether you actually want the Recordset to be returned. This step not only saves building a Recordset, it also saves executing the additional SQL query unless it's really wanted.

```
CREATE PROCEDURE sp_LargestWord4 (
            @part varChar(20),
            @LargestWord Int OUTPUT,
            @WithRecords as TinyInt)
  AS
  SELECT @LargestWord = MAX(wordLength) FROM Words
      WHERE part = @part

  if @WithRecords > 0            ◀─────────── if @WithRecords > 0,
      SELECT distinct word FROM Words         create a Recordset as well
          WHERE part = @part and wordLength = @LargestWord
```

The code to call this stored procedure is shown next. While it looks (and is) straightforward, there is one potential catch.

```
Dim pm As Parameter
With cd
 .CommandText = "sp_LargestWord4"
 Set pm = .CreateParameter("Part", adVarChar, , 20, "CLAUDIO")
 .Parameters.Append pm
 Set pm = .CreateParameter("Largest", adInteger, adParamOutput)
 .Parameters.Append pm
 Set pm = .CreateParameter("Type", adTinyInt, , , 1)
 .Parameters.Append pm
 Set rs = .Execute
 While Not rs.EOF
   Print rs(0)
   rs.MoveNext
 Wend
 rs.Close
 Print "LENGTH:", !Largest.Value
End With
```

this (>0) parameter value requests a Recordset

SQLServer7 requires the Recordset to be closed before the output parameter is accessed

prints

```
double-dealer
over-kindness
unconstrained
LENGTH:        13
```

The main point you should note here is the need to close the Recordset before reading the output parameter value. In fact, if you read the parameter value and then close the Recordset, the parameter value will still be unavailable even after the Recordset is closed. This is because ADO only fetches it once from the Provider. Subsequent reads use the value cached by ADO.

The need to close the Recordset before reading the output parameter is a limitation of SQLServer 7, but one that is fairly common when server-side cursors are used (it won't be a problem with client-side cursors). You can test for this behavior by checking the dynamic Connection property called "Output Parameter Availability." It can have the values shown in Table 5-1.

Table 5-1. Output Parameter Availability Dynamic Property Values

VALUE	DESCRIPTION
1	Output parameters are not supported.
2	Output parameters are available immediately after cd.Execute.
4	Output parameters are available only after the Recordset has been closed.[9]

Stored Procedure Example

Stored procedures are often used to handle database modifications. Let's take a look at a typical "update" stored procedure and address one or two stored procedure features not yet covered.

There are a large number of records in the Words table, and using a stored procedure to insert words is not only efficient, but it allows us to encapsulate some standard logic in a centralized location.

By using a stored procedure, we can remove the need for a client program to worry about whether a word already exists for a given part, act, and scene. If it does exist, the stored procedure will increment the existing word count, otherwise, an insert is generated. In addition, this stored procedure should:

1. Return the primary key of the new or updated record. The primary key for the Words table is an AutoIncrement field. SQLServer uses a built-in variable to hold the last AutoIncrement number generated anywhere in the database. This variable is called @@IDENTITY.

2. Tell us whether a record was updated or inserted.

3. Allow us to prevent either an insert or update from taking place. This would allow the client program to add some consistency checking if it wants.

The first of these requirements can be met by making use of the return value from the stored procedure. When using return values from stored procedures, the ADO Parameter object should have its `Direction` property set to `adParamReturnValue`. The return value Parameter must always be the first one added to the Parameters collection.

The second and third requirements can be met by adding an adParamInputOutput parameter called "@new". The caller can set this argument to the following values:

---

9. If the command generates multiple Recordsets, each Recordset must be retrieved and closed before output parameters can be read.

- **−1**: The stored procedure must update an existing record and not create a new record.

- **0**: The caller doesn't care whether an update or insert takes place.

- **1**: The stored procedure must create a new record and not update an existing record.

On return from the stored procedure, @new will be one of the following values:

- **−1**: An existing record was updated (no new record).

- **0**: An error occurred.

- **1**: A new record was created.

Here's the stored procedure code:

```
CREATE PROCEDURE sp_AddWord (
        @word varChar(50),
        @part varChar(20),
        @act tinyint,
        @scene tinyint,
        @new smallint OUTPUT)
    AS
    declare @id Int          ◄──────────────    declare a local variable
                                                for the stored procedure

    SELECT @id = id FROM Words WHERE
        word = @word and part = @part and
        act = @act and scene = @scene

 /* if @new is not 0, perform the required consistency check */

if  (@new = 1 and not (@id is Null)) Or    ◄──────┐
    (@new = -1 and @id is Null)                   │
    begin                                 @id will be Null if no existing
        set @new = 0                      record is found, otherwise, it
        return 0                          will contain a primary key
    end
```

```
if @id is Null
    begin  /* create a new record */
      set   @new = 1
      insert into Words
          (word, part, act, scene, wordCount, WordLength)
          values (@word, @part, @act, @scene, 1, LEN(@word))
       return @@identity        ◄──────────────  return the new primary key
    end                                           created for the AutoIncre-
else                                              ment id field
    begin  /* update existing record */
       set @new = -1
     update Words set wordCount = wordCount + 1 where id = @id
      return @id       ◄───────────────  return the existing primary key
    end
```

The following VB code will call this stored procedure. The variables sWord, sPart, iAct, and iScene can be assumed to have been initialized appropriately.

```
Static cd As Command
Const DONT_CARE As Long = 0


If cd Is Nothing Then     ◄───────────────  only set up the Command
    Set cd = New Command                     object once
    cd.CommandText = "sp_AddWord"
    cd.CommandType = adCmdStoredProc
    cd.Parameters.Append cd.CreateParameter( _
                "PKey", adInteger, adParamReturnValue)
    cd.Parameters.Append cd.CreateParameter( _
                "Word", adVarChar, , Len(sWord), sWord)
    cd.Parameters.Append cd.CreateParameter( _
                "Part", adVarChar, , Len(sPart), sPart)
    cd.Parameters.Append cd.CreateParameter( _
                "Act", adTinyInt, , , iAct)
    cd.Parameters.Append cd.CreateParameter( _
                "Scene", adTinyInt, , , iScene)
    cd.Parameters.Append cd.CreateParameter( _
       "New", adSmallInt, adParamInputOutput, , DONT_CARE)
Else
    cd("Word").Size = Len(sWord)
    cd("Word").Value = sWord
    cd("Part").Size = Len(sPart)
    cd("Part").Value = sPart
    cd("Act").Value = iAct           New is both an INPUT and an
    cd("Scene").Value = iScene       OUTPUT parameter, so it
    cd("New").Value = DONT_CARE  ◄── should be reset each time
End If                               it's used
```

```
Set cd.ActiveConnection = cn

cd.Execute

Print cd("PKey").Value, cd("New").Value
Set cd.ActiveConnection = Nothing
```

In this routine, cd is defined as a static local variable. The first time the routine is called, a Command object is created and initialized with all the required Parameter objects. On subsequent calls, only the parameter values and the size of the parameters with variable length data types need to be set. Even though we are using the DONT_CARE flag on each call, the New parameter needs to be set each time. This is because New is both an INPUT and an OUTPUT parameter, and the stored procedure sets it during each call.[10]

Stored Procedures with Multiple SELECT Statements

It's sometimes convenient to write multifunctional stored procedures capable of outputting more than one Recordset. Here's an example:

```
CREATE PROCEDURE sp_WordUsage (
        @word varChar(50),
        @usageType tinyint)
  AS
  if (@usageType = 1) Or (@usageType = 3)
      SELECT part, sum(wordCount) as wordCount FROM Words
          WHERE word = @word
          GROUP BY part ORDER BY part

  if (@usageType = 2) Or (@usageType = 3)
      SELECT act, scene, sum(wordCount) as wordCount FROM Words
          WHERE word = @word
          GROUP BY act, scene ORDER BY act, scene
```

sp_WordUsage takes a word argument. It also takes a usageType argument which has the following effect on the data returned by the stored procedure:

- usageType = 1: Returns a Recordset listing each part that uses @word, and its word count.

---

10. Note that in the stored procedure @New is simply defined as an OUTPUT parameter. T-SQL assumes that all parameters can be used for input. This isn't true for ADO, however. If you set the direction of New to adParamOutput, any value you assign to it will be ignored.

- usageType = 2: Returns a Recordset listing each act and scene in which @word appears, and its word count.

- usageType = 3: Returns both Recordsets.

When this stored procedure is used to return more than one Recordset, the rs.NextRecordset method can be used to retrieve the next Recordset, as soon as it's finished with the previous one. The full description of this technique is in Chapter 3. This is one situation in which NextRecordset can be very useful.

Stored Procedures and Temporary Tables

Stored procedures are limited in the types of data supported by their parameters. For example, you have just seen a stored procedure that takes a single word as an argument, and returns some usage information. What if you wanted to pass several words to the procedure and get all the usage information for these words at one go?

If you were designing a VB procedure to handle this, you would use a collection, an array, or some similar compound structure to pass in the list of words. You can't do this with stored procedures because the necessary data types don't exist. While you could call the stored procedure once for each word in the list, this approach is cumbersome and inefficient. Something better is required.

Temporary tables provide one way to pass a list into a stored procedure. There are two types of temporary tables supported by SQLServer: global and local. *Local* temporary tables look and feel just like any standard table except that they are only visible on the connection that created them, and they are automatically dropped when the connection is closed. *Global* temporary tables are visible to all users of a database.

Local temporary tables present an "acceptable" technique for passing lists between stored procedures, or from an application to a stored procedure.[11] Because it is possible to perform SQL joins that include temporary tables, manipulating temporary tables is very efficient once they have been created.

In the example that follows, VB code will be used to create a temporary table called #TempWords (local temporary table names always begin with a single #) and insert one row for each word in a "word list." It will then call a stored procedure that will join that temporary table with the Words table to

---

11. They are acceptable only because they are the least bad technique to operate on lists without suffering major performance penalties. From a structured programming perspective, the example presented here is fairly ugly because it creates a dependency between a routine in VB and a stored procedure. The caller of the stored procedure must know about the expected structure and existence of the temporary table.

create "parts" and "scenes" Recordsets containing the usage data for all the words in the temporary table, and then drop the temporary table. Just for a change, let's see the VB code first (the code assumes that cn is an open Connection):

```
Dim cd As New Command
Dim rs As Recordset
Const GET_BOTH As Long = 3

cn.Execute "CREATE TABLE #TempWords (word varchar(50))"
cn.Execute "INSERT INTO #TempWords values('horn')"
cn.Execute "INSERT INTO #TempWords values('terrible')"
cn.Execute "INSERT INTO #TempWords values('buy')"
cn.Execute "INSERT INTO #TempWords values('maiden')"


cd.CommandType = adCmdStoredProc
cd.CommandText = "sp_WordUsage1"
cd.ActiveConnection = cn
Set rs = cd.Execute(, GET_BOTH )


cd.ActiveConnection = Nothing
Print "PARTS"
While Not rs.EOF
    Print rs!word, rs!part, rs!wordCount
    rs.MoveNext
Wend
Set rs = rs.NextRecordset
Print vbCr & "SCENES"
While Not rs.EOF
    Print rs!word, rs!act, rs!scene, rs!wordCount
    rs.MoveNext
Wend
```

use cn to create the temporary table and insert some words into it

initialize the Command object and execute the stored procedure

get the second Recordset

The stored procedure code is

```
CREATE PROCEDURE sp_WordUsage1 (@usageType tinyint)
 AS
if (@usageType = 1) Or (@usageType = 3)
  SELECT Words.word, Words.part,
           sum(Words.wordCount) as wordCount
      FROM Words, #TempWords
      WHERE Words.word = #TempWords.word
      GROUP BY Words.word, Words.part
      ORDER BY Words.word, Words.part
```

join Words and #TempWords

187

```
if (@usageType = 2) Or (@usageType = 3)
  SELECT Words.word, Words.act, Words.scene,
           sum(Words.wordCount) as wordCount
      FROM Words, #TempWords
      WHERE Words.word = #TempWords.word
      GROUP BY Words.word, Words.act, Words.scene
      ORDER BY Words.word, Words.act, Words.scene


DROP TABLE #TempWords    ◄───────────────    drop the temporary table
```

The net result of running the VB code that calls sp_WordUsage1 is

PARTS			
buy	BENEDICK		1
buy	CLAUDIO		1
horn	BENEDICK		3
maiden	BEATRICE		1
maiden	DON PEDRO		1
maiden	FRIAR FRANCIS		1
maiden	HERO		1
terrible	BENEDICK		1
SCENES			
buy	1	1	2
horn	2	3	1
horn	5	2	1
horn	5	4	1
maiden	3	1	1
maiden	4	1	3
terrible	2	1	1

Local temporary tables created inside stored procedures are automatically dropped by SQLServer when the stored procedure exists. When they are created outside stored procedures, they are dropped when the connection closes. In a world which exploits Connection Pooling (see Chapter 4), physical connections won't necessarily close when you close or release your ADO Connection objects, and there is a danger that useless but resource-consuming temporary tables will accumulate over time. Therefore, it makes sense to drop temporary tables created outside stored procedures explicitly, especially if you are writing code for use in middle-tier applications or Web servers.

Command Optimizations

You have already seen one technique for optimizing Command object usage, which is simply to avoid triggering the cd.Parameters.Refresh method anywhere in the finished code. There is one other major technique to consider—the use of prepared statements—and a few less frequently used methods.

When you send a raw SQL command to a data source, there are several steps the server must go through before it can do your bidding. These are shown in the following diagram:

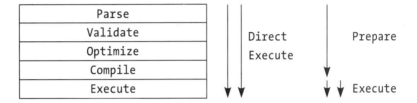

Figure 5-1. Direct and prepared execution of an SQL command

When a server receives a command, it first parses it to identify its contents. It then validates that the tables and fields and their data types are as they should be, and goes on to optimize the query, which typically means working out which indexes to use to make it run as efficiently as possible. Once all this is done, the execution plan is compiled and only then can the command be executed. This process is often called *direct execution*. It's entirely possible for the first four steps to take longer than the actual command execution. More often than not, the server throws away all this work as soon as the command has been executed and the results have been returned.[12]

What this means is that when you next execute the same command, the whole process begins again. With parameterized commands, it's only the execution step that changes when the parameter values are changed—the execution plan is the same each time.

cd.Prepared

If you set the cd.Prepared property to True, then the first time you call cd.Execute, the Command object will ask the server to prepare an execution plan and hold on to it. The Command object then immediately asks the server to execute the plan using any supplied arguments. Next time you call cd.Execute

---

12. One of the reasons that stored procedures are faster than dynamic SQL is that servers compile an execution plan for stored procedures when they are created, so that only the execution step is required at run time.

on the same Command object, the prepared execution plan is reused[13], meaning that the first four steps in Figure 5-1 don't need to be repeated, and time savings can result. This approach is often called *prepared execution*.

Enabling prepared statements is as simple as setting the `cd.Prepared` property to `True`. However, the technique raises two major questions:

1. *What happens when Connection Pooling is also being exploited?* As soon as you set `cd.ActiveConnection = Nothing`, the Command object releases its reference to the execution plan. Therefore, even if you get back the same physical connection next time you retrieve one from the pool, you won't be able to reuse the previously prepared execution plan. You can only exploit prepared execution while you are holding on to an ADO Connection object. While it isn't true to say that prepared statements and pooling are incompatible, the opportunities to exploit them both in a satisfactory way are few and far between. Given the choice between prepared statements and pooling, most developers would opt for pooling[14] (and use stored procedures instead of prepared statements).

2. *How much faster are prepared statements?* There is no straightforward answer to this question. There is an overhead in having a two-step process the first time you call Execute. If the database doesn't fully support prepared statements[15], then quite often, the Provider creates temporary stored procedures when you request a prepared statement. Alternatively, the Provider simply caches the command string so that it can simulate the preparation process, in which case the server generates a new execution plan each time anyway. When temporary stored procedures are used, there is an additional one-time overhead because it takes longer to generate a stored procedure than to simply compile an execution plan. As a general rule, you won't see any benefit (and may in fact lose out) from prepared statements unless you expect the Command to be executed at least four or five times or possibly more if temporary stored procedures are used. If you expect to execute the Command dozens of times the savings can be significant.

To summarize, prepared statements can be very worthwhile if you want to execute the same (possibly parameterized) command repeatedly on the

---

13. Unless you change the CommandText, in which case the new command will be prepared and the old execution plan released.

14. There are exceptions. For example, if you know you only have a few users and have a highly repetitive task such as a bulk update operation, prepared statements would be advantageous—although stored procedures would be better still.

15. This is the case for SQLServer 6.5 and Sybase.

same connection and if you wish to avoid using stored procedures to prevent database tie-in. Otherwise, don't bother.

One or two other optimization techniques are worth mentioning. We first met adExecuteNoRecords as a value that could be used for the Execute method when executing non-row–returning commands. In those cases its benefit was mostly theoretical, but it does come into its own with stored procedures. If you wish to call a stored procedure that generates a Recordset, but you don't want the Recordset (only some other effect brought about by the stored procedure), then adExecuteNoRecords can have measurable benefits.

In Chapter 3 we discussed the benefits of using the rs.CacheSize method. When using Command objects, you can still benefit from CacheSize optimizations by using the Command object as the Source argument to rs.Open, instead of calling cd.Execute, as discussed earlier in the chapter.

Summary

This chapter has focused on Command objects. Most developers use Command objects to work with stored procedures, and you have seen several examples of calling SQLServer stored procedures from ADO using Command objects.

Command objects:

- Make it possible to work with parameterized commands, which include both SQL and stored procedures

- Provide support for prepared statements, although in these days of Connection Pooling, prepared statements are less useful than they used to be.

- Allow you to centralize database access that would otherwise be distributed around many parts of a program. By hiding data access issues behind the central resource of Command objects, this approach can make data access management more straightforward and allow developers with different skill sets to do what they do best. These commands can even be compiled as a separate DLL and shared between applications, creating a corporate data access library.

You have now seen all the ADO objects that existed prior to ADO 2.5. However, you haven't seen everything they can do, and before moving on to look at semistructured data access using Records and Streams, it's worth looking at some of the remaining major pieces of ADO functionality. In the next chapter, we'll explore ADO Events and asynchronous processing.

CHAPTER 6

The ADO Event Model and Asynchronous Processing

Connection Events

Recordset Events

Strategies for Using Events

Asynchronous Processing

Summary

ADO 2.0 INTRODUCED a comprehensive set of events on the Connection and Recordset objects. One of the most common questions developers ask when learning about ADO events is—interesting, but why would I use them?

Every VB programmer is familiar with events because the process of creating user interfaces in VB involves placing controls, which define their own set of events, on a form and writing code in event procedures. The VB code window lists each control in the Objects dropdown list and the developer can select an event in the Procedures dropdown list. Code can then be written that will execute when these events fire.

VB5 introduced the ability to receive events from standard *COM* classes, as well as controls. When an object variable is declared using the WithEvents keyword, the object variable name is treated like a control name. The variable name appears in the Objects dropdown list, and its events are listed in the Procedures dropdown list. They can be coded just like a control's events.

A control fires events to allow its client to respond to something that has happened. The client can then tailor its behavior (and therefore the application or its user interface) appropriately. If controls did not raise events they would be far less useful. Imagine writing VB programs using a CommandButton that did not raise a Click event!

You should think about the events raised by the ADO Connection and Recordset objects in the same way as you think about the events raised by a control and exploit them for the same reasons.

Many of ADO's events come in pairs. For example, one of the most important things a Connection object does is to connect to a data source. ADO provides two events associated with this operation. The cn_WillConnect event fires before a Connection object starts the process of connecting to a data source, and the cn_ConnectComplete event fires once the connection process is completed. Event pairs give you a substantial degree of control over key ADO tasks.

ADO allows certain processes to be started asynchronously, which means a client program can continue working even while the process of connecting or fetching data is taking place. Events allow code to receive notifications when a task is complete, and it's reasonably easy to see how they can be useful in asynchronous tasks. However, it would be unfortunate to equate event processing to asynchronous operations. If you did, you would miss out on the very high level of control they give you over any ADO program, asynchronous or not. My aim in this chapter is to set out some broader scenery in which the role of events can be evaluated and understood. For sure, we'll look at asynchronous processing, but only after considering the full picture.

Connection Events

To demonstrate what can be achieved by using events, let's look at how to add an ADO Connection as an event monitor to an ADO application. The monitor can be used to diagnose ADO errors in a compiled application, or even to change the connection string so that the monitored application connects to a test database. The monitor itself will be written as a DLL that exploits ADO Connection events. The beauty of this technique is that

1. To use the monitor requires adding only six lines of code to the application being monitored.

2. When the monitor isn't being used, there is no performance overhead in the application, and no special coding is required (apart from the six lines of code).

3. You can add and remove monitors to a compiled program without making any coding changes. You can switch between multiple monitors, and the monitor doesn't even need to have been written when the "client" application is compiled and distributed.

4. The monitor will work with any ADO application that uses explicit Connection objects and includes the six lines of code or their equivalent.

I promise not to let the details of this sample program get in the way of finding out about events. It so happens that it's an easy way of creating a dramatic example of what they can be used for. First, however, let's take a look at how a Connection object's events are organized.

Table 6-1. Connection Events

PAIRED EVENTS	
Before Operation	*After Operation*
WillConnect	ConnectComplete
WillExecute	ExecuteComplete
UNPAIRED EVENTS	
BeginTransComplete	
CommitTransComplete	
RollbackTransComplete	
Disconnect	
InfoMessage	

I won't be describing each event formally. Instead, code samples and associated narrative will contain all the details required.

Each event has its own set of arguments, but there is some common ground that makes understanding events a little easier. Every event has an argument called adStatus whose value is taken from the EventStatusEnum enumeration when the event fires. It has these values defined:

adStatusOK
adStatusErrorsOccurred
adStatusCantDeny
adStatusCancel
adStatusUnwantedEvent

adStatusOK means that the operation is moving along fine, while adStatusErrorsOccurred means the opposite. Nearly every event has a pError argument, which is set to an ADO Error object when adStatus equals adStatusErrorsOccurred. You can use this Error object to find out more about any error that occurs.

In many cases, you can use the event to cancel a pending operation by setting adStatus to adStatusCancel inside the event procedure of a "Will..." event. However, if adStatus equals adStatusCantDeny then the operation can't be cancelled (in a "...Complete" event, adStatusCantDeny means that the operation has already been cancelled). If you cancel an event in this way, an error will be raised in the procedure that triggered the event, and therefore, adequate error handling will be required.

Setting adStatus to adStatusUnwantedEvent allows you to instruct ADO to stop firing that particular event. There is a cost associated with raising events,[1] so blocking unwanted ones has some performance benefit.[2]

In addition to adStatus and pError arguments, the events provide references to Connection, Command, and Recordset objects where appropriate, as well as some event-specific arguments.

cn_WillConnect
cn_Connect-
Complete
cn_Disconnect
cn_InfoMessage

Let's begin by looking at the WillConnect, ConnectComplete, Disconnect, and InfoMessage events. The first three should be self-explanatory. InfoMessage is raised when an ADO Error object is created, and when the error is not so severe as to cause a run-time error in VB.

In my sample applications, all ADO event monitoring is performed in an ActiveX DLL called ADOLogger, which contains a Public class called ADOConnection (and therefore its *ProgID* is ADOLogger.ADOConnection).

You'll see that the client program's code uses a standard VB global variable called Command. This is nothing to do with ADO's Command objects. The Command variable holds any command-line argument that is provided when the application is executed. For example, if the client was compiled as c:\myapp.exe, then running it as c:\myapp.exe ADOLogger.ADOConnection would allocate the Logger's ProgID to the Command variable, which could then be used in the CreateObject call. During development, you can simulate using a command-line argument in the VB IDE via the Make tab of the Project Properties dialog.

---

1. You are unlikely to notice the cost of Connection object events. However, the cost of Recordset events becomes significant when iterating through a client-side Recordset. Setting an event as unwanted can easily reduce this overhead by half.

2. Readers familiar with COM may be aware that events in VB are always handled using early binding. While this is more efficient than the late binding that results from declaring a variable "As Object," it's far less efficient than the vTable binding that can be used for methods and properties when variables are defined as a specific class.

Here's how the client application communicates with the Logger:

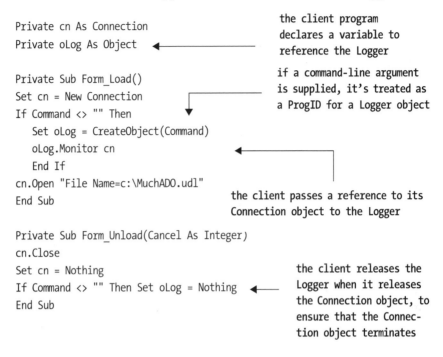

```
Private cn As Connection
Private oLog As Object
```
the client program declares a variable to reference the Logger

```
Private Sub Form_Load()
Set cn = New Connection
If Command <> "" Then
    Set oLog = CreateObject(Command)
    oLog.Monitor cn
    End If
cn.Open "File Name=c:\MuchADO.udl"
End Sub
```
if a command-line argument is supplied, it's treated as a ProgID for a Logger object

the client passes a reference to its Connection object to the Logger

```
Private Sub Form_Unload(Cancel As Integer)
cn.Close
Set cn = Nothing
If Command <> "" Then Set oLog = Nothing
End Sub
```
the client releases the Logger when it releases the Connection object, to ensure that the Connection object terminates

From this point on, the Logger can monitor all activity on the cn Connection through its events without any additional Logger-related code in the client program. The Logger is only used when the built-in VB global variable Command indicates that a command-line argument was provided when the application was executed. By using CreateObject, the client doesn't have any dependencies on the Logger compiled into it other than the expectation that the Logger (if used) will support the Monitor method. This, of course, means that I could write different Loggers for different tasks and connect to any such Logger at run time.

Now let's look at the Logger. Remember that this is written as an ActiveX DLL, which is compiled separately from the main EXE (although you could incorporate the Logger code into the main client EXE if you wanted to). Here's the code for the ADOLogger.ADOConnection class (the event argument lists are shown in gray to make it easier to identify the actual code):

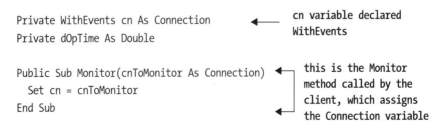

```
Private WithEvents cn As Connection
Private dOpTime As Double
```
cn variable declared WithEvents

```
Public Sub Monitor(cnToMonitor As Connection)
  Set cn = cnToMonitor
End Sub
```
this is the Monitor method called by the client, which assigns the Connection variable

```
Private Sub cn_InfoMessage( _
        ByVal pError As ADODB.Error, _
        adStatus As ADODB.EventStatusEnum, _
        ByVal pConnection As ADODB.Connection)
  MonitorEvent adStatus, "Info Message: " & pError.Description
End Sub


Private Sub cn_WillConnect( _
        ConnectionString As String, _
        UserID As String, _
        Password As String, _
        Options As Long, _
        adStatus As ADODB.EventStatusEnum, _
        ByVal pConnection As ADODB.Connection)
  MonitorEvent adStatus, "Connecting to: " & ConnectionString
  dOpTime = Timer
End Sub


Private Sub cn_ConnectComplete( _
        ByVal pError As ADODB.Error, _
        adStatus As ADODB.EventStatusEnum, _
        ByVal pConnection As ADODB.Connection)
  dOpTime = Timer - dOpTime
  If adStatus = adStatusErrorsOccurred Then
    MonitorEvent adStatus, pError.Description
  Else
    MonitorEvent adStatus, "Connection succeeded in " & _
        Format(dOpTime, "0.00") & _
        " seconds to " & pConnection.ConnectionString
  End If
End Sub


Private Sub cn_Disconnect( _
        adStatus As ADODB.EventStatusEnum, _
        ByVal pConnection As ADODB.Connection)
  MonitorEvent adStatus, "Disconnected"
End Sub
```

This code listing doesn't show the code for the `MonitorEvent` subroutine, which simply converts `adStatus` to a printable form, and prints it to the Debug window in the VB IDE. When using the compiled version of the Logger, MonitorEvent writes data to the NT Event Log (or a file on Windows 9.x).

When the client application is run with no command-line argument, the Logger is never started, no events get processed, and nothing is printed. However, if the client application is run with the Logger's ProgID in the command line, the following is printed:

```
OK:          Connecting to: File Name=c:\MuchADO.udl
OK:          Connection succeeded in 0.16 seconds to
Provider=SQLOLEDB.1;Integrated Security=SSPI;Persist Security
Info=False;Initial Catalog=MuchADO;Data Source=POLECAT;Use Procedure for
Prepare=1;Auto Translate=True;Packet Size=4096;Workstation ID=WEASEL
OK:          Disconnected
```

If I change the connection string to use an ODBC-based connection, I'll see an example of the InfoMessage event firing, as in the following printout:

```
OK:          Connecting to: DSN=MuchADO
OK:          Connection succeeded in 0.55 seconds to
Provider=MSDASQL.1;Extended Properties="DSN=MuchADO;UID=;APP=Visual
Basic;WSID=WEASEL;DATABASE=MuchADO;Trusted_Connection=Yes"
OK:          Info Message: [Microsoft][ODBC SQL Server Driver][SQL
Server]Changed database context to 'MuchADO'.
OK:          Disconnected
```

If you take a look at some of the arguments to the various events in the Logger code, you'll get an idea of the flexibility you can achieve when handling events. For example, let's assume that the client uses a hard-coded connection string, but you want to divert the client to a test database during monitoring.[3] Inserting the line

```
ConnectionString = "File Name=c:\MuchAdoJet.udl"
```

into the WillConnect event will cause the ConnectionString argument to be changed, and will result in a different data source connection being created:

```
OK:          Connecting to: DSN=MuchADO
OK:          Connection succeeded in 0.32 seconds to
Provider=Microsoft.Jet.OLEDB.4.0;User ID=Admin;Data
Source=D:\ADOBook\Data\muchado.mdb; (etc)
OK:          Disconnected
```

---

3. This example demonstrates the potential security loophole that can result from using a Logger like this. You'll probably want a real-life Logger to implement appropriate security measures.

cn_BeginTrans-
Complete
cn_CommitTrans-
Complete
cn_RollbackTrans-
Complete

The Connection object also supports events for transaction processing commands. There are no "Will…" events in this case, just "…Complete" events. Incorrect transaction processing can result in surprising errors, and analyzing what is really going on with transactions can be complex. Long-running transactions can cause serious concurrency problems in multiuser applications. In such situations, an activity logging mechanism can be invaluable.

Here's the transaction monitoring code in the Logger:

```
Private Sub cn_BeginTransComplete( _
        ByVal TransactionLevel As Long, _
        ByVal pError As ADODB.Error, _
        adStatus As ADODB.EventStatusEnum, _
        ByVal pConnection As ADODB.Connection)
Dim sTX As String

  If adStatus = adStatusOK Then
    dOpTime = Timer
    sTX = "Beginning TX (Isolation Level " & _
        pConnection.IsolationLevel & ") at " & _
            Format(Now, "hh:mm:ss")
  Else
    sTX = "Begin Transaction Error:" & pError.Description
  End If
  MonitorEvent adStatus, sTX
End Sub
```

print the time the transaction started, and the isolation level (available through the pConnection argument)

```
Private Sub cn_CommitTransComplete( _
        ByVal pError As ADODB.Error, _
        adStatus As ADODB.EventStatusEnum, _
        ByVal pConnection As ADODB.Connection)
Dim sTX As String
  If adStatus = adStatusOK Then
    dOpTime = Timer - dOpTime
    sTX = "Committing TX (" & Format(dOpTime, "0.00") & " seconds)"
  Else
    sTX = "Commit Transaction Error:" & pError.Description
  End If
  MonitorEvent adStatus, sTXEnd Sub

Private Sub cn_RollbackTransComplete( _
        ByVal pError As ADODB.Error, _
        adStatus As ADODB.EventStatusEnum, _
        ByVal pConnection As ADODB.Connection)
```

```
Dim sTX As String
  If adStatus = adStatusOK Then
    dOpTime = Timer - dOpTime
    sTX = "Rolling back TX (" & Format(dOpTime, "0.00") & " seconds)"
  Else
    sTX = "Rollback Transaction Error:" & pError.Description
  End If
  MonitorEvent adStatus, sTX
End Sub
```

Note that the cn_BeginTransComplete event has an argument called Transaction-Level. It tells you the nesting level of the new transaction. This is only really useful when you are using a Provider that supports nested transactions, such as the Jet Provider.

The following client code

```
cn.BeginTrans
cn.Execute "update Parts set description = 'bit part' " & _
                "where part = 'BOY'"
cn.RollbackTrans
```

generates

```
OK:          Beginning TX (Isolation Level 4096) at 17:53:40
OK:          Rolling back TX (0.04 seconds)
```

The transaction events fire only when the relevant ADO methods are explicitly called. This means

- Statements not bracketed by explicit ADO Connection transaction methods will be updated inside an implicit transaction and no event traffic will be generated.

- None of the events will fire when transactions are being managed by MTS or COM+.[4]

cn_WillExecute
cn_Execute-
Complete

Let's finish this section by looking at the WillExecute and ExecuteComplete events. Here's an example from the Logger DLL:

---

4. Although these products have their own event mechanisms for logging transactional activity.

```
Private Sub cn_WillExecute( _
        Source As String, _
        CursorType As ADODB.CursorTypeEnum, _
        LockType As ADODB.LockTypeEnum, _
        Options As Long, _
        adStatus As ADODB.EventStatusEnum, _
        ByVal pCommand As ADODB.Command, _
        ByVal pRecordset As ADODB.Recordset, _
        ByVal pConnection As ADODB.Connection)
Dim sObjects As String
If pCommand Is Nothing Then sObjects = "No Command Object:"
If pRecordset Is Nothing Then sObjects = _
        sObjects & "No Recordset Object:"
MonitorEvent adStatus, sObjects & vbCrLf & vbTab & _
        "(" & CursorType & "," & LockType & ") " & Source
End Sub
```

It's interesting to note that although this event belongs to a Connection object, it will fire when rs.Open or cd.Execute is called, if cn is the active connection. Therefore, the following client code

```
Dim rs As New Recordset
Dim cd As New Command
cn.Execute "SELECT * FROM Parts"
cd.CommandText = "SELECT * FROM Scenes"
cd.ActiveConnection = cn
cd.Execute
rs.Open "SELECT * FROM SceneContents", cn
```

will generate

```
OK:     No Command Object:No Recordset Object:
            (-1,-1) SELECT * FROM Parts
OK:     No Recordset Object:
            (-1,-1) SELECT * FROM Scenes
OK:     No Command Object:
            (0,-1) SELECT * FROM SceneContents
```

This sample illustrates a number of points. The pCommand and pRecordset arguments will only contain objects if you supply them. This is a "Will…" event, so unless you are calling rs.Open, the Recordset is created during the Execute operation and isn't available when the "Will…" event fires. This has an understandable but unfortunate consequence for the CursorType and

LockType arguments of the WillExecute event. CursorType and LockType are properties of a Recordset object. If there is no Recordset object, it doesn't make much sense to set these properties. This sad fact rules out the chance of exploiting WillExecute to change Recordset properties when cn.Execute or cd.Execute is used.[5]

You can however, set the cn.CursorLocation property to force a client-side (and therefore static) cursor. And of course, there is nothing to stop you from changing the Source argument if a worthwhile reason comes to mind.

After the execution completes, the cn_ExecuteComplete event fires. Here's an example from the Logger:

```
Private Sub cn_ExecuteComplete( _
        ByVal RecordsAffected As Long, _
        ByVal pError As ADODB.Error, _
        adStatus As ADODB.EventStatusEnum, _
        ByVal pCommand As ADODB.Command, _
        ByVal pRecordset As ADODB.Recordset, _
        ByVal pConnection As ADODB.Connection)
Dim sObjects As String

If pCommand Is Nothing Then sObjects = "No Command Object:"
If pRecordset Is Nothing Then _
    sObjects = sObjects & "No Recordset Object:"

MonitorEvent adStatus, "(" & RecordsAffected & ")" & sObjects
End Sub
```

And here's the printout that results from this event, using our existing client code, and with all other event logging suppressed:

OK:	(-1)
OK:	(-1)
OK:	(-1)

This is not very exciting. It does show that a Command object and a Recordset object have been created during each execution process, and it also shows that RecordsAffected returns –1 for a SELECT statement.

To seek out some more exciting output, I used the following client code against the Jet Provider:

---

5. You probably don't need to know this, but when there is no Recordset object, ADO passes the same memory address for both the CursorType and LockType arguments, so setting one automatically sets the other. This is the kind of worthless fact that gets you noticed at parties.

```
Dim rs As New Recordset
Dim cd As New Command
cn.Execute "UPDATE Parts SET description = Null " & _
           "WHERE part = 'BOY'"     , , adExecuteNoRecords
cd.CommandText = "SELECT * FROM Scenes"
cd.ActiveConnection = cn
cd.Execute
rs.Open "Parts", cn, , , adCmdTableDirect
```

which resulted in

```
OK:                  (1)No Recordset Object:
OK:                  (0)
Errors Occurred:     (0)No Command Object:
```

Without the adExecuteNoRecords argument, cn.Execute would have generated a closed Recordset. Using adCmdTableDirect is the only way of not creating a
Command object. It has the interesting effect of reporting an error via adStatus,
even though no Error object is created and the client code proceeds perfectly.

Recordset Events

Recordset objects also have a comprehensive set of events that can be received
by a variable declared using WithEvents,[6] as shown in the following table.

Table 6-2. Recordset Events

PAIRED EVENTS	
Before Operation	*After Operation*
WillChangeField	FieldChangeComplete
WillChangeRecord	RecordChangeComplete
WillChangeRecordset	RecordsetChangeComplete
WillMove	MoveComplete
UNPAIRED EVENTS	
EndOfRecordset	
FetchProgress	
FetchComplete	

---

6. The ADO Data Control provides a very similar set of events for developers who use it.

cn_WillChangeField
cn_FieldChange-
Complete
cn_WillChange-
Record
cn_RecordChange-
Complete
cn_WillChange-
Recordset
cn_Recordset-
ChangeComplete
cn_WillMove
cn_MoveComplete

The paired events are almost, but not quite, self-explanatory. Fetch-Progress and FetchComplete are only relevant to asynchronous processing, and they will be discussed in a later section. EndOfRecordset is an unusual event—we'll take a look at it shortly.

First however, let's look at the paired events. These allow you to respond to many standard Recordset operations is a very fine-grained way. Apart from writing logging or monitoring applications, one of the primary reasons for using these events is to separate navigation and user interaction from the underlying processing, validation, and business logic associated with a particular Recordset.[7]

As an example, consider the following VB Class. It returns a Recordset based on the Parts table and implements validation code so that only an administrator can delete records or change the part name, but any user can change a part description.

```
'********** CODE FOR CLASS PARTS *****************
Public WithEvents rs As Recordset
Private msUser As String

Public Sub GetData(cn As Connection)
Set rs = New Recordset
rs.CursorLocation = adUseClient
rs.LockType = adLockOptimistic
rs.Open "SELECT * FROM parts", cn
msUser = rs.ActiveConnection.Properties("User ID")
End Sub


Private Sub rs_WillChangeField( _
        ByVal cFields As Long, _
        ByVal Fields As Variant, _
        adStatus As ADODB.EventStatusEnum, _
        ByVal pRecordset As ADODB.Recordset)
On Error GoTo ErrH
Dim vField As Variant          ◄─────── don't do any checks for
If msUser = "sa" Then Exit Sub         the administrator; she
For Each vField In Fields              can do anything she likes
  If vField.Name = "part" Then adStatus = adStatus
Next
ErrH:
End Sub
```

---

7. Visual programming approaches (Data Control, Data Environment, Data Repeater, DHTML) work by taking care of the navigational and user interaction aspects of a Recordset, leaving you with the event model to control functionality.

```
Private Sub rs_WillChangeRecord( _
        ByVal adReason As ADODB.EventReasonEnum, _
        ByVal cRecords As Long, _
        adStatus As ADODB.EventStatusEnum, _
        ByVal pRecordset As ADODB.Recordset)
If msUser = "sa" Then Exit Sub
If adReason = adRsnDelete Then adStatus = adStatus
End Sub
```

don't do any checks for the administrator; she can do anything she likes

In this class, GetData must be called to create a Recordset, which is then available as a property on the object. By implementing Recordset events, the class effectively provides a Recordset with extended functionality, customized to serve the needs of a particular Recordset (in this case, cancelling certain operations unless the user name is "sa").

Using this class with the following code works fine:

```
On Error GoTo ErrH
Dim cn As New Connection
Dim oPart As New Parts
cn.Open "DSN=MuchADO", "user", "user"
With oPart
  .GetData cn
  .rs.Filter = "part = 'BOY'"
  '.rs!part = "GIRL"
  .rs!Description = "a young male"
  .rs.Update
End With
Exit Sub
ErrH:
Print Err.Description
```

this line is commented out

However, restoring the line that is commented out results in

```
Operation was cancelled.
```

unless the user is changed to "sa". Similar behavior results if a Delete is attempted.

Now that you have seen an example of the paired events in operation, let me add a bit more detail. You may be thinking that record-level events fire for every Field-level event and record-level event, and that Recordset-level events fire for just about every operation. This isn't how it works. The Field-level events fire only when you perform a Field object operation, such as setting a Value property. The record-level events fire only for those operations relevant to a whole record, while Recordset-level events fire only for operations that affect the entire Recordset. With the exception of the Field-level events, each paired Recordset-level event carries an adReason argument, which contains a value from the EventReasonEnum enumeration. This provides additional information about which operation caused an event to fire. The following table lists the operations that cause events to fire at a particular level, and where appropriate, gives the reason code associated with the operation.

Table 6-3. Events Fired by Different Recordset Operations

ADO OPERATION	REASON	FIELD-LEVEL EVENTS	RECORD-LEVEL EVENTS	RECORDSET-LEVEL EVENTS
fd.Value	adRsnFirstChange	Yes	Yes[8]	
rs.Update, rs.UpdateBatch	adRsnUpdate	Yes[9]	Yes[10]	
rs.AddNew	adRsnAddNew		Yes	
rs.Delete	adRsnDelete		Yes	
rs.CancelUpdate, rs.CancelBatch	adUndoUpdate, adUndoAddNew, adUndoDelete		Yes	
rs.Requery	adRsnRequery			Yes
rs.Resync	adRsnReSynch			Yes
rs.Close	adRsnClose			Yes

The EventReasonEnum also contains values used to indicate the type of Move operation that triggered a Move event. Any operation that changes the current cursor position can trigger a Move event, notably including rs.Open and rs.Filter.

The fact that the first edit operation on the current record raises a record-level event with adRsnFirstChange as the reason code can be very helpful. For example, consider the situation when you have a Clone of a Recordset, and the Clone is pointing at a different record than the original Recordset was pointing at. When the original Recordset updates a Field, the Field-level

---

8. The first time a field is updated after a Move operation, the record-level events and the Field-level events will fire.

9. When Update is called with field name and value arrays, the Field-level events and the record-level events fire.

10. Update doesn't trigger a record-level event when in batch update mode.

events will fire on both the original Recordset and the Clone. However, the Field-level events don't tell you which record has just been updated, only which Fields are affected. This doesn't matter for the original Recordset, because it knows which record it has updated. However, the Clone doesn't have this knowledge. Fortunately, when the record-level events fire on the Clone (for the first update only), the pRecordSet argument has a filter applied that identifies the current record.

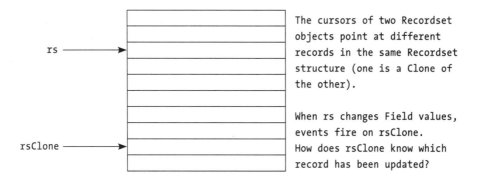

The cursors of two Recordset objects point at different records in the same Recordset structure (one is a Clone of the other).

When rs changes Field values, events fire on rsClone. How does rsClone know which record has been updated?

Figure 6-1. Events can help a Recordset identify which record a Clone has updated.

The following code demonstrates this. It assumes that rsClone has been declared using WithEvents as a module-level variable.

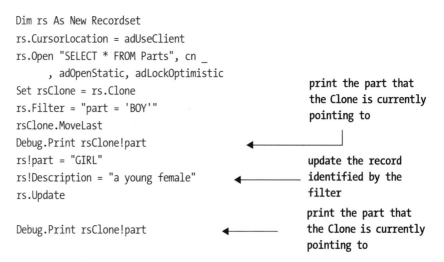

```
Dim rs As New Recordset
rs.CursorLocation = adUseClient
rs.Open "SELECT * FROM Parts", cn _
        , adOpenStatic, adLockOptimistic
Set rsClone = rs.Clone
rs.Filter = "part = 'BOY'"
rsClone.MoveLast
Debug.Print rsClone!part
rs!part = "GIRL"
rs!Description = "a young female"
rs.Update

Debug.Print rsClone!part
```

print the part that the Clone is currently pointing to

update the record identified by the filter

print the part that the Clone is currently pointing to

```
Private Sub rsClone_WillChangeRecord( _
        ByVal adReason As ADODB.EventReasonEnum, _
        ByVal cRecords As Long, _
        adStatus As ADODB.EventStatusEnum, _
        ByVal pRecordset As ADODB.Recordset)
Debug.Print "EVENT SAYS", pRecordset!part & _
            "(" & adReason & ")"
End Sub
```

← print the part that the
event filter identifies
← as the changed record

It prints

RHETT BUTLER		
EVENT SAYS	BOY	(11)
EVENT SAYS	GIRL	(3)
RHETT BUTLER		

← 11 = adRsnFirstChange

← 3 = adRsnUpdate

Stepping through this in your mind will identify that `rsClone_WillChangeRecord` is called twice—once when the record is first changed, and once when the `rs.Update` takes place. The filter is applied only during the event procedure, and it allows the Clone to know which record has changed, even when it's currently pointing at a different record.

cn_EndOfRecordset

Let's close this section by looking at the EndOfRecordset event. This ADO event allows you to populate a fabricated Recordset incrementally. Assume that you have a potentially large source of data that you want to present as a Recordset. A user of your Recordset might only want to use the first few records or may want to see thousands. It might take you some time to populate a Recordset with thousands of records. The EndOfRecordset event allows you to return with just a handful of records initially. When the user attempts to read past the last record, it allows you to add the next handful into the Recordset when the EndOfRecordset event fires, potentially ad infinitum.

For example, consider the following Recordset in which each record contains a random number (assuming `rsRandom` has been declared using WithEvents as a module-level variable).

```
Private Sub Form_Load()
Set rsRandom = New Recordset
rsRandom.Fields.Append "Next", adSmallInt
rsRandom.Open
End Sub
```

```
Private Sub rsRandom_EndOfRecordset( _
        fMoreData As Boolean, _
        adStatus As ADODB.EventStatusEnum, _
        ByVal pRecordset As ADODB.Recordset)
pRecordset.AddNew "Next", CInt(Rnd * 100)
pRecordset.AddNew "Next", CInt(Rnd * 100)
fMoreData = True                              ◄───────────
End Sub
```

Setting fMoreData to True tells ADO that more data can now be read. Leaving it as False means that the Recordset has genuinely reached its end.

```
Private Sub Command1_Click()
Print rsRandom!Next, rsRandom.RecordCount
rsRandom.MoveNext
End Sub
```

Repeatedly hitting the Command1 button yields these results:

71	0
53	2
58	4
29	4
30	6
77	6
1	8
76	8
81	10
71	10
5	12

In this case, you don't really know how many records are going to be required, and you don't want to create more than necessary. The EndOf-Recordset event can help you in such situations.

Strategies for Using Events

Unless you are using asynchronous operations (see next section) it's unlikely that you'll make much use of ADO events in small applications. There is little need in such applications to take on board the extra discipline required, because the benefits are not sufficient. You may start to think differently however, if you are involved in large, component-based systems. In these situations, ADO events can be helpful because they allow you to

1. Separate data processing from user interface and navigation.

2. Centralize common operations.

3. Achieve greater consistency and reuse, and reduce maintenance costs.

Even in a medium-sized application, there may be several places where you need to work with the same basic Recordset (for example, the Parts table, or more likely, a parameterized SQL query). Now, you know there are certain security rules that must always be applied to this data (for example, only administrators should be allowed to delete records from the table or change a primary key). You might choose to apply these rules in each place where the Recordset is used. Doing so means that the code in each location must be tested to see that the rules are applied consistently. Worse still, if the rules change, you must find each use of the Recordset and be sure to change each one. However, if the Recordset carries those rules around with it (coded into its events), then you can be sure that the rules are applied consistently.

Now scale up a bit and assume that your team manages several applications, all based on the same database. The same rules apply across applications. By coding your Recordsets as Active DLLs, you can reference the DLLs from each application and have the same consistency applied across all applications. A change in the rules can be deployed without even needing to recompile the applications that use the DLL—all that is required is that the DLL is recompiled and deployed.[11]

You may be thinking that using triggers and stored procedures in the database can achieve the same benefits. To a large degree this is true, and there are many reasons to use both triggers and stored procedures. However, consider the following benefits of using ADO events:

1. Not all Recordset sources support triggers and stored procedures, and it's rare to be able to port them from one database to another in a straightforward way.

2. Visual Basic provides a more productive programming environment than databases do.

3. ADO events allow you to validate and process data before it's sent to the database. You wouldn't think of using database techniques to perform Field-level validation. This is easily achieved using ADO events.

---

11. This assumes that you know how to maintain binary compatibility between compilations of an ActiveX DLL.

There are some downsides to using events in this way, principally:

1. *Although you can use adStatus to cancel operations, you can't return your own error messages and codes through the ADO event model.* Instead, you need to provide your own error handling model. In the example just presented, I created a class called Parts to represent a Parts Recordset. This class can be extended to have another property called Error. You can then set this property in the event that cancels the operation, and read it in the client procedure's error handler. It isn't hard to set this up, but it's a shame that you can't provide your own errors through ADO.

2. *Users of your Recordset need to know that the object that implements the events must be kept alive in order for the events to fire.* While the Recordset object raises the events, the code that handles them has a separate existence.[12]

3. *There is a performance penalty for handling Recordset events.* While you can reduce this by marking events as unwanted (the Move events would be good candidates), the penalty is noticeable on large Recordsets where the cost of scrolling is measurable.

As another example, think about what happens when you use the same user interface to display different updateable Recordsets. This user interface may be handcrafted or based on an ADO Data Control. If you do this, it's quite likely that you use a Select...Case statement to apply different data processing rules for each Recordset you present. This might be fine for two or three Recordsets, but it becomes hard to manage as the number increases. It also means that you have to go back and fiddle with the user interface code each time you use it to display a new Recordset. If you let the Recordsets handle this data processing logic through their events, you can avoid this mess and keep your application much more maintainable.

Finally, think back to what we did with the Logger example. For the cost of adding six lines of code into a client application, we created the ability to introduce a program that can intercept all Connection events. We didn't even have to write the Logger to create this option—the Logger only becomes necessary when we want to exercise the option. Once established, this option creates a number of opportunities, including the abilities to:

1. Create a Logger for performance or bug analysis.

---

12. There are various ways of overcoming this, which include using the Data Environment and writing your own Provider—both of which are covered later in the book.

2. Prevent disasters by screening out certain operations to keep a production system alive

3. Divert the application to a test or demonstration database.

If you decide to use events in any of these ways, you are hardly on your own. The VB6 Data Environment was designed to help you create centralized, "intelligent'" Recordsets, containing their own data processing logic kept separate from the user interface. We'll be looking in more detail at the Data Environment in Chapter 13.

Asynchronous Processing

Computing has been full of talk about parallel processing for as long as I can remember. It's easy to forget that just about every client-server database application is a potentially parallel system. This potential is not commonly exploited, as the following diagram shows:

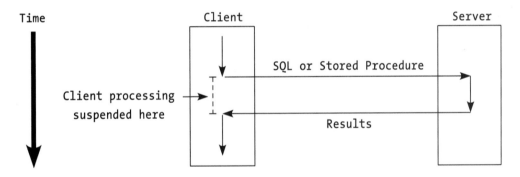

Figure 6-2. Synchronous processing

Although both the client and server have separate CPUs, typically only one is doing anything for a particular client at any point in time. This is because the client has to wait for the server to respond. While it's waiting, the client is doing nothing useful and appears frozen to the user. Figure 6-2 shows synchronous processing; the potential for parallelism isn't exploited.

The following diagram shows how asynchronous processing works using ADO:

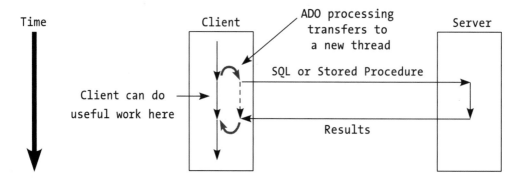

Figure 6-3. Asynchronous processing

If you ask ADO to carry out an operation asynchronously, ADO creates a separate ***thread*** in your client's process to perform the operation.[13] This thread will call the server and wait for it to respond. Meanwhile, the main thread of your application can continue doing whatever it wishes (although of course it can't use the data that the other thread is waiting for). When the server returns, the waiting thread notifies the main thread via an event, and that thread then terminates. Depending on the operation, the waiting thread may be able to report interim progress back to the main thread, again via events. This all sounds very clever, but when might you use it?

1. *If you do something worthwhile while the operation is executing.* For example, starting an application often means loading a main form and establishing a database connection, each of which can take several seconds. In synchronous processing, these operations are performed one after the other. In asynchronous processing, you can request the connection asynchronously. While you are waiting, you can load the main form, and then check that the connection has been established after the main form has loaded. The result is you could cut your application startup time by half.

---

13. You can see the thread being created and destroyed using the Task Manager's Processes tab if your operating system allows.

2. *If you have queries that take anywhere from several seconds to several minutes to execute.* Using asynchronous processing, you can provide users with a Cancel button. If they choose to cancel, not only can they carry on working, but also the server is informed that it can stop working on that query. If the user is waiting for the query (assuming they haven't cancelled) you can present them with a progress indicator showing how many records have been fetched so far.

3. *If you have a dialog with three tabs, each tab presenting the results of a separate query.* You could fire the query for the default tab synchronously, and use it to populate the dialog. You could then fire the other two queries asynchronously. This way, the user can be using the dialog while data loads in the background. If the user selects one of the other tabs, chances are that the data will already be loaded and that it can be displayed immediately. Here you are trading possibly unnecessary network and server traffic for potential responsiveness. I have certainly worked on applications where the tradeoff was considered worthwhile.

Let's see how to make asynchronous processing work in ADO. There are three operations that can be performed asynchronously:

1. Opening a Connection, Record, or Stream.[14]

2. Executing a Command.

3. Fetching records into (populating) a client-side Recordset.

In each case, asynchronous processing is enabled by providing the appropriate value from the ConnectOptionEnum and ExecuteOptionsEnum enumerations in the Open or Execute methods of Connection, Command, and Recordset objects. The relevant values from the enumerations are shown in Table 6-4.

Table 6-4. Values for Asynchronous Processing

CONNECTOPTIONENUM	EXECUTEOPTIONENUM
adAsyncConnect	adAsyncExecute
	adAsyncFetch
	adAsyncFetchNonBlocking

The difference between the two fetch options will be explained shortly.

---

14. Record and Stream objects are discussed in Chapter 9.

Opening a Connection Asynchronously

First, let's look at a simple application that loads its main form while its database connection is being established. This approach is appropriate for a connection-oriented application where creating the connection and the main form might take a measurable amount of time. If either of these operations is near-instantaneous, there would be no point in using the asynchronous approach.

This application kicks off using a `Sub Main()` routine in a .BAS module. Here's its code:

```
Private oStart As AppStarter

Sub Main()
Set oStart = New AppStarter
oStart.Begin
End Sub
```

Note that the `Sub Main()` routine doesn't do much. Any asynchronous processing must be kicked off from a COM object if you want to receive events. Either a Form or a VB class will do, because they can both receive COM notifications, but a standard .BAS module can't declare a variable using WithEvents. So instead, `Sub Main()` simply creates an instance of the `AppStarter` class and asks it to begin. Here's the complete code for the `AppStarter` class:

```
Private WithEvents mcn As Connection

Public Sub Begin()                              async call will
Set mcn = New Connection               ↓        return immediately
mcn.Open "File Name=c:\MuchADO.udl", , , adAsyncConnect
Load Form1                    ←───────────────  Form1 is loaded, but not shown
Set Form1.Connection = mcn
End Sub


Private Sub mcn_ConnectComplete( _
        ByVal pError As ADODB.Error, _
        adStatus As ADODB.EventStatusEnum, _
        ByVal pConnection As ADODB.Connection)
Form1.Display                 ←───────────────  Form1 is asked to display
Set mcn = Nothing                               itself, via a custom method
End Sub
```

cn.Open

The key to understanding this piece of code is to realize that the adAsync-Connect option will cause the mcn.Open method to terminate immediately, before the connection is ready. The Begin method then goes on to Load the form, and assign it the connection via a custom property. The Load Form operation will not display the form, but it will load it and all its controls into memory and execute the Form_Load event procedure code (if any). These are typically the most expensive tasks. Actually displaying the form is usually very quick.

When the mcn_ConnectComplete event fires, the form is already loaded. The event code asks the form to display itself (via the custom Display method) and then sets mcn to Nothing. After this point, no more events will fire on the connection. Although the Form holds a reference to the connection, the Form's connection variable was not declared using WithEvents.

Looking at the following code for the Form completes the picture:

```
Public Connection As Connection

Private Sub Form_Load()
Label1 = "(1) " & Now
End Sub

Public Sub Display()
Label2 = "(2) " & Now
Label3 = "(3) " & Me.Connection.Properties("Data Source")
Me.Show                          ◄─────────────  make the form visible when
End Sub                                          everything is ready for use
```

The form has a public property, a public method, and it's own private Form_Load. On running this application, the Form might appear as shown here:

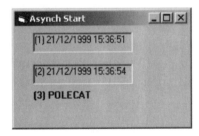

Figure 6-4. Asynchronous processing gives you time to load a Form while the server is busy building a Connection.

The display shows that Form_Load executed three seconds before the connection was ready for use, even though the connection request was fired off before the form was loaded. In other words, the client was able to carry on doing something (loading the form) while the server was preparing the connection. This is what asynchronous processing is all about.

cn.Execute
cn.Cancel

For a Connection object, both cn.Execute and cn.Open support asynchronous operations, and in both cases, the cn.Cancel method can be used to stop the current asynchronous process.

Cancelling an Asynchronous Command

Another reason for using asynchronous processing is to allow a pending command to be executed. This is especially useful when you know certain queries might take a considerable amount of time to execute.

In the following two-button application, a query is made that will typically execute fairly quickly. However, it does need to scan the entire Words table, which means that it's subject to being blocked by any transactions from other programs locking the table. To counter this potential problem, the program executes its query asynchronously, using a Command object. It also presents the user with a Cancel button. Here's the code:

```
Private WithEvents cn As Connection  ◄─────── Command objects don't
Private cd As New Command                     support events, so trap
                                              the notification using
Private Sub Form_Load()                       the Connection object
Set cn = New Connection
cn.Open "File Name=c:\MuchADO.udl"
End Sub


Private Sub cmdExecute_Click()
If (cd.State And adStateExecuting) = 0 Then
  cd.CommandText = "select * from Words where wordCount > 10"
  cd.ActiveConnection = cn
  cd.CommandTimeout = 50

                                         Execute the Command
  cd.Execute , , adAsyncExecute  ◄────── asynchronously, and
  cmdCancel.Enabled = True               enable the Cancel button
  Print "Operation Started"
End If
End Sub

Private Sub cmdCancel_Click()     ◄─┐
If (cd.State And adStateExecuting) <> 0 Then
    cd.Cancel                         if the user hits the
  cmdCancel.Enabled = False           Cancel button, cancel
End If                                the operation
End Sub                           ◄─┘
```

```
Private Sub cn_ExecuteComplete( _
        ByVal RecordsAffected As Long, _
        ByVal pError As ADODB.Error, _
        adStatus As ADODB.EventStatusEnum, _
        ByVal pCommand As ADODB.Command, _
        ByVal pRecordset As ADODB.Recordset, _
        ByVal pConnection As ADODB.Connection)
cmdCancel.Enabled = False
If adStatus = adStatusOK Then Print "Operation Complete"
If adStatus = adStatusErrorsOccurred Then Print "Operation Cancelled"
End Sub
```

cd.Execute

If the Words table was locked for a considerable period of time, and the `cd.Execute` was performed synchronously, then the user would be forced to wait until the command timed out (at which point `cn_ExecuteComplete` would fire) or restart the application. This wouldn't be a problem with a short time out, but if you suspect the operation might take some time, you may well have set the `CommandTimeout` higher. Catch 22.

When the command is executed asynchronously, a separate thread is started to support communication with the data source. This leaves the thread running the user interface free to service user requests, which could include pressing the cmdCancel button. `cmdCancel` calls `cd.Cancel` to unwind the operation.

cn.State
cd.State
rs.State
rd.State
st.State

Note that both the cmdExecute and cmdCancel buttons test the value of cd.State. We met the State property right back in Chapter 2 (in that case we saw rs.State, but there is also a State property on all the other major ADO objects). These tests ensure that the cmdExecute button doesn't try to start another asynchronous process on the same Command object,[15] and the cmdCancel button doesn't accidentally try to cancel a command that isn't executing. The State property can have a combination of the following values from the ObjectStateEnum enumeration:

> adStateClosed
>
> adStateOpen
>
> adStateConnecting
>
> adStateExecuting
>
> adStateFetching

Any controls on your user interface that refer to ADO objects that use asynchronous operations can use the State property to guard against errors. Remember that the results aren't ready for use until the cn_ExecuteComplete

---

15. If you need to have more than one asynchronous operation running in parallel, you'll need to create multiple Command objects to do this. You'll also need to use the cd.Name property to distinguish between the different Commands when the cn_ExecuteComplete event fires.

event fires, so this event must be used to start the process of working with any Recordset returned by the operation.

Asynchronous Fetch with Client-side Cursors

When server-side cursors are used, the command executes on the server, and any server-side cursor structures are created. This all happens as part of the Execute operation. When client-side cursors are used, all the Records are fetched into the client as part of the Open or Execute operation. This accounts for the additional time it takes to open client-side cursors and also for the enhanced speed of navigation once they have been created.

This fetch process can be performed asynchronously. It's even possible to start using the data at the beginning of the Recordset before all the data at the end is available. This will give you the benefits of client-side cursors, without the pain of having to wait for a client-side cursor to be completely populated[16].

rs_FetchProgress
rs_FetchComplete

The short program that follows illustrates the basics and shows the rs_FetchProgress and rs_FetchComplete events in action. The program has one button, two labels, and some space for printing.

```
Dim WithEvents rs As Recordset
Dim dTimer As Double

Private Sub Command1_Click()
dTimer = Timer
Set rs = New Recordset
rs.CursorLocation = adUseClient
rs.ActiveConnection = "File Name=c:\MuchADO.udl"
rs.Open "select word,sum(wordCount)from Words group by word" _
            , , , , adAsyncFetch           asynchronous fetch

Print "First Record Ready:", Format(Timer - dTimer, "0.00")
While Not rs.EOF
   Label1 = rs.AbsolutePosition & ":" & rs!word      DoEvents makes sure that
   DoEvents                                           the form gets updated
   rs.MoveNext                                        during the print loop
Wend
End Sub

Private Sub rs_FetchComplete( _
         ByVal pError As ADODB.Error, _
         adStatus As ADODB.EventStatusEnum, _
         ByVal pRecordset As ADODB.Recordset)
```

---

16. Although the overall fetch time will be longer.

```
Print "All Records Ready:", Format(Timer - dTimer, "0.00")
Print "Current Record:", rs.AbsolutePosition
End Sub


Private Sub rs_FetchProgress( _
        ByVal Progress As Long, _
        ByVal MaxProgress As Long, _
        adStatus As ADODB.EventStatusEnum, _
        ByVal pRecordset As ADODB.Recordset)
Label2 = Progress
End Sub
```

The rs_FetchComplete event fires when the last record has been fetched into the client-side cursor. Beforehand, the rs_FetchProgress event fires while the client-side cursor is being populated. The frequency with which it fires depends on the Provider. The current SQLServer Provider fires the event after every fifteen records have been read. The sequence of events when running the fetch program is as follows:

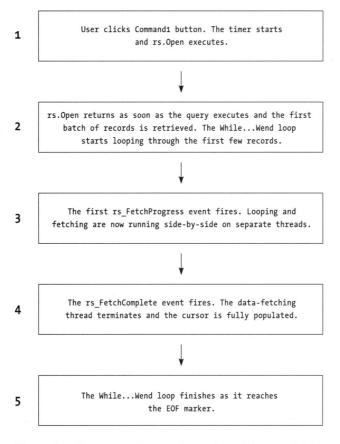

Figure 6-5. Sequence of events in an Asynchronous fetch operation

Here's the application's user interface before anything happens:

Figure 6-6. Asynchronous fetch before execution

and here it is at the beginning of Step 3 (in Figure 6-5):

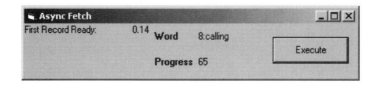

Figure 6-7. Asynchronous fetch before Step 3

Note that the first eight records have already been processed through the loop, just as the first progress event fires indicating that sixty-five records have been added into the Recordset. The two threads are now racing to complete their tasks. On my test machine, the race was won by the data-fetching thread. Here's the window at the beginning of Step 4 (in Figure 6-5):

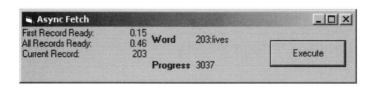

Figure 6-8. Asynchronous fetch before Step 4

Here we see that the Recordset has now been fully populated. The program has fetched 3037 records into the Recordset and has already processed the first 203 records. After this point, the program will carry on until the While…Wend loop is finished.

If this program were run on a heavily used network, it's quite likely that there would be two differences:

1. Both data retrieval times would be significantly higher.

2. The user interface (main) thread might win the race.

This raises a question: What would happen if the main thread attempted to read a record that was not yet in the Recordset? The answer depends on whether the adAsyncFetch option or the adAsyncFetchNonBlocking option is used:

-   **adAsyncFetch:** The main thread is blocked until the operation it's attempting is safe to complete. This can mean waiting until the Recordset is fully populated.

-   **adAsyncFetchNonBlocking:** The main thread is never blocked. Instead, the cursor is positioned to the last currently available record and processing continues.

To demonstrate what this means, I have modified the rs_FetchProgress event to do the following:

```
Label2 = Progress & "(" & rs.RecordCount & ")"
```

This operation requires knowing about the end of the Recordset. If we place a breakpoint immediately after this line of code and look at the form at that point, this is what we'll see (with Options still set to adAsyncFetch):

Figure 6-9. adAsyncFetch blocks when reading rs.RecordCount.

There was a noticeable delay waiting for this breakpoint to appear. This is because as soon as the main thread attempted to read the RecordCount, the thread blocked until the data-fetching thread completed. Progress still has the value it had when the event procedure was entered, but the Recordset is fully populated.

If I change the execution option to adAsyncFetchNonBlocking, the following information is displayed at the break point:

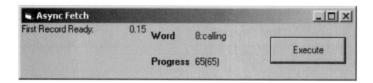

Figure 6-10. adAsyncFetchNonBlocking doesn't block when reading rs.RecordCount.

In this case, the RecordCount shows only the number of records currently in the Recordset. The RecordCount increases each time rs_FetchProgress fires, until the final figure is displayed.

Asynchronous fetching can be extremely useful when building large Recordsets with client-side cursors. You can use the technique either to display a progress bar while the user waits for the Recordset to populate, or to actually begin processing with a Recordset before it's fully populated. You can even combine the adAsyncFetch option with the adAsyncExecute option and have both the fetching and execution steps operate asynchronously.

You would probably choose not to bother with asynchronous fetching if the Recordset turned out to be unexpectedly small. By default, the Recordset fetches the first fifty records as part of the execute operation, and only begins asynchronous fetching after this.[17] However, you can change this initial fetch size by setting a dynamic Recordset property provided by the Client Cursor Engine, as follows:

```
rs.Properties("Initial Fetch Size") = 1000
```

In this case, if the Recordset has less than 1000 records, there will be no asynchronous fetching and no rs_FetchProgress or rs_FetchComplete events.

Summary

This chapter explored Recordset and Connection events and its two very distinct themes. Events can be used in:

- Synchronous processing, as a design aid for creating more reusable and maintainable software by centralizing data processing and separating it from user interface and Recordset navigation code.

17. This explains why the first rs_FetchProgress event fires after sixty-five records have been retrieved (bearing in mind that my Provider fires FetchProgress events every fifteen records).

- Asynchronous processing, using the traditional ADO objects. Client-server applications are inherently parallel, and asynchronous techniques can be used to exploit this parallelism. This allows us to get applications started more quickly and to overcome one of the main weaknesses of client-side cursors—the need to wait for the cursor to be fully populated before the Recordset can be used. Asynchronous fetching removes this constraint.

CHAPTER 7

Disconnected Recordsets

ADO in an N-Tier Environment

The Mechanics of Disconnecting

Batch Updating

Resynchronizing Disconnected Recordsets

Disconnected Recordsets and Stored Procedures

Recordset Marshalling

Recordset Persistence

Summary

WAY BACK IN CHAPTER 2, you saw how Recordsets can be created and manipulated with no explicit data source. Such Recordsets (called fabricated Recordsets) are highly portable and flexible. They can be saved to file and then reinstantiated, and they are fully updateable. Later in this chapter, you'll see how such Recordsets can be moved easily and efficiently across process and machine boundaries, and even across the Internet using HTTP.

Since Chapter 2, the chapters have focused on Recordsets that are connected to a data source. These Recordsets allow us to execute sophisticated commands to retrieve Recordsets that meet our query requirements. They allow us to save data back into shared data stores, and exploit transactional capabilities built into those data stores. However, connected Recordsets have two drawbacks:

1. *They are not highly portable.* Because a connected Recordset has a dependency on a data source connection established between the connecting process and the server process, the Recordset can't easily be passed around (except within the connecting process), and it can't sensibly be saved. There is a cost for being attached to an intelligent data source.

2. *They consume server resources while they are open.* Even if we all we do is read data after the Recordset is created, a connected Recordset is still a drain on its server and a potential scalability bottleneck.

ADO would only be half as interesting as it is if these limitations could not be overcome. As you shall see, it's very easy to disconnect a Recordset from its data source and then continue to use it. Whenever it becomes necessary to communicate with the data source again, the Recordset can be reconnected and the data source exploited. This is typically only necessary when the data source itself needs to be updated or resynchronized. A Recordset without a connection is still a fully featured data structure.

In an environment where some form of connection pooling is provided, reconnecting for updates and then disconnecting again is an efficient process. Even so, ADO supports a mechanism that allows updates to be submitted in batches to speed up the updating process. This is particularly important in environments where Recordsets are passed between processes, as it allows multiple changes to be "recorded" by the Recordset before it's returned to the process responsible for updating the data source. Even though the task of passing Recordsets between processes is highly optimized, it's still a comparatively expensive task. ADO's batch updating mechanism helps to keep this cost to a sensible minimum.

The ability of a Recordset to provide an amazing amount of functionality in both disconnected and connected mode and to be highly portable, efficient, yet routinely easy-to-use is at the heart of ADO, and at the heart of what makes ADO so different from DAO, RDO, and most other data access technologies. If you are an experienced DAO or RDO programmer, most of what has been discussed prior to this chapter will have had a familiar feel to it. Working with disconnected Recordsets is fundamentally different. But it so happens that I have already laid down much of the foundation: Recordset navigation, filters, and client-side cursors form the basis of disconnected Recordset processing. The main aim of this chapter is to introduce a new working practice based on these techniques.

The true home of the disconnected Recordset is in n-tier applications, and we'll discuss what this means in the very next section. However, we'll then explore the intricacies of disconnected Recordsets and batch updating in a traditional client-server setting, before returning to fit our new understanding into the n-tier model, by considering Recordset marshalling and persistence.

ADO in an N-Tier Environment

There are several good texts on n-tier development using VB[1] and also on Microsoft's particular n-tier vision.[2] In its most basic form, an n-tier model is one in which

1. The user interface (platform-specific, browser-based, or both) is developed as a separate element, with little or no business or application logic apart from that which is dedicated to data presentation and user interaction.

2. The algorithmic guts of the application are developed as one or more separate tiers, based on multiple binary components (the middle tier). Components are interchangeable and reusable, and each one typically represents a small, discrete processing task. These components are typically (but not necessarily) configured as MTS Packages or COM+ Applications in Microsoft architectures and compiled as separate DLLs. In the best designs, components are reused in several applications.

3. Data management forms one (or more) data tier(s), typically based on the type of product that can act as an OLE DB data source.

For the purpose of this chapter, we'll assume that each tier is running on a separate machine (or at least in a separate process). While you can apply the n-tier design mentality to systems in which the middle-tier components run in the same process as the user interface, the broader challenge and wider-reaching benefits of the n-tier approach result from having the middle tier completely independent of the client process.

It isn't hard to understand how an application can be configured as n-tier. However, despite the fact that many organizations are now routinely building all but the simplest applications (and sometimes even those) using the n-tier model, many developers remain resistant to its charms. This is partly because it involves additional complexity and a steeper learning curve before the benefits can be realized, and partly because many of the standard arguments put forward in favor of the n-tier approach are not all that convincing. Here are the reasons why I use the n-tier approach for virtually all my real applications:

---

1. Many n-tier systems have three tiers. On larger systems, the middle (and other) tier(s) is/are often split into multiple tiers, so that the three-tier label doesn't strictly apply. Think of standalone applications as being single-tier, conventional client-server applications (such as the VB front end to SQLServer) as two-tier, and anything more fancy as n-tier.

2. Microsoft's n-tier model is called DNA 2000. We'll discuss this in more detail in Chapter 14.

1. You can't avoid the n-tier approach when building Web sites (at least using Microsoft Web Server technology). While it's possible to build ASP applications using a two-tier (client-server) mentality, you are still building an n-tier system, and it makes sense to exploit the n-tier architecture and build systems based on components. The world of Web Services is explicitly n-tier.

2. Two-tier applications run into problems as the user base increases. As a very crude guideline, the closer you get to one hundred concurrent users the more difficult and expensive it gets to remain two-tier.[3] Once you cross that boundary, you are almost undoubtedly wasting money if you remain two-tier.

3. Many applications require the use of two or more databases.[4] The pain of installing drivers and/or Providers, and maintaining connection information for one data source on every client is quite offputting. Doing it for multiple data sources verges on masochism. Maintaining security information for each user in each database is hardly a rewarding endeavor either. If your client application performs updates on multiple data sources, you may have no choice but to handle a distributed transaction.[5] A properly designed n-tier model completely removes these headaches.

4. If you want to exploit the many benefits of MTS Packages or the even greater range of benefits of COM+ Applications, you have to go n-tier.

5. Deploying client-server applications into production environments is painful, even if you discount Point 3. We all know that, on average, 80%–90% of all programming is maintenance work, and therefore, deployment can't be seen as a one-time throwaway task—all that maintenance work requires deployment too. Typically, all users have to be upgraded at the same time, especially when database changes are involved. In an n-tier application, anything up to 100% of urgent maintenance releases affect one server only, with no client deployment at all.

---

3. Most two-tier applications are permanently connected to data sources. This means that one hundred users often means one hundred concurrent users, even though only a few users may be actively using the application at any point in time. Ironically, n-tier applications are typically designed to manage server resources more economically (for example, by exploiting connection pooling), and therefore, many never reach the server loading experienced by the two-tier applications they were written to replace.

4. Even a modestly sized organization is likely to have its product inventory stored separately from its customer database. Therefore, to process a purchase order online requires updating two or more databases.

5. ADO can't do this by itself. MTS or COM+ do it in their sleep.

6. At the risk of offending some readers, it's a fact that object orientation (OO) never really delivered the promises it made of widespread reusability. Even though component-based development is comparatively new, it has already enabled massive reuse (think of all the reuse you get out of ActiveX Controls). Building components is part of the n-tier mentality, while creating massive EXEs (with or without OO) is part of the two-tier mentality. Well-designed binary components are genuinely reusable.

7. After a while, you stop seeing n-tier as a big hurdle. It becomes the natural way to build applications.[6]

ADO has a specific and important part to play, at least in the Microsoft view of n-tier development, over and above its role in retrieving data from data sources. In a two-tier model, pretty much all the interprocess communication that is required is achieved by ADO or an equivalent. One of the reasons that two-tier development became popular is that all the complexity of interprocess communication was wrapped up in SQL and an appropriate networked carrier mechanism such as OLE DB or ODBC (as shown in Figure 7-1). Equally important, the fact that all data was delivered in a more or less standard format made it possible to exploit reusable user interface components such as data-bound controls.

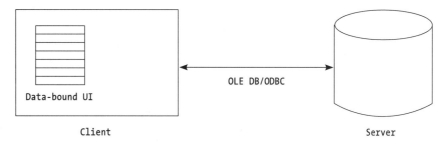

OLE DB/ODBC

Data-bound UI

Client   Server

Figure 7-1. A traditional two-tier system

One of the challenges in creating an n-tier design is knowing how to handle communication between the middle tier(s) and the client tier.[7] The nuts and bolts of communication are commonly handled either by DCOM

---

6. I am convinced that within ten years, generous-minded people will look back on two-tier client-server systems as a necessary, but fundamentally limited, stepping stone to n-tier distributed transactional systems. Less generous folks will look back on it as a mistake.

7. Another major challenge is how to handle all the software management issues (security, resource pooling, threading) that data sources traditionally create, now that you need those services in the middle tier. This is where MTS and COM+ come in.

or HTTP, but neither of these protocols defines the communication at a level that application programmers work. As a result, developers have been forced to produce a communication scheme of their own using either DCOM or HTTP as a carrier mechanism.

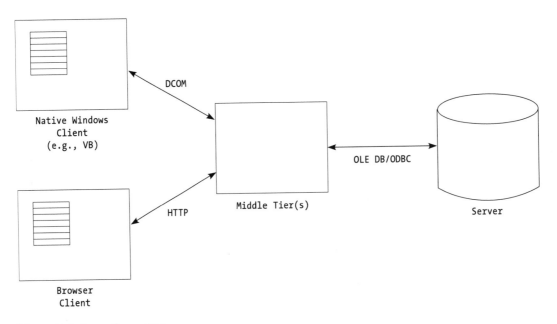

Figure 7-2. An n-tier system

In Figure 7-2, the middle tier continues to use ADO to communicate with data sources. The middle tier receives requests for data from the client, turns them into SQL or stored procedure calls, and sends them to the server. The server returns a Recordset to the middle tier, which then prepares results to return to the client.

For browser-based clients this typically means wrapping the results up into HTML and sending the results back as part of a Web page, although increasingly, XML is forming an important part of this communication channel. For native Windows clients using DCOM, more choices are available. Passing data back to the client for a single record is not a great problem as a method can be defined to accept all the required fields as arguments. Passing a connected Recordset is not an option, as the data source connection cannot successfully be passed between processes. As a result, developers have traditionally been left to their own devices for passing Recordset data between processes and have typically chosen one or more of the following:

- **Variant arrays**: Variant arrays can be *marshalled* between processes relatively efficiently. The disadvantage is that both the client and server need code to pack and unpack the arrays into useable data structures at each end.[8]

- **Arrays of User-defined Types (UDTs)**: This technique is more efficient that using Variant arrays and adds some meaning to the data, but otherwise has the same disadvantage. It can only be used with VB6 and requires Service Pack 4 on NT4.

- **PropertyBags**: VB6 made it possible to clone an object in one process, based on the property values of an object in another process passed in the form of a PropertyBag. This approach uses a standardized technique to pack and unpack the object data. Just as with arrays, it allows complex data structures to be passed between processes in a single *roundtrip*.

- **Custom data structures**: Custom data structures can be marshalled efficiently, and their design is typically based on strings or byte arrays with a custom format. This approach requires more work than the other techniques, but can be more efficient than Variant arrays or PropertyBags. It doesn't need the most up-to-date tools or operating systems.

The advantage of using PropertyBags or arrays of UDTs is that the data arrives at the client in a form that is immediately meaningful, and the client doesn't need to use an agreed-upon interpretation to make sense of the data. However, all the approaches suffer from a lack of standardized user interface features to display them.

The fact that client programs have to be coded from scratch to interpret and display data generated in a middle tier has been one of the major factors holding back the spread of n-tier development. Compared to the ease of use of ready-to-run two-tier features, such as data binding, n-tier front ends have appeared sufficiently expensive that only reasonably large projects have been able to justify them.

Disconnected Recordsets remove these obstacles at a stroke. ADO ensures that Recordsets, once disconnected from their data sources, will marshall efficiently between processes. It also allows the client to manipulate and write updates to a disconnected Recordset without significant loss of functionality, and without incurring expensive cross-process calls. When

---

8. While arrays marshall reasonably efficiently, attempting to pass collections between processes is a disastrous undertaking, involving a large number of roundtrips between the two processes.

the client has finished, the entire Recordset structure[9] can be passed back to the middle tier, which processes the changes and updates the data. Better still:

- The client can bind the Recordset to standard user interface elements, exploiting all the productivity benefits enjoyed by two-tier systems.

- Browser-based systems utilizing DHTML can also bind the Recordset Fields directly to HTML elements, providing a richer browser experience than can be achieved through pure HTML.

- While the client has the Recordset, the middle tier can release its copy of the Recordset and its data source connection. As a consequence, the middle tier has no state management issues and need not be a resource bottleneck.

The following diagram shows OLE DB being used in client-to-middle-tier communication and in middle-tier-to-data source communication.

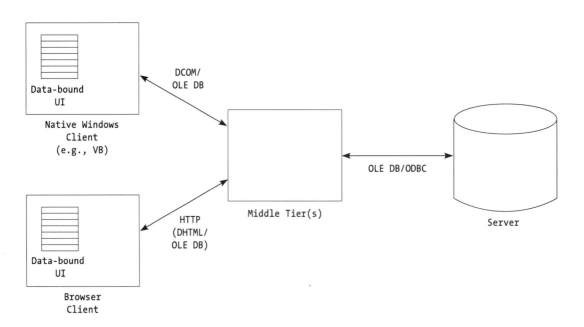

Figure 7-3. An n-tier system based on OLE DB communication

---

9. Or if required, just those records that have been changed.

Doubtless, certain questions will arise as you think this through:

- How does locking get handled?

- How does the middle tier identify which records have been changed by the client so that validation can be applied?

- How do errors get handled if the data source is updated using a batch mechanism?

- Where do stored procedures fit into all of this?

- Is this whole process safe and efficient?

The rest of this chapter is dedicated to answering these questions for the native Windows client scenario based on DCOM. Web-specific issues for the browser client scenario are covered in Chapter 15.

One other form of data exchange that we've hardly discussed is XML. Potentially, XML offers the benefits of a data exchange mechanism for n-tier systems that ADO offers, with the added advantages of being cross-platform and more generic. And XML is in the process of becoming a part of Microsoft's generic connectivity product line as part of SOAP (Simple Object Activation Protocol).

ADO will always be more efficient than XML, which has a comparatively longwinded model of data representation. XML is more generic than ADO. While this may sound like a point in favor of XML, it means that ADO has and will continue to have the edge when it comes to power and functionality. As a rule of thumb, the more general something is, the less it has to offer in specific circumstances.

As you saw in Chapter 2, ADO is already capable of persisting Recordsets in XML format, and the relationship between ADO and XML is likely to develop quickly over the next few years, and the combination of these two technologies promises some very exciting developments.

In This Section

We discussed some of the challenges faced by developers embracing the n-tier application model and saw how ADO can be used to address many of these issues. In particular, ADO presents a convenient and efficient means of passing data between clients and the middle tier(s) of an n-tier application. One major benefit of this is that, because data arrives at the client in the form of a Recordset, familiar data binding techniques can be used to present the data to users.

The Mechanics of Disconnecting

There are two steps involved in disconnecting a Recordset:

1. The Recordset's CursorLocation must be set to adUseClient.[10]

2. Once the Recordset has been populated with server data, the Recordset's ActiveConnection must be set to Nothing.

The following code is enough to achieve this:

```
Dim rs As New Recordset
rs.CursorLocation = adUseClient
rs.Open "SELECT * FROM parts", "File Name=c:\MuchADO.udl"
Set rs.ActiveConnection = Nothing
```

This is all that is required to disconnect the Recordset from its data source. The Recordset can now be sorted, filtered, iterated and have just about anything else done to it that doesn't involve changing any data. In order to make changes to the data, an appropriate lock type is required.

One locking strategy that is rarely discussed in conjunction with disconnected Recordsets, but makes perfect sense in certain situations, is to use standard optimistic locking.[11] The following piece of code is an example (you may spot the flaw):

```
Set rs = New Recordset
rs.CursorLocation = adUseClient
rs.LockType = adLockOptimistic
rs.Open "SELECT * FROM parts", "File Name=c:\MuchADO.udl"
Set rs.ActiveConnection = Nothing
rs.Filter = "part = 'BOY'"
rs!Description = "a young male"
rs.Update                    ←——————————    look Mum, no hands!
```

It looks suspiciously like this code will fail. As a result of disconnecting, there is no data source to receive the update! In fact, no error will be reported. The Recordset itself updates fine (in fact, it behaves exactly like the fabricated Recordset update we explored in Chapter 2), but for very understandable

---

10. This makes sense. You can't expect a server to provide cursor support if you are about to disconnect from it.

11. Consider a two-tier application which presents the user with a large Recordset in which to scroll around. Every now and then the user chooses to update a single record. You don't need to be connected all the time, and there are no great benefits to using batch updating. Standard optimistic locking with a disconnected Recordset is good solution.

reasons (mainly that there is no database connection), no database update takes place.

Now consider how this listing would behave if the rs variable was defined as follows:

```
Private WithEvents rs As Recordset

Private Sub rs_WillChangeRecord( _
        ByVal adReason As ADODB.EventReasonEnum, _
        ByVal cRecords As Long, _
        adStatus As ADODB.EventStatusEnum, _
        ByVal pRecordset As ADODB.Recordset)

If adReason = adRsnUpdate Then
  rs.ActiveConnection = "File Name=c:\MuchADO.udl"
End If

End Sub

Private Sub rs_RecordChangeComplete( _
        ByVal adReason As ADODB.EventReasonEnu…, _
        ByVal cRecords As Long, _
        ByVal pError As ADODB.Error, _
        adStatus As ADODB.EventStatusEnum, _
        ByVal pRecordset As ADODB.Recordset)
If adReason = adRsnUpdate Then
  Set rs.ActiveConnection = Nothing
End If
End Sub
```

a real application would want to trap inserts and deletes as well as updates

By trapping appropriate ADO events, this code conveniently supplies a data source connection just for the duration of the update process. The update will take place exactly as described in Chapter 3 for a client-side cursor. Depending on your connection management strategy, this approach can be very convenient.

As you can see, the difference between a disconnected Recordset and a connected Recordset with a client-side cursor boils down to one fact—the presence or absence of a connection—which can be changed at will at any time during a Recordset's lifetime.

In This Section

We established that disconnecting can be achieved by creating a Recordset with a client-side cursor and releasing its ActiveConnection. Disconnected Recordsets also can be used with default read-only or optimistic locking.

Batch Updating[12]

As shown in the previous section, performing an update on an "optimistic" Recordset with no active connection updates the Recordset, but quite obviously cannot update any data source. Attaching an active connection after the update will not magically result in an update to the data source. This is because once the update has completed, the Recordset has no knowledge or history of the update—it behaves as though it has always had the new value. You should have already learned enough to know exactly why this is the case:

- In Chapter 2, we studied the rs.EditMode property and the fd.Original-Value property. We saw that during an edit, rs.EditMode assumes the value adEditInProgress and fd.OriginalValue retains the old value of a field after fd.Value has been changed. After an update, `rs.EditMode` is reset to `adEditNone` while fd.OriginalValue assumes the same value as fd.Value.

- In Chapter 3, we saw how the Client Cursor Engine exploits this process to generate SQL that is used to perform an update against the active connection.

The idea of batch updating is to allow a Recordset to "record" a series of updates while disconnected, so that a whole batch of updates can be fired at the data source at once when a connection is available.[13] Why might you want to do this?

- *Batching changes is far more efficient.* Imagine a middle-tier process has passed a Recordset to a client process, which is performing multiple updates to the Recordset. The client has no access to the data source, and passing the Recordset back to the middle tier each time a single record is updated is too expensive..

- *The Recordset can be created at a time when a data source is available.* A Recordset can be saved to a file and reopened at a later date when a data source may not be available. This can occur frequently with laptop computers and mobile devices. When a data source becomes available again, the Recordset can be reconnected and the changes updated as a batch.

---

12. You should become familiar with the material on client-side cursor updates before proceeding.

13. Batch operations can be performed with a connected Recordset, although this is less common.

- *Sometimes it makes sense to preprocess a Recordset as a whole before troubling the database.* For example, you may wish to ensure that a Recordset containing a whole list of purchases doesn't exceed a credit limit before adding each record to an Orders table.

rs.LockType
rs.UpdateBatch
rs.CancelBatch

The standard Immediate mode of updates is clearly incapable of supporting this requirement. Instead, ADO allows you to switch into "batch" update mode by setting the LockType to adLockBatchOptimistic. Doing so brings about the following changes:

1. rs.EditMode and fd.OriginalValue are not reset after an update. This gives a disconnected Recordset a record of all changes that have been made to the Recordset.

2. rs.Update doesn't attempt to update a data source (even if there is one) and doesn't raise any Recordset events.

3. rs.UpdateBatch and rs.CancelBatch can be used to process the recorded changes as a batch. Transaction control can be applied to an rs.UpdateBatch to make it an atomic operation.

4. A conflict resolution mechanism is provided to resolve errors that can occur during a batch update.

To see this in action, let's revisit the code from Chapter 2 where we explored rs.EditMode and fd.OriginalValue. In the following code, the only significant change is the use of a batch optimistic cursor:

```
Dim rs As New Recordset
rs.CursorLocation = adUseClient
rs.LockType = adLockBatchOptimistic          request batch
rs.ActiveConnection = "File Name=c:\MuchADO.udl"   optimistic lock
rs.Open "SELECT * FROM parts where part = 'VERGES'"
Set rs.ActiveConnection = Nothing             disconnect here
With rs.Fields("description")
  Print "EM = " & rs.EditMode, "V = " & .Value, _
       "OV = " & .OriginalValue
  rs!Description = "a petty constable"
  Print "EM = " & rs.EditMode, "V = " & .Value, _
       "OV = " & .OriginalValue
  rs.Update                                   update takes
                                              place here
```

```
      Print "EM = " & rs.EditMode, "V = " & .Value, _
          "OV = " & .OriginalValue
      rs.ActiveConnection = "File Name=c:\MuchADO.udl"
      rs.UpdateBatch
      Print "EM = " & rs.EditMode, "V = " & .Value, _
          "OV = " & .OriginalValue
  End With
  rs.Close
```

batch update takes
place here after
reconnecting

It prints

EM = 0	V = a headborough	OV = a headborough
EM = 1	V = a petty constable	OV = a headborough
EM = 1	V = a petty constable	OV = a headborough
EM = 0	V = a petty constable	OV = a petty constable

Although this "batch" contains only a single update, it's an important example as it explains exactly how the Recordset manages a batch using its internal state.

Let's see what happens when a larger batch update takes place. In the following example, the updates are made in code, although it's more likely that they would be made through a user interface that allows records to be modified and then initiates a batch update.[14] This code uses filters, but is careful to remove all filters before calling rs.UpdateBatch.

```
Dim rs As New Recordset
rs.CursorLocation = adUseClient
rs.LockType = adLockBatchOptimistic
rs.ActiveConnection = "DSN=MuchADO"
rs.Open "SELECT * FROM parts"
Set rs.ActiveConnection = Nothing
rs.Filter = "part = 'BOY'"
rs!Description = "a young male"                 modify a record
rs.Filter = "part = 'RHETT BUTLER'"
rs.Delete                                       delete a record
rs.AddNew                                       insert a record
rs!part = "BART SIMPSON"
rs!Description = "another young male"           remove filters
rs.Filter = adFilterNone                        before batch
rs.ActiveConnection = "DSN=MuchADO"             updating
rs.UpdateBatch
rs.Close
```

---

14. The attempt to modernize the play by introducing Rhett Butler failed, so we'll try using Bart Simpson instead.

Typically, the UpdateBatch statement generates a single SQL statement. In this case it's

```
UPDATE "parts" SET "description"=? WHERE "part"=? AND "description"=?; DELETE
FROM "parts" WHERE "part"=?;
INSERT INTO "parts" ("part","description") VALUES (?,?)
```

This trace was recorded using ODBC and SQLServer 7. Note that the three SQL operations are packed into a single call to the database. This is more efficient than executing the three statements individually. By default, ADO will batch up to fifteen SQL statements into a single call. For more than fifteen statements, additional batches are made as required. This number can be changed by reference to the "Batch Size" dynamic property. Not all Providers support batched statements, and others might have a definite upper limit. Therefore, there may be times when you wish to limit the batch size to one or some other number of statements, as shown here:

```
rs.Properties("Batch Size") = 1
```

It's time to take a look at the formal syntax for UpdateBatch:

Sub UpdateBatch([AffectRecords As AffectEnum = adAffectAll])

AffectRecords is a value from the AffectEnum enumeration, which has the following values:

> adAffectCurrent
>
> adAffectGroup
>
> adAffectAll (default)
>
> adAffectAllChapters

There may be times when you need to single out a particular record and update it in isolation from the others. Because rs.Update can't be used for this when a batch optimistic lock type is specified, adAffectCurrent can be used instead to update a single record. Uses for the other two values will be presented in due course.

We've now seen the basic mechanics of batch updating. However, there are some other issues that always need attention when batch updating. We've have assumed that each update is valid and that the rs.UpdateBatch call will always succeed. This is a reckless assumption, and we need a model that allows us to validate changes and handle errors in an orderly fashion. Because such a lot of work is done in a single call to rs.UpdateBatch, it follows that we may need to take more care over these tasks than might be the case for a single update.

All of this means that you need to adopt a consistent processing scheme whenever you use batch updates. Your scheme needs to take into consideration not only preprocessing tasks, but also any errors, such as optimistic locking conflicts, that may occur when actually updating the data source.

Logically, you can think of such a model as

```
preProcessRS rs 'validate the Recordset
rs.UpdateBatch
postProcessRS rs 'handle errors and synchronization
```

although in reality, the `rs.UpdateBatch` is usually performed inside the "post-processing" routine.

The remainder of this section will explain just how sophisticated pre- and postprocessing can be. It's important to be aware of the functionality that ADO provides in this area. However, you'll soon see that pre- and post-processing code can quickly become very complicated.

Many of the most successful batch updating applications use a very simple approach, which uses transactions to ensure that the batch update is safe, but adds the barest minimum of additional processing.

I will explain soon what this safe minimum postprocessing code is, and I strongly encourage you to use it. Use of more advanced batch processing can be very powerful, but should be used sparingly.

Preprocessing a Batch Update

It's not unusual that you would want to validate a disconnected Recordset before calling rs.UpdateBatch. This would allow you to apply some business rules to the Recordset before attempting to update the database. You could then take one of the following actions:

1. If the validation succeeded, you could perform the batch update in full.

2. You could reject some of the modified records and update the remainder.

3. You could reject the entire batch and raise an error.

4. You could reject the entire batch and return the Recordset to the user or client.

Let's look at the mechanics of preprocessing. For the time being, let's assume that the rs.UpdateBatch always succeeds. As we have seen, prior to calling rs.UpdateBatch on a batch optimistic Recordset, all the records that have been modified will have an rs.EditMode value of something other than adEditNone (0). You might think you could single out modified records by applying a filter on `EditMode <> adEditNone`, but of course you can't do this—ADO would regard this filter as being based on a Field called EditMode, not on a Recordset property.

rs.Filter

Happily, ADO can help us out here. So far in this book, we've always constructed filters by applying an SQL-like WHERE clause to the Filter property. However, the Filter property can also accept values from the FilterGroupEnum enumeration, which allows it to apply filters that can't be constructed in an SQL-like manner. The enumeration has the following values:

adFilterNone

adFilterPendingRecords

adFilterAffectedRecords

adFilterFetchedRecords

adFilterConflictingRecords

We'll use most of these Filter options in the remainder of this section, as they exist largely to support "bulk" ADO operations such as batch updating and resynchronization of Recordsets. We've already encountered adFilter-None, which is the recommended way to remove all filters from a Recordset. In order to perform preprocessing, we'll exploit the adFilterPendingRecords, which allows us to see only those records that have been modified (and for which an update is therefore pending).

In the following two examples, we'll apply a business rule that prevents any records from being deleted. In the first example, we'll simply reject the batch if any records have been deleted, while in the second example, we'll allow inserts and updates to proceed. Deletes will be rejected, and a warning will be returned concerning any deletes that were canceled.

In both cases we'll write a function called preProcessRS, that will return Null if the batch update was successful and an error string otherwise. We'll also assume that the Parts table appears as it did at the start of this chapter. We'll use the following code to call `preProcessRS`. It's very similar to the code you saw earlier, but note that this code has accidentally left a filter on `'RHETT BUTLER'`:

```
Dim rs As New Recordset
rs.CursorLocation = adUseClient
rs.LockType = adLockBatchOptimistic
rs.ActiveConnection = "File Name=c:\MuchADO.udl"
rs.Open "SELECT * FROM parts"
Set rs.ActiveConnection = Nothing
rs.Filter = "part = 'BOY'"
```

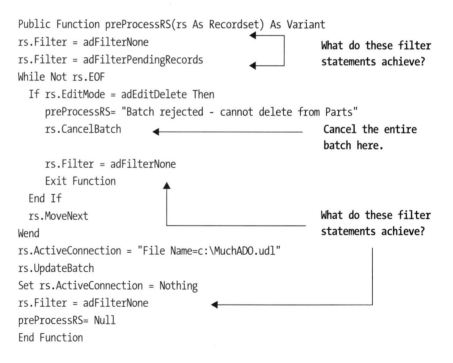

```
rs!Description = "a young male"
rs.Filter = "part = 'RHETT BUTLER'"          ◄─────┐   A filter has been left
rs.Delete                                    ◄──────┘   on a "deleted" record.


rs.AddNew
rs!part = "BART SIMPSON"

rs!Description = "another young male"
Dim vResult As Variant
vResult = preProcessRS(rs)        ◄──────────── Call preProcessRS.
If IsNull(vResult) Then
  Print "Update Succeeded"
Else
  Print vResult
End If
rs.Close
```

Here's the code for the first version of the `preProcessRS` function. Take a good look at it—it's actually more surprising than it looks:

```
Public Function preProcessRS(rs As Recordset) As Variant
rs.Filter = adFilterNone                      ◄──────┐   What do these filter
rs.Filter = adFilterPendingRecords            ◄──────┘   statements achieve?
While Not rs.EOF
  If rs.EditMode = adEditDelete Then
    preProcessRS= "Batch rejected - cannot delete from Parts"
    rs.CancelBatch        ◄─────────────────── Cancel the entire
                                               batch here.
    rs.Filter = adFilterNone
    Exit Function
  End If
  rs.MoveNext                                          What do these filter
Wend                                                   statements achieve?
rs.ActiveConnection = "File Name=c:\MuchADO.udl"
rs.UpdateBatch
Set rs.ActiveConnection = Nothing
rs.Filter = adFilterNone         ◄──────────────────
preProcessRS= Null
End Function
```

Running the code that calls this function prints

```
Batch rejected - cannot delete from Parts
```

rs.CancelBatch

CancelBatch undos the effect of all pending records in the example just shown, restoring their values to their original values and resetting their Edit-Mode property. The full syntax for CancelBatch is

Sub CancelBatch([AffectRecords As AffectEnum = adAffectAll])

Note that, like UpdateBatch, CancelBatch can take an argument from the AffectEnum enumeration, for the same reasons.[15]

Applying the adFilterPendingRecords filter means that only records with the following EditMode values are visible in the Recordset:

adEditInProgress (such as an update)

adEditAdd

adEditDelete

It also has another effect. Normally, you wouldn't expect to see a deleted record when iterating through a Recordset. However, if you couldn't see deleted records when preprocessing, you wouldn't be able to preprocess them! adFilterPendingRecords and other FilterGroupEnum options give you full access to the entire Recordset—including deleted records.[16] The caller of processRS would not expect to be able to see deleted records, so it's imperative to clear the filter after the operation[17] (although as you'll see in the next section, this isn't necessary if the caller and the function are in different processes).

Also, note that the existing filter was cleared by applying `adFilterNone` before applying `adFilterPendingRecords`. If this hadn't been done, only pending records in the existing filter would have been visible (once again, this isn't the case if the caller and the function are in different processes).

Now let's look at a less severe version of preProcessRS. In this case, we'll allow the update to continue and just remove the offending delete operation.

---

15. You need to consider whether it's advisable to call CancelBatch. If you return the Recordset to the caller after calling CancelBatch, the caller will not be able to see any changes that were made to the Recordset. In many cases, this is the safest course of action (as it keeps business processing in your middle tier—if you have one). If you don't return the Recordset to the caller, then calling CancelBatch has no real impact, as the Recordset is discarded anyway.

16. Be warned that although you can see deleted records, they don't have a valid "Value" property, although their "OriginalValue" property is intact.

17.7 A more obliging preProcessRS would actually read the filter value before changing it, and then set it back at the end of the function, rather than simply clearing it.

```
Public Function preProcessRS(rs As Recordset) As Variant
Dim lRequested As Long
Dim lActioned As Long
rs.Filter = adFilterNone
rs.Filter = adFilterPendingRecords
lRequested = rs.RecordCount
While Not rs.EOF
  If rs.EditMode = adEditDelete Then
    rs.CancelUpdate
  End If
  rs.MoveNext
Wend
rs.ActiveConnection = "File Name=c:\MuchADO.udl"
rs.Filter = adFilterPendingRecords
lActioned = rs.RecordCount
rs.UpdateBatch
Set rs.ActiveConnection = Nothing
rs.Filter = adFilterNone
If lRequested = lActioned Then
  processRS = Null
Else
  processRS = CStr(lRequested - lActioned) & _
            " delete operation(s) ignored"
End If
End Function
```

> these variables are being used to count the number of pending records before and after the preprocessing

> cancel the update for each deleted record encountered, but don't cancel the entire batch

> the validation is successful, so return a Null error

Running the code that calls this version of preProcessRS prints

```
1 delete operation(s) ignored
```

and (proving that no delete took place) generates the following SQL:

```
UPDATE "parts" SET "description"=? WHERE "part"=? AND "description"=?;
INSERT INTO "parts" ("part","description") VALUES (?,?)
```

The main thing to notice here is that instead of calling rs.CancelBatch, we simply canceled individual updates and then allowed any remaining pending updates to be performed by the rs.BatchUpdate.

Note also that we took a record count before and after the preprocessing. However, we had to reapply the adFilterPendingRecords filter in order to pick up that one of the previously pending records had been canceled.

Postprocessing a Batch Update

We've been assuming that an rs.UpdateBatch will always succeed. With appropriate preprocessing most errors can be trapped, but not all. The most common reason that a batch update fails is due to an optimistic locking error, but this is by no means the only reason.

Postprocessing is not only about error handling. It may be that making a change to one record requires other changes to be made in the database. In many databases, triggers can be used for such operations, but even so, it may be more convenient to handle them in VB code. You'll see how to achieve this in a later section, when we discuss stored procedures and disconnected Recordsets. For now, we'll focus solely on error handling.

When a batch is updated, a single operation can bring about multiple errors. The data source will typically process each SQL statement in the batch separately which means that some will succeed while others fail. This has two very important implications:

1. You'll almost certainly require transaction control.

2. You'll need a comprehensive error handling mechanism to cope with multiple errors.

Let's deal with the first of these points. Instead of using preProcessRS, we are going to use postProcessRS to handle errors that occur after the rs.UpdateBatch.[18] Our calling code is the same except for the name of the function it calls, and it's making the same changes to the disconnected Recordset. Here's some (faulty) code for postProcessRS that simply uses an error handler to trap an error should it occur:

```
'this code is not good enough
Public Function postProcessRS(rs As Recordset) As Variant
On Error GoTo ErrH

rs.Filter = adFilterNone
rs.ActiveConnection = "File Name=c:\MuchADO.udl"
rs.UpdateBatch
Set rs.ActiveConnection = Nothing
postProcessRS = Null
Exit Function
ErrH:
  postProcessRS = Err.Description
  Set rs.ActiveConnection = Nothing
End Function
```

---

18. Of course, you may have both preprocessing and postprocessing code.

Assume that after rs was created, but before `postProcessRS` was called, some other user deleted RHETT BUTLER. This would trigger the error handler, and the calling code would print

```
Row cannot be located for updating. Some values may have been
changed since it was last read.
```

You may recall this error message from Chapter 3. It's exactly what you would expect to result if you attempted to delete a nonexistent record using a client-side cursor.

There is nothing wrong with minimalistic error handling. In fact, it's often the easiest type to work with in the long run. However, the code just shown is rather too minimalistic. What you may not have noticed is that although the Delete operation failed, both the Update (which occurred before it in the SQL) and the Insert (which came after it in the SQL) succeeded.[19] This is a recipe for chaos—quite obviously, transactional control is required. Even a minimally complex batch process needs the following basic structure:[20]

```
'this is all you absolutely need
Public Function postProcessRS(rs As Recordset) As Variant
On Error GoTo ErrH

rs.Filter = adFilterNone
rs.ActiveConnection = "File Name=c:\MuchADO.udl"
rs.ActiveConnection.BeginTrans
rs.UpdateBatch
rs.ActiveConnection.CommitTrans
Set rs.ActiveConnection = Nothing
postProcessRS = Null
Exit Function
ErrH:
  postProcessRS = Err.Description
  rs.ActiveConnection.RollbackTrans
  Set rs.ActiveConnection = Nothing

End Function
```

transaction processing protects the batch operation

This is as far as many applications go with postprocessing. It's sufficient for most needs and has the virtue of being extremely simple.

---

19. When ADO builds the batch of SQL statements, updates come first, followed by deletes and then inserts.

20. Under MTS or COM+, explicit ADO transaction handling can be replaced by system services.

Advanced Postprocessing

When a batch contains a significant amount of information, it can be very annoying for users to have to re-key an entire batch of updates due to one potentially trivial error. Therefore, a number of strategies exist that allow you to handle batch update errors in a less severe way than simply dumping the Recordset:

- Generate a log or report, so that someone can identify what went wrong.

- Evaluate the severity of the error(s). It may be that your code can decide that the failed operations were not required and that the rest of the batch can complete safely (arguably, a delete that failed because the record had already been deleted may not be a cause for concern).

- Attempt to correct the error. It could be that some database integrity constraint caused the error. You may be able to apply a business rule that would allow you to avoid the constraint and retry the rs.UpdateBatch.

- Resynchronize the Recordset and return it to the caller. Optimistic locking errors can be a routine occurrence for any multiuser system. Simply returning the Recordset with the most recent underlying values (fetched using a Resync) may allow the user to decide whether the batch operation can be safely resubmitted.

Whatever strategy you decide on, it's vital to bear in mind that the batch update error most likely occurred within a transaction. Passing control back to the user within a transaction is not an option!

rs.Status

Anything more than minimal postprocessing requires information about which operations have been applied to which records, and ADO provides considerable information to assist in this task. The main source of information is provided by the rs.Status property, which can be used in conjunction with the familiar Field object value properties. rs.Status is one of the few Recordset properties we've yet to meet (because it's used mostly in bulk operations such as batch updates), and should not be confused with rs.State or rs.EditMode. rs.Status has a separate value for each record, while rs.State represents the state of a Recordset as a whole. rs.EditMode is useful before a batch update, while rs.Status is mostly used immediately after a batch update, resynchronization, or similar bulk operation.

rs.Status values are drawn from the RecordStatusEnum enumeration. They can be one or more of the following values (it's an overloaded property; the RecordStatusEnum values should be used as *bitmasks*):

adRecOK	adRecMultipleChanges	adRecMaxChanges-Exceeded
adRecNew	adRecPendingChanges	adRecObjectOpen
adRecModified	adRecCanceled	adRecOutOfMemory
adRecDeleted	adRecCantRelease	adRecPermissionDenied
adRecUnmodified	adRecConcurrencyViolation	adRecSchemaViolation
adRecInvalid	adRecIntegrityViolation	adRecDBDeleted

There are too many values to define individually[21], so I will supply the literal values of those enumerated constants that appear in the following examples:

adRecModified (2)

adRecDeleted (4)

adRecConcurrencyViolation (2048)

Two Filter options can also be used to help identify only those records which form part of the update process and to make any deleted records visible; these are:

- **adFilterAffectedRecords**: Identifies only those records affected by the last bulk operation (such as an rs.UpdateBatch or rs.CancelBatch).

- **adFilterConflictingRecords**: This filter is generally misreported as identifying only those records that failed the last rs.UpdateBatch. It so happens that it only identifies those records that failed the last rs.UpdateBatch due to an optimistic locking conflict. It doesn't include records that failed for other reasons.

By using these filters in conjunction with rs.Status, you can perform a detailed analysis of the reasons for a batch update failure. However, it should be noted that there is currently some variability between Providers concerning these features, especially when using adFilterAffectedRecords. The following

---

21. They are defined fully in the free OLE DB documentation.

example is based on the SQLServer 7 native Provider. It shows how a batch update error report might be constructed (at least one based on the Parts table):

```
Public Sub batchReport(rs As Recordset)
Dim er As ADODB.Error
For Each er In rs.ActiveConnection.Errors          process the
  Print er.Number, er.Description, er.Source       ActiveConnection's
Next                                               Errors collection


rs.Filter = adFilterConflictingRecords             process the
If rs.RecordCount = 0 Then                          conflicting records
  Print "NO CONFLICTING RECORDS"
Else
  Print rs.RecordCount & " CONFLICTING RECORD(S):"
  While Not rs.EOF
    If (rs.Status And adRecDeleted) = 0 Then        be careful with
     'record exists                                 deleted records
     Print rs!part, rs.Status
    Else
      Print "<<" & rs("part").OriginalValue & ">>", rs.Status
    End If
   rs.MoveNext
  Wend
End If


rs.Filter = adFilterAffectedRecords
If rs.RecordCount = 0 Then
  Print "NO AFFECTED RECORDS"
 Else                                               count the
  Print rs.RecordCount & " AFFECTED RECORD(S):"    affected records
 End If
 rs.Filter = adFilterNone
End Sub
```

This subroutine can be called from the error handler of the postprocessor (before releasing the ActiveConnection!).

Here are some examples of the reports produced, in all cases using the calling code we've used throughout this section.

Example 1: The Inserted Record Already Exists in the Database

```
-2147217900   Violation of PRIMARY KEY constraint 'PK_Parts'. Cannot insert
duplicate key in object 'Parts'.    Microsoft OLE DB Provider for SQL
Server
-2147217900    The statement has been terminated.       Microsoft OLE DB
Provider for SQL Server
NO CONFLICTING RECORDS
3 AFFECTED RECORD(S)
```

This example shows that errors can occur even when there are no optimistic lock conflicts. It also reminds us that the disconnected Recordset itself does not enforce primary key uniqueness (or any other database constraints), so such errors will only occur when updating to the data source. It isn't generally possible to use preprocessing to identify such errors.

Note that the source of these errors is the Microsoft OLE DB Provider for SQLServer.

Example 2: The Deleted Record Is Deleted from the Database after the Recordset Is Created, but Prior to the Update

```
-2147217864    Row cannot be located for updating. Some values may have been
changed since it was last read.     Microsoft Cursor Engine
1 CONFLICTING RECORD(S):
<<RHETT BUTLER         >>      2052
3 AFFECTED RECORD(S)
```

This is a classic example of a single conflict. Because the conflicting record was deleted, fd.OriginalValue is used to print the report instead of fd.Value, which (reasonably enough) is invalid for a deleted record.

In this case, the source of the error is the Microsoft Client Cursor Engine.

Example 3: Example 2 Error Plus the Updated Record Is
Modified by Another User after the Recordset Is Created,
but Prior to the Update

```
-2147217864   Row cannot be located for updating. Some values may have been
changed since it was last read.    Microsoft Cursor Engine
-2147217864   Row cannot be located for updating. Some values may have been
changed since it was last read.    Microsoft Cursor Engine
2 CONFLICTING RECORD(S):
BOY                        2050
<<RHETT BUTLER        >>   2052
3 AFFECTED RECORD(S)
```

Note that in this case, two Error objects are created. The conflict set can be used to identify which records are in conflict and what type of operation was performed on them.

Example 4: Example 1 Error Plus Example 3 Error

```
-2147217900   Violation of PRIMARY KEY constraint 'PK_Parts'. Cannot insert
duplicate key in object 'Parts'.    Microsoft OLE DB Provider for SQL
Server
-2147217900   The statement has been terminated.      Microsoft OLE DB
Provider for SQL Server
2 CONFLICTING RECORD(S):
BOY                        2050
<<RHETT BUTLER        >>   2052
3 AFFECTED RECORD(S)
```

In this last example, each record is responsible for one error. However, note that no errors are added to the Errors collection for the two conflicts.

These examples provide some insight into how sophisticated postprocessing of a batch update could be achieved. It's very easy for such processing to become complicated very quickly, and you should certainly resist being overly ambitious. If you wish to avoid both the severity of minimal postprocessing and the complexity of code that can result from taking the issue on yourself, there is one final option, which is to resynchronize the Recordset, roll back the transaction, and pass the Recordset back to the user. Resynchronization is covered in the next section.

Before concluding this section, it's worth observing that instead of writing explicit pre- and postprocessing code, you can use Recordset events. In this case, when a successful rs.UpdateBatch is executed:

- A WillChangeRecord event fires individually for each pending change.

- The update takes place.

- A RecordChangeComplete event fires individually for each record.

In This Section

We explored the batch update mechanism. A batch optimistic lock type suspends the normal functioning of rs.Update, so rs.BatchUpdate can be used to write all changes to the data source instead. Sane batch updating requires a planned approach to both preprocessing and postprocessing, and in particular, transaction control around the batch update is a must. The processing surrounding a batch update can be made to be very sophisticated, although in many cases a simple-but-safe approach is preferable.

Resynchronizing Disconnected Recordsets

I introduced the rs.Resync method back in Chapter 3, and you may wish to remind yourself of its basic workings. If you can't find the energy to flick back a few chapters, here's the syntax for calling Resync:

Sub Resync([AffectRecords As AffectEnum = adAffectAll],
                [ResyncValues As ResyncEnum = adResyncAllValues])

You may also recall that Resync can be triggered implicitly after an update or a batch update by setting the "Update Resync" dynamic property, as defined by the CEResyncEnum[22] enumeration.

When batch updating, there are three reasons why you might want to resynchronize a Recordset:

1. During preprocessing (such as before calling rs.UpdateBatch), you may want to refresh the underlying values before attempting the batch update. This might be so that you can perform some

---

22. This enumeration appears as ADCPROP_UPDATERESYNC_ENUM in the VB Object Browser.

validation based on the current database values, or it may be to guarantee that you won't get any conflicts when updating.[23]

2. If the batch update fails, you may wish to resynchronize as part of a recovery procedure before attempting to update again.

3. If the Recordset is going to be returned to the caller, it may be necessary to resynchronize it with the database. This can be true for both a successful and a failed batch update.

We'll focus on the third of these situations, when the Recordset is to be returned to the caller.

Resynchronization can be useful even after a successful batch update, to fill in values that can't be set in the Recordset. These might include AutoIncrement fields[24] and the results of custom resynchronization of a Recordset based on joins and the Unique Table dynamic Recordset property. The how's and why's of doing this are mostly discussed in Chapter 3. The only difference is that previously, we only considered resynchronization of one record at a time.

When batch updating, you need some way of controlling which records should be resynchronized. The number should be kept as small as possible because the resynchronization process will generate a separate SQL statement for each record to be synchronized.

rs.Resync

To resynchronize a successful batch update explicitly, the following code is typically used:

```
rs.Filter = adFilterAffectedRecords
rs.Resync adAffectGroup,adResyncAllValues
```

adAffectGroup is used to make sure that only those records that formed part of the update are resynchronized. adResyncAllValues ensures that the latest values from the data source are written into the fd.Value, fd.OriginalValue, and fd.UnderlyingValue properties of the relevant Field objects. Alternatively, adResyncUnderlyingValues can be used in place of adResyncAllValues, in which case only fd.UnderlyingValue is updated during the resynchronization process. (This approach is more likely to be used in preprocessing.)

Implicit resynchronization can be achieved by setting the Update Resync dynamic property. Implicit resynchronization gives you fine control over which

---

23. This latter reason is potentially dangerous. It's basically a way of overriding the optimistic lock control provided by ADO's QBU. If you successfully perform a Resync, QBU will use the latest values from the database to generate the WHERE clause used for the update. If you do this within a transaction, you are guaranteed to have no conflicts when updating within that transaction. At the same time, you have no idea what values you are overwriting.

24. These are resynchronized by default.

records are resynchronized, via the CEResyncEnum enumeration. These values were listed in Chapter 3 but not defined, as their full meaning applies primarily to batch updates. Here they are again, but with definitions this time.

Table 7-1. CEResyncEnum Enumeration Values and Constants

VALUE/CONSTANT	DEFINITION
adResyncNone	Does not resync after an UpdateBatch.
adResyncConflicts	Resyncs the fd.UnderlyingValues of optimistic lock conflicts, without changing fd.Values.
adResyncUpdates	Resyncs successfully updated rows.
adResyncInserts	Resyncs successful inserts, except for primary keys.
adResyncAutoIncrement (default)	Resyncs only inserts with primary keys.
adResyncAll	Resyncs all records affected by the batch update.

Certain combinations can be "Anded" together. For example, adResync-AutoIncrement and adResyncInserts can be combined to implicitly resynchronize all inserts.

The resynchronization that is required for a successful batch update will depend on the circumstances. In the vast majority of cases, it's perfectly fine to use the default value, or a combination of adResyncAutoIncrement and adResyncInserts when a Unique Table has been created.

For failed batch updates, the considerations are rather different. Once again, remember that the main reason for resynchronizing is a wish to return a Recordset to the client or user after the batch update attempt. If this is the case, there are two options:

1. *Return a valid Recordset along with a message that the user's changes have been lost forever.* If the update failed only for reasons of optimistic lock collisions, then it's generally straightforward to resynchronize using all values of the affected records. If the update failed for some other reason (such as attempting to create a duplicate primary key), it may be better to Requery the Recordset and start afresh.

2. *Return a Recordset when the user's changes remain intact, but the fd.UnderlyingValues has been resynchronized.* The problem here is that either your users will need to make changes without knowing what values they are overwriting, or you'll need both a user interface that allows users to compare the values and users who are sufficiently diligent to do so.

The approach to resynchronizing disconnected Recordsets typically depends on whether the batch update succeeded or failed. In many cases, a resynchronization isn't required at all.

Disconnected Recordsets and Stored Procedures

Here are some common myths surrounding disconnected Recordsets and stored procedures:

1. *The whole point of n-tier design is to be able to avoid writing stored procedures. All data manipulation should be written in the middle tier.* It's true that n-tier design can be used as an alternative to stored procedures. If middle-tier components run near their data sources then some of the performance requirements for using stored procedures are removed. There are certainly disadvantages to using stored procedures, so reducing the need for them is often a good thing. However, stored procedures will always be faster than raw SQL, and there will always be a need for them in high-demand scenarios. Stored procedures have an important place in n-tier designs.

2. *The big problem with disconnected Recordsets is that they depend on SQL. Therefore, you can't exploit the advantages of stored procedures, and so you can't write grown-up systems.* As we've seen, dropping the active connection of an ordinary connected Recordset with a client-side cursor creates a disconnected Recordset. There are no special requirements about the type of command string that is used. It's true that performing updates through a client-side cursor requires the data source to understand SQL. This isn't a peculiarity of disconnected Recordsets or of batch updating. It's how all client-side cursor-driven modifications take place. However, we've seen just how much control can be applied to exactly how these updates take place. We can take control of any part of the update process and do it our own way, if we wish.

Earlier in the chapter, we used the following code to create a batch-optimistic disconnected Recordset:

```
Dim rs As New Recordset
rs.CursorLocation = adUseClient
rs.LockType = adLockBatchOptimistic
rs.ActiveConnection = "File Name=c:\MuchADO.udl"
rs.Open "SELECT * FROM parts"
Set rs.ActiveConnection = Nothing
```

We then saw how to make changes to this Recordset and control the batch update statement. Here's the same code, except that the SQL has been replaced by a stored procedure call:

```
Dim rs As New Recordset
rs.CursorLocation = adUseClient
rs.LockType = adLockBatchOptimistic
rs.ActiveConnection = "File Name=c:\MuchADO.udl"
rs.Open "sp_parts", , , , adCmdStoredProc
Set rs.ActiveConnection = Nothing
```

While not all databases will return a full set of metadata for a stored procedure, SQLServer 7 certainly does. Therefore, the Recordset created using a stored procedure can be processed exactly as the one created using SQL. Because the Recordset contains all the required metadata, the QBU mechanism will generate SQL statements to make any modifications, just as it does for SQL-based commands. The same rules apply: If you don't need to update the Recordset, use a read-only lock type and no metadata will be retrieved. If updates are required, use an optimistic or a batch optimistic lock type.

Life gets a little more interesting if you want to augment (or even replace) the QBU mechanism to use stored procedures or possibly your own SQL.

In most cases, although we are working with the MuchADO database, we've been happy to ignore some of the niceties of database integrity in order to focus on ADO. For example, we've been happy to delete records from the Parts table, while still leaving words for the deleted part in the Words table. We'll be a bit more diligent in this section and tidy up the Words table whenever we delete from the Parts table. Rather than use database rules or triggers to maintain this rule, let's see how we could implement it using our batch update processing model.

Here's the definition of a stored procedure that can be used to tidy up the Words table:

```
CREATE PROCEDURE sp_deletePart (@part char(20))
AS
delete from Words where part = @part
```

We'll call this stored procedure inside a modified postProcessRS method. We'll actually call the stored procedure before the rs.UpdateBatch, but we'll need to do it inside the transaction for quite obvious reasons. Here's the new postProcessRS:

```
Public Function postProcessRS(rs As Recordset) As Variant
On Error GoTo ErrH
Dim cn As New Connection
Dim cd As New Command
cn.Open "File Name=c:\MuchADO.udl"
rs.Filter = adFilterNone
rs.ActiveConnection = cn
cn.BeginTrans
rs.Filter = adFilterPendingRecords
cd.CommandText = "sp_deletePart"          set up a Command object to
cd.CommandType = adCmdStoredProc          call the stored procedure
cd.ActiveConnection = cn
  While Not rs.EOF
    If rs.EditMode = adEditDelete Then
      cd.Execute , rs("part").OriginalValue    call the stored procedure
    End If                                     for each deleted record
    rs.MoveNext
  Wend
Set cd.ActiveConnection = Nothing
rs.UpdateBatch                            then do the batch update

cn.CommitTrans
Set rs.ActiveConnection = Nothing
cn.Close
postProcessRS = Null
Exit Function
ErrH:
  postProcessRS = Err.Description
  cn.RollbackTrans
  Set rs.ActiveConnection = Nothing
  cn.Close
End Function
```

This example shows how easily a batch update process can be augmented with additional code. As a final step, let's look at how to replace the QBU operation for deleted records completely, doing all required processing in a stored procedure. This isn't really necessary in our simple example, but there are situations in which you might need to stop the QBU process for some or all types of modification. To do this, let's first modify the stored procedure:[25]

```
CREATE PROCEDURE sp_deletePart (@part char(20))
 AS
DELETE FROM Parts WHERE part = @part
DELETE FROM Words WHERE part = @part
```

Before changing the postprocessing function, we need to decide whether the Recordset will be returned to the client or the user after the update. If we know the Recordset is going to be discarded, then the only change to the postprocessing routine is to cancel each delete prior to calling rs.Update-Batch, so that ADO doesn't try to build a delete statement for a record already deleted by the modified stored procedure. Here's the middle part of post-ProcessRS showing this trivial change:

```
cd.ActiveConnection = cn
   While Not rs.EOF
     If rs.EditMode = adEditDelete Then          cancel the update to
       rs.CancelUpdate              ◄────────    exclude it from the
        cd.Execute , rs!part                     standard batch operation
     End If
     rs.MoveNext
   Wend
Set cd.ActiveConnection = Nothing
rs.UpdateBatch
```

Note that we can now use the fd.Value property as the stored procedure parameter, as the record is restored before the stored procedure call.

This will do fine, so long as we intend to throw the Recordset away after the update process. We won't be able to continue using the Recordset because RHETT BUTLER is still in the Recordset (the rs.CancelUpdate undid the delete), even though the one in the database has gone with the wind.[26] Having canceled the delete, we would return a Recordset with a record count one higher than when we received it. This isn't consistent.

---

25. This technique can easily be extended to allow a stored procedure to handle all updates, deletes, and inserts, by passing the rs.EditMode value as an argument to the stored procedure.

26. This Recordset would be OK if your user was Scarlett O'Hara.

Showing you how to rectify this problem is simpler than explaining how to do it. The solution exploits the following two facts:

1. Calling rs.UpdateBatch on a disconnected Recordset updates the Recordset structure just as if there had been an active connection.

2. You can call rs.UpdateBatch for the current record only, by specifying the AffectRecords argument.

So, *before* you set the active connection on the Recordset, you should call rs.UpdateBatch (for the current record only) for each deleted record, and at the same time, call the stored procedure. *Then* you should set the active connection and proceed as before for the remaining pending records. This is how it looks:

```
Public Function postProcessRS(rs As Recordset) As Variant
On Error GoTo ErrH
Dim cn As New Connection
Dim cd As New Command
cn.Open "File Name=c:\MuchADO.udl"
rs.Filter = adFilterNone

cn.BeginTrans
rs.Filter = adFilterPendingRecords
cd.CommandText = "sp_deletePart"
cd.CommandType = adCmdStoredProc
cd.ActiveConnection = cn

  While Not rs.EOF
    If rs.EditMode = adEditDelete Then
      cd.Execute , rs("part").OriginalValue
      rs.UpdateBatch adAffectCurrent
    End If
    rs.MoveNext
  Wend
Set cd.ActiveConnection = Nothing
rs.ActiveConnection = cn
rs.UpdateBatch
cn.CommitTrans
Set rs.ActiveConnection = Nothing
cn.Close
postProcessRS = Null
Exit Function
```

Call UpdateBatch (for the current record only), while the Recordset is disconnected. The Recordset forgets that it needs to do a QBU for the record, allowing you to handle the delete in the stored procedure.

Set the active connection and call rs.UpdateBatch only after custom processing the deleted records.

```
ErrH:
  postProcessRS = Err.Description
  cn.RollbackTrans
  Set rs.ActiveConnection = Nothing
  cn.Close
End Function
```

From these examples you can see that it's possible to completely avoid dynamic SQL when using disconnected Recordsets. It's also possible to use stored procedures in the resynchronization process (see Chapter 3). Why might we want to go to all this trouble?

Our work with disconnected Recordsets has shown us that ADO provides a number of distinct functions:

1. It allows us to generate a freestanding Recordset structure containing data retrieved from a data source (though we have only seen some of the capabilities that this functionality gives us—the next section will take this much further).

2. When using a batch optimistic lock type, it allows us to cache multiple changes made by a user or a client and then update the data source in a single operation. ADO provides the caching features and powerful (although not necessarily simple) tools to assist in pre- and postprocessing to perform validation, error handling, and extended functionality.

3. By exploiting QBUs, ADO can generate SQL that converts Recordset changes into database updates.

4. It allows us to resynchronize Recordsets to reflect the latest database contents.

It's common to see these functions as parts of a whole package, and in many cases, it's convenient to do so. But it isn't *necessary* to do so. Many of my disconnected Recordsets start with an SQL command and exploit ADO's built in QBU and resynchronization to create a good middle-tier solution quickly. I know that I can build the Recordset faster if I need to by replacing the SQL query with a stored procedure. If I later need yet more performance, I can provide customized resynchronization and even replace QBU. None of these changes need to affect the users of my Recordset. You may be thinking that if I go as far as to replace QBU, there isn't much left of disconnected Recordsets that I am using. If so, consider the following two points:

1. Does it matter? I started out without having to write any database update code. There is every chance I could leave things like this, but if it so happens that I need to replace QBU to get more performance, I have already had considerable benefit from using it to create a usable solution quickly. The fact that my client applications won't be affected by the stored procedures I might use to enhance it is a major benefit in itself.

2. I am still benefiting from the batch update model, and in particular, the ability it gives me to write stateless n-tier applications with efficient cross-process communication, as the next section will explain.

There is one side to using stored procedure with disconnected Recordsets that is less than ideal. QBU depends on metadata retrieved alongside the Recordset data at the time the Recordset was opened. There is a measurable cost for this metadata. Once you replace QBU with stored procedures (or even custom update code) you may no longer need this metadata. However, you can't avoid having it if you want your Recordset to be updateable. All client-side Recordsets created using batch optimistic or optimistic cursors have this metadata. Only read-only Recordsets are created without it, and read-only Recordsets can't be updated—period (even if you are prepared to handle the data source updating yourself).

The net result of this is that it's always going to be more efficient to create read-only Recordsets based on stored procedures and then handle updates through direct stored procedure calls, rather than using the techniques described in this chapter. The performance savings are measurable, and in some (but by no means all) situations, significant. However, what you lose by rejecting the simple, flexible, and elegant model provided by batch updateable disconnected Recordsets is often very significant indeed.

In This Section

It's a myth that stored procedures and disconnected Recordsets can't be mixed. You can use stored procedures to generate disconnected Recordsets, and should you so wish, you can use stored procedures to perform batch updates and resynchronization with disconnected Recordsets.

Recordset Marshalling

We know how to use Recordset objects in the following two circumstances:

1. When the lifetime of the Recordset is constrained by the process or program in which it was created.

2. When all access to the Recordset takes place from inside the process or program in which it was created

Unlike most other objects, Recordsets have the built-in ability to retrieve their data from data sources and to write their changes back to data sources. Therefore, in the special case of communication with a data source, Recordsets are able to overcome these two constraints in ways that are not available to most other objects.

Nevertheless, our ability to exploit all that is great about Recordsets is sadly restricted if Recordsets can't have a life outside of the process that created them. Specifically we want to be able to:

- Move Recordsets between processes and machines as part of a distributed application. Our earlier discussion of n-tier designs explained why this is essential. The operation that makes this possible is called "marshalling."

- Store objects in various ways without relying on a data source. For example, we may want to write a Recordset to a file, place it on a message queue, or simply hold its data in memory in a stream or block of data without needing to keep a live Recordset object around to reference it. All of these tasks exploit Recordset persistence, which we'll cover in the final section of this chapter.

Marshalling makes it possible for one process to access a Recordset created in another.[27] The two processes may be on the same machine, on different machines communicating using DCOM, or connected across the world by HTTP. In all cases, marshalling performs much the same job.

To understand what this job entails, you need to consider one or two facts that are generally concealed when using a high-level language such as VB:

1. Any variable that references an object is basically a pointer to a location in memory where that object resides (more precisely, it's a pointer to an interface table exposed by the object, but we don't need to be that precise).

---

27. With a little help from its friends.

2. A pointer to a memory location has no meaning outside the process in which it resides. In fact, one of the more important responsibilities of an operating system is to prevent one process (even on the same machine) from directly accessing memory in another.

All of which means that while you may get the *illusion* that you can pass object references between processes or machines, the truth is that you can do no such thing. The illusion is maintained by the use of an agent, or a *proxy,* in the client process, which acts as a representative of an actual object in the server process. The proxy has a counterpart in the server process called a *stub,* which represents the client in the server process.[28] The proxy and the stub communicate by means of marshalling. The proxy and the stub are both standard COM objects, so both the client-reference-to-proxy and the stub-to-server-object communication are based on regular in-process COM techniques.

For example, consider an ActiveX EXE project called Server, which contains a public class called Thing. Thing has a property called Name, and method called AndAnotherThing, which returns a new Thing object. Here's Thing's definition:

```
Public Name As String

Public Function AndAnotherThing(sName As String) As Thing
Dim oThing As New Thing
oThing.Name = sName
Set AndAnotherThing = oThing
End Function
```

Now consider a client program that has a reference to Server. It can create an instance of Thing and set its Name property as follows:

```
Dim oThing As Server.Thing
Set oThing = New Server.Thing
oThing.Name = "Fred"
```

The following diagram shows the state of the two processes after this code has run:

---

28. It's a bit like communicating with someone via attorneys, except that proxies and stubs don't get paid as much.

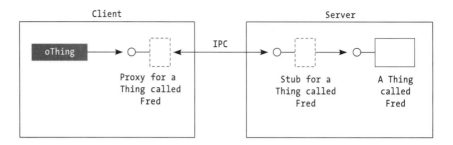

Figure 7-4. COM uses proxies and stubs to simulate an in-process call.

The code looks the same as it would if Thing objects were created in the client process, but the action behind the scenes is very different. In an in-process call, oThing refers directly to the Thing instance. In the separate process scenario, oThing refers to a proxy for the Thing instance. The proxy looks and feels exactly like a Thing instance, but it has none of the functionality or state of a Thing object. When *oThing* assigns "Fred" to the Name property, the proxy receives the assignment and passes a string containing "Fred" to the stub, which then repeats the assignment in the server process, this time actually setting the Name property on the actual instance of Thing residing in the server. The Inter Process Communication (IPC) is completely hidden from both oThing and the Thing called Fred.[29] It's important to remember that the proxy holds no state or behavior relevant to Thing objects—it's purely an agent. If the client program reads the Name property of oThing, for example:

```
MsgBox oThing.Name
```

the proxy has to ask the stub to read the value from the actual Thing instance. As you can imagine, reading many properties in this way can have a considerable overhead.

Let me put this into perspective. I am using a 400MHz single-processor PC and compiled VB6. When holding an in-process reference to a Thing object, I can read its Name property 1.5 million times in a second. When holding a cross-process reference (on the same machine), I can only read the property 4,000 times. Four thousand is still a large number, but I probably want to be sure that each cross-process call is worthwhile. Between machines, I could expect no better than three-figure performance.

---

29. If the two processes are on the same machine, the IPC uses Windows messaging. If the two processes are on separate machines, either DCOM or HTTP is used.

Now let's see what happens when the client calls the `AndAnotherThing` method, for example:

```
Dim oThing2 As Server.Thing
Set oThing2 = oThing.AndAnotherThing("Barney")
```

Here, the call on `AndAnotherThing` is received by the proxy, which passes the request to the stub, marshalling the string containing `"Barney"` across the process boundary. The instance of Thing in the server process runs its code, and creates a new instance of Thing called Barney. The client expects a reference to Barney to be returned. However, because you can't pass a reference (memory pointer) between processes, a new proxy and stub are created for Barney instead. Here's what it looks like:

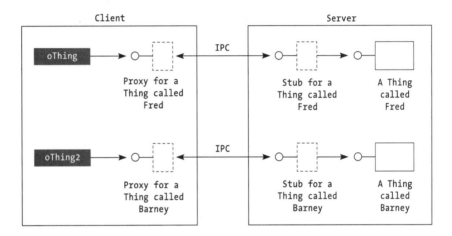

Figure 7-5. COM objects can't be passed across process boundaries.

Now let's turn our attention to Recordsets. When you pass a reference to a Recordset with a server-side cursor, the Recordset behaves in exactly the same way as Fred and Barney. The Recordset, its data, all the ADO code, and the active connection (if it has one), operate in the server process. A proxy for the Recordset is created in the client process, and all method calls and property operations performed by the client are marshalled between the proxy and the stub across the process boundary.

We'll explore Recordset marshalling using a Public class called Words implemented in an ActiveX EXE project called Server. The class's ProgID will therefore be RSServer.Words. Communication with an ActiveX EXE can be considered the same as communication with an ActiveX DLL running in an MTS Package or a COM+ Application, at least for our purposes in this chapter. All the figures I will present will be based on cross-process communication on the same machine. You can simply assume that all the cross-process effects are magnified when the processes run on separate machines, and grossly magnified when the Internet gets in the way.[30] You can perform your own tests using the companion project to this chapter which can be found on the book's CD.

The following method in the Words class creates and returns a connected server-side Recordset. The only reason for doing this is to prove that it isn't something you would ordinarily want to do in an out-of-process server.

```
'don't do this at home
Public Function getRS1(Part As String) As Recordset
Dim rs As New Recordset
rs.CursorType = adOpenStatic
rs.LockType = adLockOptimistic
rs.Source = "SELECT * FROM Words WHERE part = '" & Part & "'"
rs.ActiveConnection = "File Name=c:\MuchADO.udl"
rs.Open
Set getRS1 = rs
End Function
```

By setting a reference to the RSServer project, we can create a client EXE to call this method using the following code:

```
Dim oWords As New RSServer.Words
Dim rs As Recordset
Dim t As Double
Dim s As String
t = Timer
Set rs = oWords.getRS1("MARGARET")
rs.MoveFirst
While Not rs.EOF
    s = rs!word
    rs.MoveNext
Wend
Print "Time", Format(Timer - t, "0.000")
Print "Records", rs.RecordCount
```

This code creates an instance of RSServer.Words and uses it to create a Recordset containing all of Margaret's words. Remember that the Recordset lives in the RSServer process—the client actually references a proxy.

---

30. It isn't the purpose of this book to explain how to configure DCOM, IIS, MTS, or COM+ Applications, although we'll be discussing all these technologies from an ADO perspective.

Running this code prints

Time	5.380
Records	324

To provide a benchmark, I ran the same test with all the code in the same process. It printed

Time	0.378
Records	324

In both cases, the database work and Recordset manipulation are the same. The difference is purely accounted for by the IPC and marshalling overheads. The difference is huge, and it would be impossible to live with across a slow network link or with a large Recordset. All along, I have been saying that Recordsets marshall efficiently across process boundaries. It's time to come clean.

The good news is that I haven't been misleading you—it's just that we were doing it wrong in the example shown. Passing server-side Recordsets between processes is a bad idea (just as passing collections between processes is a bad idea), because they don't work efficiently with standard COM proxies, stubs, or marshalling.

However, whenever you use client-side cursors, a customized form of marshalling is used that is designed to marshall Recordsets efficiently. Instead of creating a proxy for the Recordset in the client process, a complete copy of the Recordset is created in the client process (so long as is the Recordset is disconnected). Therefore, instead of each method call and property access requiring an expensive cross-process call, all operations are performed on the local copy of the Recordset. These operations can include updates made to a Batch mode Recordset.

Because the client process receives a complete Recordset instead of just a proxy, the server process has no need to keep hold of the Recordset, and therefore, it can be completely stateless, helping to conserve server resources.

Here's another version of the previous method. This one returns a batch updateable disconnected Recordset:

```
Public Function getRS2(Part As String) As Recordset
Dim rs As New Recordset
rs.CursorLocation = adUseClient
rs.LockType = adLockBatchOptimistic
rs.Source = "SELECT * FROM Words WHERE part = '" & Part & "'"
rs.ActiveConnection = "File Name=c:\MuchADO.udl"
```

```
rs.Open
Set rs.ActiveConnection = Nothing
Set getRS2 = rs
End Function
```

To test this method from our client, we need only change the name of the method called from getRS1 to getRS2. Otherwise, the code is identical. This time, the client code prints

Time	0.231
Records	324

I ran another a benchmark by placing the new client and server code in the same process, to take account of the changes made to the Recordset properties. This benchmark printed

Time	0.141
Records	324

These results are far more satisfactory. We would expect some overhead to be incurred when passing a reasonably large Recordset across a process boundary, and it certainly is slower than performing the entire task in one process. However, by passing a client-side Recordset, we automatically invoke the efficient custom marshalling used by ADO and remove the need for each Recordset operation to incur an IPC overhead. As a result, it's possible to pass a complex, powerful structure between processes in a flexible, efficient fashion.

Passing Recordsets with client-side cursors across process or machine boundaries works. Passing Recordsets with server-side cursors across process or machine boundaries doesn't.

Batch Updating Using an N-Tier Model

To explore this n-tier model in more detail and to see how the client program might handle updating requirements, let's develop a complete n-tier application. Don't worry. I am going to keep it very simple. This is largely because it is very simple, but also because we'll also avoid getting into any business logic (we have already spent plenty of time seeing how this could be handled). After we build an n-tier application, we'll go on to see two useful performance enhancements.

Here are the two methods required in our server component,
RSServer.Words:

```
Public Function getWordsForPart(Part As String) As Recordset
Dim rs As New Recordset
rs.CursorLocation = adUseClient
rs.LockType = adLockBatchOptimistic
rs.Source = "SELECT word, part, act, scene FROM Words " & _
            "WHERE part = '" & Part & "'"
rs.ActiveConnection = "File Name=c:\MuchADO.udl"
rs.Open
Set rs.ActiveConnection = Nothing
Set getWordsForPart= rs
End Function
```

rs is passed in "by reference." You'll
soon see that this approach isn't
always appropriate when passing
Recordsets across process boundaries.

```
Public Function setWordsForPart(rs As Recordset) As Boolean
On Error GoTo ErrH
Dim cn As New Connection
cn.Open "File Name=c:\MuchADO.udl"
rs.ActiveConnection = cn
cn.BeginTrans
rs.UpdateBatch
cn.CommitTrans
Set rs.ActiveConnection = Nothing
SetWordsForPart = True
Exit Function
ErrH:
  cn.RollbackTrans
  Set rs.ActiveConnection = Nothing
  SetWordsForPart = False
End Function
```

There is no need to clear
filters when marshalling
client-side cursors.

There is not much new here. getWordsForPart is simply getRS2 modified
so that the primary key is not included.[31] setWordsForPart is our minimalistic postprocessing batch update routine, with no preprocessing.

The role of this server is quite clear. It prepares and returns a batch
updateable Recordset to a client, and then promptly forgets about it. When the
client passes the Recordset back, it applies the standard processing model to
oversee the batch update and returns success or failure to the client.

---

31. We don't want users to see our primary keys. We'll rely on SQLServer's Hidden Columns
(see Chapter 3) to ensure that the Recordset retains the primary keys, even though we
don't show them in the Recordset. If you are using a different database, you'll need to
return primary keys and rely on the client program not to display them.

There is one way in which our update processing is slightly simpler when custom marshalling is used. The custom marshaller is blind to filter and sort settings made in the client, so there is no need to clear these properties before processing the data. The same is true when passing Recordsets from the server to the client. There is no point in applying a filter or a sort before returning the Recordset.

For the client program, I have used the ADO Data Control and the Data Grid Control for OLE DB. We'll talk more about user interfaces in Chapter 12. However, these are standard controls and easy to use. Apart from these two controls there are three command buttons. The only properties that have been set are Name and Caption. This is what the user interface looks like:

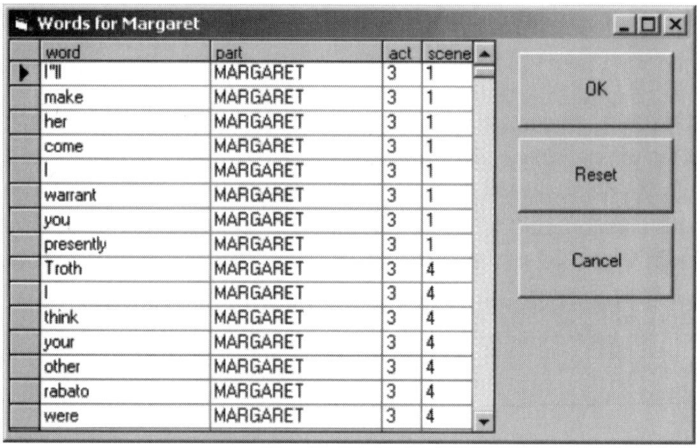

word	part	act	scene
I"ll	MARGARET	3	1
make	MARGARET	3	1
her	MARGARET	3	1
come	MARGARET	3	1
I	MARGARET	3	1
warrant	MARGARET	3	1
you	MARGARET	3	1
presently	MARGARET	3	1
Troth	MARGARET	3	4
I	MARGARET	3	4
think	MARGARET	3	4
your	MARGARET	3	4
other	MARGARET	3	4
rabato	MARGARET	3	4
were	MARGARET	3	4

Figure 7-6. ADO makes n-tier development easy.

And here's the entire code for the client program:

```
Private rs As Recordset
Dim oWords As New RSServer.Words


Private Sub Form_Load()
Set rs = oWords.getWordsForPart("MARGARET")
Set Adodc1.Recordset = rs
Set DataGrid1.DataSource = Adodc1
End Sub
```

Form_Load **calls on the server to return a Recordset. It then assigns the Recordset to the Data Control, and then sets the Data Control to be the** DataSource **for the for the** DataGrid.

```
Private Sub cmdOK_Click()
If oWords.setWordsForPart(rs) Then          ◄─────────
  MsgBox "Update OK"
Else
  MsgBox "Update Failed"
End If
Unload Me
End Sub


Private Sub cmdReset_Click()
rs.CancelBatch                              ◄─────────
End Sub


Private Sub cmdCancel_Click()
Unload Me
End Sub
```

The OK button simply passes the Recordset back to the server for update processing.

Resetting couldn't be much easier.

This is a fully functional n-tier application. It's crude in a number of ways, but it's completely usable and safe. The beauty of it is that the client is so simple. We could add validation, logging, error handling, and so on to the server without ever needing to change the client.

Rather than do this, let's instead focus on one particular part of the client-server exchange. Take a look at this code fragment from the client program:

```
oWords.setWordsForPart(rs)
```

We know that this simple-looking operation invokes ADO's custom Recordset marshaller to re-create a copy of this Recordset in the server process, so that the server process can perform the required data source updating. The wondrous thing about this operation is that passing a Recordset to a method that runs in another process or even on another machine is as easy as passing it to a method in the same process.

Think about what this means. If you pass a Recordset reference to a method running in the same process, you would expect to be able to see any changes made by that method once the method call completed. For example, if the method resynchronized the Recordset, you would expect to see the effect of the resynchronization after the method call.

If marshalling is meant to make a cross-process call look the same as an in-process call, it has to copy the Recordset back from the server process at the end of the method call, so that any changes made in the server are visible in the client. In other words, to make this method call work, the Recordset has to be marshalled between the client and server process not once, but twice. The following diagram shows this:

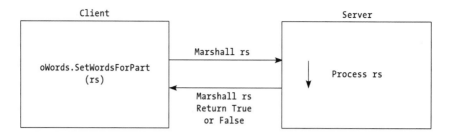

Figure 7-7. Passing a Recordset "By Reference" means marshalling twice.

To explore what this means in performance terms, let's use the following modified version of setWordsForPart in the server:[32]

```
Public Function setWordsForPart( rs As Recordset) As Boolean
setWordsForPart = True
End Function
```

and a modified client version of cmdOK_Click:

```
Private Sub cmdOK_Click()
Dim t As Double
Dim i As Integer
t = Timer
For i = 1 To 100
    oWords.setWordsForPart rs
Next
Print "Time for 100 iterations:", Format(Timer - t, "0.00")
End Sub
```

By removing all functionality from setWordsForPart we can get a feel for the cost of marshalling a 324-record Recordset 200 times (100 times in each direction). Clicking OK will print

```
Time for 100 iterations:     4.27
```

Not especially troubling, but then there is no network involved, and only one user. The frustrating part is that our client doesn't use the Recordset that is so lovingly marshalled back after the method call (and it doesn't know that the server hasn't even modified the Recordset!). This effort is in vain, and not without cost.

---

32. You can always improve your chances of writing bug-free code by writing code that doesn't do anything!

It's standard practice in VB to pass arguments by reference, largely because this is the default. We can of course define methods that pass arguments by value, using the ByVal keyword. When we pass an argument by value, we don't see any changes made to the argument by the method. Cross-process marshallers know this and use the fact to avoid marshalling arguments back to the caller after the method call.

Here's what setWordsForPart looks like when we pass by value:

```
Public Function setWordsForPart(ByVal rs As Recordset) As Boolean
setWordsForPart = True
End Function
```

And here's what the same client code prints using this new method definition:

```
Time for 100 iterations:    2.24
```

It takes almost half the time, because it performs almost half the work.

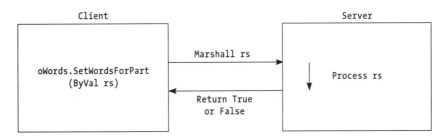

Figure 7-8. Passing a Recordset "By Value" is more efficient.

Application designers who are experienced at working with marshalling tend to define all method arguments as ByVal, unless they positively want changes to be marshalled back to clients at the end of the call. The same design rule applies equally to Recordsets. This is one aspect of how designing interfaces to be called across process boundaries is very different from designing interfaces to be called within a process.

Passing Recordsets by value is one easy way of improving performance in n-tier applications. There is one additional technique we can apply. Our client Recordset has 324 records. It's unlikely that a user will change more than half a dozen or so records, so it seems a shame to marshall all 324 records to the server. Most server processing schemes are only interested in pending changes, so the remaining 318 records don't need to be marshalled.

rs.MarshalOptions   The client can very easily ensure that only pending changes are marshalled to the server by setting the appropriately named rs.MarshalOptions property.

It can have one of two self-explanatory values, defined by the MarshalOptions-Enum enumeration:

adMarshalAll

adMarshalModifiedOnly

Here's the client program, changed to marshall only pending changes:

```
Private Sub cmdOK_Click()
Dim t As Double
Dim i As Integer
t = Timer
rs.MarshalOptions = adMarshalModifiedOnly
For i = 1 To 100
    oWords.setWordsForPart rs
Next
Print "Time for 100 iterations:", Format(Timer - t, "0.00")
End Sub
```

and here's what it prints if I change six records before hitting OK:

```
Time for 100 iterations:    0.52
```

Predictably, it's much, much faster than marshalling the entire Recordset.

One minor annoyance is that the server can't tell what marshalling option the client selected (because this information doesn't make it as part of the custom marshalling). There may be situations in which the server's preprocessing needs to check the entire Recordset, not only the pending changes. In these cases, the server is reliant on the client to choose the appropriate marshalling option.

Note that setting rs.MarshalOptions in the server makes no sense. It has no impact on how the server interacts with the data source. For one thing, we've already seen that only pending changes have SQL generated for them, and for another thing, data source interaction does not involve marshalling—because databases don't use Recordset objects.

In This Section

We examined how Recordsets can be passed between processes and computers. Passing method arguments across process boundaries is called marshalling, and ADO employs a custom marshalling scheme for Recordsets with client-side cursors. Marshalling Recordsets with server-side cursors is a painful experience. Recordsets can be used to make n-tier applications easier to write, and passing Recordsets by value and using MarshalOptions can enhance performance.

Recordset Persistence

Persistence allows you to create a durable form of a Recordset, which outlives the Recordset object itself. The most obvious durable form is a file, but there are many other ways to store a Recordset as well. Let's look at some of them in this section.

ADO 2.5 introduced the Stream object. Stream objects extend the opportunities for persisting Recordsets. While we'll discuss Stream objects formally in Chapter 9, I'll introduce them in this chapter in the context of their role in persistence. We'll also look at a persistence technique that can approximate the use of Stream objects, for pre-ADO 2.5 scenarios.

Whichever technique is used, persistence works by turning a Recordset's data into a format that has two attributes:

1. It's easily stored and transmitted as a block of data.

2. It can be used to reconstruct the Recordset back into an identical copy.[33]

ADO supports two formats for persisting Recordsets: Advanced Data Table Gram (ADTG) and XML. ADTG is an efficient but proprietary format. ADO 2.1 introduced XML as an alternative. XML is more verbose than ADTG, but its benefits hardly need mentioning.

rs.Save

You may recall that we had a brief look at Recordset persistence back in Chapter 2 when we used the Open and Save methods to read and write Recordsets from and to a file. All we are doing in this section is expanding on that earlier experience.

Here again is the formal syntax for the Save method:

Sub Save([Destination As Variant],
             [PersistFormat As PersistFormatEnum = adPersistADTG])

This isn't how the Save method looked prior to ADO 2.5. Previously, it was:

Sub Save([FileName As String],
             [PersistFormat As PersistFormatEnum = adPersistADTG])

---

33. This isn't the same as cloning. Two Clones use the same internal data. Add a record from one and it's visible to the other Clone. A Recordset reconstructed from a persisted block of Recordset data is a completely separate object with its own internal data.

With ADO 2.5, it became possible to use to rs.Save to write a Recordset's contents to certain types of objects, as well as to a file specified by a file name. Long ago, COM defined a set of interfaces to handle streams of data and data persistence.[34] One of these interfaces is called IStream. Any COM object that implements IStream can be used as a target for the rs.Save method. These include

- An ADO Stream object (as you might expect)

- The Active Server Pages (ASP) Response object

What is less well known is that well before ADO 2.5, ADO Recordsets had themselves implemented another of these persistence interfaces, called IPersistStream. This means that even if you don't have ADO 2.5, you can persist a Recordset through any medium that understands IPersistStream, including

- PropertyBags

- MSMQ (Microsoft Message Queue) Message Bodies[35]

Since we previously discussed persisting a Recordset to a file, let's take a look at these other persistence techniques.

Persisting with a Stream Object

The following code writes a Recordset into a Stream object:

```
Dim rs As New Recordset
Dim sm As New Stream
rs.CursorLocation = adUseClient
rs.ActiveConnection = "File Name=c:\MuchADO.udl"
rs.Open "select * from parts where part > 'T'"
rs.Save sm, adPersistXML          ◄──────────  Save the Recordset
Print sm.ReadText                                to the Stream
```

---

34. These interfaces form part of "Structured Storage," the technology that allows you to embed one object's data (such as an Excel spreadsheet) inside another object's data (such as a Word document). This is how compound documents get stored.

35. MSMQ is Microsoft's messaging product. It has been considered part of Windows' DNA for some time, and it's an essential part of COM+ because it supports COM+ Queued Components.

It prints

```
<xml xmlns:s='uuid:BDC6E3F0-6DA3-11d1-A2A3-00AA00C14882'
    xmlns:dt='uuid:C2F41010-65B3-11d1-A29F-00AA00C14882'
    xmlns:rs='urn:schemas-microsoft-com:rowset'
    xmlns:z='#RowsetSchema'>
<s:Schema id='RowsetSchema'>
    <s:ElementType name='row' content='eltOnly'>
        <s:AttributeType name='part' rs:number='1' rs:writeunknown='true'>
            <s:datatype dt:type='string' rs:dbtype='str' dt:maxLength='20'
                rs:fixedlength='true' rs:maybenull='false'/>
        </s:AttributeType>
        <s:AttributeType name='description' rs:number='2'
rs:nullable='true'
            rs:writeunknown='true'>
            <s:datatype dt:type='string' rs:dbtype='str' dt:maxLength='50'/>
        </s:AttributeType>
        <s:extends type='rs:rowbase'/>
    </s:ElementType>
</s:Schema>
<rs:data>
    <z:row part='URSULA                ' description='gentlewoman attending
on Hero'/>
    <z:row part='VERGES                ' description='a petty constable'/>
    <z:row part='WATCHMAN              '/>
</rs:data>
</xml>
```

You may recognize this as XML. Note that the XML has a *Schema* element which defines the metadata for the Recordset, and a *data* element which contains the actual Recordset data.

From this point, you could write the XML to a file, which would be equivalent to calling rs.Save with a file name instead of an object. The advantage to using the Stream object is that you don't need to touch a disk file if you don't want to. From this point on, what you do with the streamed representation of the Recordset is entirely up to you. For example, you could make a carbon copy of the original Recordset, as follows:

```
Dim rs As New Recordset
Dim rsCopy As New Recordset
Dim sm As New Stream
```

```
rs.CursorLocation = adUseClient
rs.ActiveConnection = "File Name=c:\MuchADO.udl"
rs.Open "select * from parts"
Print "Records before filter", rs.RecordCount
rs.Filter = "description = Null"            ◄─────────  apply a Filter to rs
Print "Records after filter", rs.RecordCount
rs.Save sm, adPersistXML
rs.Close
Set rs = Nothing                            ◄─────────  release rs
rsCopy.Open sm                              ◄─────────  Open a new Recordset
Print "Records in Copy", rsCopy.RecordCount            from the Stream
```

which prints

Records before filter	27
Records after filter	7
Records in Copy	7

rs.Open

There are a couple of things to note here. rsCopy is a brand new Recordset with no links to rs. The rsCopy.Open method populates the Recordset based on the streamed XML data stored in the Stream object. Note also that the Save operation takes into account the Filter that was applied to rs. One final point to make is that all my examples are based on client-side cursors. Some Providers allow you to persist Recordsets created with server-side cursors.

Persisting Using the ASP Response Object

The following ASP page will write an XML-formatted Recordset to the ASP Response object, and set the Response type to XML:

```
<%
set rs = Server.CreateObject("ADODB.RecordSet")
rs.CursorLocation = 3                       ◄─────────  3 is the literal
rs.ActiveConnection = "File Name=c:\MuchADO.udl"        value of adUseClient
rs.Open "select * from parts where part > 'T'"
Response.ContentType = "text/xml"
rs.Save Response, 1                         ◄─────────  1 is the literal value
%>                                                     of adPersistXML
```

I have used literal values here for simplicity. Experienced ASP programmers would use an include statement to make the ADO constants available.

After publishing this page to my Web site as getRS.asp, I can navigate to this ASP page from IE5, as shown here:

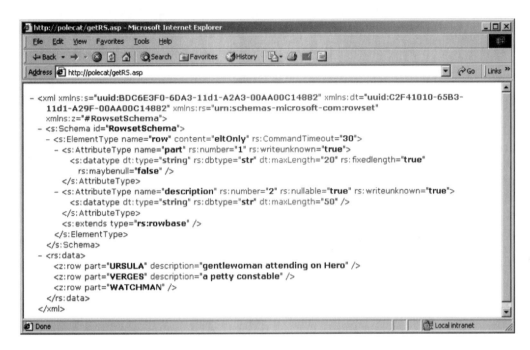

Figure 7-9. IE5 displaying an ADO Recordset as XML

This example actually achieves rather more than just demonstrating IE5's ability to render raw XML. One example of the power of persistence is that a standard VB program can access this Recordset across the Web, as shown here:

```
Dim rs As New Recordset

rs.Open "http://polecat/getRS.asp"
While Not rs.EOF
  Print rs!part, rs!Description
  rs.MoveNext
Wend
```

This prints

URSULA	gentlewoman attending on Hero
VERGES	a petty constable
WATCHMAN	Null

Persisting with a PropertyBag

PropertyBags use the IPersistStream form of Recordset persistence, and therefore, work slightly differently than rs.Save and IStream. Most VB programmers who have written ActiveX controls are familiar with PropertyBags because they are used to pass information about properties between controls and their containers. For example, when a VB Form writes its controls' properties to an .frm file, it uses PropertyBags to get the property values from each individual control, and it then writes into the file. If you have ever inspected an .frm file, you'll know how this looks.

PropertyBags can also be used in other situations in which it's desirable to turn an object into a persistable form. VB6 introduced a new Persistable property on all Public classes, which allows objects to write themselves into PropertyBags and to be re-created from a PropertyBag. When you set the Persistable property on a VB class, VB adds the IPersistStream interface to the class, and provides some additional events that can be used to decide which properties to persist. Because ADO Recordsets already support IPersistStream, they have built-in the ability to write themselves to a PropertyBag.

The following code can be used to make a carbon copy of a Recordset. It's the PropertyBag equivalent of the Stream-based copy program shown previously:

```
Dim rs As New Recordset
Dim rsCopy As Recordset
Dim oBag As New PropertyBag
rs.CursorLocation = adUseClient
rs.ActiveConnection = "File Name=c:\MuchADO.udl"
rs.Open "select * from parts"
Debug.Print "Records before filter", rs.RecordCount
rs.Filter = "description = Null"          ◄───────────  apply a Filter to rs
Debug.Print "Records after filter", rs.RecordCount
oBag.WriteProperty "RS", rs
rs.Close
Set rs = Nothing               ◄───────────────────  release rs
set rsCopy = oBag.ReadProperty("RS")  ◄───────────  create a new Recordset
Debug.Print "Records in Copy", rsCopy.RecordCount    from the PropertyBag
```

It prints

```
Records before filter     27
Records after filter      7
Records in Copy           27
```

In this code, `oBag.WriteProperty` is used to persist `rs` into the Property-Bag. Anything written into a PropertyBag is given a property name which can be used to extract it later. In this case, the property name is `"RS"`.

You can extract the contents of a PropertyBag by using its Contents property. This returns a byte array, which can be written to a file, saved in a database, or used in some other way that is to your liking.[36] You can then reassign this array to the Contents property of a new PropertyBag and re-create a copy of the original object. This is a very convenient and easy way to move any persistable object around.

In our case, we are simply using the `ReadProperty` method of the PropertyBag to re-create a copy of the original Recordset and assign it to `rsCopy`. In this sense, `oBag.ReadProperty` is acting rather like the New statement or CreateObject function, except that instead of creating a new but uninitialized object, it returns one already populated with the data stored in the PropertyBag.

As an alternative to

```
set rsCopy = oBag.ReadProperty("RS")
```

the following code could be used to achieve the same effect:

```
Set rsCopy = New Recordset
rsCopy.Open oBag.ReadProperty("RS")
```

This shows just how versatile rs.Open has become!

It's worth making a few comparisons between the use of PropertyBags and Streams:

1. Streams give you a choice of persistence formats. The PropertyBag approach does not support XML.

2. PropertyBags can be used in situations where ADO 2.5 is not available.

3. A Stream is an ADO object, while a PropertyBag is a generic COM facility for persisting objects. In addition to storing an object's contents, a PropertyBag also stores the object's ClassID (or GUID) in its Contents property. This is what allows the ReadProperty method to know what type of object to create.

4. When you write a Recordset to a PropertyBag, the Filter property does not apply.[37]

---

36. However, I won't show you what it looks like. It's a byte array and not very pretty.

37. This may just remind you of what happens when Recordsets are marshalled.

Persisting with an MSMQ Message Body

It isn't the purpose of this book to describe Microsoft Message Queue. The next few paragraphs are strictly for MSMQ users.

The following sample shows how a Recordset can be persisted directly onto the body of an MSMQ Message. The code assumes the existence of an open Queue object called oQueue, representing a physical queue managed by MSMQ.

```
Dim rs As New Recordset
Dim oMessage As New MSMQMessage

rs.CursorLocation = adUseClient
rs.ActiveConnection = "File Name=c:\MuchADO.udl"
rs.Open "select * from parts"

oMessage.Body = rs
oMessage.Send oQueue
oMessage.Close
```

A program could re-create this Recordset by reading it from the physical queue using code such as the following, which uses a receiving queue object called oQueue:

```
Dim rs As New Recordset
Dim oMessage As New MSMQMessage

Set oMessage = oQueue.Receive
Set rs = oMessage.Body
oMessage.Close
```

Just like the PropertyBag, the MSMQ Message object exploits the Recordset's implementation of IPersistStream to make this possible.

Explicit Persisting

In ADO, Recordset persistence is achieved using an OLE DB Service Component, which goes by the name of MSPersist. While it usually does its work behind the scenes, it's possible to use it explicitly.

For example, the following three code segments all open a Recordset previously persisted into a file called words.rs using rs.Save:

```
Dim rs As New Recordset
rs.ActiveConnection = "Provider=MSPersist"
rs.Open "d:\adobook\data\words.rs"
Print rs.RecordCount
```

adCmdFile **can be used in the** Options **argument of** rs.Open

```
Dim rs As New Recordset
rs.Open "d:\adobook\data\words.rs", , , , adCmdFile
Print rs.RecordCount
```

```
Dim rs As New Recordset
rs.Open "d:\adobook\data\words.rs"
Print rs.RecordCount
```

All of these code segments print

```
11385
```

The first two code segments are kind enough to provide ADO with a clue to their intentions.

In This Section

We considered Recordset persistence. The ability to persist objects (including Recordsets) opens up many design possibilities, and ADO has provided two techniques for persisting Recordsets. Traditionally, Recordsets have supported the COM IPersistStream interface, which (for example) has allowed Recordsets to be persisted to PropertyBags and MSMQ Message Bodies. More recently, support for IStream has been added, and Recordsets can be persisted using the Save method to ADO Streams and other IStream-capable sources, in either XML or the ADTG format.

Summary

This chapter has addressed disconnected Recordsets and the related topics of:

- Batch updating

- N-tier design

- Marshalling

- Persistence

It pulled together many of the different strands of ADO we've been pursuing in recent chapters, and highlighted the features of ADO that make it such a central part of Microsoft's vision for distributed and Web-based systems.

We've seen that ADO:

- Is much more than a data access technique.

- Is much more suited to modern software requirements than its predecessors, such as DAO and RDO.

- Makes it possible to use traditional user interface designs based on data binding in an n-tier world where client programs don't have access to data sources.

- Allows stored procedures to be used with disconnected Recordsets.

- Is at home in the world of distributed computing.

It's easy to be overwhelmed by the features available for disconnected Recordsets or to become disappointed that favored techniques such as stored procedures don't appear to have a place in the n-tier model based on ADO. Neither of these factors should be a concern. While the facilities for pre- and postprocessing batch updates are indeed complex, it isn't essential to employ them in most cases. Simple validation and an error model based on transactional processing is all that is required. While ADO exploits SQL to make our lives considerably easier when batch updating, we can at all times override the SQL behavior should we have the need to employ stored procedures.

In many ways, this chapter has told only half the story. While the techniques described can be used simply as a way to create VB programs, their real home is as part of Microsoft's DNA or DNA 2000 application architecture. In Chapter 14, we'll explore how ADO fits in with MTS and COM+. It's hard to begin looking at these topics without the background we've covered in this chapter. Once these ideas feel comfortable, the brave new world of distributed computing will appear much less daunting.

CHAPTER 8

Recordset Recursion and Data Shaping

The Idea of Data Shaping

Creating the Connection String

Relation-based Hierarchies

Extending and Fabricating Recordsets Using Data Shaping

Parameterized Data Shaping

Group-based Hierarchies

Summary

As ADO HAS MATURED, it has expanded its range to include models of data that it originally could not represent. Early versions of ADO presented all data in the form of tabular Recordsets. While it was possible for Providers to stretch the tabular model by placing compound data structures such as arrays in a single Recordset cell, ADO Recordsets were pretty much two-dimensional.

The first extension of ADO beyond this model was the introduction of Data Shaping. Its ability to embed Recordsets within Recordsets, popularly known as *hierarchical Recordsets*, is the subject of this chapter. All Data Shaping takes place using the MSDataShape Provider that is a standard part of an ADO installation.

A degree of mystique has developed around Data Shaping, mostly generated by authors who find any syntax that involves more than placing a dot between an object and a property or method name confusing or counterintuitive. We have come to realize that OLE DB Providers can expose command languages of their own making, and the MSDataShape Provider is just one of a growing number of Providers to do so. You'll see that the syntax of the SHAPE language is far, far simpler than the syntax of SQL, and that while the combinations it supports can result in rather convoluted statements, its very small number of keywords and syntax forms make it easy to learn.

In Chapter 13 you'll also see that VB comes with a built-in wizard for creating MSDataShape commands, so there is little excuse for not embracing this technology, especially as a number of user interface components, including the VB6 Report Designer and the Hierarchical FlexGrid control, have been created to exploit it.

The major challenge presented by Data Shaping is to learn when it's applicable and what it gives us that is new. The answer to both of these questions arises from the main purpose of Data Shaping, which is to take two or more logically tabular structures and combine them into a single Recordset that maintains the structural relationship between the original sets of data.

If this sounds a little too abstract, think about what happens when you use SQL to execute a standard join. An SQL join takes two or more logically tabular structures (for example, records from two tables), and as a result of combining them, flattens them into a single tabular structure. This is what joins are meant to do, and often it's exactly what we want. In contrast, Data Shaping doesn't flatten the data sets it combines. Instead, it maintains their hierarchical relationship (assuming they have one). When this is what we want, it's time to use Data Shaping.

The Idea of Data Shaping

Data Shaping allows you to create two types of Recordset hierarchies:

- *Relation-based hierarchy*: Two Recordsets that share a common key are formed into a parent-child hierarchy indexed on that key.

- *Group-based hierarchy*: One Recordset becomes a child of its own aggregated data. In other words, you can view its totals, averages, and other statistics at one level, and drill down to see the base data when required.

These two basic types of hierarchies can be combined with each other or with themselves to create sophisticated drill-down structures. Relation-based hierarchies can be parameterized, which causes data lower down in the hierarchy to be retrieved on an "as needed" basis. This is particularly useful when creating deeply nested hierarchies of the type that might be used in a management information system.

All Recordsets created using the MSDataShape Provider have client-side cursors. Hierarchical Recordsets can be updateable, with updates supported at any level in the hierarchy. While this sounds a bit magical, once you have seen how a hierarchical Recordset is constructed, you'll see exactly how updating works.

One easy way to visualize how Data Shaping works is to simulate a hier-archical Recordset using regular ADO techniques. Consider the following two Recordsets:

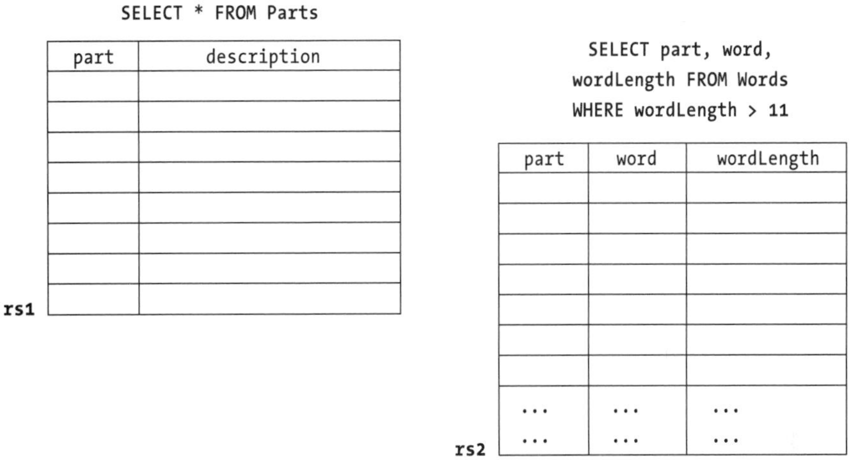

SELECT * FROM Parts

part	description

rs1

SELECT part, word,
wordLength FROM Words
WHERE wordLength > 11

part	word	wordLength
...	...	...
...	...	...

rs2

Figure 8-1. Simulating Data Shaping using regular Recordsets

Now consider using the rs1_MoveComplete event to set a filter on rs2 so that the only records visible in rs2 are those that have the same "part" field as the currently selected record in rs1. Here's the code that would achieve this:

```
Dim cn As New Connection
Dim WithEvents rs1 As Recordset
Dim rs2 As Recordset

Private Sub cmdFilter_Click()

cn.CursorLocation = adUseClient        ◄──────────  use client-side cursors
cn.Open "File Name=c:\MuchADO.udl"
Set rs1 = cn.Execute("SELECT * from Parts")
Set rs2 = cn.Execute("SELECT part, word, wordLength " & _
                "FROM Words WHERE  wordLength > 11")
rs2("part").Properties("OPTIMIZE") = True
                                  ▲            build an index on the
                                  └──────────  part field of rs2
End Sub
```

289

```
Private Sub rs1_MoveComplete( _
        ByVal adReason As ADODB.EventReasonEnum, _
        ByVal pError As ADODB.Error, _
        adStatus As ADODB.EventStatusEnum, _
        ByVal pRecordset As ADODB.Recordset)
rs2.Filter = "part = '" & rs1!part & "'"
End Sub
```
← `filter rs2 according to`
`the current record in rs1`

This is a pretty good simulation of a simple relation-based hierarchy. You could bind these two Recordsets to two Data Grid Controls using two ADO Data Controls, and create a display such as this:[1]

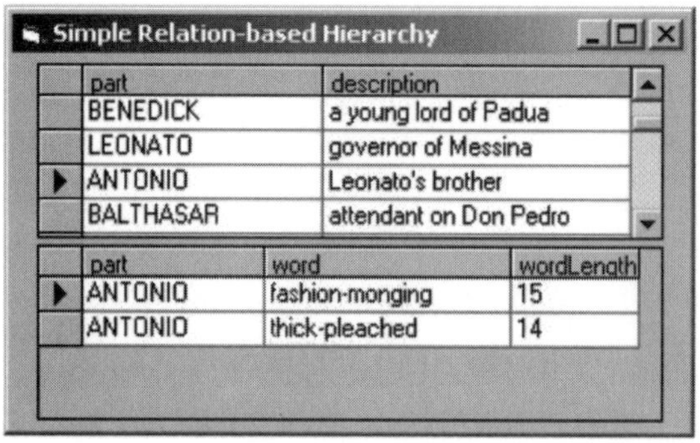

Figure 8-2: Form displaying simulated Data Shaping

Clicking a row in the upper grid (rs1) causes the lower grid (rs2) to display the big words of the selected part. For the sake of completeness, here's the binding code for four appropriately named controls:

```
Set dgRS1.DataSource = adcRS1
Set dgRS2.DataSource = adcRS2
Set adcRS1.Recordset = rs1
Set adcRS2.Recordset = rs2
```
← `bind the Data Grids to`
`the Data Controls`

← `bind the Recordsets to`
`the Data Controls`

Now that you have seen how to simulate Data Shaping, it's time to look at the real thing, and make use of the MSDataShape Provider. When you use Data Shaping to create a hierarchical Recordset based on the two previous queries, the resulting structure looks like this:

---

1. Which shows that Antonio can only construct long words by applying some blatantly thick-pleased fashion-monging.

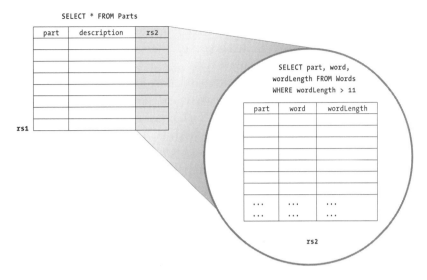

Figure 8-3. Structures created by a Data Shaping command linking two simple Recordsets

What is happening here is that MSDataShape creates the two Recordsets based on a single command that contains both SQL statements, along with a relationship statement that links the part fields in the two Recordsets. MSDataShape automatically indexes the part field in the child Recordset (rs2), and then appends a new field onto the parent Recordset (rs1) with a name of your choice (which in this case is "rs2").

This appended rs2 field has a data type of adChapter. A *chapter* is a subset of records from the child Recordset that relate to a single record in the parent Recordset. If you printed the chapters for each record in the parent Recordset, you would print the entire child Recordset, or at least all those records in the child for which a related record exists in the parent.

However, the child Recordset always has a filter applied to it, based on the value of the part column in the parent Recordset. This filter makes it look as though there is a different child Recordset associated with each record in the parent Recordset, when in reality, there is only one child Recordset. Regardless of the record you are positioned on in the parent, the Chapter-type Field always exposes the corresponding records in the child according to the defined relationship. The filter is internal to the hierarchical Recordset, and so it can't be modified using rs.Filter (which leaves rs.Filter free to be used to create subsets of the currently visible child records).

Assuming the resulting hierarchical Recordset has been assigned to rs1, the following code would access the (filtered) child Recordset for the current parent record:

```
Dim rs2 as Recordset
Set rs2 = rs1("rs2").Value
```

Now rs2 can be used like a regular Recordset (because it is one). Note that it's important to use .Value explicitly, because otherwise, VB would attempt to assign a Field object to a Recordset variable, which would result in a type mismatch error.

To manipulate all the data in this hierarchical Recordset, you need to know about its hierarchy so that you can use the Chapter-type Field to drill down to the detail. The hierarchical Recordset maintains the natural relationship between the two Recordsets, whereas a standard SQL join flattens the resulting data, destroying the natural relationship. In cases where it makes sense to maintain this relationship, the Data Shaping approach is often a better way to manage the data than using an SQL join. The scenario just discussed provides a good example. It's a master-detail relationship, and making the relationship explicit is a positive advantage.[2]

You could retrieve the same data using a standard SQL join, as follows:

```
SELECT P.part, P.description, W.word, W.wordLength
FROM Parts P,Words W
WHERE  W.wordLength > 11
AND P.part = W.part
```

The natural structure of the resulting Recordset is the standard, flat, tabular form. It isn't very easy to present this representation of the data in a master-detail style of user interface.

However, consider which approach is the most convenient if the user wants to list all the big words from the play and the parts that are responsible for speaking them. Given this requirement, the flat structure represented by the join is more appropriate. The user may want to be able to sort all the big words alphabetically, for example. This won't be possible using the hierarchical Recordset because the child Recordset (which contains all the Words) is always filtered by the parent (which is based on Parts). Of course, you could always reverse the relationship and make the Parts query into a child of the Words query. This means that you would have to drill down just to see the single part description for the current word, which is an unnecessary complexity. For this type of usage, the hierarchy just gets in the way.

Data Shaping is not a replacement for joins. It's an alternative to be used when it makes sense to preserve and exploit the natural relationship between two sets of data. It so happens that this is often exactly what you want to do. You'll also see that it can do things that are very awkward to do using standard SQL.[3]

---

2. In Chapter 13 you'll see how both the VB6 Data Environment and the Microsoft Hierarchical FlexGrid make the task of creating user interfaces that reflect this hierarchical relationship almost trivial.

3. At the same time, there are things you can do in SQL that can't be done by Data Shaping. One example is an outer join.

One final point worth noting from the previous comparison of a joined and a hierarchical Recordset is that in the joined Recordset, the description column appears in every record, whereas in the hierarchical Recordset, it appears only once for each part rather than once for each word. In some cases, the hierarchical approach can be more efficient because it involves less duplication of data, although this fact is balanced by the need to issue two SQL statements to the database instead of one.

The beauty of the hierarchical approach becomes clear when you start creating more complex structures of Recordsets. For example, a single command (and therefore a single Recordset variable) can provide access to the following type of structure:

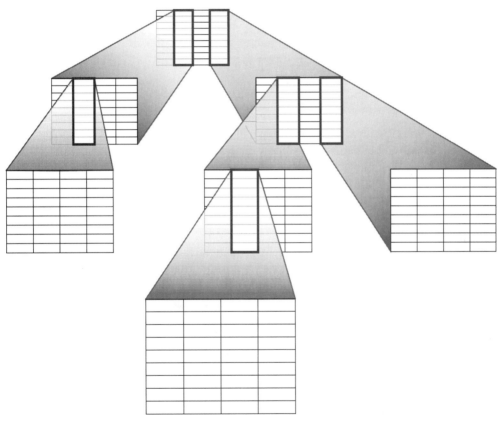

Figure 8-4. A single hierarchical Recordset can represent a complex data structure.

By passing an appropriate command to MSDataShape, it will execute the seven embedded commands required to construct this structure, build and index seven client-side Recordsets, and append six Chapter-type Fields to four Recordsets. The entire data structure can be held in memory for highly responsive drill-down and disconnected or persisted efficiently as a single structure.

Alternatively, a parameterized approach can be taken, in which case MSDataShape only builds the parent Recordset and the children are constructed as needed on a chapter-by-chapter basis. This type of hierarchy can't be disconnected (for obvious reasons), but it requires less memory and takes less time to create initially.

Either way, changes made by users at any level in the hierarchy are automatically saved back to the data source, using standard client-side modification techniques on the appropriate Recordset.

You have seen how you can *almost* simulate relation-based hierarchies by using filters. However, the standard model provided by Data Shaping is more convenient, more amenable to standard processing and data binding techniques, and provides the added power of being able to parameterize child Recordsets to provide "just-in-time" data retrieval, which is highly appropriate for larger, connected hierarchical Recordsets. We'll look at group-based hierarchies later in the chapter.

In This Section

We examined how hierarchical Recordsets are constructed, and we compared the hierarchical approach to a more traditional type of query such as an SQL join.

Creating the Connection String

We discussed the *idea* of hierarchical Recordsets in the last section. Let's now go about creating them.

The first challenge is to create the required Connection object. The Provider name for Data Shaping is always MSDataShape. The issue here is that MSDataShape doesn't have any data of its own—it merely provides a service based on Recordsets retrieved from somewhere else. Therefore, as part of the connection process, we have to tell MSDataShape about the Provider that will be used to source the data.

There are several ways of doing this, and fortunately, all of them are simple. Here's some code for one such option:

```
Dim cn As New Connection
cn.Provider = "MSDataShape"
cn.Properties("Data Provider") = "SQLOLEDB"
cn.Properties("Data Source") = "POLECAT"
cn.Properties("Initial Catalog") = "MuchADO"
cn.Open , "sa", ""
```

use the Data Provider property to set the underlying Provider name

Any reasonable combination of dynamic properties, connection string key-value pairs, and cn.Open arguments can be used. The key points are to make the Provider MSDataShape, use the Data Provider dynamic property to set the underlying data source, and set all other required Data Provider properties as though they were properties of MSDataShape. MSDataShape will then forward these on to the Data Provider.

You can also use the Data Link Properties window to create a .udl file. The following steps explain how:

1. Select MSDataShape in the Provider tab.

2. Select the All tab. Double-click the Data Provider property and set the appropriate Data Provider name (or leave MSDASQL as the default, if appropriate).

3. Either fill in the remaining properties as you normally would if the Data Provider were the Provider, or fill in the remaining properties via the All tab.

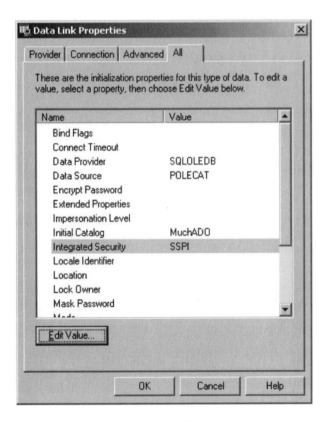

Figure 8-5. Configuring a .udl file for the MSDataShape

As soon as you open a Connection to MSDataShape, a connection to the Data Provider is created, and it's kept open until the MSDataShape connection is closed or released. You can therefore apply the same connection management and pooling rules to an MSDataShape connection as you would to the underlying Data Provider.

In This Section

We saw how to create a connection to MSDataShape and configure the Data Provider.

Relation-based Hierarchies

Now that we have a connection, we can start looking at the SHAPE language.

The basic form of a SHAPE command for creating a relation-based hierarchy is this:

```
SHAPE {<parent-command>}
    APPEND ({<child-command>}
        RELATE field TO field
        )
```

MSDataShape doesn't care about the command substrings within the curly brackets. It simply lifts them out of the command and fires them separately at the Data Provider. The APPEND statement has two parts, both contained within parentheses. The first is the child command. The second is a RELATE statement, which identifies the fields in the parent Recordset and the child Recordset that are linked. The field names don't need to be the same, but the data types must correspond. There can be multiple pairs of related fields for a "compound key."

As you have seen, MSDataShape will use the child field to index the child Recordset, and it will use the parent field to build the internal filter on the child Recordset, based on comparing the parent field to the child field. It will also append a Chapter-type column to the parent Recordset with the default name "Chapter1".

This is a very simple syntax, wrapped around some command strings embedded in curly brackets. It's common to give names or aliases to each Recordset, which makes the overall command string clearer to follow, if more verbose. Here's the general form with aliases:

```
SHAPE {<parent-command>} as ParentName
    APPEND ({<child-command>} as ChildName
            RELATE field TO field
            ) As ChapterFieldName
```

With this form, it becomes possible to identify the individual Recordsets by name, and you'll see how these names can be used shortly. By placing a ChapterFieldName after the APPEND statement, you can override the default name allocated to the Chapter-type Field with your own name. If you don't provide a ChapterFieldName, but do provide a ChildName, this ChildName will be used as the ChapterFieldName.

Here then, is some code using an actual SHAPE command, using the same SQL queries that were used in the Data Shaping simulation presented earlier in the chapter:

```
Dim sCommand As String
Dim rs As New Recordset
Dim cn As New Connection

cn.Open "File Name=c:\shape.udl"
sCommand = "SHAPE {SELECT * FROM Parts}" & _
              "APPEND ({SELECT part, word, wordLength " & _
                       "FROM Words WHERE  wordLength > 11 }" & _
              "RELATE part TO part ) As Words"

rs.Open sCommand, cn
```

This code creates a hierarchical Recordset, but it doesn't do anything with it. We could assign it to the Recordset property of a Microsoft Hierarchical FlexGrid (HFlexGrid) control (covered in Chapter 12), in which case we might end up with a display that looks like Figure 8-6.

There you can see the two Fields from the parent Recordset, and the three Fields from the child Recordset. The key to understanding this screen is to look at the left-most grid column, containing the + and – boxes. A + box is used to expand the parent record to show the child records (and therefore indicates that the child records are not currently being shown). A – box can be used to collapse a currently expanded parent to remove the child records from the display. A parent record that doesn't have a box has no child records.

We'll look at two ways of processing this Recordset in code. The first technique will be specific to this particular Recordset. The second technique is a generic version of the first technique, and can be used to navigate the structure of any hierarchical Recordset.

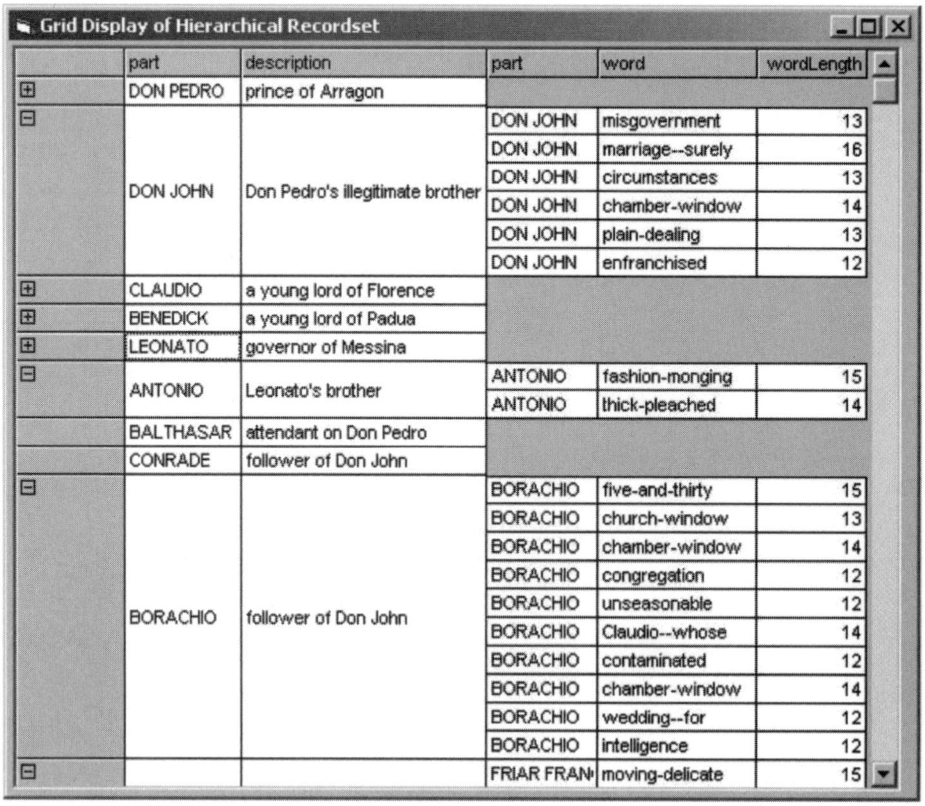

	part	description	part	word	wordLength
⊞	DON PEDRO	prince of Arragon			
⊟	DON JOHN	Don Pedro's illegitimate brother	DON JOHN	misgovernment	13
			DON JOHN	marriage--surely	16
			DON JOHN	circumstances	13
			DON JOHN	chamber-window	14
			DON JOHN	plain-dealing	13
			DON JOHN	enfranchised	12
⊞	CLAUDIO	a young lord of Florence			
⊞	BENEDICK	a young lord of Padua			
⊞	LEONATO	governor of Messina			
⊟	ANTONIO	Leonato's brother	ANTONIO	fashion-monging	15
			ANTONIO	thick-pleached	14
	BALTHASAR	attendant on Don Pedro			
	CONRADE	follower of Don John			
⊟	BORACHIO	follower of Don John	BORACHIO	five-and-thirty	15
			BORACHIO	church-window	13
			BORACHIO	chamber-window	14
			BORACHIO	congregation	12
			BORACHIO	unseasonable	12
			BORACHIO	Claudio--whose	14
			BORACHIO	contaminated	12
			BORACHIO	chamber-window	14
			BORACHIO	wedding--for	12
			BORACHIO	intelligence	12
⊟			FRIAR FRAN	moving-delicate	15

Figure 8-6. Relation-based hierarchy in an HFlexGrid

Hierarchical Recordset Navigation

Here's the code for the first technique, which relies on the knowledge that the "Words" column in rs is a Chapter-type Field providing filtered access to the child Recordset:

```
Public Sub printHRS(rs As Recordset)
If Not rs.EOF Then Set rsChild = rs("Words").Value
While Not rs.EOF
  Print rs("part"), rs("Description")
  While Not rsChild.EOF
     Print vbTab, rsChild("word"), rsChild("wordLength")
     rsChild.MoveNext
  Wend
  rs.MoveNext
Wend
End Sub
```

get hold of the child Recordset from the Chapter-type Field called Words

Here are selected highlights from its output:

```
DON PEDRO                    Tarragon
                Transgression           13
                pleasant-spirited       17
                unhopefullest           13

                . . .
                chamber-window          14
DON JOHN              Don Pedro's bastard brother
                Marriage--surely        16
                circumstances           13
                chamber-window          14
                misgovernment           13
                plain-dealing           13
                enfranchised            12

. . .
ANTONIO                  Leonato's brother
                thick-pleached          14
                fashion-monging         15
BALTHASAR             attendant on Don Pedro
CONRADE              follower of Don John
BORACHIO             follower of Don Corleone
                Unseasonable            12
. . . etc
```

Note that the rsChild variable was assigned only once. It would have been possible to set it inside the loop for each record, but it was done outside the loop to emphasize the way that chapters work. There is only one child Recordset, and its internal filter is updated automatically whenever the parent Recordset's current record changes. This process makes sure that the correct chapter for the current parent record is always exposed.

rs.StayInSync

While the process of updating the internal filter is automatic, it isn't forced upon you. You can switch this process off by setting the rs.StayInSync property to False. If rs.StayInSync is True, then any references you obtain to children of rs will be kept synchronized as rs is navigated. If rs.StayInSync is False, then any references to child Recordsets will keep the internal filter that applied when the reference was obtained.[4]

This means that if the rs.StayInSync setting is important to you, you should set it before obtaining any child references. By default, rs.StayInSync

---

4. It may help to think of the child reference you obtain as being a clone of the child Recordset maintained by the Chapter-type Field. If rs.StayInSync is True, rs keeps the Filter property on your child Recordset updated as rs is navigated. If rs.StayInSync is False, it leaves the clone alone (isn't that the name of a movie?).

is True, and this is almost always how you'll want it. However, there are occasions when you'll want the child records you are looking at to stay constant, regardless of what is happening to the parent.

As an example of using rs.StayInSync, if I introduce

```
rs.StayInSync = False
```

as the first line in printHRS (before the rsChild reference is obtained), it prints the following:

```
DON PEDRO                        Prince of Arragon
                  Transgression                13
                  pleasant-spirited            17
                  unhopefullest                13

                  . . .
                  chamber-window               14
DON JOHN                    Don Pedro's bastard brother

. . .
ANTONIO                     Leonato's brother
BALTHASAR                   attendant on Don Pedro
. . . etc
```

At first sight, this doesn't make sense, as it looks like all the child records have disappeared, except for DON PEDRO's. You were probably expecting to see DON PEDRO's big words appear after each parent record. If you were, your thinking was correct, but referring back to the code will pay dividends. With rs.StayInSync set to False, moving on to DON JOHN has no effect on rsChild—and that is exactly the point. The cursor is still at the end of the Recordset, and so no further child record printing will occur before a Move* operation on rsChild resets the Recordset cursor.

Generic Hierarchical Recordset Navigation

In about as many lines as it took to write printHRS, it's possible to write a completely generic procedure that will print any hierarchical Recordset, regardless of the number and arrangement of children. This code relies on identifying the adChapter data type and calling itself recursively when it finds a chapter. Here it is:

```
Public Sub printHRS1(    rs As Recordset, _
                    Optional iLevel As Integer)
Dim fd As Field
```

print an indent based on the depth (level) of rs in the hierarchy

```
While Not rs.EOF
  If iLevel > 0 Then Print String(iLevel, vbTab),
  For Each fd In rs.Fields
   If fd.Type = adChapter Then
      Print
      printHRS1 fd.Value, iLevel + 1
    Else
      Print fd.Value,
   End If
  Next
  Print
  rs.MoveNext
Wend
End Sub
```

printHRS1 calls itself recursively when a Chapter-type Field is identified, passing in the child Recordset and incrementing the level

Recursion was made for traversing generalized tree structures, and it's completely at home with hierarchical Recordsets. Note that setting rs.StayInSync won't affect this procedure, as a new child reference is acquired with a new filter setting each time it's needed.

Updating Hierarchical Recordsets

As long as you remember that MSDataShape creates separate Recordsets for each SQL statement embedded within the SHAPE command, and that all Recordsets built using MSDataShape have client-side cursors, then it's fairly easy to understand the mechanics of inserts, deletes, and updates performed through hierarchical Recordsets.

However deep you are in a Recordset hierarchy, you are always operating on a straightforward Recordset. Your main responsibility is to make sure you create the Recordset using an optimistic or batch optimistic lock type. However, the following observations apply:

1. Calling transactional methods on the MSDataShape Provider results in the method calls being passed on to the Data Provider— so it's business as usual with transactions.

2. rs.Update statements apply individually to each internal Recordset.

3. rs.UpdateBatch statements also apply individually to each internal Recordset. To cause all internal Recordsets to be batch updated together, it's necessary to visit each Recordset in turn and call rs.UpdateBatch. This is readily achieved using a recursive function called within a transaction. We've already seen how recursive code can traverse through a hierarchical Recordset. The AffectRecords argument of rs.UpdateBatch can take a value of adAffectAllChapters, and it's important to use this value when batch updating child Recordsets. If you don't, then only records in the current chapter (that is, those identified by the internal filter) will be updated.

4. If the hierarchical Recordset has been disconnected (for example, if it has been marshalled between a client and server process), each internal Recordset should be separately reconnected to MSDataShape with the required Data Provider settings, before attempting any updates.[5] When disconnecting a hierarchical Recordset, you need to disconnect each Recordset individually.

Let's look at an example. You may have noticed from the results shown previously that DON JOHN's longest word ("marriage--surely") is a bit of a cheat—it's really two words joined together by a pair of dashes. You may also have noticed that his relationship with DON PEDRO is defined in rather stark terms. The following code addresses both these points by making changes at two levels in the hierarchy using batch updating:

```
Dim sCommand As String
Dim rs As New Recordset
Dim rsChild As Recordset
Dim cn As New Connection
```

Same command as before.

```
cn.Open "File Name=c:\shape.udl"
sCommand = "SHAPE {SELECT * FROM Parts} " & _
             "APPEND ({SELECT part, word, wordLength " & _
                    "FROM Words WHERE  wordLength > 11 } " & _
             "RELATE part TO part) As Words "
```

```
n sCommand, cn, , adLockBatchOptimistic      ◄──────  Set the LockType.
Child = rs("Words").Value
d "part = 'DON JOHN'"    ◄─────────────
rsChild.Find "word like 'marr*'"
```

Locate DON JOHN in the parent. Doing so sets the Chapter in the child so that the offending word can be identified.

---

5. It's currently possible to perform updates with only the parent Recordset connected, but this is acknowledged as a bug by Microsoft, and you should not rely on it.

```
cn.BeginTrans
rs!Description = "Don Pedro's illegitimate brother"
rsChild!word = "surely"
rsChild!wordLength = 6
rs.UpdateBatch
rsChild.UpdateBatch adAffectAllChapters
cn.CommitTrans
```

← Perform the batch updates and commit.

This example also shows how to use batch updating on a connected Recordset. Even if disconnected Recordsets aren't appropriate, batch updating provides a convenient way to ensure that all changes made by a user are handled as part of the same transaction, without needing to keep a transaction open for a long period of time.

I used an ODBC-based connection and traced the activity. Here's the SQL generated by the two batch statements:

```
UPDATE "Parts" SET "description"=?
        WHERE "part"=? AND "description"=?
UPDATE "Words" SET "word"=?,"wordLength"=?
        WHERE "word"=? AND "wordLength"=? AND "id"=?
```

This is business as usual for client-side cursor updates. Note that for the child Recordset, SQLServer has silently included the primary key as a hidden column so that it can be used to generate updates correctly. As we have previously discussed, if your Provider doesn't support hidden columns, you'll need to make sure the primary key is part of the Recordset for updates to work effectively.

Creating Complex Shapes Using Reshaping

MSDataShape remembers that each parent and child Recordset that is created on a live Connection object. This means that if you give a name or alias to the Recordset inside the SHAPE command string, you can reuse that Recordset by referring to it by name in a later SHAPE command. This has benefits for both performance and complexity management. This process of reusing a previously shaped Recordset in a new SHAPE command is called *Reshaping*.

You can also programmatically identify a shaped Recordset by examining its Reshape Name dynamic property. You can't write to this property directly because it is under the control of MSDataShape, but it can be used as you traverse a hierarchical Recordset to identify a particular child by name.

To explore these ideas with a more complex hierarchy, consider a hierarchical Recordset with the following overall structure:

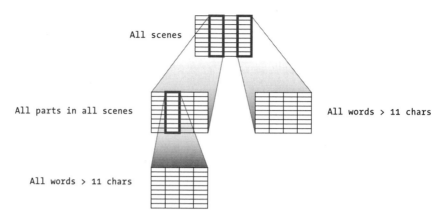

All scenes

All parts in all scenes

All words > 11 chars

All words > 11 chars

Figure 8-7: A hierarchical Recordset before Reshaping

This hierarchy will allow you to start looking at scenes. You can either drill down and see all the parts in each scene and then drill down again to see all the big words for each part (by part, rather than scene), or look at all the big words organized by scene.

This stretches the SHAPE language a good bit further than we have done so far, as it involves appending two children to a parent, and appending a grandchild to one of those children. The resulting SHAPE command does look complex, but it follows a regular syntax pattern. Also, we'll see how using Naming and Reshaping allows us to manage the complexity.

Here's the SHAPE command:

```
SHAPE {SELECT * FROM Scenes}
    APPEND
      ((SHAPE{SELECT DISTINCT P.part, W.act, W.Scene
          FROM Parts P, Words W WHERE P.part = W.part}
            APPEND ({SELECT * FROM Words WHERE worLdLength > 11}
                  RELATE part to part))
          RELATE act to act, scene to scene),
      ({SELECT * FROM Words WHERE  wordLength > 11}
          RELATE act to act, scene to scene)
```

children to append

grandchild to append

And here's the single SQL statement that results from executing the preceding code:

```
SELECT * FROM Scenes;SELECT DISTINCT P.part, W.act, W.Scene FROM Parts P,
Words W WHERE P.part = W.part;SELECT * FROM Words WHERE wordLength >
11;SELECT * FROM Words WHERE wordLength > 11
```

This compound string is passed as a single request to the Provider. There are two things to note about it. The first is that it contains a join. Joins and shaping can be mixed. The second thing to note is that exactly the same query was executed twice. This is wasteful, and we'll see shortly how to prevent it from happening.

This command becomes much less scary if we build it up in sections. We can start with the query that gets all the big words:

```
SHAPE {SELECT * FROM Words WHERE wordLength > 11} as Words
```

We can create this query as a standalone shaped Recordset. Because we have named the record that this command will generate (we called it Words), we can use its name in place of an embedded command when creating the child Recordset for the "parts in scenes" query:

Words Recordset used to create
child of Parts Recordset

```
SHAPE {SELECT DISTINCT P.part, W.act, W.Scene
      FROM Parts P, Words W WHERE P.part = W.part} as Parts
          APPEND (Words RELATE part to part)
```

We've also named this hierarchical Recordset, calling it Parts. We can use both of these names to create the complete four-Recordset command:

```
SHAPE {SELECT * FROM Scenes}
      APPEND
          (Parts RELATE act to act, scene to scene),
          (Words RELATE act to act, scene to scene)
```

All of this is very unscary indeed. Let's take a look at the complete program that creates this hierarchy:

```
Dim cn As New Connection
Dim rsWords As New Recordset
Dim rsParts As New Recordset
Dim rs As New Recordset
Dim sCommand As String

cn.Open "File Name=c:\Shape.udl"
rsWords.Open "SHAPE {SELECT * FROM Words " & _
             "WHERE  wordLength > 11} as Words", cn
rsParts.Open "SHAPE {SELECT DISTINCT P.part, W.act, W.Scene " & _
             "FROM Parts P, Words W " & _
             "WHERE P.part = W.part}as Parts " & _
             "APPEND (Words RELATE part to part) ", cn
```

```
sCommand = "SHAPE {SELECT * FROM Scenes}  " & _
             "APPEND (Parts RELATE act to act, scene to scene)," & _
             "(Words RELATE act to act, scene to scene)"

rs.Open sCommand, cn
```

Now that we've created this complex hierarchy, it's time to do some things with it. For example, we can traverse through all its individual Recordsets and print out their names and record counts using the following recursive program:

```
Public Sub traverse(rs As Recordset, Optional iLevel As Integer)
Dim fd As Field
If iLevel > 0 Then Print String(iLevel, vbTab),
Print rs.Properties("Reshape Name"), rs.RecordCount
For Each fd In rs.Fields
  If fd.Type = adChapter Then
      traverse rs(fd.Name).Value, iLevel + 1
  End If
Next
End Sub
```

With the exception of the parent Recordset, the output of this routine will vary depending on the current record, because the current record determines the size of each chapter in a chapter field. Here's the output of passing rs to traverse, with each internal Recordset pointing at its first record:

```
DSRowset1        16
      Parts           8
           Words          7
      Words           7
```

It's pure coincidence that both uses of the Words Recordset report the same record count. As proof, here's the printout after moving to the third row:

```
DSRowset1        16
      Parts          12
           Words         19
      Words          18
```

What's interesting is that there are only three physical Recordset structures created for this command. The following listing shows the SQL generated when executing the preceding code. Each statement was executed separately by MSDataShape.

```
SELECT * FROM Words WHERE  wordLength > 11
SELECT DISTINCT P.part, W.act, W.Scene
       FROM Parts P, Words W WHERE P.part = W.part
SELECT * FROM Scenes
```

The SQL shows us that there is only one physical Recordset providing the Word data. But the hierarchy contains Words Recordsets that have different record counts. How do we make sense of this? Once again, what we've previously learned about Clones may help here. We know that it's possible to maintain two different views of the same physical data using Clones, which is exactly what is happening in this hierarchical Recordset, where we have two separate representations of the same Words data.

Reshaping is a great way of simplifying the construction of complex hierarchies. However, the following limitations should be borne in mind:

- You have to keep the Recordsets and the Connection open if MSDataShape is to remember existing Recordset names.

- You can't use one Connection to reshape Recordsets created with another.

- You can't Append children onto an existing shaped Recordset, so you can't reuse any Recordset as a parent.

- You can't Reshape parameterized Recordsets.

Chapterless Child Recordsets

There are times when you might want to perform an operation on all chapters within a child Recordset. This can easily be achieved by Reshaping a named Recordset. For example, this code:

```
Dim rsChild As New Recordset
rsChild.Open "SHAPE Words", cn
```

will extract a child Recordset named Words from a hierarchical Recordset, and provide access to all its records.

Avoiding Command Objects

Unless instructed otherwise, MSDataShape uses Command objects to execute the commands within curly brackets. If you are working with a Provider that doesn't support Command objects, you can avoid them by using the SHAPE language's TABLE keyword. For example, you can replace this statement:

```
SHAPE {SELECT * FROM Scenes}
```

with this one:

```
SHAPE TABLE Scenes
```

This approach can be useful with Simple Providers (see Chapter 11), which don't use Command objects.

In This Section

We looked at relation-based hierarchies in depth. We saw how to use the SHAPE language to create hierarchical Recordsets, and various approaches for navigating them, including the use of recursion. We also explored how to modify hierarchical Recordsets, which can be done at any level in the hierarchy. Finally, we looked at Reshaping and Naming and how these can make our code less complex and more efficient.

Extending and Fabricating Recordsets Using Data Shaping

Once you start becoming comfortable with the basic idea of Data Shaping, some interesting possibilities become apparent. For example, we've seen that the APPEND statement appends new Fields to an existing Recordset. All the Fields we have appended so far have been of type adChapter. However, if we can append one type of Field, then why not another?

There are many times when I want to add Fields to existing Recordsets so that I can add data that may not be in the database and continue to exploit the convenience of working with a single Recordset. While you can do a hatchet job on SQL to simulate additional Fields, they rarely work out the way you want them to, and you know in the back of your mind that what you have done is a bit of a hack.[6]

---

6. It's been fortunate for my career that the back of my mind is not especially smart.

The SHAPE language provides an elegant way to extend existing Recordsets. For example, consider the following syntax:

```
SHAPE {SELECT * FROM Parts}
      APPEND NEW adChar(1) AS sex
```

If this were legal, you would think that this command would create a Recordset based on the Parts table, and extend it by adding a Field called sex. It's legal. You can do it.

The following function returns a disconnected Recordset with a sex Field added to Parts and populated with "F"s or "M"s.

```
Public Function getExtendedParts() As Recordset
Dim rs As New Recordset
Dim cn As New Connection
Dim sCommand As String

cn.Open "File Name=c:\Shape.udl"
sCommand = "SHAPE {SELECT * FROM Parts} " & _
             "APPEND NEW adChar(1) AS sex"

rs.Open sCommand, cn, , adLockOptimistic
While Not rs.EOF
  Select Case Trim(rs!part)
   Case "BEATRICE", "HERO", "MARGARET", "URSULA"
    rs!sex = "F"
   Case Else
    rs!sex = "M"
  End Select
  rs.MoveNext
  Wend
rs.Sort = "sex"          ⟵——————————    sort the Recordset using
Set rs.ActiveConnection = Nothing             the new Field
Set getExtendedParts = rs
End Function
```

Note that I had to make the Recordset updateable in order to be able to populate the new column. To return a read-only Recordset, I would need to make a read-only Clone.

The following code iterates through this Recordset:

```
Dim rs As Recordset
Set rs = getExtendedParts

While Not rs.EOF
  Print rs!part, rs!sex, rs!Description
  rs.MoveNext
Wend
```

and it prints this:

HERO	F	daughter to Leonato
BEATRICE	F	niece to Leonato
MARGARET	F	gentlewoman attending on Hero
URSULA	F	gentlewoman attending on Hero
DON PEDRO	M	prince of Arragon
DON JOHN	M	Don Pedro's illegitimate brother
. . .		

This approach isn't without its limitations. Ideally you would have control over Field attributes and could append populated columns of standard data types to read-only Recordsets, just as you can with chapters. This isn't a replacement to writing your own Providers. However, it's an easy and elegant way to extend an existing Recordset.

Fabricated Hierarchical Recordsets

You don't have to use a Data Provider with MSDataShape. Instead you can create wholly fabricated Recordsets using the same syntax you have just seen for appending new Fields to existing Recordsets, and set the Data Provider to NONE.

In the following example, I decided to enhance my reputation as a stage director and try a Shakespearean tragedy. Not having a handy database, I chose to fabricate a hierarchical Recordset with a parent containing Scene information and a child containing Parts in Scene. Here's the code for creating and populating this Recordset:

```
Dim cn As New Connection
Dim rs As New Recordset
Dim rsChild As Recordset
Dim sCommand As String                          set the Data Provider
Dim vScene As Variant                           to NONE
Dim vPart As Variant
cn.Open "Provider=MSDataShape;Data Provider=NONE;"
```

```
sCommand = _
            "SHAPE APPEND NEW adTinyInt AS act," & _
              " NEW adTinyInt AS scene," & _
              " NEW adVarChar(50) AS description," & _
            " ((SHAPE APPEND NEW adChar(20) AS part," & _
                     " NEW adVarChar(50) AS description," & _
                     " NEW adTinyInt AS act," & _
                     " NEW adTinyInt AS scene) " & _
                " RELATE act TO act, scene TO scene) as Parts"
```

create the
parent
Recordset

append a child Recordset

```
rs.Open sCommand, cn, , adLockBatchOptimistic

vScene = Array("act", "scene", "description")
vPart = Array("part", "description", "act", "scene")

rs.AddNew vScene, Array(1, 1, "An Open Place")
Set rsChild = rs("Parts").Value
With rsChild
 .AddNew vPart, Array("Witch 1", "First Witch", 1, 1)
 .AddNew vPart, Array("Witch 2", "Second Witch", 1, 1)
 .AddNew vPart, Array("Witch 3", "Third Witch", 1, 1)
End With
```

parent requires a
record before you can
access a Field

```
rs.AddNew vScene, Array(1, 2, "A Camp")
With rsChild
 .AddNew vPart, Array("Duncan", "King of Scotland", 1, 2)
 .AddNew vPart, Array("Malcolm", "Duncan's son", 1, 2)
End With
Set HFlex.Recordset = rs
```

which will display

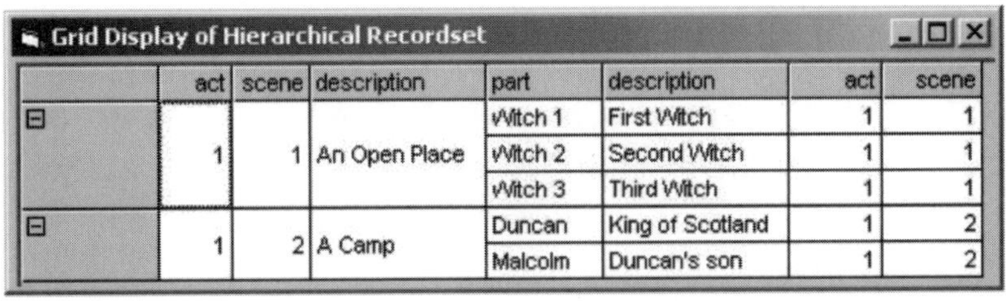

	act	scene	description	part	description	act	scene
⊟				Witch 1	First Witch	1	1
	1	1	An Open Place	Witch 2	Second Witch	1	1
				Witch 3	Third Witch	1	1
⊟				Duncan	King of Scotland	1	2
	1	2	A Camp	Malcolm	Duncan's son	1	2

Figure 8-8. Fabricated hierarchy in an HFlexGrid

Once you have fabricated a hierarchical Recordset, you can do the usual kinds of things with it.

Combining Provider and Fabricated Recordsets

Finally, you can mix Provider-generated and fabricated Recordsets in the same hierarchical Recordset. We'll see this technique in the following code. I need to start casting for *Much ADO about Nothing,* and I have an external source of information about actors who may be suitable for certain parts. I can insert this data as a fabricated Recordset, created as a child of a Recordset based on the Parts table. Here's some code to do this:

```
Dim rs As New Recordset
Dim rsChild As Recordset
Dim cn As New Connection
Dim sCommand As String
Dim vActors As Variant

cn.Open "File Name=c:\Shape.udl"
sCommand = "SHAPE {SELECT * FROM Parts} " & _
           "APPEND ((SHAPE APPEND NEW adChar(20) AS part
                      " NEW adVarChar(50) AS actor," & _
                      " NEW adBoolean AS available," & _
                      " NEW adChar(6) AS price)" & _
                 " RELATE part To part) as actors"
vActors = Array("part", "actor", "available", "price")

rs.Open sCommand, cn, , adLockOptimistic
Set rs.ActiveConnection = Nothing
Set rsChild = rs("actors").Value
With rsChild
  .AddNew vActors, Array("DON PEDRO", "Tom Hanks", False, "high")
  .AddNew vActors, Array("DON PEDRO", "Gary Cornell", True, "low")
  .AddNew vActors, Array("DON JOHN", "Russ Lewis", True, "free")
End With
```

append a fabricated Recordset to one retrieved from the MuchADO database

Here's what it looks like in an HFlexGrid:

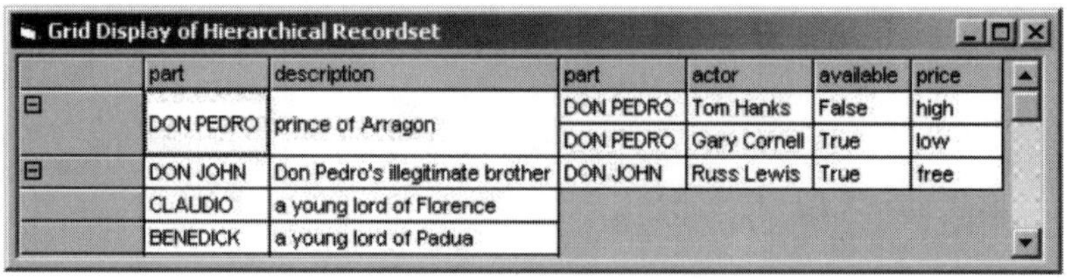

		part	description	part	actor	available	price	
⊟				DON PEDRO	Tom Hanks	False	high	
		DON PEDRO	prince of Arragon	DON PEDRO	Gary Cornell	True	low	
⊟		DON JOHN	Don Pedro's illegitimate brother	DON JOHN	Russ Lewis	True	free	
		CLAUDIO	a young lord of Florence					
		BENEDICK	a young lord of Padua					

Figure 8-9: A fabricated child of a Provider-generated parent

In This Section

The SHAPE language can add Fields of any data type (not just adChapter) to an existing Recordset, which has some useful data management opportunities. We can take this idea to its logical conclusion and fabricate entire Recordsets, which can be mixed with Provider-generated Recordsets if required.

Parameterized Data Shaping

There are two ways of using parameters with Data Shaping:

- **External parameters**: These make use of ADO Command and Parameter objects and work in exactly the same way as parameters do when working directly with a Data Provider. As long as you don't mix external and internal parameters, you can include external parameters at any level in a SHAPE command hierarchy.

- **Internal parameters**: These are used by the SHAPE language internally and don't require or use ADO Parameter objects. They are what most developers are referring to when discussing parameterized Data Shaping. Their purpose is to allow child Recordsets to be constructed, one chapter at a time, on an as-needed basis. This can have major performance implications. For example, if a parent Recordset has one hundred records and the typical user only wants to drill down to half a dozen at any one time, the total amount of data retrieved will be far less when data is fetched one chapter at a time. You cannot disconnect or marshall internally parameterized hierarchical Recordsets.

The two types can be mixed, although as we shall see, certain rules apply if you want to mix external and internal parameters and stay sane.

External Parameters

Because we previously discussed parameterized ADO commands at some length, there is little that needs to be added about using external parameters with Data Shaping. A simple example will show you all you need to know:

```
Dim sCommand As String
Dim rs As New Recordset
Dim cd As New Command
```

```
sCommand = "SHAPE {SELECT * FROM Parts WHERE part > ? } " & _
            "APPEND ({SELECT part, word, wordLength " & _
                    "FROM Words WHERE  wordLength > ? }  " & _
            "RELATE part to part)"
cd.CommandText = sCommand
cd.ActiveConnection = "File Name=c:\shape.udl"     pass two parameters to
Set rs = cd.Execute(, Array("L", 12))     ◄──────  the command, using
                                                   standard ADO techniques

printHRS1 rs
```

Here, we are using parameter place markers to control which parts we retrieve in the parent, and the size of words required for the child. Note that the construction of the child Recordset is independent of how many parts are retrieved by the parent. This is potentially wasteful. You'll see that there are ways to address this shortcoming—the simplest is to add another subclause (based on part) to the child's WHERE clause and to use another parameter for its value.

The preceding code uses our generic print routine to print the results, which look like this:

```
LEONATO         governor of Messina
                LEONATO             candle-wasters      14
                LEONATO             advertisement       13
LORD            Null
MARGARET        gentlewoman attending on Hero
                MARGARET            ill-qualities       13
MESSENGER       Null
. . .
```

Internal Parameters

Internal parameters cause the MSDataShape to behave very differently from external parameters. Internal parameters are defined by using the PARAMETER keyword in the RELATE clause of a SHAPE command. Here's an example, based on the simple SHAPE command we've been using all along:

```
Dim sCommand As String
Dim rs As New Recordset
```

```
sCommand = "SHAPE {SELECT * FROM Parts}" & _
              "APPEND ({SELECT part, word, wordLength " & _
                "FROM Words WHERE  wordLength > 11 " & _
                " and part = ? }" & _
              "RELATE part TO PARAMETER 0 ) as Words"
```

create an
internal parameter

```
rs.Open sCommand, "File Name=c:\shape.udl"
```

The only SQL that is *executed* when rs is opened is this:

```
SELECT * FROM Parts
```

However, MSDataShape also *prepares*[7] the following statement:

```
SELECT part, word, wordLength FROM Words
WHERE  wordLength > 11  and part = ?
```

As you might expect, opening rs with an internally parameterized command will be much faster than opening it with a standard relation-based command, because no Words data needs to be retrieved.

The first time any Chapter-type Field's data is accessed[8], MSDataShape executes the child command, substituting the parameter marker with the value of the related field in the current record of the parent. For example, this line:

```
Print rs("part"), rs("Words").Value.RecordCount
```

will fetch the nine child records associated with DON PEDRO, and then print

```
DON PEDRO                       9
```

These records are added into the child Recordset. When a new parent record is visited and the Words field accessed, the prepared statement will be executed again, and the retrieved records will be added into the same child Recordset.

---

7. The difference between executing and preparing a statement was discussed in Chapter 5. Preparing a statement asks the data source to get ready to execute, but returns no data.

8. Simply visiting the Field won't trigger the retrieval of the chapter's data. That will only happen when chapter data is read.

This is a very neat way of limiting the amount of data retrieved, and it's almost essential when creating a very large hierarchy with many drill-down options and many records at each level. However, note that although it's faster at opening the Recordset, it will be less responsive once opened than a nonparameterized query, because of the need to retrieve data each time a new parent record is visited.

By default, ADO caches each chapter as it's being retrieved. This is a good default because it has performance benefits, but there may be times when you want the prepared statement to be reexecuted when you return to a previously visited record and access a Chapter-type Field. You can make this happen by setting the `Cache Child Rows` dynamic property to `False`. You have to do this before opening the Recordset, and because this dynamic property is added by the Client Cursor Engine, you have to make the Recordset use a client-side cursor explicitly, rather than rely on MSDataShape to do it for you; for example:

```
rs.CursorLocation = adUseClient
rs.Properties("Cache Child Rows") = False
rs.Open sCommand, "File Name=c:\shape.udl"
```

It's pointless using internally parameterized commands if you intend to iterate through each parent record and inspect its Chapter-type Fields as soon as the Recordset is opened. It's far, far more efficient to retrieve all the child Recordset's data in one query, than to fetch it a chapter at time. It's only when chapters are retrieved on an as-needed basis that the internally parameterized approach can be more efficient than retrieving all the data at once.

Unfortunately, the Microsoft HFlexGrid control attempts to populate the entire Recordset in order to display it, and therefore, should not be used with internally parameterized commands.

Combining Internal and External Parameters

There is significant scope for confusion between ADO and MSDataShape when you try to mix internal and external parameters. However, good results can be achieved by following these two rules:

1. Never attempt to mix both types of parameter in the same internal Recordset.

2. Use external parameters in parents and internal parameters in children.

In the following code, an external parameter controls which parts are created, while an internal parameter in the child Recordset ensures that Word chapters are created only when needed:

```
Dim sCommand As String
Dim rs As New Recordset
Dim cd As New Command                              ┌─── external parameter

sCommand = "SHAPE {SELECT * FROM Parts where part > ? } " & _
              "APPEND ({SELECT part, word, wordLength " & _
                    "FROM Words WHERE  wordLength > 11 " & _
                          "and part = ? }  " & _
              "RELATE part to PARAMETER 0)"
cd.CommandText = sCommand                           └─── internal parameter
cd.ActiveConnection = "File Name=c:\shape.udl"
Set rs = cd.Execute(, 13)
```

ADO sees only the external parameter.

Some interesting results can be quickly achieved by combining parameterized queries and extended Recordsets. For example, consider the user interface here:

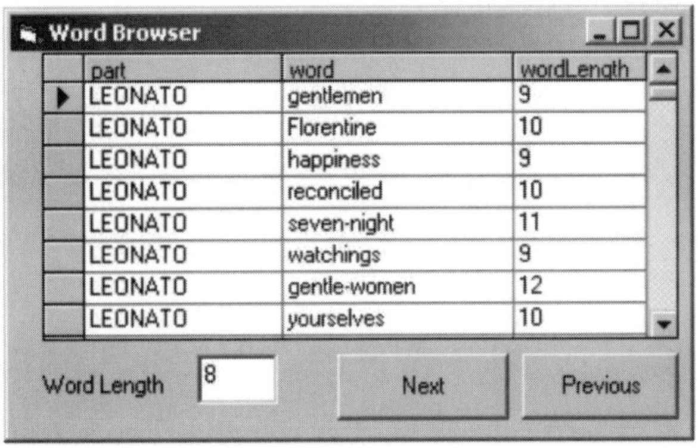

Figure 8-10: A simple word browser using a parameterized SHAPE command

Users can use the Next and Previous buttons to move around an externally parameterized Parts Recordset. Each time they navigate, the form shows all words larger than wordLength for the current part. wordLength can be adjusted as the user scrolls. The form uses a standard ADO Data Grid (not an HFlexGrid) and an ADO Data Control that is hidden. Apart from that, there are two command buttons, a textbox, and a label. Here's the complete code:

```
Private rs As New Recordset

Private Sub Form_Activate()
Dim sCommand As String                              append a standard Integer
Dim cd As New Command                               Field and a Chapter-type
sCommand = _                                        Field to Parts
  "SHAPE {SELECT * FROM Parts where part > ? } " & _
    "APPEND " & _
       "NEW adInteger as wordLength," & _
       "({SELECT part, word, wordLength " & _
           "FROM Words WHERE  wordLength > ? and part = ? } " & _
         "RELATE wordLength TO PARAMETER 0, part TO PARAMETER 1) As Words"
cd.CommandText = sCommand
cd.ActiveConnection = "File Name=c:\shape.udl"
cd.Parameters(0).Value = "L"                        create a parameterized
rs.Open cd, , , adLockBatchOptimistic     ←         Command and use it as the
                                                    source to rs.Open

rs("wordLength") = CInt(txtWordLength.Text)  ←      set the value of the
                                                    newly appended wordLength
Set rsChild = rs("Words").Value                     Field on the parent's
Set DataGrid1.DataSource = Adodc1                   first record, then assign
Set Adodc1.Recordset = rsChild                      the child to the grid
End Sub

Private Sub cmdNext_Click()                          move to the next
rs.MoveNext                                          record, set the
rs("wordLength") = CInt(txtWordLength.Text)          parent's wordLength
Set Adodc1.Recordset = rs("Words").Value            Field from the
End Sub                                              TextBox, and rebind

Private Sub cmdPrevious_Click()
rs.MovePrevious
rs("wordLength") = CInt(txtWordLength.Text)
Set Adodc1.Recordset = rs("Words").Value
End Sub
```

The key to this example is the use of an appended Integer Field to the parent Recordset, which controls how much data the child retrieves. Rebinding the grid forces the child data to be requeried each time. Note that it was necessary to use an external parameter and to create an updateable Recordset. Calling cd.Execute doesn't return an updateable Recordset. Therefore, we applied the ADO 2.5 technique of using a Command object as the source of an rs.Open.

Parameters can be either external to MSDataShape (in which case they are used like standard ADO Parameter objects) or internal to MSDataShape. Internal parameterized commands retrieve a child Recordset's data, chapter-by-chapter and on an as-needed basis, instead of retrieving all the child's data when the hierarchical Recordset is first created.

Group-based Hierarchies

The basic form of a SHAPE command for creating a group-based hierarchy is

```
SHAPE {<child-command> } as Alias
        COMPUTE <parent-fields>
        BY <child-fields>
```

This is a very different structure from relation-based commands. The key point to keep in mind is that the command that appears after the SHAPE keyword becomes the child Recordset in a group-based hierarchy, rather than the parent. The parent is defined by the COMPUTE statement. This makes perfect sense, because the COMPUTE statement defines aggregated data based on the child Recordset, and the aggregated data appears at the top of the hierarchy, with the detail (chapters of the child Recordset) appearing below. MSDataShape builds an internal filter to create chapters in the child Recordset, and the filter is based on the Fields named in the BY statement.

The parent Recordset needs a Chapter-type Field in order to provide access to the child, therefore, the COMPUTE statement must contain the child Recordset referenced by its name or alias. This will then be split up into chapters according to the BY statement. The remainder of the COMPUTE statement contains whichever aggregates are required in the parent. Let's look at an example:

```
Dim rs As New Recordset
Dim sCommand As String
sCommand = "SHAPE " & _
    "{SELECT * FROM Words } as Words " & _
        "COMPUTE Words , SUM (Words.wordCount) As WordCount, " & _
                    " AVG (Words.wordLength) As AveLength " & _
        "BY act, scene"
```

```
rs.Open sCommand, "File Name=c:\shape.udl"

Print "Act", "Scene","Count","Ave"
While Not rs.EOF
   Print rs!act, rs!scene, rs!WordCount, _
             FormatNumber(rs!AveLength, 2)
   rs.MoveNext
Wend
```

There are three Fields defined in the COMPUTE statement (one is a Chapter-type Field), and these combined with the two in the BY statement means that the parent will have five Fields. Here's the printout as the code iterates through the parent:

Act	Scene	Count	Ave
1	1	2464	4.90
1	2	215	4.32
1	3	560	4.83
2	1	2931	4.82
2	3	2092	4.78
3	1	1327	5.02
3	2	918	4.70

And here's what it looks like in an HFlexGrid with some rows collapsed:

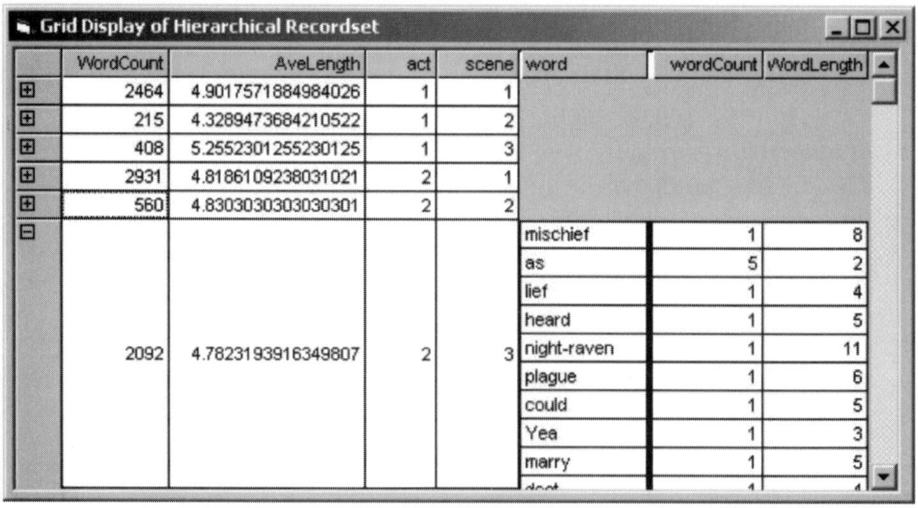

Figure 8-11. Group-based hierarchy in an HFlexGrid

It's possible to create complex group-based hierarchies, and once again, Reshaping and Naming can come to your rescue. For example, consider the following highly useful way of looking at the Words table:

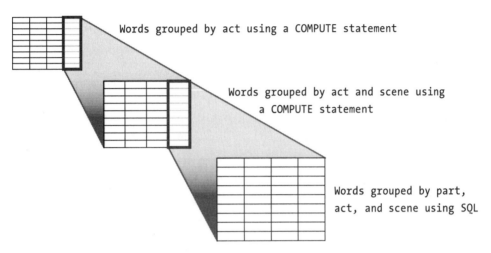

Figure 8-12. A complex group-based hierarchy

The following code builds up this group-based hierarchical Recordset using Reshaping to keep the complexity under control. Because the SQL for the grandchild is nontrivial, it's created first as a separate SQL statement and then concatenated into the SHAPE command for the child. The child is named, and its name is used in the parent Recordset to assemble the complete structure.

```
Dim rsChild As New Recordset
Dim rs As New Recordset
Dim cn As New Connection
Dim sCommand As String
```

Pure SQL creates the Parts (within a scene)-level data. wordLength is converted to a Float to get an average with decimal places.

```
cn.Open "File Name=c:\shape.udl"
sCommand = "SELECT  act, scene, part, " & _
               "Sum(wordCount) as PWordCount, " & _
               "Avg(CONVERT(float,wordLength)) as PAveLength " & _
           "FROM Words group by part, act, scene"

sCommand = "SHAPE(SHAPE {" & sCommand & " } as rs " & _
               "COMPUTE rs, " & _
               "SUM (rs.PWordCount) as SWordCount, " & _
               "AVG (rs.PAveLength) as SAveLength BY act, scene )" & _
           "as Scenes"
```

Create an aggregate parent (called Scenes) based on the SQL.

```
rsChild.Open sCommand, cn
sCommand = "SHAPE Scenes " & _
            "COMPUTE Scenes, " & _
                "SUM (Scenes.SWordCount) as AWordCount, " & _
                "AVG (Scenes.SAveLength) as AAveLength BY act"

rs.Open sCommand, cn        ◄────────────
```

Create an aggregate parent
containing act-level data
using Scenes as a child.

That code creates rather a nice HFlexGrid display:

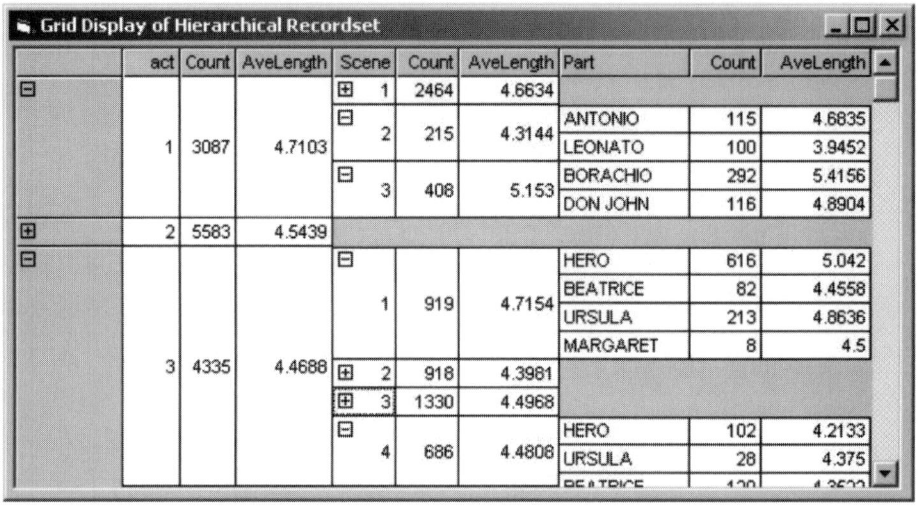

	act	Count	AveLength	Scene		Count	AveLength	Part	Count	AveLength
⊟				⊞	1	2464	4.6634			
	1	3087	4.7103	⊟	2	215	4.3144	ANTONIO	115	4.6835
								LEONATO	100	3.9452
				⊟	3	408	5.153	BORACHIO	292	5.4156
								DON JOHN	116	4.8904
⊞	2	5583	4.5439							
⊟	3	4335	4.4688	⊟	1	919	4.7154	HERO	616	5.042
								BEATRICE	82	4.4558
								URSULA	213	4.8636
								MARGARET	8	4.5
				⊞	2	918	4.3981			
				⊞	3	1330	4.4968			
				⊟	4	686	4.4808	HERO	102	4.2133
								URSULA	28	4.375
								BEATRICE	120	4.3622

Figure 8-13. Complex group-based hierarchy in an HFlexGrid

Functions Supported by the COMPUTE Statement

We've seen that in addition to referencing the child Recordset, the COMPUTE statement can include SUM and AVG aggregations. Here are all the aggregation functions supported by the SHAPE language:

> SUM
>
> AVG
>
> MIN
>
> MAX
>
> COUNT
>
> STDEV
>
> ANY
>
> CALC

All but ANY and CALC are self-explanatory. ANY allows you to include a noncalculated Field from the child as part of the Recordset. CALC allows you to apply VBA functions and calculations to any Field appearing on the COMPUTE line. For example, changing the parent Recordset's definition to

```
SHAPE Scenes
    COMPUTE Scenes,
        AVG (Scenes.SAveLength) as AAveLength,
        SUM (Scenes.SWordCount) as AWordCount,
        CALC (Format(AAveLength, '0.00')) as AveLength,
        CALC (CLng(AWordCount * AAveLength)) as Chars BY act
```

allows the number of characters in an act to be calculated, and it adds a formatted average length field. By hiding AAveLength, the following HFlexGrid display can be created:

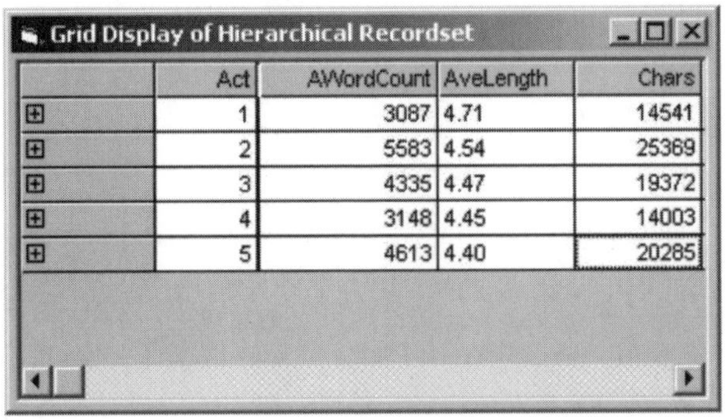

	Act	AWordCount	AveLength	Chars
⊞	1	3087	4.71	14541
⊞	2	5583	4.54	25369
⊞	3	4335	4.47	19372
⊞	4	3148	4.45	14003
⊞	5	4613	4.40	20285

Figure 8-14. A group-based hierarchy showing CALC Fields

Combining Group-based and Parameterized Relation-based Hierarchies

And for our last trick … we'll extend the preceding three-layer hierarchy with a fourth layer containing all the Words for each act/scene/part. Ideally, you would want this final layer to be parameterized, to avoid shipping the entire Words table across the network and building a client-side cursor on it.

Although a group-based parent Recordset can't have parameterized child Recordsets, it can have parameterized grandchild Recordsets (see Figure 8-15).

In our current example, the third layer is an SQL command, which is itself aggregated. We'll add a simple parameterized child to this command that draws records directly from the Words table.

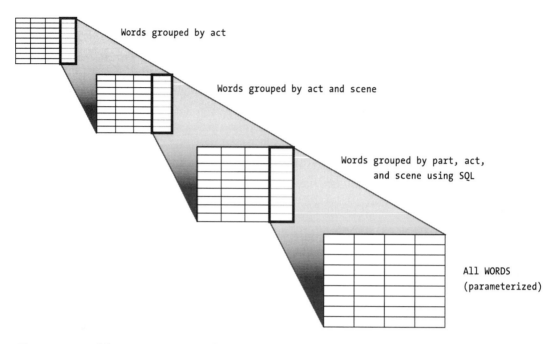

Words grouped by act

Words grouped by act and scene

Words grouped by part, act, and scene using SQL

All WORDS (parameterized)

Figure 8-15: Adding a parameterized child to the existing hierarchy

Here's the code that creates the Scenes Recordset and assigns it to rsChild. The rest of the code from the preceding example is unchanged:

```
cn.Open "File Name=c:\shape.udl"
sCommand = _
  "(SHAPE " & _
    "{SELECT  act, scene,part, " & _            the same SQL
      " sum(wordCount) as PWordCount, " & _      as before ...
      " Avg(CONVERT(float,wordLength)) as PAveLength " & _
      " FROM Words group by part, act, scene} as rs  " & _
    "APPEND ({SELECT * FROM Words WHERE " & _
            "part = ? and act = ? and scene = ?} " & _
    " RELATE part TO PARAMETER 0, act TO PARAMETER 1, " & _
        "scene TO PARAMETER 2)as Words)"


sCommand = _
  "SHAPE (SHAPE " & sCommand & " as rs " & _
    "COMPUTE rs, " & _
      "SUM (rs.PWordCount) as SWordCount, " & _
      "AVG (rs.PAveLength) as SAveLength BY act, scene )" & _
    "as Scenes"

rsChild.Open sCommand, cn
```

... now with child

The end result here is complex, but each individual step is straightforward. What makes it complex is the nature of the relationships we are modeling. You could spend a week building an application that provided users with this amount of power. Data Shaping will make your life a great deal easier.

In This Section

We looked at group-based hierarchies. You learned how to use the COMPUTE statement to create powerful structures and displays and saw how group-based and relation-based hierarchies can be combined.

Summary

Data Shaping is often automatically associated with the Microsoft Hierarchical FlexGrid. It's generally claimed that Data Shaping is obscure and complicated, but both of these viewpoints are mistaken.

- Data Shaping can do a great deal more than create hierarchical displays. It can extend and fabricate Recordsets and weave them into relationships that are natural for certain types of uses.

- How this data is presented is a completely separate issue, and the HFlexGrid is not always the most appropriate vehicle.

- The SHAPE language is simple, although the representations of data that it allows can be very sophisticated, resulting in complex-looking command structures. These can nearly always be broken down into more manageable chunks.

- What makes Data Shaping ultimately very accessible is that it introduces surprisingly little that is new.

Data Shaping creates standard tabular Recordsets and exploits filters and cloning to combine them in a powerful, flexible fashion, based on the concept of chapters. It provides viable alternatives, but not replacements, for certain types of more powerful SQL statements.

The key difference between Data Shaping and SQL joins and aggregation is that SQL always flattens data back into a tabular structure, whereas Data Shaping maintains or even extends the natural hierarchical relationship in the data it uses. Neither approach is best—each has its place. Deciding which to use is the primary challenge that Data Shaping introduces.

Data Shaping provides powerful new data representations, but they are still based on an essentially tabular form. In the next chapter, you'll see how ADO 2.5 allows you to leave behind the tabular model of data representation, should you so wish.

CHAPTER 9

Working with Documents— Records and Streams

Semi-structured Data

The Internet Publishing Provider

The Record Object

Using Records and Recordsets

Streams

Summary

THE ADO PROVIDERS WE'VE WORKED WITH until now have all returned tabular data. Even hierarchical Recordsets are strongly wedded to this potent form of data representation. No one who has worked in computing for long needs to be persuaded that manipulating data in the form of tables has many advantages.

At the same time, it's well known that a large amount of the data that is important to organizations is not highly amenable to tabular representation. Most of the data that isn't stored in "databases" (and here I am using a looser term than relational databases, to include products such as Indexing Services and Active Directory) is stored in documents of some form.

I am also using "document" very loosely, to include anything that has a set of external properties (such as name and size) and some internal content that is typically stored in a proprietary way. Documents are also frequently stored and organized in a hierarchical structure. This definition of a document clearly includes a Word document, an Excel spreadsheet, and a source code file, but also includes an email message or a file held on a Web site (Microsoft uses the term *Web Store* to describe the ability to refer to the many types of documents in a Web site as a searchable database of semi-structured data).

ADO is the application developer's entry point into Microsoft's Universal Data Access package, and to be universal, ADO needs to be able to give developers access to documents. It so happens that ADO's Recordset provides much of what is needed for accessing and manipulating document stores, but it doesn't support everything that is required. The most obvious new features of ADO 2.5 are the Record and Stream objects. Used in conjunction with the existing Recordset object, they add document management to ADO's repertoire.

In this chapter, we'll explore document management with ADO. We won't be working with a relational database in this chapter. Instead, we'll use a set of Word and HTML documents containing the text of *Much ADO about Nothing*, organized as a small Web site.

We'll not only introduce a new Provider, the Microsoft OLE DB Provider for Internet Publishing, but a whole new class of Providers known as Document Source Providers.

Semi-structured Data

If relational databases are *highly* structured, then document stores are *semi*-structured. The term semi-structured is often used in ADO when Record and Stream objects are discussed. The easiest way to grasp the model used by ADO for dealing with semi-structured data is to think about a traditional file system.

Consider the file space in the following figure:

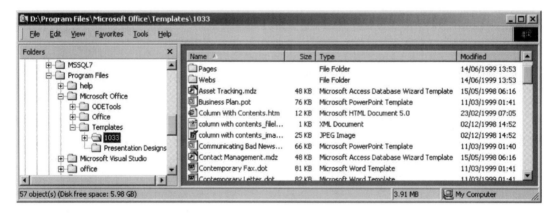

Figure 9-1. A file space is a good example of semi-structured data.

Using Recordsets to work with this data presents some problems. The contents of the current folder (displayed in the list view) could be modeled as a Recordset, with Fields representing Name, Size, Type, etcetera. As we'll see, there are times when this is entirely valid. However, the records in a Recordset typically have the same structure, whereas the items in the folder have a diverse range of characteristics; for example:

- Some of the items are themselves folders, which have their own lists of files and form part of the hierarchical structure of the file space. In an MSDataShape hierarchical Recordset, the same hierarchical relationship applies to each record. This is clearly not the case with the contents of a folder in a file space.

- Some are very simple files, such as HTML or XML files, with a small set of external properties (such as file size, creation, and modification dates), while others are Microsoft Office documents with a much wider set of external properties. When you right-click a file in Windows Explorer and select Properties, the Properties dialog box contains more tabs for some files than for others. Those with more tabs have more properties. There is a big dilemma representing this folder's contents as a Recordset. Should you have a small set of properties and ignore the extra information that is available, or a large set of properties and carry around a great deal of wasted space? Files can have custom properties, so it will never be possible to devise an appropriate Recordset that will provide the essential information about every conceivable document type.

- All of the files have content, which doesn't appear in the folder list. While it's possible to consider the content as just another property, this is not a natural way to represent such data. The content differs widely among different files.

What this implies is that there are different ways of viewing a file or folder. Sometimes it's convenient to think of a file or folder as part of a list with a standard set of properties. Other times you'll want to think of it as a node in a hierarchy, possibly with a parent and with children. Still other times you'll want to think about it in isolation and manipulate its properties in a way that isn't constrained by the common set of shared properties of other files in the same folder. Finally, you'll want to be able to do things with its contents.

Because there are other types of semi-structured data apart from file spaces, ADO uses the more general term *resource*. ADO's solution to the multifaceted views of resources that semi-structured data sources require is to support three different ways to represent the same resource:

1. **As a record in a Recordset**: This view of a resource places it in the context of its siblings—for a file, this means in the context of the other files in the folder, in which case the entire Recordset would represent the folder's contents. Recordsets are extremely efficient ways of representing data when you have many records, each with exactly the same characteristics. This representation is more than just efficient, it's also convenient for developers and users alike.

2. **As a Record object**: A Record object can have whatever Fields it likes. It knows about its position in a hierarchy and has access to its parent and its children, when appropriate. As a resource, it can easily be copied, moved, or deleted. It also knows whether it's a resource that itself has children (in which case it's known as a *collection*), whether it's a *structured OLE document*, or whether it's a simple leaf node representing a single document.

    It isn't efficient or convenient to create Record objects for every resource in a list, but then it's unlikely that you would want to use every resource in this way at a single point in time. Recordsets can be used to represent a long list of resources. Records can be used when it's time to single out and manipulate a single resource.

3. **As a Stream object**: Stream objects concentrate on the contents of a resource rather than its external properties.

ADO makes it very easy to switch between using a resource through a Recordset and using it directly through a Record object. It's also very easy to take a Record object and access its contents via a Stream object. Your task is to decide which representation is most appropriate at any point in time and to realize that different ADO structures can represent the same physical resource.

The concept of a Connection changes slightly when dealing with semi-structured data. With a relational database, the data source is a very discrete entity. In the case of SQLServer, you are connecting to a physical process that knows precisely where its boundaries lie.

However, when the data source is a hierarchy, such as a file space, the data source could potentially be all the files within a particular domain. This would be a cumbersome and expensive hierarchy to manipulate, and instead, part of the connecting process involves identifying the root of the particular file space of interest. This is typically achieved using *URLs* to identify a resource at the root of a *name space*.

Not all Providers support Record objects, and it's likely that many will continue not to, simply because the semi-structured approach is not relevant to the data they manage. Two major Providers that do support this approach are:

- Microsoft OLE DB Provider for Internet Publishing (MSDAIPP.OSP)

- Microsoft OLE DB Provider for Exchange (ExOLEDB)

Both of these Providers belong to a special group of Providers known as Document Source Providers. Among other things, all Recordsets and Records returned by these Providers are required to include a common set of Provider-supplied Fields, which are listed in the following table.

Table 9-1. Fields Available on All Recordsets Generated by Document Source Providers

FIELD NAME	DESCRIPTION
RESOURCE_PARSENAME	The resource's URL.
RESOURCE_PARENTNAME	The URL of the resource's parent record.
RESOURCE_ABSOLUTEPARSENAME	The absolute URL of the resource.
RESOURCE_ISHIDDEN	True if the resource is hidden.
RESOURCE_ISREADONLY	True if the resource is read-only.
RESOURCE_CONTENTTYPE	The *MIME* type of the document (e.g., text or HTML).
RESOURCE_CONTENTCLASS	The likely use of the document, which could correspond to the Office template used to create it.
RESOURCE_CONTENTLANGUAGE	The language in which the content is stored.
RESOURCE_CREATIONTIME	The time the resource was created.
RESOURCE_LASTACCESSTIME	The time that the resource was last accessed.
RESOURCE_LASTWRITETIME	The time that the resource was last updated.
RESOURCE_STREAMSIZE	The size of the resource's content stream, in bytes.
RESOURCE_ISCOLLECTION	True if the resource is a collection (has children).
RESOURCE_ISSTRUCTUREDDOCUMENT	True if the resource is a structured OLE document.
DEFAULT_DOCUMENT	Contains a URL to the default simple document of a parent Record or a structured OLE document.
CHAPTERED_CHILDREN	References the chapter of the Recordset containing the children of the resource. This Field is optional.
RESOURCE_DISPLAYNAME	The display name of the resource.
RESOURCE_ISROOT	True if the resource is a root resource.

Theoretically, you should be able to identify a Document Source Provider by reading the DataSource Type dynamic property of a Connection object. However, many Providers won't support this dynamic property, so check for its existence first.

Next, we'll explore semi-structured data using the Microsoft OLE DB Provider for Internet Publishing.

In This Section

We examined the characteristics of semi-structured data and the features that ADO provides to manipulate it and learned what a Document Source Provider is.

The Internet Publishing Provider

The Microsoft OLE DB Provider for Internet Publishing (MSDAIPP.DSO) is an OLE DB Provider that is installed when Internet Explorer 5.x, Office 2000, or Windows 2000 (with Internet Explorer 5) is installed. Its purpose is to make it easy to manage resources over the Internet.

The MSDAIPP.DSO Provider talks to Web servers that support an extension to *HTTP* known as WebDAV (Web Distributed Authoring and Versioning), or that support the FrontPage Web Extender Client (WEC) protocol. Of the two, WebDAV is the more interesting because it's an accepted industry standard with wide support. Although all the examples in this chapter use IIS 5 as a Web server, WebDAV (and therefore MSDAIPP.DSO) is supported by a range of leading Web servers including Apache, IIS 4, Netscape Enterprise Server, and Netscape FastTrack Server.[1]

As you'll see, WebDAV is extremely powerful and makes proper Web security of paramount importance. Using WebDAV, you can access and edit any Web site that gives you the appropriate access rights, and you can easily delete whole directory structures or replace photos of corporate VIPs with Dilbert cartoons.[2] Although WebDAV is quite a low-level protocol, we have the luxury of being able to use it via ADO, thanks to the MSDAIPP.DSO Provider.

In order to explore this Provider, I have created a virtual directory on my server called MuchADO. This contains a subdirectory for each act in *Much ADO about Nothing*, and each subdirectory holds files containing the text for each scene in Word and HTML formats. There are also a few other supporting files, and we'll create more.

---

1. You should consult appropriate documentation for versions and configuration requirements.

2. Subject to permission from Scott Adams.

The standard ADO way of opening a connection using the Internet Publishing Provider is as follows:

```
Dim cn As New Connection
cn.Provider = "MSDAIPP.DSO"
cn.Open "http://POLECAT/MuchADO/"        ◄───────    the root of the
                                                     required name space
```

However, Microsoft places sufficient importance on the use of this Provider to have introduced a new keyword into the connection string syntax. As a result, the following code performs the same task:

```
Dim cn As New Connection
cn.Open "URL=http://POLECAT/MuchADO/"    ◄───────    URL keyword identifies the
                                                     Provider as MSDAIPP.DSO
```

In both of these cases, the connection is opened using an absolute URL to identify the root resource of a resource *name space*. From this point on, further resources can be accessed using a relative URL that implicitly uses the root resource's absolute URL to uniquely identify a particular resource. We'll see how shortly.

In This Section

You were introduced to WebDAV and the Microsoft OLE DB Provider for Internet Publishing (MSDAIPP.DSO).

The Record Object

A Record object represents a single resource in a name space, which knows about its place in the name space hierarchy, and knows about its contents. It can get confusing distinguishing between a record in a Recordset, and a Record object. I'll always use the capitalized "Record" when I mean a Record object. A Record object can be created in a number of ways:

- Using a relative URL, within the context of an open Connection or another open Record.

- Using an absolute URL, in which case the Connection object is created implicitly.

- Using the current record of an open Recordset.

rd.Active-
Connection
rd.Fields
rd.Properties
rd.Mode
rd.ParentURL
rd.RecordType
rd.Source
rd.State

We'll see examples of all three methods in this section and the next. Let's begin with a simple example that shows all the properties of a Record object:

```
Dim rd As New Record
rd.Open "Act 1/", "URL=http://POLECAT/MuchADO/"
Print "Connection", rd.ActiveConnection
Print "Fields", rd.Fields.Count
Print "Properties", rd.Properties.Count
Print "Mode", rd.Mode
Print "Parent", rd.ParentURL
Select Case rd.RecordType
  Case adCollectionRecord
    Print "Type", "Collection"
  Case adSimpleRecord
    Print "Type", "Simple"
  Case adStructDoc
    Print "Type", "Structured Document"
End Select
Print "Source", rd.Source
Print "State", rd.State
rd.Close
```

open the Record using a relative URL and a connection string

The code prints

```
Connection    Provider=MSDAIPP.DSO.1;Data Source=http://POLECAT/MuchADO/;
Bind Flags=0;Mode=Read;Lock Owner="";User ID="";Password="";
Ignore Cached Data=False;Cache Aggressively=False;
Treat As Offline=False;Mark For Offline=0;
Protocol Provider={00000000-0000-0000-0000-000000000000}
Fields        26
Properties    0
Mode          1
Parent        http://polecat/MuchADO
Type          Collection
Source        Act 1/
State         1
```

Alternatively, you could open the Record using an absolute URL and no connection string, in which case the first two lines of code would be:

```
Dim rd As New Record
rd.Open "http://POLECAT/MuchADO/Act 1/"
```

and the printout would be identical, except that the Source property of the Record and the Data Source value in the connection string would both be:

```
http://POLECAT/MuchADO/Act 1/
```

As you can see, this Record has twenty-six Fields, eighteen of which are required for a Document Source Provider. The remainder are Fields that are required by the WebDAV protocol. Most of these map directly onto Document Source Provider Fields, therefore, there are pairs of Fields containing identical data. The Fields can be treated like any other ADO Field objects. Here's a selected list of this Record's Field names and values:

```
RESOURCE_PARSENAME             Act%201
RESOURCE_PARENTNAME            http://polecat/MuchADO
RESOURCE_ABSOLUTEPARSENAME     http://polecat/MuchADO/Act%201
RESOURCE_ISHIDDEN              False
RESOURCE_ISREADONLY
RESOURCE_CREATIONTIME          25/01/2000 17:22:43
RESOURCE_LASTWRITETIME         25/01/2000 18:48:52
RESOURCE_ISCOLLECTION          True
RESOURCE_DISPLAYNAME           Act 1
DAV:ishidden  False
DAV:iscollection               True
```

Records are far less protective about Fields than Recordsets. The following code is perfectly legal:

```
Dim rd As New Record
rd.Open "http://POLECAT/MuchADO/Act 1/"
Print rd.Fields.Count
rd!AppendedField = "Made up value"   ◀——————  create a new Field by
Print rd!AppendedField                        referencing one that
Print rd.Fields.Count                         doesn't exist
rd.Close
```

and it prints

```
26
Made up value
27
```

fds.Append

As you can see, Fields can be appended to individual Record objects. While it's more transparent to do this using the fds.Append method, ADO allows you to create new Fields for Record objects simply by referencing a nonexistent Field name. There is no Option Explicit to defend your honor here, so take care!

Opening and Closing Records

rd.Open

The formal syntax for rd.Open is

Sub Open([Source As Variant],
             [ActiveConnection As Variant],
             [Mode As ConnectModeEnum],
             [CreateOptions As RecordCreateOptionsEnum =
                 adFailIfNotExists],
             [Options As RecordOpenOptionsEnum =
                 adOpenRecordUnspecified],
             [UserName As String],
             [Password As String])

We've already seen Source and ActiveConnection in action. UserName and Password are especially useful when an implicit connection is used. The remaining three arguments require some explanation.

rd.Mode

Mode uses the same enumeration as the Connection object's Mode property. However, the available values make considerably more sense in the context of a Record object representing a single resource in a hierarchical name space. The values defined by the ConnectModeEnum enumeration are

adModeUnknown

adModeRead

adModeWrite

adModeReadWrite

adModeShareDenyRead

adModeShareDenyWrite

adModeShareExclusive

adModeShareDenyNone

adModeRecursive

These values determine whether you requested read and/or write access to a resource (such as a file), and whether and how the resource should be locked while you have it open. These values are *bitmasks,* so sensible combinations of them can be "Or"ed together. adModeRecursive needs to be handled with care, as it controls whether the locking strategy requested by an adMode-Share* value should be propagated to all children of the current resource.[3]

By default, an attempt to open a resource that doesn't exist will fail. However, by specifying a value for CreateOptions from the RecordCreate-OptionsEnum enumeration, rd.Open can be used to create a new resource. The enumeration offers the following options:

adFailIfNotExists (default)

adOpenIfExists

adCreateOverwrite

adCreateCollection

adCreateStructDoc

adCreateNonCollection

Specifying either adOpenIfExists or adCreateOverwrite determines whether an existing resource should be opened, if one is present, or whether a new one should always be created (overwriting any existing resource). You can then choose from the remaining three values to determine which type of resource is created.

For example, the following code will create a file in the Act 1 directory called summary.htm:

```
Dim rd As New Record
Dim cn As New Connection
cn.Open "URL=http://POLECAT/MuchADO/"
rd.Open "Act 1/summary.htm", cn, , _
            adCreateNonCollection Or adCreateOverwrite
```

whereas the following code will create a subdirectory of Act 1 called Critical Reviews, so long as one doesn't already exist:

```
Dim rd As New Record
Dim cn As New Connection
cn.Open "URL=http://POLECAT/MuchADO/"
rd.Open "Act 1/Critical Reviews", cn, , _
            adCreateCollection Or adOpenIfExists
```

---

3. Everything you have previously learned about lock management (and its effects on concurrency) for databases applies to document resources.

This is what Internet Services Manager displays for the MuchADO virtual directory after both of these operations:

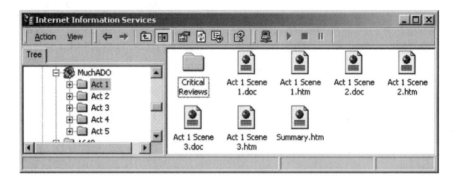

Figure 9-2. Using a Record object to create Web resources

Finally, the Options argument makes some additional possibilities available via the RecordOpenOptionsEnum enumeration:

adOpenRecordUnspecified

adOpenSource

adOpenAsync

adDelayFetchFields

adDelayFetchStream

rd.Cancel

adOpenSource is useful when the resource is an executable resource, such as an Active Server Pages file, because it can be used to return the source code for the file, rather than the results of executing it, as long as the appropriate access permissions are in place. adOpenAsync can be used to open the Record asynchronously, although in ADO 2.5, the Record object has no events, so identifying when the operation is complete is less straightforward than it might be.[4] A more appropriate way to improve responsiveness may be to use one of the adDelay* options to postpone the retrieval of the Record's Fields or data stream until it's needed. One benefit of an asynchronous rd.Open is that you can cancel it using an rd.Cancel.

rd.Close

It's a good idea to explicitly close Records using rd.Close when they are no longer needed, before allowing them to go out of scope.

---

4. It's made even less straightforward by the fact that the MSDAIPP.DSO Provider doesn't support asynchronous operations.

Deleting, Moving, and Copying Resources

The Record object has four other methods:

- DeleteRecord

- MoveRecord

- CopyRecord

- GetChildren

As we'll see shortly, rd.GetChildren returns a Recordset of all the children of the current resource, and along with the rd.ParentURL property, can be used to navigate a hierarchical name space.

The other three methods are concerned with managing resources. In conjunction with Stream objects, they provide full functionality for editing and manipulating a resource name space. It's important to realize that (by default) the document server itself performs the operations that these methods initiate. This means that you can execute a copy or move operation over a slow link without having to download and upload the resource. Alternatively, should the server not support the requested operation, or if you wish to move resources between servers, the client resident Provider software can emulate the server operation.

rd.DeleteRecord   The rd.DeleteRecord method looks like this:

Sub DeleteRecord([Source As String],
                       [Async As Boolean])

The most natural way to use rd.DeleteRecord is with no arguments. For example, to delete the Critical Reviews folder created earlier, use the following code:

```
Dim rd As New Record
rd.Open "Act 1/Critical Reviews/", "URL=http://POLECAT/MuchADO/"
rd.DeleteRecord
rd.Close
```

However, you can use rd.DeleteRecord to delete a resource other than the one that the current Record object has open by providing a relative URL for the Source argument.

| rd.MoveRecord | rd.MoveRecord and rd.CopyRecord are very similar, differing mainly in the choices available for the Options argument. Here's the syntax for rd.MoveRecord: |

Function MoveRecord([Source As String],
                      [Destination As String],
                      [UserName As String],
                      [Password As String],
                      [Options As MoveRecordOptionsEnum =
                        adMoveUnspecified],
                      [Async As Boolean]) As String

The Options available via the MoveRecordOptionsEnum enumeration are

adMoveUnspecified

adMoveOverWrite

adMoveDontUpdateLinks

adMoveAllowEmulation

By default, rd.MoveRecord will fail if the destination already exists, but adMoveOverWrite will overwrite any destination resources if they exist. Some document servers will update hypertext links in a moved resource to correct any relative URLs. You can stop this behavior if necessary. The last option allows you to permit the client resident Provider to perform the move operation if the document server is unable to.

The example that follows moves the summary HTML file, created earlier, from \\POLECAT\MuchADO\Act 1\ up one level to \\POLECAT\MuchADO\:

```
Dim rd As New Record
rd.Open "Act 1/summary.htm", "URL=http://POLECAT/MuchADO/"
rd.MoveRecord , "../../summary.htm"
```

As with rd.DeleteRecord, the current resource is moved, so there is no need to specify the source argument. As well as moving a resource, rd.MoveRecord can be used to rename a resource by keeping its parent URL the same, but changing its name via the destination argument.

| rd.CopyRecord | rd.CopyRecord looks like this: |

Function CopyRecord([Source As String],
                      [Destination As String],
                      [UserName As String],
                      [Password As String],
                      [Options As CopyRecordOptionsEnum =
                        adCopyUnspecified],
                      [Async As Boolean]) As String

and the CopyRecordOptionsEnum enumeration contains the following values:

adCopyAllowEmulation

adCopyNonRecursive

adCopyOverWrite

adCopyUnspecified

adCopyNonRecursive allows you to copy a resource without copying any of its children. A recursive copy will copy an entire hierarchy. For example, this code:

```
Dim rd As New Record
rd.Open "MuchADO/", "URL=http://POLECAT/"
rd.CopyRecord , "../TooMuchADO"
```

copies the entire MuchADO virtual directory to a new location on POLECAT.

The GetChildren Method

rd.GetChildren

The remaining Record object method to study is the GetChildren method. It returns a regular ADO Recordset with a record for each child of the current Record. It's a simple method with no arguments:

Function GetChildren() As Recordset

This function will always return a server-side, forward-only Recordset. The LockType will be read-only unless the Record is itself updateable, in which case an optimistic lock will be applied.[5]

Because the Recordset is forward-only, Recordset navigation is limited to rs.MoveNext. This is less of a problem than you might think, because the MSDAIPP.DSO Provider intelligently caches any collection information retrieved for an open Record, so the penalty for calling GetChildren again to reposition the cursor on the first record is barely measurable. The main inconvenience you'll encounter is the lack of an rs.RecordCount.

Here's an example of GetChildren in action:

```
Dim rd As New Record
Dim rs As Recordset

rd.Open "Act 1/", "URL=http://POLECAT/MuchADO/"
Set rs = rd.GetChildren
```

---

5. Non-SQL Recordsets are typically server-side, because the client-side update mechanism is based on Providers understanding SQL. There is, in fact, an SQL-like command language associated with WebDAV. Its purpose is to support more complex queries, and it has a syntax rather like Indexing Services SQL.

```
While Not rs.EOF
   Print rs!RESOURCE_DISPLAYNAME, _
         rs!RESOURCE_ISCOLLECTION, _
         rs!RESOURCE_STREAMSIZE
   rs.MoveNext
Wend
```

a selection of Provider-supplied Fields for Document Source Providers

and it prints

Act 1 Scene 3.htm	False	9647
Act 1 Scene 3.doc	False	19968
Act 1 Scene 2.htm	False	4665
Act 1 Scene 2.doc	False	19968
Act 1 Scene 1.htm	False	34454
Act 1 Scene 1.doc	False	50688
Act 1	True	0

You've seen how it's possible to navigate *up* a hierarchy using the Parent-URL property of a Record, and now you've seen how to go *down* one level by generating a Recordset for a Record's children. To be able to navigate down an arbitrary number of levels, you need to know how to create a Record object based on one of the records in the Recordset of children. You'll see how to do this in the next section.

In This Section

We examined the Record object and saw how it allows a resource to be copied, deleted, moved, and created, and how it provides access to its parent resource and child resources.

Using Records and Recordsets

To complete the story of how Record and Recordset objects work together to manipulate semi-structured data, we'll develop a small Web management tool (without any security awareness). This will allow us to browse through a WebDAV-capable name space, viewing, deleting, copying, adding, and moving resources as we go. This is what it looks like:

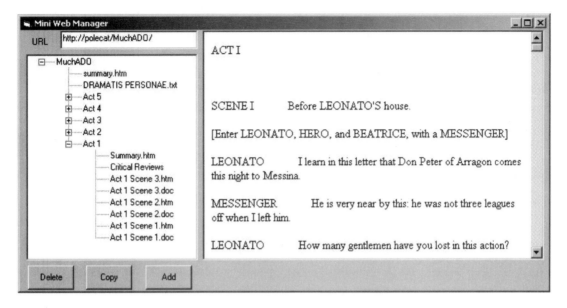

Figure 9-3. A Mini Web Manager, using ADO

In addition to about fifty lines of code, this application uses a TextBox, three CommandButtons, a TreeView control, and a WebBrowser control.[6] Delete, Copy, and Add buttons perform as expected, while Move is supported via drag-and-drop. The complete application is available on this book's companion CD.

In the "Streams" section later in this chapter, we'll use Stream objects to add editing capabilities.

rd.Open

The only new piece of ADO knowledge required to construct this program is how to create a Record object for a record in a Recordset. This is very easy with a Provider that supports Record objects. After you position the Recordset cursor on the required record, you can simply use the Recordset as an argument to the rd.Open method; for example:

```
Dim rdChild As New Record
rdChild.Open rs
```

This Record object will have all the Fields that the Recordset record had and may also have other Fields added by the Provider that are specific to this Record. More important, the Record object is hierarchy-aware and has the ability to navigate up or down a semi-structured hierarchy.

---

6. The TreeView control is available when you select "Microsoft Windows Common Controls" from the Components dialog box. The WebBrowser control is available by selecting "Microsoft Internet Controls" from the Components dialog box.

This means you can call rd.GetChildren on this new Record object and thereby continue the drill-down process. To see this technique at work, let's develop the code that populates the TreeView control (called tvwDocs) in our sample application. If you are not familiar with using TreeView controls, it's worth knowing that a Node object is created to represent each entry in a TreeView control. Collectively, the Node objects are called Tree. A Node object has a Text property, which determines what is seen in the TreeView, and a Key property, which is a string that uniquely identifies a Node. We'll set the Key of each node to be the absolute URL of the resource it represents.

The TextBox uses the following code to rebuild the Tree whenever the Enter key is pressed:

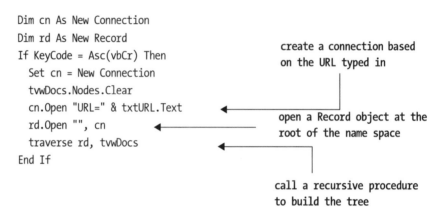

```
Dim cn As New Connection
Dim rd As New Record
If KeyCode = Asc(vbCr) Then
  Set cn = New Connection
  tvwDocs.Nodes.Clear
  cn.Open "URL=" & txtURL.Text
  rd.Open "", cn
  traverse rd, tvwDocs
End If
```

create a connection based on the URL typed in

open a Record object at the root of the name space

call a recursive procedure to build the tree

It's probably no surprise that a recursive procedure is required to fully navigate the Tree structure.[7] The traverse procedure gets passed a Record object and the TreeView control. Its job is to walk through the name space hierarchy, adding Node objects to the TreeView control as it goes.[8]

Here's the code for traverse:

```
Private Sub traverse( rd As Record, _
              tvw As TreeView, _
              Optional sParentKey As String)
Dim rs As Recordset
Dim rdChild As New Record

If sParentKey = "" Then
    tvw.Nodes.Add , , CStr(rd!RESOURCE_ABSOLUTEPARSENAME), _
              rd!RESOURCE_DISPLAYNAME
End If
```

if rd has no parent, create a root Node in the TreeView

---

7. "Required" is too strong a word. Any recursive function can be written to use plain old iterative loops—it just requires considerably more complex code.

8. For an explanation of how tvw.Nodes.Add works, search for "Add Method (Nodes Collection)" in VB Help with the Search Titles Only option.

```
If rd.RecordType = adSimpleRecord Then Exit Sub  ◄─────────────┐
Set rs = rd.GetChildren                          if rd has no children, stop
                                                 recursing; otherwise, get the
While Not rs.EOF                                 child Recordset
    tvw.Nodes.Add CStr(rd!RESOURCE_ABSOLUTEPARSENAME), _
                  tvwChild, _
                  CStr(rs!RESOURCE_ABSOLUTEPARSENAME), _
                  rs!RESOURCE_DISPLAYNAME


    If rs!RESOURCE_ISCOLLECTION Then
        rdChild.Open rs
        traverse rdChild, tvw, CStr(rs!RESOURCE_ABSOLUTEPARSENAME)
        rdChild.Close  ▲                         if the current record in
    End If             └─────────────────────    rs is a collection, open
    rs.MoveNext                                  a Record object on it and
Wend                                             recurse using the Record
End Sub
```

create a child Node in the Tree, for each record in rs (annotation for `tvw.Nodes.Add` block)

The two key elements of this procedure both take place inside the While … Wend loop. The first is the creation of Node objects for each record in rs. Node; the absolute URL from rd (the parent Record to the Recordset) is used to identify the parent Node in the Tree for each new Node created in the loop. Each new Node is then given the absolute URL from a record in the Recordset to define its unique key.

The second key step is what happens when a record (in a Recordset) is identified as a collection. This tells "traverse" that it needs to find out about the record's children. Therefore, we create a new Record object based on the current record in the Recordset. We then call traverse again, this time passing the child Record object so that the whole process is completed at the next level down in the name space hierarchy.

Because each Node in the Tree knows the absolute URL of the resource it represents, displaying this resource in the WebBrowser control is simple:

```
Private Sub tvwDocs_NodeClick( _
            ByVal Node As MSComctlLib.Node)
                                             ┌─────── an absolute URL
If Node.Children = 0 Then wbrDoc.Navigate Node.Key
End Sub
```

The NodeClick event on the TreeView receives a Node object as an argument, which of course is the Node that the user clicked. We can therefore simply pass the Node's Key to the WebBrowser control's Navigate method to display any HTML or ActiveX Document.[9]

The code for the Delete and Copy buttons is simple, and it uses methods of the Record object that you have seen already. It reads the SelectedItem property of the TreeView control to identify the currently selected Node:

```
Private Sub cmdDelete_Click()
Dim rd As New Record
rd.Open tvwDocs.SelectedItem.Key
rd.DeleteRecord
rd.Close
End Sub

Private Sub cmdCopy_Click()
Dim rd As New Record
rd.Open tvwDocs.SelectedItem.Key
rd.CopyRecord , rd.ParentURL & _
           "/Copy of " & rd!RESOURCE_PARSENAME
rd.Close
End Sub
```

an absolute URL

Both of these operations should refresh the TreeView after the changes are made. The efficient way to do this is to rebuild only the subtrees affected by the operation. Such functionality is readily supported by the TreeView control, but it involves writing more user interface code than is justified for the purposes of this chapter. Instead, clicking in the TextBox control and pressing the Enter key will rebuild the entire Tree structure.

The Move operation is achieved using drag-and-drop and requires both the OLEDragMode and the OLEDropMode properties of the TreeView to be set to 1. The following code uses the TreeView control's HitTest method to identify the Node under the mouse at the time the OLEDragDrop event fires. This identifies the target of the drag-and-drop operation, while the Selected-Item property serves to identify the source of the operation. Here's the code:

```
Private Sub tvwDocs_OLEDragDrop( Data As MSComctlLib.DataObject, _
              Effect As Long, _
              Button As Integer, _
              Shift As Integer, _
              x As Single, _
              y As Single)
```

---

9. Most Microsoft Office documents are ActiveX Documents. It's also possible to create ActiveX Documents using VB.

```
Dim oSource As Node
Dim oTarget As Node
Dim rd As New Record
Set oSource = tvwDocs.SelectedItem
Set oTarget = tvwDocs.HitTest(x, y)
If oTarget Is Nothing Or _
    oSource Is Nothing Or _
    oTarget Is oSource Then Exit Sub
```
don't attempt the MoveRecord
unless the source and target
are different and valid Nodes

```
rd.Open oSource.Key
rd.MoveRecord , oTarget.Key & "/" & oSource.Text
rd.Close
End Sub
```

Finally, the Add operation comes in two parts. The first simply adds a new Node to the Tree as a child of the selected item and with a default name of New Resource. The second allows the user to edit the Node's text and to use this new text to create a new resource in the server. Here's the code for the first part:

create a new Tree Node
with no key

```
Private Sub cmdAdd_Click()
Dim oNode As Node
Set oNode = tvwDocs.Nodes.Add(tvwDocs.SelectedItem.Key, _
                tvwChild, , "New Resource")
Set tvwDocs.SelectedItem = oNode
End Sub
```

make it the selected node

Figure 9-4 shows the application after a new node has been added, and while it's in the process of having its label edited. Because no real resource is associated with this Tree Node, the WebBrowser control is unable to display it.

As soon as the label editing is finished, the TreeView control's AfterLabel-Edit event fires. We can trap this event and use it to create a new resource for a Node that has no key. If the edited Node already has a key, we can use rd.MoveRecord to rename the resource:

```
Private Sub tvwDocs_AfterLabelEdit( Cancel As Integer, _
                NewString As String)
Dim oNode As Node
Dim rd As New Record
Dim sParentURL As String
Set oNode = tvwDocs.SelectedItem
sParentURL = oNode.Parent.Key & "/"
```

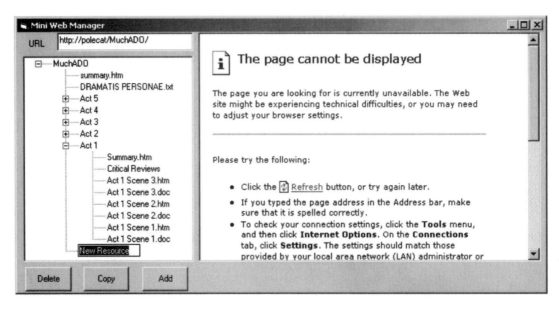

Figure 9-4. The Mini Web Manager during the process of adding a new resource

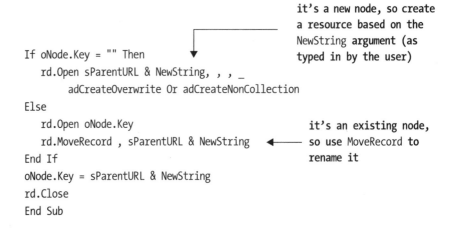

```
                                                    it's a new node, so create
                                                    a resource based on the
                                                    NewString argument (as
If oNode.Key = "" Then                              typed in by the user)
    rd.Open sParentURL & NewString, , , _
        adCreateOverwrite Or adCreateNonCollection
Else
    rd.Open oNode.Key                               it's an existing node,
    rd.MoveRecord , sParentURL & NewString          so use MoveRecord to
End If                                              rename it
oNode.Key = sParentURL & NewString
rd.Close
End Sub
```

As you can see, this code will only create leaf Nodes—it won't create new collections. However, this could easily be achieved by creating another Add button.

The program we've built in this section is not a finished product, but it does demonstrate very clearly how Record and Recordset objects work together to manage a semi-structured document name space.

One final difference between Records and Recordsets is worth noting. All Record objects have two Fields that we've yet to mention. The intriguing thing about these two Fields is that they have negative ordinal numbers. The FieldEnum enumeration defines the following two values:

adDefaultStream = –1

adRecordURL = –2

rd(adRecordURL).Value returns the same value as the RESOURCE_ABSOLUTE-PARSENAME Field and is merely a convenient way of referring to this frequently used Field. rd(adDefaultStream).Value returns a Stream object containing the actual content of the resource and provides one way to manipulate a resource's innards. The next section explores Stream objects in some detail.

In This Section

We saw how Record and Recordset objects work together to navigate and manipulate a name space hierarchy. We constructed a simple application to explore this capability and exploited what we learned in the previous section to Web site browsing and management functionality.

Streams

Streams are unlike any other type of ADO object. A Stream is nothing more specific than an arbitrary sequence of bytes. You can think of a Stream as being rather like a file, but without being tied to a location on a hard disk. Whereas a file is a sequence of bytes stored on a disk, a Stream is a sequence of bytes held in memory.[10] In fact, you'll see that Stream processing is very similar to file processing.

Although you can use an ADO Stream object purely as an in-memory file having no association with other ADO objects, our primary focus will be on how to use Streams in conjunction with Recordsets and Records. In Chapter 7 you saw how Streams can be used to persist Recordsets as XML without needing the overhead of a disk file. At the end of the last section, you saw how a Stream object provides access to the contents of a resource as represented by a Record object. Stream objects represent data in a very general way. This is handy, because in Universal Data Access, we need a structure that can hold any form of data.

Let's begin by looking at the properties of a Stream object stored in the adDefaultStream Field of a Record object:

---

10. Many object-oriented languages and tools implement a Stream object first, and then implement a file as a specialization of a Stream.

```
Dim rd As New Record
rd.Open "http://POLECAT/MuchADO/Act 1/Act 1 Scene 1.htm"
With rd(adDefaultStream).Value   ◄──────────────  a Stream object
  Print "State", .State
  Print "Mode", .Mode
  Select Case .Type
     Case adTypeText
        Print "Type", "Text"
     Case adTypeBinary
        Print "Type", "Binary"
  End Select
  Print "Charset", .Charset
  Print "LineSeparator", .LineSeparator
  Print "Size", .Size
  Print "Position", .Position
  Print "EOS", .EOS
End With
rd.Close
```

It prints

State	1
Mode	1
Type	Text
Charset	Unicode
LineSeparator	-1
Size	34454
Position	0
EOS	False

sm.State
sm.Mode
sm.Type
sm.Charset

The sm.State and sm.Mode properties use the ObjectStateEnum and ConnectModeEnum enumerations that we discussed before. sm.Type comes from the StreamTypeEnum enumeration and is either adTypeText or adTypeBinary. If it's adTypeBinary, the Charset property has no meaning. For an adTypeText Stream, the sm.Charset property can have one of many possible values, as defined under the Registry key HKEY_CLASSES_ROOT\ MIME\Database\Charset. Internally, the Stream stores text in *Unicode* format. The format you are most likely to want to use is ASCII. Both sm.Type and sm.Charset are read/write for closed Streams and for open Streams when sm.Position = 0. They are read-only at other times.

sm.LineSeparator

When sm.LineSeparator = -1, each line in a text file is separated by vbCrLf. Other possible values are defined by the LineSeparatorEnum enumeration.

sm.Size
sm.Position
sm.EOS

sm.Size tells you the number of bytes in the Stream, and sm.Position tells you where the Stream cursor is currently pointing. Note that when a Stream is opened, sm.Position is 0. sm.EOS is the Stream equivalent of rs.EOF.[11]

The Stream object's methods fall into three categories:

- Opening, closing and saving Streams.

- Uploading and downloading using Streams.

- Stream content manipulation.

Opening, Closing, and Saving Streams

sm.Open

Streams can be opened using:

- sm.Open, when the Source is a URL prefixed by the "URL=" keyword.

- sm.Open, when the Source is an open Record object.

- sm.Open with no Source (a fabricated Stream).

- A Stream object as an argument to a Recordset's Save method (see Chapter 7).

Here are examples of the first two of these options (sURL is a URL):

```
Dim rd As New Record
Dim sm As New Stream
rd.Open sURL
sm.Open rd, adModeRead, adOpenStreamFromRecord
```

and

```
Dim sm As New Stream
sm.Open "URL=" & sURL, adModeRead
```

The resulting Stream objects are functionally identical. If the Record already exists, then (by default) its contents will already be in client memory. Fetching them again would be wasteful. If you need to navigate up or down

---

11. It's ironic that a Stream (which is very file-like) doesn't use EOF (EndOfFile), whereas a Recordset (which is very un-file-like) does.

from the resource identified by the URL, you are going to need a Record object. In either of these cases, it makes sense to use the first option. Otherwise, it's just as easy to use the second option and create a Stream object directly.[12]

Here's the formal syntax for sm.Open:

```
Sub Open(   [Source As Variant],
            [Mode As ConnectModeEnum = adModeUnknown],
            [Options As StreamOpenOptionsEnum =
                adOpenStreamUnspecified],
            [UserName As String],
            [Password As String])
```

The only argument that needs further explanation is Options. The StreamOpenOptionsEnum has the following values:

> adOpenStreamAsync
>
> adOpenStreamFromRecord
>
> adOpenStreamUnspecified

sm.Cancel

As we saw at the start of this section, adOpenStreamFromRecord is required when the Source is a Record object. Stream objects support asynchronous operations, which can be canceled by the sm.Cancel method. As with Record objects, however, the MSDAIPP.DSO Provider doesn't support asynchronous retrieval, so we can't explore this feature with the current Provider.

sm.Close
sm.Flush

Once a Stream is no longer needed, it can be closed using sm.Close. Where a Source argument was specified when the Stream was opened, the Stream will automatically save itself back to its Source when closed, so there is no specific Save method for Streams. While a Stream is open, it's possible to force its contents to be saved by calling the sm.Flush method. However, it's generally not necessary to call this explicitly, as ADO has its own scheme for taking care of interim saves.

Uploading and Downloading Using Streams

To demonstrate some of the other features of Stream objects, we are going to extend our Mini Web Manager to give it download and upload functionality, and to support in-place editing of text and HTML documents. This requires adding four extra CommandButtons, an additional TextBox called txtContent, and a CommonDialog control called cdgDoc. This is what the upgraded application looks like:

---

12. A Record object also provides the RESOURCE_LASTWRITETIME Field, which can be used to provide optimistic locking control, if required.

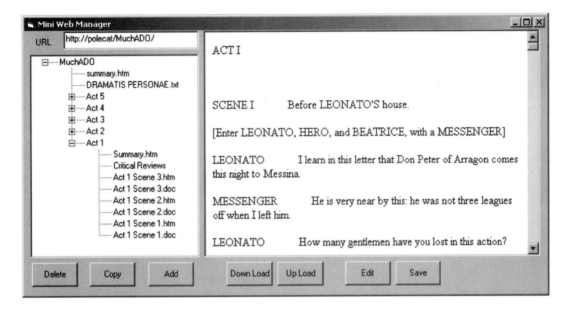

Figure 9-5. Mini Web Manager with Stream-related functionality

sm.SaveToFile
smReadFromFile

Using the Stream object's SaveToFile and ReadFromFile methods, downloading and uploading are very straightforward.

What will happen here is that HTTP and WebDAV will be used to access a resource, which will then be saved to a local disk file with a *UNC* filename. This (or another) file can then be modified locally and uploaded back to the Web server.

Here's the code behind both of the DownLoad and UpLoad buttons:

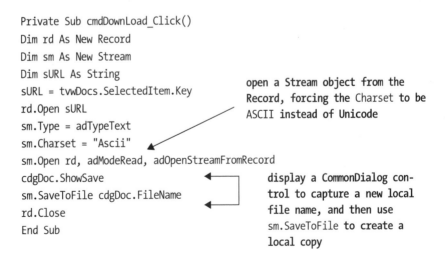

```
Private Sub cmdDownLoad_Click()
Dim rd As New Record
Dim sm As New Stream
Dim sURL As String
sURL = tvwDocs.SelectedItem.Key          open a Stream object from the
rd.Open sURL                             Record, forcing the Charset to be
sm.Type = adTypeText                     ASCII instead of Unicode
sm.Charset = "Ascii"
sm.Open rd, adModeRead, adOpenStreamFromRecord
cdgDoc.ShowSave                          display a CommonDialog con-
sm.SaveToFile cdgDoc.FileName            trol to capture a new local
rd.Close                                 file name, and then use
End Sub                                  sm.SaveToFile to create a
                                         local copy
```

```
Private Sub cmdUpLoad_Click()
Dim rd As New Record
Dim sm As New Stream
Dim sURL As String
sURL = tvwDocs.SelectedItem.Key
rd.Open sURL, , adModeReadWrite
sm.Type = adTypeText
sm.Charset = "Ascii"
sm.Open rd, adModeReadWrite, adOpenStreamFromRecord
cdgDoc.ShowSave
sm.LoadFromFile cdgDoc.FileName        ◄─────────  LoadFromFile replaces the
rd.Close                                          existing contents of the
End Sub                                           Stream with the contents from
                                                  the local file
```

Using the DownLoad button, I can make a local copy of Act 1 Scene 1.htm. I can then edit the file offline to introduce a grown-up BART SIMPSON instead of MESSENGER to respond to LEONATO's opening line. After uploading the file back to the Web server using the UpLoad button, I can use the Mini Web Manager to inspect the changes:

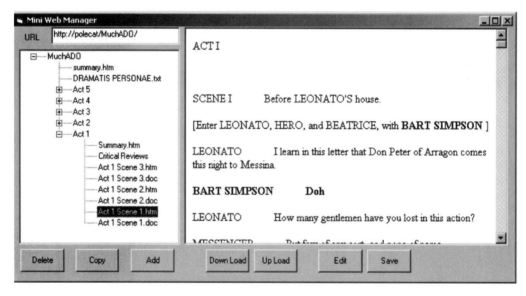

Figure 9-6. Editing the Web using the Mini Web Manager

Will Shakespeare—eat your heart out.

Stream Content Manipulation

While uploading and downloading are useful, the whole point in using Streams is to perform operations on a resource's content without needing to involve the file system. Stream objects have a set of methods that, when used in conjunction with the sm.Position, sm.EOS, and sm.LineSeparator properties, provide basic but useful Stream-processing capabilities. More elaborate processing can easily be performed by passing the Stream's contents to an appropriate processor.

Stream processing is very simple. A binary Stream is simply a sequence of bytes. A text Stream is also a sequence of bytes, but ADO provides Read-Text and WriteText methods that recognize line separators and allow you to work in characters instead of bytes when manipulating the Stream's contents. This is useful when using character sets, such as Unicode, that use two bytes per character.

Let's take a look at the properties and methods that support Stream navigation:

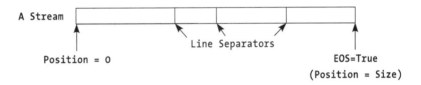

Figure 9-7. The structure of a typical Stream

sm.Position
sm.Size
sm.EOS

Read and write operations take place at the Stream's cursor, which is determined by the Position property. When Position is 0, the cursor is pointing at the beginning of the Stream. The EOS property can be used to determine when the cursor is at the end of the Stream. Position is always measured in bytes, regardless of the Stream type. Therefore, sm.EOS is simply a more convenient way of testing `sm.Position` = `sm.Size`.

Read and write operations change the current position. If Position starts at 0 and you read 100 bytes, Position will then be 100 unless the Stream has less than 100 bytes, in which case `sm.Position` will equal `sm.Size` and the number of bytes returned by the read operation will be less than requested. This means that you can't read beyond the end of the Stream.

sm.SetEOS

However, you can make the Stream smaller by calling sm.SetEOS. This makes the current position the end of the Stream, and all bytes following this new end of Stream are lost forever. For example, the following code clears the current Stream's contents:

```
sm.Position = 0
sm.SetEOS
```

Stream objects provide four approaches for reading and writing bytes of Stream data:

- You can read or write the entire Stream's contents in a single operation.

- You can read or write a specified number of bytes or characters.

sm.CopyTo

- You can copy all the contents from one Stream object to another using sm.CopyTo.

sm.SkipLine

- For text Streams, you can read and write whole lines, as well as a specified number of bytes. The sm.LineSeparator property determines how lines are delimited. The sm.SkipLine method can be used to skip a line while reading a Stream's contents.

sm.Read
sm.ReadText

Reading data from a Stream is performed using either sm.Read or sm.ReadText, depending on the Stream type (adTypeBinary or adTypeText). Here are the formal definitions of both methods:

Function Read([NumBytes As Long = -1]) As Variant

and

Function ReadText([NumChars As Long = -1]) As String

The argument to both functions is either a positive number of characters or bytes (depending on the function used) or one of the following values from the StreamReadEnum enumeration:

adReadAll (default)
adReadLine

sm.Write
sm.WriteText

Similarly, writing data to a Stream is performed using either sm.Write or sm.WriteText, depending on the Stream type. Here are the formal definitions of these methods:

Sub Write(Buffer As Variant)

and

Sub WriteText(Data As String,
                [Options As StreamWriteEnum = adWriteChar])

sm.Write takes a Variant array of bytes and writes it to a binary Stream. sm.WriteText takes a string and writes it to a text Stream. The Options argument to WriteText determines whether a line separator should be written to the stream. It has one of the following values from the StreamWriteEnum enumeration:

adWriteChar
adWriteLine

Neither sm.Write nor sm.WriteText truncate any data that remains after their own writing operation. This means that you can make changes in the middle of a Stream by using these methods. If you want to be sure the Stream has no data appearing after the data written by Write or WriteText, you need to perform an sm.SetEOS either immediately before or immediately after the operation. The same is true for the sm.CopyTo method.

We'll finish this section by adding in-place editing of text Streams to our Mini Web Manager application. We'll make use of the txtContents TextBox and the two remaining CommandButtons added earlier. txtContents has the same size and position as the WebBrowser control but is normally invisible. It supports multiple lines and is scrollable. The code for the Edit button that follows uses ReadText to take the contents of the current Record and write it to txtContents:

```
Private Sub cmdEdit_Click()
Dim rd As New Record
Dim sm As New Stream
Dim sURL As String
sURL = tvwDocs.SelectedItem.Key
rd.Open sURL
sm.Type = adTypeText
sm.Charset = "Ascii"
sm.Open rd, , adOpenStreamFromRecord
txtContent.Text = sm.ReadText
txtContent.Visible = True
End Sub
```

Read all the Stream's text and assign it to txtContent. Then make txtContent **visible.**

With the txtContents TextBox initialized and visible, the user can then edit the data. In the following screenshot, the user is editing the DRAMATIS PERSONAE file to change VERGES' description as shown in Figure 9-8.

When happy with the changes, the user can click the Save button, which executes this code:

```
Private Sub cmdSave_Click()
Dim rd As New Record
Dim sm As New Stream
Dim sURL As String
sURL = tvwDocs.SelectedItem.Key
rd.Open sURL, , adModeReadWrite
sm.Type = adTypeText
sm.Charset = "Ascii"
sm.Open rd, adModeReadWrite, adOpenStreamFromRecord
sm.WriteText txtContent.Text
sm.SetEOS
txtContent.Visible = False
End Sub
```

Write txtContent's new text into the Record's Stream. Call sm.SetEOS in case the original Stream was larger than the new one, and then make txtContent **invisible** again.

357

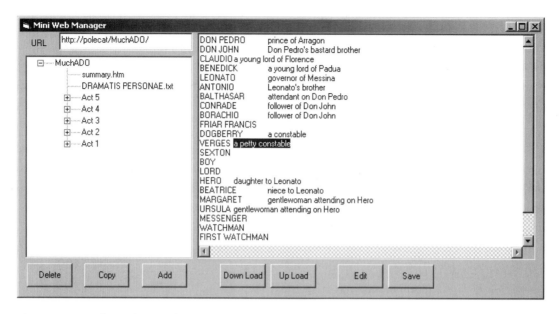

Figure 9-8. In-place editing of a Web page using the Mini Web Manager

Note that both the Record and the Stream were opened in read/write mode. Note also that we exploited the fact that the Stream was opened with `Position = 0`. A common error with Stream objects is to write the new data after the old data, instead of repositioning the cursor to the beginning of the Stream and overwriting the old content.

In This Section

Stream objects allow us to manipulate the contents of a resource. Streams make it convenient to process a resource's content either as a whole or as a series of bytes.

Summary

This chapter has shown that:

- ADO is breaking out beyond the boundaries of tabular data to deliver the promise of Universal Data Access.

- By adding the Record object to ADO 2.5, ADO acquired an object that was aware of the hierarchical structure typical of semi-structured data, and this is central to ADO's ability to manage documents.

- The Stream object adds a generalized way of manipulating the contents of documents.

Although the Provider we used in this chapter was specifically for Internet Publishing, it's clear that concepts such as URLs, which are strongly associated with the Internet, are at the heart of ADO's vision of document management, regardless of the Provider used. Both Stream and Record objects understand URLs and the nature of the name spaces they occupy.

While document management is different from database management in many ways, we've seen that:

- The new ADO features designed for document management have a distinctly ADO feel to them.

- Recordsets, the ADO workhorses, play a central role in this wider field of data access.

This is important, because Recordsets are becoming extremely well understood by many developers, and as we've seen throughout this book, are unmatched by other data structures in terms of their power, performance, and flexibility.

We can expect to see both the integration and the extension of ADO features to continue.

CHAPTER 10

The ADO Data Definition Language and Security Model (ADOX)

The Death of DAO

Using ADOX

ADOX and Jet

Summary

ONE OF THE REASONS WHY the ADO object model is small compared to previous data access models is that it has no specific objects to represent a data source's schema. This is partly explained by the fact that ADO does not assume that a data source has a schema that in any way resembles the kind of design model that a relational database might have. Instead, ADO provides a single, powerful method (OpenSchema) to allow data sources to provide whatever schema information is appropriate.

MDAC 2.1 introduced a new object model called ADOX that provides a strongly object-oriented approach to schema manipulation and management. The full name of ADOX is "ADO Extensions for Data Definition and Security," which reveals ADOX's ambitions for going well beyond the functionality supported by OpenSchema. Specifically, ADOX is designed to allow for the creation and modification of schemas in addition to providing read-only schema details, and it also has security features that allow a database's security to be maintained programmatically.

I say "ambitions" because (at the time of writing) the number of OLE DB Providers that goes anywhere near fully supporting ADOX is extremely limited.[1] It's reasonable to expect rapid progress in this area, at least in

---

1. Limited, in fact, to one—the Provider for Jet.

Providers written by Microsoft, although some limitations will remain. ODBC, for example, was never designed to provide a standard interface for creating and modifying schemas, although it does define standard functions for retrieving table, column, and stored procedure data. There is, therefore, limited scope for performing schema modification through the default ADO Provider, which uses ODBC. It's equally hard to imagine non-SQL Providers embracing ADOX enthusiastically, simply because ADOX is designed to work with relational database schemas.

In previous chapters, I paid considerable attention to performance issues. This level of attention is not appropriate for ADOX, simply because it's rare to have a situation in which large numbers of users are concurrently modifying (or even reading) schemas. While the role played by ADOX is important, most application developers (let alone end users) will spend only a small amount of their time using it.

The Death of DAO

I hope I am not being contentious by saying that the writing is on the wall for DAO. The reason for mentioning this here is that ADOX is several paragraphs of that writing.

As described in Chapter 3, Microsoft found itself with two data access models (DAO and RDO). One reason behind the creation of ADO was to replace these models with a single, all-purpose one. Supplanting RDO with ADO was a relatively simple process, but replacing DAO was trickier, due to its vast user base and significant Jet bias. In particular, ADO itself could not replace the programmatic features for data definition and security that are heavily used in some DAO programs. You only need to compare the ADOX features and objects to the DAO object model to see that ADOX was influenced by DAO. This has two implications:

1. Microsoft is determined that, in time, there should be no reason to continue using DAO. It's no coincidence that the Jet OLE DB Provider was the first one to fully support ADOX.[2]

2. Suspicious folk may get to thinking that the function of ADOX as a generic Data Definition and Security model may have been compromised by this influence.

---

2. Further evidence of this determination exists in the form of the JRO (Jet and Replication) object library. While this library is presented as part of ADO, its sole purpose is to provide all those other Jet features that aren't covered by ADODB and ADOX.

However, DAO isn't the only legacy system ADOX could potentially kill off. Another set of objects, the Distributed Management Objects (DMO), has for some years been the primary model for performing schema manipulation for SQLServer. The SQLServer OLE DB Provider doesn't currently provide all the functionality via ADOX that is required to retire DMO, but we can only speculate as to when this objective also will be achieved.

Using ADOX

Because of the difference between the ADOX functionality supported by the Jet Provider and the ADOX functionality currently supported by other Providers, let's split ADOX into two parts and deal first with those ADOX features supported by at least two Providers. Please keep in mind that ADOX functionality will be introduced into Providers as new releases become available, and that any restrictions mentioned in this discussion may well not exist by the time you read this.[3] This is less likely to be true for the ODBC Provider, due to the static nature of the ODBC API specification.

Although its scope is fairly constrained, ADOX has no shortage of classes defined in its object model, and Figure 10-1 shows a cut-down version that includes only the most-used classes.

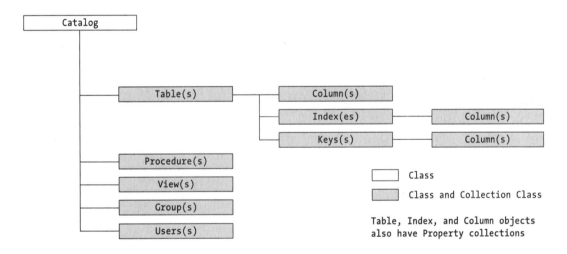

Figure 10-1. Major components of the ADOX object

---

3. And if the restrictions still exist today, they might not tomorrow.

cg.Active-
Connection

At the root of ADOX is the Catalog object. This is initialized either by providing an ADODB Connection object or a connection string for its Active-Connection property. The Catalog object can in theory be used to create new databases, but only the Jet Provider currently supports this feature.

cg.Tables
cg.Procedures
cg.Views
cg.Groups
cg.Users

Using the model to work your way around the schema is almost self-explanatory to any programmer who is familiar with collections. For example, the following code lists all the tables in the MuchADO SQLServer database (remember to set a reference to the ADOX Type Library):

```
Dim cg As New Catalog
Dim tb As Table
cg.ActiveConnection = "File Name=c:\MuchADO.udl"
For Each tb In cg.Tables
  If tb.Type = "TABLE" Or tb.Type = "VIEW" Then
    Print tb.Name, tb.Type, tb.DateCreated
  End If
Next
```

After adding a database View called MGWords, the code prints this:

Parts	TABLE	20/08/1999 14:34:46
SceneContents	TABLE	08/10/1999 10:36:13
Scenes	TABLE	20/08/1999 14:41:40
Words	TABLE	20/08/1999 14:49:32
MGWords	VIEW	03/12/1999 15:02:31

Note that the SQLServer Provider holds Views in the Tables collection. This is partly explained by the fact that the Provider doesn't support the Views collection. Let's see what happens when you try to access it. The following code:

```
Dim cg As New Catalog
Dim vw As View
cg.ActiveConnection = "File Name=c:\MuchADO.udl"
For Each vw In cg.Views          ◄──── error occurs when attempt-
  Print vw.Name, vw.DateCreated         ing to access the Views
Next                                    collection with the SQL OLE
                                        DB Provider
```

generates a run-time error:

```
3251 Object or provider is not capable of performing requested operation.
```

Sadly, there are no properties or attributes on a Catalog object that you can test to find out which ADOX features are supported based on the current Provider. This is particularly frustrating given the variable degree of support from different Providers. Be aware that this isn't the only error message that can result when using ADOX features that your Provider doesn't support, and that such errors can occur at the level of individual methods or properties, and not just when trying to create or enumerate objects. The net result of these facts is that any attempt to write robust, data source–independent code based on ADOX is either littered with complex error handling or doomed to failure, for all but the simplest applications.

The design of ADOX allows both the Views and Procedures collections to support creating and editing Views and Stored Procedures from an ADOX client. To permit this, they each have a Command property to hold a standard ADODB Command object, which is used to represent the actual view or stored procedure.

Working with Table Objects

It's reasonable to assume that if a Provider supports ADOX at all, it will provide basic support for the Tables collection. With the SQLServer OLE DB Provider, this includes being able to add and delete tables to and from an existing database.

A Table object has the following properties:

tb.Name	Name
tb.Type	Type
tb.ParentCatalog	ParentCatalog
tb.DateCreated	DateCreated
tb.DateModified	DateModified
tb.Columns	Columns (default)
tb.Indexes	Indexes
tb.Keys	Keys
tb.Properties	Properties

The last four of these properties are collections.

The only real difficulty in using the Table object arises from handling the many inconsistent errors raised by different Providers. To create a reasonably robust program, each property access on any ADOX object needs to be error handled. The only sane way to perform this is to exploit the VB6 Call-ByName[4] function, which allows you to pass in an object and a member

---

4. This is an extremely useful function, but by its very nature it uses late binding to access an object, thus significantly reducing performance.

(property or method name) as arguments. I used the following code to handle a property whose return type is not an object:

```
Public Function GetProperty(oADOXObj As Object, _
   sProperty As String) As Variant
On Error GoTo ErrH
GetProperty = CallByName(oADOXObj, sProperty, vbGet)
Exit Function
ErrH:
GetProperty = "***"
End Function
```

vbGet **is a constant specifying the member type—in this case, a property read**

And I wrote a similar function for a property with an object return type (called GetPropertyObj).

I also wrote a subroutine uses the functions to print out the name and value of each item in the collection. This subroutine (called printCollection) can be applied to Properties and Columns collections in the ADOX object model. I then wrote the following code to print a report of a table called sTableName:

```
Dim tb As Table
Dim cl As Column
Dim ky As Key
Dim ix As Index
Dim py As Property


On Error GoTo COLUMNSLABEL
Set tb = cg.Tables(sTableName)
Print "TABLE:", GetProperty(tb, "Name")
Print "Type:", GetProperty(tb, "Type")
Print "DateCreated:", GetProperty(tb, "DateCreated")
Print "DateModified:", GetProperty(tb, "DateModified")


printCollection GetPropertyObj(tb, "Properties")

COLUMNSLABEL:
Print "COLUMNS"
On Error GoTo KEYSLABEL
For Each cl In tb.Columns
    Print cl.Name, cl.Type
    printCollection GetPropertyObj(cl, "Properties")
Next
```

print out the table's static properties

print out the table's dynamic properties

print the static and dynamic properties in the Columns collection

```
KEYSLABEL:
Print "KEYS"
On Error GoTo INDEXLABEL
For Each ky In GetPropertyObj(tb, "Keys")  ◄────── print each key in the
    Print ky.Name, ky.Type                         Keys collection, along
    printCollection GetPropertyObj(ky, "Columns")  with its columns
Next
INDEXLABEL:
Print "INDEXES"                                     print each index in the
On Error GoTo ENDLABEL                     ┌──────  Indexes collection, along
For Each ix In GetPropertyObj(tb, "Indexes")        with its columns
    Print ix.Name, ix.Unique, ix.Clustered
    printCollection GetPropertyObj(ix, "Columns")
Next
ENDLABEL:
```

While not perfect, this code works with SQLServer and Access, using both native and ODBC-based connections. However, only the Jet OLE DB Provider was able to handle all the program's requests. Its (rather substantial) output for the Parts table is as follows:

```
TABLE:        Parts
Type:         TABLE
DateCreated:  20/08/1999 15:44:29
DateModified: 11/10/1999 15:00:41
              Temporary Table                False
              Jet OLEDB:Table Validation Text
              Jet OLEDB:Table Validation Rule
              Jet OLEDB:Cache Link Name/Password       False
              Jet OLEDB:Remote Table Name
              Jet OLEDB:Link Provider String
              Jet OLEDB:Link Datasource
              Jet OLEDB:Exclusive Link    False
              Jet OLEDB:Create Link       False
              Jet OLEDB:Table Hidden In Access         False
COLUMNS
description   202
              Autoincrement False
              Default
              Description
              Nullable      False
              Fixed Length  False
              Seed          1
              Increment     1
```

```
                    Jet OLEDB:Column Validation Text
                    Jet OLEDB:Column Validation Rule
                    Jet OLEDB:IISAM Not Last Column          False
                    Jet OLEDB:AutoGenerate        False
                    Jet OLEDB:One BLOB per Page False
                    Jet OLEDB:Compressed UNICODE Strings     False
                    Jet OLEDB:Allow Zero Length False
                    Jet OLEDB:Hyperlink           False
        part        202
                    Autoincrement False
                    Default
                    Description
                    Nullable      True
                    Fixed Length  False
                    Seed          1
                    Increment     1
                    Jet OLEDB:Column Validation Text
                    Jet OLEDB:Column Validation Rule
                    Jet OLEDB:IISAM Not Last Column          False
                    Jet OLEDB:AutoGenerate        False
                    Jet OLEDB:One BLOB per Page False
                    Jet OLEDB:Compressed UNICODE Strings     False
                    Jet OLEDB:Allow Zero Length False
                    Jet OLEDB:Hyperlink           False
        KEYS
        PrimaryKey    1
        INDEXES
        PrimaryKey    True          False
```

The SQLServer OLE DB Provider generates only the following output for the same table:

```
        TABLE:      Parts
        Type:       TABLE
        DateCreated: 20/08/1999 14:34:46
        DateModified: Null
                    Temporary Table          False
        COLUMNS
        part        129
                    Autoincrement False
                    Default
                    Fixed Length  False
                    Nullable      True
```

	Primary Key	
	Unique	
description	200	
	Autoincrement	False
	Default	
	Fixed Length	False
	Nullable	False
	Primary Key	
	Unique	
KEYS		
PK_Parts	1	
INDEXES		
PK_Parts	True	False

ADOX contains the required enumerations to make sense of the numerical values shown for data type and key type in the preceding examples.

Adding Tables into SQLServer

You currently can't create new databases in SQLServer, but you can add new tables to existing databases (catalogs). The only benefit you gain from doing so is that you can exploit an object model instead of writing standard SQL-DDL.[5] The following very simple code will create a three-column table called "test" and add it to a Catalog called "cg", opened using the SQLServer OLE DB Provider:

```
Dim tb As New ADOX.Table
tb.Name = "test"
tb.Columns.Append "Column1", adInteger
tb.Columns.Append "Column2", adInteger
tb.Columns.Append "Column3", adVarWChar, 50

cg.Tables.Append tb
```

---

5. DDL stands for Data Definition Language, and it represents those elements of SQL used to create, alter, and drop tables, indexes, and the like. For most purposes, DDL is standard across many databases so it already provides a standardized way of building databases. One notable exception to this is Jet, which uses nonstandard field names.

which represents the following CREATE TABLE DDL statement:

```
CREATE TABLE [dbo].[test] (
    [Column1] [int] NOT NULL ,
    [Column2] [int] NOT NULL ,
    [Column3] [nvarchar] (50) NOT NULL )
```

cls.Append
kys.Append
ixs.Append

This is reasonably straightforward, but using the Append method doesn't allow full control over how columns are created. The tb.Keys and tb.Indexes collections also support the Append method, but again with limited control over how indexes and keys are specified. For greater control, you'll need to create Column, Key, and Index objects explicitly, and then append these objects to the appropriate collection after setting their properties.

Here's a more realistic example of creating the same "test" table, where Column1 is an AutoIncrement primary key, and Column2 allows Null values:

```
Dim tb As New Table
Dim ix As Index
Dim cl As Column
tb.Name = "test"
Set cl = New Column
Set cl.ParentCatalog = cg          ←——— setting the ParentCatalog allows Pro-
cl.Name = "Column1"                      vider-specific dynamic properties to
cl.Type = adInteger                      be assigned
cl.Properties("Autoincrement") = True  ←——— create Column1 as an
tb.Columns.Append cl                        Autoincrement column

Set cl = New Column
Set cl.ParentCatalog = cg
cl.Name = "Column2"
cl.Type = adInteger
cl.Properties("Nullable") = True   ←——— create Column2 as an
tb.Columns.Append cl                     Nullable column

Set cl = New Column
Set cl.ParentCatalog = cg
cl.Name = "Column3"
cl.Type = adVarWChar
cl.DefinedSize = 50
tb.Columns.Append cl
```

```
Set ix = New Index
ix.Name = "test_pkey"
ix.PrimaryKey = True
ix.Clustered = True
ix.Columns.Append "Column1"
tb.Indexes.Append ix

cg.Tables.Append tb
```

use an Index object to create
a clustered primary key

This code represents the following DDL:

```
CREATE TABLE [dbo].[test] (
    [Column1] [int] IDENTITY (1, 1) NOT NULL ,
    [Column2] [int] NULL ,
    [Column3] [nvarchar] (50) NOT NULL )

ALTER TABLE [dbo].[test] WITH NOCHECK ADD
    CONSTRAINT [test_pkey] PRIMARY KEY  CLUSTERED
    ([Column1])
```

At the time of writing, the SQLServer OLE DB Provider doesn't support adding keys to the tb.Keys collection, and as a result, the primary key must be created using an Index, with its ix.PrimaryKey property set to True. Lack of support for true Key objects prevents foreign key constraints from being declared, although you can choose between clustered and nonclustered primary keys.

cl.ParentCatalog   The main point to note here is the use of the cl.ParentCatalog property. Some Column properties (including dynamic ones) can't be modified once the Column has been appended to a Table, and fewer still once the Table has been appended to a Catalog. This creates a problem for setting dynamic Column properties. These properties are Provider-specific, and yet they can't be set once the Column has been attached to a Catalog via its Table, which is the point at which the Table and Column objects become tied to a specific Provider. The ParentCatalog property solves this problem by making the Column object aware of the dynamic properties supported by its eventual Provider before losing its writability.

ADOX and Jet

This section provides some examples of how to create Jet databases, add "procedures," and manipulate security, which should prove useful if you use Jet. If you don't use Jet, this section will allow you to experience a wider range of ADOX functionality in anticipation of more fully featured Providers.

cg.Create

The Jet Provider allows you to create new databases from scratch. For example, the following code creates a new database and adds the "test" table to it:

```
Dim cg As New Catalog
Dim tb As New ADOX.Table
cg.Create "Provider=Microsoft.Jet.OLEDB.4.0;" & _
          "Data Source=c:\Serious ADO\testnew.mdb;"

tb.Name = "test"

tb.Columns.Append "Column1", adInteger
tb.Columns.Append "Column2", adInteger
tb.Columns.Append "Column3", adVarWChar, 50

cg.Tables.Append tb
```

The Jet Provider supports a huge range of dynamic properties on all relevant objects. These are amply documented and will be immediately meaningful to Jet aficionados.

While Jet doesn't support stored procedures in the way that the major relational database engines do, it does allow stored queries to be saved and treated like a limited form of stored procedure.[6]

For example, the parameterized Word Usage query we used back in Chapter 5 can be turned into a procedure using the Jet Provider and an open Catalog object variable:

```
Dim cd As New Command
Dim sSQL as String
sSQL = "SELECT Words.word, SUM(Words.wordCount) AS total" & _
    " FROM Words INNER JOIN Parts ON Words.part = Parts.part" & _
    " GROUP BY Words.word, Parts.part, Words.WordLength" & _
    " HAVING (Parts.part = ?)AND (SUM(Words.wordCount) > ?)" & _
      " AND (Words.WordLength > ?)" & _
    " ORDER BY SUM(Words.wordCount) DESC"
cd.CommandText = sSQL
cg.Procedures.Append "WordUsage", cd   ◄——————  create the new Procedure
```

---

6. Jet runs as a set of DLLs in the client process. As a result, the performance benefits typically attributed to stored procedures (reduced network traffic, and using the server's CPU to run queries) don't apply to Jet-based applications. Also, Jet stored queries are pure SQL—there is no programming language equivalent to the T-SQL used in SQLServer or Sybase.

pcs.Append
vws.Append

The usage in this code is interesting. The code creates an ADODB Command object, which is used in the Append method to the cg.Procedures collection, along with a procedure name. It isn't possible to create a Procedure object and append it in the way that other ADOX objects are used.[7]

pc.Name
pc.DateCreated
pc.DateModified
pc.Command

The Procedure object has Name, DateCreated, DateModified, and Command properties. The Command property provides a standard ADODB Command object. Reading this object's CommandText property provides an easy way to display and edit the text of a procedure. The Command object could even be executed as follows:

```
Set rs = cg.Procedures("WordUsage").Command.Execute _
                    (, Array("DON PEDRO", 4, 4))
```

but it would be more likely that it would be used in a standard ADODB project, using exactly the same techniques discussed in Chapter 5. Just to prove that Jet Procedures can be called using standard ADO syntax, here's an example:

```
Dim cd As New Command
Dim rs As Recordset
cd.CommandType = adCmdStoredProc
cd.CommandText = "WordUsage"
cd.ActiveConnection = "File Name=c:\MuchADOJet.udl"
Set rs = cd.Execute(, Array("DON PEDRO", 4, 4))
While Not rs.EOF
    Print rs!word, rs!total
    rs.MoveNext
Wend
```

vw.Name
vw.DateCreated
vw.DateModified
vw.Command

Jet treats Views just as it does Procedures. In fact, as far as Jet is concerned, Procedures are stored queries that contain parameters, and Views are stored queries with no parameters. If you append a command with no parameters to the Parameters collection, it will initially appear in the Procedures collection. However, if you then Refresh the Views and Procedures collections (or restart the program), the previously created Procedure will now appear only in the Views collection.

Using ADOX Security Features with Jet

gp.Users
gps.Append
ur.Groups
urs.Append

ADOX security is based around a collection of Group objects and a collection of User objects. A Group object has a gp.Users property that can be used to enumerate all the Users belonging to the Group, and to Append new Users.

---

7. In fact, both Procedure and View are marked as PublicNotCreatable—you can't use New to create them.

A User object has a ur.Groups property, which can be used to enumerate all the Groups to which a given user belongs, and to add a User to a Group.

ur.ChangePassword

Working with Groups and Users will be familiar to anyone who has ever administered security on a Windows NT file space; the same design guidelines apply.[8] The User object supports a ur.ChangePassword method, and the Group object supports gp.GetPermissions and gp.SetPermissions methods.[9]

Jet stores all security information in a Workgroup Information File (with a .mdw extension), which is kept separately from any Jet database file (.mdb). To use Jet security with ADOX or ADO, you must reference the appropriate .mdw file when connecting. You can do this in the connection string; via cn.Properties; or through the All tab on the Data Link Properties dialog box used to create .udl files. Whichever approach you use, you are setting the Jet OLEDB:System database dynamic property to the fully qualified filename for the .mdw file. An error will occur if you don't specify this property correctly.

The following code creates some Users and Groups, and sets up some Group memberships:

```
cg.ActiveConnection = "File Name=c:\MuchADOJet.udl"
cg.Users.Append "Rob", "Robpw"
cg.Users("Rob").Groups.Append "Users"
cg.Users.Append "Gary", "Garypw"
cg.Users.Append "Russ", "Russpw"
cg.Groups.Append "Readers"
cg.Groups("Readers").Users.Append "Gary"
cg.Groups("Readers").Users.Append "Russ"
```

This code creates three new Users and allocates passwords to them. Jet databases come with Admins and Users groups predefined, so I have added one extra group (Readers). It then shows two different ways to allocate Users to Groups. Both the Groups and Users collections also support Delete methods.

ur.GetPermissions
gp.GetPermissions

To find out which permissions a Group (and therefore its Users) has, the GetPermissions method can be used:

```
Function GetPermissions( Name As Variant,
                         ObjectType As ObjectTypeEnum,
                         [ObjectTypeId As Variant])
                         As RightsEnum
```

---

8. By this I mean allocate all permissions to Groups, and then add Users to those Groups, instead of allocating permissions to Users. For enhanced security, change the administrator's password to something other than your mother's maiden name. Also, it's a good idea to periodically remove all Post-It password lists from users' computers and to wipe clear the passwords section of the office whiteboard from time to time. If you know more rules of thumb than this, you are a security expert.

9. The User object also supports these methods, but see the preceding footnote.

Name is either the name of a database object (of a table, column, etcetera) or Null if you want to see permissions for all objects of a particular type. ObjectType is defined by the ObjectTypeEnum enumeration, which has the following values:

adPermObjColumn

adPermObjDatabase

adPermObjProcedure

adPermObjProviderSpecific

adPermObjTable

adPermObjView

The optional ObjectTypeId argument can be used to handle Providerspecific types, therefore allowing nonrelational concepts to be managed by ADOX security.

The return value of getPermissions is typically an overloaded value that is unpacked using bitwise operations. The RightsEnum enumeration contains the following *bitmasks* for this purpose:

adRightCreate

adRightDelete

adRightDrop

adRightExclusive

adRightExecute

adRightFull

adRightInsert

adRightMaximumAllowed

adRightNone

adRightRead

adRightReadDesign

adRightReadPermissions

adRightReference

adRightUpdate

adRightWithGrant

adRightWriteDesign

adRightWriteOwner

adRightWritePermissions

The following code will return the permissions on the Parts table for a Group name stored in `sGroupName`:

```
Dim gp As Group
cg.ActiveConnection = "File Name=c:\MuchADOJet.udl"
Set gp = cg.Groups(sGroupName)
Print gp.GetPermissions("Parts", adPermObjTable)
```

When `sGroupName` = `"Readers"`, this code prints:

```
0
```

showing that Russ and Gary have no permissions,[10] whereas `sGroupName` = `"Users"` prints

```
-1072706304
```

I'll spare you the code that uses bitwise operations and the RightsEnum to make sense of this value.[11] What matters are the results of unpacking it, which show that Rob has the following permissions (as a member of the predefined Users group):

> adRightCreate
> adRightUpdate
> adRightReadDesign
> adRightDrop
> adRightInsert
> adRightWriteDesign
> adRightReadPermissions
> adRightDelete
> adRightWriteOwner
> adRightWritePermissions

Members of the Admin group have full permissions.

---

10. This is how I like it.

11. Handling overloaded values was explained way back in Chapter 2. The full code is available on the book's CD in the companion program for this chapter.

I have used the following code to test the impact of these security settings:

```
On Error GoTo ErrH
Dim cn As New Connection
Dim rs As New Recordset
Dim sMDB As String
Dim sMDW As String
sMDB = "C:\Serious ADO\muchado.mdb"
sMDW = "d:\Program Files\Microsoft Office\Office\system.mdw"

cn.Provider = "Microsoft.Jet.OLEDB.4.0"
cn.Properties("Data Source") = sMDB
cn.Properties("Prompt") = adPromptAlways          force the user to log
                                                  on at a prompt
cn.Properties("Jet OLEDB:System Database") = sMDW
cn.Open                                           set the WorkGroup
rs.CursorType = adOpenStatic                      Information File
rs.LockType = adLockOptimistic
rs.Open "SELECT * FROM Parts WHERE part = 'BOY'", cn    read some data
Print rs!part, rs!Description
rs!Description = "a young male "           update some data
rs.Update
Print rs!part, rs!Description
Exit Sub
ErrH:
Print Err.Number, Err.Description
```

Logging on as Russ or Gary prints:

-2147217911   Record(s) cannot be read; no read permission on 'Parts'.

In other words, an error occurred when trying to execute the SELECT statement.

Logging on as Rob prints

BOY	Null
BOY	a young male

I'll finish this section by showing you how to change permissions. This is achieved using the SetPermissions method on the Group and User objects:

```
Sub SetPermissions( Name As Variant,
                    ObjectType As ObjectTypeEnum,
                    Action As ActionEnum,
                    Rights As RightsEnum,
                    [Inherit As InheritTypeEnum = adInheritNone],
                    [ObjectTypeId])
```

This method introduces two new enumerations. ActionEnum is fairly straightforward, but it requires a little explanation to expose the differences between some of the options:

- **adAccessGrant**: The Group or User will have at least the requested permissions.

- **adAccessSet**: The Group or User will have exactly the requested permissions.

- **adAccessDeny**: The Group or User will be denied the specified permissions.

- **adAccessRevoke**: Any explicit access rights the Group or User has will be revoked.

The key point here is to appreciate the difference between Deny and Revoke. Deny can be used to specifically deny access to a particular resource. Revoke can revoke this denial, thereby restoring any default rights, and it also can be used to revoke additional permissions. When using Revoke, there is no point specifying any values in the Rights argument, as these will be revoked!

The InheritTypeEnum enumeration makes it possible to control how permissions changes bubble down to objects contained within the target database object of the method call. Our example will use the default value (adInheritNone). The various options are shown here:

adInheritBoth
adInheritContainers
adInheritNone (default)
adInheritNoPropagate
adInheritObjects

The following code will allow Readers to have read access to the Parts table:

```
Dim gp As Group
cg.ActiveConnection = "File Name=c:\MuchADOJet.udl"
Set gp = cg.Groups("Readers")

gp.SetPermissions "Parts", adPermObjTable, adAccessGrant, adRightRead
```

Rerunning the test code and logging on as Russ or Gary now displays these results:

```
BOY                          a young male
-2147217911   You do not have the necessary permissions to use
the 'Parts' object.  Have your system administrator or the person who
created this object establish the appropriate permissions for you.
```

This shows that they can read the data, but an error occurs when they attempt to update it. This is an appropriate response for a member of a Readers group. One day, I'll give Russ and Gary update permissions too.

Summary

In Chapter 4 we explored the Connection object's OpenSchema method. Although OpenSchema provides read-only data, it has the following advantages over using ADOX:

- It's more widely supported by OLE DB Providers and will undoubtedly remain so, at least in the near to middle future.

- It provides a wider range of schema information with more detail than ADOX does.

- It has a more manageable error model.

- For read-only purposes OpenSchema is more efficient and easier to manage than ADOX because of the ability to provide restrictions (for example, restricting the type of table returned).

- OpenSchema returns Recordsets. As discussed in Chapter 2, Recordsets provide a more efficient, powerful, flexible, easy-to-use— and most important—consistent model for manipulating two-dimensional data than Collection-based object models in many circumstances.

Most of the schema manipulation applications I have used or written are read-only, and OpenSchema appears to offer significant benefits for such applications. It's reasonably easy to make schema changes using SQL-DDL statements with cn.Execute.

ADOX offers potential for providing a generic way of managing database schemas and security, but only when there is sufficient Provider support, and on the assumption that its longer-term ambitions haven't been confounded by any Jet bias. More seriously, ADOX suffers from a lack of run-time information concerning which features a given Provider supports. A Supports property on the Catalog object would address all my concerns here.

CHAPTER 11

Creating Simple Providers

A MAJOR CONSTRAINT ON THE USE of ADO is the availability of Providers. As long as we can get data from a Provider, ADO provides a programming model that is richer and easier to use than just about any data structure imaginable. However, there are many sources of data that would be amenable to ADO's charm if only we had access to a Provider that could create Recordsets and Records from the data. Consider the following types of data, all of which have the tabular structure required to be held as a Recordset:

- Subkeys and values of a Registry key

- The NT Event Log

- Type libraries

- Processes currently running on your computer

- Projects and files stored by SourceSafe

- OLE DB Providers registered on your computer

- All the data in your Personal Digital Assistant

- TV listings

- Sports results and statistics

- Those mainframe files with the really useful data in a weird format

- Those PC files with the really useful data in a weird format

The chances are that you don't have a Provider for these data formats, and therefore, you don't use them as much as you should, because each one requires learning a new API for accessing the data. Alternatively, each programming team you know has written their own wrapper that turns a complex proprietary interface into a simple proprietary interface with obscure proprietary bugs that require frequent proprietary fixes.

Of course, you can see what's coming. I'm going to tell you that you can write your own Provider that offers a standard ADO interface to whatever tabular form of data you can think of, and that you can do any manner of wondrous ADO things with the resulting Recordset. Too right!

In this chapter, you'll see how you can combine VB with Microsoft's Simple Provider Interface for OLE DB to roll your own Recordsets. Instead of using any of the preceding examples, you'll create a Provider that makes a VB form look like an ADO Recordset, containing a record for each control on the form, and Fields to describe its name, type, position, and so forth. You'll even see how you can use ADO to add to, delete from, and modify a form's controls.

Why Do It?

Here's a VB form:

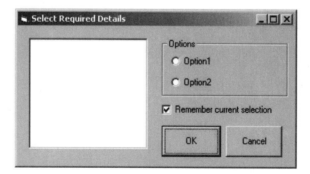

Figure 11-1. A simple VB form

and here's a VB program showing that form's controls as a Recordset bound
to a standard ADO Data Control and ADO Data Grid. The VB program
shown in this figure has no lines of code—only property settings—and is
fully updateable.

Name	DataType	Parent	Caption	Index	Left	Top	Width	Height	TabIndex
▶ frmSelect	VB.Form		Select Required Details	0	0	0	0	0	0
chkRemember	VB.CheckBox	frmSelect	Remember current selection	0	3000	1500	2595	315	6
fraOptions	VB.Frame	frmSelect	Options	0	3000	240	2595	1155	3
optDetails	VB.OptionButton	fraOptions	Option2	1	180	720	2175	315	5
optDetails	VB.OptionButton	fraOptions	Option1	0	180	300	1995	315	4
lstDetails	VB.ListBox	frmSelect		0	240	240	2475	2205	2
cmdCancel	VB.CommandButton	frmSelect	Cancel	0	4320	1980	1155	615	1
cmdOK	VB.CommandButton	frmSelect	OK	0	3000	1980	1215	615	0

Figure 11-2. A VB form viewed as an ADO Recordset

As you can see, there is a record here for each control on the previous
form. By clicking in the grid, I can edit the Caption for cmdCancel to say "give
up". This automatically modifies the source file for the form, so that the next
time I open it from the VB IDE it looks like this:

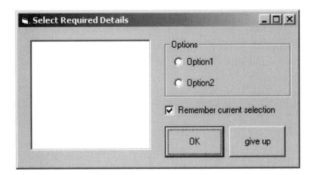

Figure 11-3. A Simple VB form, after being edited using ADO

While you may never choose to use a data grid to modify VB source code,
the potential that this demonstration shows should be clear. The only
component I haven't explained is the simple Provider that turns VB source
into a Recordset, and we'll spend our time in this chapter seeing how to write
this Provider. VB source isn't very amenable to being turned into a Recordset,
so if you can write a Provider for VB source code, it should be possible to do
it for other types of data too.

Before going any further, we should look at what a Simple Provider is exactly. There are three ways to generate Recordsets when you don't have an existing Provider:

- *Write a full-blown OLE DB Provider using C++.* Although Microsoft provides development kits to assist in this task, it's a major undertaking. You can't build a full-blown Provider in VB because it requires using COM in ways that are beyond VB.

- *Use fabricated Recordsets.* Building read-only fabricated Recordsets is very easy. However, while a user of a fabricated Recordset can also write changes to the Recordset, the user is typically responsible for saving those changes using Recordset persistence techniques. Expecting the user to save and load Recordsets takes away some of the feel of working with ADO—ADO users typically expect Recordsets to have (or be able to have) an active connection that takes care of reading and writing changes. This isn't possible with fabricated Recordsets. Also, there is no such thing as a fabricated Connection. Therefore, you can't get hold of fabricated Recordsets by using standard cn.Execute or rs.Open techniques. Some interface other than regular ADO is required for getting hold of fabricated Recordsets.

- *Use Simple Providers if you don't like the sound of the first two options.* Creating a trivial Simple Provider takes about ten times longer than creating a trivial fabricated Recordset. Creating a moderately complex Simple Provider is no harder than creating a moderately complex fabricated Recordset, and it's a far more satisfying experience for both the developer and user.

- *The Simple Provider interface is simple.* Many of the complexities of full-blown Providers are removed, so that the Provider is easier to write. This means, however, that some ADO features won't be available to users of your Provider. These include:

  - **Transaction processing:** While Simple Providers expose Connection objects, you can't do transaction processing with them. In fact each individual cell update (for example, setting one Field on one row) is treated as a separate operation, and there is no way to link together multiple updates. Your Provider is even hidden from rs.Update and rs.UpdateBatch statements—all you hear about are changes to individual cells.[1] You need to think carefully whether you can live with this limitation.

---

1. There are ways in which you can overcome this limitation, which we'll discuss later.

- **Metadata**: All Fields generated by a Simple Provider are Variants, so apart from Field Names and the adFldUpdatable attribute, there is no metadata available from Recordsets. This can be particularly annoying when you want to perform tests on data types in client code. C++ programmers using Simple Providers can add data type information, but this is off limits to VBers.

- **Sorting**: ADO Sort won't work with Simple Providers, although Find and Filter will.

- **Command and Parameter objects**: Neither Command nor Parameter objects can be used with Simple Providers.

- **Record objects**: Simple Providers are strictly limited to tabular data. However, you can save a Recordset created with a Simple Provider to a Stream object, so long as you use a client-side cursor.[2] This is a neat way of getting XML for free.

If you can live with these constraints and you want to see data appear on client programs or Web pages as ADO Recordsets, then writing a Simple Provider can be very worthwhile. It's a particularly easy and suitable technique for read-only data, enabling you to take weird data formats or even data from multiple sources, and produce a regular Recordset for client programs to consume. Handling updateable Recordsets is a bit more of a challenge, especially given the lack of transactional and batch update features, but it can be made to work well. Later in the chapter, you'll get to see what is involved.

> **In This Section**

We considered the place of Simple Providers in system designs and some of the constraints they impose.

The Simple Provider Interface

You create a Simple Provider by writing an ActiveX DLL in VB. While this chapter and its companion program on the book's CD contain all you need to know to put a Simple Provider together, I'll assume some familiarity with writing DLLs.

---

2. This is an exception to the rule that most Simple Provider Recordsets work better with a server-side cursor.

Simple Providers work like this: Microsoft supplies a Provider known as the Microsoft OLE DB Simple Provider, or MSDAOSP. MSDAOSP becomes the Provider that your ADO code connects to, although you can substitute your own Provider name, as you'll see. This Provider supports the many low-level OLE DB interfaces that Providers are required to implement and takes care of most of the OLE DB housekeeping and plumbing that supports ADO. In order to make use of your custom Provider calls, MSDAOSP makes calls through to your DLL, using an agreed-upon interface. Because MSDAOSP takes care of many routine tasks, this agreed-upon interface is much simpler than all the OLE DB interfaces that a full-blown Provider is required to implement. This agreed-upon interface is actually two separate COM interfaces: one for inbound calls (called OLEDBSimpleProvider), and one for outbound notifications (called OLEDBSimpleProviderListener). You get hold of their definitions by setting a reference to "Microsoft OLE DB Simple Provider Library 1.5", which comes from a type library called SIMPDATA.TLB.[3] The type library also contains some useful enumerations, although you may also want to set a reference to the "OLE DB Errors Type Library" to be able to raise standard OLE DB errors when necessary.

The following diagram shows the relationship between these different components:

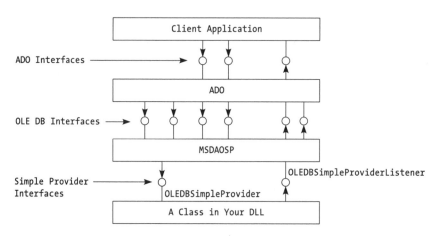

Figure 11-4. Components involved in using a Simple Provider

Your job as a Simple Provider writer is to write code that responds correctly to the calls that MSDAOSP makes to your DLL through the OLEDB-SimpleProvider interface, and to make calls back to MSDAOSP through the OLEDBSimpleProviderListener interface when you are required to raise notifications (or events), which in the case of a simple read-only Provider is never.

---

3. If SIMPDATA.TLB doesn't appear in your References box, locate the file and then register it using the Browse button on the Project-References dialog box.

We'll call an object that implements this functionality, a *Record Source Object*. With the help of MSDAOSP, it will appear as a regular ADO Recordset to client programs using your Provider. We'll also need to create an object that will represent an ADO Connection object, which is used to serve up Record Source Objects. This is known as the *Data Source Object*. We'll see that writing the Data Source Object's class is very simple.

We'll start by writing a simple read-only Provider, so we can ignore the OLEDBSimpleProviderListener interface for the time being. The OLEDB-SimpleProvider interface has fourteen methods for which we need to provide implementations. While this sounds like a lot of code, we can provide dummy implementations for many of these methods, as only updateable or asynchronous Providers require them. The following table defines all the methods in the Simple Provider interface.

Table 11-1. Simple Provider Interface Methods

METHODS USED IN ALL RECORD SOURCES

getRowCount	Returns the number of rows (records).
getColumnCount	Returns the number of columns (Fields).
getVariant	Retrieves the value of the cell for a specified row and column.
getRWStatus	Returns the read/write status of a column, row, cell, or record source.
find	Searches for a specified set of values.
getLocale	Indicates the locale of the data.

METHODS USED IN UPDATEABLE RECORD SOURCES[4]

setVariant	Sets the value of the cell at the row and column indicated.
insertRows	Inserts a specified number of empty rows.
deleteRows	Deletes a specified number of rows.
addOLEDBSimpleProviderListener	Registers an event handler.
removeOLEDBSimpleProvider-Listener	Unregisters an event handler.

---

4. Asynchronous Providers also need to implement the OLEDBSimpleProviderListener methods so that they are able to raise events during the data retrieval process.

Table 11-1. Simple Provider Interface Methods (Continued)

METHODS USED IN ASYNCHRONOUS RECORD SOURCES	
isAsync	Indicates whether data is being populated asynchronously.
stopTransfer	Requests that the Simple Provider discontinue asynchronous transfer of data.
getEstimatedRows	Returns the estimated number of rows.

As you can see, to create a synchronous read-only Provider, there are just six methods to implement, none of which is a major challenge. In fact, the major task in creating a Simple Provider is preparing the data that is to be returned when the getVariant method is called. The complexity of this depends on how much your data looks like a table. If it's already a two-dimensional structure, writing getVariant shouldn't be too much of a problem.

In This Section

We met the Simple Provider Interface. In order to create a read-only Provider, there are only six methods for which we need to write code.

Creating a Read-only Provider

There are three tasks to address when writing a Simple Provider:

1. Prepare the underlying data for Recordset processing.

2. Create a Record Source Object (custom Recordset) class.

3. Create a Data Source Object (custom Connection) class.

We are going to build a Provider that reads VB .frm files and creates a Recordset based on the Controls that appear on the form. This means we need a short diversion to discuss the structure of .frm files and the code required to parse the file. If you are not interested in these details, you can skip over this discussion.

If you are interested, please be aware that this isn't a book about source-code parsing, so the code that performs this task is only of prototype quality—I know that there are situations in which it may fail. However, I want to focus on the Simple Provider functionality. (At the same time, it works reasonably nicely, and I have often considered extending it to create Recordsets based on the procedures defined inside a VB source file, with Fields describing the arguments, return values, lines of code, and other interesting properties of procedures.)

Reading VB Source Code

A VB 6 .frm file begins rather like this:

```
VERSION 5.00
Begin VB.Form frmSelect
    Caption         =   "Select Required Details"
    ClientHeight    =   2760
    ClientLeft      =   60
    ClientTop       =   345
    ClientWidth     =   5715
    LinkTopic       =   "Form2"
    ScaleHeight     =   2760
    ScaleWidth      =   5715
    StartUpPosition =   3   'Windows Default
    Begin VB.CheckBox chkRemember
        Caption         =   "Remember current selection"
        Height          =   315
        Left            =   3000
        TabIndex        =   6
        Top             =   1500
        Value           =   1   'Checked
        Width           =   2595
    End
    . . .
    . . .
End
' code, etc
```

After a version stamp (which shows that this VB6 form is VB5 compatible) the definition of the Form starts with a Begin statement, containing the class name and the object name, followed on subsequent lines by the Form's properties. When another Begin statement appears, this is the definition of a control contained within the form. The control's layout follows the same pattern, and is terminated by an End statement, after which other control definitions appear.

Note that the Form also has an End statement, and that the control definitions appear within the Form's Begin and End delimiters. Similarly, controls that act as containers for other controls (such as Frame controls) can have other control definitions nested between them. Any code for the Form appears after the Form's End statement.

This simple, regular structure means that writing a parser for a .frm file shouldn't be too hard (although it does need to be recursive to cope with the nesting of controls within controls). In fact, I have been able to package it up into a class called vbObject, created in my DLL.

The idea is that one instance of vbObject gets created for the Form and one instance for each of the Form's Controls. Each instance of vbObject in my Provider will correspond to a record in the Recordset seen by clients.

The main method on vbObject is called ReadObject, which gets passed a TextStream object[5] positioned at the first line of a Form or a Control's definition in the .frm file. ReadObject reads the Form or Control's definition from the file and returns when its End is reached. After calling ReadObject, each instance of vbObject adds itself into a collection of vbObject objects.

The following code uses a helper method called asTokens that splits a line of source code up into convenient tokens, so that white space and text within quotes is handled properly. Here's the definition of vbObject:

```
Public Name As String
Public DataType As String
Public Parent As String          these are the properties of
Public Caption As String          vbObject that will become the
Public Index As Integer           Fields of each record in the
Public Height As Long             custom Recordset
Public Width As Long
Public Top As Long
Public Left As Long
Public TabIndex As Long


Public Sub ReadObject(oFile As TextStream, _
    colRecords As Collection, _         ReadObject gets passed the tokens on
    sName As String, _                  the Begin statement line, as well as a
    sType As String, _                  TextStream and a Collection
    sParent As String)
On Error GoTo ErrH

Dim sLine As String
Dim oVB As vbObject
Dim colData As Collection

Me.DataType = sType
Me.Name = sName
Me.Parent = sParent
```

---

5. To use TextStream objects, set a reference to "Microsoft Scripting Runtime."

```
Do                                          the Do loop reads new lines from the
  sLine = oFile.ReadLine                    TextStream and uses asTokens to convert
  Set colData = asTokens(sLine)             the text into a collection
  Select Case colData(1)
    Case "Begin"                                     if ReadObject hits a Begin,
      Set oVB = New vbObject                         it calls itself recursively
      colRecords.Add oVB
      oVB.ReadObject oFile, colRecords, colData(3), colData(2), Me.Name
    Case "Caption","Index","Left","Height","Top","Width","TabIndex"
      CallByName Me, colData(1), vbLet, colData(3)
  End Select                                         if a control's property
Loop Until colData(1) = "End"                        matches a vbObject prop-
                                                     erty, set the vbObject's
                                                     property with the con-
ErrH:                                                trol's property value
End Sub


Public Function asTokens(sLine As String) As Collection

                                            asTokens takes a line of VB source
On Error GoTo ErrH                          and turns it into a collection of
Dim sToken As String                        tokens, such as:
Dim v As Variant                            'Caption', '=', and 'Hello Rob'

Dim colTokens As New Collection
Dim iCurPos As Integer
Dim iNextPos As Integer
Dim sDelim As String
Dim bQuoted As Boolean


iCurPos = 1
iNextPos = 1
While iNextPos <> 0
  If Mid(sLine, iCurPos, 1) = """" Then
      'treat everything in quotes as a single token
    iCurPos = iCurPos + 1  ' skip over the first quote
    sDelim = """"          ' and look for the next one
    bQuoted = True
  Else
    sDelim = " "
  End If
  iNextPos = InStr(iCurPos, sLine, sDelim)
```

```
    If iNextPos > 0 Then
        sToken = Mid(sLine, iCurPos, iNextPos - iCurPos)
        sToken = Trim(sToken)
        If Len(sToken) > 0 Then colTokens.Add sToken
        iCurPos = iNextPos + 1
    Else
        sToken = Right(sLine, Len(sLine) + 1 - iCurPos)
        sToken = Trim(sToken)
        If Len(sToken) > 0 Then colTokens.Add sToken
    End If
Wend

Set asTokens = colTokens
ErrH:

End Function
```

The most important thing about this code is that it can be used to create a collection of vbObject objects, each of which will represent a record in my Recordset. It's mostly grungy file processing. The one detail worth noting is the use of CallByName. The following two statements:

```
CallByName vbOject, "Caption", vbLet, "Hello Rob"
```

and

```
VbObject.Caption = "Hello Rob"
```

are functionally equivalent. While CallByName is less efficient than directly setting a property, it saves me from having a large Select Case statement, with one Case for each property.

Creating the Record Source Object Class

We are now ready to put together the Record Source Object class that represents a custom Recordset. This object won't look much like an ADO Recordset. It's the job of MSDAOSP to implement the required OLE DB interfaces. Instead, our class will implement the OLEDBSimpleProvider interface, as required by MSDAOSP.

After adding a class called CustomRecordset to my VB DLL, I need to give it two sets of functionality:

1. It needs to prepare a collection of vbObject objects, based on a supplied file name. Most of this work will be done by the vbObject class.

2. It needs to implement the required methods from the OLEDB-SimpleProvider interface.

The ADO client program using our Provider will supply a command string, just as it would with any OLE DB Provider. The difference is, we can define our own syntax instead of SQL. Our Provider will use a command string like this:

```
select Controls from c:\frmselect.frm
```

which, although SQL-like, isn't any SQL you will have seen before.[6]

Let's look at the preparation phase first. Here's the code for Custom-Recordset, *minus* the implementation of OLEDBSimpleProvider:

```
Implements OLEDBSimpleProvider
```

the `Implements` statement declares our promise to implement all the metods in the OLEDBSimpleProvider interface

```
Const COLUMN_COUNT As Long = 10
Dim arrColumns(1 To COLUMN_COUNT) As String
Dim colRecords As New Collection
Dim sFileName As String


Private Sub Class_Initialize()
arrColumns(1) = "Name"
arrColumns(2) = "DataType"
arrColumns(3) = "Parent"
arrColumns(4) = "Caption"
arrColumns(5) = "Index"
arrColumns(6) = "Left"
arrColumns(7) = "Top"
arrColumns(8) = "Width"
arrColumns(9) = "Height"
arrColumns(10) = "TabIndex"
End Sub
```

this array will be used to map column numbers (as supplied by getVariant) to Field names and vbObject properties

```
Public Sub processFile(sCommand As String)
```

---

6. You need to think carefully about defining Command languages. For this Provider, we could have simply used the source code file name, but by extending the command structure, we'll be able to supply different types of Recordsets in future extensions. It's important to avoid creating a complex syntax that is difficult to parse and difficult for users to learn. Many custom Provider writers are using XML to avoid these two dangers, because XML parsers are two a penny.

```
On Error GoTo ErrHandler
Dim oFileSys As New FileSystemObject
Dim oFile As TextStream
Dim sLine As String
Dim colData As Collection
Dim oVB As New vbObject

sFileName = Split(sCommand)(3)
```

◄—— use the `Split` function to unpack the command string, and take the file name as the last element in the array returned by `Split`

```
Set oFile = oFileSys.OpenTextFile(sFileName, ForReading)
Do
  sLine = oFile.ReadLine
```

◄—— the `Do` loop reads lines from the file until a `Begin` statement occurs, at which point control passes to `ReadObject`

```
  Set colData = oVB.asTokens(sLine)
  If colData(1) = "Begin" Then
    colRecords.Add oVB
    oVB.ReadObject oFile, colRecords, colData(3), colData(2), ""
  End If
Loop
```

◄—— the loop is terminated by an error when there are no more lines to read

```
ErrHandler:
oFile.Close
End Sub
```

Once processFile is called, CustomRecordset has a collection of vbObject objects stored in colRecords, ready to serve up Recordset data on demand.

We are now ready to implement the methods from the OLEDBSimple-Provider interface. We are only going to put meaningful code in the six methods that are required for read-only purposes. However, VB insists that we provide an implementation for all of the methods in an interface that we have promised to implement, so we must provide something for the remaining eight methods. Fortunately a simple comment will suffice. Here's an example for the isAsync method:

```
Private Function OLEDBSimpleProvider_isAsync() As Long
'not needed
End Function
```

Of the remaining six methods, four are trivial. Here they are:

```
Private Function OLEDBSimpleProvider_getColumnCount() As Long
OLEDBSimpleProvider_getColumnCount = COLUMN_COUNT
End Function
```

```
Private Function OLEDBSimpleProvider_getRowCount() As Long
OLEDBSimpleProvider_getRowCount = colRecords.Count
End Function

Private Function OLEDBSimpleProvider_getLocale() As String
OLEDBSimpleProvider_getLocale = "en-us"
End Function

Private Function OLEDBSimpleProvider_getRWStatus( _
    ByVal iRow As Long, _
    ByVal iColumn As Long) As MSDAOSP.OSPRW
 OLEDBSimpleProvider_getRWStatus = OSPRW_READONLY
End Function
```

Of these, only getRWStatus requires any explanation. When this method is called, our Provider is required to return the read/write status according to the row and column supplied by MSDAOSP. The Simple Provider type library defines an enumeration called OSPRW, which contains the legal return values. These are:

OSPRW_READONLY = 0

OSPRW_DEFAULT = 1

OSPRW_READWRITE = 1

OSPRW_MIXED = 2

iRow refers to a row (record) in the custom Recordset (in our case, it refers to a specific vbObject in the colRecords collection), and iColumn refers to a column (Field) in the custom Recordset (which, in our case, maps onto a property of a vbObject object, the mapping being handled by the arrColumns array defined in the preceding code). As our Recordset is going to be read-only, we can simply return READONLY in all cases.

If the iRow is –1, we need to return the read/write status for the entire column specified by iColumn, and vice versa. If they are both –1, we return the status for the entire Recordset. In any of these cases, we might want to return the value OSPRW_MIXED.

We are left with two methods to implement, and we can cheat with one of these if we wish. The most important method by far is getVariant. getVariant is called to return a cell of data.

When getVariant is called with iRow = 0, we are expected to provide a column (Field) name associated with iColumn. Otherwise we provide the data for record iRow, column iColumn. Because all our data is in a suitable format, returning the required value is easy. Here's the code:

```
Private Function OLEDBSimpleProvider_getVariant( _
    ByVal iRow As Long, _
    ByVal iColumn As Long, _
    ByVal format As MSDAOSP.OSPFORMAT) As Variant
Dim oVB As vbObject
Dim vValue As Variant
If iRow = 0 Then
    vValue = arrColumns(iColumn)
Else
    Set oVB = colRecords(iRow)
    vValue = CallByName(oVB, arrColumns(iColumn), VbGet)
End If
If format = OSPFORMAT_FORMATTED Then
    OLEDBSimpleProvider_getVariant = CStr(vValue)
 Else
    OLEDBSimpleProvider_getVariant = vValue
 End If
End Function
```

This code does two jobs. First it gets the requested data into vValue. Getting the column name (iRow = 0) is as easy as using iColumn to read it from the arrColumns array. Getting the data simply requires us to locate the appropriate vbObject object (using iRow as an index into the colRecords collection) and the appropriate property based on iColumn. I have made life easier by using VB's CallByName function as explained earlier. Finally, the code converts the data into the required format, as defined by the format argument. The format argument uses a value from the OSPFORMAT enumeration, which will be one of these:

> OSPFORMAT_DEFAULT = 0
>
> OSPFORMAT_RAW = 0
>
> OSPFORMAT_FORMATTED = 1
>
> OSPFORMAT_HTML = 2

In most cases, the default is used. The exceptions are column names, which are requested using OSPFORMAT_FORMATTED, meaning a string must be returned. Handling OSPFORMAT_HTML as a special case is optional.

As you can see, implementing getVariant is not hard, as long as you have prepared your data appropriately. The main requirement is being able to translate row and column numbers into meaningful data. Actually, it isn't essential to have prepared the data in advance. So long as you can provide a row count, you could leave the task of processing the data for each row until the client requests it. This is usually more complicated than preparing all the data in advance, but it may allow you to respond more quickly to the rs.Open or cn.Execute that creates the Recordset.

It's worth noting that getVariant returns a Variant. While this is self-evident, its implications may not be. There is no reason to limit your columns (Fields) to basic data types—anything that fits into a Variant is valid. This could include an array, a collection, a file object, or even another Recordset.[7]

The last method we need to implement is the find method. This is called when a client application calls rs.Find.[8] The find method call provides you with a column number, an operator, and a value to search for, along with a start position and flag combining a search direction with a case-sensitivity indicator. Your task is to return a row (record) number where the first match occurs, or return –1 if no match is found. Writing code to cover all these options can take some time, and if your users are unlikely to use rs.Find, you may be tempted to return an error code instead. I have gone for a compromise solution in this example. The following Find code works as long as the operator used in the search is equals (=). For any other operator, our Provider will squawk. Here's the code:

```
Private Function OLEDBSimpleProvider_find( _
    ByVal iRowStart As Long, _
    ByVal iColumn As Long, _
    ByVal val As Variant, _
    ByVal findFlags As MSDAOSP.OSPFIND, _
    ByVal compType As MSDAOSP.OSPCOMP) As Long
Dim lCounter As Long
Dim iStep As Integer
Dim lRunTo As Long
Dim oVB As vbObject


If compType = OSPCOMP_DEFAULT Then    ◄──── take care of the search direction
  If    findFlags = OSPFIND_UP Or _
     findFlags = OSPFIND_UPCASESENSITIVE Then
    iStep = -1
    lRunTo = 1
  Else
    iStep = 1
    lRunTo = colRecords.Count
  End If
```

---

7. It's entirely possible for getVariant to call your Simple Provider recursively, returning custom Recordsets as cells. Sadly, this isn't the same as a hierarchical Recordset. You can't create Chapters, and even if you could, you couldn't set a Field's data type to adChapter, because you can't control data types with Simple Providers. Nonetheless, you can create some impressive functionality.

8. Simple Providers work automatically with rs.Filter, although you can only use one Filter criterion at a time. With full-blown Providers, a Filter can have multiple criteria.

```
                                                  ──────── run the search loop
For lCounter = iRowStart To lRunTo Step iStep          ↓
    Set oVB = colRecords(lCounter)    ←──────────────     get hold of the
        If    findFlags = OSPFIND_CASESENSITIVE Or _     correct vbObject
        findFlags = OSPFIND_UPCASESENSITIVE Then
         If val = CallByName(oVB, arrColumns(iColumn), VbGet) Then
           OLEDBSimpleProvider_find = lCounter   ←──── do the case-sensitive
           Exit Function                                comparison
         End If
       Else
         If UCase(val) = UCase(CallByName(oVB, _
arrColumns(iColumn), VbGet)) Then
             OLEDBSimpleProvider_find = lCounter  ←──   do the case-insensitive
             Exit Function                               comparison
             End If
       End If
    Next                      ──────────────────────  give up unless its an
Else                             ↓                        '=' operator
  Err.Raise DB_E_NOTSUPPORTED, "VBReader", _
          "Only '=' comparison supported for Find operation"
End If
OLEDBSimpleProvider_find = -1  ←────────   return -1 if there is no match
End Function
```

The find function argument list includes two enumerations defined by the OLEDBSimpleProvider type library. The first is OSPFIND, which has the following values:

OSPFIND_DEFAULT = 0

OSPFIND_UP = 1

OSPFIND_CASESENSITIVE = 2

OSPFIND_UPCASESENSITIVE = 3

To make sense of this, you need to realize that the default search direction is descending (down), and the default setting is case-insensitive.

The second enumeration is OSPCOMP, which has the following values:

OSPCOMP_DEFAULT = 1

OSPCOMP_EQ = 1

OSPCOMP_LT = 2

OSPCOMP_LE = 3

OSPCOMP_GE = 4

OSPCOMP_GT = 5

OSPCOMP_NE = 6

All of these are fairly self-explanatory (for instance, OSPCOMP_LE means "less than or equals").

We have now implemented all of OLEDBSimpleProvider that is required for a read-only Simple Provider.

Creating the Data Source Object Class

Our final task is to create the Data Source Object class, which will "represent" the ADO Connection objects created by users of our Provider.

It's usual to define a separate class to provide Data Source Object functionality. An instance of this class can then be used to serve up multiple Record Source Objects in much the same way as an ADO Connection object can serve up multiple ADO Recordsets.

Using VB6, the standard way to create a Data Source Object class is to create a new class in your DLL and use the Property Box to set its DataSource-Behavior property to "1 – VBDataSource". After setting this property, the class grows a new event, which is accessible through the code window. It's called GetDataMember.

When an ADO client requests a Recordset, it supplies a command string and a connection string (or an existing Connection object). The connection string is used to identify your Data Source class and create an instance of it if one doesn't already exist (linked to an active Connection object). The command string is passed as an argument to GetDataMember, which creates and returns an instance of a Record Source class that implements the OLEDB-SimpleProvider interface.

My Data Source class is called CustomConnection. Here's its GetData-Member event procedure:

```
Private Sub Class_GetDataMember( _
                                DataMember As String, _
                                Data As Object)
Dim oCustom As CustomRecordset
Set oCustom = New CustomRecordset
oCustom.processFile DataMember
Set Data = oCustom
End Sub
```

create an instance of CustomRecordset and call its processFile method, passing in the command string ——→ (points to `Set oCustom = New CustomRecordset`)

return a reference to the initialized Record Source Object ←—————— (points to `Set Data = oCustom`)

A more complex Data Source Object might parse the command string (DataMember) in order to decide which type of Record Source object to create. Our (very) Simple Provider has only one type of Record Source Object, making our Data Source Object very simple.

By now you are probably itching to see this custom Simple Provider in use. Just before doing so, let's review what we've achieved in this section.

We've created a VB ActiveX DLL (I set the DLL's Project Name to VBReader) and built three classes:

- **vbObject**: This turns the underlying VB source data into a collection, which is convenient for Recordset processing.

- **CustomRecordset**: This is a Record Source Object class that implements OLEDBSimpleProvider.

- **CustomConnection**: This is a Data Source Object class that implements the GetDataMember event made visible by setting its design-time DataSourceBehavior property to "1 – VBDataSource".

We also have references in our DLL to the following:

- Microsoft OLE DB Simple Provider Library 1.5, which is compulsory.

- Microsoft Data Source Interfaces, which is optional, but it's added automatically by VB when setting the DataSourceBehavior property to "1 – VBDataSource".

- OLE DB Errors Type Library, which is optional; it defines error constants.

- Microsoft Scripting Runtime, which is optional; it provides file-processing objects.

Note that we don't have a reference to ADO! That's because we don't consume any ADO resources. It's up to an ADO client program to do that.

In This Section

We saw how to put together a DLL for a read-only Simple Provider. We addressed the separate stages of preparing the source data, implementing the OLEDBSimpleProvider interface in a Record Source Object class, and creating a Data Source Object class. The most complex task is often the find method. It's possible to cheat and simply set a flag to say that find is not implemented.

Registering and Using Simple Providers

We can use our Provider just as it is. Let's do so. You can either add a Standard EXE project to the VB IDE to create a project group, or compile the DLL and start a new Standard EXE project.

You should have the Standard EXE project set a reference to ADO as you normally would. Don't set a reference to our DLL from within the EXE. You'll use a connection string to reference it, just like any other OLE DB Provider.

Here's some client code:

```
Dim cn As New Connection
Dim rs As New Recordset
cn.Provider = "MSDAOSP"          ←──────── specify Provider and Data Source
cn.Open "Data Source=VBReader.CustomConnection"
rs.Open "select Controls from c:\frmselect.frm", cn

While Not rs.EOF
  Print rs!Name, rs!DataType, rs!Caption
  rs.MoveNext
Wend
```

You don't need to create an explicit Connection. The following code will do just as well:

```
Dim rs As New Recordset
rs.ActiveConnection = "Provider=MSDAOSP;" & _
    "Data Source=VBReader.CustomConnection"

rs.Open "SELECT Controls FROM c:\frmselect.frm"
While Not rs.EOF
  Print rs!Name, rs!DataType, rs!Caption
  rs.MoveNext
Wend
```

Either way, the code prints this:

```
frmSelect     VB.Form             Select Required Details
chkRemember   VB.CheckBox         Remember current selection
fraOptions    VB.Frame            Options
optDetails    VB.OptionButton     Option2
optDetails    VB.OptionButton     Option1
lstDetails    VB.ListBox
cmdCancel     VB.CommandButton    Cancel
cmdOK         VB.CommandButton    OK
```

You can just as easily create an ADO Data Control and connect it to the Provider, as described earlier in the chapter. You can then bind data-aware controls to the Provider in completely standard ways.[9]

As you can see, specifying MSDAOSP as the Provider name and using the ProgID of the Data Source Object as the Data Source property forms the connection string in the previous examples. While this is fine, you can go one step further and create a full set of Registry entries for your Provider. This means you can:

- Use your own Provider name directly, without needing to reference MSDAOSP in client programs that use your Provider.

- See the Provider name in the Data Link Properties window's Connection tab.

- Learn a bit more about how Providers are registered, which can be useful in solving configuration errors.

There are eight Registry entries that need to be made in total, and the easiest way to create them is to construct a .reg file. Double-clicking this file will then create the Registry entries for you.[10]

You need four bits of information to build the .reg file:

- **FullName**: A friendly name for the Provider.

- **GUID**: A unique COM identifier.

- **Component**: The short name for the Provider (the VB Project Name).

- **Connection**: The ProgID of the Data Source Object.

Of all these pieces of information, the only one that might present a problem is creating a new GUID. Visual Basic generates GUIDs by the bucket-load, so you could create a component in VB, and then throw it away (being sure that you do) after salvaging a GUID. However, a more sensible approach is to run the UUIDGEN.exe[11] command line utility. This ships with Visual Studio, but it isn't included as part of a "Visual Basic only" installation. It also

---

9. However, Simple Providers do not provide enough metadata to work with the VB6 Data Environment.

10. Deployment tools, such as the Visual Studio Package and Deployment Wizard, will automatically register .reg file entries on installation.

11. This isn't a typo. Microsoft use the term Global Unique Identifier (GUID) to represent what is more commonly known in the IT world as a Universal Unique Identifier (UUID). This is a rare example of Microsoft demonstrating restraint over its ambitions.

ships with the Microsoft Windows Platform SDK. If you have UUIDGEN, you can run it at a command line prompt like this:

```
uuidgen /i /oc:\guid.txt
```

which will create a file called c:\guid.txt, containing something like this:

```
[
uuid(9d54063f-cf61-4582-a8c5-8212c6a46dad),
version(1.0)
]
interface INTERFACENAME
{

}
```

From this you can extract the GUID[12], namely

```
9d54063f-cf61-4582-a8c5-8212c6a46dad
```

These four pieces of information can then be inserted into the template.reg file shown next. This template file can be found in the same directory as the book's CD companion program to this chapter. You can simply replace each occurrence of the four template keys (for example, **FullName**) in template.reg with your own values, using search and replace. Here's the template file:

```
REGEDIT4
[HKEY_CLASSES_ROOT\**Component**]
@="**FullName**"
[HKEY_CLASSES_ROOT\**Component**\CLSID]
@="{**GUID**}"
[HKEY_CLASSES_ROOT\CLSID\{**GUID**}]
@="**Component**"
[HKEY_CLASSES_ROOT\CLSID\{**GUID**}\InprocServer32]
@="c:\\Program Files\\Common Files\\System\\OLE DB\\MSDAOSP.DLL"
"ThreadingModel"="Both"
[HKEY_CLASSES_ROOT\CLSID\{**GUID**}\ProgID]
@="**Component**.1"
[HKEY_CLASSES_ROOT\CLSID\{**GUID**}\VersionIndependentProgID]
@="**Component**"
```

---

12. if you run UUIDGEN, your GUID should be different from mine. If it isn't, email me now, assigning all rights of legal representation.

```
[HKEY_CLASSES_ROOT\CLSID\{**GUID**}\OLE DB Provider]
@="**FullName**"
[HKEY_CLASSES_ROOT\CLSID\{**GUID**}\OSP Data Object]
@="**Connection**"
```

And here are the four values (showing my GUID) along with the number of replacements required for each key:

TEMPLATE KEY	OCCURRENCES	EXAMPLE
FullName	2	VB Source Reader
GUID	7	9d54063f-cf61-4582-a8c5-8212c6a46dad
Component	5	VBReader
Connection	1	VBReader.CustomConnection

Once this .reg file has been run, you can create the same Recordset using this code:

VBReader is now a fully registered Provider

```
Dim rs As New Recordset
rs.ActiveConnection = "Provider=VBReader"

rs.Open "SELECT Controls FROM c:\frmselect.frm"
```

An alternative way of using the .reg file is to miss out the very last Registry entry:

```
[HKEY_CLASSES_ROOT\CLSID\{**GUID**}\OSP Data Object]
@="**Connection**"
```

If you do this, you can still use your own Provider name, but allow the ADO client to specify the ProgID of its choice by adding a Data Source property to the connection string:

```
rs.ActiveConnection = "Provider=VBReader;" & _
    "Data Source=VBReader.CustomConnection"
```

This approach allows you to have multiple DLLs behind the same Provider registration. If you choose to specify the OSP Data Object Registry key, you can still use this approach. The ProgID held in the Registry key will become the default Data Source, but it's overridden if an explicit Data Source property is supplied.

You can also create a Data Link File using the Data Link Properties window to select the friendly name of the Provider from the list of available Providers, as shown in Figure 11-5.

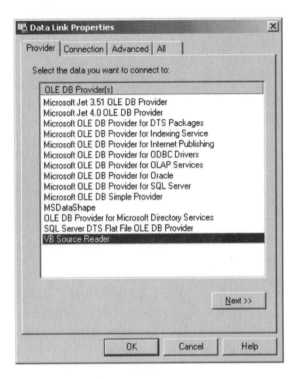

Figure 11-5. Creating a UDL file for a Simple Provider Connection

In This Section

You saw how to use the Simple Provider from a VB client program and how to create your own Provider name using Registry entries and a GUID.

Creating an Updateable Provider

At one level, making a Simple Provider updateable is a fairly straightforward task—you just implement a few more methods of the OLEDBSimpleProvider interface. However, in reality, it often works out to be quite a bit harder than creating a read-only Provider, or it at least forces you to accept a few more compromises than you would otherwise wish to.

This is largely a result of the limited semantics of the setVariant method—you have to be able to identify the correct data to update using only a row number. This sounds easy, but you need to bear in mind that a Delete operation affects the row number of all records that follow the deleted row in the

Recordset. This makes holding the data internally as an array very hard work, although, fortunately, Collections are made for this task.[13]

You also have to treat each cell update as a separate operation. You won't get the equivalent of an update statement saying that the user has finished with a particular row (record). This makes it difficult to wait for all the changes to be made to the current row and then update the underlying data in a single operation, which would typically be much more efficient. If you absolutely need to perform row-level operations, there are two fallback techniques you can use, although neither of them is perfect:

- *You can "trap."* Move operations by keeping track of changes to iRow in getVariant and setVariant calls. This isn't exactly the same as trapping a Move operation, because it relies on the client application reading or writing data, instead of just navigating. However, it can provide an acceptable "update complete" signal, as long as you also code the class Terminate event to respond correctly when the Recordset is released.

- *You can assign "special behavior" to a particular column (Field).* In other words, you only perform the update functionality when the user sets a nominated field, which could be the primary key, or a field introduced specifically for the purpose. If you choose the latter approach, you can even start using this special field as a status field to handle other unsupported Simple Provider functionality, such as transaction control. The problem with this approach is that users of your Provider have to know about this special field in order to use your Provider, which is rather at odds with the reasons for creating a Provider in the first place.

If these issues don't daunt you, then you can start addressing the mechanics of writing the update code. Here again are the OLEDBSimpleProvider methods that you need to implement:

    setVariant

    insertRows

    deleteRows

    addOLEDBSimpleProviderListener

    removeOLEDBSimpleProviderListener

You'll also need to revisit the getRWStatus method, so that you don't report each cell as read-only!

---

13. Ironically, there is another data structure that is ideal for storing data sets inside a Simple Provider. Fabricated Recordsets are easily hooked into the OLEDBSimpleProvider interface, and the Simple Provider mechanism provides a pure ADO interface for accessing them. These two seemingly competing parts of OLE DB are actually made for one another.

Supporting OLEDBSimpleProviderListeners

One final complexity of supporting updates is the need to handle Listeners. MSDAOSP simply won't play ball with update operations unless you provide proper support for Listeners.

A Listener is nothing more than a means by which you can raise events from within your DLL to inform MSDAOSP about what is going on. MSDAOSP will then turn the events you raise via a Listener into ADO events that clients of your Provider expect from an ADO Recordset. The Listener events are also important for MSDAOSP's own internal housekeeping.

If you have written ActiveX Controls using VB or written classes that raise events, you may be familiar with declaring events and calling RaiseEvent to fire the events. Conceptually, this is exactly how a Listener operates. A Listener is an object that has a set of methods defined on it. These methods are the equivalent of the list of events declared in an ActiveX Control, and calling the Listener's methods is equivalent to calling RaiseEvent from within the control. Another way of thinking about a Listener is simply as a predefined callback mechanism.

One of the problems with declaring events in VB is that you can't share a set of events between multiple classes in a safe and predictable way. MSDAOSP wants all notifications to be made in a standard way through the same interface, and therefore, the VB event mechanism can't be used. Listeners get around this limitation, but in a slightly more long-winded way.[14]

What happens is that MSDAOSP hands your Record Source Object a Listener object via the addOLEDBSimpleProviderListener method. Your Record Source Object then stores this object and calls methods on it to notify MSDAOSP when certain things happen. When MSDAOSP no longer needs notifications from your Record Source Object, it calls removeOLEDBSimpleProviderListener so that you can release your reference to the Listener object.

It is possible that MSDAOSP may pass your Record Source Object more than one Listener, and therefore, you need to store Listener objects in a collection and notify each one whenever a notifiable event occurs. Here's a list of Listener methods:

- aboutToChangeCell, cellChanged (called during setVariant)

- aboutToInsertRows, insertedRows (called during insertRows)

- aboutToDeleteRows, deletedRows (called during deleteRows)

- rowsAvailable, transferComplete (called during asynchronous operations when supported)

---

14. Long-winded for the Provider programmer, that is. Performing callbacks via a Listener is actually considerably more efficient than using events.

and here's the code that is needed to support Listeners:

```
Dim colListeners As New Collection  ◄───── declare a Collection of Listeners
                                           in general declarations

Private Sub OLEDBSimpleProvider_addOLEDBSimpleProviderListener( _
    ByVal pospIListener As MSDAOSP.OLEDBSimpleProviderListener)

If Not (pospIListener Is Nothing) Then
colListeners.Add pospIListener
End If
End Sub

Private Sub OLEDBSimpleProvider_removeOLEDBSimpleProviderListener( _
    ByVal pospIListener As MSDAOSP.OLEDBSimpleProviderListener)

Dim iCounter As Integer
For iCounter = 1 To colListeners.Count
  If colListeners(iCounter) Is pospIListener Then
    colListeners.Remove iCounter
    Exit Sub
  End If
Next
End Sub
```

With Listener management under control, we can now start implementing the updating methods.

Implementing deleteRows

To make delete operations work, we need to be able to identify that part of a VB form's source code that defines a control and cleanly remove it from the file. This task is actually quite straightforward, apart from the complexity of objects that contain other objects, such as a frame control or even a VB.Form object. I'll present you with a less-than-complete implementation that ignores this complexity.[15] The code that does this file mangling logically

---

15. The full implementation adds a dozen or so lines of code. It involves rejecting the deletion of any object that contains other objects and involves looking for the next Begin before the next End.

resides in the vbObject class, and here's its RemoveFromFile method that performs just this task:

```
Public Sub RemoveFromFile(sFileName As String)

Dim sFile As String
Dim sNewFile As String
Dim sFind As String

Dim lPosStart As Long
Dim lPosEnd As Long
Dim oFileSys As New FileSystemObject
Dim oFile As TextStream

Set oFile = oFileSys.OpenTextFile(sFileName, ForReading)
sFile = oFile.ReadAll
oFile.Close

sFind = "Begin " & Me.DataType & " " & Me.Name
lPosStart = InStr(1, sFile, sFind) - 1
lPosEnd = InStr(lPosStart, sFile, "End") + 2

sNewFile = VBA.Left(sFile, lPosStart) & _
    VBA.Right(sFile, Len(sFile) - lPosEnd)


oFileSys.DeleteFile sFileName
Set oFile = oFileSys.OpenTextFile(sFileName, ForWriting, True)
oFile.Write sNewFile
oFile.Close

End Sub
```

open the source file, read all its contents into a string called sFile, and close the file

reconstruct the Begin statement for this object, and identify its position in the string and the end of the corresponding End statement

form a new string containing everything before and after the source for this object

delete the existing source file, create a new file with the same name, and write the new string into the file

This is basic string and file manipulation. You may be wondering why I have prefixed the standard VB Left and Right string functions with their library name. This is simply because I have a property in my class called Left, which conflicts with the name of the Left function. The library name prefix avoids this conflict, and the code looks better if I use it for Right too.

Now that the code for handling the underlying data is in place, I can write the deleteRows method. Note that it's called deleteRows, not deleteRow. Although ADO doesn't allow you to delete multiple contiguous records with a single call, OLE DB permits this. The iRow argument to deleteRows tells you where to start deleting from, while cRows tells you how many rows to delete.

If you don't want to support multiple deletes, you could always return an error if cRows is greater than 1. deleteRows should return the number of rows deleted.

```
Private Function OLEDBSimpleProvider_deleteRows( _
    ByVal iRow As Long, _
    ByVal cRows As Long) As Long
Dim oVB As vbObject
Dim lCounter As Long
Dim oListener As MSDAOSP.OLEDBSimpleProviderListener

For lCounter = 1 To colListeners.Count              first, call each Listener
    Set oListener = colListeners(lCounter)  ←——     to tell it you are about
    oListener.aboutToDeleteRows iRow, cRows          to delete
Next


For lCounter = iRow + (cRows - 1) To iRow Step -1
    Set oVB = colRecords(lCounter)      ←——┐        locate the vbObject, call
    oVB.RemoveFromFile sFileName           │         its RemoveFromFile
    colRecords.Remove lCounter             │        method, and then remove
Next                                    ←——┘        it from the Collection


For lCounter = 1 To colListeners.Count
    Set oListener = colListeners(lCounter)           finally, call each
    oListener.deletedRows iRow, cRows  ←——————        Listener to tell it
Next                                                 what you have done
OLEDBSimpleProvider_deleteRows = cRows
End Function
```

Note that my iteration loop runs backward, from iRow + (cRows - 1) to iRow. When there is only one row (record) to delete, this makes little difference. However, if there were more than one row to delete, then after deleting colRecords(iRow), the next vbObject along would have its index changed to colRecords(iRow) from colRecords(iRow+1). By deleting objects from the Collection in reverse order, I can avoid having to handle the index shuffle. While this wouldn't be hard, it would make the code look counterintuitive, as it would appear that I was repeatedly deleting the same object.

Implementing insertRows

Like deleteRows, insertRows takes an iRow and a cRows argument. What it doesn't take is any data. In this sense, it's a direct response to rs.AddNew, called without any arguments. insertRows is only required to allocate space for a new row, which in our case simply means adding a new object into colRecords in the correct location. This means we don't have to extend vbObject to cope with insertRows. Of course, we'll pay for this simplicity when we get to implement setVariant, as it will be required to identify whether it is updating a new or an existing row (record).

Here's the code for insertRows. Just like deleteRows, it has to notify the Listeners before and after the operation and return the number of rows (records) successfully inserted:

```
Private Function OLEDBSimpleProvider_insertRows( _
    ByVal iRow As Long, _
    ByVal cRows As Long) As Long

Dim oVB As vbObject
Dim lCounter As Long
Dim oListener As MSDAOSP.OLEDBSimpleProviderListener
For lCounter = 1 To colListeners.Count
    Set oListener = colListeners(lCounter)
    oListener.aboutToInsertRows iRow, cRows          ← tell the Listeners what
Next                                                    you are about to do

For lCounter = iRow To iRow + (cRows - 1)
    Set oVB = New vbObject                            ⎤
    colRecords.Add oVB, After:=lCounter - 1           ⎦ do it
Next

For lCounter = 1 To colListeners.Count
    Set oListener = colListeners(lCounter)
    oListener.insertedRows iRow, cRows               ← tell them that you
Next                                                    have done it
OLEDBSimpleProvider_insertRows = cRows
End Function
```

Implementing *setVariant*

As with deleteRows, setVariant requires us to process the VB source code so that any changes are recorded. The approach I have taken is that whenever a property is changed, the code will begin in much the same way as deleteRows, by deleting the control's source (if it exists). Then, before writing out the new file, the source for the new version of the control will be inserted into the gap left by the deletion. If the control is a new one, it will be inserted immediately before the End statement for the VB.Form object. Once again, I have made the same assumptions and simplifications as were made for deleteRows.

Let's quickly look at the code required to update the VB source file. There are two procedures involved. The first generates the source for a control in VB format. It's called asString:

```
Public Function asString() As String
Dim sMe As String
sMe = vbCrLf & "  Begin " & _
    Me.DataType & " " & Me.Name & vbCrLf
sMe = sMe & vbTab & "Caption" & vbTab & _
    "=    """ & Me.Caption & """" & vbCrLf
sMe = sMe & vbTab & "Height" & vbTab & _
    "=   " & Me.Height & vbCrLf
sMe = sMe & vbTab & "Left" & vbTab & _
    "=   " & Me.Left & vbCrLf
sMe = sMe & vbTab & "TabIndex" & vbTab & _
    "=   " & Me.TabIndex & vbCrLf
sMe = sMe & vbTab & "Top" & vbTab & _
    "=   " & Me.Top & vbCrLf
sMe = sMe & vbTab & "Width" & vbTab & _
    "=   " & Me.Width & vbCrLf
sMe = sMe & "  End"
asString = sMe
End Function
```

The second procedure, UpdateFile, performs the search and replace and the file handling:

```
Public Sub UpdateFile(sFileName As String)

Dim sFile As String
Dim sNewFile As String
Dim sFind As String

Dim lPosStart As Long
Dim lPosEnd As Long
Dim oFileSys As New FileSystemObject
Dim oFile As TextStream

If Len(Me.DataType) = 0 Or Len(Me.Name) = 0 Then Exit Sub

Set oFile = oFileSys.OpenTextFile(sFileName, ForReading)
sFile = oFile.ReadAll
```

exit immediately if the Name and DataType have not been set

```
sFind = "Begin " & Me.DataType & " " & Me.Name
lPosStart = InStr(1, sFile, sFind) - 1


If lPosStart > 0 Then
    lPosEnd = InStr(lPosStart, sFile, "End") + 2
  Else
    lPosStart = InStr(1, sFile, vbCrLf & "End")
    lPosEnd = lPosStart
End If

sNewFile = VBA.Left(sFile, lPosStart - 1) & _
    Me.asString & VBA.Right(sFile, Len(sFile) - lPosEnd)

oFile.Close
oFileSys.DeleteFile sFileName
Set oFile = oFileSys.OpenTextFile(sFileName, ForWriting, True)
oFile.Write sNewFile
oFile.Close


End Sub
```

include the result of calling asString in the new source

UpdateFile will be called every time a client program assigns a value to a Field on a record (via setVariant, described next). This quite nicely highlights one of the key weaknesses of writing updateable Simple Providers, as well as showing the kind of solution that is required to address the weakness.

The Provider has to treat each cell update as an independent operation. Therefore, it has to completely reconstruct the source file, even though the very next line of client code might update another field on the same record and virtually repeat the same process. This is quite extravagant, yet as we have seen, only partial solutions exist.

What's more, before generating the source for the control, we need to know its name and data type in order to build a valid Begin statement. We can prevent the source file from being corrupted simply by refusing to process an update unless these two properties have genuine values, which is the approach used in the preceding code. However, it's hard to communicate this information to client programs or users, who may expect a new control to have been created once they have called rs.AddNew and set some field values.

It isn't possible to raise an error, simply because setting a Field on a new record that doesn't yet have a name and a data type is a legitimate activity. Therefore, there is little option but to handle the situation in the way we've done here, unless you introduce some proprietary scheme for communicating with client programs. You may be thinking that the same situation must occur with an SQL-based Provider when the client program doesn't set a primary key for a new record. However, in this case the error can be generated on a row-level operation, such as rs.Update, at which point it's appropriate to raise an error if required fields have not been set. The Simple Provider interface doesn't allow for row-level operations. This is the primary challenge of the Simple Provider writer—ensuring that updates are consistent and that client programs receive sensible error messages. Unfortunately, there is frequently no perfect solution.

This concern aside, we are ready to implement setVariant using what by now will be very familiar techniques. Here it is:

```
Private Sub OLEDBSimpleProvider_setVariant( _
    ByVal iRow As Long, _
    ByVal iColumn As Long, _
    ByVal format As MSDAOSP.OSPFORMAT, _
    ByVal Var As Variant)

Dim oVB As vbObject
Dim lCounter As Integer
Dim oListener As MSDAOSP.OLEDBSimpleProviderListener
For lCounter = 1 To colListeners.Count             tell the Listeners
    Set oListener = colListeners(lCounter)         what you are about
    oListener.aboutToChangeCell iRow, iColumn      to do
Next

Set oVB = colRecords(iRow)
CallByName oVB, arrColumns(iColumn), VbLet, Var
oVB.UpdateFile sFileName                            do it


For lCounter = 1 To colListeners.Count
    Set oListener = colListeners(lCounter)         tell them that you
    oListener.cellChanged iRow, iColumn            have done it
Next

End Sub
```

The new value arrives in the Var argument, and once again I have used CallByName to remove the need for a lengthy Case statement. Most of the real work is handled by the vbObject.

Our updateable Simple Provider is now complete.

We added insert, delete, and update functionality to our Provider. This required that we implement Listener management and also modify the getRWStatus method accordingly. The update model for Simple Providers is where its major weaknesses are exposed, but when these weaknesses aren't too limiting, making Simple Providers updateable isn't too demanding of a task.

Data Shaping with Simple Providers

It's just about possible to perform Data Shaping with Simple Provider Recordsets, although some tricks are required to achieve it. Simple Providers create two problems for Data Shaping:

- MSDataShape generally expects to use Command objects with a Provider, which aren't supported by Simple Providers. This can be overcome by using the SHAPE language's TABLE keyword.

- The RELATE keyword used in Data Shaping needs to be able to determine the data type of the related Fields, and it won't accept Variants. Overcoming this requirement is a little more tricky. It can be done using the SHAPE language's NEW keyword to append an additional Field to the Simple Provider Recordsets being linked together in the hierarchy. These can be given data types and can therefore be RELATEd. You then need an easy way to populate these new Fields using data from the Field that would have been RELATEd, had it an appropriate data type.

In order to demonstrate this technique, I have added a new Custom Recordset class to the VBReader DLL that creates a record for each type of control used in a Form. I have also modified the Data Source Object to be able to determine whether a Control Recordset or a Types Recordset has been requested.

With support for this new type of Recordset, this client code:

```
Dim rs As New Recordset
rs.Open "SELECT Types FROM c:\frmselect.frm", "Provider=VBReader"
While Not rs.EOF
    Print rs!DataType
    rs.MoveNext
Wend
```

request Types instead of Controls

prints this:

```
VB.Form
VB.CheckBox
VB.Frame
VB.OptionButton
VB.ListBox
VB.CommandButton
```

I can now create a hierarchical Recordset with Types as a parent and Controls as a child.

However, before doing this, I need a subroutine that copies data from one Field to another for all records in a Recordset at any level in the hierarchy. This will allow me to take data from a Variant-type, Provider-generated Field, and copy it into a strongly data-typed appended field. The following subroutine will do this for a named Recordset:

```
Private Sub copyFields(     cn As Connection, _
    srsName As String, _
    sCopyFrom As String, _
    sCopyTo As String)
Dim rs As New Recordset
rs.Open "SHAPE " & srsName, cn      ◄———   use a SHAPE command to create a
While Not rs.EOF                           chapterless Recordset reference
  rs(sCopyTo).Value = rs(sCopyFrom).Value
  rs.MoveNext
Wend

End Sub
```

With copyFields in place, I can now create the hierarchical Recordset:

```
Dim rs As New Recordset
Dim cn As New Connection
Dim sCommand As String
cn.Open "Provider=MSDataShape;Data Provider=VBReader;"

sCommand = _
  "SHAPE TABLE 'select Types from c:\frmselect.frm' as Types " & _
  "APPEND NEW adVarChar(20) as Type ," & _
      "((SHAPE TABLE 'select Controls from c:\frmselect.frm' " & _
                                          as Controls " & _
          " APPEND NEW adVarChar(20) as Type) " & _
      "RELATE Type TO Type)"
```

append strongly typed Fields

```
rs.Open sCommand, cn, , adLockBatchOptimistic
copyFields cn, "Controls", "DataType", "Type"          copy data from
copyFields cn, "Types", "DataType", "Type"    ◄───────  Variant to strongly
                                                        typed Fields
```

This isn't a wholly satisfying experience, and the copyFields process has a measurable overhead. Nonetheless, it does allow you to use your Simple Provider to create a display like this:

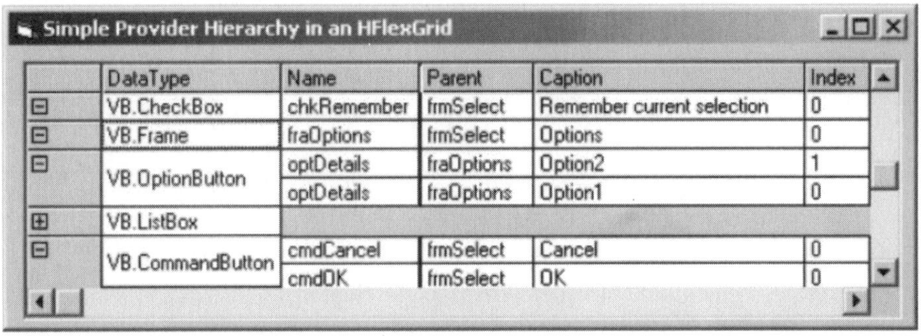

Figure 11-6. Displaying a hierarchical Recordset using a Simple Provider

In This Section

We saw that it's possible to create hierarchical Recordsets based on Simple Providers.

Summary

In this chapter we saw how to extend the list of available OLE DB Providers by creating our own. Simple Providers:

- Make it possible to wrap up your own data formats, or even complex business-object processing, and expose it through standard ADO interfaces.

- Are of huge benefit to client programmers who can start using your customized resources without needing to learn new programming interfaces, and who can exploit the many high productivity features that exist to create user interfaces based on ADO data.

- Are easy to create for read-only data.

Creating updateable Simple Providers is more complicated, and it's in this area that some of the limitations that result from simplifying the many OLE DB interfaces down to a single interface become most apparent.

The limitations of Simple Providers would be largely overcome if the following additional features were available:

- The ability to add additional metadata, such as data type. Specifically, by adding enough metadata to allow the VB Data Environment and the Data Shaping engine to work property with Simple Providers, their applicability would be extended enormously.

- Support for Recordset sorting, which requires data-type metadata.

- Row-level Update and CancelUpdate methods.

- Three additional methods to allow transactional commands to be passed to the Provider.

These omissions aside, the Simple Provider mechanism has many applications. The fact that you can code something as seemingly complex and embedded as an OLE DB Provider in VB opens up whole new opportunities to developers who previously saw themselves as applications programmers.

Part Two

ADO AT LARGE

CHAPTER 12

Binding and Data-aware Objects

Binding with Controls

Binding with Classes

The Data Repeater Control

Binding Hierarchical Recordsets

Summary

THE BASIC TECHNIQUES OF BINDING DATA to controls will be familiar to just about every Visual Basic programmer, and there is little to be gained from rehashing well-worn material. Instead, this chapter will look at how both VB6 and ADO have generalized the binding model to give significant new power and applicability.

Data binding is loved by many programmers for its ability to create user interfaces quickly with minimal code. At the same time, many other developers have shunned data binding because of its dependence on a two-tier system design, because it exposes users to raw data, because of the lack of control it provides for highly customized functionality, or simply out of dislike of "data controls." None of these objections are valid today, as they can all be addressed without losing the undeniable ease of use that binding provides.

Note that the title of this chapter refers to data-aware objects, and not just to controls. The ability to write classes whose instances can be either data sources or consumers of data (resulting in nongraphical equivalents of data controls and data-aware controls) provides some interesting and powerful design options. Understanding how classes can be made data aware also provides useful insights into the topic of the next chapter—using Data Environments.

This chapter will also explore some more advanced data-binding techniques using controls, such as the Data Repeater control (which allows you to create your own customized grid control with very little pain) and binding with hierarchical Recordsets.

Despite the major changes in data binding over the past few years, it still won't suit all developers. However, if you have tried and rejected binding techniques in the past, it's certainly worth reevaluating your opinion. If you are an enthusiastic user of bound controls, the newer features simply extend the techniques you already know and love.

Binding with Controls

This section will begin with a very quick review of the ADO Data Control (ADC) in normal operation, before looking at how binding can be performed programmatically using Binding Collections and at how to bind to controls that are not data aware.

The ADC follows in the tradition of the intrinsic (DAO-based) Data Control and the Remote Data Control (RDC) introduced with VB4, which exploits RDO data access. In all cases, these data source controls have the abilities to create Recordsets based on a connection and a command (or SQL) string and to support navigation and updating of the Recordset. Many standard ActiveX controls can be linked (or bound) to one or more fields on the Recordset managed by the data source control, and can become data consumers. While data consumers (typically called data-aware controls) are responsible for displaying and editing a particular value, the data source control looks after everything else.

It's easy to build a simple application with no code using this technique. For example, the application shown here is created entirely by adding controls to a form and setting their properties:

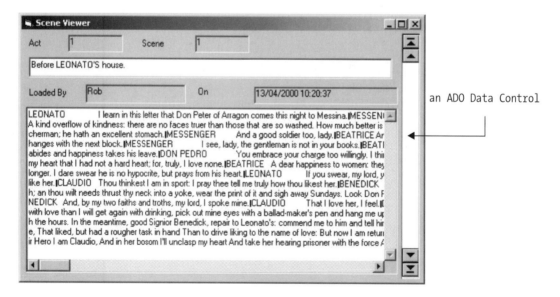

Figure 12-1. A codeless application using data binding

We'll see how to smarten this application up shortly, but as it stands, it's serviceable as a way of viewing a scene's contents and of editing its description or the content held in the SceneContent table.

In addition to standard Label and TextBox controls, this application uses a single ADC, which in this case, has been given a vertical orientation to make it look like a scroll bar.[1] The ADC doesn't appear on the VB toolbox by default—you need to add it using the Project–Components menu.

It's worth spending just a little while looking at how this application was constructed. If you examine an ADC, you'll see that it has a set of methods and properties selected from those available on ADO Connection, Command, and Recordset objects. These exist mainly to allow the Control to be initialized via the standard VB Properties box or its own Property Pages, thus justifying the "look Mum—no code" attraction of Data Controls. It also supports the WillChange and ChangeComplete Recordset events, which can be coded for control and validation purposes as described in Chapter 6. Just in case you were worried about missing your favorite ADO feature, the ADC has a read/write Recordset property, which provides complete control and access to the Recordset that it creates, and can even have a separately generated Recordset assigned to it. It also has a Refresh method that can be used to re-create the Recordset, if required.

For the preceding code-free example, I simply set the ConnectionString property to my Data Link File for the MuchADO database and set the RecordSource property to the following SQL string:

```
SELECT S.act, S.scene, s.Description,
C.dateTimeLoaded, C.loadedBy,C.content
FROM Scenes S, SceneContents C
WHERE S.act = C.act and S.scene = C.scene
```

By default, the ADC creates a client-side optimistic cursor with a cache size of 50, although these and other properties are controllable.

An ADC is not of much use by itself. To be of service, it needs data consumers to be linked to it. Controls that can be bound to a data source fall into four groups:

- **Single Record–Single Field**: This simple form of data binding is supported by most of the built-in VB controls, including TextBox, Label, and CheckBox, among others. They basically show one piece of Recordset data at a time.

---

1. It's common practice to make the ADC invisible to create a more pleasing interface that makes method calls into the hidden Data Control to provide navigation. An alternative approach, which I'll introduce later in this chapter, is to create a custom Data Control with the user interface of your choosing.

- **Single Record–Multiple Field**: These are typically custom-written controls designed to provide a consistent presentation of a single record based on a predefined query.

- **Multi Record–Single Field**: These are typically list or combo type controls, which display one item for each record in a Recordset.

- **Multi Record–Multi Field**: This is the realm of data grids. In addition to the standard ones provided for free with VB, there is a very healthy market in third-party products of this type.

Single Record–Single Field controls generally have four data-related properties:

PROPERTY	DESCRIPTION
DataSource	Used to specify the data source that the control is bound to. This can be an ADC, a DataEnvironment object, or a custom Data Source Object.
DataMember	Used when the same data source can serve multiple Recordsets simultaneously. DataEnvironment objects can do this, but data controls can't, so the property can be ignored when using the ADC.
DataField	Used to specify the field from the DataSource/DataMember's Recordset that the control will display and edit.
DataFormat	Used to specify a data format for the selected data.

In the preceding example, the DataSource for the two TextBox controls and the four inset Label controls was set to refer to the same ADC, while the DataField property was set to the relevant field name from the SQL query.

One of the biggest hassles with data binding in the past was formatting data to give a pleasing appearance on the form. The DataFormat property can be used to make formatting much, much easier. Behind the scenes, it makes use of a special DataFormat object, which can be exposed to provide any kind of formatting you can think of. You'll see how to do this later, but for most formatting needs, the DataFormat can be set via Property Pages.

For example, by selecting the Label control showing the loadedBy date Field, I can display the Property Page via its DataFormat property in the VB Properties Box (see Figure 12-2).

If none of the many available options are to your liking, you can choose the Custom option and provide any format string supported by the VB Format function.

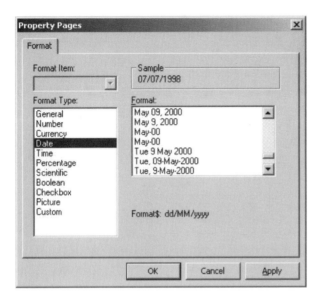

*Figure 12-2. Change DataFormat for a data-bound control using
a Property Page*

Binding Programmatically

The code-free approach can be made to work when the query or command is known
at design time. Most applications don't have this luxury (especially because the
ADC doesn't understand about Command parameters), so some kind of coding is
usually required.

If the query is supplied at run time, then generally speaking, binding is
performed at run time as well. While you can assign values directly to the DataSource
and DataField properties of data-aware controls, a more convenient and powerful
approach is to use a Binding Collection. To use Binding Collections, you need to
set a reference to "Microsoft Data Binding Collection."

A BindingCollection object maintains a collection of Binding objects. It has a
DataSource property, a DataMember property, and standard collection features
for adding and removing objects. A Binding object maintains
a relationship between a property on an object (such as a control) and a Field in
the BindingCollection's Recordset (as defined by the DataSource and DataMember
properties). It also holds a Format object that can be used for formatting Recordset
data for display and unformatting display data for updating the Recordset.

The following code re-creates the original code-free program, but instead of binding the controls to the ADC at design time, all the binding is done at run time:

```
Private bc As New BindingCollection          ◄────────   define a BindingCollection
                                                         object with module-level scope

Private Sub Form_Load()
Adodc1.ConnectionString = "File Name=c:\MuchADO.udl"
Adodc1.RecordSource = _
    "SELECT S.act, S.scene, s.Description," & _
    "C.dateTimeLoaded, C.loadedBy,C.content " & _
    "FROM Scenes S, SceneContents C " & _
    "WHERE S.act = C.act and S.scene = C.scene"

Set bc.DataSource = Adodc1              ◄────────   specify the data source
bc.Add lblAct, "Caption", "act"                    for the BindingCollection
bc.Add lblScene, "Caption", "scene"
bc.Add txtDescription, "Text", "description"
bc.Add lblLoadedBy, "Caption", "loadedBy"
bc.Add lblLoadedOn, "Caption", "dateTimeLoaded"    bind the content Field of the
bc.Add txtContent, "Text", "content"   ◄────────   DataSource's Recordset to
End Sub                                            the Text property of the
                                                   txtContent object (control)
```

Keyboard-phobic readers will no doubt prefer the design-time approach to all the typing that this code requires. However, the following points are relevant:

- It can be argued that this code is more maintainable than setting properties on each control. You can see at a glance which data is bound to which fields, and you are less likely to inadvertently change a data-binding property when tuning the user interface's look and feel.

- The binding code used here is portable. You only need to change the bc.DataSource property to connect this user interface to any other data source, such as a DataEnvironment or custom data source serving up the same Recordset.

- You can create dynamic forms by creating controls and then binding controls at run time.

- BindingCollections have some other benefits too, such as highly customizable formatting and binding to controls or properties that aren't even data aware.

An alternative to specifying the ADC's RecordSource and ConnectionString properties is to assign an ADO Recordset directly to the control's Recordset property. For example, the first two lines of the preceding Form_Load event procedure could be replaced by this:

```
Dim rs As New Recordset
rs.ActiveConnection = "File Name=c:\MuchADO.udl"
rs.Source = "SELECT S.act, S.scene, s.Description," & _
            "C.dateTimeLoaded, C.loadedBy,C.content " & _
            "FROM Scenes S, SceneContents C " & _
            "WHERE S.act = C.act and S.scene = C.scene"
rs.Open
Set Adodc1.Recordset = rs
```

Using this approach, an existing Recordset could be attached to the ADC, or existing code could be used to create the Recordset. An explicit ADO reference is required if this approach is taken.

Using Format Objects

With a reference to the "Microsoft Data Formatting Object Library" you can programmatically control formatting as part of the binding process. For example, I can replace this line of code:

```
bc.Add lblLoadedOn, "Caption", "dateTimeLoaded"
```

with this:

```
Dim ft As New StdDataFormat
ft.Type = fmtCustom
ft.Format = "dddd, dd MMMM yyyy"
bc.Add lblLoadedOn, "Caption", "dateTimeLoaded", ft
```

which adds a DataFormat object to the BindingCollection. This will achieve exactly the same effect as the formatting added through Property Pages in the earlier example. Alternatively, if you prefer to bind at run time but specify formatting declaratively at design time, the following approach can be used:

```
bc.Add lblLoadedOn, "Caption", _
        "dateTimeLoaded", lblLoadedOn.DataFormat
```

This simply makes sure that the design-time formatting object is assigned to the correct location in the BindingCollection.

Format objects can be used to achieve formatting effects that could never be specified declaratively. For example, if you look back a few pages to Figure 12-1, you'll notice that my Scene Viewer looks a bit messy. This is because the content Field of the SceneContent table uses vbCr characters to represent a line break, whereas the TextBox control expects a vbCrLf pairing. As a result, the TextBox is littered with vertical bars where proper formatting should be applied.

You can use programmed formatting to correct this problem. The DataFormat object can raise events to request formatting and unformatting whenever they are required. To make use of these events, you need to declare module-level objects using the WithEvents keyword. The following code uses the Format event to replace each vbCr with a vbCrLf. The complete code for the program is now:

```vb
Dim bc As New BindingCollection
Private WithEvents ft As StdDataFormat          ◄────────  declare the DataFormat
                                                            object WithEvents, and
                                                            initialize i
Private Sub Form_Load()
Set ft = New StdDataFormat          ◄──────────────────────┘
Adodc1.ConnectionString = "File Name=c:\MuchADO.udl"
Adodc1.RecordSource = _
    "SELECT S.act, S.scene, s.Description," & _
    "C.dateTimeLoaded, C.loadedBy,C.content " & _
    "FROM Scenes S, SceneContents C " & _
    "WHERE S.act = C.act and S.scene = C.scene"
Set bc.DataSource = Adodc1
bc.Add lblAct, "Caption", "act"
bc.Add lblScene, "Caption", "scene"
bc.Add txtDescription, "Text", "description"
bc.Add lblLoadedBy, "Caption", "loadedBy"
bc.Add lblLoadedOn, "Caption", _
        "dateTimeLoaded", lblLoadedOn.DataFormat
bc.Add txtContent, "Text", "content", ft   ◄────────  include ft in the
End Sub                                                binding collection

Private Sub ft_Format(ByVal DataValue As StdFormat.StdDataValue)  ◄──┐
DataValue = Replace(DataValue, vbCr, vbCrLf)                         │
End Sub                                    ▲──────────────  format the data
                                                            for presentation
```

With this code, the form appears as follows:

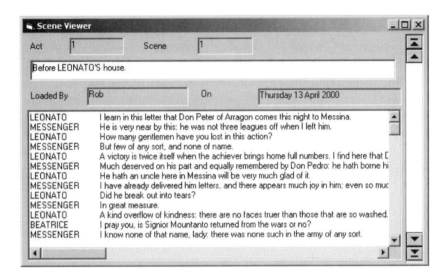

Figure 12-3. Use custom formatting to improve data presentation.

Binding to Controls and Properties
That Are Not Data Aware

Windows 2000 comes with the "Microsoft Direct Text-to-Speech" control. This impressive control generates audio output from a string input, but has a potentially irritating user interface. Therefore, I have wrapped it in my own ActiveX control called Speak, which has a single property called Speech and a user interface that looks like this:

Figure 12-4. The Speak control, midway through reading a scene

As you can see, it fits nicely into the top-right corner of my Scene Viewer application. When you click the Play button, it reads whatever text is currently in the Speech property through the computer's audio system.[2] The progress bar lets you see how far the reading has progressed.

---

2. You can find the code for this control on the CD in the MuchADOControls project associated with this chapter. However, it only has about ten lines of code—the real work is done using the embedded Microsoft Direct Text-to-Speech control.

The Speak control is not data aware, but by using a BindingCollection, its Speech property can be bound to a data source. Here's the extra code that is required in Form_Load:

```
bc.Add Speak1, "Speech", "content"
```

For this small amount of effort, I can have each scene read aloud. Any control can be incorporated into the BindingCollection in exactly the same way. It's just as easy to bind different data fields to properties of the same control. For example, you could bind a product code to a Label's Caption property and a product description to its ToolTipText property.

In This Section

We saw how the traditional techniques of binding using controls have been extended to include the use of Format objects and how programmatic binding can be performed using BindingCollections. BindingCollections are powerful, because they allow you to bind to any property of a control and to use controls that aren't data aware.

Binding with Classes

You have already seen that by using BindingCollections and Format objects, you can achieve more flexible binding and presentation results than have traditionally been possible with data-binding techniques. However, there are still some limitations of binding that we need to address, namely:

> *To exploit data binding in many modern programming scenarios, we need to be able to work in an n-tier fashion.* The ADC insists that either it connects directly to a Provider, or we generate a Recordset separately and attach it to the Control. Unless we decide to write our own Provider, the former approach makes our application a two-tier one: the user interface is directly dependent on the internal design of the data source. While this is fine for some people, it's definitely not for others. You can overcome this problem by attaching a Recordset directly to the ADC, but in doing so, the benefit of encapsulation is lost. The client program must first create the data it requires and then pass the resulting Recordset to a "dumb" ADC. A more sensible approach would be to create our own data sources capable of fetching data in a manner of our choosing, and then the data consumer needs only bind to this custom data source without being responsible for building Recordsets.

Being dependent on controls for both data sources and data consumers is limiting. For one thing, it means you have to be using Forms. This more or less rules out the use of binding in middle-tier components. (You may be wondering what benefit binding offers in a nonvisual situation— I'll address this issue shortly.) For another thing, many developers simply don't like the idea of using a control to represent a data source. Fundamentally, a data source is not part of a user interface, and therefore, using a control to represent it doesn't make too much sense. Arguably, the only reason for having a control as a data source is historical. Prior to VB5, controls were the only VB feature capable of raising events. Programming with events is very convenient, and therefore, many components were historically packaged as controls, simply to allow events to be processed. However, this is no longer an issue, and the only benefit that such nonvisual controls offer is the ability to work declaratively with properties at design time.

VB6 allows any object to be a data source or a data consumer. This allows you to construct the system design of your choice without losing the convenience of data binding.

Turning a class into a data source is extremely easy. Each class in VB6 has a property called DataSourceBehavior. If you set this property to "1–vbDataSource" your class acquires a new event, GetDataMember, and it's ready to be a custom data source. The signature for the new event is

```
Private Sub Class_GetDataMember(DataMember As String, Data As Object)
```

This event will be fired when data is needed. The `DataMember` argument can be used to tell the data source which data is required. The primary task of the data source is to create a Recordset (possibly based on the information provided via DataMember) and to assign this Recordset to the Data argument.

We saw an almost identical technique in Chapter 11, when we created a Data Source Object for a custom Simple Provider. In fact, the only difference is that when we are creating a Provider, GetDataMember returns an object that implements the OLEDBSimpleProvider interface, whereas when we are just creating a Data Source Object for binding purposes, it returns a Recordset. Note that VB adds a reference to "Microsoft Data Source Interfaces" when you set DataSourceBehavior.

In the same way that an ADC exposes a Recordset property, it makes sense for a custom data source to expose a Recordset property. This will allow a client program to operate directly on the Recordset if required. Here then, is some code that be used to create a Data Source Object (of class CustomDataSource) to replace all but the visual aspects of the ADC used previously:

```
Private WithEvents rs As Recordset

Private Sub Class_GetDataMember( DataMember As String, _
Data As Object)
  Dim sSQL As String
  sSQL = "SELECT S.act, S.scene, s.Description," & _
         "C.dateTimeLoaded, C.loadedBy,C.content " & _
         "FROM Scenes S, SceneContents C " & _
         "WHERE S.act = C.act and S.scene = C.scene"
  Set rs = New ADODB.Recordset
  rs.CursorLocation = adUseClient
  rs.Open sSQL, "File Name=c:\MuchADO.udl", , _
  adLockOptimistic
  Set Data = rs              ◄──────────────     assign rs to the Data argument
End Sub

Public Property Get Recordset() As Recordset
Set Recordset = rs    ◄──────────────    expose rs as a read-only
End Property                             property called Recordset
```

This code ignores the DataMember argument because it's a single Recordset data
source with no need for parameterization.

Note that the **rs** variable was defined using **WithEvents**. The ADC uses delega-
tion to expose the events of the Recordset it manages. You may wish to do the same
thing for Data Source Objects you create, in which case you would need to add
Event declarations to the CustomDataSource class that have the same name and
arguments as the Recordset events. You can then trap the Recordset events on the rs
variable and pass them on through your own events. To show you what this looks
like, here are the event declarations for the WillChangeField and FieldChangeCom-
plete events:

```
Public Event WillChangeField( _
            ByVal cFields As Long, ByVal Fields As Variant, _
            adStatus As ADODB.EventStatusEnum, _
            ByVal pRecordset As ADODB.Recordset)
Public Event FieldChangeComplete( _
            ByVal cFields As Long, ByVal Fields As Variant, _
            ByVal pError As ADODB.Error, _
            adStatus As ADODB.EventStatusEnum, _
            ByVal pRecordset As ADODB.Recordset)
```

And here's the code that raises these events at the appropriate point:

```
Private Sub rs_WillChangeField( _
            ByVal cFields As Long, ByVal Fields As Variant, _
            adStatus As ADODB.EventStatusEnum, _
            ByVal pRecordset As ADODB.Recordset)
RaiseEvent WillChangeField _
        (cFields, Fields, adStatus, pRecordset)
End Sub


Private Sub rs_FieldChangeComplete( _
            ByVal cFields As Long, ByVal Fields As Variant, _
            ByVal pError As ADODB.Error, _
            adStatus As ADODB.EventStatusEnum, _
            ByVal pRecordset As ADODB.Recordset)
RaiseEvent FieldChangeComplete _
  (cFields, Fields, pError, adStatus, pRecordset)
End Sub
```

raise your own events based on those raised by rs

Of course, you could implement as many or as few events as required.

With the CustomDataSource object implemented, we can now remove the ADC from our Scene Viewer user interface and instead bind the controls to the Data Source Object. We are then free to add whatever user interface we require, and for demonstration purposes, I have chosen to use a vertical scroll bar. This is what the user interface now looks like (also showing the Speak control introduced in the last section):

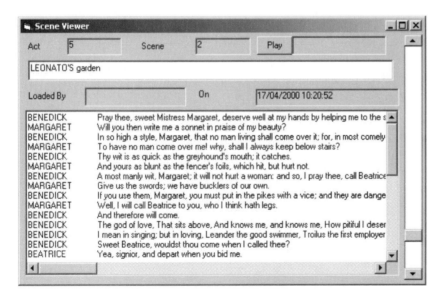

Figure 12-5. Scene Viewer application with a Speak control and scroll bar

The client code now looks like this:

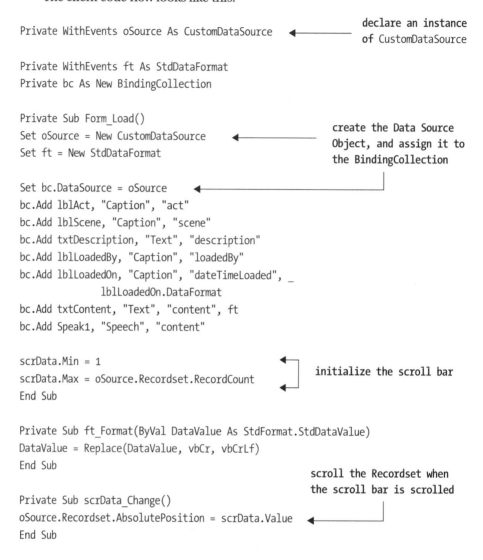

```
Private WithEvents oSource As CustomDataSource          declare an instance
                                                       of CustomDataSource

Private WithEvents ft As StdDataFormat
Private bc As New BindingCollection


Private Sub Form_Load()                                create the Data Source
Set oSource = New CustomDataSource                     Object, and assign it to
Set ft = New StdDataFormat                             the BindingCollection

Set bc.DataSource = oSource
bc.Add lblAct, "Caption", "act"
bc.Add lblScene, "Caption", "scene"
bc.Add txtDescription, "Text", "description"
bc.Add lblLoadedBy, "Caption", "loadedBy"
bc.Add lblLoadedOn, "Caption", "dateTimeLoaded", _
              lblLoadedOn.DataFormat
bc.Add txtContent, "Text", "content", ft
bc.Add Speak1, "Speech", "content"

scrData.Min = 1
scrData.Max = oSource.Recordset.RecordCount            initialize the scroll bar
End Sub

Private Sub ft_Format(ByVal DataValue As StdFormat.StdDataValue)
DataValue = Replace(DataValue, vbCr, vbCrLf)
End Sub
                                                       scroll the Recordset when
                                                       the scroll bar is scrolled
Private Sub scrData_Change()
oSource.Recordset.AbsolutePosition = scrData.Value
End Sub
```

As you can see, the binding code is identical to that used when the data source was an ADC. In fact, the data-aware controls are oblivious to the change of data source.

You now have a data source that is completely free from any user interface restrictions and can create Recordsets any way it wants, without the data consumer needing to worry about how this was achieved. By using the DataMember property, your data sources can become highly configurable, returning many different types of data. You can also use the same techniques to create your own Data Control if you like the visual metaphor it supports, but wish to hide data access code from GUI developers. VB UserControls have a DataSourceBehavior property just like classes do, and you can use the same coding techniques described in this section to create a Custom Data Control. Either way, the source of the data is entirely up to you.

Creating a Nonvisual Data Consumer

Now that you know that you can replace a Data Control with a nonvisual class, it seems natural to see whether a nonvisual data consumer can be created that can be bound to a data source.

The answer is yes, but you might also want to ask why this is worth doing. While it's easy to see why binding controls to a data source means that user interface features are kept synchronized with Recordset navigation, it's less easy to see why keeping a nonvisual object synchronized with a Recordset has any merit.

One of the themes of this book is that Recordsets are an extremely useful data structure in their own right, regardless of their other virtues. Compared to (for example) a collection of objects, Recordsets provide some major advantages. At the same time, two obvious disadvantages come to mind:

1. When you access the properties of a standard object, VB's IntelliSense and COM's early binding come to your assistance. These features aren't available when specifying a Field name from a Recordset.

2. While it's true that Recordsets have a wide range of built-in methods, properties, and events, you can't extend them. Therefore, you can't add custom functionality to a Recordset.

You can overcome these shortcomings by making a class into a data consumer. A data consumer class is much like a set of data-aware controls bound to a data source, except that it doesn't have a visual component. This means that it can be used in the middle tier of an n-tier system to provide middle-tier programmers with a supercharged form of Recordset.

You can make any class into a data consumer by setting the class's `DataBinding-Behavior` property to `vbSimpleBound` via the VB Property Box. This allows you to map the properties of an object onto individual fields in the current row of a Recordset. In fact, you can use a BindingCollection to create such an object without setting the DataBindingBehavior property, but when you set this property, VB adds a number of features to the class that are especially useful if you want your objects to update the Recordset when their properties are changed. These features include a PropertyChanged method that functions rather like the PropertyChanged method in UserControls. You can call the PropertyChanged method in a Property Let procedure to inform the BindingCollection that a data value has been updated.

There are many ways to create data consumer classes, and if the idea grabs you, you'll no doubt think of some suitable design approaches. As an example, I will show you an approach that wraps a data consumer around the CustomData-Source class just created. This CustomConsumer class will have a property for each Field in the underlying Recordset and also a WordCount method, which will provide a rough-and-ready count of the words in the content field of the current Record. It's usual to write a few standard navigation methods in a data consumer class, but for the sake of brevity, CustomConsumer simply exposes the Recordset object to allow the base client to navigate. Here's the code for CustomConsumer with some of the Property Get and Let procedures removed to prevent code overdose:

```
Private oSource As New CustomDataSource
Private bc As BindingCollection

Private msAct As String
Private msScene As String
Private msDescription As String
Private msLoadedBy As String
Private msDateTimeLoaded As Date
Private msContent As String

Public Sub GetData()

Dim fd As Field
Set bc = New BindingCollection
Set bc.DataSource = oSource

For Each fd In oSource.Recordset.Fields
  bc.Add Me, fd.Name, fd.Name
  Next
End Sub
```

GetData **is called to initialize the data consumer**

use a For Each **loop to bind each Field to a property with a** BindingCollection

```
Public Property Get Recordset() As Recordset
Set Recordset = oSource.Recordset
End Property

Public Property Get Act() As String
Act = msAct
End Property

Public Property Let Act(ByVal vNewValue As String)
msAct = vNewValue
PropertyChanged "Act"
End Property
```

call PropertyChanged **to inform the** BindingCollection **that data has been updated**

```
. . .

Public Property Let Content(ByVal vNewValue As String)
msContent = vNewValue
PropertyChanged "Content"
End Property
```

```
Public Property Get Content() As String
Content = msContent
End Property

Public Function WordCount() As Long
Dim vArray As Variant
vArray = Split(Me.Content, " ")
WordCount = UBound(vArray)
End Function
```

WordCount **counts the space-delimited words in** Me.Content

This code uses a shortcut approach to creating the bindings. A more sophisticated consumer could make use of Format objects to give each property pretty print capability. Here's the code that allows a client program to make use of the CustomConsumer:

```
Dim oData As New CustomConsumer
With oData
 .GetData
While Not .Recordset.EOF
  Print .Act, .Scene, .WordCount
  .Recordset.MoveNext
Wend
End With
```

The client program prints

1	1	2370
1	2	207
1	3	548
2	1	2822
2	2	400
2	3	2040
. . .		

While you may be thinking that this took quite a lot of code to achieve, it's worth comparing the data consumer approach to the frequently used approach of converting a Recordset into a custom collection. The custom collection approach involves even more coding and is significantly less efficient, requiring a great deal of up-front copying and object creation.

The data consumer is also considerably more flexible. For example, you could add a property that gives users of the data consumer a number of different format options. When they change the format option, the data consumer simply rebinds the properties to the data fields using a different set of Format objects. This would make it very easy to generate different HTML output for a Web page, or content for a report, according to a user's preferences.

In This Section

You learned how to create your own data sources—either as a regular, nonvisual VB object or as a control that can be used in place of the ADC. Custom data sources can be more powerful than the ADC because they can have multiple DataMembers. More importantly, they hide away the details of how Recordsets are created, and in doing so, provide the flexibility to work in n-tier as well as traditional two-tier environments. You also saw how nonvisual data consumers can be written to exploit binding in a middle-tier component.

The Data Repeater Control

VB5 introduced the ability to create custom ActiveX controls using the UserControl designer. It also provided the ability to make custom controls data-aware (in other words, turn them into custom data consumers), so that they could be bound to Data Controls. While making controls data-aware can make them easier to use in binding scenarios, the arrival of BindingCollection has removed the necessity of doing so.

Creating user interfaces incorporating custom controls that display a single record at a time is a very straightforward process. However, it has always been a far greater challenge to make customized displays that show multiple records. While there are several high-quality data grids on the market offering ever-increasing levels of customization, there are still limits to their flexibility.

Creating highly tailored gridlike displays presents developers with a major challenge. Either you take an existing grid control and risk customizing it beyond its limits, or you try to build your own scrollable grid control. Both approaches are likely to take far more programming resources than most projects can justify.

The Data Repeater control offers a solution to the dilemma. It allows you to concentrate on designing a control that represents one record. It then takes that control and automatically uses it to create each row in a scrollable grid. When you use the Data Repeater, it looks as though your "single row" control has been duplicated enough times to create a copy of itself for each record in a Recordset. In reality, the Data Repeater is far more efficient than this—it only ever creates one instance of your control and creates and manages bitmaps to fill the grid area with what look like copies of your control. It handles all the scrolling, binding, and other tasks that make writing grids a major endeavor.

The usual approach for working with the Data Repeater control is to use the ADC as the data source and to use a data-aware custom control whose properties can be bound to the data source's fields. There is nothing wrong with this approach, and in fact, the Data Repeater control provides a user interface for the binding task via its Property Pages. However, once you have learned to program with a Binding-Collection, there is no real need to create a data-aware control—a standard custom control will do.[3]

To show the Data Repeater in action, I have created a control to represent a single record of the query we've been using throughout this chapter. Because this control is going to be used as a row in a grid, it makes sense to make it disproportionately short and fat. The control displays the act, scene, description (which is editable), and word count, and it displays a Speak control for reading out the scene's contents. If the word count is less than 500, it's displayed in a bold, red font as an indication that this is a very short scene that may require special stage directions.

Figure 12-6. The SceneView control, representing one record in a Recordset

Here's the complete code for the control, which is little more than a few standard Property Procedure definitions:

```
Public Property Get Act() As String
Act = lblAct.Caption
End Property

Public Property Let Act(ByVal sNewValue As String)
lblAct.Caption = sNewValue
End Property

Public Property Get Scene() As String
Scene = lblScene.Caption
End Property

Public Property Let Scene(ByVal sNewValue As String)
lblScene.Caption = sNewValue
End Property

Public Property Get Description() As String
Description = txtDescription.Text
End Property
```

---

3. Personally, I find VB's user interface for making controls data-aware rather fiddly. Unless I am producing a control for sale, I prefer to leave it up to the user of my control to bind programmatically using a BindingCollection.

```
Public Property Let Description(ByVal sNewValue As String)
txtDescription.Text = sNewValue
UserControl.PropertyChanged "Description"
End Property

Public Property Get Content() As String
Content = Speak1.Speech
End Property

Public Property Let Content(ByVal sNewValue As String)
Speak1.Speech = sNewValue
lblWordCount.Caption = UBound(Split(sNewValue, " "))
If CLng(lblWordCount.Caption) > 500 Then
   lblWordCount.ForeColor = vbBlue
   lblWordCount.Font.Bold = False
Else
   lblWordCount.ForeColor = vbRed
   lblWordCount.Font.Bold = True
End If
End Property

Private Sub txtDescription_Change()
UserControl.PropertyChanged "Description"
End Sub
```

Before you can attach a control to the Data Repeater, it must be compiled and registered. My control is called SceneView, and it's part of the MuchADOControls project. Once it has been compiled, you can use it as part of a VB Project Group and test it interactively just like any regular control. This is what it looks like when linked to a Data Repeater:

Figure 12-7. The SceneView control, operating inside a Data Repeater control

This display shows six rows—there is one instance of the SceneView control (used for the current row) and five bitmaps. The scroll bar lets us scroll through the entire Recordset of scenes.

Let's see how this display was put together.

The first step was to use the Project–Components menu to reference "Microsoft Data Repeater" and then to add a Data Repeater control to a form. The Data Repeater control has a property called RepeatedControlName which has a dropdown box that you can use to select the *ProgID* for your control. At this point, if you are using the ADC and a data-aware custom control, you can use the VB Properties Box to set the data source and perform the bindings graphically.

However, we are going to perform these operations programmatically, using our existing data source class and the (data-unaware) SceneView control. The Data Repeater control has DataSource and DataMember properties that can be set programmatically. It also has a RepeaterBindings property, which behaves exactly like a BindingCollection object. Here's the complete code required to do the binding business:

```
Dim oSource As New CustomDataSource          ←——————   use an instance of the
With DataRepeater1                                     previously created data
  Set .DataSource = oSource                            source class
  .RepeaterBindings.Add "Act", "Act"
  .RepeaterBindings.Add "Scene", "Scene"
  .RepeaterBindings.Add "Description", "Description"
  .RepeaterBindings.Add "Content", "Content"
End With
```

At this stage, we have a scrollable grid that performs perfectly as a read-only display. It should also work as an updateable grid, but sadly, a bug in the current version of the Data Repeater means that an additional step is required. Both the Data Repeater control and its internal BindingCollection maintain a pointer to the current record in the data source's Recordset. These two pointers should be kept in synchronization, but they aren't. As a result, unless we add some synchronization code, any updates we make via the Data Repeater disappear in a puff of blue error handling. The most frequently used approach to re-establish the required synchronization is to add a Save button to the form containing the grid and to instruct the user to click this button after making changes to a row and before scrolling to or selecting another Record. The Save button basically forces a move operation on the data source, thus resynchronizing the BindingCollection to which it's attached, using code such as this:

```
Dim oSource As CustomDataSource
Set oSource = DataRepeater1.DataSource
oSource.Recordset.Move 0
```

An alternative approach, which many users find quite natural, is to code the Data Repeater control's KeyPress event to perform the synchronization whenever the Enter key is pressed:[4]

```
Private Sub DataRepeater1_KeyPress(KeyAscii As Integer)
Dim oSource As CustomDataSource
If KeyAscii = Asc(vbCr) Then
  Set oSource = DataRepeater1.DataSource
  oSource.Recordset.Move 0
  End If
End Sub
```

For relatively little effort, the Data Repeater control allows us to create exactly the type of grid display that we want. It's also an elegant demonstration of the power of component-based development.

In This Section

We used the Data Repeater control to create a highly customized data grid, without needing to write any grid management code.

Binding Hierarchical Recordsets

Chapter 8 introduced the concept of hierarchical Recordsets, in which a Chapter-type Field is appended to a Recordset to allow drilling down into a Recordset to a lower level of detail. To provide a ready-to-run user interface for displaying hierarchical Recordsets, VB6 delivers a new data grid control, the Hierarchical FlexGrid (HFlexGrid), designed to display hierarchical Recordsets automatically.

It's all too easy to assume that the HFlexGrid is the only way to display hierarchical Recordsets using data grids. It so happens that this isn't the case and that there are situations where other approaches work better.

There is no doubt that the HFlexGrid works well when the hierarchical Recordset contains two constituent Recordsets in a traditional master-detail type of arrangement. For example, consider the following SHAPE command, which has a child Recordset containing all words greater than eleven characters in length, and a parent that provides a word count for each scene:

```
SHAPE {SELECT  word, wordCount, wordLength,
 act, scene FROM Words WHERE wordLength > 11} as Words
      COMPUTE Words , SUM (Words.wordCount) As WordCount
      BY act, scene
```

---

4. Being the obliging folk that they are, users typically get great comfort from hitting the Enter key. Just for once, here's a situation where it pays us to indulge them.

Remember that because this is a COMPUTE SHAPE command, the child Record-set is defined before the parent, which is based on the COMPUTE statement.

You can attach a Recordset directly to the HFlexGrid's Recordset property and manipulate its bindings programmatically. This is relatively straightforward, so long as you realize that the HFlexGrid organizes the hierarchical display into bands. Each band represents one constituent Recordset, and therefore, has its own set of bindings.

While gaining familiarity with the control, you may prefer to create an ADC based on the SHAPE command statement and set the DataSource property of the HFlexGrid to this ADC. The reason for doing this is that you can then use the HFlexGrid's design-time menu to retrieve the structure of the hierarchical Recordset, after which you can manipulate the bands graphically using the control's Property Pages, shown here:

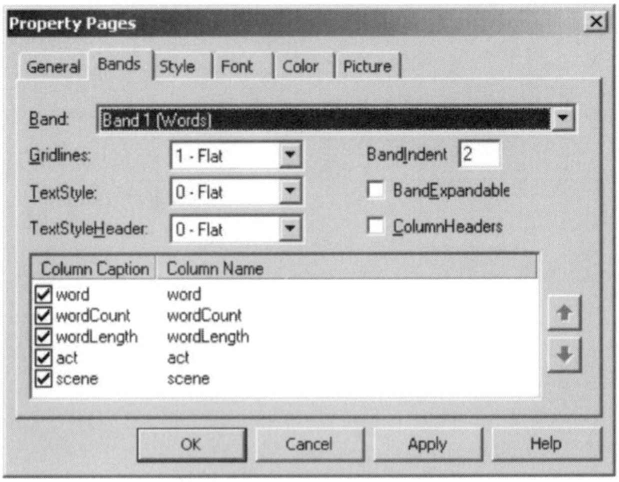

Figure 12-8. Configuring an HFlexGrid using its Property Pages

You can then very easily create a display such as the one shown in Figure 12-9, where the bands are displayed in a vertical configuration (one appearing beneath another). It's almost essential to provide buttons, such as the Collapse All, Expand All, Hide Headers, and Show Headers, to allow the user to create a reasonable display. Fortunately, they are very easy to code:

```
Private Sub cmdCollapseAll_Click()
HFlex.CollapseAll
End Sub

Private Sub cmdExpandAll_Click()
HFlex.ExpandAll
End Sub
```

```
Private Sub cmdHideHeaders_Click()
HFlex.ColHeader(0) = flexColHeaderOff
HFlex.ColHeader(1) = flexColHeaderOff
End Sub
```

the ColHeader **property is an array indexed by band number—this code removes all column headers for bands 0 and 1**

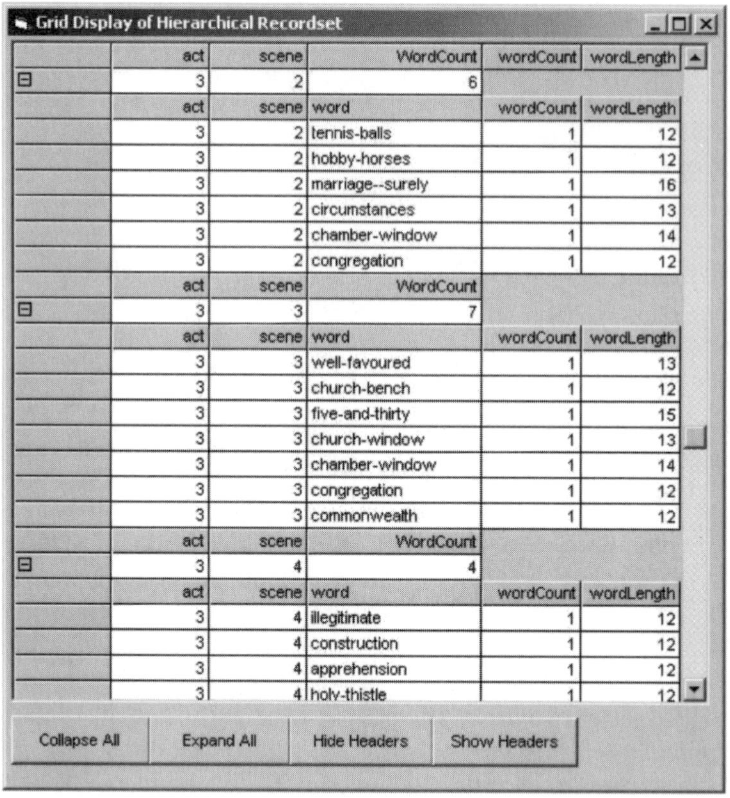

```
Private Sub cmdShowHeaders_Click()
HFlex.ColHeader(0) = flexColHeaderOn
HFlex.ColHeader(1) = flexColHeaderOn
End Sub
```

Grid Display of Hierarchical Recordset

	act	scene	WordCount	wordCount	wordLength
⊟	3	2	6		
	act	scene	word	wordCount	wordLength
	3	2	tennis-balls	1	12
	3	2	hobby-horses	1	12
	3	2	marriage--surely	1	16
	3	2	circumstances	1	13
	3	2	chamber-window	1	14
	3	2	congregation	1	12
	act	scene	WordCount		
⊟	3	3	7		
	act	scene	word	wordCount	wordLength
	3	3	well-favoured	1	13
	3	3	church-bench	1	12
	3	3	five-and-thirty	1	15
	3	3	church-window	1	13
	3	3	chamber-window	1	14
	3	3	congregation	1	12
	3	3	commonwealth	1	12
	act	scene	WordCount		
⊟	3	4	4		
	act	scene	word	wordCount	wordLength
	3	4	illegitimate	1	12
	3	4	construction	1	12
	3	4	apprehension	1	12
	3	4	holy-thistle	1	12

| Collapse All | Expand All | Hide Headers | Show Headers |

Figure 12-9. A highly configured HFlexGrid display

Displaying Complex Hierarchies

As hierarchies become more complex, the HFlexGrid becomes increasingly more unwieldy as a display mechanism. For example, consider the following four-level SHAPE command borrowed from Chapter 8:

```
SHAPE (SHAPE (SHAPE
  {SELECT  part, sum(wordCount) as PWordCount,
   Avg(CONVERT(float,wordLength)) as PAveLength, act, scene
        FROM Words group by part, act, scene} as Parts
APPEND ({select * from Words where part = ? and act = ? and scene = ?}
  RELATE part TO PARAMETER 0, act TO PARAMETER 1,
   scene TO PARAMETER 2)as Words)
  COMPUTE Parts,
  SUM (Parts.PwordCount) as wordCount ,
  AVG (Parts.PAveLength) as wordLength BY act, scene) as Scenes
    COMPUTE Scenes,
    SUM (Scenes.wordCount) ,
         AVG (Scenes.wordLength) BY act
```

This command allows you to see word count and average length by act, and then to drill down to see the data by scene, then by part, and then to see the words used by a part in each scene.

Binding an HFlexGrid using the SHAPE command raises two serious issues:

1. The benefits of parameterization are lost, as the HFlexGrid tries to retrieve as much data as it can to build the grid display.

2. It's extremely hard to create a manageable display that gives users flexible data management options. For example, the grid in Figure 12-10 looks impressive, but it will be more confusing than useful for many users.

Once the data becomes this complex, it can be more effective to create a display using a more traditional type of grid control for each constituent Recordset in the hierarchy. Figure 12-11 shows how this looks.

Because of the way hierarchical Recordsets work (see Chapter 8), these grids appear to be automatically linked with no additional coding required. For example, clicking a new row in the upper-left grid causes the other three to refresh automatically. Each grid is a standard DataGrid, available after you check "Microsoft DataGrid Control 6.0 (OLEDB)" in the Project–Components dialog box. Most modern grids are smart enough to know they can't display chapter columns, so they simply don't bother. As an added benefit, this display will exploit the parameterization used in the SHAPE command, retrieving data on an as-needed basis. Therefore, the initial display will be created far more quickly than with the HFlex-Grid approach, and in most cases, the overall network demand will be lower.

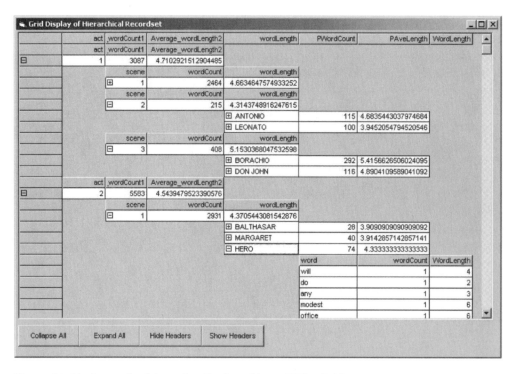

Figure 12-10. A complex hierarchy displayed in an HFlexGrid

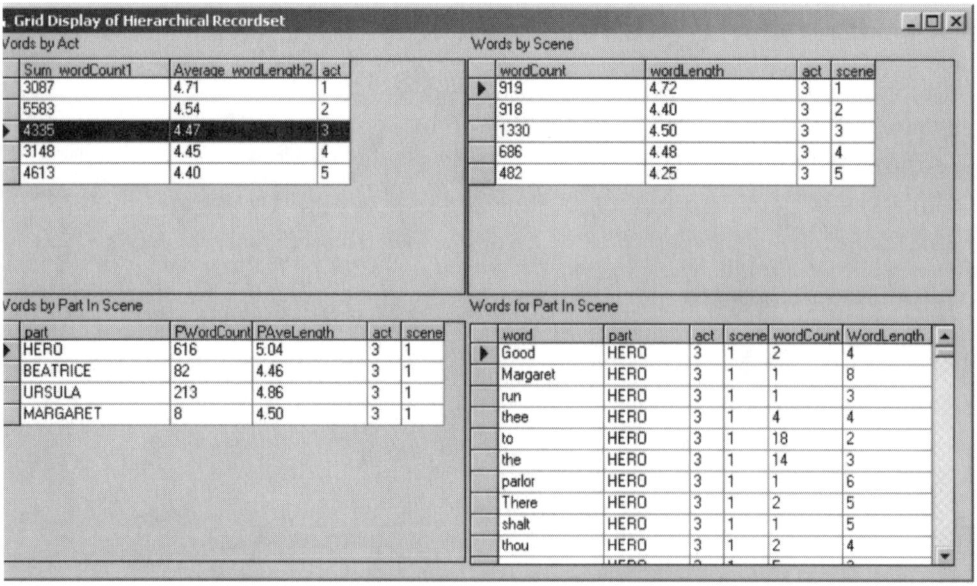

Figure 12-11. A complex hierarchy displayed using conventional DataGrids

This display could be created by using four different ADCs and setting the Recordset property of each one to the appropriate Recordset in the hierarchy. However, following the theme of this chapter, let's use a more elegant solution based on a custom data source. This data source makes use of the DataMember argument of the GetDataMember event. When there is no DataMember, the data source builds the hierarchical Recordset and returns a reference to it. When the DataMember is one of Scenes, Parts or Words, it returns the appropriate child Recordset. It's assumed that the hierarchy is created before the children are requested. Here's the code for this custom data source class, which is called WordsData:

```
Private rs As New Recordset
Private rsScenes As Recordset          declare a Recordset variable for the
Private rsParts As Recordset           hierarchy and one for each child
Private rsWords As Recordset


Private sSQL as String


Private Sub Class_GetDataMember( DataMember As String, _
                                 Data As Object)


Dim sCommand As String
Select Case DataMember
  Case "Scenes"
    Set Data = rsScenes
  Case "Parts"                         return a child (assuming the
    Set Data = rsParts                 variable has been set)
  Case "Words"
    Set Data = rsWords
  Case Else
     << initialize sSQL to the command shown above >>
    sCommand = sSQL
    rs.Open sCommand, "File Name=c:\Shape.udl"
    Set rsScenes = rs("Scenes").Value        open the hierarchical
    Set rsParts = rsScenes("Parts").Value    Recordset and assign the
    Set rsWords = rsParts("Words").Value     child variables
    Set Data = rs
End Select


End Sub
```

Once the Data Source Object is created, the code for setting up the grids is trivial. The following code sets the DataSource and DataMember properties of four data grids, and sets the Format objects on their BindingCollections (available through the DataFormats property) to show the "average word count" columns to two decimal places:

```
Dim oSource As New WordsData
Set DataGrid1.DataSource = oSource
DataGrid1.DataFormats(1).Format = "0.00"
DataGrid2.DataMember = "Scenes"
Set DataGrid2.DataSource = oSource
DataGrid2.DataFormats(1).Format = "0.00"
DataGrid3.DataMember = "Parts"
Set DataGrid3.DataSource = oSource
DataGrid3.DataFormats(2).Format = "0.00"
DataGrid4.DataMember = "Words"
Set DataGrid4.DataSource = oSource
```

When a DataMember is specified, it must be assigned before the DataSource property to ensure it gets passed through to the GetDataMember event on the Data Source Object.

In This Section

We explored the use of the HFlexGrid control and alternative ways of displaying hierarchical Recordsets. You also saw how to create a custom data source with multiple DataMembers.

Summary

Data binding has been a part of Visual Basic for as long as data access has been available. VB6 and ADO provide all the traditional data-binding facilities through OLE DB, and they also extend the binding model to overcome some of the limitations that have made data binding less than ideal in many people's minds. In this chapter, we've seen that:

- It's still possible, and in some ways easier than ever, to build the traditional style of data-bound VB program in which a data control links the user interface directly to the database.

- It's now also possible to create more elaborate and controllable designs by creating custom data sources.

- Data binding can be used in both the front end and middle tiers of an n-tier application.

- The benefits of component-based design are clearly shown by the Data Repeater control, which links an ADO Recordset or data source to a "single-row" component and adds in all that is required to create a highly customized data grid.

These new features, coupled with the extra control provided by ADO's event model, are enough to make a reevaluation of data binding essential for even the most ardent skeptic. At the same time, developers who fear that the inevitable migration to n-tier development will mean that the benefits of binding will be lost forever, should also think again. Creating sophisticated, yet bindable, custom data sources is a straightforward process that may be enough to persuade two-tier diehards that componentization is not necessarily an antidote to rapid application development.

In the next chapter, we'll explore the extent of Microsoft's commitment to flexible data binding by examining one of the major new features provided in VB6, the Data Environment.

The Data Environment

What Is a Data Environment?

Using Parameterized Commands

Defining Hierarchical Recordsets

Making Data Environments into Components

Summary

IN THE LAST CHAPTER, you saw how to create custom data sources and perform data binding without placing a Data Control on a form. You saw the potential that custom data sources have for organizing all data access code into a centralized location, freeing user interface developers from the need to wade through the details of database schemas, and providing consistent access to data through a convenient interface.

A custom data source creates and manages a set of Recordsets known as its DataMembers. A user of a custom data source simply requests a DataMember by name, without needing to know anything about how to create it.

Before rushing off and writing data sources to encapsulate all your business requirements though, spare a moment to investigate the Data Environment. The Data Environment provides a graphical tool for building and using one or more data source classes. Using the Data Environment designer, you can create Data-Members using point-and-click techniques, Property Pages, and a powerful graphical SQL builder. You can also add custom code, event handling, and new methods and properties to extend the set of DataMembers created graphically by the Data Environment designer.

A user of a Data Environment can make use of its DataMembers in any of three ways:

- DataMembers can be dragged and dropped directly onto Forms or Reports, in which case the Data Environment designer will create a control for each selected field and automatically bind it.

- Controls can be bound manually to a DataMember's fields, either through the VB Properties Box or by coding a BindingCollection.

- DataMembers can be used programmatically in unbound mode by using dynamically created methods and properties of a run-time Data Environment object.

In one sense, you can think of a Data Environment as a superior alternative to using the ADO Data Control. However, the reality is rather more profound. A Data Environment is a highly productive way of writing a Data Access Layer, where all data-oriented code is located in a centralized component. An application's user interface can then call into this Data Environment to receive data services. Of course, designing a Data Access Layer means spending more time up-front on design and planning, so that the separation between presentation (user interface) and data management is maintained. While this overhead seems to work against the principle of rapid application development, it's important to consider the development effort spent on an application over its entire lifetime. For any successful application, more development effort is expended after the application goes into production than during the additional development phase.[1] Maintaining an application with a centralized Data Access Layer is far and away easier than maintaining one in which SQL is spread around many different modules. Converting a form-based application into a browser-based application is also much easier, because none of the code in the Data Access Layer needs to be modified.

If you start using a Data Environment to create a Data Access Layer, you have taken the first step to writing an n-tier application. As you'll see, most people use a Data Environment simply as an object within their front-end application. In this case, the application is n-tier in spirit,[2] but no one is going to believe you, and you won't be able to exploit an environment such as MTS or COM+. However, you can also make a Data Environment into a public COM object and compile it into a separate EXE or DLL, in which case, it's visibly and functionally a middle-tier component.

In this chapter we'll explore the basic workings of the Data Environment, which will build upon what you learned about data sources in the previous chapter. You'll see how to successfully use parameterized queries with Data Environments and learn how to compile a Data Environment into a middle-tier component using both connected and disconnected Recordsets.

What Is a Data Environment?

If you think of the design-time Form designer (used for laying out controls) in conjunction with its associated code window as a "Form Environment," then it's fairly easy to imagine what a Data Environment is.

---

1. Industry commentators differ on their estimates of the ratio of effort expended between (pre-release) development and (post-release) maintenance on an average production system, but most estimates fall between 30:70 and 10:90, with the majority being maintenance work in all cases.

2. This is because you have met the entry condition for an n-tier design, which is to separate presentation logic from business and data access logic.

At design time, the Data Environment designer provides a window that is used to manage and create data access services graphically and a code window that is used to programmatically customize the Data Environment. At run time, a Data Environment object is a data source with multiple DataMembers, each of which can be bound to data consumers such as controls. The same Data Environment object can also be used programmatically when binding is not appropriate.

A Data Environment provides objects, such as Connection, Command, and Field. However, these aren't ADO objects. Instead, they are objects that are used to capture and persist your Data Access Layer's design. They automatically generate genuine ADO objects on demand at run time. The Data Environment prefixes its own class names with "DE" (for example, DECommand) in order to distinguish them from their ADO counterparts.

At design time, you can create a Data Environment by selecting "Add Data Environment" from the Project menu. If it isn't there, it may be available by selecting "More ActiveX Designers" from the Project menu. If you still can't find it, go to the Project–Components dialog box and select the Designers tab. After putting a checkmark against "Data Environment," the option should then become visible on the Project menu.

A new Data Environment will display a designer, which will be similar to one of the two screen shots shown in Figure 13-1. Both show a single Data Environment object (DataEnvironment1), containing a single DEConnection object (Connection1), the only difference being the layout style, which is determined by the two right-most buttons on the Designer's toolbar.

Figure 13-1. Two views of the Data Environment designer

As soon as it's created, the Data Environment designer may display the Data Link Properties window to allow you to specify the connection properties for Connection1. Right-clicking Connection1 and selecting Properties will also bring up this window. If you wish to use an existing Data Link File, it's better to set this directly using the ConnectionSource property of Connection1 in the VB Properties Box.

You should immediately change the names of DataEnvironment1 and Connection1 to something more meaningful—this is especially important for the DataEnvironment, as you'll refer to it frequently in code. If you examine the

DEConnection object's properties, you will see that it has two sets of security-related properties: one for design time and one for run time. These are extremely useful. For example, you may want your end users to log on to a database when they start the application, but you find constant log-on prompts during development to be irritating. Use these properties to reduce your irritation.

To show the basic operation of the Data Environment, let's build a Data Member using the same SQL we used in the previous chapter, which is basically a join on the Scene and SceneDetail tables. The first step is to add a DECommand to the DEConnection object (mine is now called MuchADO) via its pop-up menu. Selecting Add Command will display the following dialog box:

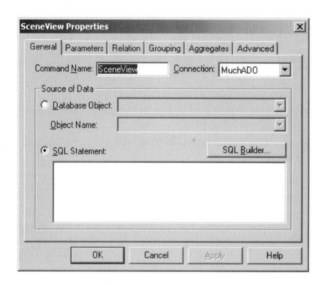

Figure 13-2. The Command Properties dialog box

Here I have changed the Command Name to SceneView and selected SQL Statement as the Source of Data. Rather than type in the SQL query, I am going to use the SQL Builder button. This will display a Data View window and a Query Builder. You can use the Data View window to drag fields or whole tables from your connection's schema onto the Query Builder, from which you can tailor the query to your heart's content. The SQL that you are building graphically is always on display, and you can run the query at any time to see the results. Overall, it's a pleasant experience. Figure 13-3 shows what the display looks like once I have created and tested my query.

Closing the Query Builder will prompt you to save the DECommand (Data Member) definition, after which, the Data Environment designer will look like Figure 13-4.

At run time, this DECommand object will be used to create a Recordset with default properties, which means that it will be read-only. Several properties (including Lock Type) can be changed via the Advanced tab on the DECommand's Properties window.

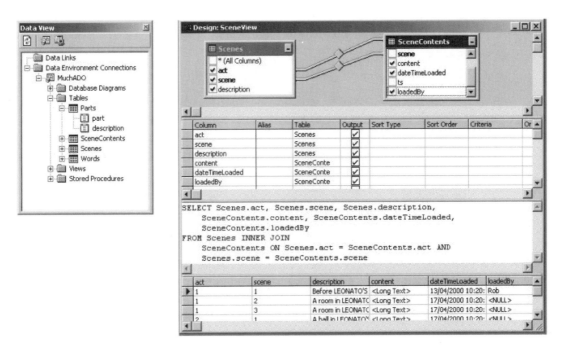

Figure 13-3. The Data View window and the Query Builder window

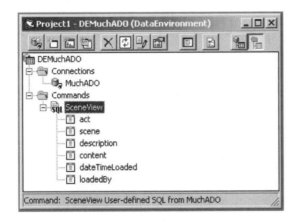

*Figure 13-4. The Data Environment designer showing
a newly created DECommand*

The SceneView Data Member is now ready to be used in application code.
You'll see three different ways of using it, the most impressive of which is by drag-
ging and dropping it on a form.

Building a Form Using Drag-and-Drop

By having the Data Environment designer and a standard VB Form both visible at the same time, you can drag SceneView directly onto the Form. The result of this trivial operation is a Form which at run time looks like this:

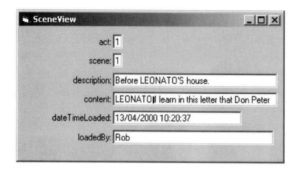

Figure 13-5. A Form created by the Data Environment designer

To find out what has happened here, you need do no more than inspect the properties of one of the controls created by the drag-and-drop operation. For example, the dateTimeLoaded TextBox control has the following properties:

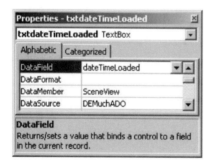

Figure 13-6. VB Properties Box showing settings created by the Data Environment designer

In other words, the Data Environment has automatically set the binding properties of the data-aware TextBox control that it created. Note that the Data Environment has also given this TextBox a meaningful name. It would be easy to use the DataFormat property to set some formatting at this point, but instead, I am going to exploit the Field Mapping feature of the Data Environment, which allows me to specify which type of control I want the drag-and-drop process to create. To do this,

I will right-click the dateTimeLoaded field displayed in the Data Environment designer and select Properties. The following dialog box is displayed:

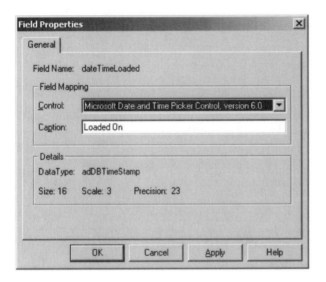

Figure 13-7. Field Mapping using the Field Properties dialog box

With this dialog box I can achieve two things: I can select the control I want to use whenever an automatic binding is created for this field, and I can also specify the Caption to be used for the associated Label control. The same approach can be used to make selected fields read-only by replacing the default TextBox control with a Label control. These settings will take effect next time I drag these fields (or the command they belong to) onto a Form, resulting in this:

Figure 13-8. Creating a Form after Field Mapping

Impressive this is. Fully functional it isn't. We need to be able to add navigational capability to this form so that we can scroll through the records, which means having access to the Recordset behind the query.

Whenever you add a DataMember that returns a Recordset to a Data Environment, the Data Environment object grows a new property that references the Recordset created by that DataMember. This gives full programmatic access to the underlying Recordset. The property name is the DataMember (DECommand) name prefixed by "rs", and it's fully supported by IntelliSense.

You can, therefore, easily add command buttons that call MoveNext and MovePrevious on this property to add scrolling. For demonstration purposes, I'll use the same technique that I used in the last chapter and use a vertical scroll bar to set the Recordset's AbsolutePosition. Here's the code:

```
Private Sub Form_Load()
VScroll1.Min = 1
VScroll1.Max = DEMuchADO.rsSceneView.RecordCount    ◄——————— The Recordset created
End Sub                                                        by the DE


Private Sub VScroll1_Change()
DEMuchADO.rsSceneView.AbsolutePosition = VScroll1.Value
End Sub
```

And here's what it looks like:

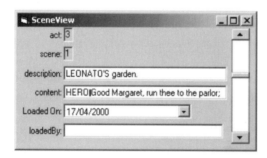

Figure 13-9. Scrolling added by programming the Data Environment

The Data Environment performs updates when a move operation occurs. An unpleasant consequence of this is that if the Recordset is not scrolled, it's likely that any changes made won't be saved. You can address this problem by including the following code in the Form's Unload event procedure:

```
Private Sub Form_Unload(Cancel As Integer)
DEMuchADO.rsSceneView.Move 0
End Sub
```

In addition to specifying a control for a specific field, you can use the Options button on the Data Environment designer to specify the default control to be used for each data type supported by a Provider.

The Data Environment's drag-and-drop feature is an excellent way of creating Forms based on bound controls. Even if all the controls have to be moved to create the results you are after, all the tedious binding operations are performed for you automatically. There are two other impressive binding features that the Data Environment supports:

1. You can also drag and drop command objects onto the VB6 Data Report designer. This provides a very easy way to build simple but attractive reports, using a report building user interface that is similar to that found in Access.

2. You can bind the DECommand to a data-aware grid control, instead of creating an interface that displays one record at a time. To do this, drag the DECommand on to the Form using a the right mouse button instead of the more standard left mouse button.

Building a Form Using Explicit Binding

If the automatic layout and binding resulting from drag and drop doesn't suit you, then there is no reason not to lay out the Form's controls manually and bind via the VB Properties Box. This would allow you to bind using a control other than the one defined in the Data Environment's field mapping.

If you bind manually, the available binding options are easily selected using the Data Source dropdown control in the VB Properties Box, just as though you were binding using a Data Control, although you do need to remember to select the required Data Member as well.

Because your data source is not linked to a particular Form, you can achieve some interesting effects. For example, you can have controls on different Forms bound to the same Data Member. As you scroll on one Form, the other Form automatically updates itself. This can lead to some impressive and attractive user interfaces, especially in MDI applications.

Alternatively, you can write explicit binding code using a BindingCollection. This makes it possible to bind to controls that are not data aware, such as the Speak control introduced in the last chapter; for example:

```
Private bc As New BindingCollection

Private Sub Form_Load()
bc.DataMember = "SceneView"
Set bc.DataSource = DEMuchADO
bc.Add lblact, "Caption", "act"
bc.Add lblscene, "Caption", "scene"
bc.Add txtdescription, "Text", "description"
bc.Add txtcontent, "Text", "content"
bc.Add ctldateTimeLoaded, "Value", "dateTimeLoaded"
bc.Add txtloadedBy, "Text", "loadedBy"
bc.Add Speak1, "Speech", "content"
VScroll1.Min = 1
VScroll1.Max = DEMuchADO.rsSceneView.RecordCount
End Sub

Private Sub VScroll1_Change()
DEMuchADO.rsSceneView.AbsolutePosition = VScroll1.Value
End Sub

Private Sub Form_Unload(Cancel As Integer)
DEMuchADO.rsSceneView.Move 0
End Sub
```

As you saw in the last chapter, binding programmatically allows you to use programmed Format objects to apply nonstandard formatting. In the next section, you'll also see that there are times when it's necessary to write binding code in order to make full use of the Data Environment's capabilities.

Using the Data Environment Programmatically

It's entirely possible to use the Data Environment without performing any binding. We've already seen that the Recordsets generated by the Data Environment object at run time can be accessed as a property of the object, so all that remains is to see how to ensure that the Recordsets get built when we want them to be built.

Each Data Environment run-time object has three properties associated with it:

- Connections

- Commands

- Recordsets

These are collections that contain all the relevant ADO objects known to the Data Environment object, and you can use these properties to access the run-time ADO objects. You can also use a For ... Each loop to iterate through the collections, but you can't add or remove items to or from them at run time—they are strictly controlled by the Data Environment designer.[3]

You can therefore easily access a Command object via the Commands property and execute it in order to make a Recordset available. However, there is a more satisfying way. Just as the Data Environment creates a property (prefixed "rs") for each Recordset it knows about, it also creates a method for each Command it knows about, giving the method the same name as the Data Member. The following two pieces of code, which print the description of each scene loaded into the database by Gary, are functionally identical:

```
With DEMuchADO
  .Commands("SceneView").Execute
  .Recordsets("SceneView").Filter = "loadedBy = 'Gary'"
  While Not .Recordsets("SceneView").EOF
    Print .Recordsets("SceneView")!Description
    .Recordsets("SceneView").MoveNext
  Wend
.Recordsets("SceneView").Close
End With
```

and

```
With DEMuchADO
  .SceneView
  .rsSceneView.Filter = "loadedBy = 'Gary'"
  While Not .rsSceneView.EOF
    Print .rsSceneView!Description
    .rsSceneView.MoveNext
  Wend
.rsSceneView.Close
End With
```

both print

```
A room in LEONATO's house.
A hall in LEONATO'S house.
```

3. In fact, by referencing the "Microsoft Data Environment Extensibility Objects" library, you can create run-time components that manipulate Data Environments. This allows you to create or add to Data Environments entirely programmatically. One application would be to create a simple wizard that builds a Data Member for each table in a Connection's schema. You could even build your own Data Environment designer and install it in VB as an add-in, should you wish.

Note that calling `DEMuchADO.SceneView` will raise an error if the `DEMuchADO.rsSceneView` Recordset is open at the time. This behavior is designed to protect you by making sure that you don't discard open Recordsets, but it's just as likely to cause you irritation at times. As a consequence, it's always a good idea to be explicit about closing Recordsets. When you reexecute the Command by referencing the Commands collection, no such checks are performed. Shortly, you'll see how to ensure that all Recordsets are closed in a simple, centralized way before being discarded.

Adding Code to the Data Environment

Right-click any item in the Data Environment window and you'll gain access to a code window. The code window can be used to add public properties, methods, and events to the Data Environment as if it were a Form, Class, or UserControl.

From the Objects dropdown list box in the code window, you can select each Connection or Recordset (as defined by a DECommand object) known to the Data Environment and program its events. Using ADO events was described in some detail in Chapter 6. To provide an example of how useful this ability can be, I will show you how the WillExecute event of the ADO Connection object created by the MuchADO DEConnection object can be used to ensure that each Recordset is closed before an attempt is made to execute its associated Command.

When the DEMuchADO.SceneView method is called, the SceneView Command is executed, but as you have seen, an error will occur if the DEMuchADO.rsSceneView Recordset is open when it's overwritten by the new Recordset that results from executing the Command.

The following code uses the WillExecute connection event to read a Command object's Name property before the Command is executed, and it looks in the Data Environment's Recordsets collection to see if the associated Recordset is open. If it is, it closes it.

```
Private Sub MuchADO_WillExecute( _
                Source As String, _
                CursorType As ADODB.CursorTypeEnum, _
                LockType As ADODB.LockTypeEnum, _
                Options As Long, _
                adStatus As ADODB.EventStatusEnum, _
                ByVal pCommand As ADODB.Command, _
                ByVal pRecordset As ADODB.Recordset, _
                ByVal pConnection As ADODB.Connection)

Dim sName As String
sName = pCommand.Name
If DEMuchADO.Recordsets(sName).State = adStateOpen Then
    DEMuchADO.Recordsets(sName).Close
    End If
End Sub
```

This code will ensure no errors occur when calling a Command method on a Data Environment. If the Data Environment contained Commands that didn't return Recordsets, an additional check would be required, but otherwise, this code is completely general.

The availability of ADO events in the Data Environment is powerful. However, it's worth noting that it has a performance penalty. With events firing on every move operation, there will be a measurable time penalty as you scroll through a very large Recordset. You can, of course, switch off unwanted events (see Chapter 6) but you have to code this explicitly. When using pure ADO, you only get events if you ask for them by using the WithEvents keyword.

At the beginning of this section, I likened the Data Environment designer to the all-too-familiar Form designer. There is another way in which Data Environments work very much like Forms. In object-oriented terms, when you add a new form to a project (for example, Form1) you are actually creating a new class called Form1. When you refer to Form1 in code (for instance, Form1.Show) you appear to be performing an operation on a class, rather than on a class instance or object. In fact, since the early days of VB, VB has created a hidden instance of Form1, which it uses whenever you refer to Form1 in code. Developers who are familiar with object orientation regard this as something of a hack (which of course it is, albeit a generally benign one), and tend to always create explicit (rather than hidden) instances of Form1 by using the New operator. While some people regard this as a little overzealous (or even downright nerdy), it's actually a necessary technique when you want to use events added to Forms or create multiple instances of a Form in an MDI application.

Data Environments work in a very similar way. When you create a new Data Environment and give it a name, you are creating a new class of that name. When you refer to that name in code, you are working with a hidden instance of that class. If you would prefer (or need) to work with an explicit Data Environment object, you can declare a variable to refer to it.

In This Section

We took a tour around the Data Environment designer and saw three different ways of using the ADO objects it creates at run time. We also saw how code can be added to the Data Environment so that its behavior can be extended or customized at run time.

Using Parameterized Commands

Real-life applications can rarely rely on static SQL. In many cases, however, the use of parameters in Command objects provides sufficient extra flexibility. This is good, because it means we can still build Command objects for most of our needs and simply provide parameter values at run time as needed.

The Data Environment offers some nice features for building parameters into Commands. Nonetheless, many inexperienced users of Data Environments run into problems when using parameterized Commands. The reasons for this are two-fold:

1. *Parameter values need to be set before the Command is executed.* While this is not news to you, one of its implications may be. When you use bound controls, loading a Form causes the data source to execute the Command. The problem is that the Form-loading process provides no means of supplying the parameter values. Trying to execute the Command in the Form_Load event is too late—the binding has already taken place with the wrong data. It's essential that you execute the Command with the correct parameter values before the Form-loading process takes place; otherwise, the Form will load but won't display any data.

2. *When you reexecute a query, a new Recordset is generated.* If you reexecute a query without reloading a Form, the Form's controls will not be bound to the new Recordset. Once again, there is a tried and tested solution.

Before dealing with these issues, let's see how to make a parameterized Command in a Data Environment.

The SceneView Command that we've used so far in this chapter currently returns a record for each scene. We are going to change this to retrieve data for just one scene at a time by adding parameters to it. We'll then use a new Command that reads only the Scene table to allow us to choose which scene we want to look at using the newly parameterized SceneView Command. This will be considerably more efficient than loading the entire SceneDetails table.

There are two steps involved in converting our SceneView Command into a parameterized Command. The first requires us to go back into the Query Builder by right-clicking SceneView in the Data Environment designer and selecting Design. You can then type =? into the Criteria column of the Query Builder for those fields that you want to be parameterized. Figure 13-10 shows what it looks like.

The second step is not compulsory but it's highly recommended. By going back to the Properties window for the SceneView DECommand, you can give meaningful names to the two parameters just created via the Parameters tab (see Figure 13-11).

In this case, I renamed Param1 as Act and Param2 as Scene, and I changed the host data type to Integer (from Byte). The payback for doing this comes as soon as I try to execute this Command as a method on the Data Environment object (see Figure 13-12).

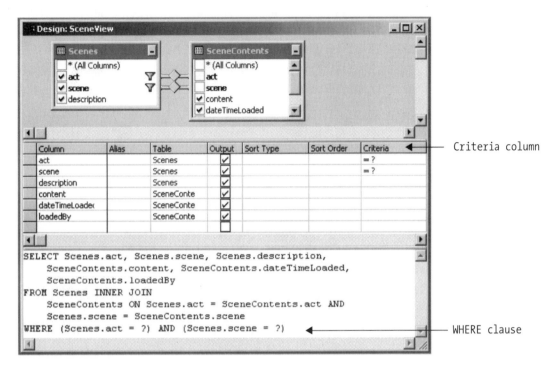

Figure 13-10. Creating a parameterized Command in the Query Builder

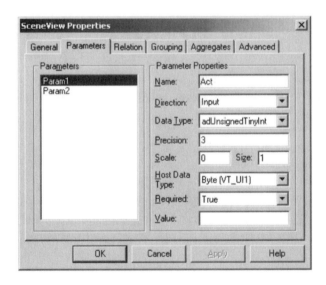

Figure 13-11. Assigning names to parameters

```
DEMuchADO.SceneView
    SceneView(Act As Byte, Scene As Byte)
```

Figure 13-12. Parameter names appear in IntelliSense.

As you can see, the parameter settings are carried through to IntelliSense and even into the Object Browser.

Let's now consider ways of using this parameterized command, bearing in mind the issues raised earlier in this section. There are two scenarios to consider: executing the Command before loading a Form whose controls are bound to the Form, and executing the Command after loading the Form.

Executing Before Loading the Form

If you can execute the Command before the Form is loaded, then the control binding that takes place during the Form loading will bind to the correct Recordset. With this approach, you can use controls that are bound to a DataMember at design time, as long as you ensure that the query runs, using the correct parameters, before the Form loads. Consider the situation in which a Form (Scenes) that contains a list of records from the Scenes table has a button that when clicked, displays another Form (Scene Details) that displays details of the record selected in Scenes.

Here's a simple example. The Scenes Form lists all the available scenes. Clicking the View button displays details of the selected Scene:

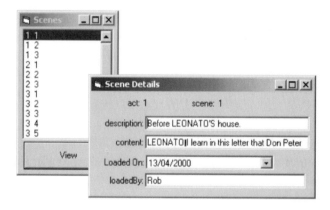

Figure 13-13. Displaying a Form with a parameterized Command

```
Private Sub cmdView_Click()
Dim iAct As Integer
Dim iScene As Integer
iAct = CInt(Left(lstScenes.Text, 1))
iScene = CInt(Right(lstScenes.Text, 1))

DEMuchADO.SceneView iAct, iScene
frmSceneView.Show vbModal
End Sub
```

As you can see, this is hardly rocket science. The appropriate act and scene numbers are extracted from the text of the selected item in the ListBox lstScenes. These numbers are then passed as arguments to the SceneView method on the DEMuchADO Data Environment object, causing the Command to execute and the correct Recordset to be created. When the SceneDetails Form is loaded, its control will be bound to this Recordset when VB loads the Form. Because this Form is modal, it has to be unloaded before any new scene is selected, and therefore, the process repeats each time the View button is clicked.

The only other code that this application requires is to tidy up correctly when the SceneDetails Form is closed. Here's its Form_Unload event procedure, which ensures that any updates are processed and then closes the Recordset:

```
Private Sub Form_Unload(Cancel As Integer)
DEMuchADO.rsSceneView.Move 0
DEMuchADO.rsSceneView.Close
End Sub
```

This does the job, but it isn't very elegant. This approach requires that any piece of code that wants to use the SceneDetails Form must remember to execute the correct Command beforehand. It would be better to have the SceneDetails Form execute the Command so that all the required processing is encapsulated into one module. What you can't do is use the SceneDetails Form's Form_Load event procedure to do this, for reasons already stated.

The solution is to add a method to the Form that makes the required data request and then loads itself. Here's such a method:

```
Public Sub Display(iAct As Integer, iScene As Integer)
DEMuchADO.SceneView iAct, iScene
Me.Show vbModal
End Sub
```

The code for the View button on the Scenes form can then be changed to this:

```
Private Sub cmdView_Click()
Dim iAct As Integer
Dim iScene As Integer
iAct = CInt(Left(lstScenes.Text, 1))
iScene = CInt(Right(lstScenes.Text, 1))
frmSceneView.Display iAct, iScene        ◄─────────  call the Display method
End Sub                                               on the SceneDetails Form
```

Executing After Loading the Form

When you can't be sure that a Form is always loaded after the Command is executed, a different solution is required. The following screen shot shows a single Form combining the function of the two Forms shown in the last example:

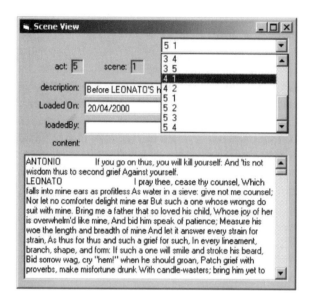

Figure 13-14. A consolidated Scene Viewer

Here, a dropdown ListBox is used to select the scene. Each time a new scene is selected, the parameterized SceneView command is reexecuted, generating a new Recordset. It isn't acceptable to unload and reload the Form each time, and therefore, it will be necessary to regenerate the bindings. The only sensible way to do this is to do all the binding for this Form programmatically via a BindingCollection object. The Click event procedure on the dropdown ListBox can then rebind all the controls after reexecuting the Command with a new set of parameters. As you have already seen in this chapter and the last one, BindingCollection code is simple, if slightly tedious, to write. Here's the complete code for the single-form application shown in Figure 13-14 (assuming the DECommands and Will_Execute event code have been set up in the Data Environment, as discussed earlier in this chapter):

```
Private bc As BindingCollection
Private WithEvents ft As StdDataFormat

Private Sub Form_Load()
DEMuchADO.AllScenes
With DEMuchADO.rsAllScenes
  While Not .EOF
    cboScene.AddItem !act & "   " & !scene
    .MoveNext
  Wend
End With
cboScene.ListIndex = 0
End Sub
```

Form_Load triggers the AllScenes **DECommand that returns the contents of the Scenes table.**

⟵ **Populate the Combo.**

⟵ **Setting** ListIndex **triggers the Combo's Click event.**

```
Private Sub cboScene_Click()
Dim iAct As Integer
Dim iScene As Integer
iAct = CInt(Left(cboScene.Text, 1))
iScene = CInt(Right(cboScene.Text, 1))
DEMuchADO.SceneView iAct, iScene
bindToRS
End Sub
```

Get the Act and Scene numbers from the clicked row, and call the SceneView **DECommand. Then call the** bindToRS **routine to construct a new** BindingCollection.

```
Public Sub bindToRS()
Set bc = New BindingCollection
Set ft = New StdDataFormat
bc.DataMember = "SceneView"
Set bc.DataSource = DEMuchADO
bc.Add lblact, "Caption", "act"
bc.Add lblscene, "Caption", "scene"
bc.Add txtdescription, "Text", "description"
bc.Add txtcontent, "Text", "content", ft
bc.Add ctldateTimeLoaded, "Value", "dateTimeLoaded"
bc.Add txtloadedBy, "Text", "loadedBy"
bc.Add Speak1, "Speech", "content"
End Sub
```

standard binding code

```
Private Sub ft_Format(ByVal DataValue As StdFormat.StdDataValue)
DataValue = Replace(DataValue, vbCr, vbCrLf)
End Sub

Private Sub Form_Unload(Cancel As Integer)
DEMuchADO.rsSceneView.Move 0
End Sub
```

We saw how the DataMembers in a Data Environment can be parameterized, providing significantly more power than can be achieved with data binding based on controls. The primary requirement when using parameterized Commands is to make sure that the Command executes with the correct arguments before binding takes place. This means it's sometimes necessary to write binding code using a BindingCollection.

Defining Hierarchical Recordsets

One of the most popular uses of the Data Environment is for creating hierarchical Recordsets. Fear of the SHAPE language has encouraged a belief that it's too complex for anyone with a regular life to be able to understand. As we saw in Chapter 8, the SHAPE language is actually quite straightforward once you break it down, but it can still be a challenge getting brackets in the correct place and so on. The Data Environment provides a graphical tool for building SHAPE commands, which is undoubtedly more palatable than writing the commands by hand, especially for more complex hierarchies.

As an example, consider the first SHAPE command we encountered in Chapter 8:

```
SHAPE {SELECT * FROM Parts}
    APPEND ({SELECT part, word, wordLength
            FROM Words WHERE  wordLength > 11 }
         RELATE part TO part ) As Words
```

To re-create this command using the Data Environment, first create two individual DECommands, one for the `SELECT * FROM Parts` query (called Parts) and one for the `SELECT part, word, wordLength FROM Words WHERE  wordLength > 11` query (called Words).

You can then right-click the Words DECommand and select Properties. The Relation tab can then be configured as shown in Figure 13-15.

This tab allows you to use point-and-click methods to say that the Words DECommand has a parent (Parts) and to specify which fields should be related between the two Recordsets. You can then select Hierarchy Info from the Parts DECommand (which is now the parent of a hierarchy) and display the SHAPE command that the Data Environment generates, as follows:

```
SHAPE {SELECT * FROM "dbo"."Parts"}  AS Parts
    APPEND ({SELECT part, word, wordLength
        FROM Words WHERE  wordLength > 11}  AS Words
      RELATE 'part' TO 'part') AS Words
```

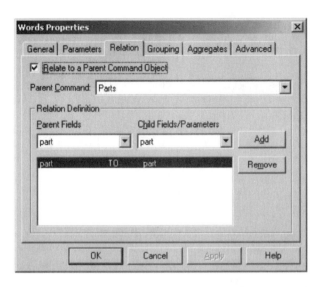

Figure 13-15. Building a SHAPE Command graphically

This is very similar to its hand-coded predecessor. You can certainly take this string and use it in a non-Data Environment application should you wish to do so, and claim intimate knowledge of the SHAPE language at the same time.

When you drag the Parts DECommand onto a Form, the Data Environment automatically creates a master-detail display using standard controls for records in the Parts Recordset, and a Hierarchical FlexGrid for records in the Words Recordset (which will be filtered according to the selected record in Parts). To create the display shown in Figure 13-16, I simply dragged the Parts DECommand onto a Form and added a vertical scroll bar and three lines of code to scroll the rsParts Recordset (which is the Recordset that the Data Environment creates based on the Parts DECommand).

Note that I did not need to specify MSDataShape as the Provider. The Data Environment takes care of this. Just for completeness, here's the full code for this application:

```
Private Sub Form_Load()
VScroll1.Min = 1
VScroll1.Max = DEMuchADO.rsParts.RecordCount
End Sub

Private Sub VScroll1_Change()
DEMuchADO.rsParts.AbsolutePosition = VScroll1.Value
End Sub
```

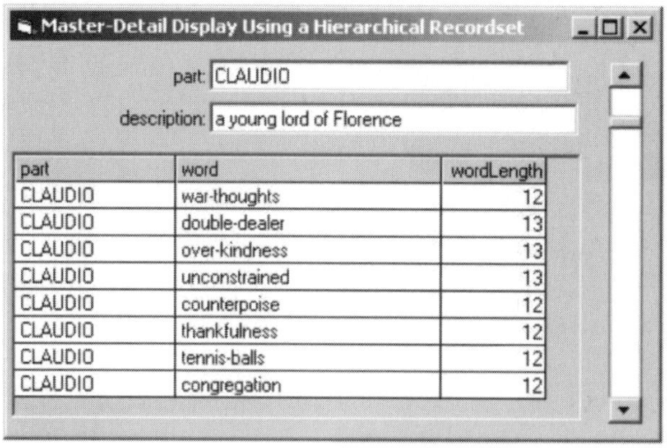

Figure 13-16. A drag-and-drop master-detail Form

Group-based hierarchies are just as easy to build. Here's the first group-based hierarchy we constructed in Chapter 8:

```
SHAPE
    {SELECT * FROM Words } as Words
      COMPUTE Words , SUM (Words.wordCount) As WordCount,
                      AVG (Words.wordLength) As AveLength
          BY act, scene
```

There are three stages to constructing a group-based hierarchy using the Data Environment:

1. Create a new DECommand based on SELECT * FROM Words.

2. Create the group relationship (using the BY clause).

3. Define the aggregates (the SUM and AVG clauses) to use in the group.

All of these tasks can be performed using the Properties dialog box for the DECommand. Assuming that the query has been specified, the groupings can be specified using the Grouping tab as shown in Figure 13-17.

You can then move to the Aggregates tab and set up the SUM and AVG elements of the Command as shown in Figure 13-18.

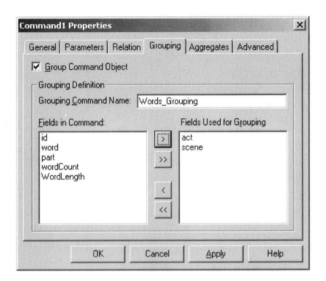

Figure 13-17. *Defining the group for a group-based hierarchy*

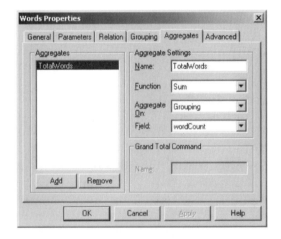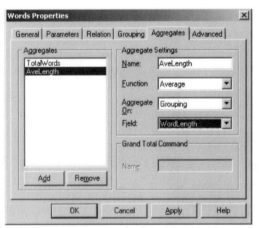

Figure 13-18. *Defining aggregates for a group-based hierarchy*

The resulting command is this:

```
SHAPE
    {SELECT * FROM Words }  AS Words
        COMPUTE Words, SUM(Words.'wordCount') AS TotalWords,
        AVG(Words.'WordLength') AS AveLength
        BY 'act','scene'
```

which creates the following display with minimal effort:

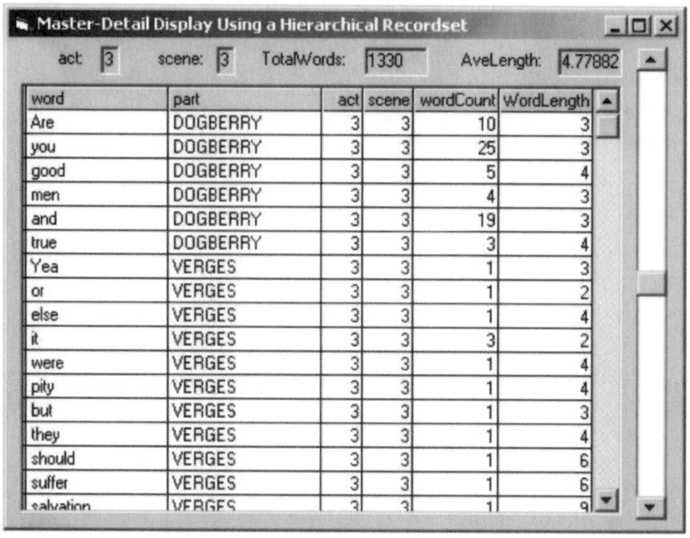

Figure 13-19. A drag-and-drop Form for a group-based hierarchy

In This Section

You saw how to tame the SHAPE language and use the Data Environment to create hierarchical Recordsets.

Making Data Environments into Components

If you intend to share a Data Environment between projects, it makes sense to compile it into a DLL rather than risk having the code base modified in uncontrollable ways by different project teams. Perhaps more importantly, if you intend to run the Data Environment with an MTS Package or a COM+ Application, then you'll certainly need to compile it into a DLL.

Each Data Environment has a Public property that is False by default, but which you can easily change to True. However, there are several issues you should be aware of when making components out of Data Environments:

- When you make a Data Environment Public, you get a stern warning that the methods and properties that are exposed automatically by the Data Environment will be changed to private members. Therefore, they won't be available to any users of your Data Environment component. What this means is that you need to design your own public interface (just as you would for a regular VB class) to expose the features of the Data Environment that you want users able to access. The Commands, Connections, and

Recordsets collections won't be available, nor will the dynamically generated Command and Recordset methods and properties. It may seem a little mean of the Data Environment to behave like this, but the Data Environment's standard interface is designed for use as an in-process object. Giving users of a Data Environment access to its Connections and server-side Recordsets across a process boundary would have unpleasant side effects.[4] By forcing you to expose your own interface, you are being made responsible for your own mistakes.

- The compiled component will contain the run-time Data Environment objects, but won't contain the design-time objects or provide a Data Environment designer. Therefore, design-time binding won't be possible. Also, binding isn't designed to work across process boundaries, so most developers use Data Environment components in unbound mode.[5]

- If you intend to use MTS or COM+ to host your component, be sure that it only exposes client-side Recordsets. By default, the Data Environment is configured for client-side operations, so you just need to be sure that you don't change these defaults. If the Recordsets are updateable, you'll most likely want to handle them using batch mode updating. In this case, you'll need to change their LockType via the Properties dialog box.

- DEConnection objects have two properties called DesignPromptBehavior and RunPromptBehavior, which are set to `adPromptComplete` by default. These are used to set the Prompt dynamic Connection property, as discussed in Chapter 4. There is a danger that the default setting could cause a logon prompt to be displayed when the Data Environment starts work. As your component may be running on a server some distance from the user's client PC, this would be undesirable. Change both properties to `adPrompt-Never` for peace of mind, and be sure to provide a full connection string.

- Data Environments have their own ideas about Connection management, and corrective action is typically required. I'll address this issue shortly.

There are two ways to provide a public interface to a Data Environment component. The first is to provide separate public methods for creating and batch updating each Recordset. This involves work for each Recordset the Data Environment generates, but it provides the user of the component with IntelliSense support. The second approach is to code generic getRS and setRS methods where the user specifies the DataMember required and supplies any arguments. This approach

---

4. If you are not sure what these are, see Chapter 7.

5. If you are very keen on using binding techniques in clients, you can create an in-process data source that requests Recordsets from the Data Environment component. Client programs can then bind to this in-process data source using BindingCollection at run time.

is easier to code from the component writer's viewpoint and makes it easier to centralize any specific code handling that is required to make the Data Environment component work. I'll show you the second approach. The final choice is up to you.

The code that follows supports a Data Environment called DEMuchADO, which has three DataMembers: Parts and Scenes, which simply return the relevant tables, and Words, which has two parameters—one for wordLength and one for act. Its SQL is as follows:

```
SELECT * FROM Words WHERE wordLength > ? and act = ?
```

Each Command is defined to use BatchOptimistic locking and is client-side. The getRS method code in the Data Environment designer's code window is as follows:

```
Public Function getRS( DataMember As String, _
    ParamArray Parameters() As Variant) _
    As Recordset
Dim iParam As Integer
Dim cn As Connection
Dim cd As Command
Set cd = DataEnvironment.Commands(DataMember)
Set cn = DataEnvironment.Connections("MuchADO")
If cn.State = adStateClosed Then
    cn.Open                        ◄──────────────── make sure the Connection is open
    Set cd.ActiveConnection = cn ◄──── make sure the Command has a valid Connection
    End If

For iParam = 0 To UBound(Parameters)          ◄─┐
    cd(iParam).Value = Parameters(iParam)        │  initialize all Parameters
    Next                                       ◄─┘

Set getRS = DataEnvironment.Recordsets(DataMember)
If getRS.State = adStateOpen Then getRS.Close
getRS.Open cd                      ◄────────────── pass the Command object
                                                   to the Recordset
Set getRS.ActiveConnection = Nothing
Set cd.ActiveConnection = Nothing
cn.Close
End Function
```

This is a small segment of code, but there is quite a lot going on, so it's worth spending a little while understanding it. The function takes a DataMember and a *ParamArray* as arguments. The ParamArray is used to supply any parameter values to the Command.

Left to its own devices, a Data Environment will automatically create and maintain an open Connection throughout an application session. This is fine in many circumstances, but it's not fine if you want to install the component in MTS or COM+, or make use of connection pooling. Therefore, it's important to check that the Data Environment's Connection object is open before trying to use it, if you intend writing pooling-enabled code. If the Connection needs to be opened, then the Command object will need to have its ActiveConnection property reestablished.

There are several different ways you could execute the Command specified in the DataMember argument and retrieve the Recordset. For example, you could use a Select...Case statement to write code for each DataMember that executes the Command using the "Command as method" approach.[6] This will work, but it requires adding a new Case each time a new DataMember is created. Alternatively, you could use the Data Environment's Commands collection to execute the Command associated with DataMember. This works fine, but it means that any Recordset-specific properties (such as LockType) will be ignored by the Command object.

The approach used in the preceding code is to pass the Command object as the Source argument to the Recordset object, thus preserving the configuration of both objects. The first task is to get hold of the required Command object and set its Parameter values, if any. In Chapter 5 we saw that setting a Parameter object's values as shown in the code, results in a request to the server to retrieve Parameter information, which is generally a bad idea. However, when you first access a Command object in a Data Environment, the Data Environment automatically generates the Parameter objects based on information captured at design time. Therefore, there is no request to the server at run time. You can happily work directly with the Parameter objects with no performance concerns when using a Data Environment. The For...Next loop will take any parameter values supplied in the Parameters argument and pass them on to the Parameters collection of the Command. If there are no parameters, the upper bound of the Parameters array will be –1, so the For...Next loop will never run.

Once any parameters have been initialized, you can get hold of the Recordset object associated with DataMember, close it if necessary, and then open it based on the newly initialized Command object. You can then disconnect the Connection from both the Recordset and the Command object, and then close the Connection. The disconnected Recordset is then returned.

A client would call this function using code like this:

```
Dim oSource As New DEServer.DEMuchADO
Dim rs As Recordset
Set rs = oSource.getRS("Words", 11, 3)
```

---

6. Visual Basic won't let you use the CallByName function to invoke the dynamic "Command as method" methods, so there is no alternative to coding each one separately.

The code for the setRS function follows the basic plan we developed for updating disconnected Recordsets back in Chapter 7:

```
Public Function setRS(rs As Recordset) As Variant
On Error GoTo ErrH
Dim cn As Connection
Set cn = DataEnvironment.Connections("MuchADO")
cn.Open
Set rs.ActiveConnection = cn
cn.BeginTrans
rs.UpdateBatch
cn.CommitTrans
Set rs.ActiveConnection = Nothing
cn.Close
setRS = Null
Exit Function
ErrH:
  setRS = Err.Description
  cn.RollbackTrans
  Set rs.ActiveConnection = Nothing
  cn.Close
End Function
```

perform a transactional batch update

This code uses transactions explicitly. As you'll see in the next chapter, you would handle transactions rather differently if the component were to be installed in MTS or COM+.

As you can see, the main chore in writing a Data Environment component is Connection management, because of the need to override the built-in features the Data Environment provides. If you are intending for the component to run in MTS or COM+, it's absolutely essential to manage connections in a stateless fashion and leave everything to a connection pooling mechanism. Failure to do so will lead to very undesirable results.

In This Section

You saw how to make a component out of a Data Environment. This is a straight-forward process, as long as you provide an explicit means for clients to create and update DataMembers and to take control of Connection management.

Summary

The Data Environment makes it easy to develop an n-tier mindset by providing you with a set of convenient tools for developing a Data Access Layer in your projects. One of the drawbacks of the Data Environment is that its user needs to code in a slightly different way than is appropriate for use with regular ADO objects. However, the changes are relatively few and you can easily to become accustomed with them.

Data Environments are useful for a number of reasons:

- If you are a developer who is used to working with bound controls, using a Data Environment makes it possible for you to hold your head up high and legitimately claim that you have taken a component-based approach, without throwing away the treasured benefits of data binding.

- They give you the chance to mix data binding with parameterized Commands, which can significantly reduce coding.

- They are also handy if you don't like grappling with command languages. This is true for SQL, but especially true for creating hierarchical Recordsets based on the SHAPE language.

- They can readily be compiled into binary components, although you do need to take a little control to support connection pooling.

Data Environments are easy to work with, and they don't create additional database or network overhead—a sacrifice that often accompanies graphical productivity features.

In the next chapter, we'll take the theme of components and n-tier design one step further by exploring the role of ADO in applications based on MTS and COM+.

CHAPTER 14

ADO, DNA, MTS, and COM+

What Are MTS and COM+?

Creating Transactional Components Using ADO

Distributed Transactions

Summary

WE INTRODUCED THE IDEAS behind n-tier design in Chapter 7, and this chapter will assume that you are familiar with n-tier development concepts, disconnected Recordsets, and related ADO topics, such as Recordset marshalling and batch updating that we covered there. We also discussed transaction concepts in Chapter 4, which are very relevant here. All of these concepts fall into place in the DNA world.

DNA (Distributed interNetworking Architecture) and DNA 2000, which is its latest lifeform, are at the heart of Microsoft's model for distributed and Internet-based systems, e-commerce, and mobile devices. DNA is built firmly around the n-tier model, where thin front ends receive data in the form of Recordsets, XML, or other data formats from middle tiers designed for high scalability.

The design and management of middle-tier components is the most crucial aspect of a good DNA-based system, where in order to create scaleable and robust software solutions, resource management becomes a key consideration. While it's all very well to talk about such aims, achieving them is another matter completely, and over the past few years Microsoft has developed products to make this task easier. These products are core elements in the DNA and DNA 2000 architectures. Specifically, Microsoft has developed

1. *An environment where components can be installed, run, and managed, such that they can exploit essential services that would otherwise take a great deal of time to develop.* Such services include thread and connection pooling, and a security model that is component-friendly. To support scalability, the environment can be installed on many computers, and makes it easy for components to communicate with other computers or to be moved from one computer to another.

2. *A tool that makes it easy to create and manage complex transactions and encourages developers to write transactions that have a short lifetime.* As we've seen, an active transaction can maintain a large number of database

locks. Locks are not only expensive; they have a negative impact on high concurrency. Transactions are the building blocks of e-commerce systems, and many real-world systems require a transaction to apply the ACID rules (see Chapter 4) to a unit of work that involves more than one database. By itself, ADO doesn't support this form of distributed transaction, but as we shall see, the DNA approach removes this limitation from ADO.

3. *A system that guarantees message delivery, even when the recipient is not running or is too busy to provide a timely response.* Most communication between software objects (as typified by COM) assumes that both parties are in a fit state to communicate directly with each other. Communication based on message queues allows work to continue even when a receiver is not able to receive. The message queue stores messages securely and forwards them when the receiver is able to process them. This capability is increasingly important in environments (such as Web-based applications) in which peak loading is almost impossible to predict, or where vital business operations such as order capturing, need to keep going even if one or more servers is unavailable.

For systems based on Windows NT, Microsoft Transaction Server (MTS) provides the first two of these products. The transactional services are actually provided by a separate product, the Distributed Transaction Coordinator (DTC), but this is so tightly integrated into MTS that it makes sense to think of them as the same product. Nevertheless, MTS is typically regarded as a product that acts as a component host, providing a range of general middle-tier services, as well as specific transaction services.

Windows NT users make use of message queues using Microsoft Message Queue (MSMQ), which also offers tight integration into MTS, but is more obviously a separate product.

All components hosted by MTS are COM components. However, because MTS was developed after COM appeared, it has to provide its services as a separate layer on top of COM. While MTS is transparent to client programs, COM components installed inside MTS need to talk to each other in a specific way if they want to make full use of MTS's services.

Windows 2000 ships with a new version of COM, called COM+. COM+ is similar in many ways to "classic" COM, but it has been extended to include component hosting features as an essential part of the COM+ architecture. COM+ has also been specifically designed to allow additional services to be woven into its fabric, and these services include transactions and message queuing "out of the box." It's expected that Microsoft will provide further COM+ add-ons as COM+ matures.

DNA and COM+ deserve several books in their own right, and while this chapter provides an introduction to MTS and COM+ features, it focuses on the role that ADO can play in DNA applications and on how to create DNA-enabled applications. Specifically, it addresses the important changes to the way transactions are handled when ADO and MTS or COM+ come out to play.

The examples presented in this chapter are based on COM+. In many cases however, identical or almost identical code will work in an MTS environment, and when I refer to MTS/COM+, the explanations given will apply to both environments. Where there are important differences between the two, these will be made clear.

What Are MTS and COM+?

Much can be said about MTS. Indeed, much has been said about MTS, but all too often, the wrong much.[1] Put simply, MTS provides a sensible place to stick middle-tier components. These are in-process COM objects (in our case VB objects) that don't have user interfaces and that typically provide an access layer to shared resources (such as databases, files, and message queues) and any necessary business logic.

The main unit of organization in MTS is a Package. In COM+, the same unit is called a COM+ Application.[2] A Package/Application typically "hosts" many components for which the Package/Application supplies a common set of facilities. In most cases, a Package/Application is a single NT/Windows 2000 process. It therefore provides the physical space within which the in-process components will run. A reasonably sized system could employ several Packages/Applications, quite possibly spread around a number of computers. Components *within* a Package/Application can communicate with each other very quickly, are administered (that is, imported, exported, or shut down) as a unit, and share common security, identity, and other characteristics. Communication between Packages/Applications is easy, but much slower than intra-Package/Application communication because of the overhead imposed by marshalling.

For most purposes, it's convenient to identify two types of MTS/COM+ components:

- Non-transactional

- Transactional

---

1. Microsoft is generally considered masterful when it comes to marketing new products. However, the product positioning of MTS was shambolic by any standards. Fearing the task of really explaining the purpose of MTS, early product literature created the impression that MTS achieved scalability by switching inactive objects out of memory in order to save RAM. The truth is that MTS achieves its aims through other means (as you'll see) and is typically far more RAM-hungry than the objects it manages.

2. The COM+ term can easily cause confusion. Our standard notion of an application is something that has a front end to it. This is not how COM+ sees it. Front ends are things that call into a COM+ Application; they are not part of a COM+ Application.

Non-Transactional Components

Components that don't use transactional services can be any standard VB DLL. They don't need to be coded in any special way, but you do need to bear in mind that although they are in-process components, clients will typically be in a separate process because the DLL runs in the process space of the Package/Application. Therefore, marshalling considerations apply.

There are no specific coding requirements for non-transactional components; the specters of statelessness and activation/deactivation that frequently arise in MTS/COM+ design discussions need not apply (unless you choose to exploit them). Of course, you do need to consider the effects of clients creating thousands of objects running in one Package/Application at the same time. You need to be sure that you are not introducing any resource bottlenecks. Non-transactional components are unlikely to be contending for database locks, but they will still be sharing the same thread, memory, and other resources.

If the components aren't making use of transactional services, what benefits of MTS/COM+ will they enjoy? Well, for one thing, the entire Package/Application can be managed as a unit. MTS/COM+ provides a simple management tool that allows you to administer Packages/Applications in a convenient graphical way. For example, if something has gone wrong with a component on a remote server, you can shut down the Package/Application from your desktop with a few mouse clicks. You can also create a simple Windows Installer file (or an .exe when using MTS) that can be run on client computers to create the registration entries required to allow the clients to access all the components in the Package/Application via DCOM. This removes the need for a great deal of messy configuration.

Perhaps more importantly, MTS/COM+ provides a sophisticated resource management service. This means you can write components as though they were for a single user and allow MTS/COM+ to manage those components in a multiuser environment. Specifically, MTS/COM+ will look after threads and connections to ensure that resources are managed efficiently (so long as you don't fight against it). In addition to creating pools of threads and connections, COM+ (but not MTS) has the ability to create pools of custom-coded COM objects. This feature isn't available to VB6 programs because of the way that threads work with VB6 objects. It can be used with C++ and Java objects today. Pre-release details of VB7 suggest that it will provide a far more flexible approach to thread management than VB6.

All versions of Internet Information Server (IIS) since version 4 have been entirely dependent on MTS/COM+ to provide an environment in which components can be run. Even components that are not installed in a Package or Application are loaded into one when called from IIS. This provides another reason for understanding MTS/COM+ services—they are available to components used in a Web server.

Components running on Windows 2000 have access to additional services that COM+ provides, which aren't available in MTS. These include Queued Components and a publisher/subscriber Event model. These features are an important part of DNA 2000, and they make it very easy (and cheap) to design the kind of system previously only possible with far more expensive products and larger development budgets.

In short, any middle-tier components that are not designed to run in the process space of a client (and are therefore able to run on a separate server) should really be installed in an MTS Package or a COM+ Application. There are many benefits in doing so and only a few drawbacks. In the past, debugging with MTS was problematic, but with VB6 and NT4 Service Pack 4 (or COM+), such problems are history.

As an example of a non-transactional component, consider the following method, which returns the HTML representation of a scene from *Much ADO about Nothing*, using Record and Stream objects, as described in Chapter 9:

```
Public Function getScene(Act As Integer, Scene As Integer) As String
Dim rd As New Record
Dim cn As New Connection
Dim sm As New Stream
cn.Open "URL=http://polecat/MuchADO/Act " & Act & _
    "/Act " & Act & " Scene " & Scene & ".htm"
rd.Open "", cn
sm.Type = adTypeText
sm.Charset = "Ascii"
sm.Open rd, adModeRead, adOpenStreamFromRecord
getScene = sm.ReadText
End Function
```

This method belongs to a class called FullText in a DLL called AnyDLL. In MTS/COM+ terms, the class (which has a *ProgID* of AnyDLL.FullText) is considered a component, and the DLL is a component DLL. AnyDLL has been compiled with *binary compatibility*.

To install AnyDLL.FullText in COM+, you would first need to create a COM+ Application. To do this, start the Component Services Administrative Tool[3] from the Start menu, which displays a window rather like that shown in Figure 14-1.

MTS has a similar tool called the MTS Explorer, which is available from the NT4 Option Pack menu on NT servers (the Option Pack is widely available as a free installation for NT4).

By right-clicking COM+ Applications under My Computer, you can create an empty COM+ Application called Any. When you create a Package/Application you are prompted for its identity. For development purposes, it's convenient to use the "Interactive User" setting, but this should be changed to a nominated account for deployment.

---

3. This tool is typically referred to as the Component Services "snap-in" because it is hosted by the Microsoft Management Console (MMC), a generic management tool into which specific management features are loaded or "snapped in."

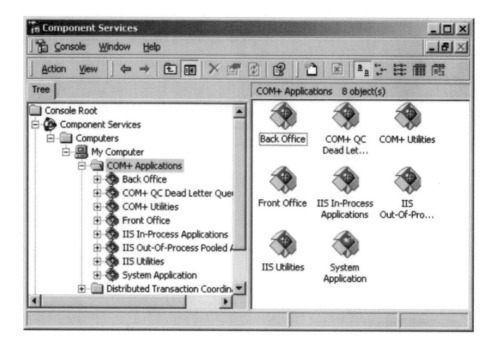

Figure 14-1. The Component Services snap-in

By expanding the "Any" node just created, you can right-click Components to add a new component. It's easiest to use the "Install New Component" option provided by the wizard that appears and then locate the AnyDLL DLL. This will automatically install the AnyDLL.FullText component and leave the window looking like the one shown in Figure 14-2.

This component is now installed in a COM+ Application. A client application can call this component without knowing that it's managed by COM+. When the first client application requests a component from the COM+ Application, the Application's process will be started (if it isn't already running), and the requested component will be created. As you'll see shortly, the client is actually connected to the COM+ Application, although it believes it's connected directly to the component.

Client code such as this:

```
Dim oText As New AnyDLL.FullText
MsgBox oText.getScene(3, 1)
```

can be run on the computer that the Application/Package is running on, simply by setting a reference to AnyDLL in the usual way. To access the Application/Package from a remote client, an easy-to-use export process is provided.

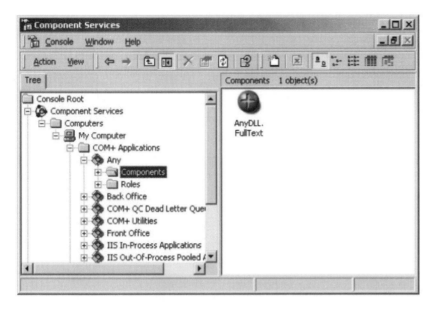

Figure 14-2. Installing a COM DLL into a COM+ Application

It's important to note that although AnyDLL is compiled as a DLL, communication between a client and a FullText object will be process-to-process or machine-to-machine. This is because the client is really talking to the COM+ Application, which by default (and in most configurations), runs in its own process space. You shouldn't attempt to install EXEs in a COM+ Application.

Transactional Components

Much of the confusion that has been created by MTS/COM+ results from the implications of its transaction-processing environment. We discussed the ACID requirements for transactions and saw the implications of transactions on database locks in Chapter 4. We know that transactions are an essential part of business systems, because of the need to provide the type of commercial guarantees that business customers expect. We also know that to make it easy to meet these requirements, it's usual to consider a transaction as involving (at least) two elements:

1. A system such as a database that manages data and contains the sophisticated logic and systems required to guarantee the ACID requirements. In MTS/COM+, such systems are called Resource Managers, to allow systems other than databases to be included in the definition.

2. Application code (stuff that we write) that uses simple instructions like BeginTrans, CommitTrans, and RollbackTrans to tell a Resource Manager how to manage a transaction. MTS/COM+ transactions are constructed slightly differently, but they still have a start point and are ultimately either committed or rolled back. One of the major innovations of MTS/COM+ is that it considers our application code (the components we install in Packages/Applications) to be part of a transaction if we choose to use its transactional services.

The requirements of scalable, robust multiuser systems place special demands on both of these elements:

1. It's often necessary to run transactions that involve more than one Resource Manager. For example, you may have a product inventory on one database and a customer accounting system on another. It's quite likely that these systems were developed separately, but in an e-commerce system, an automated customer purchase transaction will need to update both the inventory and the accounting system under the ACID rules. Even if both databases were originally on the same server, throughput may demand that they be split onto separate machines. MTS/COM+ provides the DTC, which makes it possible for a transaction to be split over several Resource Managers. Without using the DTC, it would be impossible to use ADO to write a transaction that used more than one connection.

   It may also be necessary for the code that controls the transaction to be split between several machines (or at least, between several Packages/Applications). MTS/COM+ is able to keep track of the complexities of such an arrangement, receiving instructions for the same transaction from different computers.

2. The application code that we write must also meet stringent requirements. To allow applications developers to focus on applications rather than on complex system plumbing, MTS/COM+ looks after these requirements as long as we abide by two very important rules:

   • *Keep transactions as short as possible.* MTS/COM+ uses serializable transactions,[4] and therefore, all shared resources accessed during the transaction are locked for its duration. The MTS/COM+ programming model encourages us to keep transactions short, which is essential for maintaining high concurrency—other users will want to access those locked resources.

---

4. This is the highest and safest level of transaction isolation (see Chapter 4).

• *Obey the Consistency rule of the ACID test.* A complex transaction may involve several components and several Resource Managers. MTS/COM+ contains the programming logic required to keep track of these different transactional elements and makes the final decision as to whether the transaction as a whole commits or rolls back. The Resource Managers are informed of this decision and are expected to manage their internal state accordingly. However, it would be far too messy for our components to respond correctly to this decision. If a transaction rolls back, our components may contain values in their properties (such as in their internal state) that are inconsistent with the data in the Resource Managers. A client program accessing these properties would therefore get inconsistent information, breaking the ACID rules. To avoid this highly dangerous situation, MTS/COM+ deactivates all components involved in a transaction when the transaction finishes. This means that the internal state of all transactional components is lost at this point and must be regenerated from an external source (typically, but not necessarily, from a Resource Manager) next time it's needed.[5]

Connection-oriented vs. Transaction-oriented Systems

Conventional client-server systems are connection-oriented. Figure 14-3 shows the resources used at one point in time by a typical three-tier client-server system with three clients.

When clients start, they request connections to middle-tier resources (such as COM objects). DCOM connections take time to establish, so the client hangs on to the connection, and therefore, to the middle-tier objects. Typically these objects are not expensive to create; it's the cost of establishing the remote connection to them that is measurable.

Middle-tier components request connections to Resource Managers. For similar reasons, they tend to hang on to the Resource Manager connections. However, Resource Managers typically carry an overhead for each live connection and are highly dependent on middle-tier components releasing locks in order to offer high concurrency.

---

5. This requirement is responsible for the fact that MTS/COM+ components are often described as "stateless." Statelessness has been described as a scalability feature, but in fact scalability results partly from keeping transactions short and partly from allowing MTS/COM+ resource management to work its magic. The purpose of statelessness is to keep transactions consistent, and this is necessary because transactional components are considered part of a transaction and are therefore affected by the ACID rules. Non-transactional components are not required by MTS/COM+ to handle state in any special way. Statelessness is sometimes associated with the design principle of having no properties on MTS/COM+ components. However, this is no different from the design of any out-of-process COM object, in which allowing clients to set individual properties has expensive marshalling implications when compared to providing several values via a single method call.

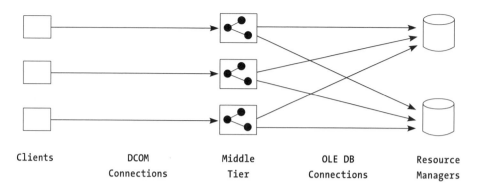

Figure 14-3. A connection-oriented system

Such systems are fine for small numbers of users, but they start to become unmanageable as the number of users exceeds a few dozen. Problems can occur because locks are retained for too long and because computers often accumulate more resources than they can efficiently cope with. The sad thing is that in most cases, these resources aren't being used for the vast majority of the time they are being maintained. For these and other reasons, this architecture is not scalable— it won't support hundreds or thousands of users.

An alternative to the connection-oriented model is the transaction-oriented model. In this model, each request for data or each update instruction is considered a separate transaction. Once a transaction is completed, all that remains of it are the data returned to the client as a result of the transaction, and the durable results of executing the transaction (which are held by Resource Managers). A transaction-oriented solution looks like this:

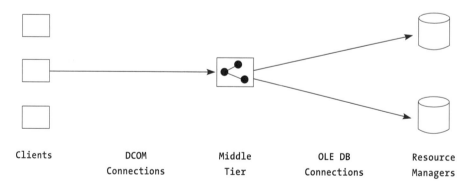

Figure 14-4. A transaction-oriented system

Here, the architecture is typified by transactions. At any one time, only clients that are actively executing transactions are consuming system resources. This model is highly scalable because it minimizes the demand on shared resources. However, the pure transaction-oriented model has two shortcomings:

1. It forces clients to be continually creating and destroying references to middle-tier services, and it makes client programs responsible for critical aspects of system maintenance and correctness. If client programs forget to release resources, the whole system clogs up.

2. Each transaction has the overhead of reestablishing two sets of connections for each and every request: from client to middle tier, and from middle tier to Resource Manager. This time is measurable and often significant.

The DNA/DNA 2000 model is essentially a transaction-oriented model with features built into MTS/COM+ to address the weaknesses of a pure transaction-oriented model. DNA programming requires a mind shift from connection-oriented design to transaction-oriented design.[6] This point is so important that it's worth repeating: *DNA programming requires a mind shift from connection-oriented design to transaction-oriented design. It's in the nature of mind shifts to cause concern and confusion until they are completed and everyone is happy with the new approach.*[7]

The DNA/DNA 2000 model is highly influenced by the Internet and the use of browser-based front ends. However, before considering the impact of the Internet, let's take a look at how DNA works in an application fronted by DCOM connections, as shown in Figure 14-5.

The DNA/DNA 2000 model is different from the pure transaction-oriented model in two important ways:

1. *Clients never connect directly to the middle-tier objects they request.* Instead, a connection point known as a context wrapper intercepts the client requests. MTS/COM+ makes sure that the context wrapper exposes exactly the same interface as the requested object, so that it looks to the client as though it's talking directly to the requested object. This process of interception makes a number of things possible. It means that when a transaction is finished and transactional objects are deactivated, the client remains connected to the context wrapper. Therefore, although the object may actually be destroyed,[8] the DCOM connection from the client to the middle tier is maintained. This saves time when another call is made to

---

6. This shift goes hand-in-hand with the transition from object orientation to interface orientation that is equally disturbing for many developers.

7. In more flowery literature, this type of transition is referred to as a paradigm shift. Psychologists and management consultants have written shelves full of books on the subject.

8. Under MTS, deactivated objects are always destroyed. Under COM+, objects with a suitable threading model can be reused. VB6 doesn't have a suitable threading model.

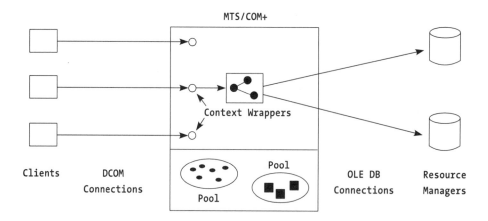

Figure 14-5. A DNA system

launch a new transaction and removes responsibility from the client for creating and destroying objects. Interception also means that the context wrapper can *do things* before and after every client call. The most fundamental thing the context wrapper does is to create a new object if the last one was deactivated and pass the client call on to the object. In both MTS and COM+ the context wrapper also checks whether any transactional services are required before and after each client call, as you'll see shortly. In COM+, interception is used to provide a host of additional features too. It's a very powerful way of letting the operating system (such as COM+) do things for an object, so that applications developers can concentrate on application issues.

2. *MTS/COM+ manages resources efficiently by using pooling techniques.*
   This applies automatically to threads and to Resource Manager connections. So long as you don't try to hold on to ADO Connections in your code, they will be looked after for you. COM+ allows component objects to be pooled as well, although not VB6 ones. While you may think that not being able to pool objects is a big performance hit, in fact, it generally isn't. Creating COM objects is one of the faster things your application can do.

When the Internet is introduced into the equation, diagrams usually get far more complicated, but the issues themselves don't. Web communication is based on HTTP, and HTTP requests from browsers are received by IIS. If any COM objects are required to service these requests,[9] IIS communicates with MTS/COM+ using

---

9. Requests for components are typically determined by an ASP page. This may be one that has been written, or it may be the generic ASP page created by a VB6 IIS Application.

standard COM or DCOM calls. Therefore, as far as MTS/COM+ is concerned, the client is IIS rather than the browser.

ADO hasn't featured heavily in the past few pages, yet it has a significant role to play in DNA-based systems. It's the primary technology available for getting data out from Resource Managers and for executing transactional updates. And, as we saw in Chapter 7, ADO, along with XML, is a key player in moving data between clients and the middle tier. In order to use MTS/COM+ transactional services, ADO applications should avoid using the Connection object's transaction methods. As you'll see in the next section, MTS/COM+ provides a more powerful and convenient alternative.

In This Section

This section introduced a load of new concepts. If most of this was new to you, it's unlikely that you took it all in. The first time many people hit this material, their response is, "Why should I hurt my brain learning all this just to use a new product?" However, DNA isn't about a new product, it's about writing code that works in a world that isn't connection-oriented, that allows many different front ends to be bolted onto the same core software, and that supports anything from one to one million users.

MTS/COM+ provides many of the facilities that this new world demands of our code. Middle-tier components can be considered to be either non-transactional or transactional. Transactional components must meet very tough requirements, but as long as you keep transactions short and understand why MTS/COM+ deactivates objects when it does, then MTS/COM+ looks after everything else. This is how it should be. It isn't that MTS/COM+ programming is hard, it's just that you need to have an appreciation of what it does for you in order to be able to use it profitably. Gaining that appreciation takes time, but like learning to drive, it's a one-time investment that, once made, can take you to new places.

Creating Transactional Components Using ADO

We are getting near the end of the book, so it's high time we started selling tickets for our production of *Much ADO about Nothing*.

Our theater's booking office makes heavy use of two separate databases. The Reservations database keeps track of how many seats are available for each performance put on at the theater. It has only one table of interest to us, called Seats:

Seats				
Column Name	Condensed Type	Nullable	Identity	▲
⚷ performanceID	int	NOT NULL		
⚷ type	char(1)	NOT NULL		
available	smallint	NOT NULL		
price	money	NULL		
				▼

Figure 14-6. The Seats table in the Reservations database

The theater has four types of seating:

- Budget (B)

- Standard (S)

- Special (P)

- Box (X)

There is a record in the Seats table for each type of seat for a given performance, specifying the price charged for the type of seat and the number of seats (or boxes) available. We are interested only in next Thursday's performance of *Much ADO about Nothing*, which has a performanceID of 101.

The other database is called Accounts. This database has a table called Balances that contains a running total of how much is owed to the theater by each customer and what their credit limit is:

Balances				
Column Name	Condensed Type	Nullable	Identity	▲
⚷ customerID	int	NOT NULL		
name	varchar(50)	NOT NULL		
balance	money	NOT NULL		
creditLimit	money	NULL		
				▼

Figure 14-7. The Balances table in the Accounts database

Be clear that we are not talking about two tables in the same database. *These tables are in different databases on different servers.* Without MTS/COM+ we wouldn't be able to write a transaction involving both of these tables. In the next section you'll see how this is done. In this section however, we'll concentrate on what is involved in reading and writing from and to the Seats table in the Reservations database using ADO in a COM+ Application.

To do this we'll create a component with a ProgID of Reservations.Numbers. This component will provide two transactions:

1. A method called getRS will return a disconnected Recordset containing details of seat availability and cost for a given performanceID.

2. A method called setRS will receive a disconnected Recordset generated by getRS. It will examine any changes made to this Recordset to make sure that there is no negative availability. It will then perform a transactional batch update and return Null for success or an error string in case of failure.

Reservations.Numbers differs from other components we've written in that it allows COM+ to take care of its transactional requirements. In fact, transactional components don't begin and end transactions themselves. Instead, they give information to COM+ about how the work they do should be treated from a transactional perspective. COM+ uses this information to determine when to start a transaction and when to commit it or roll it back. It takes a little while to get used to this idea, but it not only makes your life easier, it also makes your components more flexible.

For example, if an object starts a transaction explicitly in one of its methods (for instance, by calling cn.BeginTrans), then that method can never be called as part of a bigger transaction—as soon as it was called, a new transaction would be started. Therefore, the caller's work and the method's work couldn't form a new logical unit of work. If the caller's work is in a transaction, it's a different one from the method's transaction. The COM+ approach overcomes this limitation—it makes transaction reuse a possibility.

Each COM+ component has a transactional attribute. This is usually set in the Component Services snap-in via a component's Properties dialog box, after the component has been installed in a COM+ Application. Components developed using VB6 provide an alternative. Every Public class module in VB6 has a property called MTSTransactionMode, which can be set using the VB Properties Box. It has the same meaning in both COM+ and MTS and is used to set the component's transactional attribute.[10] The settings available for this property are:[11]

- **NotAnMTSObject**: This is the default. It means that you won't be installing this component in COM+, or if you do, VB6 won't allow you to debug it while running in COM+.

---

10. It's better to use this approach for VB components, as it makes interactive debugging easier for components while they are running under COM+/MTS.

11. Some of the settings have slightly different names in the COM+ snap-in. The translation between the two is straightforward, and their effects are identical.

- **NoTransactions**: This component will be installed in a COM+ Application, but it doesn't require or use any transactional services.

- **RequiresNewTransaction**: Every time an object is activated, a new transaction must be started. In other words, this object can never be enlisted into another object's transaction.

- **RequiresTransaction**: Objects must always run inside a transaction. If an object is activated directly by a client request, a new transaction will be started by COM+. However, if it's called by another COM+ object that is already running in a transaction, the object can become part of the other object's transaction (for example, become enlisted into it).

- **UsesTransactions**: The object will make use of a transaction if one already exists, but it doesn't require one, and it won't create a new one when activated.

Whenever a method is called on a COM+ object, COM+ intercepts the call. If the object is not already running inside a transaction,[12] COM+ will look at its transactional attribute to determine whether to create a new transaction, enlist the object in an existing transaction, or ignore transactions altogether. When the method returns, COM+ needs to know if the object has completed its transactional work, and whether it was successful or not.

For every active object, COM+ creates what is called a context object. A COM+ component can get access to its context object by calling the GetObjectContext function and can use it for a number of purposes. One of the most important uses is to communicate the status of its transactional work. Let's consider just two ways in which a COM+ object can tell COM+ about its transactional status:

1. **GetObjectContext.SetComplete**: When a COM+ object calls this method on its context object, it's saying, "My transactional work is done, and I am happy about it."

2. **GetObjectContext.SetAbort**: When a COM+ object calls this method, it's saying, "My transactional work is done, but I am not happy about it."

After each method call, COM+ looks at the transactional status of each object enlisted into the transaction and decides whether to commit, abort, or keep the transaction open. If any object calls SetAbort, the entire transaction is doomed. However, no single object can force a commit. COM+ needs every enlisted object to be happy before it will attempt to commit a transaction.

If an object calls SetComplete or SetAbort, one thing is certain: its work is done and it can be deactivated. Transactional COM+ objects that are created directly by

---

12. For a transactional component, this means that it's currently inactive. Because VB6 components can't be pooled, being inactive means that they always need to be created by a context wrapper.

client applications (known as *root objects*) should always call SetComplete or SetAbort in every Public method. The reason for this is that otherwise the transaction would stay open (and the database locks would be maintained) after control has been returned to the client application. This is a bad thing, because it means that the concurrency of our system is determined by the behavior of the client. If the client keeps hold of its object reference and doesn't call another method on the object, which has a chance of finishing the transaction, the transaction and all its resources will stay open until COM+ decides it has had enough, automatically deactivates all objects participating in the transaction, and rolls it back. By default, COM+ waits sixty seconds before timing out a transaction.

Let's apply all this knowledge to our Reservations.Numbers component. Its MTSTransactionMode will be set to RequiresTransaction. In addition to a reference to ADO, the Reservations project has a reference to "COM+ Services Type Library," which provides the GetObjectContext function, among other things.[13] Its getRS method is coded as follows:

```
Public Function getRS(ByVal PerformanceID As Long) As Recordset
On Error GoTo ErrH
Dim sSQL As String
Set getRS = New Recordset
sSQL = "SELECT * FROM Seats WHERE performanceID = " & _
       PerformanceID

With getRS
    .CursorLocation = adUseClient
    .LockType = adLockBatchOptimistic
    .ActiveConnection = "File Name=c:\Reservations.udl"
    .Source = sSQL
    .Open
    Set .ActiveConnection = Nothing
End With
GetObjectContext.SetComplete        ◄────────  I am happy and I am done
Exit Function
ErrH:
    Set getRS = Nothing
    GetObjectContext.SetAbort        ◄────────  I am not happy and I am done
End Function
```

This is standard disconnected Recordset stuff, with the addition of two calls to the component's context object. If the method succeeds, SetComplete is called; if it fails, SetAbort is called. The setRS function follows a more or less familiar pattern:

---

13. MTS applications should reference "Microsoft Transaction Server Type Library." This provides a subset of the functionality provided in COM+, but offers the same GetObjectContext function.

```
Public Function setRS(ByVal rs As Recordset) As Variant
On Error GoTo ErrH

rs.Filter = "available < 0"
If rs.RecordCount > 0 Then
    setRS = "There are not enough seats available"
    GetObjectContext.SetAbort
    Exit Function
Else
    rs.Filter = adFilterNone
End If


rs.ActiveConnection = "File Name=c:\Reservations.udl"
rs.UpdateBatch
Set rs.ActiveConnection = Nothing
GetObjectContext.SetComplete
setRS = Null
Exit Function
ErrH:
    setRS = Err.Description
    GetObjectContext.SetAbort

End Function
```

a business rule has failed;
the transaction cannot succeed

The Reservations project can now be compiled (as Reservations.dll), made binary compatible, and installed in a COM+ Application. COM+ will see that Reservations.Numbers requires a transaction.

Before taking a closer look at what is going on, let's consider a simple client made up of a data grid, an ADO Data Control, and a Command button. This is what it looks like:

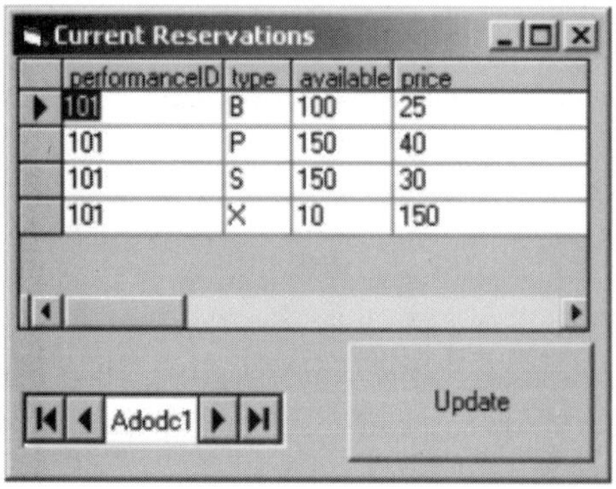

Figure 14-8. A simple client for Reservations

This client uses a reference to the Reservations DLL, its complete code is this:

```
Private oNumbers As Reservations.Numbers

Private Sub Form_Load()
Set oNumbers = New Reservations.Numbers
Set Adodc1.Recordset = oNumbers.getRS(101)
Set dgdNumbers.DataSource = Adodc1
End Sub

Private Sub cmdUpdate_Click()
Dim vResult As Variant
Adodc1.Recordset.MarshalOptions = adMarshalModifiedOnly
vResult = oNumbers.setRS(Adodc1.Recordset)
If Not IsNull(vResult) Then MsgBox vResult
Unload Me
End Sub
```

When the client's Form_Load runs, it requests a new Numbers object. This request is picked up by COM+ and causes a context wrapper to be created. The context wrapper creates the Numbers object, but it doesn't activate the object, and it doesn't create the object's context object at this point. Only when the client calls a method (getRS) is the context object created and the object activated. At this point, COM+, knowing that the object requires a transaction, asks the DTC to start a transaction and enlists the Numbers object into it. The context wrapper then passes the call onto the Numbers object, which executes all of its code within the transaction.

As long as nothing goes wrong, the method calls SetComplete and returns (to the context wrapper). The context wrapper notices that SetComplete was called, and it therefore deactivates the object (because all its work is done), commits the transaction (because the object is happy), releases all locks held by the database, and returns to the client.

The client displays the data in the grid and allows the user to work on it. All of the activity just described will typically take a fraction of a second to execute. Note that while the user is working with the data (which could take minutes), only the context wrapper remains consuming resources in the server environment. Objects, connections, and locks have all been released.

The client still believes it's connected to a Numbers object however, and when the user clicks the Update button, it sets the MarshalOptions property to ensure that only changed records get sent back to the client and then calls setRS. The call to setRS proceeds in exactly the same way as the call to getRS. A transaction is started, a Numbers object is activated (created) within the transaction, and work begins.

Notice how setRS handles the task of ensuring that no overbooking has taken place. If any record has a negative value, it simply calls SetAbort and gives up.

COM+ will tidy up for it. Because a transaction is an all-or-nothing affair, error processing is actually very black and white. Either everything works or nothing gets done.

The batch update process follows our usual model. Don't be alarmed that there are no calls to BeginTrans, CommitTrans, etcetera. There shouldn't be. This is a transactional COM+ object. Transactions are handled automatically. Our task is simply to do our work and call SetComplete or SetAbort accordingly.

While the COM+ approach to transactional processing is different from a more conventional approach, it's not especially harder. It may seem that there are many new things to learn about, but this is only because there are many services and features available for us that need to be understood. The real benefit of these features only becomes apparent when our applications become more complex or the number of users increases. The beauty of COM+ is that if we take a few extra steps now, we are creating components capable of running under those more demanding conditions. In the next section, we'll gear up our complexity by one small step. You'll see how you can put the DTC to work to write a transaction that includes two databases in one logical unit of work.

In This Section

You saw how to create a transactional component for use with COM+. You have learned how to set a component's transactional attribute and how to write code that gives COM+ transactional status information. A client application that uses COM+ is no different from any other client application.

Distributed Transactions

In the last section, you saw how to write a transaction that would allow you to make changes to the Seat table in the Reservations database. A real booking for theater seats would be a little more involved. You would need to record who the tickets were sold to and check that the customer is able to pay the ticket price.

We already have a component that can book the seat reservations using the Reservations database. In this section, we'll add a new component called Accounts.Names to update the Balances table of the Accounts database and check the customer's credit limit. We'll also add a third component called Request.Booking to coordinate the task of making a booking. Request.Booking will oversee the two tasks of reserving the seats and updating the customer's balance as part of a single transaction. Figure 14-9 shows all the objects and connections involved in the transaction.

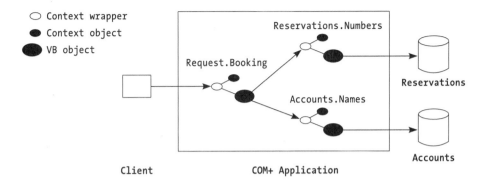

Figure 14-9. A distributed transaction with multiple components

The client has a reference to a context wrapper representing a root object. During the transaction, the root object is active and is enlisted into the transaction (assuming its transaction attribute is RequiresTransaction or RequiresNewTransaction). At various points during the transaction, a Reservations.Numbers object and an Accounts.Names object will be created. Objects created as part of a transaction that aren't root objects are called *secondary objects*. Note that each of the secondary objects also has a context wrapper and a context object, and Request.Booking is connected to the context wrappers of these objects, not to the objects themselves. As a reminder, this is what the context wrapper and context object are for:

- The context object allows the VB object to call SetComplete and SetAbort. It also provides the VB object with other information, such as the identity of the client who started the transaction. Each transaction has a unique identifier called the TRID (which is a *GUID*). Each context object involved in a transaction knows its TRID. TRIDs allow COM+ to keep track of all activities concerning a transaction. Like transactional component objects, context objects don't survive the ending of a transaction.

- The context wrapper provides a connection point to clients to give the impression that an object is still there after it has been deactivated. It provides the interception services before and after a method call.

Database connections will be acquired and released by each object that needs them during a method call. The connections will be pooled by COM+ for performance reasons and also to ensure that locks are maintained after an object has released a connection and until the transaction ends.

If any object calls SetAbort, then the transaction will roll back when the root object is deactivated or when control is returned to the client. There are two situations that must be avoided if a secondary object calls SetAbort:

1. *The root object should not call SetComplete after a secondary object has called SetAbort.* Once SetAbort has been called, the transaction cannot succeed. COM+ raises an error if the root object tries to call SetComplete for a doomed transaction. This means that each secondary object must provide a way of letting the root object know whether it succeeded or failed. This is typically done using either a return value or an error-handling scheme.

2. *If any secondary object calls SetAbort, the root object should call SetAbort too.* If it doesn't, then the transaction will be aborted when control is returned to the client, but the root object won't be deactivated. However, it can't join in a new transaction while it's active, therefore, it's a lame duck and of no use to the client.

If all secondary objects have called SetComplete, then the transaction will be committed, as long as the root object also calls SetComplete. Because the transaction involves multiple Resource Managers (databases), the DTC uses a special scheme to control the transaction execution.

A Resource Manager should only need to look after its own transactional resources. Writing Resource Managers is tough enough without needing to worry about other Resource Managers that may be part of the same distributed transaction. What happens instead is that the DTC looks after the transaction using a protocol called "two-phase commit." Two-phase commit is rather like a wedding ceremony. If the transaction wants to commit, the DTC asks each Resource Manager involved in the transaction to say that they are prepared to commit. Once they do this, they can't go back. This is rather like the minister at a wedding getting the bride and groom to say, "I do." This marks the end of the first phase. In the second phase, the DTC instructs each Resource Manager to complete the commit process that it has already prepared, and the transaction is a done deal. This is like the minister saying, "I pronounce you man and wife." When the transactional components are on different computers, the process is a little more complicated, but COM+ and the DTC take care of all this—it doesn't affect your code. In fact, the whole two-phase commit process is invisible to your components.

Now let's take a look at the code for our transactions. The Reservations component already exists. In the last section we used it as a root object, but for our current purposes, it will be a secondary object without any changes being required. The other secondary object is defined by the Accounts.Names component, which has two methods. It has a getRS method, which returns a Recordset containing the name and customer ID of each customer in the Balances table. Its purpose is to allow a user to select a customer to book some tickets for. The second method is updateBalance. It takes a customer ID and a sum of money representing the value of tickets purchased, and it updates the Balance table appropriately.

Accounts.Names has its transactional attribute set to RequiresTransaction. Its code is as follows:

```
Public Function getRS() As Recordset
On Error GoTo ErrH
Dim sSQL As String
Set getRS = New Recordset
sSQL = "SELECT customerID, name FROM Balances"
With getRS
    .CursorLocation = adUseClient
    .LockType = adLockReadOnly
    .ActiveConnection = "File Name=c:\Accounts.udl"
    .Source = sSQL
    .Open
    Set .ActiveConnection = Nothing
End With
GetObjectContext.SetComplete
Exit Function
ErrH:
    Set getRS = Nothing
    GetObjectContext.SetAbort
End Function


Public Function updateBalance(ByVal ID As Long, _
    ByVal Amount As Currency) _
    As Variant
On Error GoTo ErrH
Dim rs As New Recordset
Dim sSQL As String
sSQL = "SELECT customerID,balance, creditLimit FROM Balances " & _
        "WHERE customerID = " & ID

With rs
    .CursorLocation = adUseClient
    .LockType = adLockOptimistic
    .ActiveConnection = "File Name=c:\Accounts.udl"
    .Source = sSQL
    .Open
```

```
    If (rs!balance - Amount) < (rs!creditLimit * -1) Then
        GetObjectContext.SetAbort
        updateBalance = "Credit Limit Exceeded"
        Exit Function
    End If
    rs!balance = rs!balance - Amount
    rs.Update
End With
updateBalance = Null
GetObjectContext.SetComplete
Exit Function
ErrH:
    GetObjectContext.SetAbort
    updateBalance = "Error updating balance"
End Function
```

Accounts.Names is slightly different from Reservation.Numbers, because it doesn't use batch updating. There is no rule that says it should. Because balances only tend to be updated one at a time, it makes more sense simply to pass it a customer ID and an amount, and let it perform a standard Recordset update (or indeed, it could call a stored procedure). That aside, it uses the same basic scheme for rejecting an update that would exceed a credit limit.

The Accounts project will compile as Accounts.dll. Once compiled, it can be installed in a COM+ Application. We can then concentrate on the new root object, Request.Booking.

Request.Booking creates Accounts.Names and Reservations.Numbers objects and calls their methods. In MTS, a special technique is required when creating secondary objects. In COM+ this isn't necessary, although the older MTS approach is still supported. You'll see how it's done in COM+ first, and then deal with MTS's requirements.

Before doing either of these things, let's take a quick look at the client that will reference Request.Booking. Its user interface, which wins no prizes for ergonomic design, looks like that shown in Figure 14-10.

Its role is to display a list of customers and the current reservations (retrieved by calling getDetails on a Request.Booking object). The user selects a customer, adjusts the reservations to reflect the customer's purchase request (if the customer wants two budget seats, reduce B from 100 to 98), and presses Update, which calls confirm-Booking to do the business. The ADO Data Controls, which would normally be invisible, have been left visible to show you what is going on. Here's the code:

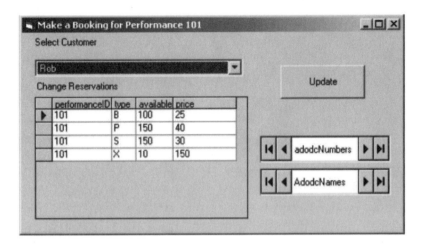

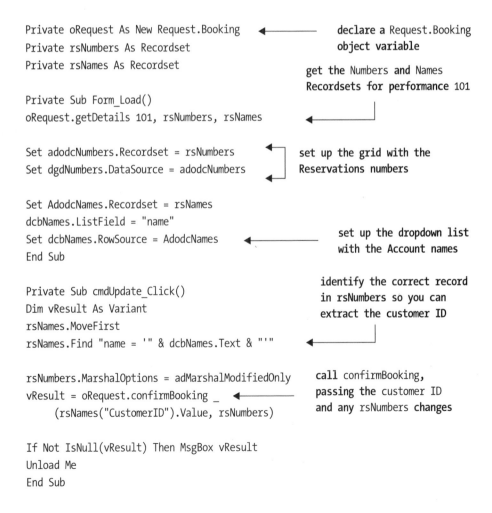

Figure 14-10. A simple client for a booking

```vb
Private oRequest As New Request.Booking          ◄──────  declare a Request.Booking
Private rsNumbers As Recordset                            object variable
Private rsNames As Recordset
                                                 get the Numbers and Names
                                                 Recordsets for performance 101
Private Sub Form_Load()
oRequest.getDetails 101, rsNumbers, rsNames      ◄──────┐

Set adodcNumbers.Recordset = rsNumbers           ◄──┐   set up the grid with the
Set dgdNumbers.DataSource = adodcNumbers         ◄──┘   Reservations numbers

Set AdodcNames.Recordset = rsNames
dcbNames.ListField = "name"
Set dcbNames.RowSource = AdodcNames              ◄──────  set up the dropdown list
End Sub                                                  with the Account names

                                                 identify the correct record
Private Sub cmdUpdate_Click()                    in rsNumbers so you can
Dim vResult As Variant                           extract the customer ID
rsNames.MoveFirst
rsNames.Find "name = '" & dcbNames.Text & "'"    ◄──────┘

rsNumbers.MarshalOptions = adMarshalModifiedOnly  call confirmBooking,
vResult = oRequest.confirmBooking _              ◄──────  passing the customer ID
    (rsNames("CustomerID").Value, rsNumbers)            and any rsNumbers changes

If Not IsNull(vResult) Then MsgBox vResult
Unload Me
End Sub
```

Controlling Secondary Objects in COM+

We've already discussed all the rules required to write our controlling root component in COM+. Our root component, Request.Booking, will have its transactional attribute set to RequiresTransaction. Here's its first method, getDetails:

```
Public Sub getDetails(ByVal PerformanceID As Long, _
                      Numbers As Recordset, _
                      Names As Recordset)
On Error GoTo ErrH
Dim oNumbers As New Reservations.Numbers          create a Numbers object and a
Dim oNames As New Accounts.Names                  Names object, and make them
Set Numbers = oNumbers.getRS(PerformanceID)       both return Recordsets
Set Names = oNames.getRS
If (Numbers Is Nothing) Or (Names Is Nothing) Then    if either of them fail
    GetObjectContext.SetAbort                         call SetAbort; otherwise,
Else                                                  be happy
    GetObjectContext.SetComplete
End If
Exit Sub
ErrH:
    GetObjectContext.SetAbort
End Sub
```

getDetails cuts down on roundtrips by requiring the caller to pass two Recordset variables as arguments. As a result, one method call can return two Recordsets, and we can provide all the data required for the booking screen in a single roundtrip. Of course, this means we can't define these two arguments as ByVal.[14] Once the user has selected a customer and made changes to the reservations grid, the confirmBooking function is called. This function executes the main business transaction of the application. It looks like this:

```
Private Const ERR_TASKFAILED = vbObjectError + 512


Public Function confirmBooking( _
            ByVal CustomerID As Long, _
            ByVal Numbers As Recordset) As Variant
On Error GoTo ErrH
Dim oNumbers As New Reservations.Numbers          create new Numbers
Dim oNames As New Accounts.Names                  and Names objects
Dim cAmount As Currency
```

---

14. Visual Basic allows input parameters (ByVal) and input/output parameters (ByRef), but unlike some languages, it doesn't allow output parameters, apart from a return value. The closest we can get to having multiple output parameters is to pass in uninitialized ByRef variables, which are initialized on return.

```
Dim fdAvailable As Field
Set fdAvailable = Numbers("available")
While Not Numbers.EOF
    cAmount = cAmount - _
        ((fdAvailable.Value - fdAvailable.OriginalValue) * _
            Numbers("price").Value)
    Numbers.MoveNext
Wend


confirmBooking = oNumbers.setRS(Numbers)
If Not IsNull(confirmBooking) Then Err.Raise ERR_TASKFAILED


confirmBooking = oNames.updateBalance(CustomerID, cAmount)
If Not IsNull(confirmBooking) Then Err.Raise ERR_TASKFAILED


confirmBooking = Null
GetObjectContext.SetComplete
Exit Function
ErrH:
    If IsEmpty(confirmBooking) Then
        confirmBooking = "A Booking error occurred"
    End If
    GetObjectContext.SetAbort
End Function
```

iterate through the Recordset, working out the cost of purchased tickets

update the Reservations database (within the transaction)

update the Accounts database (within the same transaction)

The simplicity of this code belies the underlying complexity of coordinating its work, which is performed for us by COM+ and the DTC. As far as this method is concerned, a transaction is started for it, it performs a simple calculation, and then it calls two other objects to do some work for it as part of that transaction. It does some error handling and then winds up.

This is how it should be. The fact that two Resource Managers were involved in the transaction is not an issue. It would be a huge issue if we relied on an ADO Connection object to handle the transaction, because we could never achieve the required outcome. It so happens that both the Numbers and the Names components are installed in the same COM+ Application as the Request component. However, if we needed to move either or both of these components to different computers, the code would run the same. This is a major scalability benefit. We can split the load on an overworked server across two or more machines without needing to make code changes. The Component Services snap-in makes this a straightforward administrative task.

Note that this root object uses a transactional attribute of RequiresTransaction, rather than RequiresNewTransaction. It also uses the error-handling convention by which its caller always knows whether it's happy or sad. Therefore, a more complex transaction could be written that uses Request.Booking as a secondary object, enabling us to reuse transactional components and achieve greater consistency along the way.

Controlling Secondary Objects in MTS

If you are familiar with MTS, you may well be thinking that the preceding code contains a glaring error. I know what you are thinking, but relax, COM+ is just more sophisticated than MTS, and so it makes your life easier. In case you have no idea what I am going on about, I had better explain.

There is a golden rule of MTS programming that states when one MTS object wants to enlist another MTS object into its transaction, it should avoid creating the object using the New operator or by calling the CreateObject function.

When a client application creates an MTS (or a COM+) object, the object gets a context wrapper and is allocated to a thread from the thread pool. This is how it should be. However, if this root object attempts to create a secondary object in the same Package using New or CreateObject, MTS behaves very differently from COM+. This is what happens:

- *If the root object uses New to create an object defined in the same DLL as the root object, VB takes sole responsibility for creating that object.* Because VB doesn't make an external call to COM's Service Control Manager to create the COM object, MTS doesn't get the chance to create a context wrapper for the object, and so it can't supply the object with interception services. It therefore doesn't behave in a predictable MTS way.

- *If the root object uses CreateObject or New to create an object defined in a different DLL from the root object, then VB uses COM's Service Control Manager to create the new object.* This allows MTS to get a look in, but MTS treats this as another request from a client application to create a new root object. The new object will be allocated to a thread by MTS, which will most likely be a different thread from the one used by the real root object. This means that communication between the two objects will be slow because all calls to an object running on a different thread need to be synchronized and marshalled. It also means that one of MTS's basic rules will be violated, which states that all objects taking part in a transaction should use the same logical thread.[15]

---

15. MTS uses the term "activity" to describe a logical thread. Each transaction runs in exactly one activity. Because a transaction's objects can run in different processes and on different computers, the objects may physically run on different threads, but MTS manages their work as a single logical thread (activity), providing all the required synchronization between different processes and computers. This makes the developer's work much easier, because there is never any need to worry about synchronization, even if the components are distributed.

MTS solves this problem by providing a method called CreateInstance on the context object. When you use CreateInstance to create the object, MTS knows that the request is coming from inside an MTS Package, and therefore, handles it correctly. CreateInstance takes a ProgID as an argument. Both the getDetails and the confirmBooking methods would need to use CreateInstance to create the secondary objects in an MTS environment. Here's what confirmBooking looks like in this case:

```
Public Function confirmBooking(CustomerID As Long, _
                ByVal Numbers As Recordset) As Variant
On Error GoTo ErrH
Dim oNumbers As Reservations.Numbers          variables for secondary objects
Dim oNames As Accounts.Names                  should not be declared As New
Dim cAmount As Currency
Dim fdAvailable As Field
Dim oContext As ObjectContext
Set oContext = GetObjectContext
Set fdAvailable = Numbers("available")
While Not Numbers.EOF
    cAmount = cAmount - _
        ((fdAvailable.Value - fdAvailable.OriginalValue) * _
          Numbers("price").Value)        call CreateInstance to ensure that
    Numbers.MoveNext                     secondary objects are created correctly
Wend

Set oNumbers = oContext.CreateInstance("Reservations.Numbers")
Set oNames = oContext.CreateInstance("Accounts.Names")

confirmBooking = oNumbers.setRS(Numbers)
If Not IsNull(confirmBooking) Then Err.Raise ERR_TASKFAILED
confirmBooking = oNames.updateBalance(CustomerID, cAmount)
If Not IsNull(confirmBooking) Then Err.Raise ERR_TASKFAILED

confirmBooking = Null
oContext.SetComplete
Exit Function
ErrH:
    If IsEmpty(confirmBooking) Then
        confirmBooking = "A Booking error occurred"
    End If
    oContext.SetAbort
End Function
```

Here, you can see the use of CreateInstance to create secondary transactional objects. To avoid calling GetObjectContext several times in this method, it was called once, and the context object was assigned to a variable. It's common practice to create a module-level variable to hold the context object so that it's easy to reference from all code. Although the variable can be declared at a module-level, it will need to be instantiated on each method call for a stateless object. While it's true that the object's Initialize event will fire prior to each method call (because it's reactivated each time), it's important to avoid calling GetObjectContext in the object's Initialize event procedure. Initialize runs before the object's context is created, and so GetObjectContext won't work at this point. MTS provides an additional interface called ObjectControl that raises events when an object is activated and deactivated, and which can safely be used to initialize and release context object variables.[16]

To encourage MTS developers to use CreateInstance, it's sometimes said that you should never use New or CreateObject inside an MTS component. This is a misleading view. CreateInstance should only be used to create objects that are installed in an MTS Package, which therefore need a context wrapper and a context object to work properly. Any object that is not installed in a Package (which includes any ADO object) should be created using standard techniques. This sometimes leads developers to worry that ADO objects won't display the required transactional behavior because they aren't explicitly invited into the MTS transaction. Don't worry. This isn't your problem—it's ADO's problem, and ADO handles it perfectly.[17]

COM+ programmers never need to worry about CreateInstance. A major part of the transition from COM to COM+ was to make COM+ aware of the kind of things that MTS wanted to do. Whereas MTS bolts interception on top of COM by performing some fancy Registry footwork, interception is built into the fabric of COM+. Not only does this make COM+ a great deal more powerful, it makes it a more natural programming environment for working with services that use interception. COM+ continues to support the CreateInstance approach for backwards compatibility.

In This Section

We created a distributed transaction. Using COM+, it's easy for a root object to call a secondary object and enlist the secondary object into its transaction. COM+ components don't care where secondary objects run, and they don't care how many Resource Managers are involved in a transaction. COM+ looks after all of this. MTS is almost as obliging, but it requires us to use CreateInstance to control secondary objects correctly.

---

16. To use this interface, you need to use the VB Implements keyword.

17. ADO is one example of what is known as an MTS Resource Dispenser. This basically means it has been specifically coded to know how to manage a connection between MTS and Resource Managers. When you use ADO outside MTS, this functionality isn't used. When you use ADO within MTS, it automatically knows how to behave.

Summary

The 1990s were characterized by the shift to client-server models. Even while client-server was establishing itself, it was the inevitable first step toward a more distributed type of system architecture, typically referred to as n-tier. While the impact of browser-based front ends and mobile devices may not have been predicted, the n-tier model gives system architects the flexibility to move into these new and exciting worlds.

This flexibility has come at the cost of vastly more complex middle-tier software. MTS and COM+ (and MSMQ) have been developed to prevent each organization from needing to write essentially the same complex system plumbing. By following the rules of MTS/COM+, we can write applications that can exist in the challenging middle-tier environment, but still think about our components as single-user software most of the time.

To provide a road map for moving into this brave new world, Microsoft created DNA and then DNA 2000 as n-tier development frameworks, which are based on the concept of transaction-oriented processing and are heavily dependent on MTS/COM+ and ADO.

In this chapter, we looked at what working in this environment means, at least from the perspective of an ADO programmer. We looked at

- How transactional components can be written.

- How transactional components can be linked together to form bigger transactional components and to lay a foundation for reusable transactions.

- Some of the key issues that have made developers wary of using MTS/COM+. Although it takes time to embrace the methodology, it ultimately makes it much easier to write the kinds of systems all businesses and organizations are screaming for.

CHAPTER 15

RDS and DHTML

RDS and DHTML in Action

RDS Components and Architecture

RDS Customization Handlers

Using RDS with Custom Business Objects

Summary

REMOTE DATA SERVICES (**RDS**) and Dynamic HTML (DHTML) are two technologies that work together to deliver ADO data from Web servers into Web browsers. In fact, both technologies can work together without any input from ADO, but ADO is the glue that makes them flow together to give users a more responsive and productive Web experience than can be delivered by ASP or CGI alone.[1]

In this chapter, you'll see how to deliver Recordsets to the browser, where they can be bound to HTML elements. This way, users can scroll through data much like they would on a standard VB Form, and without needing to refresh the Web page each time. You'll see how a page can request new data from a Web server and update itself without needing to be rebuilt, and you'll see how the Web server can be configured to control access to the databases that manage this data and to limit the amount and type of data that is returned to browsers. You'll also see how any COM object can be accessed from a Web page through the RDS architecture.

There is a catch to using this technology. DHTML is currently a Microsoft-specific technology that is only built into Internet Explorer 4 and above (IE4+). It relies on COM technology being available to the browser, which restricts it to Windows client platforms. Similarly, RDS will only work with COM-aware browsers. You must decide for yourself whether these constraints are acceptable. It's true that a very large number of users have access to IE4+, but there are also users who don't or won't use it. In intranet situations, you have much more control over which type of browser users work with. However, for Internet situations, DHTML and RDS raise genuine business issues, if only because they don't work with Netscape browsers.

While many people have some idea of what RDS does, there is little consensus on what it actually is. While this may sound strange, it's linked to the history of RDS

---

1. This chapter is heavily Web-oriented. It assumes the reader has some general familiarity with topics such as HTML, HTTP, CGI, ASP, and IIS.

and its relationship with ADO. Originally, RDS and ADO were separate products with some common concerns. Both addressed data access, but while ADO dealt mostly with traditional two-tier applications, RDS addressed n-tier applications, and in particular, the Web-enabling of data access. You have seen in earlier chapters that ADO is fully equipped to deal with n-tier applications, and in truth, some of this capability is based on technology originally developed for RDS. However, the time when people considered disconnected Recordsets (for example) as an RDS technology is long gone.

The defining feature of RDS is an architecture that allows data (usually, but not exclusively Recordsets) to be returned from an IIS Web server via HTTP in a way that doesn't upset too many firewalls. On the client side, RDS handles the data returned from the Web server and, through DHTML, allows it to be bound to HTML elements on the Web page. When I refer to RDS, it's this architecture that I will be discussing.

Microsoft provides two classes, DataSpace and DataFactory, to coordinate this HTTP-enabled exchange. Understanding the role of these classes is important, but as you'll see, it's entirely possible to use RDS without ever referring to them explicitly. A third component, the RDS.DataControl, is responsible for binding ADO data into DHTML elements.

We've discussed so much of the technology relevant to RDS in previous chapters (for example, disconnected Recordsets, marshalling, transactions, and n-tier design) that the fundamentals of RDS can be discussed in a relatively short chapter such as this one.

We'll begin this by exploring a simple RDS-enabled application, before looking in more detail at the architecture of RDS. We'll then examine the RDS Customization Layer, a generally underused feature of RDS that adds sanity into the server-side administration and control of RDS data access. Finally, we'll see how the RDS architecture allows you to access just about any COM object over HTTP.

RDS and DHTML in Action

In this section, we'll develop some simple Web pages that demonstrate the power of RDS and DHTML.[2]

We'll begin by creating a simple Web page that allows the user to look at each part in the Parts table, one at a time. A pure ASP application performing this task would either need to present all the information as part of the same page or build a separate page for each part. The RDS approach is somewhat sweeter. Our first attempt at an RDS Web page will do a few things that RDS programmers wouldn't normally do. However, it works perfectly well and uses familiar ADO knowledge. I'll address the differences between this and "standard RDS" in later sections.

---

2. All the pages used in this chapter were written using the Microsoft Script debugger. Any HTML viewer from Notepad upward can be used to edit the companion files to this chapter located on the CD.

We'll break the HTML page into three sections. The first section looks like this:

```
<html>                                                          class ID for
<head>                                                          RDS.DataControl
<object classid="clsid:BD96C556-65A3-11D0-983A-00C04FC29E33"
           id="oDCParts"  width="0"  height="0">
</object>
```

This code marks the beginning of the HTML page and defines an RDS.DataControl using the HTML object tag. The control is given the name oDCParts. Because it's invisible at run time, its dimensions are set to 0. Objects referenced in HTML object tags are known by their *GUID* (CLASSID) rather than a more convenient *ProgID*.

The remainder of the header section of the page defines the page's scripts (using VBScript):

```
<script LANGUAGE=VBScript>
Sub Window_OnLoad()
  Set rs = CreateObject("ADODB.Recordset")
  rs.LockType = 4                                   create a batch optimistic
  rs.ActiveConnection = _                           ADO Recordset
    "Provider=MS Remote;" & _                       use a Provider called MS Remote
    "Remote Server=http://POLECAT;" & _
    "Remote Provider=SQLOLEDB;Database=MuchADO;UID=sa;PWD=;"
  rs.source = "SELECT * FROM Parts"
  rs.open                                           attach the Recordset to
  Set oDCParts.SourceRecordset = rs                 the DataControl's
End Sub                                             SourceRecordset property


Sub MoveNext()
  If Not oDCParts.Recordset.EOF Then oDCParts.Recordset.MoveNext
End Sub


Sub MovePrevious()
  If Not oDCParts.Recordset.BOF Then oDCParts.Recordset.MovePrevious
End Sub


Sub SubmitChanges()
  oDCParts.Recordset.UpdateBatch
End Sub
</script>
<title>DHTML with elements bound to a Recordset</title>
</head>
```

Most of the action here takes place in the OnLoad event, which fires when the page is first processed by the browser.[3] The first line of code creates an ADODB.Recordset.

Many RDS programmers, if they create Recordsets in this way, would use the ADOR.Recordset, rather than the ADODB.Recordset. Both Recordsets expose the same interface, and the use of ADOR is largely historical. ADOR differs from ADODB in that it doesn't expose Connection and Command objects. In earlier versions of ADO, it was intended that client programs that only need Recordset functionality wouldn't need the overhead of the ADODB library. They wouldn't need Connection or Command objects because the middle tier (typically the Web server) handled connections and commands. At one time, ADOR used a different DLL from ADODB with a smaller footprint. However, in ADO 2.0, both ADOR and ADODB Recordsets have the same class ID and both use the same DLL for their code. All Windows 2000 machines have the full ADODB library installed as part of the operating system. There is no difference between the ADOR and ADODB Recordsets whatsoever.

The ActiveConnection for this Recordset is

```
"Provider=MS Remote;" & _
"Remote Server=http://POLECAT;" & _
"Remote Provider=SQLOLEDB;Database=MuchADO;UID=sa;PWD=;"
```

Note that the Provider is MS Remote. This Provider uses an RDS.DataSpace object to communicate with a DataFactory on a remote server using HTTP. The Remote Server key provides the URL of the remote server. The Remote Provider key contains information passed to the remote DataFactory (which resides on the remote server) to create an ADO Connection.

This connection string has a serious flaw—it contains a user ID and password. Anyone using this page can take this information and have unwanted access to your database. Shortly, you'll see how customization handlers provide a simple and elegant way to control such access.

It's important to understand that the remote OLEDB Provider (in this case, SQLOLEDB) and the database specified in the Remote Provider key do not need to be accessible on the client. No client software needs to be installed to run the code on the client, other than ADO itself. All database access is performed via the Web server, using a DataFactory object. The client merely passes a connection string for the server to execute. RDS uses a default DataFactory object on the Web server to handle ADO commands, so there is no need to create a DataFactory yourself, although we'll see that there are good reasons for doing so in some circumstances.

When the Recordset calls rs.Open, the client's Provider (MS Remote) creates a DataFactory object on the specified Web server and passes it the connection and command string. The DataFactory creates the Recordset and returns. DataFactory

---

3. ASP programmers should note that this is not server-side script. It executes in the browser. The normal rules about not using VBScript in browser code don't apply because RDS code is limited to IE browsers anyway.

objects are stateless and are released by the server once the Recordset is returned. This tells you that the Recordset will always be client-side, because all server resources are released.

Finally, the Recordset is attached to the SourceRecordset property of the RDS.DataControl. This will use the Recordset in very much the same way that a standard ADO Data Control uses it, except that it binds it to HTML elements on a page, instead of to controls on a form.

The rest of the preceding script code contains simple routines that are triggered by buttons on the Web page. Before discussing these routines, let's look now at the remainder of the HTML:

```
<body>
    PARTS
    <BR>
    Part Name
    <INPUT type="text" datasrc="#oDCParts" datafld="part" id="Part">
    <BR>
    Description
    <INPUT type="text" datasrc="#oDCParts" datafld="description"
            id="description" size= "50">
    <BR>
    <INPUT type="button" value = "   Next   " onclick="MoveNext">
    <INPUT type="button" value = "Previous" onclick="MovePrevious">
    <INPUT type="button" value = "Update" onclick="SubmitChanges">
</body>
</html>
```

The body section of the page is very simple. It contains two input boxes and three buttons. The buttons have onclick parameters that tie them to routines in the script code. The input boxes have datasrc and datafld attributes. These attributes are responsible for binding the input boxes to the RDS.DataControl. DHTML binding is very similar to regular Form binding.

The resulting page looks like Figure 15-1.

The Next and Previous buttons call the script routines that use standard ADO methods to scroll through the records. Because the HTML input boxes are bound to the RDS.DataControl, they are automatically updated when the Recordset scrolls, without needing to refetch the page. The Recordset is held in the browser's memory, so scrolling is instantaneous.

When the Update button is clicked, the changes are marshalled to the Web server, where a new instance of the DataFactory handles the update process. The MS Remote Provider ensures that the UpdateBatch takes place under transactional control.

Before finishing this section, let's take our RDS page one step further. Take a look at Figure 15-2.

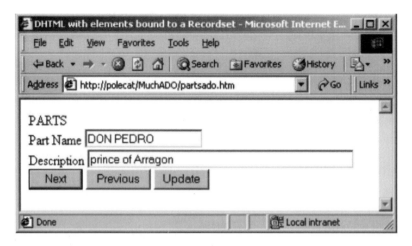

Figure 15-1. A simple DHTML/RDS Web page

Figure 15-2. A more sophisticated DHTML/RDS Web page

This is the same as the previous page, except that a Words button has been added. When the Words button is clicked, it fetches a new Recordset containing all the Words used by the current Part that have a word count and a word length greater than 5. All of this happens within the same page. The Words button fetches a new Recordset, and DHTML dynamically rebuilds the HTML table.

Extending this functionality to our previous page involves three simple steps. First, create another RDS.DataControl (called oDCWords) to handle the additional Recordset, as follows:

```
<OBJECT CLASSID="clsid:BD96C556-65A3-11D0-983A-00C04FC29E33"
  id="oDCWords" width="0" height="0">
</OBJECT>
```

Then add a new script that will fire when the Words button is clicked:

```
Sub Words()
  Set rs = CreateObject("ADODB.Recordset")
  rs.LockType = 4
  rs.ActiveConnection = _
    "Provider=MS Remote;" & _
    "Remote Server=http://POLECAT;" & _
    "Remote Provider=SQLOLEDB;Database=MuchADO;UID=sa;PWD=;"
  rs.source = "sp_WordList ('" & Part.Value & "',5,5)"
  rs.open
  Set oDCWords.SourceRecordset = rs
End Sub
```

This script calls a stored procedure called sp_WordList that we met in Chapter 5, which takes a part name, a word count, and a word length as input. The resulting Recordset is bound to oDCWords.

Finally, add some more DHTML:

```
<BR><BR>
  <INPUT type="button" value = "Words" onclick ="Words">
  <BR>
  <TABLE id="tblWords" border = "1" datasrc="#oDCWords" width="200">
    <TR>
      <TD><SPAN datafld="word"></SPAN></TD>
      <TD><SPAN datafld="total"></SPAN></TD>
    </TR>
  </TABLE>
```

This adds the Words button (which triggers the Words subroutine) and an HTML table. The table is bound to the oDCWords DataControl, just as a grid would be bound to a data control in a VB program. Each column within the table is bound to a Field in the Recordset using a SPAN HTML element. Note that we only need to define one row in the table. DHTML does the rest, according to the number of records in the Recordset.

Suppose you want to allow the user to sort the words into alphabetical order without going back to the Web server. Just add a button that calls the following script subroutine:

```
Sub Sort()
  oDCWords.Recordset.Sort = "word ASC"
End Sub
```

and it's done. This is a client-side ADO Recordset. We expect it to behave.

It looks and feels like we've been developing a two-tier application in this section, with data coming straight from a database into our browser-based applications. This impression is created and maintained by RDS. In fact, all the previous examples employ an n-tier approach, in which a Web server–based DataFactory receives our remote requests for data and executes them from the Web server. This default DataFactory behavior is deliberately transparent in order to make RDS easy to use. Using a DataFactory in this transparent fashion is sometimes referred to as *implicit remoting*, whereas adding code that creates a DataFactory is called *explicit remoting*.

The DataFactory's existence should never be ignored, for as we shall see, the presence of this middle-tier component is only critical to the ability of RDS to support remote access over HTTP. Furthermore, we can make use of the DataFactory by adding increasing levels of control into the middle tier, starting with simple security switches and checks via the RDS Customization Layer, and resulting in a highly customized and controlled Web server environment.

In This Section

We saw how DHTML and RDS work together to create a dynamic Web page with elements on the page bound directly to ADO Recordsets. The Recordsets are delivered to the browser by RDS and held in client memory to permit a highly responsive Web interaction.

RDS Components and Architecture

RDS allows Web servers to deliver Recordsets over HTTP to browsers that are able to use them. Figure 15-3 shows the various communication paths involved. Programmable RDS components are shown with a gray background.

RDS clients always communicate through a DataSpace object. The DataSpace object can be created implicitly, as in the previous section, or it can be programmed

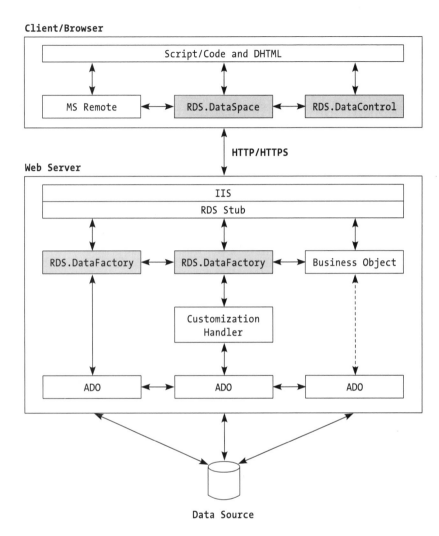

Figure 15-3. The RDS architecture

explicitly. You'll see how to do this later in this section. You'll also see how the RDS DataControl can itself be used to create a DataSpace implicitly, without any help from the ADO MS Remote Provider.

Whatever programming technique the client uses, RDS data flows through a DataSpace via HTTP or HTTPS.[4] Data is marshalled between client and Web server using the same marshalling techniques (based on proxies and stubs) that we discussed in Chapter 7, although in RDS, data is packaged for marshalling in a Web-friendly way.

On the Web server, there are basically three techniques for working with RDS.

---

4. You can also use RDS to communicate using COM or DCOM, although as we've seen, this is easily achieved using ADO and without the RDS architecture.

The most straightforward is a direct path through the default RDS.DataFactory object to the data source of your choice. This is the path we used in the last section. The client-side DataSource object creates a client-side proxy to represent a DataFactory object on the server (DataFactory objects always run on the server). The DataFactory receives the connection string and command string over HTTP and uses them to create a Recordset, which is then marshalled back to the Data-Source object on the client. The Recordset is unmarshalled to reveal a full-fledged client-side Recordset. If updates take place on the client, these are marshalled back to the server in true disconnected Recordset fashion, along with a connection string. The server creates a new DataFactory object to handle the update. The details of this process were hidden behind the MS Remote Provider in the last section.

This approach of working directly through a data factory on the server has the virtue of simplicity, but otherwise suffers badly from lack of control and, in particular, from the potential it gives for browser users to learn how to sabotage your database by getting connection and security information from the HTML source that should be for your eyes only.

The second technique is to use the RDS Customization Layer, which makes it easy to overcome these weaknesses. When a customization handler is used, the data factory passes all requests for Recordsets and updates through a handler. Microsoft supplies a default handler, which can be controlled by a server administrator making changes to an .ini file on the Web server. This allows you to override connection strings and, more crucially, to replace connection strings that don't contain logon details with connection strings that do. As a result, scripts that get sent to browsers need only contain benign connection details that can be replaced with the real McCoy within the server environment. You can also configure users and specify permitted SQL queries in the same way.

You can either make it compulsory for all RDS requests to specify the use of a customization handler, or simply enable a default handler to be used in all cases. Alternatively, you can write custom handlers. These allow you to track and modify any aspect of a data factory request. You could, for example, specify the maximum number of records to be included in all Recordsets returned by RDS. As you'll see in the next section, it isn't hard to write a customization handler in VB. Microsoft supplies a sample project to get you started.

The third RDS technique is to write your own COM business objects to take the place of the DataFactory. The DataSpace object can create proxies for just about any VB-generated COM object. Typically, such RDS custom business objects return Recordsets (Provider-generated or fabricated) but this shouldn't be seen as a restriction—other types of data can also be returned. Security checks ensure that browsers can't create any kind of COM object on your Web server via RDS. Access rights must be given specifically to each type of business object that can be accessed in this way. (By default, access is already set up for the RDS.DataFactory class.)

Having looked at the architecture of RDS, let's now look at the different RDS components, beginning with the RDS DataControl.

The RDS DataControl

The last section described the data binding capabilities of the RDS DataControl, as well as its Recordset (read-only) and SourceRecordset (write-only) properties. In one sense, ADO programmers need to know little more about the DataControl (because they can do everything else they need via the Recordset itself), but it does have a number of other properties and methods, some of them remaining from a time before ADO Recordsets became as fully featured as they are today.

Let's explore some of the broader RDS DataControl features by taking a look at a DataControl-oriented version of the partsado.htm page we looked at earlier (the one without the Words button and table).

The object definition and HTML body for this version of the page are identical to the previous version. Only the script section is different. Here it is:

```
<script LANGUAGE=VBScript>

Sub Window_OnLoad()
  oDCParts.Server = "http://POLECAT"
  oDCParts.SQL = "SELECT * FROM Parts"
  oDCParts.Connect = "Provider=SQLOLEDB;Database=MuchADO;UID=sa;PWD=;"
  oDCParts.Refresh
End Sub

Sub MoveNext()
  If not oDCParts.Recordset.EOF Then oDCParts.Recordset.MoveNext
End Sub

Sub MovePrevious()
  If not oDCParts.Recordset.BOF Then oDCParts.Recordset.MovePrevious
End Sub

Sub SubmitChanges()
  oDCParts.SubmitChanges
End Sub
</script>
```

There are two things to note about this version of the code. The first is that we don't need to create a Recordset object explicitly. We can simply set properties on the oDCParts DataControl and call its Refresh method. The second thing to note is the behavior of the SubmitChanges subroutine. Instead of calling UpdateBatch on its Recordset, this code uses the DataControl's SubmitChanges method. This performs the same job as UpdateBatch, with MarshalOptions automatically set to adMarshalModifiedOnly (as described in Chapter 7). Like MS Remote, the update instructs the server to perform the update under transactional control so that either all changes work, or all fail.

This code is about as simple as it can be. The DataControl uses a DataSpace object (and a DataFactory on the server) implicitly, hiding the details from the programmer. The next three tables give a full list of the methods, properties, and events of the DataControl.

Table 15-1. DataControl Methods

NAME	DESCRIPTION
Cancel	Cancels a Refresh that is executing asynchronously.
CancelUpdate	Cancels pending changes made to the Recordset prior to calling SubmitChanges.
CreateRecordset	Creates an empty Recordset based on an array of column details (same as building a fabricated Recordset using fds.Append).
Refresh	Requests a new Recordset from the Web server, based on the control's current property settings.
Reset	Applies Filter and Sort settings made using the control's properties (alternatively, the Recordset's Sort and Filter can be used).
SubmitChanges	Marshalls the Recordset to the Web server and triggers a transactional batch update.

Table 15-2. DataControl Properties

NAME	DESCRIPTION
Connect	A connection string to be used on the Web server to connect to a data source.
DataSpace	Not used; maintains backwards compatibility.
ExecuteOptions	One of adcExecSync or adcExecAsync (members of the ADCExecuteOptionEnum enumeration). The default is adcExecAsync.
FetchOptions	One of adcFetchAsync, adcFetchBackground, or adcFetchUpFront (members of the ADCFetchOption-Enum enumeration). The default is adcFetchAsync.
FilterColumn, FilterCriteria, FilterValue	Assigns filter properties to the Recordset, which are applied using Reset (alternatively, the Recordset's Filter can be used).

Table 15-2. DataControl Properties (Continued)

Handler	Specifies a customization handler.
InternetTimeout	A timeout (in milliseconds) for Refresh and SubmitChanges.
ReadyState	Indicates the state of the Recordset during an asynchronous operation. One of adcReadyStateComplete, adcReadyStateInteractive, adcReadyStateLoaded (members of the ADCReadyStateEnum enumeration).
Recordset	Provides read-only access to the control's Recordset.
Server	Identifies the Web server.
SortColumn, SortDirection	Assigns sort properties to the Recordset, which are applied using Reset (alternatively, the Recordset's Sort can be used).
SourceRecordset	Allows a Recordset to be assigned to the control.
SQL	SQL to be passed to the Web server for execution.
URL	URL to an ASP page that returns a Recordset through the ASP Response object (see Chapter 7). This provides one way to hide connection details from the user.

Table 15-3. DataControl Events

NAME	DESCRIPTION
onError	Fires when an error occurs in a DataControl operation.
onReadyStateChange	Fires when the ReadyState property value changes.

The RDS DataSpace

The sole purpose of the DataSpace object is to create a local proxy for a remote object.[5] While it can be used to create proxies using regular COM and DCOM communication, its primary use is to create proxies that can communicate with a stub over HTTP.

The DataSpace object is used by both the RDS DataControl and the ADO MS Remote Provider, so more often than not, it isn't used explicitly. To see it in action, the following script code for our Web page uses a DataSpace object to create a proxy for a DataFactory, which is then used to create the Recordset required by the DataControl:

---

5. Proxies, stubs, and marshalling were described in Chapter 7.

```
<script LANGUAGE=VBScript>
Dim oFactory
Dim sConnect
Sub Window_OnLoad()
  Dim oSpace
  Dim sSQL

  Set oSpace = CreateObject("RDS.DataSpace")
  Set oFactory = oSpace.CreateObject _
              ("RDSServer.DataFactory", _
               "http://POLECAT")
  sSQL = "SELECT * FROM Parts"
  sConnect = "Provider=SQLOLEDB;Database=MuchADO;UID=sa;PWD=;"
  set oDCParts.SourceRecordset = oFactory.Query( sConnect, sSQL)
End Sub

Sub MoveNext()
  If Not oDCParts.Recordset.EOF Then oDCParts.Recordset.MoveNext
End Sub

Sub MovePrevious()
  If Not oDCParts.Recordset.BOF Then oDCParts.Recordset.MovePrevious
End Sub

Sub SubmitChanges()
  oFactory.SubmitChanges sConnect, oDCParts.Recordset
End Sub
</script>
```

Create a local DataSpace **object.**

Use its CreateObject **method to create a remote object over HTTP. Assign a proxy to the remote object to oFactory.**

Call the DataFactory's Query **method to get a Recordset.**

Call the DataFactory's SubmitChanges **method to update the server.**

As you can see here, once the DataSpace has done its job, it can retire from the scene, leaving the browser with a reference to the DataFactory, which can be used to create data and call SubmitChanges. Note that SubmitChanges is being called on the DataFactory object here, rather than on the DataControl. Both support the SubmitChanges method. The DataControl merely passes the call through to the implicit DataFactory object it uses when the Refresh method is called.

The DataSpace has just one method and one property, identified in the following tables.

Table 15-4. DataSpace Method

NAME	DESCRIPTION
CreateObject	Returns a reference (via a proxy) to a remote object.

Table 15-5. DataSpace Property

NAME	DESCRIPTION
InternetTimeOut	A time out (in milliseconds).

The RDSServer DataFactory

Unlike the DataControl and the DataSpace, DataFactory objects always live on the server. The last code example showed pretty much what DataFactory objects do, which is to respond to Query and SubmitChanges method calls. The DataFactory supports two other methods that aren't meant to be used from clients, and the need for them has rather disappeared. The full list of DataFactory methods is listed in the following table.

Table 15-6. DataFactory Methods

NAME	DESCRIPTION
ConvertToString	Allows server-side components to convert a Recordset into a string format for inclusion in an HTML page.
CreateRecordset	Creates an empty Recordset, based on an array of column details (same as building a fabricated Recordset using fds.Append).
Query	Returns a disconnected Recordset.
SubmitChanges	Performs a transactional batch update.

DataFactory objects have no properties or events. They are stateless and are destroyed after each method call. They are managed MTS-fashion within IIS, so that client references are maintained between method calls even though the objects themselves are not.

RDS allows clients to create DataFactory objects, which can be used to retrieve any data available through ADO. If you are happy to allow people to access your servers like this, or you have set up appropriate security by other means, then this is fine. If you want to stop anyone from being able to create DataFactory objects, then the Registry key shown in Figure 15-4 should be removed from your server.

The subkeys of ADCLaunch define those ProgIDs that the server will allow remote DataSpaces to use to create objects; in Figure 15-4 this means RDSServer.DataFactory. After making changes, IIS needs to be restarted for the changes to take effect.

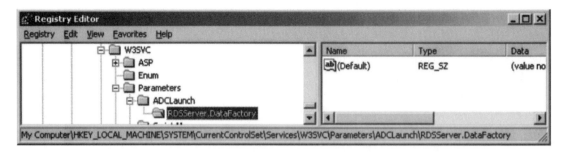

Figure 15-4. Enabling and disabling the DataFactory component

The MS Remote Provider

ADO developers can avoid using RDS components by using the MS Remote Provider, which creates Recordsets through the RDS architecture using a familiar ADO programming style. This means that RDS can be used in standard VB programs if required, and this allows Recordsets to be returned to any client that has access to your Web server.

This is an immensely powerful way to provide data to any users who have Internet access, even if you don't want to provide a browser-based front end. If you built a VB application that retrieved data using MS Remote, you would still need to distribute your VB program, but you wouldn't need to set up database access, install Providers, or worry about additional networking or communication issues.

When MS Remote first appeared in ADO, it wasn't a genuine Provider, but just a switch that persuaded Recordsets to behave in a different way. Since ADO 2.1, it has functioned properly as a Provider, and it supports a number of dynamic Connection properties that can either be added into a connection string or accessed via cn.Properties. MS Remote provides the following dynamic properties:

Table 15-7. MS Remote Provider's Dynamic Connection Properties

DYNAMIC PROPERTY	DESCRIPTION
DFMode	Used to specify which version of DataFactory should be created. Can be one of the following valid string values: "25", "21", "20", or "15" which map to a version of ADO (for example "25" maps to ADO 2.5).
Current DFMode	The actual version number of the DataFactory used on the server.
Handler	The name of a server-side customization handler to be used.
Internet Timeout	Timeout in milliseconds. (The default is five minutes.)

Table 15-7. MS Remote Provider's Dynamic Connection Properties (Continued)

DYNAMIC PROPERTY	DESCRIPTION
Remote Provider	The name of the Provider to be used on the server.
Remote Server	The name of the server and protocol to be used to connect to the server.

Any of these properties can be used in connection strings used with DataFactory Query or DataControl Refresh, as well as with MS Remote.

In This Section

We explored the architecture of RDS on both the client and the Web server. We also looked at the RDS.DataControl, RDS.DataSpace, and RDSServer.DataFactory components, as well as the workings of the MS Remote Provider.

RDS Customization Handlers

Like so many powerful things, RDS is open to abuse, and wise people will want to control how users can make use of the default DataFactory object. This is particularly true in Internet scenarios where literally anyone can potentially access your server. Dishing out user IDs and passwords in HTML files is going to disappoint some hackers (it's the challenge of breaking into your database that appeals to them, rather than the pleasure of dropping tables arbitrarily), but others will think you are asking for trouble and will be happy to oblige.

RDS allows you to place customization handlers between the DataFactory and any Connections and Recordsets it creates. This makes it very simple to control access and to substitute connection strings and command strings for strings of your own. This functionality is provided by the default customization handler that Microsoft provides. You can go further and create your own customization handler to provide a very high level of control over what can and cannot be done using the DataFactory object.

First let's to look at how customization handlers are invoked, and then let's see what you can do with them.

Handlers can be specified in an HTML file or in ADO code that connects using MS Remote. For example, an RDS DataControl's Handler property can be set with the ProgID of the Handler to use

```
dc.Handler = "MSDFMAP.Handler"
```

or an ADO connection string can include a Handler key and value; for example:

```
rs.ActiveConnection = _
    "Provider=MS Remote;" & _
    "Remote Server=http://POLECAT;" & _
    "Remote Provider=SQLOLEDB;Database=MuchADO;UID=sa;PWD=;" & _
    "Handler=MSDFMAP.Handler"
```

In either of these cases, the DataFactory will use the Handler ProgID to create a Handler object that will have the opportunity of performing various checks and modifications before the target Provider is contacted. MSDFMAP.Handler is the default handler provided when either ADO 2+ or SQLServer 7+ is installed. Handlers can also be provided with parameters as part of the handler specification, permitting another level of customization, if required.

Specifying handlers in this way makes it possible for different pages or applications to use different handlers. However, it also makes it look like the use of a handler is optional, which rather defeats the purpose of using handlers to apply control. On the Web server, Registry settings can be used to insist that handlers are used.

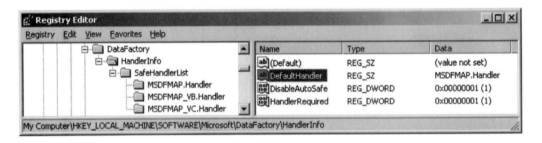

Figure 15-5. Configuring customization handlers

Here you can see that the HandlerInfo Registry key can be used to specify that a handler is required by setting the HandlerRequired property. All DataFactory method calls will then go through a handler. It can also provide the ProgID of a default handler that will be used if a handler isn't explicitly specified. If the Disable-AutoSafe property is set, then only handlers listed under the SafeHandlerList key will be permitted.

Now that we know how to make sure that a handler is always used, it's time to look at what can be done with the default handler, MSDFMAP.Handler.

The default handler is configured using an INI file called MSDFMAP.INI, located in the c:\WINNT directory. The file can have a number of different sections. A very simple INI file might look like this:

```
[connect default]
Access=ReadOnly
Connect="Provider=SQLOLEDB;Database=MuchADO;UID=sa;PWD=;"
```

This means that all access to any data through a DataFactory will be read-only and will use the connection string specified (regardless of what the request asks for).

My HTML page can now be coded without needing to provide a connection string:

```
sSQL = "SELECT * FROM Parts"
sConnect = ""
Set oDCParts.SourceRecordset = oFactory.Query( sConnect, sSQL)
```

The handler will simply replace the connection string supplied to the DataFactory with one of its own. Because I have set access to be read-only, any attempt to update via RDS will fail.

I am now in control of my server and am no longer sending logon information out to unknown users. However, it's more likely that I want to have different types of access for different applications or databases. I can do this by defining names for different connection requirements. For example, if I change my INI file to this:

```
[connect default]
Access=NoAccess

[connect PARTS]
Access=ReadWrite
Connect="Provider=SQLOLEDB;Database=MuchADO;UID=sa;PWD=;"
```

I can ensure that only requests for a connection called PARTS will be permitted. All other requests will be refused. If the PARTS connection is requested, read-write access will be permitted and the specified connection string will be substituted for PARTS.

To use this PARTS data source, my connection string would look like this:

```
sSQL = "SELECT * FROM Parts"
sConnect = "Data Source=PARTS"
Set oDCParts.SourceRecordset = oFactory.Query( sConnect, sSQL)
```

As you can see, I can very simply set up different data source sections in the INI file, hide all connection details, and be in control of all connection requests.

We can just as easily apply control over which command strings are permitted. For example, adding the following section to the INI file will ensure that only "named" commands are allowed:

```
[sql default]
sql = " "
```

This section effectively says, "If there is no section in the INI file for a given command string, replace it with an invalid string that is going to fail when executed."

We can then add sections to the INI file for the command strings we wish to succeed. For example:

```
[sql getAllParts]
sql = "SELECT * FROM Parts"
```

will perform a valid command string substitution for the following HTML code:

```
sSQL = "getAllParts"
sConnect = "Data Source=PARTS"
Set oDCParts.SourceRecordset = oFactory.Query( sConnect, sSQL)
```

The handler will convert `getAllParts` into the appropriate SQL string. All other command strings will be rejected. No user is given information about the structure of our database because we don't show them any SQL. This approach will also cope with parameterized statements and stored procedures.

Currently, while our parts query works, the words query on the page that calls the sp_WordList stored procedure will fail. This is because it isn't a recognized command, and therefore, the default substitution will take place.

We can correct this by adding the following section to the INI file:

```
[sql getWordsForParts]
sql = "sp_WordList (?,?,?)"
```

We can then recode the Words subroutine as follows:

```
Sub Words()
 RDCWords.SQL = "getWordsForParts ('" & Part.Value & "',6,6)"
 RDCWords.Refresh
End Sub
```

The INI file will permit this call and will substitute `getWordsForParts` with the stored procedure name before contacting ADO.

In addition to the "connect" and "sql" sections, the default handler can also process "user" sections in the INI file to control access for different users, and a "logs" section to record errors.

Instead of exploring these options, we'll complete this section by taking a look at what is involved in writing your own customization handler. This may sound as though it's likely to be a daunting task, but in fact, it's easy for two reasons:

1. The interface that customization handlers need to implement is very simple.

2. Microsoft provides a sample VB customization handler that works with the same INI file structure that the default handler uses.

ADO 2.1 introduced some important changes to the way that customization handlers work. Prior to 2.1, customization handlers were required to return a Recordset when called during a DataFactory Query method, and they were passed a Recordset during a DataFactory SubmitChanges method. This gave considerable scope to the handler writer to modify and process each Recordset. ADO 2.1 introduced a simpler mechanism whereby the handler is only responsible for creating the Connection object. Using this approach, only the command string, and not the entire Recordset, could be manipulated by the handler. This simplified approach has some modest performance gains but comes at the cost of losing some of the original flexibility of handlers.

The new approach is used by default for clients using ADO 2.1 or greater. However, the original approach is still supported—you simply need to include the DFMode argument in the RDS connection string (as discussed earlier) with a value of "20". To see what can be achieved through handlers, let's explore the original (still supported) functionality. If you want to use only the newer approach, you'll need to write a custom DataFactory to do what we'll be doing in the remainder of this section.

To see what can be achieved via customization handlers, let's extend the existing functionality of the sql section in the INI file to allow us to place an upper limit on the number of records that a given query can return. This is a useful feature in its own right, as it's often inappropriate to return thousands of records over a dial-up connection, but it also demonstrates how many other types of customizations could be handled, including (but not limited to):

*   Setting other Recordset properties to control or optimize the application.

*   Performing update validation. Your handler could call a COM object that performs validation on a batch update Recordset before allowing the update to take place. You could store the ProgID of the object in the INI file and pass a Recordset to it during the update process.

*   Performing query validation. Using the same technique as for update validation, you could check or modify arguments passed to stored procedures or parameterized SQL statements.

*   Writing your own logging and security features.

A handler is called either when a handler is specified in a connection string or when a default handler is specified via Registry settings on the Web server. A handler is required to implement three methods as defined by the MSDFHDL.IDataFactory-Handler interface. To use this interface, you need to set a reference to MSDFHDL, which resides in c:\mssdk\samples\dbmsg\dataaccess\rds\handler\vb\msdfhdl.tlb.[6] The interface contains the following three methods:

- **GetRecordset(conn As String, args As String, query As String) As Recordset**: This method is called during a DataFactory Query method. It returns the Recordset that goes back to the browser. GetRecordset is called only for ADO 2.0 clients or where DFMode = "20".

- **Reconnect(conn As String, args As String, pRS As Recordset)**: This method is called during a DataFactory SubmitChanges method. Its task is to connect pRS to an active Connection so that it can be updated by the DataFactory. Reconnect is called only for ADO 2.0 clients or where DFMode = "20".

- **OpenConnection(conn As String, args As String, lFlags As Long, pQuery As String) As _Connection**: This method is called when an ADO Connection object is requested using the MS Remote Provider. OpenConnection is the default method used (instead of GetRecordset and Reconnect) for ADO 2.1+ clients.

As you can imagine, it doesn't require very many lines of code to implement these three methods and to create a simple handler. However, to provide the kind of functionality that the default handler provides would involve a fair amount of INI file-processing code. We can avoid writing this code by using the sample VB customization handler provided by Microsoft. It resides in the same directory as the MSDFHDL type library mentioned previously.

When working with this sample code, be aware of three things:

1. *It assumes that all command strings (such as getAllParts) have brackets after them.* Therefore, you will either need to change command strings in HTML to getAllParts() or modify the ParseSql subroutine supplied in the code that makes this assumption.

2. *The sample code has a debug flag that is on by default.* You can change this in the Initialize event procedure for the Handler class.

3. *The project has the Unattended Execution option set on.* This means that the MsgBox statements used by the debug code get written to the NT Event Log.

---

6. You'll need the Microsoft Platform SDK to have access to this type library.

These points aside, the code is pretty simple. There are three source files in addition to the VB Project file (.vbp):

1. **The Handler Class**: This class implements the MSDFHDL.IDataFactory-Handler interface and is the Public class of the project.

2. **Module1**: This is a support library used by the Handler class.

3. **The Events Class**: This class exists to allow you to write ADO Event code for the Recordsets and Connections processed by the Handler.

In order to make our required change (to impose an upper limit on the size of a Recordset), we need to modify the Recordset returned by the Handler so that it only creates a specified number of records. The request for the Recordset comes through the GetRecordset method (described earlier), which itself calls an internal method called Execute. Here's Microsoft's code for this Execute method (the debug code has been stripped out):

```
Private Sub Execute(ByVal CommandText As String)
    Dim origCommand As String

    origCommand = CommandText
    ModifySqlViaIni CommandText

    evh.rs.CursorLocation = adUseClient
    evh.rs.Open CommandText, evh.conn,, adLockBatchOptimistic
End Sub
```

Execute calls the ModifySqlViaIni subroutine, which will use the INI file to replace a command string with a modified SQL string in the manner we've been exploring in this section. It then uses this modified command to execute a Recordset stored in the rs property of an Event object (evh). This will be the Recordset that is returned to the RDS client.

Our version of Execute will pass an extra argument to ModifySqlViaIni so that we can retrieve a MaxRecords value from the INI file in the same section as the replacement SQL. We'll then use this value to set the rs.MaxRecords property prior to opening the Recordset. Here's our modified Execute code (changes in bold):

```
Private Sub Execute(ByVal CommandText As String)
    Dim origCommand As String
    Dim lMax As Long

    origCommand = CommandText
```

```
                    ModifySqlViaIni CommandText, lMax

                    evh.rs.CursorLocation = adUseClient
                    If lMax > 0 Then evh.rs.MaxRecords = lMax   ◄────── set the Recordset's
                                                                         MaxRecords property

                    evh.rs.Open CommandText, evh.conn, , adLockBatchOptimistic

                End Sub
```

The Microsoft-supplied ModifySqlViaIni looks like this:

```
Public Sub ModifySqlViaIni(ByRef sql As String)
        Dim section As String
        Dim str As String
        Dim func As String
        Dim args As String
                                                        extract the command name
                                                        and the arguments into
        ParseSql sql, func, args   ◄───────────────     separate strings

        'Compute the section name.
                                                        work out the INI file section
        section = "sql " + GetSqlSectionName(func) ◄─── to use either func or default

        'Modify the sql string.
        str = GetIniString(section, "Sql") ◄──────      get the SQL substitution
        If str <> "" Then                               from the INI file

            sql = SubstituteParameters(str, args) ◄───  add back any arguments

        End If
End Sub
```

Our modified version is this:

```
Public Sub ModifySqlViaIni(ByRef sql As String, _
                Optional ByRef MaxRecords As Long)
        Dim section As String
        Dim str As String
        Dim func As String
        Dim args As String

        Call ParseSql sql, func, args

        'Compute the section name.
        section = "sql " + GetSqlSectionName(func)
```

```
    'Modify the sql string.
    str = GetIniString(section, "Sql")
    MaxRecords = CLng(GetIniString(section, "MaxRecords"))
    If str <> "" Then
        sql = SubstituteParameters(str, args)
    End If
End Sub
```

This code simply reads a MaxRecords key from the appropriate section in the INI file.

Once this project is compiled, three further changes are required before the new feature can take effect. First we need to modify the INI file:

```
[sql getWordsForParts]
sql = "sp_WordList (?,?,?)"
MaxRecords = 5                    ◀─────────────  include a MaxRecords key
```

Here, we ensure that the word list is never more than five items in length.

Next we need to change the default handler via the Registry (to use our new component) and restart IIS. Finally, we need to include the DFMode argument in the HTML page's connection strings:

```
Sub Window_OnLoad()
  RDCParts.Server = "http://POLECAT"
  RDCParts.SQL = "getAllParts()"
  RDCParts.Connect = "Data Source=PARTS;DFMode=20"
  RDCParts.Refresh

  RDCWords.Server = "http://POLECAT"
  RDCWords.Connect = "Data Source=PARTS;DFMode=20"
End Sub
```

We are now able to control how much data is returned for any or all Recordsets generated via RDS, simply by configuring an INI file.

We can choose whether to make this behavior optional by choosing how the handler is coded. If we only want to apply this check for certain pages, we can include DFMode=20 in the connection strings for those pages. All other pages that come from clients with ADO 2.1 or greater installed will bypass the restriction by calling OpenConnection. If we want to insist that this restriction is applied, then OpenConnection can be coded to reject any request for Recordsets where a MaxRecords value has been specified in the INI file. Those pages would then need to be changed to use DFMode=20 before they could be used.

We saw how the default customization handler can be used to control access to our Web site and to hide passwords and user IDs from users. We also saw how to write customized handlers.

Using RDS with Custom Business Objects

If the default RDSServer.DataFactory(with or without a customization handler) proves not to provide the functionality you require, RDS supports the creation of custom business objects, accessible from IIS via RDS.DataSpace objects.

A custom business object is nothing more than a standard in-process COM or COM+ component hosted by IIS. It's accessible over HTTP from a DataSpace object in exactly the same way that DataFactory objects are accessible.

Custom business objects typically provide a set of methods that return disconnected ADO Recordsets and a set of methods that receive ADO Recordsets containing changes, which optionally perform some preprocessing on the Recordset before performing a batch update under transactional control. However, they aren't limited to exchanging Recordsets and can communicate using a very wide range of data types and structures.

All custom business objects accessed via RDS run in a COM+ or MTS context provided by IIS, and therefore, have access to a ContextObject . This is true even if you don't explicitly install the business objects in COM+ or MTS. By default, they are not transactional and do need to be installed in a COM+ Application or an MTS Package in order to make use of the transactional services provided by these environments. However, regardless of whether or not they are transactional, custom business objects are deactivated after each method call—they are, therefore, stateless objects.

If the last two paragraphs haven't made too much sense to you, then it's probably because you haven't read Chapter 7 (Disconnected Recordsets) and Chapter 14 (ADO, DNA, MTS, and COM+). Ninety-nine percent of what you need to know about RDS custom business objects was covered in those chapters, and everything in them is relevant to RDS. The only additional piece of information you require is how to create Registry entries that inform IIS that it's safe to create these objects via an RDS.DataSpace request.

To see RDS custom business objects in action, let's create a COM class with a ProgID of RDSCustomServer.MuchADO. The MuchADO class will have two methods: getParts and updateParts. Here's the code for getParts:

```
Public Function getParts() As ADODB.Recordset
On Error GoTo ErrH
Set getParts = New ADODB.Recordset
getParts.CursorLocation = adUseClient
```

```
getParts.LockType = adLockBatchOptimistic
getParts.ActiveConnection = _
    "Provider=SQLOLEDB;Database=MuchADO;UID=sa;PWD=;"
getParts.Source = "select * from Parts"

getParts.Open

If GetObjectContext.IsInTransaction Then
  GetObjectContext.SetComplete
End If
Exit Function
ErrH:
If GetObjectContext.IsInTransaction Then
  GetObjectContext.SetAbort
  Set getParts = Nothing
End If
End Function
```

This is standard disconnected Recordset code. The updateParts code has no surprises either. The project has an MTS/COM+ reference set and uses the context object to test whether or not the component is running as part of a transaction. If it is, it behaves in the expected manner.

It's entirely up to you to decide whether or not to install the compiled component in a COM+ Application or MTS Package. As we discussed in Chapter 14, there is little to be lost in doing so and a lot to be gained.

Either way, we have one final step to take before the component can be called using RDS. We need to register the component as being safe for RDS to create, which we can do by creating the following Registry key:

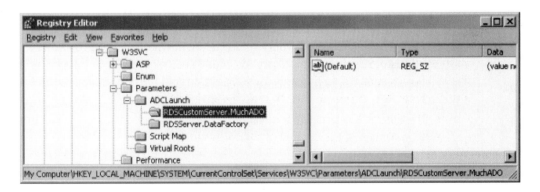

Figure 15-6. Enabling and disabling the custom business objects

The component's ProgID is RDSCustomServer.MuchADO. Creating a key for it under the ADCLaunch key as shown marks it as safe for use by RDS. Once IIS is restarted, it will know that this is a creatable component.

The following HTML script code shows how this component can be called:

```
Sub Window_OnLoad()
  Dim oSpace
  Dim sSQL

  Set oSpace = CreateObject("RDS.DataSpace")
  Set oCustom = oSpace.CreateObject _
                    ("RDSCustomServer.MuchADO", _
                     "http://POLECAT")

  set oDCParts.SourceRecordset = oCustom.getParts
End Sub
```

In this case, we've assigned the Recordset returned by getParts to the RDS.Data-Control. In a similar manner, we could exploit DHTML capabilities and request other data types (such as strings and numbers) from the business object, which could be assigned to HTML buttons and text elements in a very dynamic way.

Programming with DHTML and RDS is not so very different from program-ming a standard VB Form, except that the data services are being provided over HTTP via a Web server. Visual Basic 7 takes this concept a great deal further.

In This Section

We saw how the RDS architecture can be used with a wide range of server-based COM objects to supply data to browsers over HTTP.

Summary

ADO cements together two Web-based technologies:

- RDS allows Web pages to request Recordsets and other data over HTTP from IIS servers.

- DHTML allows a Web page's elements to be modified dynamically without needing to rebuild the page. Specifically, it allows Recordset data to be bound to Web page elements in much the same way that data aware con-trols can be bound on a standard VB Form.

The combination of DHTML and RDS is a very powerful way of delivering COM-based services over the Internet. The ability of ADO Recordsets to be marshalled and updated in batches extends this capability significantly.

In one sense, RDS is a smaller technology than it used to be. This is only because much of the functionality that was originally built for RDS is now a central part of ADO. Many of the methods and properties of the RDS.DataControl and the RDSServer.DataFactory no longer have a role because ADO code can be used instead.

In a different sense though, RDS has been a pioneering, revolutionary technology. You have seen how easy it is for a Web-enabled client to talk to a server-based object over HTTP using the RDS architecture. The result is a far more interactive and responsive experience for a user than can ever be achieved through an ASP-based approach. It's also a stepping stone to a broader model of distributed computing.

CHAPTER 16

Multidimensional ADO (ADOMD)

WHEN YOU ARE CARRYING OUT an operational task, it's good to focus on just those things that are needed to get the task done. Taking a booking for theater tickets requires knowledge of seat availability, ticket price, and a customer's ability to pay. You don't want to be worrying about what types of ice cream to sell at the time; otherwise you may make a mistake ("That's two seats for next Tuesday in row J, with chocolate sauce"). When writing a computer program to support the booking process, it makes sense to write the specific queries and transactions required for that process.

There comes a time though, when you need to sit back and really think about what you want the theater to be doing next year: What types of shows should be put on? What about pricing? Where should advertising appear? Is the Web site really working? Where are the bottlenecks? Hopefully, you have been collecting the data needed to make these decisions, but even if you have, you still will have certain problems:

- More than likely, you have so much data that you don't know where to start. You have data about every sale, every production, every customer. You can't possibly start analyzing data at this raw level. You need to start with a high-level view and have the ability to drill down to examine areas of interest in detail.

- There are so many dimensions to this data. You could ask the IT department to run some huge queries to generate high-level reports, but which way should the data be sliced? Do you break it down by production, time of year, price, customer profile, advertising money spent, or purchase method? Any of these dimensions could yield the insights you need, but you won't really know how you want to slice the data until you have started analyzing it. And you can't start analyzing until you have decided how to slice it.

Most organizations face exactly the same problems, although typically in a more complex scenario than a single theater. Making the right decisions is essential in increasingly competitive markets. Spotting a new trend can create whole new business areas.

To solve these problems, businesses have been creating data warehouses. It doesn't make sense running huge analytical queries against production databases. For one thing, it brings the rest of the business to a halt as analytical queries gobble up server time that should be involved in selling things. For another, the data in production systems is typically not stored in a way that suits analytical processing. Therefore, data warehouses are used to create huge repositories of static data for analysis purposes, leaving production systems to get on with running the business.

The data storage and querying techniques that work so well for operational purposes (relational databases and SQL) aren't strictly appropriate for analytical work, and so over time, new technology has been developed (or just as likely, old technology has been extended) to support this task specifically. Just as it's common to use the abbreviation OLTP to describe Online Transaction Processing and the technology used to support it, so the acronym OLAP is used to describe Online Analytical Processing and the specific technology used to meet its needs.

OLAP has been around for well over a decade, but has become big business as many organizations have started to regard their data warehouses as major corporate assets and their ability to extract meaningful information from them as an essential business weapon.

Where does ADO come into all this? SQL doesn't meet the needs of OLAP systems, and two-dimensional Recordsets aren't always an appropriate means of manipulating its results. A whole new set of standards has been required to prevent the new OLAP marketplace from developing a range of incompatible tools all its own. The SQL-like language called MDX (Multidimensional Expressions) has been developed for creating OLAP queries. MDX is capable of generating results with more than just the two dimensions (records and Fields, or rows and columns) that standard Recordsets support. OLAP data is truly multidimensional, and an appropriate access and manipulation service was needed to work with it, which is what ADOMD was designed to do. As part of Microsoft's vision of Universal Data Access, ADO should be able to cope with more than just tabular data, and ADOMD was created to take ADO into the world of OLAP. The good news is that it isn't just

Microsoft that believes in ADOMD. The OLAP world knew it needed a standard, and many of the major vendors have rallied behind ADOMD.

OLAP software has traditionally been expensive. Even so, it's a growing market, and Microsoft is determined to have a presence and to reduce the cost of entry to encourage even more rapid growth. SQLServer 7 ships with a sophisticated OLAP data engine and ADOMD-compliant Provider software. Because this will be the most accessible OLAP engine for most readers, this chapter will concentrate on the use of ADOMD with SQLServer 7. Also, to avoid the need to design and create an OLAP database, we'll make use of the sample database that is set up when SQLServer 7 OLAP Services are installed.[1] In fact, Microsoft has gone to great lengths to make it as easy as possible to transform regular relational data into an OLAP data warehouse, providing wizards to simplify the process. However, this book is no more about OLAP database design than it is about relational database design. Our objective is to understand how OLAP data differs from relational data and how to use ADOMD to work with it to create entirely new types of applications.

OLAP and Multidimensional Data

OLAP allows users to manipulate data with multiple dimensions and to drill down to explore data at different levels of detail. Users can perform these tasks interactively, without having to wait for reports to run or new queries to be set up. The amount of data at low levels can be vast, which means that the quantity of calculations required to generate the higher levels of aggregations is also vast. Clearly, OLAP puts substantial demands on hardware and software, which is why special OLAP software technology is typically used in data warehouses.

While one of the aims of OLAP is to make it easy for users to experiment with different dimensions of data, manipulating multidimensional data is a challenge for developers who are more familiar with two-dimensional row and column data. The aim of this section is to explain OLAP concepts to relational database developers.

A relational database has a schema, which (among other things) describes the tables that comprise the database. Each table is a two-dimensional structure, with rows and columns. One of the strengths of SQL, however, is that many tables are involved in a query. The Recordset that the query generates will always have a two-dimensional structure, with rows and columns (or records and Fields in ADO terminology), just like the tables from which it is derived. There is, therefore, a clear relationship between the schema, queries, and Recordsets, as shown in Figure 16-1.

In OLAP databases, data is organized into dimensions. A set of dimensions is called a Cube. This is true regardless of how many dimensions there are, but it naturally makes most sense to call it a Cube when there are three dimensions of data. The sample database that is installed with SQLServer 7 OLAP Services is

---

1. The SQLServer 7 CD contains an option to install the OLAP Server and set up the sample database.

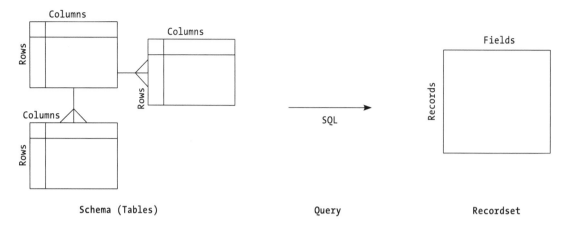

Figure 16-1. Relational data processing

called FoodMart. This database contains a Cube called Sales, which represents sales data in a large chain of grocery stores. The Sales Cube has thirteen dimensions.[2] Here are some of them:

- Product (such as food or drink)

- Time

- Store (geographical location)

- Store Type (size)

- Gender (of customer making purchase)

- Yearly Income (of customer)

At the intersection of all dimensions is a single piece of sales data. At the intersection of all but one dimension is a square containing data (basically a table). At the intersection of all but two dimensions is a cube of data, and so on.

If all this does is bring back vague and unhappy memories of geometry lessons, don't despair. Just as no one can think sensibly about all the data in a complex relational database at once, so no one can think sensibly about sales data in thirteen-dimensional space.[3] Just as we run SQL queries to get a specific cut of relational data, we can run MDX queries to get a specific cut of Cube data that we can then

---

2. This includes a special dimension called Measures, which we'll meet later.

3. No one I'd choose to have dinner with, anyway.

analyze. The only difference is that the result of running an MDX query is a multi-dimensional structure called a Cellset.

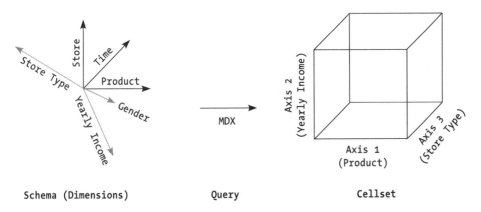

Figure 16-2. OLAP data processing

In this diagram, an MDX query has been used to create a Cellset with three dimensions. You'll see shortly what these queries look like. For now, just think of the Cellset as containing a subset of multidimensional data that we can work with, in the same way a Recordset contains a subset of data from a set of tables.

The Cellset shown in Figure 16-2 contains three axes.[4] Each cell is an intersection of the three axes. For example, if you move across the Product axis until you find Drink, then move along the Yearly Income axis until you find $70K–$90K, and then move along the Store Type axis until you find Mid-Size Grocery, you will find a single figure telling you how much drink has been sold to customers in that income bracket by mid-size grocery stores.

A single cell is not in itself very interesting. And while a three-dimensional cube of data may be easy enough to think about, it's still hard to display on a computer screen. You start developing an appreciation of what you can do with a cube when you start slicing it. Take a slice out of a cube (along any axis) and you get a square (or table) of data.

For example, the items along the Product axis include Drink and Food. If you take a slice along the Product axis at the Food item, you will get a table of Yearly Income and Store Type data, containing the sales figures for all Food items. Figure 16-3 shows what

---

4. That's the plural of axis, not the tool for chopping wood.

it looks like when the Food slice is taken out of the cube, and this table (square) of data is displayed in a conventional grid.

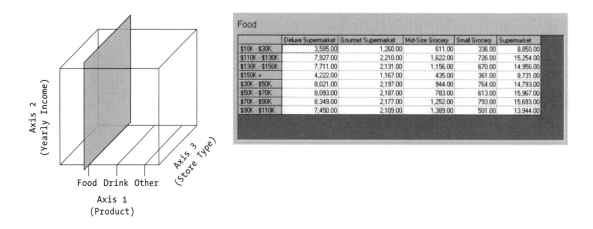

Food					
	Deluxe Supermarket	Gourmet Supermarket	Mid-Size Grocery	Small Grocery	Supermarket
$10K - $30K	3,585.00	1,260.00	611.00	336.00	8,850.00
$110K - $130K	7,927.00	2,210.00	1,622.00	726.00	15,254.00
$130K - $150K	7,711.00	2,131.00	1,156.00	670.00	14,956.00
$150K +	4,222.00	1,167.00	435.00	361.00	8,731.00
$30K - $50K	8,021.00	2,197.00	944.00	764.00	14,793.00
$50K - $70K	8,093.00	2,187.00	783.00	613.00	15,967.00
$70K - $90K	8,349.00	2,177.00	1,252.00	793.00	15,693.00
$90K - $110K	7,450.00	2,109.00	1,389.00	501.00	13,944.00

Figure 16-3. Slicing the Cellset using the Food member

The next slice contains a table of data for Drink sales:

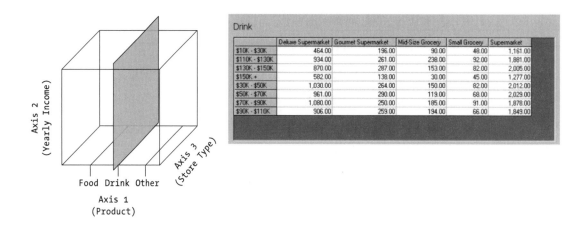

Drink					
	Deluxe Supermarket	Gourmet Supermarket	Mid-Size Grocery	Small Grocery	Supermarket
$10K - $30K	464.00	196.00	90.00	48.00	1,161.00
$110K - $130K	934.00	261.00	238.00	92.00	1,881.00
$130K - $150K	870.00	287.00	153.00	82.00	2,005.00
$150K +	582.00	138.00	30.00	45.00	1,277.00
$30K - $50K	1,030.00	264.00	150.00	82.00	2,012.00
$50K - $70K	961.00	290.00	119.00	68.00	2,029.00
$70K - $90K	1,080.00	250.00	185.00	91.00	1,878.00
$90K - $110K	906.00	259.00	194.00	66.00	1,849.00

Figure 16-4. Slicing the Cellset using the Drink member

The same Cube can be sliced along any axis. For example, a slice along the Yearly Income axis would look like this:

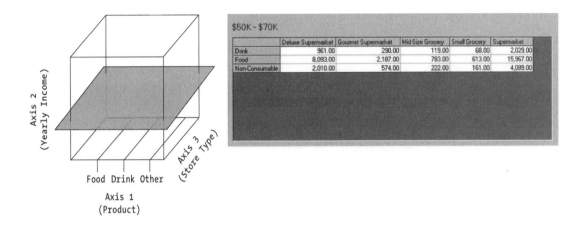

$50K - $70K					
	Deluxe Supermarket	Gourmet Supermarket	Mid-Size Grocery	Small Grocery	Supermarket
Drink	961.00	290.00	119.00	68.00	2,029.00
Food	8,093.00	2,187.00	783.00	613.00	15,967.00
Non-Consumable	2,010.00	574.00	222.00	161.00	4,089.00

Figure 16-5. Slicing the Cellset using the $50K–$70K member

The key to the success of OLAP is that while IT folk worry about the implications of multidimensional data and manipulation, users just mix and match the dimensions they are interested in and get on with analyzing data and making better business decisions. The multidimensional nature of the data simply makes manipulating data in this flexible way very easy.

The other aspect of OLAP that users really appreciate is the ability to drill down through different levels of detail on any dimension. When a Cube is set up, all the dimensions are defined for it. For each dimension, one or more hierarchies are created. A hierarchy consists of a number of levels, each level representing a finer level of detail in the data. When an MDX query is generated, the query specifies which level or levels of data are required.

For example, the hierarchy for the Product dimension contains the following levels:

- Product (top level)

- Product Family (such as Food or Drink)

- Product Department (such as Produce, Meat, Dairy, or Canned Foods)

- Product Category (such as Specialty, Fruit, or Vegetables)

- Product Subcategory (such as Nuts)

- Brand Name (such as Ebony, High Top, or Tell Tale)

- Product Name (such as Ebony Almonds or Ebony Walnuts)

A query that takes the $30K–$50K Yearly Income slice and expands the Food item on the Product axis would look like this:

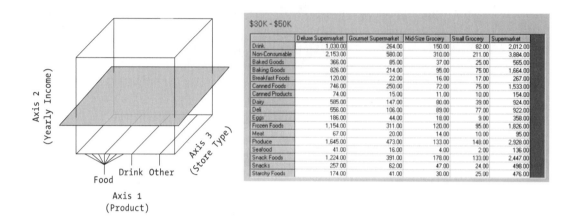

$30K - $50K

	Deluxe Supermarket	Gourmet Supermarket	Mid-Size Grocery	Small Grocery	Supermarket
Drink	1,030.00	264.00	150.00	82.00	2,012.00
Non-Consumable	2,153.00	580.00	310.00	211.00	3,884.00
Baked Goods	366.00	85.00	37.00	25.00	565.00
Baking Goods	826.00	214.00	95.00	75.00	1,664.00
Breakfast Foods	120.00	22.00	16.00	17.00	267.00
Canned Foods	746.00	250.00	72.00	75.00	1,533.00
Canned Products	74.00	15.00	11.00	10.00	154.00
Dairy	585.00	147.00	80.00	39.00	924.00
Deli	556.00	106.00	89.00	77.00	922.00
Eggs	186.00	44.00	18.00	9.00	358.00
Frozen Foods	1,154.00	311.00	120.00	95.00	1,826.00
Meat	67.00	20.00	14.00	10.00	95.00
Produce	1,645.00	473.00	133.00	148.00	2,928.00
Seafood	41.00	16.00	4.00	2.00	136.00
Snack Foods	1,224.00	391.00	178.00	133.00	2,447.00
Snacks	257.00	62.00	47.00	24.00	498.00
Starchy Foods	174.00	41.00	30.00	25.00	476.00

Axis 2 (Yearly Income)

Axis 3 (Store Type)

Food Drink Other

Axis 1 (Product)

Figure 16-6. Drilling down the Food hierarchy

A single query can build a Cellset with data from multiple levels for the same axis. A Cellset created in this way can provide the user with a range of drill down and data aggregation options without even needing to build another query.

You may be wondering why dimensions can have more than one hierarchy. In fact, in most cases, dimensions will have a single hierarchy, but there are situations in which a user might want to break down a dimension using more than one classification scheme. For example, consider the Time dimension. One hierarchy may have levels such as Calendar Year, Calendar Quarter, and Calendar Month, while another one may contain Fiscal Year, Fiscal Quarter, and Fiscal Month.

So far, we've discussed data stored in a Cube, but we haven't said anything about what that data is. All the data we have presented so far has been Unit Sales data for the FoodMart grocery chain. However, you may wish to present other types of sales information, such as Profit, Cost, and Net Sales. This is possible by using Measures. The Sales Cube in the FoodMart database defines the following measures:

- Profit

- Sales Average

- Sales Count

- Store Cost

- Store Sales

- Store Sales Net

- Unit Sales

Any of these measures can be chosen when creating a Cellset, although we'll be working with the default measure, Unit Sales, most of the time. The full set of Measures simply form another dimension to the Cube, which can be included in MDX queries just like any other dimension.

Part of the process of coming to terms with the OLAP concept is realizing that most Cubes will have huge computational demands. You can do the math yourself. Seven dimensions with ten items along each dimension require ten million cells. Make that thirteen dimensions and we're talking a lot of data. Now add in a few hierarchies. Does a query that returns data for a Food slice have to recurse through every level to add up the sales figures for each product, or does the OLAP server precalculate all the required aggregations? Needless to say, OLAP vendors have produced clever solutions to deal with these issues, and a description of them is well beyond our scope. However, it's worth bearing in mind that due to various optimization techniques, the explosion of data and calculations that results from having many dimensions and levels is not as devastating as you might think, although it does still pose challenges for Cube designers.

In This Section

You were introduced to the basic concepts and terminology of multidimensional data. A Cube can be made up of many dimensions and running an MDX query generates a Cellset with multiple axes. Cube data can be sliced in different ways, and hierarchies provide drill-down capability.

The MDX Command Language

MDX is a powerful language that would easily require two or three chapters to describe in detail. For our purposes, a simple overview will be sufficient, but don't finish this chapter thinking that you have seen all there is to MDX.

MDX is an SQL-like command language that is used for building Cellsets from Cubes. You use it to specify which data you want to see on each axis you create, and to add filters, calculated items, and functions as required. This is the basic form of an MDX command:

```
SELECT  {Data Set 1} ON AXIS (1),
        {Data Set 2} ON AXIS (2),
        {Data Set 2} ON AXIS (3)
  FROM [Cube]
  WHERE {Slice Set}
```

MDX allows names to be used instead of numbers for the first five axes, which cover most of the queries anyone will ever think of. These names are COLUMNS, ROWS, PAGES, SECTIONS, and CHAPTERS.

A data set lists the items that appear on an axis. For example, a data set based on all the items at the top level of the Product dimension could be defined as:

```
{[Product].[Drink], [Product].[Food], [Product].[Non-Consumable]}
```

Here, the dot notation specifies that Drink is a child of Product. This helps to identify the level at which Drink exists and to refer to the correct data in the case that Drink might exist in another hierarchy or dimension. If the individual names were unique, it would be adequate to specify the data set as

```
{[Drink], [Food], [Non-Consumable]}
```

However, even this gets unwieldy when you want many items to appear on an axis. Fortunately, you can specify all the children of an item using this notation:

```
{[Product].Children}
```

Square brackets are only required for names containing spaces. Curly brackets are only required when the data set is made up of multiple definitions. However, it's generally cleaner to use both square and curly brackets all the time.

A data set is often no more than a .Children specification, therefore, a Cellset based on three dimensions can be generated by

```
SELECT {[Product].Children} ON COLUMNS,
       {[Yearly Income].Children} ON ROWS,
       {[Store Type].Children} ON PAGES
  FROM [Sales]
```

This query generates a three-dimensional Cellset. As you'll see in the next section, you can write code to pick out the required slice from a three-dimensional Cellset. Alternatively, you can specify a slice set as part of the MDX query; for example:

```
SELECT {[Product].Children} ON COLUMNS,
       {[Yearly Income].Children} ON ROWS
  FROM [Sales]
  WHERE {[Store Type].[Mid-Size Grocery]}
```

Here, the WHERE clause specifies a particular slice of the Store Type dimension to be used to create a two-dimensional Cellset. The dot notation can be used to identify a child at any particular level; for example:

```
SELECT {[Product].[Food].Children} ON COLUMNS,
       {[Yearly Income].Children} ON ROWS
  FROM [Sales]
  WHERE {[Store Type].[Mid-Size Grocery]}
```

This query drills down the Product dimension to display all the data at the Product Department level that belongs to the Product Category called Food.

To select a Measure other than the default (for example, Unit Sales), the required Measure must be added to the WHERE clause:

```
SELECT {[Product].[Food].Children} ON COLUMNS,
       {[Yearly Income].Children} ON ROWS
  FROM [Sales]
  WHERE {[Store Type].[Mid-Size Grocery],[Measures].[Profit]}
```

A good way to explore freeform MDX queries is to use the MDX Sample Application that is installed when SQLServer 7 OLAP Services is installed, The MDX Sample Application comes with VB source code. This will allow you to type in MDX queries and see their results, so long as the query generates a two-dimensional Cellset.

In This Section

We took an introductory tour of the MDX language.

ADOMD—Dimensions and Axes

We've discussed the basic concepts of OLAP and introduced the MDX command language. It's now time to see where ADOMD fits into the picture. Whereas in regular ADO the result-manipulation object model is kept separate from the object model that describes a schema (ADOX), the ADOMD model covers both requirements. This makes it quite a large model, but having already covered the concepts, it should look quite familiar, as shown in Figure 16-7.

The Catalog class marks the top of the hierarchy of classes that describe the schema of a Cube. A multidimensional database is opened using an ADODB Connection object, which can be assigned to the cg.ActiveConnection property. Just as a relational database server can support several logical databases, so can a multidimensional database contain several Cubes. The Catalog makes these available via a collection of CubeDef objects. We've already discussed how Dimensions, Hierarchies, and Levels continue the schema description. A single level is made up of items such as Drink and Food, which are known as Members. We'll explore the Members class in more detail in a later section.

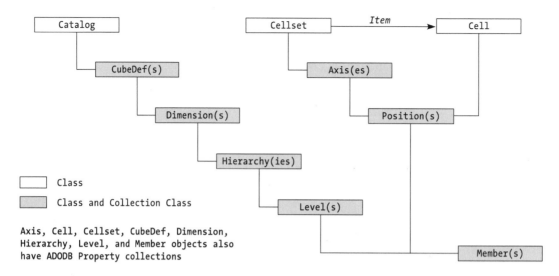

Figure 16-7. The ADOMD object model

In ADOMD, Cellsets, Axes, and Positions take the place of Recordsets and Fields. An individual data item in ADODB is simply represented by the Value property of a Field object. However, ADOMD has a distinct type of object for this purpose: the Cell object. There are far too many Cells in a typical multiaxis Cellset to create collections of Cell objects. Instead, if you need a Cell object, the Item method of the Cellset class returns one. You'll see shortly how the Item method takes a variable number of arguments, according to the number of axes that must be specified to identify an individual Cell. Each Cell object sits at the intersection of a set of Positions—one for each axis in the Cellset. A Cell has a collection of Position objects that it can use to find out about its position in a Cellset and also to find out about its location in the broader schema of the Cube it derives from, should it require schema information.

It's time to look at some code.

Working with a Three-dimensional Cellset

In this first program, we'll create a Cellset based on three dimensions from the Sales Cube in the FoodMart Catalog. We'll use an MDX query that we've already discussed:

```
SELECT {[Product].Children} ON COLUMNS,
       {[Yearly Income].Children} ON ROWS,
       {[Store Type].Children} ON PAGES
  FROM [Sales]
```

We'll provide the user with a dropdown combo box for each axis, from which a member can be selected. Whichever member is selected will be used to identify a slice of the cube, which can be displayed in a FlexGrid control. Later, we'll see how to create a slice by creating a query using a WHERE clause, but for now, we'll write code to display the chosen slice.

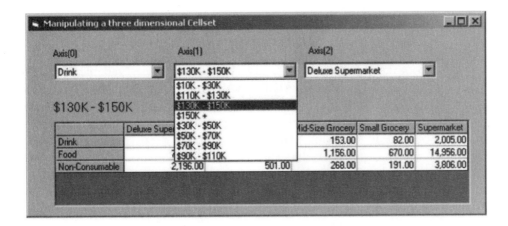

Figure 16-8. Manipulating a three-dimensional Cellset

The application has a reference to ADOMD and a reference to ADODB (to provide the Connection object). It uses two module-level variables:

```
Private cn As New ADODB.Connection
Private cs As New ADOMD.Cellset
```

Here's the Form_Load event procedure:

```
Private Sub Form_Load()
Dim sCommand As String
Dim ax As Axis
Dim ps As Position                         open an ADODB Connection
Dim i As Integer                           object using the MSOLAP
cn.Open "Data Source=POLECAT;Provider=MSOLAP;"    Provider
cn.DefaultDatabase = "FoodMart"
sCommand = " select {[Product].Children} ON COLUMNS, " & _
           "[Yearly Income].Children ON ROWS," & _
           "[Store Type].Children ON PAGES From [Sales]"
cs.Open sCommand, cn    ◄──────────  open a Cellset using the command
                                     string and the ADODB Connection
```

```
For i = 0 To 2
  Set ax = cs.Axes(i)
  lblAxis(i).Caption = ax.Name
  For Each ps In ax.Positions
     cboAxis(i).AddItem ps.Members(0).Caption
  Next
  cboAxis(i).ListIndex = -1
Next
End Sub
```

iterate through each axis, filling a ComboBox with member names for each one

This code creates a Cellset and holds it in the module-level variable, cs. It also populates an array of combo boxes with member names, so that the user can select a member from one axis that can be used to slice the remaining two axes to create a grid display. This operation is triggered by the cboAxis_Click event procedure, which receives an Index argument from VB because cboAxis is a control array.

This event procedure has the following tasks:

1. Identify the Position in the selected Axis of the chosen member (the one is used for slicing the other two). This position will remain constant in the resulting slice.

2. Identify which two axes will be used to supply the rows and columns of the grid. These will be the two axes that are not selected by the user. The Positions on each of these axes of the Cellset will be used to label the grid axes.

3. Use two For…Next loops, one nested within the other, to populate the grid. The outer loop will iterate the Rows axis selected for the slice, and the inner loop will iterate the Columns axis selected for the slice.

The grid axis labels are populated using a subroutine called labelAxes, which takes two arguments. The first is an integer identifying which axis to use for the rows, and the second is an integer identifying which axis to use for the columns. labelAxes iterates down each axis to label the grid. It looks like this:

```
Private Sub labelAxes(iRow, iCol)
Dim ax As Axis
Dim ps As Position
Set ax = cs.Axes(iRow)
For Each ps In ax.Positions
   flxData.TextMatrix(ps.Ordinal + 1, 0) = ps.Members(0).Caption
Next

Set ax = cs.Axes(iCol)
```

Select the axis to be used for the row headings.

Set the row headings.

Select the axis to be used for the column headings.

```
For Each ps In ax.Positions
  flxData.TextMatrix(0, ps.Ordinal + 1) = ps.Members(0).Caption  ◄──┐
Next                                                                │
End Sub                                              Set the column headings.
```

Here's the code for the cboAxis_Click event procedure:

```
                                             The control array's index
Private Sub cboAxis_Click(Index As Integer)  ◄────── determines the axis
Dim iPosition As Integer                     selected by the user.
Dim i As Integer
Dim j As Integer
Dim sText As String                          Get the position of the
iPosition = cboAxis(Index).ListIndex  ◄───── Member selected to slice
lblSlice.Caption = cboAxis(Index).Text       the Cellset.
If iPosition = -1 Then Exit Sub
Select Case Index
  Case 0
    flxData.Rows = cs.Axes(1).Positions.Count + 1  ◄──┐  Determine the size of the
    flxData.Cols = cs.Axes(2).Positions.Count + 1     │  grid (slice) and label
    labelAxes 1, 2                                     │  it. The Case statement
  Case 1                                               │  takes the correct action
    flxData.Rows = cs.Axes(0).Positions.Count + 1      │  for each possible
    flxData.Cols = cs.Axes(2).Positions.Count + 1      │  selected axis.
    labelAxes 0, 2
  Case 2
    flxData.Rows = cs.Axes(0).Positions.Count + 1
    flxData.Cols = cs.Axes(1).Positions.Count + 1
    labelAxes 0, 1                            ◄──┐  Iterate both axes of the slice,
End Select                                       │  populating the grid.
For i = 0 To flxData.Rows - 2
  For j = 0 To flxData.Cols - 2
    Select Case Index
      Case 0
        sText = cs(iPosition, i, j).FormattedValue
      Case 1
        sText = cs(i, iPosition, j).FormattedValue
      Case 2
        sText = cs(i, j, iPosition).FormattedValue
    End Select
    flxData.TextMatrix(i + 1, j + 1) = sText
  Next
Next
End Sub
```

A few points are required to make sense of this code. The variable "i" always refers to a row of the grid, while the variable "j" always refers to a column of the grid. The Case statement inside the nested loops maps data from the appropriate axes onto the grid. It's worth thinking this through in your mind. You have a cube of data[5] (three dimensions), from which you are taking a slice in either the vertical, horizontal, or depth plane and mapping that slice onto a flat grid display.

The code

```
sText = cs(i, iPosition, j).FormattedValue
```

could also be written as

```
Dim cl As Cell
Set cl = cs.Item(i, iPosition, j)
sText = cl.FormattedValue
```

Here, you can see that the Item method of a Cellset returns a Cell. Item is the default method on Cellset and so can be used implicitly if desired. The FormattedValue property of the Cell returns a string fit for display, based on the Cell's value. Note that in this example, Item takes three arguments. This is the correct number to identify a Cell in a Cellset with three axes. In fact, Item can take a variable number of arguments, depending on the number of axes in the Cellset. Instead of Position numbers, Member names can also be used as arguments to cs.Item to identify a specific Cell.

Creating Slices Using a WHERE Clause

In the previous example, we created a single Cellset in memory and wrote code to manipulate the Cellset to produce a two-dimensional slice. An alternative is to build a new MDX query each time the user selects a member, and create a two-dimensional Cellset, which can be easily used to populate a grid. We'll take a look at this approach now, using an almost identical user interface.

This approach makes displaying the data a good deal easier, but it shifts the complexity to the task of building the MDX query. It also means that we haven't got a Cellset available when we need to populate the dropdown combo boxes with Member names. Instead, we'll make use of the schema information available from the Catalog object. This version of the program uses the following module-level variables:

```
Private cn As New ADODB.Connection
Private cg As New ADOMD.Catalog
Private cb As ADOMD.CubeDef
Private cs As ADOMD.Cellset
```

---

5. I am using "cube" in the everyday sense here. In ADOMD terms, you have a Cellset with three axes drawn from a Cube with thirteen dimensions.

and has the following Form_Load event code:

```
Private Sub Form_Load()
cn.Open "Data Source=POLECAT;Provider=MSOLAP;"
cn.DefaultDatabase = "FoodMart"
Set cg.ActiveConnection = cn
Set cb = cg.CubeDefs("Sales")
showDimension "Product", 0
showDimension "Yearly Income", 1
showDimension "Store Type", 2
End Sub
```

which relies on a subroutine called showDimension to populate the combo box array. showDimension looks like this:

```
Private Sub showDimension(sDimension As String, iIndex As Integer)
Dim lv As ADOMD.Level
Dim mb As ADOMD.Member
Set lv = cb.Dimensions(sDimension).Hierarchies(0).Levels(1)
For Each mb In lv.Members
  cboDimension(iIndex).AddItem mb.Caption
Next
cboDimension(iIndex).ListIndex = -1
lblDimension(iIndex).Caption = sDimension
End Sub
```

showDimension does two things. First it goes to the first level in the named dimension and adds each of its Members to cboDimension (which is a ComboBox array) using the specified index number. Second, it assigns the dimension name to a Label array called lblDimension, again using the index number. Both cboDimension and lblDimension have three elements in them, all of which will be populated after Form_Load completes. Figure 16-9 shows what the user interface looks like for this version of the program.

It's very similar to the previous version, but note the labels above the Combo-Boxes. We'll use these dimension names to generate the MDX query. Here's a function called buildCommand that does just that:

```
Private Function buildCommand(        _
                iCol As Integer, iRow As Integer, _
                iSlice As Integer, sMember As String) As String
Dim sColumns As String
Dim sRows As String
Dim sSlice As String
```

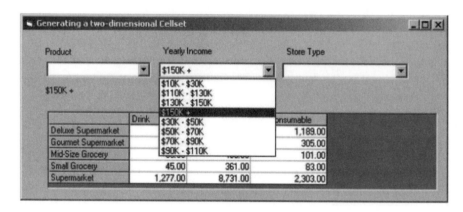

Figure 16-9. Manipulating a two-dimensional Cellset

```
sColumns = "[" & lblDimension(iCol).Caption & "]"
sRows = "[" & lblDimension(iRow).Caption & "]"
sSlice = "[" & lblDimension(iSlice).Caption & "].[" & sMember & "]"

buildCommand = "SELECT {" & sColumns & ".CHILDREN} ON COLUMNS," & _
               "{" & sRows & ".CHILDREN} ON ROWS FROM [Sales] " & _
               "WHERE (" & sSlice & ")"
End Function
```

This code gets passed the index numbers of the Dimensions to use for columns, rows, and the WHERE clause slice. It uses these index numbers to read Dimension names from the lblDimension Label array. It also gets passed the Member name, which is the text selected from the dropdown box. For example, this call to buildCommand:

```
Print buildCommand (0, 2, 1, "$150K +")
```

prints this:

```
SELECT  {[Product].CHILDREN} ON COLUMNS,
        {[Store Type].CHILDREN} ON ROWS
      FROM [Sales]
      WHERE ([Yearly Income].[$150K +])
```

The buildCommand function is called by the Click event code for the cboDimension ComboBox, which looks like this:

```
Private Sub cboDimension_Click(Index As Integer)

Dim i As Integer
Dim j As Integer
Dim sCommand As String

Dim sText As String
Set cs = New ADOMD.Cellset
lblSlice.Caption = cboDimension(Index).Text
If cboDimension(Index).ListIndex = -1 Then Exit Sub
Select Case Index
  Case 0
    sCommand = buildCommand(1, 2, 0, cboDimension(0).Text)
  Case 1
    sCommand = buildCommand(0, 2, 1, cboDimension(1).Text)
  Case 2
    sCommand = buildCommand(0, 1, 2, cboDimension(2).Text)
End Select

cs.Open sCommand, cn          ◄─────────────────  open a Cellset
flxData.Cols = cs.Axes(0).Positions.Count + 1
flxData.Rows = cs.Axes(1).Positions.Count + 1
labelAxes 1, 0
For i = 0 To flxData.Cols - 2
  For j = 0 To flxData.Rows - 2
      sText = cs(i, j).FormattedValue
      flxData.TextMatrix(j + 1, i + 1) = sText
  Next
Next
End Sub
```

This is pretty straightforward. After building the MDX command, the command is executed. The axes are labeled using the labelAxes routine from our previous example. As the resulting Cellset has only two dimensions, filling the FlexGrid is a routine task.

In This Section

We worked with ADOMD objects. You learned how to create and process Cellsets with two or three axes and how to use the ADOMD schema objects.

Using ADODB Recordsets with OLAP Servers

It's entirely possible to use an OLAP server without needing to use ADOMD. If you only ever want two-dimensional results with no drill-down capability, a standard ADODB Recordset can be used to execute an MDX query. It's even possible to get OLAP schema information without using ADOMD by exploiting an ADODB Connection's OpenSchema method.

To show how this can be achieved, let's construct an application with the same functionality as the application developed in the previous section, but without using a reference to the ADOMD library. Apart from being able to exploit your ADODB familiarity, this approach can be useful because of the many benefits of Recordsets, from binding to persistence, that have been the topic of much of this book. Nevertheless, if you rely on Recordsets alone, you won't get the full power of ADOMD, a good deal of which we have still to cover.

Way back in Chapter 4, we discussed the cn.OpenSchema method, which can be used to return all kinds of schema data. This includes OLAP schema data, and several of the options defined in the SchemaEnum enumeration are reserved specifically for use with OLAP data sources. These include

adSchemaCubes

adSchemaDimensions

adSchemaHierarchies

adSchemaLevels

adSchemaMeasures

adSchemaMembers

Chapter 4 discussed the general usage of OpenSchema and described a sample program that can be used to find out how to construct the arrays used for the Restrictions argument. None of this detail will be repeated here.

Our ADODB-only version of the program uses just one module-level variable:

```
Private cn As New ADODB.Connection
```

The Form_Load event code looks like this:

```
Private Sub Form_Load()
cn.Open "Data Source=POLECAT;Provider=MSOLAP;"
cn.DefaultDatabase = "FoodMart"
showDimension "Product", 0
showDimension "Yearly Income", 1
showDimension "Store Type", 2
End Sub
```

Clearly, a new version of showDimension is required—one that uses cn.Open-Schema instead of exploiting an ADOMD CubeDef object. This is what it looks like:

```
Private Sub showDimension(sDimension As String, iIndex As Integer)
Dim rs As Recordset
Set rs = cn.OpenSchema(adSchemaMembers, _
  Array("FoodMart", Null, "Sales", sDimension, Empty, Empty, 1))

While Not rs.EOF
  cboDimension(iIndex).AddItem rs!MEMBER_CAPTION
  rs.MoveNext
Wend
cboDimension(iIndex).ListIndex = -1
lblDimension(iIndex).Caption = sDimension
End Sub
```

This code calls cn.OpenSchema to get a Recordset containing Member details. With no restrictions, this Recordset would contain information about the entire OLAP server's members. The array argument to OpenSchema defines restrictions so that only members at Level 1 of the Dimension called sDimension are retrieved from the Sales Cube in the FoodMart catalog.

The Recordset returned is processed so that each Member's caption is added to the appropriate ComboBox.

The code for the ComboBox Click event uses exactly the same buildCommand function that we saw in the last section. However, this time, it's used as the source for a Recordset instead of a Cellset. We can therefore exploit the binding capability of a Recordset by attaching it to an HFlexGrid (which replaces the standard Flex-Grid used in the last section). This is the code:

```
Private Sub cboDimension_Click(Index As Integer)
Dim rs As New Recordset
Dim sCommand As String
lblSlice.Caption = cboDimension(Index).Text
If cboDimension(Index).ListIndex = -1 Then Exit Sub
Select Case Index
  Case 0
    sCommand = buildCommand(1, 2, 0, cboDimension(0).Text)
  Case 1
    sCommand = buildCommand(0, 2, 1, cboDimension(1).Text)
  Case 2
    sCommand = buildCommand(0, 1, 2, cboDimension(2).Text)
End Select

rs.Open sCommand, cn
Set hfxData.Recordset = rs
End Sub
```

This is pretty simple, and the result is almost perfect:

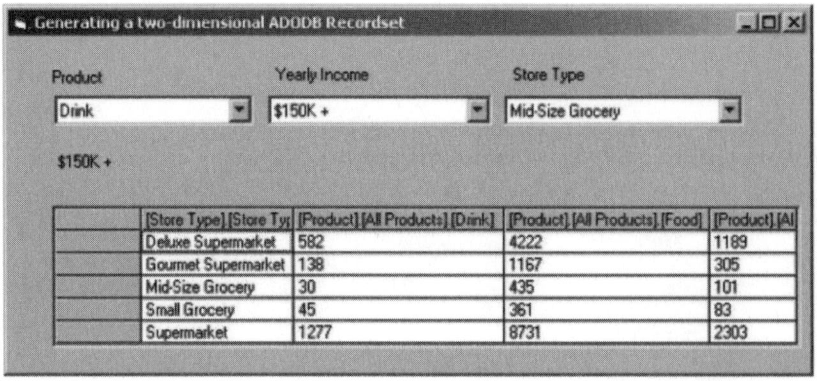

Figure 16-10. Cube processing using ADODB Recordsets (version 1)

ADODB has interpreted the OLAP Server data and built a Recordset, which has been bound to the grid. There are two problems here:

1. The Field names are fully qualified (and therefore guaranteed unique) Member names, rather than the friendly Captions we would prefer to see.

2. The first Field contains the names of the Row Members (although they are friendly Captions). It would be nicer if this data appeared as a fixed column so that it looked like row headings and would remain in view if the grid were scrolled horizontally.

Fortunately, it's quite easy to correct this. The following code reassigns the Column headings with friendly names and turns the Row names into a fixed column:

```
hfxData.FixedCols = 0                    ◄──── remove all fixed columns before the
                                               binding takes place
Set hfxData.Recordset = rs
hfxData.FixedCols = 1                    ◄──── make a new fixed column
hfxData.TextMatrix(0, 0) = ""
Dim i As Integer
Dim vArray As Variant
Dim sHeader As String
For i = 1 To hfxData.Cols - 1                          get the last section of
  vArray = Split(hfxData.TextMatrix(0, i), ".")        the fully qualified name
  sHeader = vArray(UBound(vArray))     ◄────           for each Field
  sHeader = Mid(sHeader, 2, (Len(sHeader) - 2))
  hfxData.TextMatrix(0, i) = sHeader                   strip off the square
Next                                                   brackets and update
                                                       the grid
```

Using this code to replace the

```
Set hfxData.Recordset = rs
```

line in cboDimension_Click results in this grid:

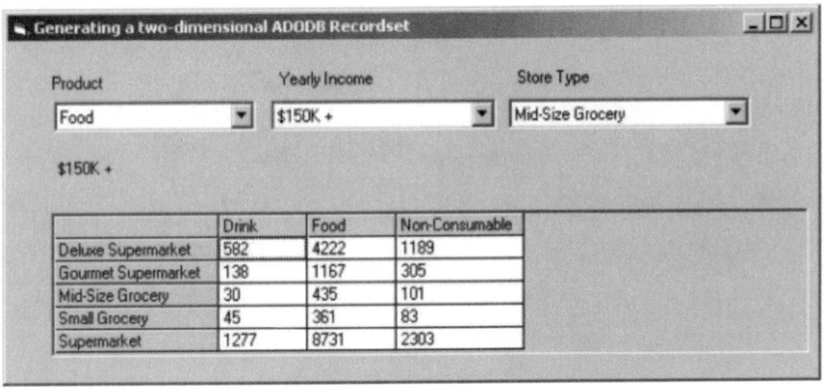

Figure 16-11. Cube processing using ADODB Recordsets (version 2)

The MDX commands passed to an ADODB Recordset need not return simple, two-dimensional structures. If a more complex command is executed, the resulting data is "flattened" into a two-dimensional structure suitable for Recordset processing.

In This Section

We saw how to use standard ADODB Recordsets to process both OLAP schema data and the results of MDX queries.

Drill Down—Hierarchies, Levels, and Members

Up to this point in the chapter, we've only dealt with one level of members in each dimension we've used. This has already given us the flexibility to take slices out of multidimensional data, cutting along any axis we choose. But ADOMD offers far more power than this. It allows us to drill down to find different levels of detail on any axis. There are two ways in which this drill-down capability can be exploited:

1. By using the schema, you can choose which level you are interested in when constructing MDX queries.

2. By exploiting MDX query capability, you can create Cellsets in which multiple levels of data exist on a single axis.

Let's begin by looking at the first of these options. We've already seen how the object model for ADOMD provides Dimensions, Hierarchies, and Levels to explore the detail of a Cube's schema. To keep things simple, we'll deal with a single hierarchy on each dimension, but we've discussed how a dimension could have multiple hierarchies.

In any hierarchy, the top level has a single member that represents all the data for that hierarchy. The children of this level (which exist at level 1) give us the first breakdown of members within the hierarchy.[6]

For example, look at the following code, which assumes cb references the Sales CubeDef:

```
Dim lv As Level
Dim mb As Member
Set lv = cb.Dimensions("Product").Hierarchies(0).Levels(0)   ◀──── level = 0
For Each mb In lv.Members
  Print mb.Caption
Next
```

The preceding code prints

```
All Products
```

while this code:

```
Dim lv As Level
Dim mb As Member
Set lv = cb.Dimensions("Product").Hierarchies(0).Levels(1)   ◀──── level = 1
For Each mb In lv.Members
  Print mb.Caption
Next
```

prints this:

```
Drink
Food
Non-Consumable
```

We can understand a bit more about how to move around inside the schema by taking a look at the Member object. This provides a significant amount of navigational information for each Member in the schema. Member objects are referenced both in the schema (through each Level object's Members collection) and in

---

6. This explains how the MDX language creates a data set using the .Children syntax.

Cellsets (through each Position object's Members collection). Some of the properties of Member objects are meaningful only in one context and raise errors if accessed via the other context. Each Member object has the properties shown in Table 16-1.

Table 16-1. Member Class Properties

PROPERTY	CONTEXT	DESCRIPTION
Name	Both	The Member's name.
Caption	Both	The Member's display name.
UniqueName	Both	The fully qualified (unique) name for the Member, which includes all of its ancestors.
Type	Level only	The Member's type, which is a value from the MemberTypeEnum enumeration, which is one of adMemberRegular, adMemberMeasure, adMember-Formula, adMemberAll, and adMemberUnknown.
Description	Level only	A description of a Measure or Formula Member.
LevelName	Both	The name of the Level to which the Member belongs.
LevelDepth	Both	The depth of a Member in its Level's hierarchy.
Parent	Level only	The Member's parent (another Member or Nothing).
ChildCount	Both	An estimate of the number of children a Member has (the exact value can be determined from the Children property).
Children	Level only	A collection of the Member's children.
DrilledDown	Position only	Where an axis has been created using multiple levels, DrilledDown returns True if a Member has children available within the current Cellset.
Parent-SameAsPrev	Position only	When iterating through Positions, ParentSame-AsPrev is True if the Member has the same parent as the previous Member in the Position.
Properties	Both	An ADODB dynamic Properties collection.

We can use this knowledge of Hierarchies, Levels, and Members to create a version of our ADOMD application that allows queries to be built at any level in any dimension. In this version of the program, dropdown ComboBoxes are replaced with TreeView controls, giving full access to each hierarchy. It looks like this:

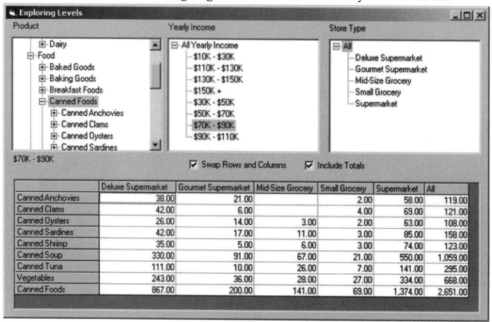

Figure 16-12. Exploring Levels

Yearly Income and Store Type have only two Levels, while Product has several.[7] This display shows a slice based on Yearly Income across the Store Type and Product Dimensions, where the Product Dimension has been drilled down to show the different Product Categories in the Canned Food Product Department, which is a child of the Food Product Family. As well as showing the breakdown for each type of Canned Food and each income group, I've included the option to show totals, illustrating that members from different levels can be included on the same axis (as illustrated in the code that follows shortly).

Drilling down is easy. A few clicks and you're looking atFigure 16-13 for different brands of Canned Anchovies for the same income group.[8]

---

7. If you are trying out using the program on the companion CD, you can swap the dimensions to include more deeply nested ones very easily.

8. Exciting, huh?

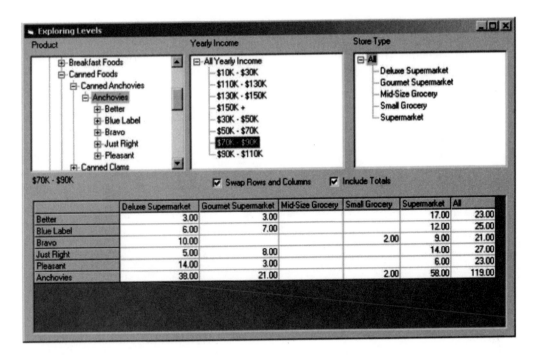

Figure 16-13. Drilling down Levels

It's time to see how this is done. The program is very similar to its predecessor. Form_Load now looks like this:

```
Private Sub Form_Load()
Dim i As Integer
Dim vDimensions As Variant
Dim sDim As String
Dim mb As ADOMD.Member
cn.Open "Data Source=POLECAT;Provider=MSOLAP;"
cn.DefaultDatabase = "FoodMart"
Set cg.ActiveConnection = cn
Set cb = cg.CubeDefs("Sales")                    create an array of
                                                 Dimension names

vDimensions = Array("Product", "Yearly Income", "Store Type")
For i = 0 To UBound(vDimensions)
   sDim = vDimensions(i)
   lblDimension(i).Caption = sDim                get hold of the top level
   Set mb = _                                    Member for each dimension
      cb.Dimensions(sDim).Hierarchies(0).Levels(0).Members(0)
   showHierarchy mb, tvwHierarchy(i)   ◄——— pass the Member and a TreeView
Next                                             control to the recursive function
End Sub                                          showHierarchy
```

As you can see, `Form_Load` basically calls on `showHierarchy` to populate the Tree-View controls. Without further ado, (but including further ADO!) let's take a look at `showHierarchy`:

```
Private Function showHierarchy(oMember As Member, _
                              tvwTree As TreeView)
Dim oChild As Member
Dim oNode As Node
If oMember.Parent Is Nothing Then
    Set oNode = tvwTree.Nodes.Add(, , _
            oMember.UniqueName, oMember.Caption)
    oNode.Tag = oMember.LevelName
    Set tvwTree.SelectedItem = oNode
Else
    Set oNode = tvwTree.Nodes.Add (oMember.Parent.UniqueName, _
        tvwChild, oMember.UniqueName, oMember.Caption)
    oNode.Tag = oMember.LevelName
End If
For Each oChild In oMember.Children
    showHierarchy oChild, tvwTree
Next
End Function
```

← if `oMember` has no parent, add it to the TreeView as a root node

← otherwise, make it a child of the node with the same key as its parent's UniqueName

← then call `showHierarchy` recursively for each of its children

TreeView nodes require a unique key to identify them. ADOMD conveniently provides the UniqueName property on each Member, which can be used as a key in the TreeView's Nodes collection. As we've seen before, recursion is a natural tool for processing hierarchies, and it hides most of the complexity of schema navigation here.

There is one other thing to note from this code. We have set each Node's Tag property to the Member's Level name. We won't be using this information just yet, but we'll see where it comes in handy shortly.

Building up the TreeViews in their entirety like this makes it easy to show you what's what, but it can take time to build the entire tree structure, which has to be retrieved from the OLAP server. If greater responsiveness were required, the program could build up the tree "on demand," as the user expanded each node.

We've seen how the TreeViews are created. All that remains to show you is the NodeClick event code on the TreeView that draws the grid. This has the added sophistication of supporting the "Totals" and "Swap" check boxes (see the previous screen shot) but is otherwise very similar to code we've already seen:

```
Private Sub tvwHierarchy_NodeClick( _
                Index As Integer, _
                ByVal Node As MSComctlLib.Node)
Dim iPosition As Integer
Dim i As Integer
Dim j As Integer
Dim sCommand As String
Dim sColumns As String
Dim sRows As String
Dim sSlice As String
Dim sText As String
Dim sTemp As String
Set cs = New ADOMD.Cellset
lblSlice.Caption = Node.Text


Select Case Index
  Case 0
    sColumns = tvwHierarchy(1).SelectedItem.Key
    sRows = tvwHierarchy(2).SelectedItem.Key
    sSlice = tvwHierarchy(0).SelectedItem.Key
  Case 1
    sColumns = tvwHierarchy(0).SelectedItem.Key
    sRows = tvwHierarchy(2).SelectedItem.Key
    sSlice = tvwHierarchy(1).SelectedItem.Key
  Case 2
    sColumns = tvwHierarchy(0).SelectedItem.Key
    sRows = tvwHierarchy(1).SelectedItem.Key
    sSlice = tvwHierarchy(2).SelectedItem.Key
End Select
If chkSwap Then
  sTemp = sColumns
  sColumns = sRows
  sRows = sTemp
End If


If chkTotals Then
  sCommand = _
  "SELECT {" & sColumns & ".CHILDREN, " & sColumns & "} " & _
        "ON COLUMNS," & _
      "{" & sRows & ".CHILDREN, " & sRows & "} " & _
        "ON ROWS " & _
            "FROM [Sales] WHERE (" & sSlice & ")"
```

grab the UniqueNames of the items selected in the TreeView

swap the rows and columns if requested

include totals on rows and columns if requested

```
Else
  sCommand = _
  "SELECT {" & sColumns & ".CHILDREN} ON COLUMNS," & _
       "{" & sRows & ".CHILDREN} ON ROWS " & _
             "FROM [Sales] WHERE (" & sSlice & ")"
End If
cs.Open sCommand, cn
flxData.Cols = cs.Axes(0).Positions.Count + 1
flxData.Rows = cs.Axes(1).Positions.Count + 1
labelAxes 1, 0              ◄──────────── call existing labelAxes code
For i = 0 To flxData.Cols - 2
  For j = 0 To flxData.Rows - 2
    Select Case Index
      Case 0
        sText = cs(i, j).FormattedValue
      Case 1
        sText = cs(i, j).FormattedValue      populate the grid as usual
      Case 2
        sText = cs(i, j).FormattedValue
    End Select
    flxData.TextMatrix(j + 1, i + 1) = sText
  Next
Next
End Sub
```

The only bit of this that is really new is the creation of the MDX command. The command used to create Figure 16-13 was

```
SELECT {[Store Type].[All].CHILDREN,
       [Store Type].[All]}
    ON COLUMNS,
       {[Product].[All Products].[Food].[Canned Foods].    ◄─┐ first element of
          [Canned Anchovies].[Anchovies].CHILDREN,          ─┘ ROW data set
       [Product].[All Products].[Food].[Canned Foods].    ◄─┐ second element of
          [Canned Anchovies].[Anchovies]}                   ─┘ ROW data set
    ON ROWS
  FROM [Sales]
  WHERE ([Yearly Income].[All Yearly Income].[$70K - $90K])
```

While this looks frightening, it's actually equivalent to this:

```
SELECT {[Store Type].CHILDREN, [Store Type]} ON COLUMNS,
       {[Anchovies].CHILDREN,[Anchovies]} ON ROWS
    FROM [Sales] WHERE ([$70K - $90K])
```

The difference is that the command used in the program is based on unique, fully qualified Member names, while the shorter, handcrafted query relies on the fact that the Member names that are used happen to be unique in this Cube. Obviously, where you can use software to generate the query, it's better to use fully qualified names.

Defining Axes with Multiple Levels

All the queries used so far have either named the Members in the data set used to create an axis or have used the .Children notation. MDX has a more flexible way of constructing queries for drill-down purposes, based on the DESCENDANTS function.

The DESCENDANTS function returns not just the children of a Member (for example, Members at the next level down) but all descendants (for example, Members at all levels below the specified Member that have the specified Member as an ancestor) when a value of AFTER is specified for the Flags argument.

The syntax for the DESCENDANTS function is

```
DESCENDANTS (Member Name, Level Name, Flags)
```

This is an example of just one of the many powerful functions defined in MDX. There is a complete program showing how to work with this function, included on the CD as a companion project to this chapter. Rather than show the full code, I will just pull out the highlights here. As you saw earlier in this section, we've stored the Level Name in the Tag property of each TreeView Node. This means we can access both the Member Name and the Level Name at any time, allowing us to construct the arguments for the DESCENDANTS function for any Member.

For example, the NodeClick event can be used to store the Level Names for both the row and column axes using code such as this:

```
. . .
Select Case Index
  Case 0
    sColumns = tvwHierarchy(1).SelectedItem.Key
    sRows = tvwHierarchy(2).SelectedItem.Key          extract the Level names
    sSlice = tvwHierarchy(0).SelectedItem.Key          from the Node's Tag as
    sColLevel = tvwHierarchy(1).SelectedItem.Tag       set in the showHierarchy
    sRowLevel = tvwHierarchy(2).SelectedItem.Tag       function declared
. . .                                                  WithEvents
```

A command string can then be constructed as follows:

```
sCommand = "SELECT " & _
  "{ DESCENDANTS (" & sColumns & "," & sColLevel & ",AFTER)} " & _
     "ON COLUMNS," & _
  "{ DESCENDANTS (" & sRows & "," & sRowLevel & ",AFTER)} " & _
     "ON ROWS " & _
  " FROM [Sales] WHERE (" & sSlice & ")"
```

Executing this query will create axes with Members from different Levels on the same axis. By using the LevelDepth property of each Member, the grid labels can be drawn on different rows or columns to reflect the structure of the data. The resulting display looks like this:

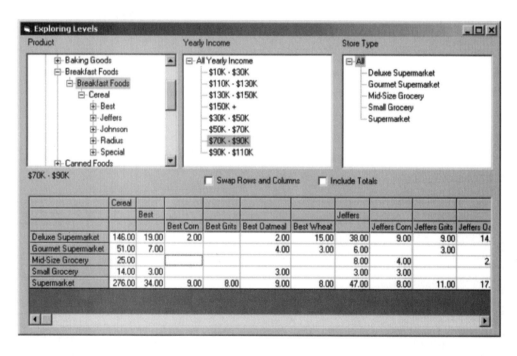

Figure 16-14. Showing multiple Levels on the same grid

As you can probably imagine, handling this kind of Cellset requires some fairly tricky user interface code, especially if you consider that the grid display would really benefit from expand and collapse options on the row and column headers. You'll see in the next section that there are already some Controls available to specifically handle this type of OLAP presentation requirement.

In This Section

We exploited the drill-down capability of ADOMD by navigating Member objects through different Levels of a hierarchy.

ADOMD-aware Controls

One of the benefits of using ADODB Recordsets to create OLAP data is the availability of a wide range of mature data aware controls. The downside, of course, is that none of them capture the spirit of multidimensional, drill-down data. Controls are now available for working specifically with Cubes and Cellsets, and we'll take a look at two of them in this section.

The first is the OLAP Manager Cube Browser. The purpose of this control is to give users full access to a Cube for which they can construct their own data displays.

The following code is all you need on a form that has a Cube Browser control:

```
Dim cn As New ADODB.Connection
cn.Open "Data Source=POLECAT;Provider=MSOLAP;"
cn.DefaultDatabase = "FoodMart"
CubeBrowser1.Connect cn, "Sales"
```

It's enough to present an interface like this:

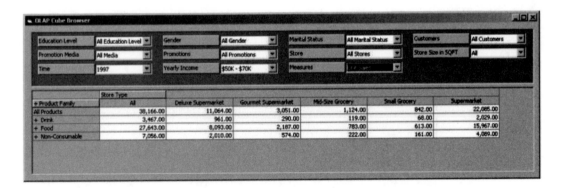

Figure 16-15. The OLAP Cube Browser

The top part of the display contains buttons labeled with all available dimensions and includes dropdown lists for selecting Members from them. The bottom part contains a data display. The user interface offers the following (undocumented) functionality:

- The buttons displaying dimension names support drag-and-drop onto the grid headings to configure the grid display.

- Unwanted dimensions can be dragged from the grid back into the top part of the display.

- The dropdown lists can be used to create slice expressions (in the WHERE clause).

- Column and row headings support double-click expand and collapse to allow flexible drill-down.

For example, expanding the Drink row results in this:

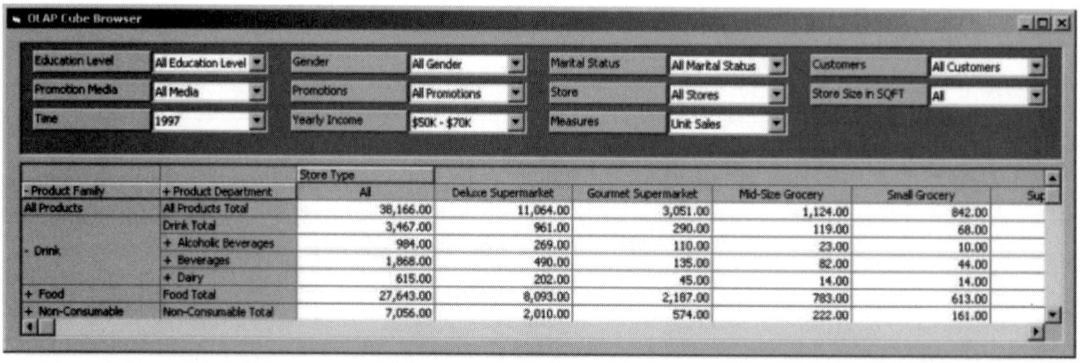

Figure 16-16. Drilling down with the OLAP Cube Browser

There is no real programmability possible with this Control, which makes it impractical to tailor the user interface using code. One technique that can be used is to create a Virtual Cube. The SQLServer 7 OLAP Manager provides a simple wizard for creating a Virtual Cube that is a customized view onto one or more existing Cubes. It allows you to select the dimensions you want to appear in the Virtual Cube, making it possible to create subsets and supersets of existing Cube data. Like a relational database View, a Virtual Cube doesn't create more data; it's just an alternative way of looking at existing data:

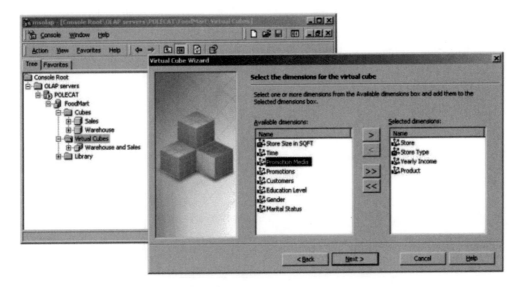

Figure 16-17. Creating a Virtual Cube

By creating a Virtual Cube called SimpleSales containing only the dimensions shown in Figure 16-17, you can present a simpler interface via the CubeBrowser control:

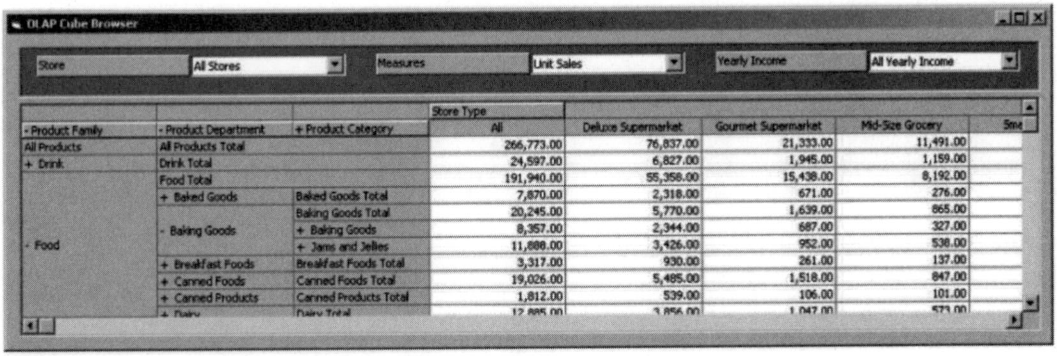

Figure 16-18. Displaying a Virtual Cube

Using the Microsoft Office Web Components, which contain a PivotTable control, you can create an altogether more sophisticated type of display. This makes a large object model available that includes several events, which can be used to customize the presentation. It only requires a small amount of code to get started. For example, this code:

```
With PivotTable1
  .DisplayToolbar = False
  .ConnectionString = "Provider=MSOLAP;" & _
          "Data Source=POLECAT;Initial Catalog=FoodMart;"
  .DataMember = "Sales"
  .DisplayFieldList = True
End With
```

will create the following display. (The PivotTable Field list can be used to drag Levels and Measures onto the grid).

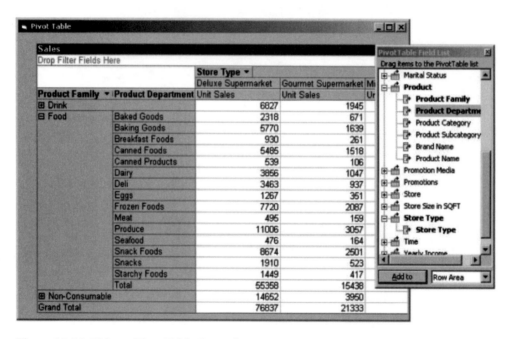

Figure 16-19. Using a Pivot Table Control

No doubt a wider range of controls will be developed as ADOMD matures.

Summary

This chapter introduced the use of ADOMD and the concept of Online Analytical Processing. OLAP is aimed squarely at decision-support applications, rather than process-oriented applications, which are the focus of much ADO programming.

OLAP has been considered important by many businesses for a long time, but the lack of tools and the high cost of entry has made it viable for only the largest businesses. This has changed recently, and ADOMD is a large part of the increasing accessibility of OLAP technology.

Working with multidimensional data is fundamentally different from working with relational data. In this chapter we:

- Developed an understanding of the way multidimensional data can be used.

- Learned how ADOMD provides us with the features to use multidimensional data.

- Saw that the ADOMD library contains support for processing both the schema of an OLAP Cube and the Cellsets that result from running MDX queries against the Cube.

- Saw that standard ADO Recordsets can be used for certain types of OLAP processing.

ADOMD is interesting, not only because of the role it plays in a rapidly expanding field of computing, but because it signifies ADO's overall ambition of providing a universal model for data access.

GLOSSARY

binary compatibility

When a VB class is compiled as a component in an ActiveX DLL or ActiveX EXE, it's given two names, both of which are stored in the Registry so that they can be identified by client programs. One of these names is called a ProgID (see **ProgID** in this glossary). ProgIDs are easy for humans to read, but are not guaranteed to be unique. An example is "MyServer.MyClass". The other name is called a ClassID. A ClassID is a type of GUID (see **GUID** in this glossary). It isn't easy for humans to read, but it's guaranteed to be unique.

When you refer to a Class or Interface name in code, you use its ProgID (or more likely, the second part of the ProgID), but VB stores the ClassID, which is safer because of its uniqueness. This is fine until you go to recompile the component containing the Class. Left to itself, VB will retain the Class's ProgID but generate a new ClassID, which means that any compiled client will be left holding an old ClassID that is no longer supported. You can ask VB to retain the old ClassIDs by setting its binary compatibility via the Project Properties dialog box. Here, you give the file name of the previously compiled DLL or EXE, and VB will check that all the old methods and properties are still part of the new one, and have not been modified in any way (it allows you to add new methods and properties to Classes). If there are no compatibilities, VB will retain the old ClassIDs, thereby ensuring that it's safe for existing clients to call the new component without themselves needing to be recompiled.

bitmask

Bitmasks are often used to allow a single property to represent a large number of Boolean flags. It's common to have a large number of these flags associated with an object. These are important, but may not be used all the time. It would be inconvenient to have individual properties on a Class to represent each of these flags.

The fd.Attributes property in ADO is a good example of this. It can have one of more of the values defined by the FieldAttributeEnum enumeration. Here are some this enumeration's values:

ATTRIBUTE NAME	VALUE	BINARY VALUE (LAST SIX BITS)
adFldMayDefer	2	000010
adFldUpdatable	4	000100
adFldUnknownUpdatable	8	001000
adFldFixed	16	010000

The key to understanding how a single property can hold multiple values is to look at the binary value of each attribute. Notice that for each of the binary values, only one bit is set, and this bit is a different one from any of the other values. The preceding table only shows the last six bits of a value. In reality, fd.Attributes is a Long and therefore, provides thirty-two bits to play with.

Now, assume that fd.Attributes actually holds the value 20. In binary, this is represented as

```
010100
```

If you place this binary number beneath the binary value adFldUpdatable and do a logical "And" operation on each pair of binary digits, you get the following results:

```
000100
010100
------
000100
```

This is a non-zero result. If we now repeat the process using the adFldMayDefer value the result is

```
000010
010100
------
000000
```

which is a zero result. In these examples, we've used the values from the Field-AttributeEnum as bitmasks to perform a bitwise comparison against the value of fd.Attributes. Using this technique, you could store up to thirty-two different Boolean values in fd.Attributes.

When you use the And operator on two numbers in VB, you perform exactly this type of bitwise comparison. Here's a code example:

```
Print fd.Attributes And adFldUpdatable
```

It prints

```
4
```

"And" can therefore be used to extract individual values from a property with multiple values (sometimes called an overloaded property). You can do the opposite by using the "Or" operator on two or more values from the FieldAttributesEnum to create an Attrib argument for the fds.Append method.

collection

In most circumstances, a Collection has a specific meaning to a VB developer—it's an object that can contain a dynamic list of other objects. In ADO, "collection" has another meaning when applied to Record objects. A Record object represents a node in a tree. A Record object representing a node that has children is called a collection Record because it represents (in the general sense of the word) a collection of child Records. In the case of a tree that is representing a file structure, a collection Record equates to a folder or directory, rather than a file.

COM

COM (Component Object Model) makes it possible for programs to communicate in a "plug-and-play" fashion (which is at the very heart of Windows). It's sometimes confused with the terms OLE and ActiveX, but these are simply specific aspects of COM technology. Programs may be written in different languages by programmers who know nothing of each other. COM makes this level of interoperability possible by using a formal definition of *interfaces*. An interface defines a service that an object provides. A client who knows about the interface can use the object without caring how it works. The object can be on the same machine as the client, or on a different machine—the client neither knows nor cares.

VB uses COM extensively. Every form, control, and object in VB is a COM object. While VB is wholly dependent on COM, it does a great job of hiding many of the complex details of COM from programmers.

Windows 2000 uses COM+, which is an enhanced version of COM, with features suited to n-tier and Web applications.

concurrency

The concurrency of a system is a statement about its ability to handle a large number of users all accessing the system at the same time. Most multiuser systems have to deal with contention for shared resources. For example, to preserve data integrity, only one client program should be allowed to update a particular record at a time. A program will acquire a lock on that record before updating it, and release the lock when the update has taken place. To achieve high concurrency (many users) a program must be designed to hold locks for as short a time as possible. Holding on to locks for a long time (which can happen with pessimistic locking, for example) results in low concurrency.

fabricated Recordset

In ADO, most Recordsets are built by Providers in response to command strings supplied by client programs. However, a fabricated Recordset is a Recordset that is created directly by client programs that specify the Fields the Recordset should have and supply all its data. The ADO Client Cursor Engine aids the client in this task. Fabricated Recordsets have nearly all the capabilities of regular Provider-generated Recordsets.

fat client

Most early (and many current) client-server systems use servers simply to supply Recordsets and process data updates. In this case, the client program contains all the user interface, validation code, business functionality, and algorithms used by the system. Such systems are often called fat client systems because most of their substance is in the client portion of the system.

GUID

In a system built of many components, where the components are typically developed by different teams (or even companies), programs need a reliable way of uniquely identifying the different components they use. Microsoft's COM(+) makes use of an industry standard algorithm which efficiently generates identifiers that are guaranteed anywhere in the world. These identifiers are 128-bit integers called GUIDs (Globally Unique Identifiers).

HTTP

HTTP (Hypertext Transfer Protocol) was originally developed as a protocol to allow Web browsers to request and retrieve Web pages (written in HTML [Hypertext MarkUp Language]) from Web servers. HTTP is rapidly becoming a standard protocol for many types of data transfer around the Internet and between distributed systems, especially between systems that run on different operating systems.

ISAM

ISAM (Indexed Sequential Access Method) is a way of representing data in files, where each file has a regular, fixed-length record structure. Records in the file can be read sequentially or can have an ordering applied to them by an index, which is typically stored in a separate file. ISAM is the database technology used by desktop databases such as dBase and Paradox, and is also used in a more sophisticated way by Access and FoxPro.

ISAM databases work well for single-user applications. However, when many users share the same database they are less appropriate. Another feature of ISAM databases is that they are typically used by programmers who have a detailed knowledge of the physical structure of files and indexes. This means that if a new index is created to increase search speeds, programs need to be modified to use the new index.

ADO is optimized for client server databases that typically use a query language such as SQL and are based on the relational model of data management.

Marshalling/marshalled

When objects in the same process communicate, they can directly access each other's memory. This makes programming with these objects easy. If the same objects were in different processes or on different machines, they would not be able to see each other's memory. This could make programming with these objects far more difficult. Programmers can ignore these complications if they use marshalling.

In marshalling, when one object calls another, the data in method arguments and return values is automatically transported between processes and machines. Marshalling is also used in multithreaded applications that use the apartment-threading model for communication between apartments.

Marshalling means that the same code can be used to allow objects to communicate regardless of whether they run in the same process. However, marshalling can add a considerable overhead to the time it takes two objects to exchange data.

middleware

Middleware is the name for all kinds of "glue" software that joins clients to servers. This includes ADO, OLE DB, ODBC, COM(+), and HTTP.

MIME

MIME (Multipurpose Internet Mail Extensions) was designed as a means for transmitting non-text files through Internet e-mail, which was originally designed to handle only ASCII text. The most common predefined MIME types include GIF and JPEG files, sound files, movie files, postscript programs, and non-ASCII character sets.

Name space

A Name space is an abstract concept. Just as people operate in three-dimensional physical space, a Name space provides a context in which Names can operate. For example, the names of all the computers in a network operate within a Name space. Within that space, all names must be unique, and there is room for other Names to be introduced so long as they adhere to certain naming conventions. In ADO terms, a Connection object representing a set of documents (in a Web site, for example) defines a Name space. The Connection object will represent a folder at the top of a set of files and subdirectories. The file and subdirectories within that folder occupy a Name space. To create a Record object based on a document in that Name space, it isn't necessary to specify a full URL (Uniform Resource Locator) (defined in this glossary)—it's only necessary to specify the document's location within the Name space defined by the Connection.

ParamArray

If a VB method is defined as having a ParamArray argument, it can receive a variable number of arguments. The caller of the method simply supplies as many arguments as they want. The method itself receives these arguments as an array of values that can be processed within the method code using standard array processing techniques.

primary key

In relational database theory, each record in a database table should be unique. It may have a single field that makes it unique (an ID, for example), or it may require multiple fields to make it unique (a venue and date, for example). Either way, the field or fields that make it unique are called the primary key. When a table is defined, its primary key should also be defined, so that the database can index the records. ADO requires a table to have its primary key defined in order to perform data modifications safely.

process

Windows allows many programs to run concurrently on the same computer. To prevent programs from interfering with each other's resources, Windows uses the concept of a process. A process is like a virtual machine. It has its own virtual memory, which no other program can access directly. It also has files, windows, and other resources.

Because a process can't directly access the resources of another (this feature happens by design, as a safety measure for programs), when two processes need to communicate, special protocols are required. The task of communication between processes is known as Inter Process Communication and several established IPC protocols exist. One of these protocols is COM, which makes Intra Process and Inter Process Communication look identical to programmers, as a result of a technique called marshalling (defined in this glossary).

A process also has one or more threads (defined in this glossary) that are responsible for executing code using the computer's CPU(s).

ProgID

Every class in ADO, and every Public class created in VB, is given two names by COM. One of these is a unique ID known as a GUID (defined in this glossary). The other is a human-friendly name called a ProgID. For example, "ADODB.Recordset" is a ProgID. If you create a Public class called "MyClass" in a VB project called "MyServer", its ProgID will be "MyServer.MyClass". You can use the CreateObject function in VB to create objects based on their ProgID.

resource

When using ADO with a Document Source Provider, you are typically dealing with semistructured data in the form of a hierarchy. The hierarchy can be viewed as a tree of nodes. Each node represents a resource. Resource is a very loose term, because many types of data can be represented in a hierarchy. In ADO, a resource is typically a file, a folder, or an email message, but given the right Provider, it could be virtually anything. A resource may be represented in ADO by a Record object, or (at the same time) by a record in a Recordset, or by a Stream object.

roundtrip

When two objects talk to each other in the same process, the communication between them is very quick. Most of the time is spent actually doing the work that was requested, and a relatively small amount of time is spent handling the communication between objects.

However, when the objects are in different processes or on different machines, the amount of time spent handling the communication is often much more than the time spent doing the actual work.

The process of making a call from one process to another, having the work done in the other process, and then waiting for the results to come back, is known as a roundtrip. In designing distributed systems, it's a good idea to avoid too many roundtrips and to make sure that each one does a useful chunk of work.

A good analogy is preparing a meal. It's no big deal to go to the fridge each time you need an ingredient. However, if you had to get all the ingredients from a nearby grocery store, you would get them all at once rather than going for each ingredient separately.

scalability

Scalability is one of the most overused words in IT at the moment. However, it's an important concept, especially in a world that is embracing Web servers as a means of providing services to a user base whose size is very hard to predict.

If houses were scalable, it would be easy to add new rooms when a family grows. Because they are not scalable, families often go through the cost and inconvenience of moving to a new house when they outgrow their old one.

Programs that aren't scalable need to be rewritten or extensively modified when their user base hits a certain limit. It isn't possible to throw hardware at them because they have hit a bottleneck that their design didn't take into consideration. A typical example is a program that holds a database connection open all the time it's running. This is fine for five users. It may be fine for fifty users. But it will never work for five hundred or five thousand users. Worse is a program that uses pessimistic locking to lock whole tables for long periods of time. Such programs may not scale beyond two or three users.

Scalable programs are designed not to hog resources that will become a bottleneck as the number of users grows. Writing scalable programs is hard, and for this reason, Microsoft has created products such as MTS and COM+ and provided development frameworks such as DNA and DNA 2000. Once you have learned how to use these products and frameworks properly, it's easy to write scalable programs.

set

Set can be both a verb (see "set a reference" next) and a noun. In math theory, a set can contain any number of things, but each thing appears in the set only once (that is, it's unique within the set). The things in a set have no implied ordering. Set theory is important in ADO because relational databases are built on set theory and the majority of ADO programs use relational databases. It's also no accident that a Recordset is called a Recordset, and not a Recordlist, Recordbag, or Record collection.

set a reference

VB handles objects differently from other types of data. You make a variable refer to an object by using the Set keyword to "set a reference" to an object. You can have many variables referring to the same object, which is something you can't do with an Integer for example. Setting a variable to Nothing doesn't necessarily destroy the object it previously referred to. If another variable also refers to the same object, the object will stay in memory. VB automatically destroys an object when the last variable to hold a reference to the object releases it.

structured OLE document

You are probably familiar with the technique of placing an Excel object in a Word document. The technology that allows one document to contain data that was generated by a completely different program is called OLE structured storage. Such a document is called a structured OLE document. OLE DB Providers such as Microsoft OLE DB Provider for Internet Publishing can recognize structured OLE documents.

thread

A thread is a unit of execution. In Windows, processes are allocated a share of memory, but they don't actually get to use CPU time directly. Instead, each process has (at least) one thread, and CPU time is shared out (more or less evenly) among all the current threads. By default, each thread gets twenty milliseconds of CPU at a time before it gets suspended, and any other thread wanting to run gets its share in turn. This way, even on computers with a single CPU, the system gives the appearance that all programs are running at the same time.

transaction

A transaction is a logical unit of work. Transactions are used to make sure that a single real-world task that is made up of multiple computer tasks (such as processing a bill payment) gets treated as a single task, and doesn't fail halfway through (either all the tasks in a transaction succeed or they all fail). Transactions are defined in detail in Chapter 4.

UNC

UNC is a convention for naming files and other resources that allows you to refer to resources anywhere in a network. UNC names use the \\ComputerName\ShareName syntax, where ComputerName is the server's name and ShareName is the name of the shared resource.

Unicode

ASCII uses eight bits (one byte) to represent characters. While this is enough memory to represent the characters in the English language, one byte isn't big enough to represent languages that have very large character sets. Unicode uses two bytes per character, which provides enough space to represent the character sets of nearly all the world's languages.

URL

A URL (Uniform Resource Locator) is a string that uniquely identifies the location of a computer, directory, or file on the Internet. The URL also specifies the appropriate Internet protocol, such as HTTP or FTP. Examples include `www.apress.com` and `www.salterton.com/hill`.

Variant array

A Variant array is an array stored in a Variant, rather than one that has been explicitly declared as an array. Any Variant can be dimensioned (using the ReDim statement) to contain an array. Variant arrays are frequently used when an argument can take either a single value or an array.

XML

XML stands for Extensible Markup Language. It's a format for structured data interchange on the Web. XML is sometimes confused with HTML. HTML is a Web language with a specific purpose—for defining the appearance of a Web page. It has a defined set of tags (for example, <BODY>, <OBJECT>). XML is more of a meta language, because it allows users to define the tags and structure required to define a particular type of data.

Index

Apress™

License Agreement (Single-User Products)